Here's what people say about bestselling author Doug Hergert's QBasic Programming For Dummies

"By reading this book, I believe that many people can realize their full programming potential!"

— Jason B. Trum, Sterling, CO

"Loved the straightforward, top-down approach to explaining even the most difficult topics. First-rate examples!"

— Donovan Keith Harris, Old Hickory, TN

"I'm an IS person, and I can safely say that it's the best computer book I've read!"

— Kevin McClelland, Ellicott City, MD

"Excellent source code used to explain the language, plus practical tips for implementing concepts."

— Laurence Rosenberg, Houston, TX

"The flow and the examples are excellent!"

— James H. Nelson, Littleton, NH

"I liked this book's down-to-earth clarity — and the fun way it helps the layperson learn QBasic programming!"

— Reuben S. Jeffers, Oakville, Ontario

"Easy to use, easy to navigate — you won't get lost in a sea of technical jargon."

— Rich Mauru, Princeton, NJ

"The perfect QBasic book for the beginner!"

— Mike Card, Santa Ana, CA

D1501377

FOUNDATIONS™ *of*

VISUAL BASIC™ 4

for Windows® 95
PROGRAMMING

FOUNDATIONS™ *of*

VISUAL BASIC™ 4
for Windows® 95
PROGRAMMING

D O U G L A S   H E R G E R T

Foundations of Visual Basic 4 for Windows 95 Programming
Published by
IDG Books Worldwide, Inc.
An International Data Group Company
919 East Hillsdale Boulevard, Suite 400
Foster City, CA 94404

Library of Congress Catalog Card No.: 94-75062

ISBN 1-56884-320-8

Printed in the United States of America

First Printing, September, 1995
10 9 8 7 6 5 4 3 2 1

Distributed in the United States by IDG Books Worldwide, Inc.

  Published in the United States

FROM THE PUBLISHER

The *Foundations* series is designed, written, and edited by working programmers for working programmers. We asked you what you needed from a book to become productive using a programming tool, technique, or language. You told us to publish a book that

- Is written from the perspective of a professional programmer

- Provides great coding examples that can be readily applied to your programs

- Serves as a tutorial that facilitates mastery of complex techniques, features, and concepts

- Serves as a comprehensive reference, achieving "dog-eared" status on your short-shelf of must-have books

- Provides a comprehensive index (programmers always go to the index first!)

- Includes either a fully indexed and linked electronic reference for quick and portable reference or valuable software that helps you get your job done better.

Our goal is to deliver all of this and more. We offer no gimmicks; no promise of instant proficiency through repetition or oversimplification. Sure, it's okay to learn the basics of driving a car doing 20 MPH with your dad in an empty parking lot. But if you're competing the next day in the Indy 500, you need entirely different preparation. You need to know the capabilities of your machine, the idiosyncrasies of the course, and how to translate that knowledge into a competitive advantage.

Like all Programmers Press books, this book is written by professionals. It is meticulously edited for technical accuracy, completeness, and readability. It is a book you will come to trust and rely on.

Thank you for choosing our product.

Christopher J. Williams

Christopher J. Williams
Group Publisher and Vice President

Welcome to the world of IDG Books Worldwide.

IDG Books Worldwide, Inc. is a subsidiary of International Data Group, the world's largest publisher of computer-related information and the leading global provider of information services on information technology. IDG was founded more than 25 years ago and now employs more than 7,500 people worldwide. IDG publishes more than 235 computer publications in 67 countries (see listing below). More than fifty million people read one or more IDG publications each month.

Launched in 1990, IDG Books Worldwide is today the #1 publisher of best-selling computer books in the United States. We are proud to have received 3 awards from the Computer Press Association in recognition of editorial excellence, and our best-selling ...*For Dummies*™ series has more than 18 million copies in print with translations in 24 languages. IDG Books, through a recent joint venture with IDG's Hi-Tech Beijing, became the first U.S. publisher to publish a computer book in the People's Republic of China. In record time, IDG Books has become the first choice for millions of readers around the world who want to learn how to better manage their businesses.

Our mission is simple: Every IDG book is designed to bring extra value and skill-building instructions to the reader. Our books are written by experts who understand and care about our readers. The knowledge base of our editorial staff comes from years of experience in publishing, education, and journalism — experience which we use to produce books for the '90s. In short, we care about books, so we attract the best people. We devote special attention to details such as audience, interior design, use of icons, and illustrations. And because we use an efficient process of authoring, editing, and desktop publishing our books electronically, we can spend more time ensuring superior content and spend less time on the technicalities of making books.

You can count on our commitment to deliver high-quality books at competitive prices on topics consumers want to read about. At IDG, we value quality, and we have been delivering quality for more than 25 years. You'll find no better book on a subject than an IDG book.

John Kilcullen
President and CEO
IDG Books Worldwide, Inc.

WINNER
Eighth Annual
Computer Press
Awards 1992

WINNER
Ninth Annual
Computer Press
Awards 1993

IDG BOOKS WORLDWIDE

About the Author

Douglas Hergert began his current career in 1980 as an editor for a west coast computer book publisher. After helping to develop several works by other authors, he began producing his own books, initially as a staff writer. His earliest books were about Pascal and BASIC programming. When he eventually left his publishing job, he continued writing computer books from his home office. In the years since, he's published more than 40 titles with seven of the industry's major publishers. He's written extensively about spreadsheets, database management, and programming languages. He produced one of the first books on Visual Basic, when the product first came out in 1991. Several of his books have become top sellers in their categories.

For More Information...

For general information on IDG Books in the U.S., including information on discounts and premiums, contact IDG Books at 800-434-3422.

For information on where to purchase IDG's books outside the U.S., contact Christina Turner at 415-655-3022.

For information on translations, contact Marc Jeffrey Mikulich, Foreign Rights Manager, at IDG Books Worldwide; fax number: 415-655-3295.

For sales inquiries and special prices for bulk quantities, contact Tony Real at 800-434-3422 or 415-655-3048.

For information on using IDG's books in the classroom and ordering examination copies, contact Jim Kelly at 800-434-2086.

Foundations of Visual Basic 4 for Windows 95 Programming is distributed in Canada by Macmillan of Canada, a Division of Canada Publishing Corporation; by Computer and Technical Books in Miami, Florida, for South America and the Caribbean; by Longman Singapore in Singapore, Malaysia, Thailand, and Korea; by Toppan Co. Ltd. in Japan; by Asia Computerworld in Hong Kong; by Woodslane Pty. Ltd. in Australia and New Zealand; and by Transword Publishers Ltd. in the U.K. and Europe.

Dedication

To Andrew and Audrey

Credits

Group Publisher and Vice President
Christopher J. Williams

Publishing Director
John Osborn

Senior Acquisitions Manager
Amorette Pedersen

Managing Editor
Kim Fields

Editorial Director
Anne Marie Walker

Production Director
Beth A. Roberts

Project Editor
Clare Mansfield

Manuscript Editor
Susan Pink

Technical Editor
Don Hergert

Composition and Layout
Dusty Parsons

Proofreader
Carol Burbo

Indexer
Liz Cunningham

CD-ROM Production
EMS Professional Shareware

Cover Design
Draper and Liew Inc.

Acknowledgments

Many people worked hard to produce this book. Chris Williams suggested the idea and got it started. Clare Mansfield deftly guided the project through the publication process. Trudy Neuhaus and Denise Peters read early versions of the manuscript and offered their support. Amy Pedersen stepped in at key moments and helped keep the project going smoothly. Anne Marie Walker directed the editorial work and Beth Roberts managed the production of the book.

Susan Pink performed her usual editorial magic with poise and skill. Don Hergert checked the technical content of the manuscript and offered a number of excellent suggestions. Carol Burbo carefully proofread the book, and Dusty Parsons did outstanding work in the final steps of the process — composition and layout.

Throughout the project, Claudette Moore offered guidance, advice, and encouragement.

My sincere thanks to all.

The publisher would like to give special thanks to Patrick McGovern, without whom this book would not have been possible.

Contents Overview

Visual Basic 4.0 is a practical and dynamic tool for creating programs in Windows 95. Part I gives you a first look at its features and components. Along the way, you'll preview the steps of application development and discover the meaning of the event-driven programming model.

This chapter introduces you to the parts of a Visual Basic project, including forms, modules, controls, properties, and events. You'll examine and run a short program example named Travel Guide, the first of many travel-related applications you'll find in this book.

Here you take a detailed look at the steps for creating a program: selecting the appropriate controls for your project and arranging them in forms; setting the properties that will ultimately determine the appearance and behavior of controls; and writing code to define your program's reaction to specific events. As you study the details of each step, you'll create a sample project named the International Currency Exchange application.

Chapter 2 Designing an Effective Interface **35**

This is the first step. In a sequence of hands-on exercises, you'll select controls from the Toolbox and place them on a form; arrange individual controls and adjust their sizes; lock the form when you've achieved the visual design you want; and save the components of the project to disk.

Chapter 3 Defining Properties **57**

In the second step you define the properties of the forms and controls in your program. The settings you choose in the Properties window can dramatically affect your program's performance. As you'll discover, some properties change the visual appearance of your program and others establish operational features.

Chapter 4 Writing Code **81**

The third step is to write the code that conducts your application's activities. Specifically, you create event procedures to direct the program's reactions to runtime events. In this chapter you'll use the Code window to develop event procedures, and you'll see how these procedures work during the program's performance.

PART III   PROGRAMMING ESSENTIALS **109**

Here you'll master the key elements of Visual Basic programming, including variables, operations, project design, control structures, data structures, data file programming, input and output, and custom controls. You'll work with a different application in each chapter, always related to the general theme of business travel.

Chapter 5 Procedures, Variables, and Operations **111**

As you work with an expense-reporting tool called the Travel Expense Log application, you'll explore several core programming topics: writing and using procedures; declaring variables; understanding scope; selecting data types; and using arithmetic and string operations.

Chapter 6 Designing a Project **161**

Although a successful application can contain a single form, more complex projects may require a greater variety of components. In applications containing multiple forms, you need to pay close attention to form properties, data-sharing techniques, and the choice of a startup form. You'll explore these topics as you work with a project called the Restaurant Review application, which creates a database of your favorite restaurants.

A structured programming language provides lucid and practical ways to organize data (in arrays and user-defined types, for example) and to express the flow of control (as in loops and decisions). You'll investigate these topics in a project named the Meetings application, which is designed to help you keep notes about the business meetings you attend while you're on the road.

Data file programming is a key skill for developing programs that manage databases, create reports as text files, or store data for eventual use by other programs. This chapter's Phone Directory program illustrates a variety of data file techniques for creating databases and text files.

As illustrated in the International Sales program, input and output procedures can require meticulous care as you design the features of an interactive application. In this context, input is the information or instructions supplied by the user, and output is the data the application provides in return.

In addition to the intrinsic controls, such as command buttons, text boxes, lists, labels, and check boxes, Visual Basic provides a large selection of custom controls to meet special programming requirements. The Transportation Planner program illustrates a powerful custom control called the common dialog.

Here you'll examine a selection of advanced topics, including objects and classes, MDI, OLE automation, and external database connections. Each chapter presents a complete application designed to illustrate the topic at hand.

A class defines the properties and methods of an object. For example, controls are objects that belong to classes defined in Visual Basic. Here you'll, learn to create class modules of your own, and to generate objects belonging to those classes. The Travel Reminders application helps you explore this topic.

Windows programs often enable the user to work with more than one open file at a time. In Visual Basic you can develop a multiple-document interface by adding an MDI parent form to your project along with one or more child forms. You'll see how this works in the MDI version of the Transportation Planner program.

In OLE automation, a server application supplies its own objects, properties, and methods as programmable components that are available to other programs. A client application thereby takes control of the resources available in the server. You'll explore this topic in the OLE automation version of the International Sales program.

Visual Basic's data control enables you to create programs that manage databases from applications such as Microsoft Access, dBASE, Paradox, Excel, or Lotus 1-2-3. To illustrate the programming techniques for using the data control, this chapter presents a database version of the Currency Exchange program.

Table of Contents

Introduction

*I*n the world of personal computers, anyone can become a programmer. All it takes is the imagination to devise useful new applications and the initiative to master the appropriate programming tools. Programmers appear in every profession — including education, research, medicine, business, commerce, sales, accounting, consulting, law, and science. Often a programmer is first an expert in a particular field, and second an occasional designer of applications to support this expertise.

You can think of this phenomenon as *personal* programming. Wherever you work, whatever you do, you can expand your computer's usefulness by writing applications to use in your own job. To count yourself as a working programmer, you combine your professional expertise with the inspiration and energy to develop the applications you need.

Personal programming is what Visual Basic is about. Using its versatile tools, you quickly translate an abstract idea into a program design you can actually see on the screen. Visual Basic encourages you to experiment, revise, correct, reconsider, and rework your design until the new project meets your requirements. It inspires your imagination and creativity.

The Process

Visual Basic 4.0 is ideal for developing applications that run in the new Windows 95 operating system. This book is for programmers everywhere who are ready to master the tools and techniques of this popular programming environment. As you'll learn at the beginning of the book, Visual Basic prescribes a three-step approach for creating programs:

1. Design the appearance of your application. This step takes place interactively on the screen, as you select and arrange controls in the forms of your project.

2. Assign property settings to the objects of your program. Properties help you refine the appearance and behavior of your program.

3. Write the code to direct specific tasks at runtime. In Visual Basic's event-driven programming model, code is designed to respond to the activities you expect to occur during a performance. For example, you might write event procedures to respond to a mouse click, a keyboard entry, or a menu selection.

With its interactive approach to creating forms, and its lucid, structured programming language, Visual Basic helps you produce satisfying results at each step along the way.

The Programs

At the heart of this book is a collection of working program examples, ready for you to load into your computer and run. They are all built around a consistent theme: developing applications that can prove useful to the business traveler.

Think of each program as a hands-on exercise. As you work with a program — and read the text in the corresponding chapter — your goal is to master the tools and techniques illustrated in the project's design and code. Once you've seen how a program works and what it does, you should feel free to revise it in any way you like. Adjust the interface, add new features, change the steps of procedures, refine the input and output techniques, replace operations that you don't like — in short, do anything you want to make the programs conform to your own programming style.

All the program files are included on the CD-ROM attached to the back cover of this book. Look for the files in a directory named BookApps. Before you begin reading the book, your first task should be to copy all the files to the main Visual Basic directory on your hard disk. In Windows 95, use the My Computer utility to carry out the copy operation. Or, if you still prefer to perform file operations in DOS, click the Start menu, choose

Programs, and click the MS-DOS Prompt command. Then use the DOS Copy command to transfer all the programs from the BookApps directory to the \VB directory on your hard disk.

Each chapter gives you instructions for loading and running the corresponding program, and provides a complete printed listing of the program's code. The listings themselves are carefully designed as learning tools. Specifically, the following features help make the code as readable as possible:

- Each program is substantially documented with comments. In Visual Basic, a comment line begins with an apostrophe. For example, three lines of comments precede the following line of code:

```
' Read the country field from the
' current record and add the country
' name to the combo box list.
cboCountry.AddItem .Fields("Country").VALUE
```

Comment lines are ignored at runtime.

- The names assigned to controls always begin with a three-letter prefix that identifies the class of the control. For example, a label name begins with the letters *lbl*, an option button name with *opt*, and a command button with *cmd*, as in these examples:

```
lblConvCurr.Caption = "U.S. dollar(s):"
optDollarsTo.VALUE = True
cmdClear_Click
```

- Long lines of code are frequently broken up into smaller parts, through the use of Visual Basic's line-continuation character, the underscore (_). When you see a line of code that ends with a space and an underscore, you know that the next line is a continuation of the same statement. For example, the following statement is divided into three physical lines:

```
MsgBox "Problem opening or using the " & _
   dbCurrency.DatabaseName & " database.", , _
   "International Currency Exchange"
```

- Although Visual Basic allows programmers to omit *default* property names, this practice is generally avoided in this book. For example, Text is the default property of a text box; consequently your code can assign a setting to this property without referring to the property name itself:

```
Text1 = "Hello there."
```

This abbreviation is useful for programmers who don't like to type, but it can also lead to confusion. In this book, you'll see the complete property reference as follows:

```
Text1.TEXT = "Hello there."
```

Notice that the Visual Basic editor automatically displays default property names in all capital letters.

In addition to these features, the listings at the end of each chapter include many brief annotations, pointing out particularly salient lines of code.

Many programmers find that the most fruitful way to learn new programming techniques is to study working examples of code. As you read each chapter, you should focus on the programs themselves — their forms, controls, property settings, and especially their code.

I

A Profile of Visual Basic 4.0

Visual Basic 4.0 is a structured programming language and a complete application development environment, all in one package. Before you begin working with the elements of the language, you need to become familiar with the important development tools that the product supplies. Part I gives you an introductory look at these features.

The project window, the Toolbox, the Properties window, the form and code windows, the toolbar and menu commands — all of these appear on the screen while you're designing a new project. Chapter 1 explains what these tools are for, and helps you explore their use in several hands-on exercises. You'll begin to see how you can combine forms, controls, and code to build a working project. You'll also learn how to find context-sensitive help whenever you need it. Finally, this chapter presents a simple program called the Travel Guide application. You'll load the project from disk, run it, and then briefly investigate its components.

CHAPTER 1

Creating Applications in Visual Basic

A programming language gives you the tools to develop computer applications of all varieties — small or large, simple or complex, single-purpose or multifaceted. Your job as a programmer is to plan and write the code that guides the computer through basic activities such as input and output, data storage, calculations, decisions, and repetition. Programming is always intense work, requiring a solid understanding of the language in use and unwavering attention to detail. But when you complete a well-designed computer program — whatever its size or scope — the creative accomplishment yields genuine satisfaction.

Visual Basic 4.0 is a powerful application development tool for Microsoft's new Windows 95 operating system. The package includes not only a familiar and accessible programming language, but also an efficient interactive environment for designing forms and windows. With this unique combination, Visual Basic simplifies programming tasks, shortens development time, and improves the quality of the end product.

In Visual Basic you can quickly design the visual elements of any new programming project. Your program's interface may include the familiar controls that Windows users already know how to operate — such as command buttons, option lists, text boxes, and scroll bars. With just a few swift mouse actions, you can add any combination of these controls to a program. As a result, the design tasks that used to require many hours of detailed programming effort can now be completed in minutes.

In this first chapter you'll start Visual Basic and begin exploring the dynamic tools it offers. Along the way, you'll preview the three-step process of application development in Visual Basic:

1. Designing a program's visual interface

2. Defining the properties of individual objects in the interface

3. Writing the code

The brief hands-on exercises in this chapter will help you understand the basic concepts surrounding these three steps. (In chapters to come you'll learn much more about each step individually.)

At the end of this chapter you'll take a look at a sample application named the Currency Exchange Travel Guide, which you'll load from the program disk included with this book. This program is a calculation tool designed to simplify one aspect of international business travel, a recurring theme in the programming projects presented throughout this book.

Starting Visual Basic

Once installed on your computer, Visual Basic is available directly from the Start menu in Windows 95. As illustrated in Figure 1-1, you begin your work as follows:

1. Click the Start button and choose Programs from the Start menu.

2. Choose the Visual Basic group from the Programs menu.

3. Click Visual Basic to start the program.

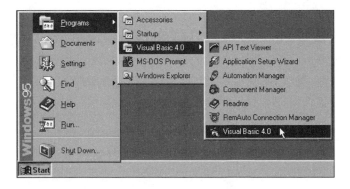

Figure 1-1
Starting Visual Basic.

Alternatively, you can easily place a shortcut to Visual Basic directly on the Windows 95 desktop. In the My Computer window or the Explorer, find and open the Visual Basic folder on your hard disk. Holding down the right mouse button, drag a copy of the Visual Basic icon from the folder to the desktop, and choose Create Shortcut(s) Here from the resulting pop-up menu. A new shortcut icon appears on the desktop (Figure 1-2). To start Visual Basic, you can simply double-click this icon.

Figure 1-2
Creating a shortcut to Visual Basic.

Either way you choose to get started, Visual Basic appears on the desktop. As you can see in Figure 1-3, the development environment includes a variety of overlapping windows. At the top of the screen you see the Visual Basic title bar. Its caption tells you that Visual Basic is ready for you to begin designing a new program with a default name of Project1:

```
Project1 - Microsoft Visual Basic [design]
```

During the design process, an application is known as a *project* in Visual Basic. An application may include multiple files on disk, all of which are available as windows on the desktop when you open the project into the Visual Basic environment. Projects may consist of several types of files; among them are *forms*, *modules*, and the *project* file itself:

- A *form* is a window that you design to play a specific role in your program's visual interface. To develop a form, you place an arrangement of buttons, options, lists, frames, or other controls within the window's borders. Each form is saved on disk as a separate file with an extension name of FRM. The FRM file also stores any code you write to orchestrate activities on the form. (In addition, Visual Basic creates FRX files to record special properties of forms.)

- A *module* is a separate code file, saved on disk with an extension name of BAS.

- The *project* file keeps track of all the files and objects included in a given application. Visual Basic 4 saves a project file on disk with an extension name of VBP. (Note that project files were identified with the extension MAK in previous versions of the development environment.) Each application includes one project file; when you open this file, the Project window provides a list of other files that are part of the application — including forms and modules.

While you're developing a program, many windows may appear on the desktop at once, resulting in a screen that's crowded with images and information. Take a moment now to examine the windows that appear initially in the Visual Basic environment.

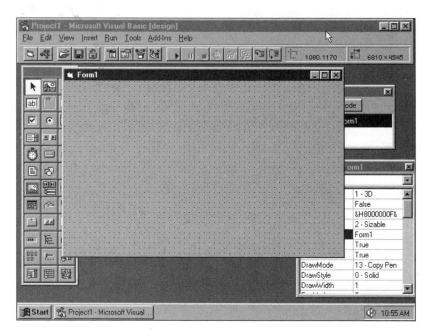

Figure 1-3

The Visual Basic development environment.

Menus and Toolbar Buttons

Just beneath the title bar at the top of the screen, you can see the menu bar, the row of buttons that make up the toolbar, and — just to the right of the toolbar — the position and size indicators, designed to help you arrange the objects of a project. (See Figure 1-4.) As in any Windows application, menu commands are designed to give you ways to perform specific operations. For example, the File menu contains commands for starting new projects, opening existing projects from disk, or saving the project that you're currently working on. The Edit menu provides a variety of familiar operations, including undo, redo, cut-and-paste, copy-and-paste, find, and replace. You'll learn more about specific menu commands as you proceed through this book.

Figure 1-4
The menu bar, the toolbar, and the position and size indicators.

The toolbar provides shortcuts for many important menu commands. As you can see, the buttons along this toolbar are arranged in four groups, identified in Figures 1-5 through 1-8:

- The first group (Figure 1-5) contains shortcuts for adding new forms and modules to the current project.

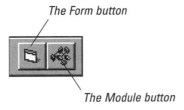

Figure 1-5
The first group of toolbar buttons are for adding files to a project.

■ The second group (Figure 1-6) contains buttons for opening a project from disk and for saving the current project. In addition, the Lock Controls button allows you to freeze controls in place when you've completed the design of a particular form.

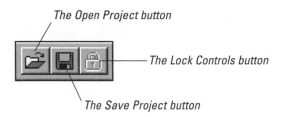

The Open Project button

The Lock Controls button

The Save Project button

Figure 1-6
The second group of toolbar buttons are for opening and saving project files.

■ The third group (Figure 1-7) includes buttons that help you sort through the jumble of windows that appear in the Visual Basic environment. For example, the Project button brings the project window to the front of the desktop, and the Properties button displays the Properties window, which you'll examine shortly.

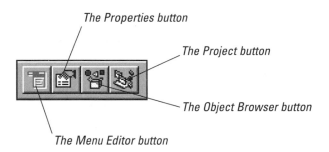

The Properties button

The Project button

The Object Browser button

The Menu Editor button

Figure 1-7
The third group of toolbar buttons are for managing windows.

- The fourth group (Figure 1-8) contains an assortment of buttons for running, stopping, and debugging a program as you complete your work on a given project.

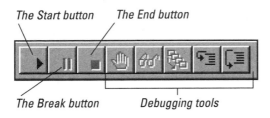

The Start button   *The End button*

The Break button   *Debugging tools*

Figure 1-8
The fourth group of toolbar buttons are for running and debugging programs.

You'll learn much more about the buttons on the toolbar as you begin creating your own Visual Basic projects. If you forget the purpose of a particular shortcut on the toolbar, you can simply position the mouse pointer over a button; Visual Basic displays a small ToolTip box showing the name of the button.

The Toolbox

At the left side of the desktop is another collection of buttons, known as the Toolbox. These buttons represent the controls you can include in any program you develop. The Toolbox is typically the main focus of your attention as you begin a new project and choose controls to depict the options, procedures, and activities you're planning for your application. The number of controls initially displayed in the Toolbox depends on the edition of Visual Basic that you are using. Three editions are available, known as Standard, Professional, and Enterprise. The Standard edition provides a basic set of intrinsic controls, as shown in Figure 1-9. The Professional and Enterprise editions extend the Toolbox with a collection of custom controls designed for special purposes. (You can see the extended Toolbox back in Figure 1-3.)

Figure 1-9
The Toolbox of intrinsic controls.

There's no need to memorize all the Toolbox buttons at this point, although you may already recognize most of the tools in the box. For example, the buttons in the top half of the Toolbox are among the most commonly used controls in most Windows applications. They include the controls you use to organize text and graphics in a window (labels, picture boxes, and frames), controls that elicit input or instructions from the user (text boxes and command buttons), and controls that provide options (check boxes, option buttons, combo boxes, and list boxes). As shown in Figure 1-10, a ToolTip displays the name of a tool when you simply hold the mouse pointer over a button in the Toolbox.

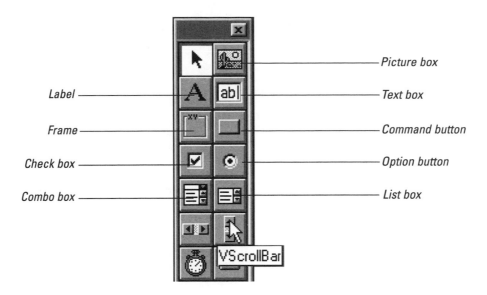

Figure 1-10
Identifying buttons in the Toolbox.

In the next section you'll discover how easy it is to place a control on a form.

Forms in a Project

In the center of the Visual Basic environment is a large window named Form1 (Figure 1-11). A form is a window you design as part of a program's interface. For example, a form can become a dialog box for eliciting information from the user, or a window in which your program displays specific information. You can develop any number of forms for use in a program, although a program may consist of a single form.

Visual Basic initially includes the Form1 file in each new project. (As you'll learn later, you can change the form's name and caption to identify the purpose of the form.) You can immediately begin the first step of your work — planning the appearance of your program on the desktop — inside Form1.

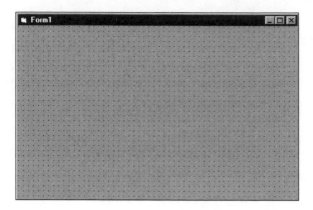

Figure 1-11
An empty form in a new Visual Basic project.

Step 1: Placing Controls on a Form

As a first experiment with forms and controls, the following exercise guides you through the steps of placing a variety of objects on Form1:

1. Move the mouse pointer to the Toolbox, and click its title bar to activate the box. Then position the pointer over the command button tool. After a brief pause, a ToolTip appears to identify the tool you've selected.

2. Double-click the left mouse button over the command button tool. In response, Visual Basic places the first control — a command button — in the middle of Form1. The caption on the control is Command1, as shown in Figure 1-12. Around the perimeter of the command button are *sizing handles*, small solid black squares that you can use to change the dimensions of the control. The appearance of these handles indicate that this first control is the *selected* object in the form.

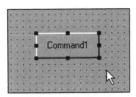

Figure 1-12
Placing a command button on Form1.

3. Position the mouse pointer over the center of the Command1 control, hold down the left mouse button, and drag the control toward the upper-left corner of Form1. As you do so, notice that the control moves in small jumps within the dotted grid shown in the background of the form. Also notice the position indicator shown at the right side of the Visual Basic toolbar (Figure 1-13). These coordinates represent the current position of any selected object. The adjacent pair of numbers — the size indicator — gives the dimensions of an object. (The position and size of an object are shown in *twips*, a standard unit of measurement for graphic objects on the Windows desktop.) Release the mouse button when you've moved the command button to its new position in the form.

Position indicator

Size indicator

Figure 1-13
The position and size indicators for a selected object.

4. Now try a slightly different technique for placing a control on a form. Position the mouse pointer over the label tool, shown as a bold uppercase **A** in the Toolbox. Then click the left mouse button once; this action selects the label control. Move the mouse pointer to a position near the top center of Form1. Hold down the left mouse button, and drag the mouse through a small rectangular area on the form. Release the mouse button, and Visual Basic places a label control in the form. The caption on this new control is Label1.

5. You can *resize* any control by dragging any one of the small black sizing handles displayed around the perimeter of the control. Try this now with Label1, as follows. Position the mouse pointer over one of the handles; the pointer becomes a two-headed arrow. Hold down the mouse button and drag the handle in any direction to change the dimensions of the control. At the right side of the toolbar you'll see the changes take place in the size indicator (Figure 1-14).

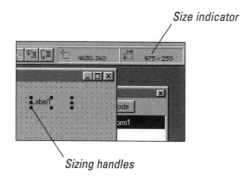

Size indicator

Sizing handles

Figure 1-14
Resizing a control.

6. Now try placing several more controls on Form1. First double-click the text box control in the Toolbox. A control named Text1 appears in the form. Drag this new control to a position just beneath Label1. Labels and text boxes are often paired in forms; the purpose of the label is to tell the user what kind of information to enter in the text box.

7. Double-click the option button tool in the Toolbox. A control named Option1 appears in the form. Then perform this same step two more times to produce the controls named Option2 and Option3 in turn. Reposition these new controls to produce a column of option buttons down the center of the form.

8. Finally, double-click the combo box button in the Toolbox. A combo box is a text box with an attached drop-down list of options. Drag this new control, named Combo1, to a position near the lower-right corner of Form1. You've now placed seven controls on the form, and your work should appear approximately as shown in Figure 1-15.

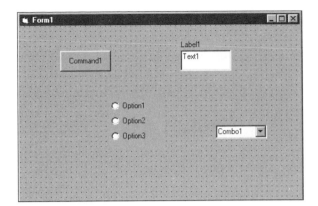

Figure 1-15
Arranging a variety of controls in a form.

Although the steps of this exercise may have seemed a little arbitrary, you can easily imagine beginning your work on a real application by placing a similar selection of controls on a form. For example, Figure 1-16 shows an actual dialog box illustrating the controls you've been working with. This example contains a text box for entering the name of an employee, a set of option buttons and a combo box for specifying information about the employee, and a command button for requesting a search for the employee's record.

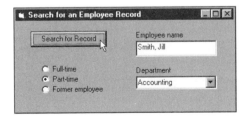

Figure 1-16
Building a real dialog box for an application.

Running a Program

Now try another experiment with the form you've created. You can run a program in Visual Basic before you've written any code. Doing so gives you an opportunity to explore the behavior of the controls you've placed on the form.

There are three simple ways to start a program:

- Click the Start button on the toolbar (Figure 1-17).
- Pull down the Run menu and choose the Start command (Figure 1-18).
- Press F5, the shortcut key for the Start command.

The Start button

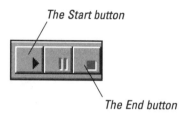

The End button

Figure 1-17
The Start button on the toolbar.

Figure 1-18
The Start command in the Run menu.

Take one of these actions now to start the project you've been building. Then follow these steps to experiment with the controls on the form:

1. Click the Command1 button several times with the mouse. Notice the visual push-button effect that takes place on the screen with each mouse click.

2. Try entering some text in the text box. A Visual Basic text box has all the built-in editing capabilities of any Windows text box. You can insert, select, delete, cut, copy, and paste text in the box, using mouse and keyboard operations that are common to all Windows applications.

3. Click any one of the three option buttons. A bold black dot appears inside the button you've chosen. Now click a different button. The previous button is cleared and the bold black dot appears inside your most recent selection. In a group of option buttons, only one option can be selected at a time.

4. Click the down-arrow icon just to the right of the Combo1 control. Although the resulting drop-down list is empty at the moment, you can still see the behavior that's built into this particular control (Figure 1-19).

5. Now click the End button on the toolbar (Figure 1-17) or choose the End command from the Run menu to stop the program.

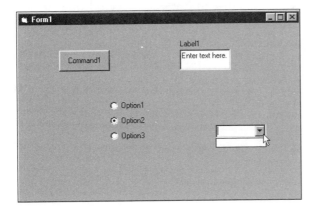

Figure 1-19
An initial run of a Visual Basic project.

The Properties Window

Once you've placed one or more controls on a form, the second step in the Visual Basic development scheme is to set the properties of your controls. Properties determine the appearance and behavior of individual controls and forms in the applications you create. Each type of control or object has its own set of properties; for example, you'll discover properties representing the name, caption, color, style, and status of a particular control.

Properties are defined in the Properties window, which is displayed on the desktop (but partly hidden behind the Form1 window) from the beginning of your work with Visual Basic. You can activate this window and bring it to the top of the desktop by taking any one of these steps:

- Click the Properties button on the toolbar.
- Pull down the View menu and choose Properties.
- Press F4, the shortcut for the Properties command.

When you do so, you'll see that the Properties window is arranged as a two-column grid (Figure 1-20). The column on the left contains the names of all the properties that apply to a selected object, and the column on the right shows the setting for each property. Each property has a *default* setting that remains in effect unless you change it.

Figure 1-20
The Properties window.

Step 2: Setting the Properties

In the following exercise, you'll select the command button that you've placed on Form1, and quickly change three of the properties of this control. You'll also take the opportunity to scroll through the entire property list to see what else it contains:

1. Click the Command1 control on the form you've been creating. Sizing handles reappear around the perimeter of the command button.

2. Press F4 or click the Properties button on the toolbar. The Properties window comes to the front of the desktop, and you can see the list of properties that apply to the command button you've selected.

3. Use the scroll bar at the right side of the Properties window to scroll through the entire set of properties. You'll find about two dozen properties that apply to this control. Among them are properties named Left and Top, which specify the position of the control in the containing form. You've changed these property settings already, just by dragging the command button to a new position inside the form. You'll also see properties named Height and Width, which determine the size of the control. You can change the size either by entering new settings for these properties in the Properties window, or — as you've seen — by selecting a control and dragging its sizing handles with the mouse.

4. Scroll back to the top of the properties list and click the Caption property. For a command button, the Caption property is the text that appears on the face of the button. As you can see, the default setting of this property is Command1 for the current control.

5. Type the new caption **Message** and then press Enter to confirm your new entry. Now look back at the command button on Form1; as you can see (Figure 1-21) the button displays the new caption that you've assigned to it.

6. Now select the Default property in the list. A Default setting of True means that the user can select a command button by pressing Enter from the keyboard; in some applications this feature provides a convenient alternative to a mouse click. The current setting for this property is False. To change the setting, select True from the drop-down list, or simply type T.

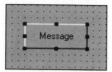

Figure 1-21
Changing the Caption property of a command button.

7. For the final change, scroll down the list again until you find the Name property. This property assigns a name by which you refer to a given control in the code of your program. As you can see, the default Name setting is Command1.

8. Select the Name property and enter **cmdMessage** as the new setting. You can assign any name you like to a control, but certain conventions will make your work easier when you begin writing code. In this example, starting the name with the letters *cmd* will help you remember later that this name refers to a command button.

9. Before you complete your work in the Properties window, notice that the window contains a list box, located just below the title bar. The box currently displays the name you've just assigned to the command button, cmdMessage. This drop-down box gives you a simple way to select a different control or form, so that you can begin changing the properties of other objects in your program. Click the down-arrow button located at the right side of the box, and you'll see a list of all the objects you've placed on Form1 (Figure 1-22). To see the list of properties that apply to any one of these controls, you simple select the name of the control in the drop-down list.

So far you've examined four windows that appear initially in the Visual Basic environment:

- The title bar window, showing the menu bar, the toolbar, and the position and size indicators

- The Toolbox, containing buttons for all the controls available to you as you create your project

- The Form1 window, which Visual Basic includes in every new project

- The Properties window, in which you can view and change the property settings for any control or form in your program

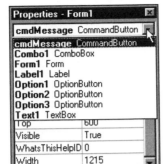

Figure 1-22
The list of controls in the Properties window.

One last window has remained partially hidden behind your other work up to this point — the Project window.

The Project Window

The Project window provides a list of the files in your current program. Each program contains one Project window, which is stored on disk with a default extension name of VBP. To view the Project window, you can simply click it with the mouse, or you can take any one of these actions:

- Click the Project button on the toolbar.
- Pull down the View menu and choose the Project command.
- Press Ctrl+R, the keyboard shortcut for the Project command.

When you do so, you'll see that the Project window lists the files contained in your current program. At the moment, the list has only one entry, Form1, as shown in Figure 1-23. But as you know already, a project may contain as many forms as are necessary in the design of your program. In addition, you can add modules to a project for storing additional code in your program.

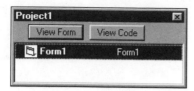

Figure 1-23
The Project window.

Without worrying too much just yet about the different roles that forms and modules play in a program, try adding some additional files to the current project:

1. Click the Form button — the first button on the toolbar — twice. Each time you do so, Visual Basic adds a new form to your project, named Form2 and Form3, respectively.

2. Click the Module button, the second button on the toolbar. In response, Visual Basic adds a module file named Module1 to your project.

3. Now click the Project button or press Ctrl+R to view the Project window. The window displays the list of three forms and one module that currently make up your project (Figure 1-24). (Note that you can resize the Project window to view the entire list of files.)

4. Your original Form1 is now hidden behind the other windows you've added to your project. The Project window gives you a quick way to return to your work on this form: Select Form1 in the list and click the View Form button at the top of the window.

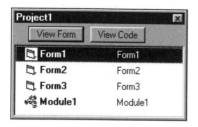

Figure 1-24
Adding new forms and modules to a project.

Once you've selected and arranged the forms and controls of your project and assigned property settings as needed, the final step of your work is to begin writing code. You can store code in individual forms or in modules. In general, the code you store in a form applies to the objects in the form; the code in a module can be defined as "public" code, available anywhere in your program. You'll learn more about this distinction in Part III.

The Event-Driven Programming Model

One of Visual Basic's most important and compelling features is a design approach known as the *event-driven programming model*. When you plan a Visual Basic program, you focus on the events that you expect to take place while the program is running. Most events correspond to actions that may be performed by the person who's running your program. For example, the user clicks a button, selects an option, chooses a menu command, highlights an item in a list, or types an entry into a text box; all of these are events that are formally defined and recognized in Visual Basic applications. Much of the code in Visual Basic projects is oriented around anticipated events like these.

Accordingly, a program contains blocks of code known as *event procedures* that you design to respond to specific events. For example, suppose you're ready to write the procedure that will be performed whenever the user clicks the cmdMessage button on Form1. Visual Basic defines the name Click for the event that takes place when the user clicks a command button with the mouse. The procedure you'll write for this event is therefore named cmdMessage_Click, combining the name of the control (cmdMessage) with the name of the event (Click).

As you'll learn in the upcoming exercise, Visual Basic gives you an efficient way to open a window for developing an event procedure.

Step 3: Writing Code

The event procedures for the controls on a given form are saved as part of the FRM file. To open the code window for a form, all you need to do is double-click any control on the form. Visual Basic automatically starts an event procedure for the control you've selected.

In the following exercise you'll create a short event procedure for the cmdMessage control:

1. In the Form1 window, double-click the command button labeled Message. In response, Visual Basic opens the Form1 code window (Figure 1-25) and creates the first and last line of the cmdMessage_Click event procedure. A flashing cursor appears between these two lines of code, indicating that Visual Basic is ready for you to enter the actual code of the procedure.

2. Type the line **MsgBox "Hello there..."** on the line where the cursor is flashing. The three lines of the procedure now look like this:

```
Private Sub cmdMessage_Click()
  MsgBox "Hello there..."
End Sub
```

3. Now click the Start button on the toolbar or press F5. Visual Basic runs your project and displays the Form1 window with the various controls you've arranged in it.

4. Use the mouse to click the Message button, or simply press the Enter key from the keyboard. Doing so triggers the cmdMessage_Click event; accordingly, Visual Basic makes a *call* to the event procedure that you've just created. The MsgBox instruction you wrote in the procedure displays a small message box on the screen with the message "Hello there..." as shown in Figure 1-26.

5. Click OK in the message box. Then click the End button on the toolbar to end the program performance.

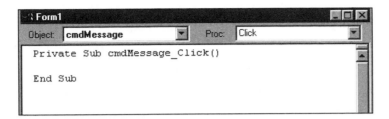

Figure 1-25
The code window for Form1.

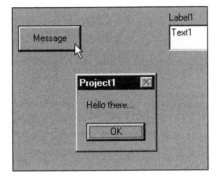

Figure 1-26
The message box resulting from a click of the Message button.

In short, you've just created and performed your first event procedure. You'll learn much more about the event-driven programming model as you continue in this book. The main point to keep in mind from this exercise is simple: Visual Basic recognizes certain events that may take place around the controls you place in a form; by writing event procedures, you define your program's reaction to those events.

Now you've finished your work with this first exercise. Because the forms you've created were merely experimental in this case, you can now abandon them without saving any files to disk. Here's how you do it:

1. Pull down the File menu and choose the New Project command.

2. A warning box appears on the desktop asking whether you want to save the files of Project1. Click No to All to abandon the entire project. In response, Visual Basic creates the elements of a new Project1, including an empty Form1 window. The environment now looks just like it did when you first started.

Getting Help

This quick tour has introduced you to the elements of the Visual Basic programming environment. The chapters ahead will fill in many more details. But before you continue, you should take a look at one more important feature — the Help window. Like all major Windows applications, Visual Basic has a useful cross-referenced help system that's never more than a few keystrokes or mouse clicks away. The Help menu provides several starting points into the system; alternatively, you can press F1 at almost any time to get *context-sensitive* help about your current activity.

Try it now. Click the Toolbox title bar to activate the window, and then press F1. In response, Visual Basic opens the Toolbox help topic (Figure 1-27), which you can scroll through to read more about the controls available for your projects. You'll see other examples of context-sensitive help later in your work.

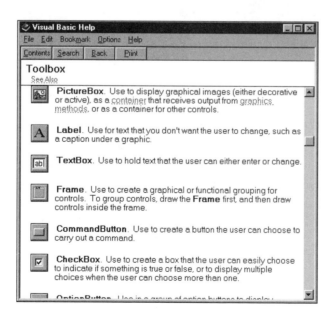

Figure 1-27
The Toolbox topic in the Visual Basic Help window.

To review what you've learned so far, the final section of this chapter takes you through the steps of opening and running a sample project from the program disk included with this book. (If you haven't copied the sample programs from the program disk to your Visual Basic directory, you should do so now.)

Running the Travel Guide Program

In the upcoming exercises you'll examine a project named the Travel Guide program, a currency exchange calculator for international business travelers. The program is designed to read a text file named CURRENCY.TXT that contains today's currency exchange rates for any number of countries. Before running the program, you need to create and store this file in the root directory of your hard disk. For example, here is a version of the file that contains rates for nine countries:

```
England, pound, 1.594500
Canada, dollar, .728700
Japan, yen, .011800
Germany, mark, .723600
France, franc, .206600
Italy, lira, .000613
Holland, guilder, .646100
Switzerland, franc, .870700
Mexico, peso, .160300
```

Notice that each line of the text file contains the name of a country, the name of the corresponding currency, and the current exchange rate in U.S. dollars. Create the file in any text editor — for example, the Windows 95 NotePad application will work just fine. On a daily basis you can download the exchange rate information from your favorite on-line service or copy it from a newspaper. But for now — if you simply want to try running the program with a typical data set — you can copy the CURRENCY.TXT file from the program disk to your root directory.

When you open a project from disk, the Project window provides access to all the form and module files that are part of the program. You can then run the program by clicking the Start button, or you can examine the program's components in the Design mode. Here are the steps for opening and running the Travel Guide project:

1. Pull down the File menu and choose Open Project, or simply click the Open Project button on the Visual Basic toolbar. The Open Project dialog box shows you a list of the project files (*.VBP) available in your Visual Basic directory (Figure 1-28). (Keep in mind that Visual Basic 4 also recognizes MAK files from previous versions of the language; for this reason, the Open Project dialog box also lists any MAK files that may be stored in your directory.)

2. Select TrvlGde and click Open. Visual Basic loads the project into memory. In the Project window (Figure 1-29) you can see that the project consists of a form (TrvlGde.Frm) and a module (CurrExch.Bas).

3. Click the Start button on the toolbar, or press F5.

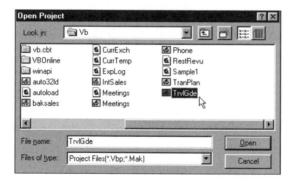

Figure 1-28
Opening a project from disk.

The program window, titled Currency Exchange Travel Guide, appears on the screen. At the upper-left corner of the window you see a combo box labeled Country. Click the down-arrow button at the right side of this box and select a country from the list, as shown in Figure 1-30. When you do so, the program window instantly fills with data, as you can see in Figure 1-31.

Figure 1-29
The Project window for the Travel Guide program.

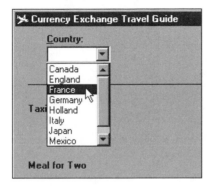

Figure 1-30
Choosing a country in the Travel Guide program.

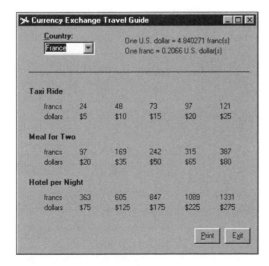

Figure 1-31
Currency exchange data supplied by the program.

The program is designed to provide currency equivalents for a variety of expenses you might incur during an international business trip. At the top of the program window, you see the basic exchange rates for the country you've selected. Below, there are three tables of exchange data, labeled "Taxi Ride," "Meal for Two," and "Hotel per Night." These categories are merely a convenient way to organize the output data; as you can see, they display currency equivalents for dollar amounts ranging from $5 to $275.

To view data for a different country, you simply pull down the Country list again and make a new selection. The data changes completely, as shown in Figure 1-32.

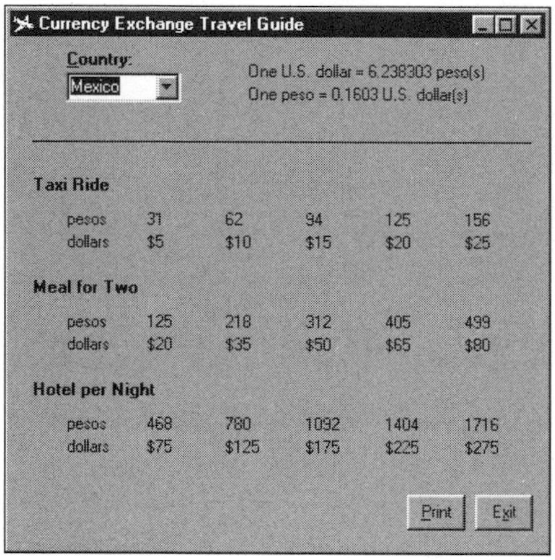

Figure 1-32

Another set of currency exchange data.

Continue experimenting with the program for a while if you want. Notice the two command buttons displayed at the lower-right corner of the program window. You can click the Print button (or press Alt+P) to print a copy of the program window and all its current data. When you're ready to stop the program, click the Exit button (or press Alt+X or simply Escape); in response, Visual Basic returns you to the Design mode.

Inside the Program

To view the program's form, select TrvlGde.Frm in the Project window and click View Form. As shown in Figure 1-33, the form contains a combo box, two command buttons, and several sets of labels. (There's also a *line control* that divides the top part of the window from the tables of data below.) Some of the labels have predefined captions that remain unchanged throughout the program run; others are blank until the program displays information in them by assigning a value to the Caption property. Like many Visual Basic properties, Caption can be set at design time in the Properties window or at runtime by your program's code.

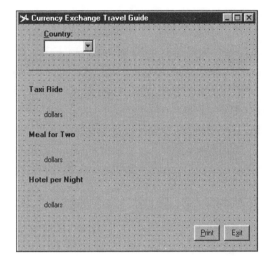

Figure 1-33
The controls in the Travel Guide project.

Among the events that the program recognizes are Click events on either of the two command buttons, and a Click event for making a selection from the Country combo box. To explore a portion of the program's code, try double-clicking the combo box now in Design mode. As you can see in Figure 1-34, the resulting code window shows an event procedure named cboCountry_Click. This procedure computes and displays the currency exchange information whenever the user selects a new country from the drop-down list.

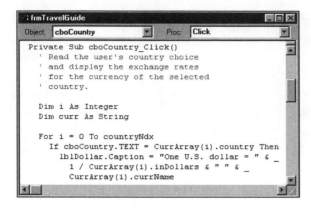

```
frmTravelGuide                                      _ □ ×
Object:  cboCountry        ▼    Proc:  Click               ▼
Private Sub cboCountry_Click()
  ' Read the user's country choice
  ' and display the exchange rates
  ' for the currency of the selected
  ' country.

  Dim i As Integer
  Dim curr As String

  For i = 0 To countryNdx
    If cboCountry.TEXT = CurrArray(i).country Then
      lblDollar.Caption = "One U.S. dollar = " & _
        1 / CurrArray(i).inDollars & " " & _
        CurrArray(i).currName
```

Figure 1-34
Exploring the code of the Travel Guide program.

In short, the Travel Guide program is a one-form project that illustrates a variety of controls, properties, and events. It gives you a first taste of Visual Basic's potential. When you're ready to close the project, pull down the File menu and choose New Project, or exit from Visual Basic altogether by choosing the Exit command.

In Chapter 2 you'll begin creating a somewhat different version of the Currency Exchange program and you'll learn more about the steps of application design in Visual Basic.

II

The Steps of Program Development

*I*n the three steps of Visual Basic program development, you arrange the controls and forms of your project, set properties of selected objects, and write the code that makes your program work. Part II introduces you to these steps in detail, and guides you through several hands-on exercises to practice the steps. As you develop a program named the International Currency Exchange application, you'll see exactly how a project looks at each stage of its design.

Chapter 2 gives you the opportunity to work through the initial design process for a new project. You'll use the Toolbox to select controls and add them to a form. You'll learn how to adjust the sizes of controls and place them at appropriate positions within the form. And finally, you'll save the components of your project to disk.

Chapter 3 explains the significance of properties in the design of a project. Each class of controls has its own list of properties that help define an object's role in your program. You'll see how various properties can change the appearance and behavior of a control, and you'll learn to use the Properties window to select their settings. You'll also investigate the properties of a form, and see how the settings affect your program.

Chapter 4 introduces Visual Basic's event-driven programming model, and shows you how to begin developing event procedures in a code window. In your first experiments with the code window, you'll notice some of the useful features of Visual Basic's built-in text editor, including color coding, syntax checking, and a direct link to context-sensitive help. After developing some simple event procedures, you'll see how they work by running your project.

2

Designing an Effective Interface

*A*n *interface* includes all the visual objects and procedural techniques that define a program's interaction with the *user*, the person sitting at the computer. How does the program get information from the user? How does the user select among the program's options? What keyboard and mouse techniques are available for giving instructions to the program? When the input data has been entered and options chosen, how does the program present the information that the user has requested? These are some of the questions you'll ask yourself as you begin designing your program's interface.

In the old days of the BASIC language — before Visual Basic appeared on the scene — programmers spent a large percentage of their time solving these particular design problems. Devising graceful ways — or practical ways, at least — to communicate with the user typically required a greater effort than any other single feature of a program. Long sections of code and many hours of programming were often devoted to the process of coordinating screen activity with the user's input from the keyboard.

But Visual Basic has changed all that, as you've already begun to learn. In the Visual Basic environment you create your program's interface by dragging controls into a form and arranging them in place. The Toolbox provides an assortment of controls that meet particular requirements in a program's design. These controls have several important benefits. They are *intuitive* — that is, a user can learn to operate them almost without any instruction. They are also *familiar*, because the same types of controls appear in all Windows applications. And — perhaps most important from your point of view as programmer — they are *ready-made;* when the program is running, the keyboard and mouse techniques for **using** those controls are built into the objects themselves. Adding these controls to your program and making them work requires little or no programming.

The first step of creating an application in Visual Basic — the step that was most time consuming in old versions of BASIC — is now the easiest and possibly the most fun: Decide how you want your program to interact with the user, and choose the best controls for carrying out that interaction. Place the controls on a form, and arrange them in a way that suits the program's requirements and satisfies your own sense of programming aesthetics. When you complete this step, your work already begins to take shape as a programming project. You can see what your program will look like and to a great extent how it will work.

This chapter guides you through the process of completing this first step for a real project. In Chapter 1 you examined the Travel Guide program, which is devoted to the arithmetic of international currency exchange. Now you'll design a second version of this program that allows the user to choose a currency and quickly calculate conversions between dollars and the selected currency. You'll begin your work by analyzing the program's purpose and choosing controls that best meet that purpose. To keep your work in perspective, you'll take a brief look at the finished project, which you'll load into Visual Basic from the program disk included with this book. Then you'll go back and work through the exercise of creating the program's interface. Along the way, you'll learn more about the Visual Basic development environment and the options it provides.

Planning the Program

Call this new project the International Currency Exchange application. Like its predecessor, this version will begin by reading a text file named CURRENCY.TXT. As you'll recall, this file contains a list of countries, the names of their currencies, and the value of each currency in dollars. For example, here's the sample data you'll find in the CURRENCY.TXT file provided on the program disk:

```
England, pound, 1.594500
Canada, dollar, .728700
Japan, yen, .011800
Germany, mark, .723600
France, franc, .206600
Italy, lira, .000613
Holland, guilder, .646100
Switzerland, franc, .870700
Mexico, peso, .160300
```

The program has only one expectation for this file. The information for each country should appear on one line in a specific order: country name, currency name, dollar value. Otherwise, you can build the file in any way you want. The countries themselves appear in no particular order. Furthermore, any number of countries can be included in the list. (As noted in Chapter 1, you can update this file on a regular basis by downloading the currency exchange information from an on-line service, or by copying it from a newspaper.)

After reading this data, the program will be ready to provide exchange rates for any country in the list, and to perform conversion calculations between dollars and any selected currency.

Choosing Controls for the Program's Features

All the program's activity will take place in a single window. Here are the features the program will offer.

A simple way to choose a country from the available list. A combo box control is a good way to provide this list, as shown in Figure 2-1. A label ("Country") just above the box identifies the purpose of the control. To use the combo box, the user starts by clicking the down-arrow icon at the right side of the box. In this program, a drop-down list of countries will appear below the box. When the user clicks an entry in the list, the selection is copied to the box itself and the list disappears.

Figure 2-1

A combo box presents a list of countries.

A clear display of the basic exchange rates, once the user has selected a country. A pair of label controls will provide this feature, as shown in Figure 2-2. Before the user chooses a country, these two labels are blank. But as soon as a country selection has been made, the program uses the labels to display two lines of text. The dollar value of the selected currency is copied directly from the information supplied in the currency text file. By contrast, the program has to calculate the value of one dollar in the selected currency. A *line control* separates this basic currency information from the calculation controls displayed in the lower half of the program window.

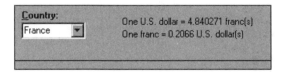

Figure 2-2

Labels display the basic currency exchange information.

A choice between currency exchange calculations. The user can choose to compute the currency equivalent of a dollar amount, or the dollar equivalent of a specified amount in the selected currency. A pair of option buttons provides this choice, as shown in Figure 2-3. Just above the buttons, a label ("Conversion:") identifies the choice to be made. The current selection is shown as a button filled with a bold dot. To change the selection, the user simply clicks the other option. Because

only one option button in a group can be selected at a time, Visual
Basic automatically clears the other button when the user makes a new
selection.

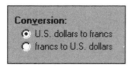

Figure 2-3
Option buttons offer a choice between calculations.

*An unambiguously labeled input box for the amount that is to be con-
verted.* As you know, a text box control is Visual Basic's tool for accepting
numeric or text input from the user at the keyboard. Figure 2-4 shows the
text box for accepting a currency amount. A flashing cursor inside the text
box indicates that the program is ready to accept an input value. Simple as
it may seem as a control, the text box is actually a full-featured editing tool.
It allows deletions, insertions, highlighting, and copy-and-paste operations.
Notice that the program labels the text box according to the selected calculation option. If the user selects the other option, the program changes the
label (Figure 2-5).

Figure 2-4
A text box for accepting a currency amount from the keyboard.

Figure 2-5
The label changes when the user select a new calculation option.

An efficient keyboard or mouse technique to instruct the program to carry out the calculation, once a monetary amount has been entered from the keyboard. A command button is the ideal control for this operation, as shown in Figure 2-6. After entering a value in the text box, the user can click the Calc button with the mouse to complete the calculation. Alternatively, if this button is designated as the *default* button control, the user can simply press the Enter key to carry out the calculation. (You'll learn more about the Default property in Chapter 3.)

Figure 2-6
A command button represents the calculation operation.

A display of the result. As soon as the user requests a new calculation, the result should appear in an obvious place in the program window. A label control located just beneath the input text box is a good solution, as in Figure 2-7. This juxtaposition gives the user a clear view of the original input value and its equivalent in the other currency.

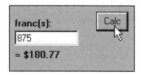

Figure 2-7
A label displays the calculated currency equivalent.

A way to clear the current data so that a new calculation can be performed. Another command button serves this purpose, as in Figure 2-8. When the user clicks the Clear button, the program clears the values from both the input text box and the label that displays the result of the calculation.

Figure 2-8
A command button that the user can click to start a new calculation.

An open-ended invitation to start the entire process over again. At any time, the user can pull down the country list to view a new set of currency exchange values. When this happens, the program immediately changes the basic exchange rates displayed in the labels to the right of the country list (Figure 2-9) and also the captions displayed next to the calculation option buttons. The user can then perform any number of calculations in the new currency.

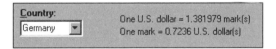

Figure 2-9
Changing the country and currency selection.

An easy keyboard or mouse technique to end the program. Another command button — typically labeled Exit — serves this purpose. To end the performance and close the program window, the user simply clicks the Exit button (Figure 2-10). Alternatively, if this button is designated as the *cancel* button, the user can simply press the Escape key on the keyboard to end the performance. (You'll learn how to define the Cancel property in Chapter 3.)

Figure 2-10
The Exit button is the user's way to stop the program.

In summary, the International Currency Exchange program will contain six types of controls, all arranged in a single form:

- A combo box that presents the list of countries
- A variety of label controls, serving either of two general purposes — identifying the purpose of other controls or displaying the results of the program's calculations
- A pair of option button controls, offering two different calculation options
- A text box control, where the user can enter a currency amount to be converted
- A set of command buttons representing three operations: completing a calculation, clearing the previous calculation, and ending the program
- A line control that divides the program window functionally into two parts

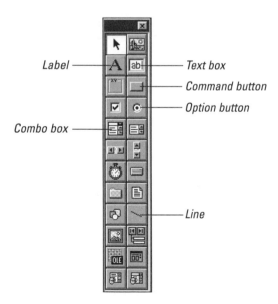

Figure 2-11
The six types of controls you'll use in the Currency Exchange project.

Figure 2-11 identifies these six controls in the Visual Basic Toolbox. (Keep in mind that the Toolbox contains additional controls and is organized differently if you are running the Professional or Enterprise editions of the product.) Once you've envisioned and planned the program's operations, the job ahead of you is clear. You need to place these controls on a form in appropriate combinations to serve the program's purposes. But before you turn to this task, take a moment now to look ahead at the program as a finished product.

Previewing the Finished Program

The International Currency Exchange application is provided on the program disk under the name CurrExch.VBP. If you've copied the contents of the program disk to your Visual Basic directory, you can follow these steps to open the program and run it:

1. Make sure you copy the CURRENCY.TXT file from the program disk to the root directory of your hard disk (or create your own currency file from today's actual currency exchange data).

2. Start Visual Basic. In Windows 95, click the Start button and choose Programs. Then choose the Visual Basic group of the Programs menu. Click Visual Basic to start the program.

3. In the Visual Basic environment, pull down the File menu and choose Open Project (or click the Open Project button on the toolbar). In the file name list, choose the CurrExch project (Figure 2-12), and then click Open to open the project into the Visual Basic development environment.

4. Take a look at the Project window for the application (Figure 2-13). The project consists of one form and one module.

5. Press F5 to start the program. When the application window (Figure 2-14) appears on the screen, you'll see that many of the program's controls are blank initially. The program doesn't fill in any specific currency information until you first select an entry from the Country list.

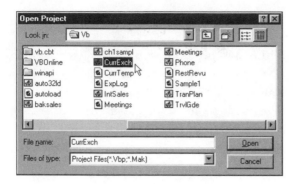

Figure 2-12

Opening the CurrExch.Mak project.

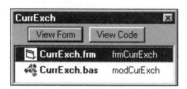

Figure 2-13

The Project window for the CurrExch.Mak program.

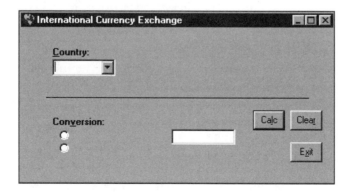

Figure 2-14

The initial appearance of the program window.

6. Start experimenting with the program. Pull down the Country list
   and select the name of a country. The program immediately displays
   the basic currency exchange information just to the right of the
   Country box. Try clicking one of the two Conversion options and
   notice the changes that take place in other controls in the program
   window. Finally, enter a currency amount in the text box and press
   Enter to instruct the program to carry out a conversion calculation.
   The result of the calculation appears just beneath the text box, in
   bold text (Figure 2-15). Continue making other selections until you
   understand exactly how the program works.

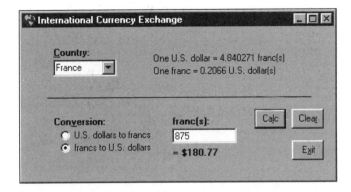

Figure 2-15
An exchange rate calculation is displayed in the program window.

7. Click the Exit button (or press the Escape key) to stop the program.
   Then pull down the File menu and choose the New Project command to clear the CurrExch program from memory. A new project
   appears, with an empty form named Form1.

In the upcoming exercise, you'll go through the steps of creating this
program's interface on your own computer. You'll use the Form1 window
currently displayed on the desktop for this exercise.

Creating the Program Window

The first step is to reposition and resize the form window itself to suit the program's design. Specifically, you'll want to decrease the dimensions of the form and approximately center the window on the desktop, as shown in Figure 2-16. To change the form's width, position the mouse pointer over the left or right side; the pointer becomes a two-headed arrow. Then drag the border line toward the center of the form to decrease the width. Likewise, drag the top or bottom border to change the form's height. To move the form to a new position on the desktop, drag the form by its title bar.

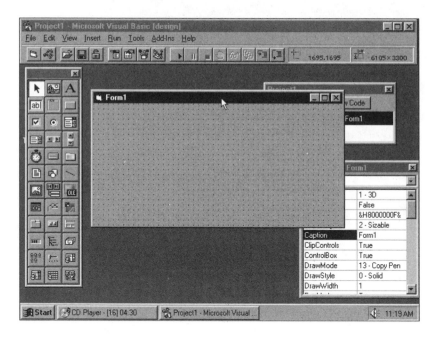

Figure 2-16
Moving the form window and decreasing its dimensions.

As you make these changes in the form window, keep in mind that you can read the current position and size measurements in the position and size indictors shown at the right side of the toolbar. Figure 2-17 shows the measurements you should attempt to achieve. The first set of numbers (1695, 1695) represents the form's position on the desktop. Specifically, the form's upper-left corner is 1695 twips across and 1695 twips down from the upper-left corner of the desktop. As you discovered in Chapter 1, these are the settings of the properties named Left and Top, respectively. The second set of measurements (6105 x 3300) represents the form's size — 6105 twips wide by 3300 twips high. These are the settings of the properties named Width and Height.

Figure 2-17
Measurements of the form's position and size.

Now you're ready to begin placing controls on the form. For each new control, you'll follow the same pattern of steps:

1. Double-click the Toolbox button that represents the control you want to add to the form. In response Visual Basic places a new control in the middle of the form, with a standard, or default, size. Sizing handles are displayed around the perimeter of the new control, indicating that the object is selected — and can be resized or moved.

2. Position the mouse pointer inside the control and drag it to a new position in the form. The position measurements (*Left, Top*) for the control are shown in the position indicator just to the right of the toolbar. These measurements represent the object's position in relation to the upper-left corner of the containing form.

3. Position the mouse pointer over any of the sizing handles displayed around the perimeter of the control, and drag the handle to change the size of the object. Again, the size measurements (*Height* x *Width*) are shown in the size indicator to the right of the toolbar.

Adding Controls to the Form

You'll begin your work by placing a line control across the middle of the form. This will help you orient the remainder of your work. Then you'll add the six labels that the program uses to identify other controls and to display calculated data in the window:

1. Double-click the line control in the Toolbox. (See Figure 2-11 if you forget where this button is located.) Visual Basic places a diagonal line in the center of Form1, as shown in Figure 2-18. A sizing handle is located at each end of the line. Drag these handles to create a horizontal line that extends across almost the entire width of the form, as in Figure 2-19. The line's position measurements are 480, 1320, and its size measurements are 5055 x 15.

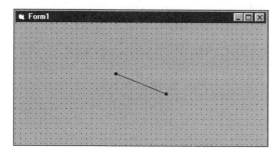

Figure 2-18
The default length and position of a new line control.

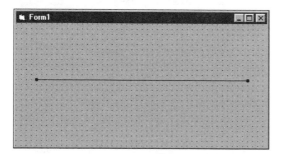

Figure 2-19
Moving and resizing the line.

2. Now double-click the label control, shown as a boldface A in the Toolbox. A new control named Label1 appears in the center of the form. Drag the label toward the upper-left corner of the form, to the position 600, 360. Then resize the label to the dimensions 735 x 255, as in Figure 2-20. Eventually this label will serve to identify the Country list.

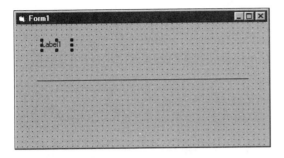

Figure 2-20
Adding the first label to the form.

3. Double-click the Label in the Toolbox two more times. In response, Visual Basic adds Label2 and Label3 to the form. (Whenever you add multiple objects of the same type to a form, the default names are numbered in this same manner — for example, Option1 and Option2, or Command1, Command2, and Command3.) These two new labels will display the basic exchange rates for a selected country. Move both labels toward the upper-right corner of the form, to positions 2520, 480 and 2520, 720, respectively. Then resize both labels to the same dimensions: 2895 x 255. Figure 2-21 shows Form1 at this stage in your work.

4. Add the three remaining labels to the form, as shown in Figure 2-22. Label4 will eventually identify the conversion options; move it to 600, 1680 and assign it dimensions of 1095 x 255. Label5 will identify the text box; its position is 2880, 1680 and its size is 1215 x 255. Finally, Label6 will display the result of each new currency exchange calculation. Drag it to 2880, 2280 and assign it a size of 2175 x 495.

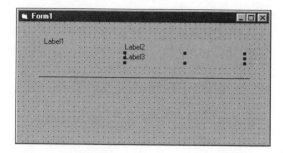

Figure 2-21
Adding labels to display currency exchange data.

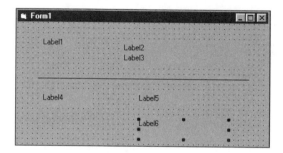

Figure 2-22
Adding the rest of the labels to the form.

5. Now your form is ready for the controls that the user can interact with in one way or another — the combo box, the option buttons, the text box, and the command buttons. Begin by double-clicking the combo box control in the Toolbox. Visual Basic places the Combo1 control in the center of the form. Drag it to its correct position (600, 600). It can retain its default dimensions of 1215 x 315, as in Figure 2-23.

6. Double-click the option button control twice in the Toolbox. Option1 and Option2 appear in the center of the form. Resize both buttons to dimensions of 2055 x 255. Drag Option1 to 720, 1920 and Option2 to 720, 2160 (Figure 2-24).

7. Double-click the text box control once in the Toolbox. Drag the Text1 control to 2880, 1920. Then resize it to the dimensions 1215 x 285 (Figure 2-25).

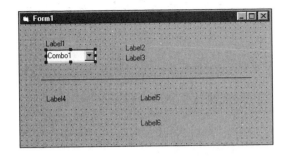

Figure 2-23
Adding a combo box to the form.

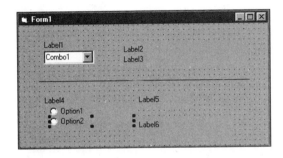

Figure 2-24
Adding two option buttons to the form.

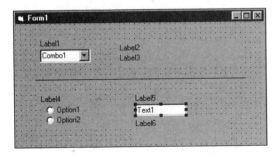

Figure 2-25
Adding a text box to the form.

8. Finally, double-click the control button in the Toolbox three times, to add Command1, Command2, and Command3 to the form. Reduce the dimensions of all three buttons to 615 x 375. Then drag Command1 to 4440, 1560, Command2 to 5160, 1560, and Command3 to 5160, 2160. Click the mouse at any blank area of Form1 to deselect all controls. Figure 2-26 shows your work.

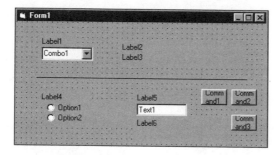

Figure 2-26
Arranging three command buttons on the form.

After all the effort of placing each control at its precise position inside the form, you'll now want to protect your work from inadvertent changes. You can do this by clicking the Lock Controls tool, the fifth button on the toolbar (Figure 2-27). In response, Visual Basic freezes all the controls on the current form. This tool is a *toggle*. Clicking the tool once turns the lock feature on, and clicking the tool again turns it off. If you later want to make changes in the position or size of a control, you can simply click the Lock Controls button to unfreeze the controls temporarily. (By the way, this button is a shortcut for the Lock Controls command in Visual Basic's Edit menu.)

Figure 2-27
The Lock Controls button can be toggled on or off.

Saving Your Work

In Chapter 3 you'll continue your work on this form, focusing on a variety of properties for each control in the program. For now, the final task remaining in this exercise is to save your work to disk. You'll begin by saving Form1 as a FRM file on disk. Then you'll save the current Project1 as a VBP file:

1. Make sure Form1 is the active window on the desktop. (If it isn't, click its title bar with the mouse.) Then pull down the File menu and choose the Save File As command. In the resulting dialog box, enter CurrTemp in the File name box, as shown in Figure 2-28. Then click Save to save the FRM file to disk.

2. Pull down the File menu again and choose the Save Project As command. In the resulting dialog box, enter CurrTemp in the File name box and click Save, as shown in Figure 2-29. Visual Basic saves your project as CurrTemp.VBP. When you want to return to your work on this project, you'll open it under this name.

3. Now pull down the File menu again and choose New Project. Visual Basic clears your work from the desktop and opens new Project1 and Form1 windows.

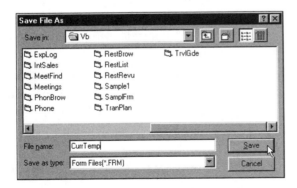

Figure 2-28
Saving the form to disk.

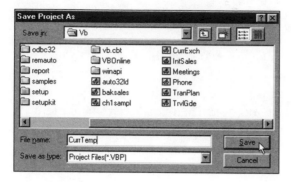

Figure 2-29
Saving the project.

Adjusting the Form Design Grid

Throughout this exercise you've arranged controls on Form1 within
Visual Basic's *standard form grid*. This grid is represented by the rows
and columns of dots that appear in the background of every form at
design time. (The grid disappears when you run a program.) As you've
noticed, all the changes you make in the size and position of a control
are aligned to this grid by default. For most projects, the grid is a great
benefit; it helps you to arrange groups of controls in relation to each
other and to resize controls appropriately.

But sometimes you may prefer to work without the grid so that
you'll have more freedom to move controls wherever you want them.
Or, you may want to change the distance between the rows or columns
of dots that make up the grid itself. Visual Basic allows you to make
both of these changes. To see how, pull down the Tools menu and
choose Options. Make sure the Environment tab is selected in the resulting dialog box. In the upper-left section of the box (Figure 2-30) you
can see the options available for changing the grid:

- To make the grid invisible, click the Show Grid check box. (The
  check disappears from the check box.)

- To change the dimensions of the grid, enter new values into the Width and Height boxes. By default, the rows and columns of the grid are spaced 120 pixels apart.

- To deactivate the grid altogether, clear the check box labeled Align Controls to Grid.

After making any changes you want in the structure of the grid, click OK to confirm your choices.

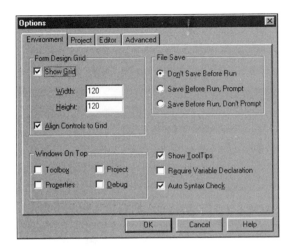

Figure 2-30
The Environment options for changing the form design grid.

Looking Ahead

You've now completed the first step of application development — arranging controls on a form, and saving your work to disk. Comparing Figure 2-26 with the final version of the program (Figure 2-15), you can see that the project is already beginning to take shape. But there's still a lot of work left to do. For one thing, you'll need to change the captions and names of almost all the controls in the form. There are also several other property settings that will help define the behavior and performance of your program. You'll learn about these properties in Chapter 3.

3 Defining Properties

*A*s you've learned, the first step of Visual Basic application development is to create and arrange the visual objects of a project — for example, to open a form and place a relevant selection of controls within its boundaries. This step takes place interactively on the desktop, almost as if Visual Basic were a special kind of Paint program in which you draw your plans for a program's visual interface.

In the second step, often just as dramatic as the first, you set the *properties* of individual objects, including forms and the controls they contain. Each type of control — command button, text box, label, option button, and so on — has its own list of properties that apply specifically to the object's design. Working with these properties, you refine your program's appearance and function, sometimes in surprisingly subtle ways. Not only can you change obvious features — such as the captions displayed on buttons, or the text fonts used in labels — but you can also modify the behavior of your program and the quality of its interaction with the user. For example, you'll find properties that determine

- What keyboard shortcut sequences a command button will respond to
- How items will be arranged in a list
- When a given control will receive the *focus* in response to repeated pressing of the Tab key
- Whether a control will be active or inactive, visible or not, at a given point in the program run

Like the controls themselves, properties are clearly intended to streamline the process of creating an application. Many features that require major programming effort in other languages are achieved in Visual Basic with the simple selection of a property setting. In this chapter you'll continue exploring the properties for specific controls, and you'll learn more about what they can mean for your applications.

Setting Properties at Design Time or Runtime

Many properties can be set at either design time or runtime. You've already had some experience with these two distinct operating modes in the Visual Basic environment. At design time, you add controls to a project, set properties, and write code. During runtime, you examine your program in action, just as an end-user will eventually see it.

You follow a familiar pattern of steps to set a property at design time:

1. Select the control or object whose characteristics you want to change.

2. Activate the Properties window.

3. Scroll to the property you want to set and select its name.

4. Enter a new setting.

You'll go through these steps many times during this chapter's hands-on exercises.

At runtime, property settings can be changed by a program's code. You accomplish this by writing a special kind of assignment statement that gives a new value to a specific property of a selected control:

```
controlName.propertyName = value
```

At the left side of this assignment statement, *controlName.property-Name* is a compound name identifying the control and the property that is to be reset. The *value* on the right side of the statement gives the new setting. When a program resets a property at runtime, the new setting overrides the value assigned at design time.

This is an important general point to keep in mind as you begin creating a new program. Design-time settings need not be permanent during a program run. For example, a label may display a particular design-time caption at the outset, but that caption may change many times during a program run, as your code assigns new values to the label's Caption property.

But for the moment, you can postpone worrying about code. In this chapter you'll concentrate instead on the simple and direct techniques for assigning property settings at design time. Your focus will be on the Properties window and its two-column list of properties and settings. To explore this feature, you'll return to the project you began designing in Chapter 2 — a version of the International Currency Exchange program that you've stored on disk as CurrTemp.Mak. To get started, follow these steps to open the project and display its form on the desktop:

1. Choose Visual Basic from the Windows 95 Start menu.

2. When the elements of the Visual Basic environment appear on the desktop, pull down the File menu. The CurrTemp.Mak program should be listed near the bottom of the menu, as shown in Figure 3-1. Click the program's name to open the project. (If the name doesn't appear in the File menu, choose the Open Project command instead and select the program's name from the resulting dialog box.)

3. If the program's Project window doesn't immediately appear on the desktop, press Ctrl+R to display it.

4. Click the View Form button to open the form named CurrTemp.Frm onto the desktop.

When you complete these steps, the form you created in Chapter 2 reappears on the desktop, as shown in Figure 3-2. In the exercises ahead, you'll change the properties of most controls on this form. In doing so, you'll make significant progress in completing the design of your program.

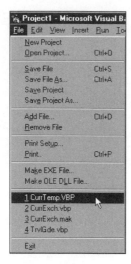

Figure 3-1
The list of recently opened projects at the bottom of the File menu.

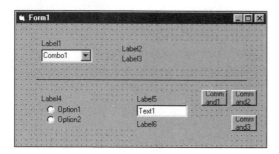

Figure 3-2
The form you began designing in Chapter 2.

Changing the Properties of Labels

This form contains six labels, currently displaying captions from Label1 to Label6. Your first job is to change these captions appropriately. As you may recall from your work with the final version of the program, shown again in Figure 3-3, several of these labels are meant to display information that may change frequently during a program run. For example, Label2 and Label3 will show the basic currency exchange rates for a selected country, and Label6 will display a calculated currency conversion. At the outset of the program, these three labels, along with Label5, should therefore have blank captions.

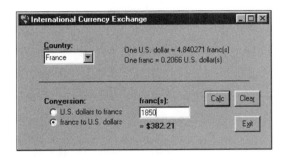

Figure 3-3
Reviewing the final version of the Currency Exchange program.

Only the captions for Label1 and Label4 remain unchanged throughout the program run. Label1 displays the word Country, identifying the purpose of the combo box below it; and Label4 displays the word Conversion, representing the choice offered in the pair of option buttons below.

But take a closer look at these two labels in Figure 3-3. Each caption contains an underlined letter — the *C* in Country, and the *v* in Conversion. This underlining identifies the *access keys* (sometimes called *keyboard shortcuts*) for the corresponding controls. During a run of the program, the user can press Alt+C to activate the Country list, or Alt+V to choose a Conversion option. This is a small but important design element for a person who prefers to use the keyboard rather than the mouse to control the action of a program.

You therefore have several tasks ahead of you in setting the captions of the program's six labels: Create blank captions for the four labels that are reserved for numeric output, supply the program's two fixed labels, and define two of the program's access keys.

Captions and Access Keys

The Caption property gives you simple ways to accomplish all these tasks. To create a caption, you choose the property and then enter the text of your caption as the new setting. (To create a blank caption, you delete the default setting and leave it empty.) To define an access key, you place an ampersand character (&) just before the letter that you want to be underlined in the text of the caption. For example, the following setting defines Alt+V as the access key:

        Con&version

In the label itself, this caption appears as

        Conversion

Starting with Label1 and Label4, then, here are the steps for setting the Caption property — first for the labels and then for several other controls in your program:

1. Click Label1, near the upper-left corner of Form1. When you do so, handles appear around the perimeter of the label. Because Form1 is currently locked, the handles are represented by unfilled squares, indicating that the control is protected from inadvertent moves or resizing.

2. Press F4 to activate the Properties window. The Caption property may be selected automatically, as shown in Figure 3-4. If it's not, click Caption in the first column of the window.

Figure 3-4
Preparing to set the Caption property.

3. Type **&Country:** and press Enter to confirm the setting. Back in Form1, notice that the label appears as <u>C</u>ountry:.

4. Now click Label4 in the form.

5. Begin typing the new Caption setting, **Con&version:**. Because you've already established Caption as the current property, Visual Basic automatically activates the Properties window and accepts your new setting. Press Enter to confirm.

6. Click Label2 and press F4 to activate the Properties window. In the column on the right, the current Caption setting, Label2, is highlighted. Press Delete. The Caption setting is now blank.

7. Repeat Step 6 for Label3, Label5, and Label6. At this point in your work, Form1 appears as in Figure 3-5. You've successfully set the initial Caption properties for the six labels.

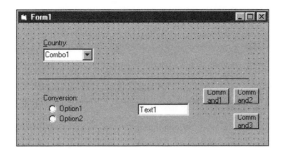

Figure 3-5
Completing the Caption settings for labels.

Because Caption is currently selected in the Properties window, this is a convenient moment to set the captions for other controls in Form1, specifically the three command buttons and the two option buttons. Note in Figure 3-3 that each of the command button captions is to include an access key; by contrast, the option button captions are initially blank.

1. Begin by clicking Command1 and typing **Ca&lc** from the keyboard. The caption on this button is displayed as Ca<u>l</u>c.

2. Reactivate Form1 and click Command2. Type **Clea&r** as the caption. Finally, select Command3 and type **E&xit**.

3. Now click Option1 in the form. Press F4 to activate the Properties window. Press Delete to create a blank caption. Press Enter to confirm.

4. Repeat step 3 for the Option2 control. Form1 now appears as in Figure 3-6.

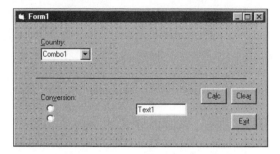

Figure 3-6
Setting the captions for command buttons and option buttons.

All the initial captions for your application are now set. But an important step remains in creating the access keys for the Country list and the Conversion options. Specifically, you need a way to link the access keys — as defined in the label captions — with the actual controls they'll activate: Alt+C for the combo box and Alt+V for the option buttons. Your tool for accomplishing this is a property called TabIndex.

TabIndex and the Focus of Controls

The Tab key is a universal shortcut for moving among the controls in a Windows dialog box. When a dialog box is open, pressing Tab moves you forward from one control to the next; pressing Shift+Tab moves you to the *previous* control. This action is sometimes called *moving the focus*.

Within a dialog box, only one control has the focus at a time. When a given control receives the focus, a small but distinctive change occurs in the control's appearance. For example, a dotted rectangle is displayed around the caption in a command button or option button; or a flashing vertical cursor appears inside a text box or a combo box. When you see this change, you know that the control is ready to record an entry or accept a selection from the keyboard.

In a Visual Basic project, you use the TabIndex property to define the *order* in which controls will receive the focus when the user presses the Tab key. By default, this property is established by the order in which you originally place controls on a form. The first control has a TabIndex setting of 0; the second, 1; the third, 2; and so on. In addition, a property called TabStop indicates whether or not a given control will receive the focus in response to tabbing.

Significantly, a label control has a TabIndex property, but no TabStop property. By definition, labels never have the focus at runtime. All the same, a label's TabIndex setting is essential for completing the definition of an access key. For example, you've used the ampersand in &Country to identify Alt+C as the access key in the Country label. Now to associate Alt+C specifically with the combo box located below the label, you have to make sure that the label and the combo box have *consecutive* TabIndex settings. If the label has a TabIndex setting of 0, the combo box must have a setting of 1.

In the following steps, you'll enter new TabIndex settings for several of the controls on Form1. You actually have two goals in this exercise: first, to make sure the access keys work the way you want them to; and second, to provide a sensible tab order for moving the focus from one control to another in the form. You'll begin your work by examining the current TabIndex setting for the Country label:

1. Click the Country label, at the upper-left corner of the form.

2. Press F4 to activate the Properties window, and scroll down to the TabIndex property. Notice that the label's default TabIndex setting is 0. (Although this label was the *second* control that you placed on the form, it is the first that has a TabIndex property. The property doesn't apply to the line control, which was the first item you placed in the form.)

3. Now select the combo box control, just beneath the Country label in the form. The current TabIndex setting for the combo box is 6.

4. Select TabIndex in the Properties window and enter **1** as the control's new setting. This consecutive tab order ensures that the label's Alt+C shortcut key will activate the Country combo box list.

5. Repeat this process to change the TabIndex settings for seven more controls on the form, as shown in the following list:

Control	*TabIndex setting*
Conversion (label)	2
Option1 (option button)	3
Option2 (option button)	4
Text1 (text box)	5
Calc (command button)	6
Clear (command button)	7
Exit (command button)	8

You've set the TabIndex property for the two label controls that define shortcut keys for other controls in the form. Other settings in the list create a convenient tab order for using the controls in the form.

At design time, the TabIndex property has no immediate visual impact on the form; its influence is evident only at runtime. For a quick demonstration, try running the project now:

1. Press F5 or click the Start button on the toolbar. A caption on the Visual Basic title bar tells you that you're now in the Run mode. A flashing cursor appears in the Country combo box, indicating that this control has the focus initially.

2. Press the Tab key five times and watch as the focus moves through the other controls in the form, in the order you've defined in the TabIndex property — first the Conversion buttons, then the text box, and then the three command buttons.

3. Now try the access keys. For example, press Alt+L. The focus moves to the Calc button. (When you later write a procedure in your program's code to define the *action* of the Calc button, Alt+L will carry out that action.) Next try pressing Alt+C. The focus moves to the Country combo box.

4. When you've finished experimenting, click the End button on the toolbar to return to the Design mode.

You still have several changes to make in the appearance of your form. For example, notice back in Figure 3-3 that four of the label captions are displayed in boldface type. To achieve this effect, you use the Font property.

The Font Property

As you might guess, the Font property gives you access to a variety of typographical effects. You can use the options of this property to select any of the available fonts in your installation of Windows. You can also change the point size and you can select styles, including boldfacing. The Font property is available for many controls that display text, such as text boxes, command buttons, option buttons, combo boxes, and labels.

Unlike the properties you've worked with so far, Font provides a range of options in a special dialog box that appears on the desktop. You'll examine this dialog box in the following steps:

1. Click the Country label.

2. Press F4 to activate the Properties window. Inside the window, scroll to and select the Font property. Notice the small button labeled **...** at the right side of the property setting box (Figure 3-7).

3. Click the **...** button once. In response, Visual Basic opens the Font dialog box, as shown in Figure 3-8. Take a moment to examine the options provided in this box. The scrollable Font list contains the names of the available fonts on your system. The Font style list contains four special typographical options (including Bold, which you'll select shortly). The Size list provides a range of point sizes for the current font selection. Additional options are available in the lower half of the dialog box.

4. In the Font style list, click the Bold option. Then click OK to confirm your selection and close the dialog box. Back in Form1, the Country caption now appears in boldface type.

5. Repeat steps 1 to 4 for three additional labels: the Conversion label and the blank labels located just above and just below the text box.

Figure 3-7
The Font property.

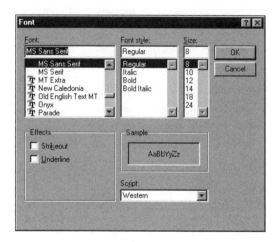

Figure 3-8
The Font dialog box.

Now Form1 appears as in Figure 3-9. You can see the boldface effect in the two non blank label captions. Boldfacing will appear in the other labels when the program displays text in them.

Next you'll turn to the Name property. As you may recall, this property defines a name by which a given control is identified in code. The default Name property for a label is the same as the caption originally displayed in the label (Label1, Label2, Label3, and so on). By supplying a more descriptive control name, you can ensure that your code will ultimately be more readable and easier to understand.

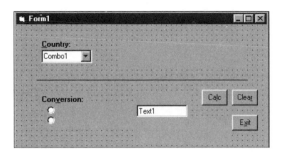

Figure 3-9
Applying the boldface style to label captions.

The two labels for which you've supplied nonblank captions (Country and Conversion) will never be referred to in your program's code, because their captions are fixed and they serve exclusively to identify the purpose of other controls. For these reason, you don't need to bother changing the default Name settings of these two labels. Conversely, the four labels that currently have blank captions will appear repeatedly in your code; specifically, the program will assign new Caption settings to these labels as a means of displaying the currency exchange information that the user requests. In the next exercise you'll change the Name settings for these four labels and other controls that need names in this project.

The Name Property

The Visual Basic documentation makes a good general suggestion regarding your choice of names for the controls in a project: Begin each name with a consistent three-letter prefix that identifies the control type. For example, begin a label name with *lbl*, a combo box with *cbo*, an option button with *opt*, a text box with *txt*, and a command button with *cmd*. As you begin writing code, this naming convention will help you keep track of the types of objects your program is working with. All the projects presented in this book follow this practice.

Here, then, are the names you'll assign to the eleven controls that will be referred to in the program's code:

Default name	New Name setting
Label2	lblDollar
Label3	lblCurrency
Label5	lblConvCurr
Label6	lblConvText
Combo1	cboCountry
Option1	optDollarsTo
Option2	optCurrTo
Text1	txtConvAmount
Command1	cmdCalc
Command2	cmdClear
Command3	cmdExit

Follow these steps to set the Name property for these controls, starting with Label2:

1. Click the blank label at the upper-right corner of the form; this control is currently named Label2.

2. Press F4 to activate the Properties window.

3. Scroll down to the Name property in the window, and click the property name to select it.

4. Type the new Name setting, **lblDollar**, and press Enter.

5. On Form1, click the next label, currently named Label3. Then type the new Name setting, **lblCurrency**. (Visual Basic automatically activates the Properties window and accepts your entry as the new Name setting.)

6. Repeat step 5 for each of the remaining controls in the list — first the labels, then the combo box, option buttons, and text box, and finally the command buttons.

The Name setting has no visible effect on the forms or controls of your project. But the meaningful control names you've created will help clarify your program's code, as you'll see in Chapter 4.

Before you continue, this would be a good time to save your work to disk. To do so, you can simply click the Save Project button on the toolbar (or choose the Save Project command from the File menu). In response, Visual Basic saves any changes you've made in any file component of your current project. In this case, Form1, saved on disk as CurrTemp.Frm, is the only file you've changed.

Next you'll look at some examples of properties that affect your program's behavior. Specifically, you'll focus on the combo box and the command button controls, and you'll examine properties that make these controls more convenient to work with from the user's point of view.

Combo Box Properties

As you'll recall, the combo box in this project provides a scrollable list of countries available in the CURRENCY.TXT file. When you first run the program, the box is empty. To select a country, you click the down-arrow button at the right side of the box. A drop-down list of countries appears on the screen, as shown in Figure 3-10. Interestingly enough, the program reads these countries and first assigns them to the combo box list in the order in which they appear in the CURRENCY.TXT file:

```
England, pound, 1.594500
Canada, dollar, .728700
Japan, yen, .011800
Germany, mark, .723600
France, franc, .206600
Italy, lira, .000613
Holland, guilder, .646100
Switzerland, franc, .870700
Mexico, peso, .160300
```

But, as you can see in Figure 3-10, the combo box displays the list in alphabetical order. Does this mean that you need to write a procedure that sorts the list before your program displays it? No, it doesn't. Visual Basic takes care of this detail automatically, in response to a simple property setting. The name of the property is Sorted.

Figure 3-10
The alphabetized list of countries in the combo box list.

To explore the Sorted property and its available settings, follow these steps:

1. Click the combo box control, near the upper-left corner of Form1.

2. Press F4 to activate the Properties window, and then scroll to the Sorted property and select its name in the property list. This property determines whether the elements of a list will appear in alphabetical order or in the original order in which they are assigned to the list. Notice that the default setting is False; this means that sorting will *not* occur.

3. Click the down-arrow button at the right side of the property setting. As you can see in Figure 3-11, there are only two settings available for the Sorted property — True and False.

4. Click the True setting.

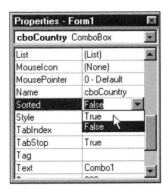

Figure 3-11
The Sorted property for a combo box.

That's all there is to it. Thanks to this simple setting, the country list will appear in alphabetical order in your program, regardless of the order of countries in the original data file. As you can see, the Sorted property is an example of a setting that enhances your program's performance without any programming effort on your part.

While you're working on the properties of the combo box, take this opportunity to select the Text property, which represents the current value displayed inside the combo box itself. (The setting of the Text property changes at runtime each time the user selects a new item in the drop-down list. Your program therefore reads the user's selection by referring to this property.) At the beginning of the program run, this control should be blank:

1. Double-click the default Text setting, displayed as Combo1.

2. Press Delete on your keyboard.

3. Press Enter to confirm. Notice in Form1 that the combo box is now empty.

4. While the Text property is selected in the Properties window, select the text box in Form1. As with a combo box, the Text property represents the current contents of a text box. Select and delete the current setting of this property, displayed as Text1. When you do so, the text box in Form1 is displayed as an empty box, as shown in Figure 3-12.

5. Click the Save Project button on the toolbar again to update your project on disk.

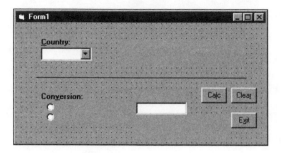

Figure 3-12
Blank Text settings for the combo box and text box.

Next you'll examine two command button properties that make your program easier to use from the keyboard.

Command Button Properties

You've already used the Caption property to supply access keys for the project's three command buttons. For example, you entered a Caption setting of **Ca&lc** for the first of the three command buttons. When the user types a numeric value into the currency text box, the purpose of clicking the Calc button is to instruct the program to perform the currency conversion — from dollars to the currently selected international currency, or vice versa. Thanks to the access key, a mouse-averse user will be able to press Alt+L from the keyboard as a substitute for clicking the Calc button.

An access key like this one is an important feature; but in many programs you may want to provide *several* ways to accomplish the same task. Redundancy in design is often the key to ease-of-use at runtime.

In this project, the most natural technique for requesting a currency calculation is perhaps to press the Enter key upon completing the input into the text box. Accordingly, you might want to add this feature to your program: Pressing Enter should be equivalent to clicking the Calc button.

Likewise, the user already has two ways of selecting the program's Exit button — click the button or press Alt+X. But because this project consists of a single dialog box, a simpler way to end the program would be to press the Escape key. Here, then, is another feature you might like to build into your program — recognizing the Escape key as a signal to terminate a run.

Visual Basic supplies two command button properties that automatically implement these two features. The properties are named Default and Cancel, and they each have two possible settings, True or False:

- A Default setting of True for a particular command button means that the user can press Enter from the keyboard to select the button.

- A Cancel setting of True for a particular command button means that the user can press Escape from the keyboard to select the button.

Each of these properties has a default setting of False for every command button you place on a form. If you decide to make use of these features, you should change the Default setting to True for only one command button and change the Cancel setting to True for a different command button.

In the Currency Exchange program, you'll designate the Calc button as the default — that is, the button that is selected when the user presses Enter. Then you'll establish the Exit button as the cancel setting — that is, the button selected when the user presses Escape. Here are the steps for accomplishing this:

1. Select the Calc button in Form1 and then press F4 to activate the Properties window.

2. Select Default in the property list.

3. Change the property's setting to True by pressing T at the keyboard. (Alternatively, you can select the True setting from the drop-down list attached to the property.)

4. Select the Exit button in Form1 and press F4 again to activate the Properties window.

5. Select the Cancel property.

6. Press T to change the setting to True.

Now activate Form1 again and take a close list at the trio of command buttons at the lower-right corner of the form. Do you notice a small change that has taken place in one of the buttons? As shown in Figure 3-13, the Calc button is now enclosed in a slightly bolder border than the other two buttons. This visual effect indicates that Calc is now the form's default button.

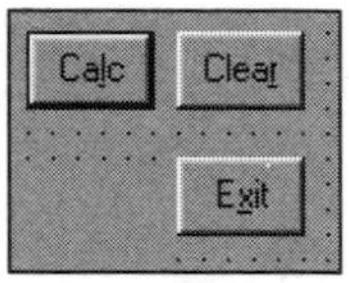

Figure 3-13
Calc has become the form's default button.

Like the Sorted property, Default and Cancel make small but important changes in your program's behavior and performance. Attention to this level of detail is what ultimately makes a program easy and inviting to use. Visual Basic encourages you to think carefully about how your user will operate the features of your program. In addition, once you've considered the best ways to design your interface, Visual Basic supplies tools and properties that make many of your design decisions very easy to implement.

Finally, take a quick look at three properties that apply to forms.

Form Properties

The Currency Exchange program uses Form1 to elicit input from the user and to display calculated information about currencies. From the user's point of view, this window *is* the program. Consequently, you'll want to identify this window as clearly and definitively as possible, by placing the program's name — and a representative icon — on the window's title bar. In a form, the Caption property specifies the text displayed on the title bar.

Furthermore, a special form property named Icon allows you to select a predesigned icon graphic (supplied on disk in the Visual Basic directory) to be displayed at the far upper-left corner of the form window.

A form also has a Name property. As with other objects in a Visual Basic property, a form's Name setting provides an identifier for the form in your program's code. In this chapter's final exercise, you'll change these three properties — Caption, Icon, and Name — for the form currently named Form1:

1. Click the mouse in a blank area of Form1 — that is, at a position where no control is displayed. (Be careful not to click inside one of the blank labels.)

2. Press F4 to activate the Properties window for the form.

3. Select the Caption property, and enter **International Currency Exchange** as the setting. Notice that this text now appears inside the form's title bar.

4. Select the Icon property, and then click the **...** button displayed at the right side of the property setting. In response, Visual Basic displays a dialog box named Load Icon, as shown in Figure 3-14.

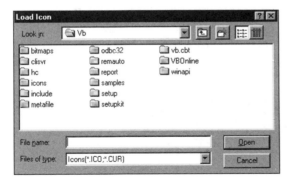

Figure 3-14
The Load Icon dialog box.

5. Double-click the Icons folder. Then scroll down the list of subfolders, and double-click the folder named elements. In response, the File Name list shows a collection of ICO files (Figure 3-15) — graphics files that can be used as icons in Visual Basic programs.

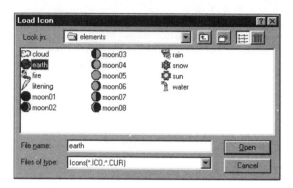

Figure 3-15
Icon files available in the Load Icon dialog box.

6. Select the earth icon in the list. This file represents a globe icon.

7. Click Open. On Form1, notice that the globe icon appears in the title bar, just to the left of the program's name (Figure 3-16). This icon represents the control menu for the form. When you click the icon (either during design time or runtime), a special menu of control commands drops down onto the window.

Figure 3-16
Adding an icon to the title bar of a form.

8. Finally, scroll down to the Name property, and select it in the property list.

9. Enter **frmCurrExch** as the new name for the form. (Notice the use of *frm* as the prefix for the form name; as before, these three letters will help you identify the object type that the name represents.)

10. Now press Ctrl+R to activate the Project window. As shown in Figure 3-17, the new form name is recorded in this window, just next to the file name for the form.

Figure 3-17
Changing the Name setting for a form.

11. Click the Save Project button on the Visual Basic toolbar to save your work to disk. (When you do so, Visual Basic creates a new file named CurrTemp.FRX to record the icon you've selected for the project's form. Although this file is not listed in the Project window, you can confirm that it has been created by examining the contents of your Visual Basic folder.) You can now exit from Visual Basic by choosing the Exit command from the File menu.

The Next Step

You've seen the effects of several important properties in this chapter. The Caption, Font, and Text properties change your project's appearance on the screen. The TabIndex, Sorted, Default, and Cancel properties define specific aspects of your program's behavior at runtime. This is only a small sampling of the many properties that apply to Visual Basic controls. You'll learn about many others as you continue in this book.

Now you're ready to develop the procedures that your program will be capable of carrying out. For that, you finally turn your attention to coding, the subject of Chapter 4.

4

Writing Code

*A*fter planning a project's appearance and features, your next step is to begin the essential activity of programming — writing code. Individual sections of code, known as *procedures*, define what your program will be able to do.

In this chapter you'll learn to use a variety of tools designed to simplify the process of developing code. Specifically, you'll look at the Code window and see how it's organized; you'll practice writing some short event procedures; and you'll see how to get help with any element of the Visual Basic language.

Of course, program development in Visual Basic is not always a strictly linear process, flowing neatly in three distinct steps. Once you start writing code, you may often find yourself going back and revising certain elements of your basic design. For example, you may want to rearrange the controls in a form, add new objects to your program, or assign new property settings to certain controls.

Even so, the code itself is always the most challenging part of the project. Fortunately, Visual Basic's *event-driven* programming model gives you a clear path for organizing the work ahead of you. Once you've arranged the forms and controls that represent your program's on-screen interface, these very objects represent the procedures you'll write to complete the project.

Planning Event Procedures

Event procedures allow your program to react appropriately to the user's activities during runtime. If the user clicks a button, selects an option, changes a setting, or enters a data item, a specific event procedure determines the program's response. Knowing this, you can easily see what procedures you need to write to complete a project. Here, then, are the general steps for planning your code:

1. Identify the controls around which the main events of your program will take place — for example, the command buttons that the user can click, the text boxes where the user can enter text, and the lists from which the user selects options.

2. Determine the specific events you expect to take place around these controls.

3. Write the procedures that define your program's action when any one of these events takes place.

As you'll recall, the name of an event procedure is a combination of two predefined identifiers:

- The Name property you've assigned to the control around which the event takes place

- The name that Visual Basic defines for the event itself

In the procedure name, these two identifiers are separated by an underscore character (_), in the following format:

```
ControlName_EventName
```

For example, consider the command button named *cmdClear* in the Currency Exchange program you've been developing. This button represents a specific operation in the program: When the user clicks the button, you want your program to clear certain parts of the dialog box in preparation for a new calculation. Visual Basic's name for the event that takes place when the user clicks a button is — simply enough — *Click*. Accordingly, you know that the procedure you need to write for this operation is named:

```
cmdClear_Click
```

This procedure will take control whenever the user clicks the Clear button.

You develop individual event procedures in a Code window. Each form in a project has a Code window that you can open at any time.

The Code Window

There are two convenient ways to open a Code window:

- Activate the Project window (press Ctrl+R) and select the form in which you want to create a new procedure. Then click the View Code button in the Project window.

- Activate the form and double-click the control for which you want to create a new event procedure. (Alternatively, select a control and press F7.) In response, Visual Basic automatically writes the first and last lines of an event procedure for you.

To get started with this chapter's exercises, you'll begin now by reopening your unfinished version of the Currency Exchange program and taking a first look at the Code window:

1. Pull down the File menu and choose CurrTemp.VBP from the list of projects at the bottom of the menu list. (Alternatively, choose the Open command to open the project.)

2. Press Ctrl+R if necessary to open the Project window. The project currently consists of a single form file, named CurrTemp.Frm.

3. Click the View Code button at the top of the Project window to open the Code window for this form. Because you haven't written any code yet, the window is empty, as shown in Figure 4-1. Near the top of the window you can see two boxes, called the Object box and the Procedure box. At the outset, these boxes are designed to help you select the controls and events for which you need to write procedures. Later they'll give you a quick way to navigate to any procedure you've written in your program.

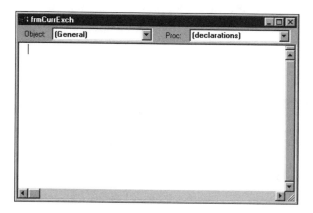

Figure 4-1
The empty Code window.

4. Click the down-arrow button just to the right of the Object box. As shown in Figure 4-2, this scrollable list displays the names of all the controls you've placed in the active form. Any one of these controls can ultimately become the object of an event procedure. For now, click the name of one of the form's command buttons, cmdClear. When you do so, Visual Basic displays the first and last lines of the *cmdClear_Click* procedure in the Code window. These lines serve as a kind of template for creating the procedure. A flashing cursor appears in the space between the two lines, indicating that Visual Basic is ready for you to begin entering additional lines of code.

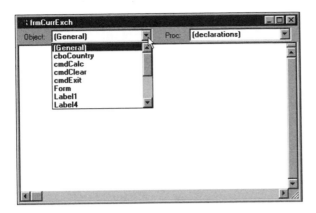

Figure 4-2
The Object list in the Code window.

5. Click the down-arrow button just to the right of the Procedure box
   (labeled *Proc*). This list displays the names of all the predefined
   events that can take place around the control you've selected in the
   Object box. As you can see in Figure 4-3, Click is only one of about
   a dozen events that apply to any command button control.

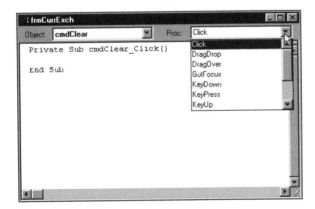

Figure 4-3
The Procedure list in the Code window.

6. Now click the Close button at the upper-right corner of the Code window. The Code window disappears temporarily from the desktop.

7. In the Project window, click the View Form button to reopen the Form window. The project's form appears on the screen, displaying the controls you've created to represent specific operations (Figure 4-4).

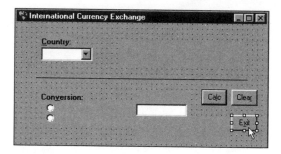

Figure 4-4

The form you've created for the Currency Exchange program.

8. Double-click the Exit button at the lower-right corner of the form. In response, Visual Basic once again opens the Code window and creates the template for yet another event procedure, this time cmdExit_Click (Figure 4-5). You can now begin writing the code for the Click procedures you've created.

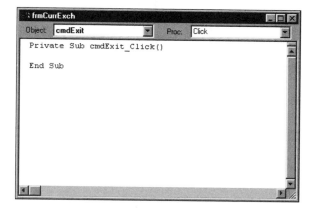

Figure 4-5

The initial template for the cmdExit_Click event procedure.

While a Code window is open, you can use the vertical scrollbar at the right side of the window — or the PgUp and PgDn keys on your keyboard — to scroll through the existing code, from one procedure to the next. Alternatively, you can make selections in the Object and Procedure boxes to go directly to any procedure; first select the name of a control from the Object box, then select the name of an event from the Procedure box. In the Procedure list, Visual Basic uses boldfacing to indicate the names of any events for which you've already written procedures, as illustrated in Figure 4-6.

Figure 4-6
Boldfacing indicates event procedures that you've already written.

Again, it's up to you to decide which event procedures to write for a given project, depending on the actions you want your program to respond to. Although Visual Basic defines many different events for a given type of control, you may decide that only a small selection of these events — one or two — are relevant to your plans for a particular program.

The Split Bar

As you begin filling in the event procedures for a particular form, you may find that the text of your program — known as the *listing* — quickly becomes long and unwieldy. Of course, you can always maximize the Code window to give yourself as much viewing space as possible. But sometimes you may want to view two distant parts of your code at once. For example, you may want to compare the techniques you've implemented in two different procedures. Or you may even want to perform a cut-and-paste or copy-and-paste operation to transfer a particular passage of code from one place to another. In this case, the Code window has a convenient tool that allows you to divide the viewing space in two. The tool is called the *split bar*, and it's initially represented by a small horizontal rectangle located just above the scroll bar. To split the Code window, follow these steps:

1. Position the mouse pointer over the split bar, shown in Figure 4-7. The pointer becomes a two-headed arrow icon.

2. Hold down the left mouse button, and drag the split bar down the vertical scroll bar. When you do so, the Code window is divided into two *panes*. Release the mouse button when the split appears where you want it.

3. Select either pane by clicking inside its code area. Then use the Object box and the Procedure box to select the event procedure that will be displayed inside the current pane. Alternatively, use the scroll bars at the right side of the Code window to scroll through each pane independently.

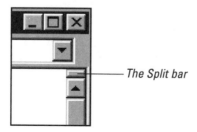

— The Split bar

Figure 4-7
The split bar.

For example, Figure 4-8 shows a Code window in which the two panes display different parts of the complete Currency Exchange program. To remove the split and restore the Code window to a single pane, you can drag the split bar back up to its original position near the top of the window. (Alternatively, try double-clicking the split bar.)

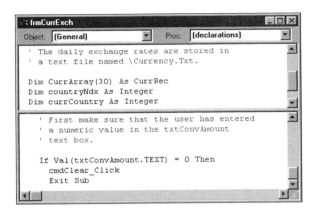

```
frmCurrExch
Object: (General)         Proc: (declarations)

' The daily exchange rates are stored in
' a text file named \Currency.Txt.

Dim CurrArray(30) As CurrRec
Dim countryNdx As Integer
Dim currCountry As Integer

    ' First make sure that the user has entered
    ' a numeric value in the txtConvAmount
    ' text box.

    If Val(txtConvAmount.TEXT) = 0 Then
       cmdClear_Click
       Exit Sub
```

Figure 4-8

Viewing two different sections of code in one Code window.

Using the Editor

A Code window represents all the built-in capabilities of the Visual Basic *text editor*, the environment in which you enter and revise the text of your code. This editor provides many important features designed to make programming as easy as it can be; for example:

- Your code is displayed in multiple colors, so you can easily pick out different elements of the program.

- You can include comments in your code to provide explanations of your program, written in your own words.

- The Code window gives you a direct link to Visual Basic's help system whenever you need quick information about a particular element of the language itself.

You'll learn more about these features in the next exercise, when you begin entering the text of two procedures into the Currency Exchange program.

As you complete individual event procedures, you'll discover another important feature of the Visual Basic development environment. You can often test the performance of a given procedure, long before you've written all the program's code. To do so, you run the program and simulate the action that triggers a specific event, resulting in a performance of the event procedure you want to test. You'll try out this process in the next exercise. The goal of the steps ahead is to create two of the program's simplest event procedures: *cmdClear_Click* and *cmdExit_Click*. As you've seen, the first of these clears the text box on the form so that the user can start a new currency calculation. The second terminates the program. Together these two procedures contain only a few lines of code, so you'll be able to complete them quickly. For now, don't worry too much about the *meaning* of the code; just concentrate on the mechanical steps required for successfully entering the code into your project:

1. Activate the Code window for the Currency Exchange form, and scroll to the *cmdClear_Click* procedure. Click the mouse on the blank line in the middle of the procedure. The flashing cursor appears on the line, indicating that the editor is ready for you to begin typing code.

2. Press Enter to create another blank line. Then press the spacebar twice to create a two-space indent for the first line of text you're about to type.

3. Type the following two lines, starting each line with a single-quote character:

```
' Clear the previous conversion
' calculation.
```

Visual Basic recognizes any line of text that begins with a single-quote character as a comment, a brief explanation that you write in plain English to help you (or others) keep track of the various parts of your code. When you run your program, Visual Basic ignores the comment lines. Comments are displayed in green to distinguish them from executable statements.

4. Type the next two lines of code, each of which assigns a new setting to a selected property of one of the program's controls:

```
txtConvAmount.Text = ""
lblConvText.Caption = ""
```

Notice the format of a statement that changes a property setting. At the left side of the equal sign, the notation *ControlName.Property-Name* identifies the control and its property. At the right side you enter the new property setting. In this passage, both the Text property of a text box and the Caption property of a label are reset to empty strings.

5. Enter two more lines of comments:

```
' Return the focus to the
' txtConvAmount text box.
```

6. Finally, enter another line of code:

```
txtConvAmount.SetFocus
```

This line is a call to a Visual Basic method named *SetFocus*. A *method* is a built-in procedure that performs an operation on a specific control or object. In this case, the control is the txtConvAmount text box; the SetFocus method returns the focus of the program to this control. (You'll learn much more about methods in later chapters.) When you've completed this final line, the *cmdClear_Click* procedure looks like Figure 4-9. On the screen you can see the color scheme that Visual Basic uses for displaying your code: comments are in green, the *keywords* of the language itself (for example, Private, Sub, and End) are displayed in blue, and other text is in black. You'll see yet another display color before you finish with this program.

II

4

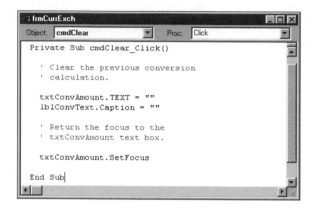

Figure 4-9
Entering the code of an event procedure.

7. Scroll down to the cmdExit_Click procedure, located just below the cmdClear_Click procedure. Position the cursor on the blank line between the first and last line of the procedure, and press Enter. Type the keyword **End** and press Enter again. This procedure will terminate your program when the Exit button is clicked.

You've written your first two event procedures, both of them designed to respond to clicks on command buttons. You can now close the Code window and then click the Save Project button on Visual Basic's toolbar to save your work to disk. You're ready to try running the program to experiment with these two procedures.

Testing Event Procedures

Even though the two procedures you've written are small parts of the whole program, they cover details that you can easily test during a program run. In the upcoming steps, you'll start the program and confirm that the *cmdClear_Click* and *cmdExit_Click* procedures are running properly:

1. Press F5 or click the Start button on the Visual Basic toolbar to start the program. The International Currency Exchange window appears on the desktop, although most of the features eventually planned for the application are not yet implemented. For example, there's no available list from which you can choose a country and a currency.

2. Press the Tab key twice to activate the text box located just to the left of the three command buttons. Type any sequence of digits into this box, as though you were planning to convert a monetary amount from one currency to another. For example, in Figure 4-10, the amount 123456789 has been entered into the box.

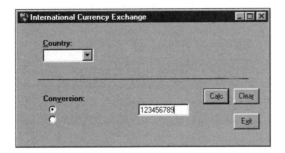

Figure 4-10
Testing the program at an early stage.

3. Click the Calc button, or press Alt+L — just as you might do if the program were fully operational at this point. The program gives no response, but your action does move the focus from the text box to the Calc button. (Two small details indicate that this is the case: The flashing cursor disappears from the text box and a dotted rectangular frame appears around the caption of the Calc button.)

4. Now click the Clear button, or press Alt+R. As you know, this action triggers a call to the cmdClear_Click procedure that you've written in the Code window for this form. The procedure performs two visible actions: First the number you've typed into the text box is erased from view; and second, the focus returns to the text box, as indicated by the reappearance of the flashing vertical cursor.

5. Finally, click the Exit button, or press Alt+X. As predicted, this action triggers a call to the *cmdExit_Click* procedure, resulting in a termination of the program performance.

From this sequence of events, you know that the code you've written so far is working as expected. Programmers are not always so lucky. The first time you try to run new code — even a small amount of code consisting of only a few lines — a great variety of problems can prevent a successful performance of your program. Fortunately, Visual Basic provides a number of tools that will help you write good code as early as possible in the process. You'll look at some of these tools in the next section of this chapter.

Syntax Checking and Keyword Help

As you write your program's code, the Visual Basic editor automatically checks the syntax of each line you enter. In this context, *syntax* refers to the basic grammatical rules of the programming language — the format Visual Basic expects you to follow for each particular statement in your code. If the editor finds that something is wrong with a given line, two distinct events tell you clearly that you've made a mistake:

- The mistyped line is displayed in red, highlighting the fact that there's some kind of syntax error in your code.

- An error message appears on the screen, briefly identifying the possible problem.

This sequence may take place many times while you're developing your program's code. The first few times you see the bright red highlighting accompanied by an abrupt error message, you may feel a bit disconcerted. But you'll soon learn to appreciate Visual Basic's direct technique for letting you know that something is wrong.

A good step to take immediately after an error message appears is to open the Visual Basic Help system for a review of the correct syntax. Fortunately, help is just a single keystroke away. With the cursor positioned next to a Basic keyword in the Code window, you simply press F1 to get help with the syntax of that keyword.

To experiment with these features, you'll try adding another few lines of code to your program in the next exercise. Specifically, you'll go to the Declarations section of your program and try entering two DIM statements to declare variables for your program. A *variable* is a name you define to represent a particular value in a program — for example, a number, a string of text, or a date. A *Dim* statement allows you to declare a variable name at the outset of your program. You'll learn lots more about variables and *Dim* statements in Chapter 5. Meanwhile, the following exercise will help you understand Visual Basic's syntax checking feature and help system:

1. Activate the Code window again and pull down the Object list from the top of the window. Scroll to the top of the list and select the entry that reads *(General)*, as shown in Figure 4-11. In response, the Visual Basic editor scrolls up to the *General Declarations* section of your code, where you can write special declarations that apply to the entire form (Figure 4-12). The Dim statement is one of the declarations that typically appears in this section.

2. Type the keyword **dim**. (Enter the word in all lowercase letters for the moment.) In the correct syntax of this statement, the keyword is followed by the name of a variable you want to declare. But in this exercise, you're going to make an intentional error, omitting any further information on the Dim line.

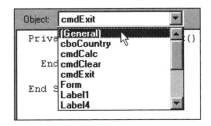

Figure 4-11

Switching to the General Declarations section of the program.

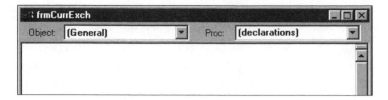

Figure 4-12
The General Declarations section.

3. Press the Enter key after typing *dim*. As you can see in Figure 4-13, Visual Basic immediately displays a small dialog box on the desktop with the error message "Expected Shared or identifier." In essence, this message means that you pressed Enter before completing the Dim statement. In the code window the keyword *dim* is now displayed in red, further emphasizing the fact that you've made a mistake.

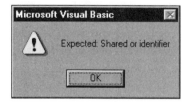

Figure 4-13
An error message appears in response to a syntax error.

4. Click OK to close the dialog box. Back in the Code window, the flashing cursor is located immediately after *dim*.

5. Press F1. In response, Visual Basic opens its Help system and immediately displays the topic that fully describes the usage and syntax of the Dim statement, as shown in Figure 4-14. You can now read this information to figure out exactly what you did wrong in your line of code.

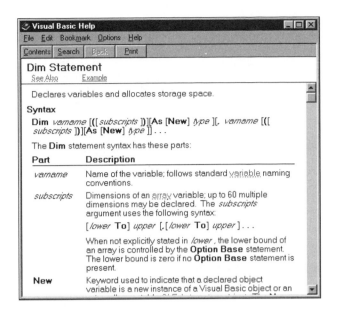

Figure 4-14
Jumping to the Visual Basic Help system.

In short, the Visual Basic editor constantly watches over your work, and is always ready to direct your attention to an error.

Press the Escape key to close the Help window. Now you can complete your code entries into the Declaration section of the program. Enter the two *Dim* statements as follows:

```
dim countryNdx as integer
dim currCountry as integer
```

If you watch closely, you'll see an additional feature that the editor uses to help you with your work — this time to confirm that you've entered the lines correctly. You've entered the code mostly in lowercase letters, but the editor automatically capitalizes the first letter of each keyword when you press Enter after each line:

```
Dim countryNdx As Integer
Dim currCountry As Integer
```

Furthermore, the Basic keywords in these statements — *Dim*, *As*, and *Integer* — appear as blue text. These small adjustments in the text of your code reassure you that you've followed the correct syntax rules for these lines. Your Declaration section now looks like Figure 4-15.

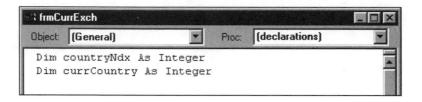

Figure 4-15
The Declaration section of the program.

Now click the Save button on the toolbar to save your work to disk. You've seen one kind of error that can occur while you're developing a program's code. A syntax error prevents a successful run of your program; accordingly, Visual Basic encourages you to correct this type of error immediately. By contrast, a *logical* error in your code may not stop you from running your program, but may instead lead to incorrect results or unexpected behavior. Logical errors can be much more difficult to correct than syntax errors. For this reason, Visual Basic supplies a collection of techniques known as *debugging tools*, designed specifically to help you find and correct logical errors in a running program. When you've had more experience with writing code, you may want to begin exploring the debugging tools.

As a final exercise, you'll now open the finished Currency Exchange Program from this book's program disk and take a brief look at the procedures the program contains. Along the way, you'll preview some of the major programming topics you'll be studying in the chapters ahead.

Examining the Code in a Finished Program

You'll find the complete code of the Currency Exchange program printed in Listings 4-1 through 4-7. Alternatively, you can look at the code directly on your screen. Open the program (CurrExch.VBP) from disk and, if necessary, press Ctrl+R to open the Project window. Then click the View Code button to open a Code window. The finished program contains a form (CurrExch.Frm) and a module (CurrExch.Bas), each with its own Code window.

PROCEDURES

Begin with a brief overview of the listing. Each event procedure in the form begins with a *Private Sub* statement; for example, here's the first line of the *cboCountry_Click* procedure:

```
Private Sub cboCountry_Click
```

The *Sub* keyword identifies this block of code as a procedure, and *Private* indicates that the procedure is available for use only within the current form. As you'll recall, Visual Basic creates this line for you when you take the steps to create a new event procedure. Visual Basic also enters an *End Sub* statement as the final line of each procedure. To create an unambiguous marker for the end of each procedure, you can append a comment to each *End Sub* line, identifying the procedure by name; for example:

```
End Sub   ' cboCountry_Click
```

Although this extra comment is optional, it helps you see clearly where one procedure ends and another begins.

LONG LINES OF CODE

Another important feature that you may notice in your first glance through the program listing is the convenient *line continuation* character. Visual Basic allows you to break very long statements into multiple lines of text in your listing. To indicate that two or more lines belong to the same statement, you place an underscore character (_) at the end of each line except the last one. For example, the following statement appears in the cboCountry_Click procedure (Listing 4-2):

```
lblCurrency.Caption = "One " & _
   CurrArray(i).currName & " = " & _
   CurrArray(i).inDollars & _
   " U.S. dollar(s)"
```

These four lines make up a single statement, whose purpose is to assign a new setting to the Caption property of the lblCurrency label. As long as you use the line continuation character correctly, Visual Basic reads these lines as a single statement. By breaking the statement into multiple lines, you avoid the printing problems that sometimes occur when a program contains very long lines of code. (In a printed listing, long lines can sometimes be broken up arbitrarily, making your code difficult to read.)

VARIABLES AND DATA STRUCTURES

As you've seen, the top of the code (Listing 4-1) contains declarations for the variables used in the program. The Currency Exchange program needs a convenient way to store and access the country names, currency names, and exchange rates it reads from the Currency.txt file. For this purpose, it declares an *array of records* called *CurrArray*:

```
Dim CurrArray(30) As CurrRec
```

An array is an indexed variable that can represent many data values at once. Each element of *CurrArray* is a structure representing the data for one country — name, currency, and exchange rate. The CurrExch.Bas module (Listing 4-7) defines this structure:

```
Type CurrRec
  country As String
  currName As String
  inDollars As Single
End Type
```

In addition, the program declares two variables to keep track of the currency data:

```
Dim countryNdx As Integer
Dim currCountry As Integer
```

The variable named *countryNdx* represents the number of countries read from the data file; and *currCountry* identifies the country that the user has chosen most recently from the Country list.

Understanding variables, data types, and data structures is essential to your success as a programmer. You'll examine these topics in detail in Chapters 5 and 7.

THE FORM_LOAD PROCEDURE

The first event procedure performed in this program is *not* triggered by a user action such as a mouse click or a data entry. Rather, the *Form_Load* procedure (Listing 4-5) is performed automatically at the beginning of the run, when the program first opens the Currency Exchange form onto the desktop. In many applications, a Form_Load procedure is a good place for you to write code that initializes your program's variables and performs any other tasks that need to take place at the outset.

In the Currency Exchange program, the Form_Load procedure opens the Currency.txt file from its storage location in the root directory of your hard disk:

```
Open "\Currency.Txt" For Input As #1
```

The procedure then reads all of the file's data into the *CurrArray* structure:

```
Do While Not EOF(1)
   Input #1, CurrArray(i).country
   Input #1, CurrArray(i).currName
   Input #1, CurrArray(i).inDollars

   ' Build the country list.

   cboCountry.AddItem CurrArray(i).country

   i = i + 1
Loop
```

After reading each record of data from the file, the procedure appends the name of the current country to the Country combo box, represented by the name *cboCountry*. (Another Visual Basic method, named *AddItem*, allows the program to build the combo box list.)

Data file programming techniques are important in any programming language because they allow you to access information from files stored on disk. You'll study this topic in Chapter 8.

THE CLICK PROCEDURES

After reading the currency exchange data from disk, the program is ready to respond to the user's selections in the dialog box. Each of the user's possible actions — selecting an entry from the Country list, changing the setting of the option buttons, or clicking a command button — triggers a particular Click procedure, which defines the program's response:

- The cboCountry_Click procedure is called when the user pulls down the Country list and selects the name of a country. In response, this procedure calculates and displays the dollar-to-currency and currency-to-dollar exchange rates in the two labels located just to the right of the Country list. It also adjusts the option button captions appropriately.

- One of the two procedures in Listing 4-6 (optCurrTo_Click or optDollarsTo_Click) is called when the user clicks a Conversion option button. These short procedures take charge of supplying an appropriate label above the text box.

- When the user enters a numeric amount in the text box and then clicks the Calc button, the cmdCalc_Click procedure (Listing 4-3) is called. This procedure performs the conversion arithmetic, and displays the result in the label located just below the text box.

- As you've seen, two additional event procedures (Listing 4-4) represent the program's response to clicks on the Clear and Exit buttons. The cmdClear_Click procedure prepares the dialog box for a new currency exchange calculation, and the cmdExit_Click procedure ends the program run.

As you examine these procedures, you'll find a variety of interesting *control structures*, designed to carry out decisions (*If*) and repetitions (*For* and *Do*) during the course of the program. You'll study these structures in Chapter 7.

In summary, the code in the Currency Exchange program illustrates many of the language structures and programming techniques covered in the remaining chapters of this book. Now that you've looked briefly at the code, you might want to take a moment to run the program again. As you make selections from the controls in the application's dialog box, you'll now have a new perspective on the meaning of the event-driven programming model.

Listing 4-1

The Declarations section

```
' Currency Exchange Program
' CurExch.mak

' Converts between dollars and
' the currencies of other countries.
' The daily exchange rates are stored in
' a text file named \Currency.Txt.

Dim CurrArray(30) As CurrRec                    ──────→  An array at records
Dim countryNdx As Integer
Dim currCountry As Integer
```

Listing 4-2

The cboCountry_Click procedure

```
Private Sub cboCountry_Click()
  ' Read the user's country choice
  ' and display the exchange rates
  ' for the currency of the selected
  ' country.

  Dim i As Integer
  For i = 0 To countryNdx
    If cboCountry.Text = CurrArray(i).country Then
      lblDollar.Caption = "One U.S. dollar = " & _
        1 / CurrArray(i).inDollars & " " & _
        CurrArray(i).currName & "(s)"
      lblCurrency.Caption = "One " & _                    Using the line
        CurrArray(i).currName & " = " & _                 continuation
        CurrArray(i).inDollars & _                        character
        " U.S. dollar(s)"
      currCountry = i
    End If
  Next i

  ' Display captions for the conversion
  ' option buttons.
```

```
optDollarsTo.Caption = "U.S. dollars to " & _
  CurrArray(currCountry).currName & "s"
optCurrTo.Caption = CurrArray(currCountry).currName & _
  "s to U.S. dollars"

lblConvCurr.Caption = "U.S. dollar(s):"
optDollarsTo.Value = True
cmdClear_Click

End Sub   ' cboCountry_Click
```

Listing 4-3
The cmdCalc_Click procedure

```
Private Sub cmdCalc_Click()

  ' Perform the currency exchange calculation
  ' that the user requests.

  ' First make sure that the user has entered
  ' a numeric value in the txtConvAmount
  ' text box.

  If Val(txtConvAmount.Text) = 0 Then
    cmdClear_Click
    Exit Sub
  End If

  ' If so, the calculation is based on
  ' the user's choice of conversion options.

  If optDollarsTo.Value Then
    lblConvText.Caption = "= " & _
      txtConvAmount.Text / _
      CurrArray(currCountry).inDollars & _
      " " & CurrArray(currCountry).currName & "(s)"
```

```
    Else
      lblConvText.Caption = "= " & _
        Format$(txtConvAmount.Text * _
        CurrArray(currCountry).inDollars, _
        "$###,###.00")
    End If

End Sub  ' cmdCalc_Click
```

Listng 4-4
Two additional Click procedures

```
Private Sub cmdClear_Click()

  ' Clear the previous conversion
  ' calculation.

    txtConvAmount.Text = ""
    lblConvText.Caption = ""
```
Assigning new settings to properties at runtime

```
  ' Return the focus to the
  ' txtConvAmount text box.

    txtConvAmount.SetFocus
```
Calling a method

```
End Sub  ' cmdClear_Click

Private Sub cmdExit_Click()

  ' Terminate the program when
  ' the user clicks the Exit button.

    End

End Sub  ' cmdExit_Click
```

Listing 4-5
The Form_Load procedure

```
Private Sub Form_Load()

   ' Open the Currency.Txt file and
   ' read its contents into CurrArray,
   ' an array of records. Also create
   ' the list of countries in the
   ' cboCountry combo box.

   Dim i As Integer
   Open "\Currency.Txt" For Input As #1
     i = 0

     ' Read the file.

     Do While Not EOF(1)
        Input #1, CurrArray(i).country
        Input #1, CurrArray(i).currName
        Input #1, CurrArray(i).inDollars

        ' Build the country list.

        cboCountry.AddItem CurrArray(i).country

        i = i + 1
     Loop
   Close #1

   ' Keep a record of the last country index.

   countryNdx = i - 1

End Sub   ' Form_Load
```

Form_Load procedure is performed at the beginning of the program run

II

4

Listing 4-6
Click procedures for the option buttons

```
Private Sub optCurrTo_Click()

    ' Change the conversion option:
    ' foreign currency to U.S. dollars.

    lblConvCurr = CurrArray(currCountry).currName & "(s):"
    cmdClear_Click

End Sub  ' optCurrTo_Click

Private Sub optDollarsTo_Click()

    ' Change the currency option:
    ' U.S. dollars to foreign currency.

    lblConvCurr = "U.S. dollar(s):"
    cmdClear_Click

End Sub  ' optDollarsTo_Click
```

Listing 4-7
Code in the CurExch.Bas module

```
' Travel Guide Program
' Module: CurExch.Bas

' Type definition for country and
' currency records.

Type CurrRec
  country As String
  currName As String
  inDollars As Single
End Type
```

III Programming Essentials

*T*he six chapters of Part III introduce the major tools and techniques of Visual Basic programming. Each chapter provides a sample application to illustrate the topics covered. You'll run the applications to explore their features, and then you'll examine each program's code in detail.

Chapter 5 explains the difference between event procedures and general procedures, and shows you how to work with both. You'll learn how to create Sub and Function procedures and how to write calls to each type of routine. You'll also study variables and data types, Dim declarations, scope, assignment statements, expressions, operations, and the order of precedence. The Travel Expense Log application, a simple tool for recording and reporting travel expenses, illustrates many of these topics.

Chapter 6 addresses some important design issues for a project that contains multiple forms. You'll learn to set properties to distinguish between different roles for the forms in your project. You'll also see the significance of the startup form, and you'll use the Options dialog box to choose a form for this purpose. The Show and Hide methods control the display of forms at runtime; you'll see examples of these methods in this chapter's Restaurant Review program. The application builds a personal restaurant database in which you can record information about restaurants you try during business trips.

Chapter 7 discusses Visual Basic as a structured programming language. On the subject of data structures, you'll learn how to work with arrays and user-defined record types. You'll also investigate a variety of control structures, including If and Select Case decisions, Do loops, and For loops. Along the way you'll learn how to use relational and logical operators in a conditional expression. Other important topics include nested loops and decisions; dynamic arrays; arrays of records; and Visual Basic's With structure, which you can use to abbreviate references to the elements of a user-defined type. This chapter's Meetings application illustrates these topics; you can use the program to keep records of the meetings you attend while on business trips.

Chapter 8 shows you how to use Visual Basic's data file commands to manage databases, create and read text files, and store data on disk for exchange with other programs. You'll master two different sets of commands and techniques for working with random-access files and text files. The Phone Directory application will help you understand these techniques; it creates a useful database of names, phone numbers, and e-mail addresses.

Chapter 9 illustrates the intricate details of input and output procedures. In particular, you'll consider the important design issues in a program that receives extensive input from the user. You'll also see several ways in which a program can supply output, including text, numbers, and graphs. The International Sales program is a small worksheet application in which the user enters numeric sales data; in response, the program calculates rows and columns of totals and displays column charts or pie charts representing the data. This program illustrates the use of menus in a Visual Basic project. You'll see how to use the menu editor to define the elements of a menu on a form.

Chapter 10 explains the distinction between Visual Basic's intrinsic controls and custom controls, and focuses on one particular tool named the common dialog control. You can use this control in a program to display Windows-style dialog boxes on the screen for opening and saving files, sending information to the printer, and a variety of other purposes. The common dialog control is illustrated in this chapter's Transportation Planner application, a tool for planning your itinerary on a multi-stop business trip.

CHAPTER 5

Procedures, Variables, and Operations

D evising effective ways to work with data is one of your first tasks in a new programming project. The decisions you make about handling data are basic to the success of your program. For example, as you begin planning your code, you'll think carefully about the following issues:

- How to represent the different types of data values that your program will use

- How to send information from one part of your program to another, given the specific data requirements of individual procedures

- How to use operations to perform calculations and to work with multiple data values

A *variable* is a name you create to represent an item of information in a program. Depending on how you use a variable, its value might remain unchanged throughout your program or it might change frequently. If you've worked with a previous version of BASIC (QBasic, for example), you know that you can create variables to represent specific *types* of data — for example, integers, floating-point numbers, or strings of characters.

In the past, BASIC programmers have traditionally used a standard set of *type-declaration characters* at the end of variable names to indicate type. For example, under this convention the variable *city$* represents a string and the variable *visits%* is an integer. The final characters in these variable names — *$* and *%* — serve as declarations of the types of data each variable will represent.

Type-declaration characters are still available in Visual Basic, but they are falling out of use, for some interesting reasons. For one thing, Visual Basic has a richer set of data types than has been available in previous versions of the language, and type-declaration characters are not defined for many of the new types.

But more importantly, many Visual Basic programmers prefer to write *formal* declarations for all variables used in a program, as is the practice in other programming languages. Although formal declarations have traditionally been optional in BASIC, long programming projects tend to become easier to manage when programmers systematically declare variables.

Variable declarations in Visual Basic take the form of Dim statements. In one of its simplest forms, a Dim declaration appears as

```
Dim variableName As dataType
```

For example, the following statement declares a string variable named *logFileName*:

```
Dim logFileName As String
```

Using Dim, you not only declare the names and types of the variables you intend to use in a program, but also establish the appropriate *scope* of each variable — that is, you specify the part of your program in which a given variable will be recognized and available. By carefully defining the scope of variables throughout your program, you avoid unexpected conflicts between variables in different procedures, a common problem in older versions of the BASIC language.

Because variable declarations are so important in large programming projects, Visual Basic gives you the option of *requiring* formal declarations throughout. To do so, you place the following statement at the top of the code in a form or module:

```
Option Explicit
```

In response, Visual Basic provides a helpful error message whenever you inadvertently omit a variable declaration.

In this chapter you'll examine the variety of data types available in Visual Basic, and you'll learn how to declare and use variables in procedures and modules. In addition, you'll look at the convenient new data type known as Variant, and you'll discover how its use can simplify data operations in a program. You'll see examples of assignments and operations using numeric and string data.

But first you'll focus on the various ways of organizing procedures in Visual Basic. You've already seen examples of event procedures, designed to respond to predefined events that take place during a program run. Now you'll learn the distinction between event procedures and *general* procedures in the organization of a project. In the category of general procedures, you'll examine the practical differences between Sub and Function procedures, and you'll learn how information can be shared between one procedure and another.

To help you examine all these essential programming topics, you'll work with a sample project named the International Travel Expense Log program. As its name suggests, this program is designed to help you keep track of travel expenses during an international business trip. To begin your work in this chapter, you'll open the project from the program disk, run it, and see what it does.

The International Travel Expense Log Program

Start up Visual Basic if you haven't done so already, and click the Open Project button on the toolbar. The Expense Log program is stored on disk as ExpLog.VBP. Choose ExpLog from the Open Project dialog box, and click OK. Then press F5 or click the Start button on the toolbar to run the program.

The program consists of one form, shown in Figure 5-1. Controls on the form are designed to elicit information about a single travel expense record: the date, the country and city where the expense was incurred, the amount spent, a description, and the currency exchange rate in effect — that is, the value of one dollar in the local currency. By default, the program saves your expense data in a text file named \ExpLog95.Txt, as indicated on the title bar; but you can specify a different file name for saving the expense records of a particular business trip if you prefer. You'll examine this feature later.

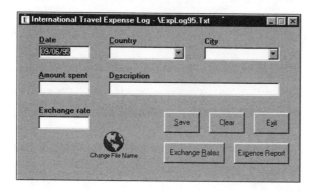

Figure 5-1
The International Travel Expense Log program.

At the lower-right corner of the dialog box, a panel of command buttons represents the operations you can perform by clicking the mouse or by pressing a keyboard shortcut:

- Click the Save button — or press Alt+S — to save the current expense record. The program requires you to enter information in each of the six fields — Date, Country, City, Amount spent, Description, and Exchange rate — before saving a record. (If you leave any field blank, an error message appears on the desktop when you click the Save button.) Once you complete a record and click Save, the program clears the Amount spent and Description boxes, to make room for the next entry.

- Click the Clear button (or press Alt+L) to abandon the current record and start over again.

- Click the Exchange Rates button (Alt+R) for information about the exchange rates you've already recorded for a selected country.

- Click the Expense Report button (Alt+P) to produce an expense report from the current data file. The program stores this report as a text file named ExpRept.Txt, which you can merge into any word processed document or send directly to your printer.

- Click the Exit button (Alt+X) to quit the program. Next time you run the program, you can continue recording expenses in the ExpLog95.Txt file or in any other expense data file you've created with the program.

Suppose you're in the middle of a two-week, three-country business trip to Europe. At the end of each day, you sit down at your laptop to record the day's expenses. Using the Expense Log program, you can quickly type the information to complete each record.

At the beginning of each new record, the program automatically provides today's date as the default value in the Date box. You can accept this default or enter a different date. From there, you press Tab to move from one box to the next, as you enter the country and city, the amount, a brief description, and today's dollar-to-currency exchange rate (Figure 5-2). Finally, you click the Save button to save the current record and begin a new one.

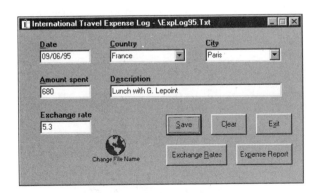

Figure 5-2

Entering an expense record.

Each time you complete a record and click Save, the program writes the information as a new line of text in the current data file — ExpLog95.Txt, by default. (You can examine this file in any text editor, such as the Windows 95 NotePad program.) For example, here's what the file might look like after several days of expense entries in three countries:

```
"09/06/95","France","Paris",2480,"l'Hotel du Pont, two nights",5.3
"09/06/95","France","Paris",680,"Lunch with G. Lepoint",5.3
"09/06/95","France","Paris",240,"Taxi to airport",5.3
"09/06/95","France","Strasbourg",475,"Dinner with C. Muller, Cafe Berthe",5.3
"09/07/95","France","Strasbourg",750,"l'Hotel Central, one night",5.45
"09/07/95","France","Strasbourg",665,"Miscellaneous supplies",5.45
"09/07/95","Switzerland","Basel",485,"Dinner with buyers",1.3
"09/08/95","Switzerland","Geneva",185,"l'Hotel du lac, one night",1.3
"09/08/95","Switzerland","Geneva",295,"Lunch with agents",1.3
"09/09/95","Italy","Florence",240000,"English Hotel, one night",1614
"09/10/95","Italy","Florence",210000,"Dinner with buyers",1614
"09/11/95","France","Paris",1850,"Car rental",5.5
"09/12/95","France","Caen",1750,"Conference room, l'Hotel du Chateau",5.45
"09/13/95","France","Caen",850,"l'Hotel du Chateau, one night",5.45
"09/14/95","France","Chartres",455,"Lunch meeting with M. Lenoir",5.55
"09/15/95","France","Chartres",825,"Grand Hotel, one night",5.55
"09/16/95","France","Paris",585,"Books and supplies",5.55
"09/16/95","France","Paris",3480,"l'Hotel du Jardin, four nights",5.6
```

Notice that each line in this file contains six items of information, corresponding to the six boxes in the Expense Log dialog box — the date, country, city, amount, description, and exchange rate. Four of the items are stored as strings, enclosed in quotation marks; and the other two are stored as numbers. Within a given line, each item is separated from the next by a comma. These storage characteristics make the file convenient to use for the program's other operations.

The dialog box has several features designed to simplify expense recording as you move from place to place on your business trip. For example, each time you start the program, it reads the current data file and develops a list of all the countries you've recorded up to now. You can view this list — and select any country from it — by clicking the down-arrow button at the right side of the Country box, as shown in

Figure 5-3. Once you've selected a country, the program searches through the data file for any cities you've already visited in the current country selection. A list of those cities appears when you click the down-arrow button at the right side of the City box, as in Figure 5-4. Thanks to these two lists, you can quickly fill in the information needed to identify the location for a given expense record.

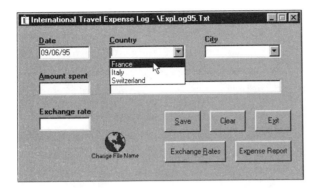

Figure 5-3
Choosing a country.

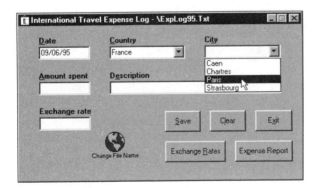

Figure 5-4
Choosing a city.

The exchange rate in a country may change from day to day. For example, one day during a trip to France you may get 5.6 francs to the dollar, and another day only 5.3. Although you record your expenses in the currency of a particular country, the actual cost of any transaction depends on how much you paid for the currency. A 500-franc business lunch is more expensive to you when the exchange rate is 5.3 francs to the dollar rather than, say, a rate of 5.6 francs to the dollar. Keeping track of exchange rates is therefore an important part of expense accounting during international travel.

The Expense Log program provides a simple way to monitor rate fluctuations as you continue your stay in a particular country. When you've selected an entry in the Country list, you can click the Exchange Rates button for quick information about the rates you've recorded during your trip, as shown in Figure 5-5. The Exchange Rates dialog box shows you the lowest and highest rates found in the current data file for the country you've selected.

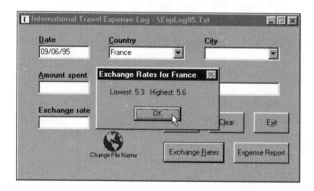

Figure 5-5

Examining fluctuations in exchange rates.

You may periodically want to generate an expense report that summarizes the expenses you've recorded up to a certain point. This document might serve as an intermediate review of expenses during a business trip or as a final report at the end of the trip. Either way, you can create the latest version of the report simply by clicking the Expense Report button on the dialog box. When you do so, you'll see a small message appear on the desktop, as shown in Figure 5-6.

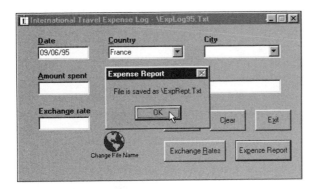

Figure 5-6
Producing an expense report.

The program always saves the expense report as a text file on disk, under the name \ExpRcpt.Txt. You can use the Windows 95 NotePad application to view the report, or you can send it directly to your printer as a text file. If you want to save the report, you can merge it into a word processed document, or assign the file a new name on disk.

Here's an example of what this report looks like:

```
                  Travel Expense Log
                  ====== ======= ===

                  \ExpLog95.Txt


Place                   Date       Amount   Description
-----                   ----       ------   -----------

Paris, France           09/06/95   $467.92  l'Hotel du Pont, two nights
Paris, France           09/06/95   $128.30  Lunch with G. Lepoint
Paris, France           09/06/95    $45.28  Taxi to airport
Strasbourg, France      09/06/95    $89.62  Dinner with C. Muller, Cafe Berthe
Strasbourg, France      09/07/95   $137.61  l'Hotel Central, one night
Strasbourg, France      09/07/95   $122.02  Miscellaneous supplies
Basel, Switzerland      09/07/95   $373.08  Dinner with buyers
Geneva, Switzerland     09/08/95   $142.31  l'Hotel du lac, one night
Geneva, Switzerland     09/08/95   $226.92  Lunch with agents
Florence, Italy         09/09/95   $148.70  English Hotel, one night
Florence, Italy         09/10/95   $130.11  Dinner with buyers
Paris, France           09/11/95   $336.36  Car rental
```

```
Caen, France              09/12/95    $321.10  Conference room, l'Hotel du Chateau
Caen, France              09/13/95    $155.96  l'Hotel du Chateau, one night
Chartres, France          09/14/95     $81.98  Lunch meeting with M. Lenoir
Chartres, France          09/15/95    $148.65  Grand Hotel, one night
Paris, France             09/16/95    $105.41  Books and supplies
Paris, France             09/16/95    $621.43  l'Hotel du Jardin, four nights

Total amount spent ...                $3,782.78
```

Unlike the original data file, the report presents expense records in neatly tabbed columns of information. The Amount column shows each expense in dollars rather than in a variety of local currencies. (The exchange rates are omitted from the expense report altogether.) The bottom line of the report shows the total amount you've spent on the business trip.

Finally, you may prefer to save your expense data under a file name that you choose, rather than the default ExpLog95.Txt. In some cases, the default file may serve as a convenient temporary storage place for data that you ultimately plan to save elsewhere. But an alternative approach is to create a new file — under a name you supply yourself — for each business trip, and to save the original data in this file.

If you prefer the latter approach, the Expense Log program allows you to change the current file name at any time during the program run. To do so, move the mouse pointer over the globe icon located just to the left of the panel of command buttons. As you can see in Figure 5-7, the caption under the icon reads "Change File Name." When positioned over this icon, the mouse pointer becomes an upward-pointing hand. Click the globe once to view the Expense Log File Name dialog box, as shown in Figure 5-8. Then enter the file name (or a complete path name) under which you want to save subsequent expense records, and click OK. The new file name appears on the title bar of the Expense Log program; for example:

```
International Travel Expense Log - \Africa95.Txt
```

Given this display, you always know the name of the file in which you're currently saving data.

Figure 5-7
The Change File Name icon.

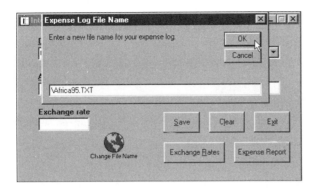

Figure 5-8
Changing the expense log file name.

In summary, the Expense Log program is easy to use for recording expenses and generating expense reports from a business trip. This project is a good place to start your study of Visual Basic programming. It provides an introduction to the structure and organization of procedures and it illustrates a variety of techniques for working with variables and data.

Inside the Expense Log Program

The project consists of one form, which contains all the program's code, shown in Listings 5.1 through 5.11. Looking through the listings, you'll find the program's major event procedures, including the six Click procedures designed to carry out specific operations when buttons are clicked:

- The cmdSave_Click procedure (Listing 5-2) confirms that a complete expense record has been entered into the program's dialog box, and then saves the record to the current data file (ExpLog95.Txt by default).

- The cmdRate_Click procedure (Listing 5-3) searches through the data file for records that match the current country selection (that is, the name displayed in the Country text box). By comparing the exchange rates stored in the file, the procedure determines the largest and smallest rates recorded for the current country, and displays these rates in a message box.

- The cmdExpRept_Click procedure (Listing 5-4) reads the current data file, and uses the information it contains to create an expense report that's easy to read and understand. The expense report is stored as a text file in ExpRept.Txt.

- The cmdClear_Click procedure (Listing 5-5) assigns blank strings to the Text properties of text boxes and combo boxes.

- The cmdExit_Click procedure (the second routine in Listing 5-5) terminates the program run.

- The picFileName_Click procedure (Listing 5-6) is called when the user clicks the Change File Name icon. The procedure displays an input box on the desktop to elicit a new file name for storing expense records.

In addition to event procedures, the program contains many important sections of code known as general procedures. Unlike event procedures, general procedures are *not* performed directly as the result of events. Rather, a general procedure is *called* from a specific place in your code. As the result of a call, Visual Basic sends control to the procedure, performs its statements, and then returns control to the location of the call.

There are several important advantages to organizing your code into a combination of event procedures and general procedures:

- General procedures allow you to isolate particular operations into small, self-contained blocks of code that are easy to identify and to revise if necessary. As a rule of thumb, you should try to limit the length of each procedure you write to about a page of code. Dividing your program into many small procedures — rather than a few long ones — results in code that is easier to maintain over time.

- A general procedure, as the term implies, can be written to carry out operations in a variety of different contexts. A given procedure might be called from several places in your program, and might accomplish slightly different tasks depending on the source of the call. As a result, general procedures help you avoid unnecessary duplication in your code.

- General procedures come in two varieties: Sub and Function procedures. A Sub procedure performs a defined operation and then returns control to the caller. A Function procedure is designed to calculate or determine a specific value, and return that value to the location of the procedure call. You'll see examples of both Sub and Function procedures as you continue examining the International Travel Expense Log program.

Because general procedures are so important to the structure of a program, Visual Basic provides convenient tools for creating and working with them. You'll examine these tools next.

Creating General Procedures

As you've seen, Visual Basic automatically creates *templates* for event procedures in a project. For example, suppose a project contains a command button that you've named cmdOpen. To create a template for the cmdOpen_Click procedure, you simply open the form that contains the button (in design mode, of course), and double-click the button. Visual Basic opens the code window for the form, and creates a template consisting of the first and last lines of the event procedure:

```
Private Sub cmdOpen_Click()

End Sub
```

To develop the event procedure itself, you begin entering lines of code between the Sub and End Sub statements.

Likewise, Visual Basic provides a tool you can use to create templates for any general procedure you want to include in the code of a project. To use this tool, you begin by deciding what kind of procedure you want to create — a Sub or Function procedure — and devising a name for the new procedure. Then follow these steps:

1. Press Ctrl+R to activate the Project window, and select the form or module in which you want to create a new procedure. Click the View Code button to open the code window.

2. Pull down the Insert menu and choose the Procedure command. The Insert Procedure dialog box appears on the screen, as shown in Figure 5-9.

3. In the Name box, enter the name of the procedure you want to create.

4. Select Sub or Function in the Type group. (Notice that there is a third type of procedure, known as a Property procedure. You'll learn about Property procedures in Chapter 11.)

5. Select Public or Private in the Scope group. A Private procedure is available for use only in the form or module that contains the procedure. A Public procedure is designed to be called from any place in a project's code.

6. Click OK. In response, Visual Basic creates a template for your new procedure in the active code window.

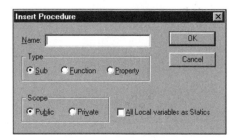

Figure 5-9
The Insert Procedure dialog box.

For example, suppose you follow these steps to create a private Sub procedure named *DoCalc*. Here is the template you see in your code window:

```
Private Sub DoCalc()

End Sub
```

By contrast, if you were take the same steps to create a Function procedure named *FindItem*, Visual Basic would supply this template in your code window:

```
Private Function FindItem()

End Function
```

In either case, you're ready to begin writing the procedure's code, between the Sub and End Sub statements or the Function and End Function statements.

A more direct way to create a new procedure is simply to enter a Sub or Function statement on a blank line in a code window. When you press Enter to complete the line, Visual Basic completes the procedure template by entering an End Sub or End Function statement.

As you develop procedures in a form or a module, you can use the code window's Object and Proc lists to locate any general procedure or to view the names of all the general procedures you've written so far:

1. Open the code window.

2. Select the *(General)* entry in the Object list at the top of the code window.

3. Pull down the Proc list to view the names of all the general procedures you've written for this form or module.

4. Click any name in the list to scroll directly to a particular procedure.

For example, Figure 5-10 shows the scrollable list of general procedures in the Expense Log program. You'll be examining a number of these procedures as you continue this chapter.

Figure 5-10

Viewing the list of general procedures in a form or module.

Understanding Procedures

A Sub procedure is designed to perform a specific, carefully defined task. The task is repeated each time your program calls the procedure. By contrast, the primary job of a Function procedure is to *return* a specific item of information.

As you've seen, every procedure has a name, which you supply when you first create the procedure. The name of the procedure is defined in the Sub or Function statement at the beginning of the code. A good procedure name indicates something essential about what the procedure is designed to do.

A *call* is a statement or expression that refers to a procedure by name and results in a performance of the procedure. A *private* procedure can be called from any other procedure in the same form or module; a *public* procedure can be called from anywhere in the project that contains the procedure. When a general procedure completes its task, control of the program returns to the location where the procedure was originally called.

A call to a Sub procedure is a statement by itself. For example, consider the Sub procedure named *DoCalc*; a call to the procedure may look like this:

```
DoCalc
```

By contrast, a call to a Function procedure always appears as part of a statement designed to use the value that the function returns. For example, a call to a function named FindItem might appear at the right side of an assignment statement:

```
newItem = FindItem
```

or in a decision statement:

```
If oldItem = FindItem Then

        . . .

End If
```

The more you learn about Sub and Function procedures, the more skillfully you can use them as the building blocks of a program. In the upcoming sections of this chapter, you'll review the structural elements of procedures and you'll focus on their use. In particular, you'll learn how to send information to a procedure in a call, and how to design a procedure to make use of the information it receives.

DESIGNING SUB PROCEDURES

Here is a general format of a Sub procedure:

```
Sub ProcedureName (argument1, argument2, ...)

   ' The statements of the procedure.

End Sub
```

As you've seen, the keyword Sub can be preceded by Private or Public, specifying the scope of the procedure.

The procedure name is followed by an optional *argument list*, enclosed in parentheses. An argument is a variable representing a data item that will be passed to the procedure at the time of a call. The argument list consists of variable names and, optionally, their type declarations. Like any variable, each argument belongs to a specified type.

You can use an As clause to define an argument's type. For example, consider the *FillCityList* procedure (Listing 5-10):

```
Private Sub FillCityList(countryName As String)
```

As its name indicates, this procedure is in charge of maintaining the list of names attached to the City box in the Expense Log program. When the user chooses an entry from the Country list, a call to FillCityList opens the current data file, finds all the city names recorded for the selected country, and adds each name to the drop-down City list. As you can see, the procedure receives one string argument, represented by the variable *countryName*. This argument tells the procedure what country to search for in the data file. In the procedure's code, this argument looks just like any other variable. Its distinct feature is that it represents data that has been passed to the procedure from the caller.

CALLING SUB PROCEDURES

A call to a Sub procedure sends items of information to the procedure's argument variables. Here is the general form of a Sub procedure call:

```
ProcedureName argument1, argument2, ...
```

Notice that the argument list is not enclosed in parentheses in the procedure call.

For example, a call to *FillCityList* sends one string argument to the procedure. The following call, which takes place from a general procedure named *ChangeCityList* (Listing 5-9), sends the current Text property of the cboCountry combo box control as the value of the argument:

```
FillCityList cboCountry.Text
```

In this particular example, the argument is represented by a property. But you can express an argument in any way that results in a value of the appropriate data type. For example, the argument might appear as a literal string value, enclosed in quotation marks:

```
FillCityList "France"
```

Keep in mind that the argument list is optional in the definition of a general procedure. If there is no argument list, a call consists simply of the procedure name itself. For example, the *ChangeCityList* procedure (Listing 5-9) arranges to rebuild the city list whenever a change occurs in the country entry. The procedure takes no arguments:

```
Private Sub ChangeCityList()
```

In the Sub statement, the procedure name is followed by a pair of empty parentheses, indicating that there is no argument list. A call to the procedure is represented simply by the name itself:

```
ChangeCityList
```

As you can see in Listing 5-9, the program calls this procedure in response to either of two events:

- A Click event occurs when the user chooses a new entry from the Country list. This event results in a call to the cboCountry_Click procedure.
- An event named LostFocus occurs when the user moves the focus from the Country list to another control (by pressing the Tab key or by clicking another control with the mouse). In this case, the corresponding event procedure is cboCountry_LostFocus. (You'll see other examples of the LostFocus event shortly.)

PASSING CONTROLS AS ARGUMENTS

Significantly enough, a procedure can also receive a reference to a control as an argument. This feature allows you to write procedures that perform general operations on different controls in your project. For example, consider the *ValidNumInput* procedure, shown in Listing 5-8:

```
Private Sub ValidNumInput(textControl As Control)
```

The purpose of this procedure is to examine and validate the contents of a text box that's meant for numeric input. The procedure examines the box just after the control loses the focus. If the control contains a valid numeric entry, the value is left intact. But if the entry can't be read as a number, the procedure clears the value from the box. The Expense Log program uses this procedure to ensure that the Amount box (which is named txtAmount) and the Rate box (named txtRate) both contain numeric values. If the user inadvertently enters a nonnumeric value in one of these boxes, the *ValidNumInput* procedure removes the entry. (You can test this procedure during a program run by entering a nonnumeric value in either of these boxes and then moving the focus to another control.)

The *ValidNumInput* procedure needs to be able to operate on a control that's specified at the time of a call. Accordingly, the textControl argument represents the control whose contents should be examined. The procedure is called when either the Amount or the Rate box loses the focus, triggering the LostFocus event for the corresponding control. In Listing 5-8 you can see the two LostFocus event procedures that handle this situation. In each case, a call is made to the *ValidNumInput* procedure to check for numeric data entry.

For example, this is the LostFocus procedure that's called when the Amount box loses the focus:

```
Private Sub txtAmount_LostFocus()

   ValidNumInput txtAmount

End Sub
```

And here is the equivalent procedure for the Rate box:

```
Private Sub txtRate_LostFocus()

   ValidNumInput txtRate

End Sub
```

In both cases, the call sends the name of a text box control as the argument of the *ValidNumInput* procedure. The procedure then performs its validation tasks on the contents of the corresponding control.

DESIGNING FUNCTION PROCEDURES

Like a Sub procedure, a function may include an argument list:

```
Function FunctionName (argument1, argument2, ...) As type

   ' The statements of the function procedure.

End Function
```

But a function procedure has several important features that distinguish it from a Sub procedure. Most obviously, the first line of the procedure is a Function statement and the last is End Function. Beyond that, however, a function is designed to return a specific value to the location of the function call:

- An optional As clause in the Function statement defines the type of value that the function will return.
- Within the function's code — often near the end — is an assignment statement that identifies the return value. At the left side of the equal sign in this assignment statement is the name of the function itself, and at the right side is an expression that gives the return value:

```
FunctionName = returnValue
```

The arguments that a function receives are often central to the algorithm that produces the result. For example, consider the *AlreadyListed* function, shown in Listing 5-11. This function prevents duplicate entries in the Country and City lists. In an expense data file, a given country and city name may be recorded many times, but each name should appear only once in the Country or City list.

The *AlreadyListed* function returns a *Boolean* value — that is, a value that the program can read as True or False:

```
Private Function AlreadyListed(listControl As Control, _
                      newItem As String) As Boolean
```

The function searches through a list for a particular entry. If the item is already in the list, the function returns a value of True; if not, False. Notice that the function takes two arguments — a Control-type argument named *listControl* and a String argument named *newItem*. The first argument tells the function which list to search through, and the second provides the string value that the function should search for.

CALLING FUNCTION PROCEDURES

In Visual Basic, a function call is always part of a statement, never a statement by itself. For example, a function call might appear in an assignment statement in the following general form:

```
variableName = FunctionName(argument1, argument2, ...)
```

Unlike the argument list in a call to a Sub procedure, the arguments sent to a function are enclosed in parentheses after the function's name. The arguments may appear as literal values, variables, or expressions, as long as each value matches the data type specified in the function definition itself.

For example, the *AlreadyListed* function is called from the *Fill-CountryList* and *FillCityList* procedures (Listing 5-10), which are responsible for building the Country and City lists. In each case, the function call appears in an If statement, designed to decide whether or not to add a new item to the list. Here is the statement in the *Fill-CountryList* procedure:

```
If Not AlreadyListed(cboCountry, countryName) _
   Then cboCountry.AddItem countryName
```

You'll learn about decision statements in detail in Chapter 7, but for now you can intuitively see how this statement works:

- The call to the *AlreadyListed* function checks to see whether a particular country — represented by the variable *countryName* — is already in the Country list. (Notice that the control name cboCountry is sent as the first argument to the function.)

- If *AlreadyListed* returns a value of False, the expression *Not AlreadyListed* is True. In this case, the program uses the AddItem method to add the country name to the list.

- If *AlreadyListed* returns a value of True — meaning that the country is already in the list — *Not AlreadyListed* is False. In this case the country is not added again to the list.

A similar statement in the FillCityList procedure checks to see whether a given city name is already in the City list:

```
If Not AlreadyListed(cboCity, city) _
   Then cboCity.AddItem city
```

Examining these two decision statements closely, you can appreciate the beauty of a function like *AlreadyListed*. Once you've created the function as a general tool, you can confidently use it in different contexts — searching through different lists for different data values. When you write a call to the function, you don't need to think about the algorithmic details of the search itself; you simply focus on sending the right combination of arguments to the function.

In summary, one important way to exchange information between different parts of your program is to pass argument values to a Sub or Function procedure. Inside the procedure, the arguments are represented by variables defined in the Sub or Function statement.

But there are other important ways to share data among procedures. You'll continue to examine this topic in the remaining sections of this chapter.

Using Variables in a Program

A program may contain many different variables to represent data. Most programmers devise *meaningful* variable names that clearly indicate the kind of information variables represent. For example, variables such as *largeRate*, *smallRate*, *country*, *exchRate*, and *boxTitle* help make a program listing easy to read and understand. But programmers who don't like to type are sometimes tempted to skimp on meaning in favor of brevity; for this reason, you may often see very short variable names like *i*, *j*, and *k* in a program. As you write your own programs, you'll develop your own style of creating variable names.

An *assignment statement* is an essential way to store a value in a variable. The item you assign to a variable can be represented as a literal value, another variable, or an expression. An *expression* is a sequence of operations that result in a particular value. When you write an expression as part of an assignment statement, Visual Basic performs the operations and then assigns the result to the designated variable.

In the Expense Log program you'll find many examples of variables, assignments, and expressions. You'll also see uses of the Dim statement to define variables at different levels of the program. Listing 5-1 contains the code known as the *general declarations* section, which starts with a series of comment lines that describe the program itself. Notice that the very first statement in the program is the following:

```
Option Explicit
```

As you know, this statement enforces the discipline of systematic variable declarations. As a result of this statement, all variables used in the program have to be declared formally. You'll see the significance of this option as you continue examining the program's code.

DECLARING VARIABLES

Visual Basic sets a few simple rules for variable names. A name must begin with a letter, and may contain any combination of letters from *A* to *Z* and digits from 0 to 9. Periods and spaces are not allowed.

As you learned at the beginning of this chapter, Visual Basic allows, but doesn't necessarily encourage, the use of the traditional type-declaration characters. You can place any one of these characters at the end of a variable name to declare the variable's data type:

$ String variable
%   Integer variable
&   Long-integer variable
!   Single-precision numeric variable
Double-precision numeric

If you decide to use more formal techniques for declaring types, however, you should avoid these five characters in variable names.

A variable name can be as long as 255 characters. But once you've created a variable, you've got to spell it consistently throughout your program; the longer the name, the harder this task becomes. You should therefore try to write variable names that are as meaningful as possible within a reasonable length. Most programmers create names that are no longer than about ten to fifteen characters.

You can use any combination of uppercase or lowercase letters in a variable name. The use of uppercase letters can help clarify the significance of a name, as in *logFileName* or *countryName*. As you type variable names into the code window, Visual Basic automatically maintains consistency in alphabetic case. For example, suppose you initially declare a variable as *cityName*. Then in another part of your program you inadvertently type the variable as *cityNAME*. Visual Basic recognizes this as an existing name and changes it to *cityName*.

In the As clause of a Dim statement, you can define a variable of any type without using a type-declaration character:

```
Dim variableName As dataType
```

In this syntax, *dataType* is one of the following keywords:

- *Byte*, for an integer in the range 0 to 255.
- *Integer*, for a whole number in the range --32768 to 32767.
- *Long*, for an integer in a range of about --2 billion to +2 billion.
- *Single*, for single-precision floating-point value.
- *Double*, for a double-precision floating-point value.
- *Currency*, for a numeric data type that supports an appropriate range and precision for large or small monetary values.
- *Date*, for values that Visual Basic recognizes as dates.
- *String*, for a string of characters, either variable length or fixed length.
- *Boolean*, for a value of True or False.
- *Object*, for a reference to an object.
- *Variant*, for Visual Basic's most versatile and general-purpose data type. (This is the default type if you omit the As clause from a Dim declaration.)

The Expense Log program illustrates many of these data types. For example, the following Dim statements declare string variables:

```
Dim logFileName As String

Dim dollarAmount As String * 11
```

The first of these statements declares a variable-length string named *logFileName*, and the second a fixed-length string named *dollarAmount*. A variable-length string can contain any number of characters, up to about 2 billion in Windows 95; this is the most commonly used type of string variable. But a fixed-length string can simplify operations in some procedures. For example, the Expense Log program uses the string variable called *dollarAmount* in the process of organizing tabbed information in the expense report.

Note the format for declaring a fixed-length string variable. After the keyword String you include an asterisk and then the length of the variable in characters:

```
Dim variableName As String * length
```

You can declare individual variables in separate Dim statements, or you can use a single Dim statement to declare several variables at once:

```
Dim expDate, country, city, amount, _
            descript, exchRate

Dim largeRate As Double, smallRate as Double
```

The first of these Dim statements declares six variables belonging to the default Variant type. The second declares two double-precision floating-point variables.

In short, Visual Basic allows you to declare variables formally or informally, with or without the use of Dim statements. Your choice between these two approaches may depend on the length of your programming project or just your own programming style. Some programmers feel strongly about declaring *all* variables, and therefore appreciate the extra security supplied by the Option Explicit statement. Other programmers believe that coding is easier and more efficient without the requirement of variable declarations; they're glad to take advantage of Basic's traditionally loose structure in this regard. You'll decide for yourself as you begin building your own programs.

Notice the use of the terms *range* and *precision* in the descriptions of Visual Basic's numeric data types. The *range* of a numeric data type indicates the largest and smallest values that can be represented in the type. The *precision* is the number of digits of accuracy provided in the type. For complete technical descriptions of Visual Basic's data types, you can consult the online Help system:

1. Pull down the Help menu and choose the Search For Help On command.

2. Enter *types, intrinsic* in the text box at the top of the Index tab.

3. Press Enter to go directly to this help topic. A help screen titled Data Type Summary provides complete information about the Visual Basic data types.

THE VARIANT TYPE

Most variable types are, by design, somewhat rigid in the ways they can be used. For example, a numeric variable can store a number, not a string; if you try to assign a string value to a numeric variable, an error results. By contrast, a Variant can represent values of almost any type, thereby providing greater flexibility in programs that work with data. As you know, variables that are not explicitly declared belong to the Variant type by default. You may ultimately find yourself favoring the Variant over other variable types because of the advantages it provides.

Perhaps the best way to understand a Variant is to compare it with a text box control in a Visual Basic dialog box. A text box accepts any type of entry from the keyboard — number, currency, string, or date. What a program *does* with the input is another question, but the text box itself accepts all types of values. Likewise, any type of value can be stored in a Variant-type variable.

You'll find many illustrations of Variant-type variables in the Expense Log program. For example, the procedures that read expense records from the data file use Variants to represent individual fields of data. In Listing 5-4, the cmdExpReport_Click procedure defines six variables for this purpose:

```
Dim expDate, country, city, amount, _
            descript, exchRate
```

These variables then appear in the Input statement that reads each record from the open file:

```
Input #1, expDate, country, city, amount, _
            descript, exchRate
```

You'll learn more about reading data from files in later chapters. For now, simply notice that the Variant-type variables can receive whatever data types are stored in the file itself, including dates, strings, and numeric values.

THE SCOPE OF VARIABLES

The *scope* of a variable determines where it is available for use in your program. In general, variables defined in a Sub or Function procedure are private to that procedure, and not available to other procedures in the same form or module. If another procedure happens to have a variable of the same name, it is a *different* variable, with its own distinct values.

Private variables are one of the great advantages of procedural programming. They allow you to develop independent procedures that don't interfere with each other's data. But occasionally you may want to establish a few central variables at the *module level* — that is, available to all the procedures in a form or module. In this case, you define the variables in the general declarations section, at the top of the code and outside any procedure.

For example, Listing 5-1 shows the general declarations section of the Expense Log program, where two module-level String variables are declared:

```
Dim logFileName As String

Dim currCountry As String
```

The variable *logFileName* represents the file name under which the expense records will be stored. As you know, this file is ExpLog95.Txt by default, but can be changed at any time by the user. Because several procedures in the program need access to this name, *logFileName* serves most usefully as a module-level variable.

The variable *currCountry* represents the current entry or selection in the Country box. Defining this as a module-level variable gives the program a simple technique for finding out when the user has changed the Country entry — and therefore when the City list has to be rebuilt.

Because the Expense Log program contains a single form, the only scope levels you need to worry about are module level and procedure level. In a project that contains multiple forms and modules, scoping rules are more complex, as you'll learn in Chapter 6.

To overdo the use of module-level variables would be counter-productive in a procedural language. As you've learned, procedures can exchange information with each other through arguments, which is generally a more elegant way to share data. But declaring a few of a form's central variables at the module-level is always a reasonable technique, especially when a majority of the procedures in the program need access to the variables.

Once you've defined the name, type, and scope of a variable, the next step is to assign it a value.

ASSIGNING VALUES TO VARIABLES

An assignment statement changes the value of a variable. An equal sign represents the assignment. At the left side of the equal sign is the name of the variable that receives the value; at the right is the value being assigned:

```
variableName = value
```

The expression on the right side of the equal sign can appear in any form that produces a value of the appropriate type. For example, it can be a literal numeric value:

```
numEntries = 0
```

a literal string value enclosed in quotation marks:

```
boxTitle = "Expense Log File Name"
```

another variable name:

```
smallRate = exchRate
```

or an expression that calculates a value:

```
totAmount = totAmount + amount / exchRate
```

In some old versions of BASIC, assignment statements always began with the keyword Let:

```
Let variableName = value
```

Although Visual Basic still allows you to write assignments in this way, the Let keyword is now optional and seldom used.

INITIALIZING VARIABLES AND DEFINING CONSTANTS

Often you may want to *initialize* certain variables — that is, to assign them their first values — at the very beginning of a program's performance. The usual place to take care of initializations is in a special event procedure named Form_Load. This event is triggered when a form is first loaded into memory.

In a project that contains only one form — such as the Expense Log program — Visual Basic automatically loads the form into memory at the beginning of the program. The first code performed is the Form_Load procedure. This procedure is therefore an ideal place for initializing the program's module-level variables and for completing any other tasks that need to be accomplished at the outset of the program's performance.

You can examine the Expense Log program's Form_Load procedure in Listing 5-1, just below the general declarations section. You'll see that this procedure does indeed initialize the program's module-level variables. For example, the *logFileName* variable receives a string value represented by the name *DefaultFile:*

```
logFileName = DefaultFile
```

DefaultFile, in turn, is a constant defined in the general declarations section. Unlike a variable, a *constant* is a name that represents an unchanging value throughout a program. You use the keyword Const to create a constant:

```
Const constantName = value
```

For example, here's the statement that defines *DefaultFile:*

```
Const DefaultFile = "\ExpLog95.Txt"
```

Constants are convenient for representing important or frequently used values in a program.

WRITING EXPRESSIONS IN ASSIGNMENT STATEMENTS

As you've seen, the value on the right side of an assignment statement can appear in the form of an expression. To carry out the assignment, Visual Basic first performs the calculation that the expression represents and then stores the result in the variable.

Visual Basic provides a variety of *operators* for forming arithmetic expressions. As you see in the following list, an operator is the symbol that represents a particular calculation:

- The ∧ operator represents *exponentiation*, which raises a number to the power of an exponent. For example, the expression $x \wedge 2$ finds the value of x squared.

- The * operator represents multiplication.

- The / operator represents division, where the number at the left of the operator is the *dividend* and the number at the right is the *divisor*. The divisor may not be zero in a Visual Basic program; division by zero is not defined and results in a runtime error.

- The \ operator (the backslash character) represents *integer division*, which divides one integer by another and drops the remainder. For example, the expression 7 \ 3 results in a value of 2. The divisor may not be zero.

- The *Mod* operator returns the remainder from the division of two integers. For example, 7 *Mod* 3 is 1. This is the only arithmetic operation that is represented by a keyword rather than a symbol. Again, the divisor may not be zero.

- The + operator represents addition.

- The -- operator represents subtraction. The minus sign is also used for negation or for a negative number.

You'll find some of these operations illustrated in the Expense Log program. For example, the following statement from the procedure called cmdExpRept_Click calculates a running total of the expense amounts recorded in the current data file:

```
totAmount = totAmount + amount / exchRate
```

To find the total, the procedure divides each expense amount by the corresponding exchange rate, and adds the result to the previous total value.

Notice that the variable *totAmount* appears on both sides of the equal sign in this assignment statement. Sometimes a program needs to assign a new value to a variable, based on the variable's *current* value. Here's a simpler example, from the cmdRate_Click procedure (Listing 5-3):

```
numEntries = numEntries + 1
```

This statement increases the value of *numEntries* by 1. The expression on the right adds a value of 1 to the current value of *numEntries*; then the statement assigns this new incremented value to *numEntries*. As always in an assignment statement, the previous value of *numEntries* is lost.

UNDERSTANDING THE ORDER OF PRECEDENCE

When an expression contains multiple operations — as in the expression *totAmount + amount / exchRate* — Visual Basic follows a default set of *precedence* rules to decide which operation to perform first. Here's the order in which arithmetic operations are performed:

1. exponentiation (^)
2. negation (-)
3. multiplication (*) and division (/)
4. integer division (\)
5. the *Mod* operation
6. addition (+) and subtraction (-)

Following this order, you can see how the total expense amount is calculated in the *cmdExpRept_Click* procedure:

```
totAmount = totAmount + amount / exchRate
```

The division is performed first and then the addition, even though the operations appear in just the opposite order in the expression itself. Clearly it's important to pay close attention to the order of precedence in arithmetic expressions. Making false assumptions about the default order can result in significant calculation errors.

You can *override* the default order of precedence by inserting *parentheses* into an expression. Visual Basic performs operations that are enclosed in parentheses first. You can even place one set of parentheses inside another (sometimes known as *nested* parentheses). In this case, Visual Basic performs the operation in the innermost parentheses first, and then works its way step by step to the outermost parentheses.

For example, suppose you want to find the average of two values, *v1* and *v2*. To carry out the calculation, you need to find the sum of the values and then divide the result by 2. Here's the assignment statement you might write:

```
average = (v1 + v2) / 2
```

The parentheses in this expression specify that the addition must be performed before the division. Without the parentheses, Visual Basic would divide *v2* by 2 and then add the result to *v1*, which could produce a very different value.

You can use parentheses even when they are not strictly needed. Sometimes parentheses can help you formulate a complex expression, even when the default order of precedence is the correct way to evaluate the expression. Alternatively, you can use parentheses when you can't remember Visual Basic's default precedence rules. Extraneous parentheses are always better than an incorrect calculation.

PERFORMING OPERATIONS ON STRINGS

Visual Basic also defines specific operations for other types of data. For example, you can use an operation known as *concatenation* to combine two strings. The preferred operator for concatenation is the ampersand character (&). Here's an example from the *cmdRate_Click* procedure (Figure 5-4):

```
boxTitle = "Exchange Rates for " & cboCountry.Text
```

The expression on the right side of the equal sign combines a literal string with the current value of the *cboCountry.Text* property. This value is then displayed in the title bar of a message box. For example, you might see the following text in the title bar:

```
Exchange Rates for France
```

Turn back to Figure 5-5 to see exactly what this message box looks like.

Significantly, the & operator can be used with data values that don't belong to the same type — for example, a string and a number. In this case, Visual Basic converts the numeric value to a string before completing the concatenation. The cmdRate_Click procedure illustrates this technique in the following statement:

```
msg = "    Lowest: " & smallRate & _
      "    Highest: " & largeRate
```

Here the variables *smallRate* and *largeRate* are both declared as double-precision values:

```
Dim largeRate As Double, smallRate As Double
```

But the concatenation successfully combines string versions of these two numeric values with two literal strings. Again, you can turn back to Figure 5-5 to see an example of the resulting string.

An alternative operator for performing concatenations is the plus symbol (+). But unlike the ampersand, the + operator works only on strings. An attempt to combine a string and a number using + results in an error.

USING OTHER TYPES OF OPERATIONS

Visual Basic has other important categories of operations:

- The *relational* operators (also known as *comparison* operators) perform comparisons between values. For example, the expression $x > y$ is true if x is greater than y, or false if y is greater than or equal to x.

- The *logical* operators (sometimes known as Boolean operators) provide ways to combine true or false values. The most commonly used logical operators are *And*, *Or*, and *Not*.

If you continue examining the code of the Expense Log program, you'll find several examples of both relational and logical operators. You'll study these operations in detail in Chapter 7.

Listing 5-1
General declarations and the Form_Load procedure

```
' International Travel Expense Log Program
' ----------------------------------------

' Files:
' ------
' Project File:   ExpLog.VBP
' Form File:      ExpLog.Frm
```

```
' Maintains expense files for international
' business trips, and produces an expense report.
' Also helps keep track of exchange rate variations.

Option Explicit   ' Declare all variables.

' The default data file name is \ExpLog95.Txt,
' but the user can save expenses for individual
' trips under other names. The expense report is
' saved on disk as a text file under the name
' ExpRept.Txt.
```

Named constants

```
Const DefaultFile = "\ExpLog95.Txt"
Const ExpenseReport = "\ExpRept.Txt"
```

```
' The current expense file name
' is represented by the global
' variable logFileName.
```

```
Dim logFileName As String
```

Module-level variable declarations

```
' The current country name is
' also a global string variable.
```

```
Dim currCountry As String
```

```
' End of general declarations.
```

Form_Load procedure is often used to initialize variables

```
Private Sub Form_Load()
```

```
    ' The Form_Load procedure opens the default
    ' travel expense log file, and fills the country
    ' list with any country names stored in the file.

    logFileName = DefaultFile
    txtDate.Text = Format$(Date, "mm/dd/yy")
    currCountry = ""

    If FileExists(logFileName) Then FillCountryList

End Sub   ' Form_Load
```

Listing 5-2
The cmdSave_Click procedure and the BlankFields function

```
Private Sub cmdSave_Click()

    ' The cmdSave_Click procedure saves the current
    ' record to the travel expense log file.

    ' Make sure all data fields have been entered.
    If Not BlankFields Then

        ' Append a record to the file.
        Open logFileName For Append As #1
            Write #1, txtDate.Text, _
                      cboCountry.Text, _
                      cboCity.Text, _
                      Val(txtAmount.Text), _
                      txtDescript.Text, _
                      Val(txtRate.Text)
        Close #1

        ' Add the country name and city name
        ' to the appropriate lists if they are
        ' not already included.
        If Not AlreadyListed(cboCountry, cboCountry.Text) _
            Then cboCountry.AddItem cboCountry.Text
        If Not AlreadyListed(cboCity, cboCity.Text) _
            Then cboCity.AddItem cboCity.Text

        txtAmount.Text = ""
        txtDescript.Text = ""
        txtAmount.SetFocus

    Else

        MsgBox "You must fill in all the fields.", _
               0, "Save"

    End If

End Sub  ' cmdSave_Click
```

A function call in a decision statement

Function calls with arguments

```
Private Function BlankFields() As Boolean

    ' The BlankFields function tests for blank
    ' fields in the current record entry. The function
    ' returns a value of true if any entry is found
    ' to be empty; or false if all fields are complete.


    BlankFields = Trim(txtDate.Text) = "" Or _
                Trim(cboCountry.Text) = "" Or _
                Trim(cboCity.Text) = "" Or _
                Trim(txtAmount.Text) = "" Or _
                Trim(txtDescript.Text) = "" Or _
                Trim(txtRate.Text) = ""

End Function   ' BlankFields
```

Listing 5-3
The cmdRate_Click procedure

```
Private Sub cmdRate_Click()

    ' The cmdRate_Click procedure finds the range of
    ' Exchange rates recorded for the current country
    ' selection, and displays the range in a
    ' message box.

    Dim numEntries As Integer
    Dim largeRate As Double, smallRate As Double
    Dim item1, item3, item4, item5              Variant  is the
    Dim country As String, exchRate As Double   default data type
    Dim msg As String, boxTitle As String

    numEntries = 0

    If FileExists(logFileName) Then
        If Trim$(cboCountry.Text) <> "" Then
```

```
' Open the expense file and
' read each record in the file.
Open logFileName For Input As #1

Do While Not EOF(1)
  Input #1, item1, country, item3, item4, _
              item5, exchRate

  ' Look for matches between the current
  ' country selection, and the countries
  ' identified in specific expense records.
  If UCase$(country) = UCase$(cboCountry.Text) Then
    numEntries = numEntries + 1

    If numEntries = 1 Then
      smallRate = exchRate
      largeRate = exchRate
    Else

      ' Compare each exchange rate to locate
      ' the smallest and largest rates on record.
      If exchRate < smallRate Then _
        smallRate = exchRate
      If exchRate > largeRate Then _
        largeRate = exchRate
    End If
  End If
Loop

Close #1

boxTitle = "Exchange Rates for " & cboCountry.Text
If numEntries > 0 Then
  msg = "   Lowest: " & smallRate & _
        "   Highest: " & largeRate
Else  ' If no country matches were found...
  msg = "No entries for " & cboCountry.Text & "."
End If
```

Increasing the value of a variable by 1

```
      Else  ' If no country is currently selected...
        msg = "Please select or enter a country name."
        boxTitle = "Exchange Rates"
      End If

    Else   ' If logFileName doesn't exist...

      msg = logFileName & " is not available."
      boxTitle = "Exchange Rates"

    End If

    MsgBox msg, , boxTitle

End Sub   ' cmdRate_Click
```

Concatenation using the & operator

Listing 5-4
The cmdExpRept_Click procedure

```
Private Sub cmdExpReport_Click()

    ' The cmdExpReport_Click procedure creates an
    ' expense report file summarizing the data stored
    ' in the current travel expense log. The summary
    ' is always stored in \ExpRept.Txt

    Dim expDate, country, city, amount, _
                 descript, exchRate
    Dim dollarAmount As String * 11
    Dim totDollarAmount As String * 11
    Dim totAmount

    If FileExists(logFileName) Then
       Open logFileName For Input As #1
       Open ExpenseReport For Output As #2

       ' Create the report title and the
       ' column headings.
```

Fixed-length string variables

```
Print #2, Tab(23); "Travel Expense Log"
Print #2, Tab(23); "====== ======= ==="
Print #2, Tab(25); logFileName

Print #2,
Print #2, "Place"; Tab(27); "Date"; Tab(39); _
           "Amount"; Tab(48); "Description"

Print #2, "-----"; Tab(27); "----"; Tab(39); _
           "------"; Tab(48); "-----------"



' Read each expense record and add
' a detail line to the report.
totAmount = 0
Do While Not EOF(1)
   Input #1, expDate, country, city, amount, _
            descript, exchRate
```

Default order of operations

```
   totAmount = totAmount + amount / exchRate
   RSet dollarAmount = Format$(amount / exchRate, _
                "$##,###.00")


   Print #2, city; ", "; country; Tab(27); expDate; _
            dollarAmount; "   "; descript

Loop

' Display the total amount spent.
RSet totDollarAmount = Format$(totAmount, "$###,###.00")
Print #2,
Print #2, "Total amount spent ... "; Tab(35); totDollarAmount

Close #1, #2

MsgBox "File is saved as " & ExpenseReport _
   , , "Expense Report"
```

```
      Else  ' If logFileName doesn't exist...

        MsgBox logFileName & " is not available." _
            , , "Expense Report"

      End If

  End Sub  ' cmdExpReport_Click
```

Listing 5-5
The cmdClear_Click and cmdExit_Click procedures.

```
Private Sub cmdClear_Click()

    ' The cmdClear_Click procedure clears the dialog
    ' box, in preparation for a new record entry.

    cboCountry.Text = ""
    cboCity.Text = ""
    txtAmount.Text = ""
    txtDescript.Text = ""
    txtRate.Text = ""
    txtDate.Text = Format$(Date, "mm/dd/yy")
    txtDate.SetFocus

End Sub   ' cmdClear_Click


Private Sub cmdExit_Click()

    ' The cmdExit_Click procedure ends the program
    ' when the user clicks the Exit button.

    End

End Sub   ' cmdExit_Click
```

Listing 5-6
The picFileName_Click procedure

```
Private Sub picFileName_Click()

' The picFileName_Click procedure gives the user
' the opportunity to open a different travel
' expense log file.

Dim inPrompt As String
Dim boxTitle As String

inPrompt = _
  "Enter a new file name for your expense log."
boxTitle = "Expense Log File Name"

' Get a new file name from the user.
logFileName = InputBox _
              (inPrompt, boxTitle, logFileName)

' If the user enters no name or clicks cancel,
' revert to the default expense file name.
If logFileName = "" Then _
  logFileName = DefaultFile

' Display the expense file name in the
' program's title bar.
frmExpLog.Caption = _
  "International Travel Expense Log - " _
    & logFileName

If FileExists(logFileName) Then
  FillCountryList
Else
  cboCountry.Clear
  cboCity.Clear
End If

End Sub  ' picFileName_Click
```

Listing 5-7
The GotFocus procedures and the HighlightContents procedure

```
Private Sub txtDate_GotFocus()

   ' The txtDate_GotFocus procedure highlights
   ' the contents of the Date text box whenever
   ' the box receives the focus.

  HighlightContents txtDate

End Sub   ' txtDate_GotFocus


Private Sub txtAmount_GotFocus()

   ' The txtAmount_GotFocus procedure highlights
   ' the contents of the Amount text box whenever
   ' the box receives the focus.

  HighlightContents txtAmount

End Sub   ' txtAmount_GotFocus

Private Sub txtDescript_GotFocus()

   ' The txtDescript_GotFocus procedure highlights
   ' the contents of the Description text box
   ' whenever the box receives the focus.

  HighlightContents txtDescript

End Sub   ' txtDescript_GotFocus


Private Sub txtRate_GotFocus()

   ' The txtRate_GotFocus procedure highlights
   ' the contents of the Rate text box
   ' whenever the box receives the focus.
```

A procedure call with one argument

```
    HighlightContents txtRate

End Sub   ' txtRate_GotFocus



Private Sub HighlightContents(target As Control)

  ' The HighlightContents procedure uses the
  ' SelStart and SelLength properties to
  ' highlight the contents of any control
  ' that has just received the focus.

  target.SelStart = 0
  target.SelLength = Len(target.Text)

End Sub   ' HighlightContents
```

Listing 5-8
The LostFocus procedures and the ValidNumInput procedure

```
Private Sub txtDate_LostFocus()

  ' The txtDate_LostFocus procedure ensures that
  ' the value entered into the Date text box is
  ' a valid date.

  If IsDate(txtDate.Text) Then
    txtDate.Text = Format$(txtDate.Text, "mm/dd/yy")
  Else
    txtDate.Text = Format$(Date, "mm/dd/yy")
  End If

End Sub   ' txtDate_LostFocus



Private Sub txtAmount_LostFocus()
```

```
' The txtAmount_LostFocus procedure ensures
' that the value entered into the Amount text box
' is a number.

  ValidNumInput txtAmount

End Sub   ' txtAmount_LostFocus



Private Sub txtRate_LostFocus()

  ' The txtRate_LostFocus procedure ensures that
  ' the value entered in the Rate text box is a
  ' number.

    ValidNumInput txtRate

End Sub    ' txtRate_LostFocus
```

A procedure that takes a control-type argument

```
Private Sub ValidNumInput(textControl As Control)

  ' The ValidNumInput procedure tests for a
  ' valid numeric input value in a text box that
  ' has just lost the focus.

  If Val(textControl.Text) = 0 Then _
    textControl.Text = "" _
  Else _
    textControl.Text = Val(textControl.Text)

End Sub    ' ValidNumInput
```

Listing 5-9

The cboCountry event procedures and the ChangeCityList procedure

```
Private Sub cboCountry_Click()

  ' Change the city list in response to
  ' a new selection from the country list.

  ChangeCityList

End Sub   ' cboCountry_Click


Private Sub cboCountry_LostFocus()

  ' Change the city list in response to
  ' possible change in the country entry.

  ChangeCityList

End Sub   ' cboCountry_LostFocus


Private Sub ChangeCityList()

  ' The ChangeCityList procedure rebuilds
  ' the cboCity list if the country name has
  ' changed.

  If UCase$(cboCountry.Text) <> _
    UCase$(currCountry) Then
      cboCity.Clear
      If FileExists(logFileName) Then _
        FillCityList cboCountry.Text
      currCountry = cboCountry.Text
  End If

End Sub   ' ChangeCityList
```

Listing 5-10

The FillCountryList and FillCityList procedures

```
Private Sub FillCountryList()

    ' FillCountryList reads the names of countries
    ' from the current log file and adds all
    ' unique country names to the cboCountry list.

    Dim item1, item3, item4, item5, item6
    Dim countryName As String

    cboCountry.Clear
    cboCity.Clear

    ' Open the expense file and
    ' read each country name.
    Open logFileName For Input As #1
      Do While Not EOF(1)
        Input #1, item1, countryName, _
          item3, item4, item5, item6

        ' Add a country name to the list
        ' if it's not already included.
        If Not AlreadyListed(cboCountry, countryName) _
          Then cboCountry.AddItem countryName
      Loop

    Close #1

End Sub    ' FillCountryList




Private Sub FillCityList(countryName As String)

  ' FillCityList reads the names of cities
  ' recorded for a selected country, and
  ' adds the city names to the City list
  ' in the cboCity control.
```

```
Dim item1, item4, item5, item6
Dim country As String, city As String

' Open the expense file and read each record.
Open logFileName For Input As #1
  Do While Not EOF(1)
    Input #1, item1, country, _
      city, item4, item5, item6

    ' Search for matches between the current
    ' country selection and the countries
    ' identified in specific expense records.
    ' Add the corresponding city names to the
    ' list if they are not already included.

    If UCase$(countryName) = _
      UCase$(country) Then _
        If Not AlreadyListed(cboCity, city) _
          Then cboCity.AddItem city

  Loop
  Close #1

End Sub  ' FillCityList
```

Listing 5-11
The FileExists and AlreadyListed functions

```
Private Function FileExists(fileName As String) _
  As Boolean

  ' Checks to see if a file exists on disk.
  ' Returns True if the file is found, or
  ' False if it is not.

  ' Set up an error trap.
  On Error GoTo noFile
```

```
' Attempt to open the file.
Open fileName For Input As #1
Close #1

' Return True if no error occurs.
FileExists = True
Exit Function
```

Assigning a boolean value to a function

```
noFile:

  ' If the file can't be opened,
  ' return False.
  FileExists = False


End Function   ' FileExists




Private Function AlreadyListed(listControl As Control, _
                          newItem As String) As Boolean

  ' The AlreadyListed function checks an existing
  ' list to see if a potential new entry (newItem)
  ' is currently in the list or not. If the item
  ' is in the list, the function returns true; if
  ' not, false.

  Dim i As Integer

  AlreadyListed = False

  ' Go through the current list and
  ' search for a match.
  For i = 0 To listControl.ListCount - 1
    If UCase$(listControl.List(i)) = _
      UCase$(newItem) Then _
      AlreadyListed = True
  Next i

End Function   ' AlreadyListed
```

CHAPTER

6

Designing a Project

*A*s you've seen, you can build a practical application around a single form. A project that presents all of its features and operations in one window can be a perfectly appropriate solution to a particular programming task. For example, in the International Travel Expense Log program (Chapter 5), all the action takes place in one dialog box, where you enter your expense records and then request information about the data you've recorded. Likewise, the two currency exchange programs (Chapters 1 to 4) provide varieties of information about international currencies in single windows.

But some applications are more complex and require more than one form to present all their features. Even if *most* of a program's activities take place in one major window, additional forms and dialog boxes may appear on the screen as the user chooses menu commands or performs other operations in the program.

To develop such a program in Visual Basic, you create a project consisting of multiple forms. One form may become the program's primary window, displaying the workspace that is most closely associated with the program's main features. But other forms may serve secondary purposes — for example, eliciting information from the user, offering specific sets of options, or presenting information in useful formats.

Visual Basic provides some important properties and methods that allow you to design and work with multiple forms in a program. For example, you can use properties to define several important characteristics of a form in your application:

- The title bar caption, which your program can change at any time during a performance

- The buttons available on the title bar, including the minimize, maximize, and close buttons, and the control-menu box

- The form's border style, which determines whether the user can resize the form during runtime

- The form's reaction to keystrokes — that is, whether specific keystrokes will trigger form events rather than control events

- The three-dimensional quality of a form's appearance

These properties help to define a form's specific role in your project.

Also central to your program's capability to manipulate multiple forms are two methods named Show and Hide:

- The Show method loads a form into memory (if it's not already loaded) and displays the form on the screen. This method gives you the option of specifying whether the form will be *modal* (the exclusive form available for use at a given time) or *modeless* (a nonexclusive form). You'll learn more about these two form styles later. The Show method triggers a form event named Activate. The Form_Activate procedure is therefore a good place to write code that initializes the conditions for a newly displayed form.

- The Hide method removes the form window from the desktop — temporarily or permanently, depending on the plan of your program.

In this chapter you'll begin learning about these and other features as you examine a project named the Restaurant Review application. The program builds a personal restaurant database for locations anywhere in the world. If you're a frequent business traveler, the database helps you keep track of restaurants you like — or don't like — wherever you go. In each restaurant record you can keep information about varieties of cuisines, food quality, price, and suitable ambiance for business meetings. Closer to home, you can also use the database to record information about favorite restaurants in your own neighborhood. The program provides several techniques for retrieving information from the database whenever you need it.

Running the Restaurant Review Program

The Restaurant program is stored on the program disk as RestRevu.VBP. Open the application now. In the Project window (Figure 6-1) you'll see that it contains two forms and one module:

- RestRevu.Frm (named frmRestRevu) is the program's main dialog box, in which the user enters individual restaurant records and retrieves records for inspection or revision.

- RestList.Frm (named frmRestList) is a secondary dialog box, enabling the user to scroll through all the restaurant records for a selected city.

- RestRevu.Bas (Module1) is a module that contains declarations and other code relevant to the entire program.

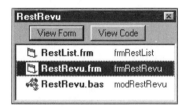

Figure 6-1
The project window for the Restaurant Review program.

THE STARTUP FORM

In this application, RestRevu.Frm is known as the *startup form*, which means it is the first window to appear on the desktop when you run the program. By default, the startup form is the first form you create when you're developing a project. Alternatively, you can designate *any* form in your application as the startup form by following these simple steps:

1. In the Visual Basic development environment, pull down the Tools menu and choose the Options command. In the Options dialog box, click the Project tab, as shown in Figure 6-2.

2. The Startup Form box contains a list of all the forms you've added to your project. Pull down the list and choose the name of the form you want to designate as the startup.

3. Click OK.

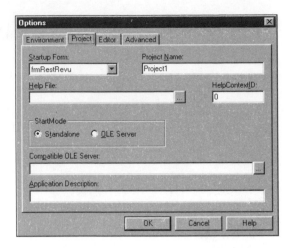

Figure 6-2

The Project tab in the Options dialog box.

When you run a program, Visual Basic immediately loads the startup form into memory, triggering the Load event for the form. If you've written a Form_Load procedure in your startup form, this is the first code to be performed.

Try running the Restaurant Review program now, by pressing F5 or clicking the Start button on the Visual Basic toolbar. The Restaurants dialog box appears on the screen, as shown in Figure 6-3. This window contains a variety of controls that allow you to enter the fields of a new restaurant record or ultimately to view the fields of an existing record:

- The City combo box is where you enter the restaurant's location. As soon as you begin entering records, the attached list shows the names of all the cities represented in your database. You'll see how this works shortly.

- The Restaurant box is for the name of the establishment. The attached list shows the restaurants recorded for a selected city, a selected food type, or both. But the Restaurant list remains empty until you choose a city or food type that's already represented in your database.

- The box labeled Type of Food is for identifying the restaurant's cuisine specialty, such as French, Mexican, Chinese, barbecue, or fast food. Again, the program develops an attached list of all food types represented in your database.

- The Comments box allows you to enter any brief notes you might want to include in a given restaurant record.
- The Quality option buttons give you the opportunity to assign a rating to the restaurant, from four stars (****) down to one star (*).
- The Price option buttons allow you to specify the price range of a meal at the restaurant, from very expensive ($$$$) down to inexpensive ($).

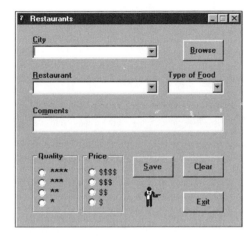

Figure 6-3
The Restaurants dialog box.

ENTERING A RESTAURANT RECORD

Suppose you've just returned from a business trip to Washington, D.C., and you want to record information about a small French restaurant you tried while you were there. You start up the Restaurant Review program and begin entering the relevant data: the city, the name of the restaurant, the type of food, and a brief description in the Comments box. You liked the food and the atmosphere, so you click the three-star option in the Quality box. The price was moderate, so you click the $$ option in the Price box. When all of these fields are complete, the Restaurants dialog box might appear as shown in Figure 6-4. To save the record, you click the Save button, or press Alt+S. In response, the program writes your new record to the database and then clears the dialog box for your next record entry.

Figure 6-4
Entering a restaurant record.

The database is saved under the file name RestRevu.DB, in the root directory of your hard disk. The program creates this file the first time you run the program, and adds a new record to it each time you click the Save button.

Significantly, the program insists that each record be complete. In other words, you have to enter information in all four text fields and you must select Quality and Price options before you click the Save button. If you omit a field, an error message appears on the screen, as shown in Figure 6-5. To continue your work, click OK and then finish the record before clicking Save again.

Figure 6-5
The error message for an incomplete record.

RETRIEVING RECORDS FROM THE DATABASE

The Restaurant dialog box serves not only as a form for entering new records, but also as a window for viewing existing records. Once you begin developing your database, the City, Type of Food, and Restaurant boxes are designed to display lists of the information you've stored.

For example, suppose you've been using the program for some time to record your reviews of restaurants in the many cities you've visited on business trips. Now you're anticipating a trip to California and you want to search for the restaurants you've recorded in your database for San Francisco. To do so, begin by clicking the Clear button, if necessary, to clear any information currently displayed in the dialog box. Then click the down-arrow button displayed at the right side of the City box. As you can see in Figure 6-6, the resulting list displays all the cities currently represented in the records of your Restaurant database. The cities are arranged in alphabetical order. Click San Francisco as your city selection. When you do so, this name is copied to the City box.

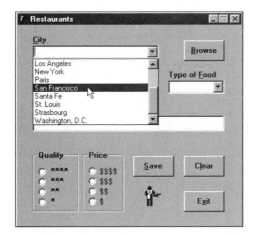

Figure 6-6
The City list.

Once you've chosen a city, the program automatically searches through the database for all the restaurants corresponding to your selection. To view the list of restaurants in San Francisco, you simply click the down-arrow button at the right side of the Restaurant box. As shown in Figure 6-7, the list of restaurants appears in alphabetical order.

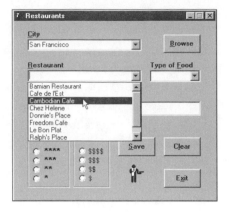

Figure 6-7
The Restaurant list for a selected city.

You can now select any entry in this list to view the entire restaurant record. For instance, if you want to see the information you've recorded about a restaurant called Cambodian Cafe, you click this name in the Restaurant list. In response, the program retrieves this record and displays all of its fields in the Restaurant dialog box, as in Figure 6-8. (Keep in mind that the program can display only the information that's actually available in your own database. You can duplicate these sample screens — or display real information of your own — only after you've saved a selection of records in the database.)

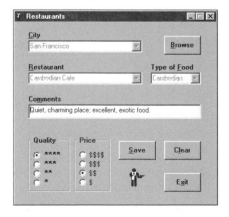

Figure 6-8
Retrieving a restaurant record from the database.

Alternatively, you can search for restaurants by cuisine type. If you want to see a list of all the French restaurants in your database, begin by clicking the Clear button to clear any existing data in the dialog box. Then pull down the Type of Food list. The program displays all the unique cuisine types that are currently represented in your database, as in Figure 6-9. Select an entry from this list. Then pull down the Restaurant list to see the names of all the restaurants in this category.

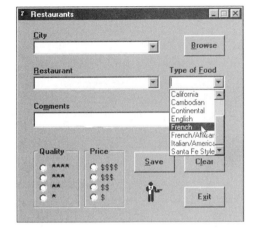

Figure 6-9
The list of cuisines.

Another option is to search for specific types of food in a selected city — in other words, to select all the records that match both a city name and a cuisine type. To do so, follow these steps:

1. Click Clear to clear the dialog box.
2. Pull down the City list and select a city.
3. Pull down the Type of Food list and select a cuisine.
4. Pull down the Restaurant list. The program displays all the restaurants that match the two criteria you've specified. (Note that the Restaurant list remains empty if the program finds no matches for the combination of City and Type of Food entries you've selected. This is an *and* condition — a record must match *both* fields to be selected.)

BROWSING THROUGH RESTAURANT RECORDS

The program gives you a convenient way to examine all the records you've recorded for a given city in your personal restaurant database. This is where the project's second form comes in: You can select a name from the City list and then click the Browse button, located near the upper-right corner of the dialog box. When you do so, the program temporarily hides the main dialog box and displays a new window in which you can quickly scroll through the restaurant descriptions for the selected city.

For example, suppose you've recently taken a short business trip to Paris, during which you recorded descriptions of three good restaurants for meeting with clients. Now, back home again, you want to take a look at these records. To do so, you follow these steps:

1. Click the down-arrow button at the right side of the City box, and select Paris from the resulting list.

2. Click the Browse button, as shown in Figure 6-10. (Alternatively, you can press Alt+B to use this feature.) In response, the program hides the Restaurants dialog box and displays a new window, entitled *Restaurants in PARIS*. This window displays one complete restaurant record at a time, in a format that's easy to read, as shown in Figure 6-11.

3. The new dialog box contains buttons labeled Previous and Next. To scroll forward to the next restaurant record, you can either click the Next button with the mouse, or simply press the PgDn key on your keyboard. Likewise, to scroll backward to the previous record, click Previous or press PgUp on your keyboard. Each time you take one of these actions, the program displays a new restaurant record in the window.

4. When you reach the last record in this selection, the program disables the Next button. As shown in Figure 6-12, the button's caption is *dimmed*, or displayed in gray text; the button no longer responds to a mouse click. (Likewise, pressing PgDn produces no response.) Press Previous repeatedly to go back to the first record in the selection; when you do so, you'll see that the program disables the Previous button.

5. When you've finished examining this particular set of records, click the Cancel button. The program closes the Restaurants in Paris box and reopens the main Restaurants dialog box.

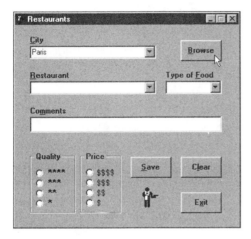

Figure 6-10
Preparing to click the Browse button.

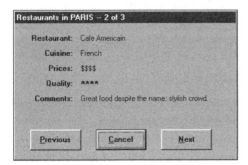

Figure 6-11
The program's second dialog box.

You can now click the Clear button to clear the dialog box so you can continue entering new records or examining existing records. By the way, if you click the Browse button at a time when the City box is empty, the program displays an error message, shown in Figure 6-13. The Browse operation is designed to display restaurant records from a particular city; you therefore can't use this feature until you select a city name.

Figure 6-12
The disabled Next button.

Figure 6-13
The Browse error message.

REVISING RESTAURANT RECORDS

Finally, the program also enables you to revise the information in any record you've already stored in your restaurant database. To do so, follow these steps:

1. To find the restaurant record that you want to revise, make appropriate selections from the City and Type of Food lists.

2. Pull down the Restaurant list and select the name of the target restaurant. The program displays the fields of the selected record in the Restaurant dialog box.

3. Make any changes you want in the Comments box, or to the Quality and Price options. (The program disables the City, Restaurant, and Type of Food boxes to prevent revisions in these fields. Although you can *view* the contents of these boxes for the record you've selected, you can't make changes.)

4. Click the Save button. In response, the program displays the Existing Record box (Figure 6-14), asking you to confirm that you want to overwrite an existing record in your database.

5. Click Yes to save the revised record. The program writes the revised record over the existing record in the database. (Alternatively, you can click No if you change your mind about revising the record.)

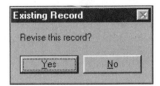

Figure 6-14
Revising a restaurant record.

When you've finished entering, examining, and revising restaurant records, click the Exit button (or press Alt+X) to end the program. As you've seen, this program makes effective use of its two forms to provide different views of the information in a database. In the upcoming sections of this chapter you'll examine the techniques for handling these forms and the controls they contain.

Inside the Restaurant Review Program

Each of the three files identified in this application's project window — the two forms and the module — contains part of the program's code. Listings 6-1 through 6-18 display the code of the entire project:

- Listing 6-1 shows the code contained in the RestRevu.Bas module. This module includes a Type statement that defines the program's central data structure — the fields of a restaurant record. It also declares a single record variable named *RestRecord* to represent individual restaurant records read from or written to the database on disk. (You'll learn much more about record structures in Chapter 7.) The constant *DatabaseFile* represents the name of the database on disk, and a string variable named *currCity* is used to communicate an essential piece of information between the program's two forms. You'll see exactly how the program uses this variable later. Finally, the module contains one general procedure, a function named *StrFix*. Like everything else defined or declared in the module, this function is available for use anywhere in the program.

- Listings 6-2 through 6-12 show the code contained in the frmRestRevu form. The code includes event procedures for all the form's command buttons and combo boxes, plus a large collection of general procedures designed to carry out specific operations on the form. Of particular interest in this chapter is the cmdBrowse_Click procedure (Listing 6-6), which takes care of hiding the Restaurant window and displaying the browse window. As you'll see, these changes are carried out by the Hide and Show methods.

- Listings 6-13 through 6-18 show the code in the frmRestList form. In addition to the Form_Activate procedure, which initializes conditions in the dialog box, these listings include Click event procedures for each command button. Significantly, there is also a Form_KeyDown procedure that enables the program to recognize the PgUp and PgDn keys while this form is displayed on the desktop. You'll learn how this feature works shortly.

As you develop a project that contains more than one form, you'll find yourself paying close attention to the properties of the forms. As you know already, some form properties define characteristics that are more cosmetic than functional. But others establish conditions that are central to the program's operations, and have significant implications for the design and content of your project's code. Before jumping directly into the code of the Restaurant program, you should therefore take a brief detour to the Properties window. You'll examine a few property settings for this program's two forms and several of the controls they contain.

Understanding the Properties of Forms and Controls

If the Restaurant Review program is still running, click the Exit button on the main dialog box now to stop the performance. To set up the Visual Basic environment conveniently for a review of form properties, follow these steps:

- Press Ctrl+R, if necessary, to display and activate the Project window.

- Select RestRevu.frm in the project list, and click the View Form button to display the form.

- Press Ctrl+R, select RestList.frm, and click View Form again. Now both forms are displayed in design mode. RestList.frm is active.

- Without selecting any individual control on the form, press F4 to view the Properties window. The list displays the property settings for the frmRestList form. With both forms open, you can easily switch between them to compare their properties.

Try scrolling through the Properties list and studying the variety of properties available for a form. Keep in mind that you can jump to a help topic for any property by selecting the property's name in the list and pressing F1. This is a very useful way to learn quickly about the properties of any object in Visual Basic.

In the upcoming sections you'll examine the settings of a half dozen form properties. At least one of them is purely visual in its effect, and several others control small but significant details in the presentation and function of a form. But two of the properties have larger effects on the program's overall design.

CHANGING THE APPEARANCE OF A FORM AND ITS CONTROLS

The first item in the Properties list, Appearance, provides a useful way to change the look of a form and many of its controls in one simple setting. This property gives the form a gray background, and adds subtle shadings to the controls in a form to enhance the three-dimensional effect of the form's display on the desktop.

The Appearance property has two possible settings, identified as Flat and 3D. (The default setting is 3D.) Figure 6-15 shows what the Restaurants dialog box would look like with Flat settings for the form and its controls. Comparing this to Figure 6-3, you can see that the 3D setting provides a richer, more typical Windows-like appearance for the form. In the Restaurant project, both forms have Appearance settings of 3D.

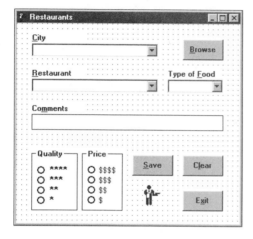

Figure 6-15
A form's look with an Appearance setting of Flat.

Keep this property in mind whenever you create a new form, and decide for yourself how you want the form to appear on the screen.

SELECTING THE CONTROL ELEMENTS OF A FORM

In Windows 95, as in previous versions of the Windows environment, a window that appears on the desktop may typically have certain visual elements that help the user manipulate the window itself:

- The control menu is represented by an icon at the left side of a window's title bar. By clicking this icon, you pull down a menu of basic control commands, which may include Restore, Move, Size, Minimize, Maximize, and Close.

- The Minimize, Maximize, and Close buttons, clustered together at the right side of the title bar, enable you to reduce a window to a button along the Windows 95 taskbar, expand a window to its maximum size on the desktop, or close a window.

By default, each new form you create in Visual Basic possesses all of these elements. But sometimes you may have reasons to exclude or disable one or more of these features, to restrict the operations available for a given window. For example, the Restaurant window contains an active Minimize button but an inactive Maximize button; this combination allows the user to reduce the window to a taskbar button, but not to expand the window's dimensions, which are initially set appropriately for the window's contents.

Visual Basic provides several form properties that you can use to define the control elements of a window, and thereby expand or restrict the user's ability to change the window's properties:

- The ControlBox property has values of True or False, for including or excluding the control-menu icon. (By the way, the Icon property enables you to select the icon that represents the control menu. The *icons* folder in the Visual Basic directory contains a large library of files that are appropriate for this use.)

- The MinButton or MaxButton properties have values of True or False to include or exclude the minimize and maximize buttons at the upper-right corner of the window.

- The BorderStyle control is somewhat more complex. For a form, it has six settings, numbered 0 to 5:

  A setting of 0, None, produces no border, no title bar, and therefore none of the elements that usually appear on the title bar.

  A setting of 1, Fixed Single, produces a fixed border and a title bar that may contain a control-menu icon and all the other usual buttons (depending on the settings of the ControlBox, MaxButton, and Min-Button properties). With a fixed single border, the window can't be resized by dragging the border with the mouse.

A setting of 2, Sizable, is the default and results in a sizable border. This means the user can drag any border with the mouse to resize the window. Under this setting, the window has a title bar that can include any of its usual control elements.

A value of 3, Fixed Dialog, gives a fixed border. The window has a title bar and may include a control-menu icon, but not a minimize or maximize button. The window isn't resizable.

A setting of 4, Fixed ToolWindow, is similar to the Fixed Single setting, except that the resulting form contains no minimize or maximize button and does not appear on the Windows 95 taskbar.

A setting of 5, Sizeable ToolWindow, is similar to the Sizable setting, except that the form has no minimize or maximize button and does not appear on the taskbar.

Take a look at the settings of these four properties for the two forms in the Restaurant program, and consider their effects on the resulting windows:

- The frmRestRevu form has a BorderStyle setting of 1, which means that the window cannot be resized, but any combination of buttons is possible on the title bar. Accordingly, the form has ControlBox and MinButton settings of True so that the window can be minimized, but a MaxButton setting of False so that the window cannot be maximized. Interestingly enough, clicking the Close button on the title bar (or choosing Close from the control menu) is an alternate way of ending the program, and has the same effect as clicking the Exit button on the form itself.

- The frmRestList form has a BorderStyle setting of 3, which means that the resulting window cannot be sized, maximized, or minimized. Although this setting does not necessarily preclude the presence of a control-menu icon, the form has a ControlBox setting of False so that the control menu will not be available. Consequently, the only way to close the browse window is to click the Cancel button, which the program takes as a signal to switch back to the main dialog box. (As you'll see later, the cmdCancel_Click procedure contains essential code for making a successful switch between these two windows.) Note that the frmRestList form has MaxButton and MinButton settings of False; but with a BorderStyle setting of 3, these other settings are redundant.

In short, you can see that these four properties — BorderStyle, MaxButton, MinButton, and ControlBox — enable you to specify exactly how much control your user will have over the shape and status of a window, and how many operations will be reserved for your program to control. In the Restaurant application, which carefully orchestrates a particular display sequence between two windows, this is an important distinction.

PROPERTIES IN CODE

When you first begin designing a new project, the Properties window, with its long lists of properties for any selected object, is always a main focus of your attention. But properties may also play prominent roles in the code you eventually write for your project. Their names may appear explicitly in expressions and statements, or their influence may implicitly affect your program's design.

As you know, a reference to a property in code generally takes the form *objectName.propertyName*. In an assignment statement, this reference may appear on the left side of the equal sign:

```
objectName.propertyName = value
```

The result of this statement is to change the property setting to a new *value*. As you learn about the properties of a given object, you'll come to recognize categories of use:

- Some property settings can be changed only at design time, not at runtime. The ControlBox, MaxButton, and MinButton properties are three examples. The settings of these properties are *read-only* at runtime; by referencing the property name, your program can read the current setting, but cannot change it.

- Conversely, a few properties are available only at runtime. For example, a property named ActiveForm supplies the name of the form that is active at a given point during runtime. ActiveForm is not listed in the Properties window, because it has no relevance at design time.

- A large selection of properties can be changed either at design time or at runtime. For example, the Caption property for a form specifies the text displayed along the form's title bar. At design time you create a form's title by selecting Caption in the Properties window and entering a line of text. In your code, you can change the caption at any time by assigning a new value to the Form.Caption property.

In the Restaurant Review program, the title of the main dialog box is simply *Restaurant*. This caption remains unchanged throughout the program. But the second dialog box is a different story. When this second window is on the screen, its title displays the name of the city you've selected, the current record number, and the total number of restaurant records for this city; for example:

```
Restaurants in PARIS -- 2 of 3
```

While the second dialog box is active, this title changes each time you click the Next or Previous button. (Look back at Figures 6-11 and 6-12 to confirm that this is the case.) As you might guess, the code responsible for this change is in cmdNext_Click and cmdPrevious_Click, the event procedures that respond to clicks of the Next and Previous buttons (Listing 6-15). Near the top of each of these procedures, the following assignment statement changes the Caption property:

```
frmRestList.Caption = "Restaurants in " _
   & currCity & " -- " & _
   currRec & " of " & recCount
```

As you can see, the caption is a concatenation of several literal strings and variables.

Incidentally, these same event procedures contain another important example of a property whose setting is changed frequently at runtime, the Enabled property. Enabled determines whether a given object will respond to the user's input activities, such as clicks of the mouse or entries from the keyboard. This property applies to forms and to most controls displayed in a form; its default value is True, which means events may occur around a given form or object.

In the frmRestList form, the Restaurant program uses the Enabled property explicitly to activate or deactivate the Next and Previous buttons. For example, examine the following code from the cmdPrevious_Click procedure (Listing 6-15):

```
If (currRec - 1) = 0 Then _
   cmdPrevious.Enabled = False
If currRec < recCount Then _
   cmdNext.Enabled = True
```

If the current restaurant record displayed in the form is the first one available for the selected city, the program sets the cmdPrevioius.Enabled setting to False. As a result, the Previous button is dimmed on the dialog box, and will no longer respond to mouse clicks. But as long as the current record is not the only restaurant available for the selected city, the setting cmdNext.Enabled is assigned a value of True, so that the user can click the Next button to examine the next record.

You'll find another important use of the Enabled property in a general procedure named FindRestaurantRecord, which is part of the frmRestRevu form (Listing 6-12). This procedure searches for a particular restaurant record when the user pulls down the Restaurant list and selects an entry. When the record is located, the procedure displays its fields in the Restaurant dialog box. At this point, the user has the option of changing certain fields in the record — the Comments entry, the Quality rating, or the Price rating — and then clicking the Save button to save a revised version of the record. But the program does not permit changes in the City, Restaurant, and Type of Food entries. To prevent the user from making changes in these three fields, the program simply switches the Enabled settings to False for the corresponding controls:

```
cboCity.Enabled = False
cboFoodType.Enabled = False
cboRestaurant.Enabled = False
```

After the user completes the save operation — or clears the record from the dialog box without revising it — the cmdClear_Click procedure (Listing 6-5) restores the original True settings of these properties:

```
cboCity.Enabled = True
cboFoodType.Enabled = True
cboRestaurant.Enabled = True
```

In short, the ability to control the property settings of forms and controls at runtime is one of the important features of Visual Basic programming. You'll see many other examples in other projects presented in this book.

PROPERTIES AND PROGRAM DESIGN

Some properties are so influential that they may affect the way you design your program, and even dictate the selection of procedures you decide to write. One obvious example of this is the form property named MDIChild. When you set this property to its nondefault True setting, it creates an instance of a *child* form in a *multiple-document interface* application. In an MDI program, a primary background window serves as the container for any number of document windows; familiar examples are spreadsheet programs such as Excel and Lotus 1-2-3, and word processing programs such as Word and WordPerfect. You'll explore the topic of MDI programming in Chapter 12.

But even in simpler applications you can find properties that have special programming significance. An interesting example is the use of the KeyPreview property in the Restaurant Review program. KeyPreview applies only to forms; it allows a form to override its own controls in intercepting and reacting to keyboard activity. This property is especially important when you're designing a form that needs to recognize certain keystrokes, regardless of the control that has the focus at a given moment.

The frmRestList form has three command buttons, any one of which might have the focus at a point when the form is displayed on the screen. Normally a keystroke event is captured by the control that has the focus. But in this case, *the form itself* needs to recognize two keys — PgUp and PgDn — as signals to move to the next or previous record in the current selection of restaurant descriptions.

The event that occurs when the user presses a key is KeyDown. A related event, KeyUp, occurs when the user releases the key. By default, these events apply to the object that currently has the focus. Because the frmRestList form has three buttons — cmdPrevious, cmdCancel, and cmdNext — that may have the focus, one approach to capturing the PgUp and PgDn keys would be to write a KeyDown event procedure for each of these objects; the procedures would be named

```
cmdPrevious_KeyDown
cmdCancel_KeyDown
cmdNext_KeyDown
```

Each procedure would have the identical task of translating the PgUp an PgDn keys into the equivalent mouse events — that is, making calls to the Click event procedures that are normally performed when the user clicks the Previous or Next button.

Fortunately, the KeyPreview property allows the program to avoid this redundancy. KeyPreview is set to True for the frmRestList form, ensuring that the PgUp and PgDn keystrokes will be captured first by the form itself rather than by any one of the controls on the form. Consequently, a single event procedure — Form_KeyDown, shown in Listing 6-17 — is enough to define the program's reaction to these keys.

The KeyDown event procedure automatically receives an argument named KeyCode:

```
Private Sub Form_KeyDown(KeyCode As Integer, _
    Shift As Integer)
```

KeyCode is an integer that represents the key that the user has pressed. The codes for the PgDn and PgUp keys are 34 and 33, respectively:

```
Const PgDn = 34
Const PgUp = 33
```

The Form_KeyDown procedure does its work in two simple statements. If the user has pressed the PgDn key and the Next button is currently available for use, a call to the cmdNext_Click procedure displays the next restaurant record:

```
      If KeyCode = PgDn _
        And cmdNext.Enabled = True _
          Then cmdNext_Click
```

Likewise, if the user has pressed PgUp and the Previous button is available, a call to cmdPrevious_Click displays the previous record:

```
      If KeyCode = PgUp _
        And cmdPrevious.Enabled = True _
          Then cmdPrevious_Click
```

Keep in mind that the form's KeyPreview property setting is partially responsible for the economy of this event procedure. The properties you set for forms and their objects are not always merely cosmetic; they sometimes have important meaning to the program as a whole.

As you continue exploring the Restaurant Review application, you'll learn more about how a program can manage forms and promote communication between them.

MANAGING MULTIPLE FORMS IN A PROJECT

When the user clicks the Browse button, the program calls the Hide method to remove the main window temporarily from the desktop, and calls the Show method to display the secondary window, which is designed for browsing through the records of a selected city. Both of these methods are easy to use; they appear in the following general formats:

```
      formName.Hide
      formName.Show
```

For example, you'll find these two statements in the cmdBrowse_Click procedure in Listing 6-6:

```
      frmRestRevu.Hide
      frmRestList.Show
```

These statements make the switch between one window and the other in response to a click of the Browse button.

Interestingly, the Show method takes an optional argument, style, an integer equal to 0 or 1:

```
formName.Show style
```

If *style* is 0, *formName* appears on the desktop as a *modeless* form. This means that the user can activate and work with any other form in the program, even while the newly displayed form is still on the desktop. No specific response to *formName* is required before another form can be activated. By contrast, a *style* value of 1 produces a *modal* form. A modal form requires the user's full attention as long as the form is displayed; no other form can be activated until the user responds to the modal form in whatever way the program requires. Only when the modal form is removed from the desktop can the user activate other forms.

The modal style is useful for creating dialog boxes in an application. Before the user can resume other activities in the application, the modal dialog box requires a response. You'll notice, though, that the Restaurant program does *not* use the *style* argument. There is no need in this case, because the program presents only one window on the screen at a time. This is an alternative approach to capturing the user's attention for a particular activity.

Note that a modal window does not prevent the user from activating a different application on the Windows desktop.

EXCHANGING INFORMATION BETWEEN FORMS

In a program that contains multiple forms and modules, the code in one form may need to read information available on a different form. There are several ways that you can conveniently exchange information between forms in a program.

For example, consider the frmRestList form. To display a selection of records from the database, it needs to know which city the user has selected on the main Restaurants window. Without this key piece of information, the secondary form has no way of knowing which set of records to read from the database.

One simple way to get information from another form is to refer directly to a specific control on the target form. The general format for this kind of reference is

```
formName.controlName.propertyName
```

or, alternatively

```
formName!controlName.propertyName
```

Either format supplies the current setting of a specific property of a control on the target form. This reference works successfully even if the target form is not currently displayed on the desktop.

For example, the frmRestList form could use the following format to read the current city selection from the City box in the Restaurant dialog box:

```
frmRestRevu.cboCity.Text
```

The first part of this reference identifies the form that contains the control, the second identifies the control itself, and the third is the name of the property that is to be read.

Another way to exchange information between the forms of a project is to establish one or more global variables — that is, variables available anywhere in the program. If one form assigns a specific value to a global variable, another form can read the value by referring to the variable.

This second approach is used in the Restaurant program to make the current city selection available to the frmRestList form. In the RestRevu.Bas module (Listing 6-1), a global variable named *currCity* is declared to represent the user's city selection:

```
Public currCity As String
```

(In previous versions of Visual Basic, the Global keyword was used to declare global variables. Although this has been changed to Public in version 4, Global is still recognized.)

When the user clicks the Browse button on the main dialog box, the program assigns the current value of the cboCity control to the variable *currCity*:

```
currCity = StrFix(cboCity.Text)
```

The *StrFix* function, defined in the RestRevu.Bas module, simply removes leading and trailing blanks from a string and converts it to all uppercase letters. This conversion results in reliable comparisons between strings throughout the program.

When the frmRestList form is activated, it uses the variable *currCity* to find out which city's restaurant records the user wants to see. It opens the restaurant database, and selects only those records whose City fields match the value of *currCity*:

```
If currCity = StrFix(RestRecord.City) Then
```

The technique you decide to use for exchanging data between forms is largely a matter of personal preference and convenience. As an exercise, you might want to try revising the Restaurant program to eliminate the global *currCity* variable and use *formName.controlName.propertyName* references instead.

Looking Further at the Restaurant Program

The Restaurant application illustrates many other programming techniques that you'll study in later chapters. Before you go on, you may want to survey a few highlights in the program's code:

- *Dynamic arrays.* An array is an indexed variable that represents a list or table of data values. A *dynamic* array is an array whose dimensions may change one or more times at runtime. The Restaurant program uses a dynamic array to represent the list of records that match any given city selection when the user clicks Browse. The array named *matchingRecords* is declared in the general declarations section of the frmRestList form (Listing 6-13) and used in a general procedure named *CountMatches* (Listing 6-14). You'll learn about arrays and other data structures in Chapter 7.

- *Random-access files.* A random-access file gives a program direct access to any record in the file, thereby simplifying operations that read, write to, or revise records. The Restaurant database is a random-access file, which streamlines the program's capability to retrieve and store restaurant records. You'll examine the various techniques of data file programming in Chapter 8.

- *Data structures and record variables.* A data structure is a way of representing the multiple fields in a record. As you've seen, the RestRevu.Bas module uses a Type statement to define a structure that matches the fields of a Restaurant record, and a Public statement to declare a variable that will represent individual records. You'll learn more about these statements in Chapters 7 and 8.

- *Control arrays.* Sometimes it's convenient to define a group of controls as an array, so that they can be identified under a single indexed name. In the Restaurant program, the two sets of option buttons (Quality and Price) are both defined as control arrays. Chapter 9 discusses this kind of array.

- *MsgBox function and statement.* As you've seen, several message boxes pop up onto the desktop at various points in the Restaurant program. (Look back at Figures 6-5, 6-13, and 6-14 to review this feature.) These boxes are not defined as individual forms in the program, but rather are created by Visual Basic's built-in MsgBox tool. MsgBox is available both as a statement and a function. In either case, it displays a modal box on the screen, and waits for a specific reaction from the user. You can see how these boxes are displayed and used by examining the cmdSave_Click procedure (Listing 6-3) and the cmdBrowse_Click procedure (Listing 6-6).

- *Other built-in functions.* Visual Basic has a large library of built-in functions that perform calculations and operations on specific types of data. These functions save time and effort; as you learn to use them, you'll avoid reinventing procedures that already exist in the language itself. Like all the programs in this book, the Restaurant application contains many illustrations of built-in functions.

You'll continue learning about these programming topics as you examine other applications presented in this book.

Listing 6-1
The RestRevu.Bas module

```
' The Restaurant Review program
' -----------------------------


' Module: RestRevu.Bas
' --------------------
' This module contains the type definition
' for the records in the restaurant database,
' along with one global function that's used
' in both of the program's forms.



' The six fields of a restaurant record.
Type RestaurantType
  City As String * 30
  Restaurant As String * 30
  FoodType As String * 15
  Quality As String * 1
  Prices As String * 1
  Comments As String * 65
End Type
```
A public constant declaration

```
' The file name of the database.
Public Const DatabaseFile = "\RestRevu.DB"
```

```
' A record variable belonging to
' the RestaurantType.
Public RestRecord As RestaurantType
```
Public variable declarations

```
' A variable representing the current
' city selection. This global variable
' is a means of communication between
' the program's two forms.
Public currCity As String
```

```
Function StrFix(s As String) _
  As String

  ' The StrFix function converts a
  ' string argument to all uppercase
  ' letters and removes any leading
  ' or trailing blanks. This ensures
  ' reliable comparisons between strings
  ' in the program.

  StrFix = UCase(Trim(s))

End Function   ' StrFix
```

Using the built-in UCase and Trim functions

Listing 6-2

General declarations for RestRevu.Frm and the Form_Load procedure

```
' The Restaurant Review program
' ----------------------------

' Files:
' ------
' Project File:   RestRevu.VBP
' Form Files:     RestRevu.Frm
'                 RestList.Frm
' Module File:    RestRevu.Bas

' Creates a database of restaurant reviews
' for the business traveler. Allows the user
' to enter individual restaurant records, and
' to find restaurants by city and cuisine type.
' User can also browse through restaurant
' listings by city.

Option Explicit   ' Declare all variables.

' The program uses the variables
' prevCity and prevFoodType to determine
' whether the user has changed the City
' and Food Type entries. (In response, the
' program rebuilds the Restaurant list.)
```

```
Dim prevCity As String
Dim prevFoodType As String
```

Module-level variable declarations

```
' The variable recNum represents the
' record number of the currently selected
' restaurant.
Dim recNum As Long
```

```
' End of general declarations.



Private Sub Form_Load()

    ' The Form_Load procedure builds the
    ' City and Food Type lists at the beginning
    ' of the program, and also initializes
    ' some important form-level variables.

    ' Build the lists.
    ListCities
    ListFoodTypes

    ' The prevCity and prevFoodType variables
    ' are used to keep track of changes in the
    ' City and Food Type boxes. They are
    ' initialized as blank strings.
    prevCity = ""
    prevFoodType = ""

    ' The recNum variables indicates whether the
    ' dialog box is currently displaying information
    ' from an existing restaurant record. An initial
    ' value of zero means it is not. (This value is
    ' important to the cmdSave_Click procedure.)
    recNum = 0

End Sub   ' Form_Load
```

Listing 6-3
The cmdSave_Click procedure

```
Private Sub cmdSave_Click()

    ' The cmdSave_Click procedure saves the
    ' current restaurant entry as a new record
    ' in the database, or as a revision of an
    ' existing record.

    Dim i
    Dim yesNo As Integer

    ' First call BlankFields to make sure the
    ' user has entered all the fields of a new
    ' record. If not, display an error message.
    If Not BlankFields Then

        ' Copy all the information to the
        ' fields of the RestRecord structure.
        With RestRecord
            .City = cboCity.Text
            .Restaurant = cboRestaurant.Text
            .FoodType = cboFoodType.Text

            ' Save the option button selections
            ' as string values from "1" to "4".
            For i = 0 To 3
                If optQuality(i).Value Then _
                    .Quality = Right$(Str$(i + 1), 1)
                If optPrice(i).Value Then _
                    .Prices = Right$(Str$(i + 1), 1)
            Next i
            .Comments = txtComments.Text
        End With

        ' A recNum value of zero indicates that
        ' this is a new record, not a revision
        ' of an existing record.
        If recNum = 0 Then
```

Local variable declarations for use only in a procedure

```
' Open the database and save
' the record at the end of the file.
Open DatabaseFile For Random As #1 _
   Len = Len(RestRecord)
     Put #1, _
        LOF(1) / Len(RestRecord) + 1, _
        RestRecord
   Close #1


' If recNum contains a value greater than
' zero, this is an existing restaurant
' record that the user is saving in a
' revised version.
Else

   ' Ask the user to confirm the save
   ' operation before writing over the
   ' previous version of the record.
   yesNo = MsgBox("Revise this record?", _
     4, "Existing Record")

   ' If the user confirms, open the
   ' database and save the record at
   ' the same position as the original
   ' version. In this case, the record
   ' position is represented by recNum.
   If yesNo = vbYes Then
     Open DatabaseFile For Random As #1 _
       Len = Len(RestRecord)
         Put #1, recNum, RestRecord
     Close #1
   End If
End If


' If the new record contains a new city and/or a
' new food type, add this information to the
' appropriate combo box list.
If Not AlreadyListed(cboCity, cboCity.Text) _
   Then cboCity.AddItem cboCity.Text
If Not AlreadyListed(cboFoodType, cboFoodType.Text) _
   Then cboFoodType.AddItem cboFoodType.Text
```

*Using MsgBox
as a function*

```
            ' Clear the dialog box in preparation for
            ' the next new record entry.
            cmdClear_Click

        Else

            ' Display an error message if the user
            ' hasn't filled in all the fields of a new
            ' restaurant record.
            MsgBox "You must fill in all the fields.", _
                0, "Save"

        End If

    End Sub  'cmdSave_Click
```

*Using MsgBox
as a statement*

Listing 6-4
The Blankfields, AllFalseOptions, and AlreadyListed functions

```
Private Function BlankFields() As Boolean

    ' The BlankFields function determines whether
    ' the user has entered all the fields of
    ' information required for a new record. The
    ' program calls this function before a save
    ' operation. The function returns a value of
    ' True or False. A value of True means that
    ' one or more fields are still blank, and the
    ' current record cannot yet be saved.

    BlankFields = Trim(cboCity.Text) = "" Or _
                Trim(cboRestaurant.Text) = "" Or _
                Trim(cboFoodType.Text) = "" Or _
                Trim(txtComments.Text) = "" Or _
                AllFalseOptions

End Function  ' BlankFields
```

```
Private Function AllFalseOptions() As Boolean

  ' The AllFalseOptions function examines the
  ' two arrays of option button controls
  ' to determine whether the user has made
  ' a selection in each group. If one or both
  ' groups remains without a selection, this
  ' function returns a value of True, which
  ' indicates that the current record cannot
  ' be saved yet. The function is called by
  ' the BlankFields function, just before a
  ' save operation.

  Dim i

  ' The Boolean variables priceOpts and
  ' qualityOpts record the current status of
  ' the option button groups.
  Dim priceOpts As Boolean
  Dim qualityOpts As Boolean

  ' Initialize both variables to False.
  priceOpts = False
  qualityOpts = False

  ' Read each group of option buttons. If either
  ' group of buttons has no selection, the
  ' corresponding variable remains False.
  For i = 0 To 3
    priceOpts = priceOpts Or optPrice(i).Value
    qualityOpts = qualityOpts Or optQuality(i).Value
  Next i

  ' If either variable is still False, the
  ' function returns a value of True.
  AllFalseOptions = Not (priceOpts And qualityOpts)

End Function   ' AllFalseOptions
```

Looping through control arrays

```
Private Function AlreadyListed(listControl As Control, _
                         newItem As String) As Boolean

  ' The AlreadyListed function checks an existing
  ' list to see if a potential new entry (newItem)
  ' is currently in the list or not. If the item
  ' is in the list, the function returns True; if
  ' not, False.

  Dim i As Integer

  AlreadyListed = False

  ' Go through the current list and
  ' search for a match.
  For i = 0 To listControl.ListCount - 1
    If StrFix(listControl.List(i)) = _
      StrFix(newItem) Then _
      AlreadyListed = True
  Next i

End Function   ' AlreadyListed
```

Listing 6-5
The cmdClear_Click and cmdExit_Click procedures

```
Private Sub cmdClear_Click()

  ' The cmdClear_Click procedure clears all
  ' the fields of information on the main
  ' dialog box, so that the user can enter
  ' a new restaurant record. (This occurs in
  ' response to a click of the Clear button.)

  Dim i

  ' Assign empty strings to the Text properties
  ' of all the combo boxes and the one text box.
  cboCity.Text = ""
  cboRestaurant.Text = ""
```

```
cboFoodType.Text = ""
txtComments.Text = ""

' Set all the option buttons to False.
For i = 0 To 3
  optQuality(i).Value = False
  optPrice(i).Value = False
Next i

' Enable the controls that
' may have been disabled in preparation
' for accepting a revision in the record.
cboCity.Enabled = True
cboFoodType.Enabled = True
cboRestaurant.Enabled = True
```

*Changing the
Enable setting
back to True*

```
' Clear the current restaurant list and
' the variables that keep track of changes
' in the city and food type entries.
cboRestaurant.Clear
prevCity = ""
prevFoodType = ""


' Move the focus to the City box.
cboCity.SetFocus

End Sub  ' cmdClear_Click



Private Sub cmdExit_Click()

  ' The cmdExit_Click terminates the
  ' program, in response to a click of
  ' the Exit button.

  End

End Sub  ' cmdExit_Click
```

Listing 6-6
The cmdBrowse_Click procedure

```
Private Sub cmdBrowse_Click()

    ' The cmdBrowse_Click procedure activates
    ' the frmRestList form so that the user can
    ' browse through the restaurants for a
    ' selected city.

    ' If the City box contains a selection,
    ' hide the program's main dialog box and
    ' activate the browse dialog box.
    If StrFix(cboCity.Text <> "") Then
      currCity = StrFix(cboCity.Text)
      frmRestRevu.Hide
      frmRestList.Show

    ' Otherwise, if the user hasn't yet
    ' selected a restaurant, display an
    ' error message.
    Else
      MsgBox "You must select a city first.", , _
         "Browse through Restaurants"
    End If

End Sub   ' cmdBrowse_Click
```

Hiding and Showing forms

Listing 6-7
The ListCities procedure

```
Private Sub ListCities()

  ' The ListCities procedure builds the list
  ' of cities represented in the records
  ' currently contained in the restaurant
  ' database.

    Open DatabaseFile For Random As #1 _
       Len = Len(RestRecord)
```

```
' Go through the database from
' beginning to end.
Do While Not EOF(1)
  Get #1, , RestRecord

  ' Add any new city to the list.
  If Not AlreadyListed _
    (cboCity, RestRecord.City) _
    And Not EOF(1) _
    Then cboCity.AddItem RestRecord.City
Loop

  Close #1


End Sub   ' ListCities
```

Listing 6-8
The ListFoodTypes procedure

```
Private Sub ListFoodTypes()

  ' The ListFoodType procedure builds the
  ' list of cuisines (for example, French,
  ' Chinese, American) in the Food Type
  ' combo box. The procedure reads the
  ' food types from the records currently
  ' contained in the restaurant database.

  Open DatabaseFile For Random As #1 _
    Len = Len(RestRecord)

  ' Go through the database from
  ' beginning to end.
  Do While Not EOF(1)
    Get #1, , RestRecord

    ' Add any new food type to the list.
```

```
    If Not AlreadyListed _
      (cboFoodType, RestRecord.FoodType) _
      And Not EOF(1) _
      Then cboFoodType.AddItem RestRecord.FoodType
  Loop

  Close #1

End Sub   ' ListFoodTypes
```

Listing 6-9

Click and LostFocus procedures for the combo boxes

```
Private Sub cboCity_Click()

  ' The cboCity_Click procedure arranges
  ' to rebuild the restaurant list if the
  ' user selects a new entry from the
  ' current city list.

  ChangeRestaurantList

End Sub   ' cboCity_Click

Private Sub cboCity_LostFocus()

  ' The cboCity_LostFocus procedure arranges
  ' to rebuild the restaurant list if the
  ' user enters a new city and then move the
  ' focus to another control.

  ChangeRestaurantList

End Sub   ' cboCity_LostFocus

Private Sub cboFoodType_Click()

  ' The cboFoodType_Click procedure arranges
  ' to rebuild the restaurant list if the
  ' user selects a new entry from the
  ' current Food Type list.
```

```
    ChangeRestaurantList

End Sub   ' cboFoodType_Click

Private Sub cboFoodType_LostFocus()

  ' The cboFoodType_LostFocus procedure arranges
  ' to rebuild the restaurant list if the
  ' user enters a new food type and then move the
  ' focus to another control.

    ChangeRestaurantList

End Sub   ' cboFoodType_LostFocus

Private Sub cboRestaurant_Click()

  ' The cboRestaurant_Click procedure searches
  ' for a restaurant record -- and displays its
  ' fields in the dialog box -- if the user
  ' selects an entry from the current restaurant
  ' list.

    FindRestaurantRecord

End Sub   ' cboRestaurant_Click

Private Sub cboRestaurant_LostFocus()

  ' The cboRestaurant_LostFocus procedure searches
  ' for a restaurant record -- and displays its
  ' fields in the dialog box -- if the user enters
  ' an existing restaurant name and then moves the
  ' focus to another control.

    FindRestaurantRecord

End Sub    ' cboRestaurant_LostFocus
```

Listing 6-10
The ChangeRestaurantList procedure

```
Private Sub ChangeRestaurantList()

  ' The ChangeRestaurantList procedure checks
  ' to see whether the conditions are right
  ' for rebuilding the restaurant list.

  ' The variables c1 and f1 represent the
  ' current City and Food Type entries. The
  ' variables c2 and f2 represent the previous
  ' entries in these two controls.
  Dim c1 As String, c2 As String
  Dim f1 As String, f2 As String
  Dim r As String

  ' Use StrFix to standardize the string
  ' formats before attempting comparisons.
  c1 = StrFix(cboCity.Text)
  c2 = StrFix(prevCity)
  f1 = StrFix(cboFoodType.Text)
  f2 = StrFix(prevFoodType)

  ' If a change has taken place in either
  ' the City or Food Type entry, then call
  ' the ListRestaurants procedure to
  ' rebuild the list.
  If (c1 <> c2) Or (f1 <> f2) Then

    ' Save the current restaurant
    ' entry, but clear the current list.
    r = cboRestaurant.Text
    cboRestaurant.Clear
    cboRestaurant.Text = r

    ' The current City and Food Type entries
    ' become the new values of prevCity and
    ' prevFoodType.
    prevCity = c1
    prevFoodType = f1
```

```
              ' Make sure that at least one of the two
              ' controls contains an entry before
              ' attempting to build the list.
              If Not (Len(c1) = 0 And Len(f1) = 0) _
                 Then ListRestaurants c1, f1
           End If


        End Sub   ' ChangeRestaurantList
```

Listing 6-11
The ListRestaurants procedure

```
        Private Sub ListRestaurants _
           (place As String, food As String)

           ' The ListRestaurants procedure builds a list
           ' of restaurants that match (1) a city selection,
           ' (2) a food type selection, or (3) a combination
           ' of city and food type. The list appears in the
           ' cboRestaurant combo box.

           Open DatabaseFile For Random As #1 _
              Len = Len(RestRecord)

              ' It the Food Type entry is blank,
              ' base the search on the City entry.
              If Len(food) = 0 Then

                 ' Search through the entire database.
                 Do While Not EOF(1)
                    Get #1, , RestRecord              Using the built-in
                                                      EOF function

                       ' Compare each City field with the
                       ' current City entry. When a match is
                       ' found, add the restaurant to the list
                       ' if it's not already there.
                       With RestRecord
                          If StrFix(.City) = place Then _
                             If Not AlreadyListed _
                                (cboRestaurant, .Restaurant) _
```

```
                    Then _
                        cboRestaurant.AddItem .Restaurant
            End With
        Loop

' If the City entry is blank, base the
' search on the current Food Type entry.
ElseIf Len(place) = 0 Then

    ' Search through the entire database.
    Do While Not EOF(1)
        Get #1, , RestRecord

            ' Compare each FoodType field with
            ' the current Food Type entry. When a
            ' match is found, add the restaurant to
            ' the list if it's not already there.
            With RestRecord
                If StrFix(.FoodType) = food Then _
                    If Not AlreadyListed _
                        (cboRestaurant, .Restaurant) _
                            Then _
                                cboRestaurant.AddItem .Restaurant
            End With
        Loop


' If the user has entered both a city and
' a food type, base the search on both entries.
Else

    ' Search through the entire database.
    Do While Not EOF(1)
        Get #1, , RestRecord

            ' When a record matches both the
            ' city and the food type, add the
            ' restaurant to the list if it's not
            ' already there.
```

```
            With RestRecord
              If StrFix(.City) = place _
              And StrFix(.FoodType) = food Then _
                If Not AlreadyListed _
                    (cboRestaurant, .Restaurant) _
                        Then _
                          cboRestaurant.AddItem .Restaurant
            End With
          Loop

        End If

      Close #1

    End Sub   ' ListRestaurants
```

Listing 6-12
The FindRestaurantRecord procedure

```
Private Sub FindRestaurantRecord()

  ' The FindRestaurantRecord procedure looks
  ' through the database for a selected
  ' restaurant name. If the record is found,
  ' the procedure displays its fields in the
  ' frmRestRevu form.

  ' Open the restaurant database.
  Open DatabaseFile For Random As #1 _
    Len = Len(RestRecord)

  ' Set recNum to zero until a record
  ' is found. (Note that the actual record
  ' numbers in the database begin with 1.
  ' A recNum value of zero therefore tells
  ' the program that no record was found.)
  recNum = 0

  ' Search through the database from
  ' beginning to end.
  Do While Not EOF(1)
```

```
        Get #1, , RestRecord

     ' Compare each Restaurant field
     ' with the current Text value of
     ' the cboRestaurant control.
     With RestRecord
       If StrFix(cboRestaurant.Text) = _
         StrFix(.Restaurant) Then

            ' If a match is found, copy
            ' the record's fields to the
            ' appropriate controls on the
            ' frmRestRevu form.
            cboCity.Text = .City
            cboFoodType.Text = .FoodType
            optQuality(Val(.Quality) - 1).Value _
              = True
            optPrice(Val(.Prices) - 1).Value _
              = True
            txtComments.Text = .Comments

            ' Store the record number in recNum.
            ' (Note that Seek supplies the next
            ' record number. Subtract 1 to find
            ' the current record number.)
            recNum = Seek(1) - 1

            ' Disable the controls that
            ' should not be edited if the user
            ' chooses to revise the record.
            cboCity.Enabled = False
            cboFoodType.Enabled = False
            cboRestaurant.Enabled = False

       End If
     End With
   Loop

   Close #1

End Sub   ' FindRestaurantRecord
```

Disabling controls by setting the Enable property to False

Listing 6-13
General declarations of RestList.Frm

```
' The Restaurant Review program
' ----------------------------


' Form: frmRestList
' -----------------


' The form allows the user to browse through
' all the restaurant reviews recorded for a
' specified city.

Option Explicit   ' Declare all variables.

' Form-level variables:
' recCount is the number of restaurants
'    recorded for the city.
' currRec is the record currently
'    displayed in the form.

Dim recCount As Long, currRec As Long

' matchingRecords is a dynamic array of
'    record numbers, representing the
'    restaurants in the selected city.

Dim matchingRecords() As Long

' End of general declarations for frmRestList.
```

Listing 6-14
The Form_Activate procedure and the CountMatches function

```
Private Sub Form_Activate()

    ' The Form_Activate procedure is called each
    ' time the frmRestList form appears on the
    ' desktop. It opens the database, finds matching
    ' records, and enables or disables the appropriate
    ' command buttons.
```

```
Open DatabaseFile For Random As #1 _
   Len = Len(RestRecord)

' If any matching records are found, adjust
' the Next and Previous buttons appropriately.
If CountMatches() > 0 Then

   cmdPrevious.Enabled = False
   If recCount = 1 Then
      cmdNext.Enabled = False
   Else
      cmdNext.Enabled = True
   End If

   currRec = 0

   ' Display the first record.
   cmdNext_Click

Else

   ' Otherwise, display a message box to tell the
   ' user that no matching records were found.
   frmRestList.Caption = ""
   MsgBox "No restaurants found for " _
      & currCity, , "Browse"
   cmdCancel_Click
End If

End Sub   ' Form_Activate



Private Function CountMatches() As Long

   ' The CountMatches function counts the number
   ' of matching records (that is, restaurants in
   ' the selected city) in the database. It also
   ' stores the corresponding record numbers in the
   ' dynamic array named matchingRecords.
```

Enabling or disabling the Next and Previous buttons

```
Dim i
recCount = 0

' Go through the database from beginning to end.
For i = 1 To LOF(1) / Len(RestRecord)
   Get #1, i, RestRecord

   ' Look for matching records.
   If currCity = StrFix(RestRecord.City) Then

      ' If a match is found, increment the
      ' record counter by 1 and change the size
      ' of the matchingRecords array.
      recCount = recCount + 1
      ReDim Preserve matchingRecords(recCount)

      ' Then store the record number in the array.
      matchingRecords(recCount) = i
   End If
Next i

' Return the record count as the
' result of the function.
CountMatches = recCount

End Function   ' CountMatches
```

Using the built-in LOF and LEN functions

III

6

Listing 6-15
The cmdNext_Click and cmdPrevious_Click procedures

```
Private Sub cmdNext_Click()

   ' The cmdNext_Click procedure displays the
   ' next restaurant record when the user clicks
   ' the Next button or presses the PgDn key.

   ' Increment the record counter.
   currRec = currRec + 1
```

```
        ' Update the form's title.
        frmRestList.Caption = "Restaurants in " _
            & currCity & " -- " & _
            currRec & " of " & recCount

        ' Display the record.
        ShowRecord

        ' Enable or disable the Next and
        ' Previous buttons appropriately.
        If (currRec + 1) > recCount Then _
           cmdNext.Enabled = False
        If currRec > 1 Then _
           cmdPrevious.Enabled = True

End Sub   ' cmdNext_Click



Private Sub cmdPrevious_Click()

    ' The cmdPrevious_Click procedure displays the
    ' previous restaurant record when the user clicks
    ' the Previous button or presses the PgUp key.

    ' Decrease the record counter by 1.
    currRec = currRec - 1

    ' Update the form's title.
    frmRestList.Caption = "Restaurants in " _
      & currCity & " -- " & _
      currRec & " of " & recCount

    ' Display the record.
    ShowRecord

    ' Enable or disable the Next and
```

```
' Previous buttons appropriately.
If (currRec - 1) = 0 Then _
  cmdPrevious.Enabled = False
If currRec < recCount Then _
  cmdNext.Enabled = True

End Sub  ' cmdPrevious_Click
```

Listing 6-16
The ShowRecord procedure

```
Private Sub ShowRecord()

  ' The ShowRecord procedure reads the record
  ' from the position represented by the variable
  ' currRec, and copies its fields to the appropriate
  ' labels on the frmRestList form.

  ' Get the correct record.
  Get #1, matchingRecords(currRec), RestRecord

  ' Display its fields as the Caption properties
  ' of the appropriate labels on the form.
  With RestRecord
    lblRestaurant.Caption = .Restaurant
    lblCuisine.Caption = .FoodType

    ' Convert the Quality and Prices values into
    ' strings of asterisks and dollar signs.
    lblQuality.Caption = String$(Val(.Quality), "*")
    lblPrices.Caption = String$(Val(.Prices), "$")

    lblComments.Caption = .Comments
  End With

End Sub  ' ShowRecord
```

*Using the built-in
String and Val
functions*

Listing 6-17
The Form_KeyDown procedure

```
Private Sub Form_KeyDown(KeyCode As Integer, _
  Shift As Integer)

  ' The Form_KeyDown procedure allows the user to
  ' scroll through a city's restaurants by pressing
  ' the PgUp or PgDn keys on the keyboard.

  ' *** Note that the form's KeyPreview property
  '      is set to True to make this event possible.

  ' Code numbers for the
  ' PgDn and PgUp keys.
  Const PgDn = 34
  Const PgUp = 33

  ' If the user presses PgDn and the Next
  ' button is currently enabled, force a call
  ' to the cmdNext_Click event procedure.
  If KeyCode = PgDn _
    And cmdNext.Enabled = True _
      Then cmdNext_Click

  ' If the user presses PgUp and the Previous
  ' button is currently enabled, force a call
  ' to the cmdPrevious_Click event procedure.
  If KeyCode = PgUp _
    And cmdPrevious.Enabled = True _
      Then cmdPrevious_Click

End Sub   ' Form_KeyDown
```

The KeyDown event for a form

Listing 6-18
The cmdCancel_Click procedure

```
Private Sub cmdCancel_Click()

    ' The cmdCancel_Click procedure clears
    ' the data displayed in the frmRestList form,
    ' closes the form, and activates frmRestRevu,
    ' the application's startup form.

    ' Begin by closing the restaurant database.
    Close #1

    ' Then clear the captions in the labels used
    ' for displaying restaurant records.
    lblRestaurant.Caption = ""
    lblCuisine.Caption = ""
    lblQuality.Caption = ""
    lblPrices.Caption = ""
    lblComments.Caption = ""

    ' Hide this form and display the startup form.
    frmRestList.Hide
    frmRestRevu.Show

End Sub    ' cmdCancel_Click
```

Using the Hide and Show methods

Data Structures and Flow of Control

*I*n a programming language, the word *structure* has several important meanings. A structured language encourages a *modular* approach to writing code, where programs are organized into small, self-contained tasks. The practical result is that programmers can confidently create longer and more elaborate projects. Although the earliest versions of BASIC were anything but structured, the language has evolved. Visual Basic has all the elements of a well-structured language, including a productive variety of data structures and control structures. These are the topics of this chapter.

A data structure gives you convenient ways to organize and store information in a program. Two commonly used data structures in Visual Basic are arrays and user-defined types. A variable belonging to a user-defined type is sometimes known as a *record* variable:

- An *array* is a list, a table, or another multidimensional arangement of data items, all represented by a single variable name. In programs that work with large amounts of interrelated information, arrays are an indespensible way of organizing data.

- A *user-defined type* enables you to create record variables that represent multiple values of different types. This type of structure is ideal for use in database applications.

A programming language also has control structures that you can use to define the direction and flow of your program. Control stuctures include procedures, loops, and decisions:

- As you know, *procedures* allow you to divide your code into small, cogent, usable blocks of code that are easy to understand and revise if necessary. A Sub procedure in Visual Basic performs a discrete well-defined task; a Function procedure produces a return value. A *call* results in a performance of a procedure.

- *Loops* are structures that perform repetition in a program. During a loop, a block of code is performed over and over until a particular condition is met or until a counter reaches a specified value. Visual Basic has several convenient loop structures, each suited to particular needs.

- *Decisions* are structures that choose among alternative courses of action available in a program. A simple decision might determine whether or not a single line of code should be performed. More complex decisions involve many alternative blocks of code and many elaborate conditions. But the idea is always the same: Given what's happened so far in a program, what direction should the action take next?

Control structures and data structures are often closely related in the code of a program. For example, certain kinds of loops are ideally designed to process all the data elements in an array. Other control structures are perfect for working with the information stored in a record variable.

The best way to explore these language elements is to examine them in working examples. This chapter's project, called the Meetings program, illustrates a variety of structures and shows how they operate together. The program is designed to help you keep records about the business meetings you conduct or attend during your travels. It saves meeting records in a database file on disk, and gives you the opportunity to retrieve records and view them on the screen.

You'll begin your work in this chapter with a close look at the Meetings program. Then you'll examine parts of the program's code in detail as you review Visual Basic's data structures and control structures.

Running the Meetings Program

The Meetings application is stored on the program disk as Meetings.VBP. When you open the project, you'll see that it contains two forms and a module:

- Meetings.Frm (named *frmMeetings*) is the program's startup form. In this form, you enter the information about a particular meeting — the place, date, and time; the names of the people who attended the meeting; the main subject or purpose of the meeting; and any brief notes that you want to store about what took place or what was discussed.

- MeetFind.Frm (named frmMeetFind) is a secondary form that allows you to search for a particular set of meeting records. The key for each search is the name of any person who attended a particular meeting.

- Meetings.Bas is a module file that contains the program's central data structure definitions, along with two short procedures available for use anywhere in the project.

Run the program now by pressing F5 or by clicking the Run button on the toolbar. A dialog box named Business Meetings appears on the screen, as shown in Figure 7-1. The window is divided into four areas. At the upper-left corner are four text boxes in which you can enter the place, date, and time of the meeting. In the area below, you can enter a list of as many as five people who were present at the meeting; there are separate boxes for each person's first and last names. Then at the upper-right corner of the dialog box you can see a space for the subject of the meeting and a large scrollable text box for your own notes and observations about the meeting. The program accepts a 400-character block of text (about 80 words) in the Notes box. As you type text in the box, word wrap takes place at the end of each line. To scroll the text in the box up and down, you can use the PgUp and PgDn keys or you can click inside the scroll bar at the right side of the box.

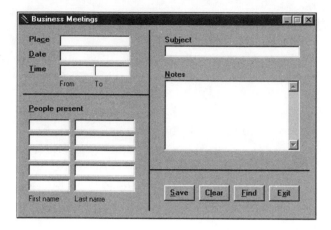

Figure 7-1

The Business Meetings dialog box.

Finally, at the lower-right corner of the dialog box you see a panel containing four command buttons:

- The Save button saves your current meeting record in the root directory of your hard disk, as part of a database file named Meetings.DB. Before you click Save, you should fill in the Place, Date, Time, Subject, and Notes text boxes, and at least one pair of boxes in the People present list. (If you click Save before filling in all the boxes, the program displays an error message: *Can't save an incomplete record*.) After a save operation, the program clears the dialog box for your next record entry.

- The Clear button erases all the information currently displayed in the dialog box. You might want to click this button if you begin an entry and then decide you want to start over without saving the current information. But as you'll see shortly, the program can also use the Business Meetings dialog box to display an existing meeting record that you've requested; in this case, the Clear button allows you to clear a record and return to data-entry mode.

- The Find button switches to a different dialog box, where you can search for specific meeting records by entering the name of a person who attended the target meetings. You'll explore this feature shortly.

- The Exit button stops the program's performance.

ENTERING AND RETRIEVING MEETING RECORDS

Figure 7-2 shows a sample record that's been entered into the Business Meetings dialog box. As you can see, this record contains a list of four people who were present at the meeting and several lines of notes about the discussion that took place. Try entering this record — or a meeting record of your own — into the Business Meetings dialog box on your screen. Then click Save to save the record. The program clears the record and moves the focus to the Place box. Continue experimenting with the program by entering several more meeting records, real or imaginary. Remember that you can click the Clear button at any time to remove the current entry from the dialog box and start over again.

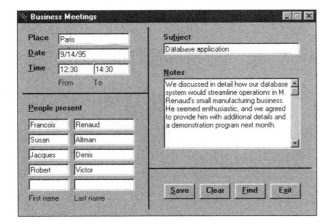

Figure 7-2
Entering a meeting record.

Once you've begun developing a database of meeting records, you'll want to be able to retrieve the information and review the notes you've kept. To do so, you begin by clicking the Find button. In response, the program displays a new dialog box titled Find a Meeting Record. As you can see in Figure 7-3, this window contains text boxes in which you can identify a person you want to search for in the Meetings database. For a successful search, you have to enter the person's first and last name in the same way you stored it in one or more database records. (The program ignores differences in alphabetic case; you can enter the name in all uppercase or lowercase letters, or any combination.) Then click the Search button, or simply press Enter.

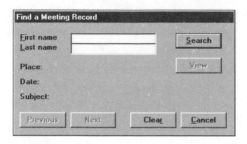

Figure 7-3
The Find a Meeting Record dialog box.

In response, the program searches for all the records in which this person's name appears, and displays information from the first record it finds. Notice that this dialog box displays only three fields of information from a given record: the place of the meeting, the date, and the subject. If the target name appears in more than one record, the program activates the Next button so you can scroll through the records that match the name you've entered.

For example, in Figure 7-4 you can see a name that the program has searched for in the database. Because the Previous and Next buttons are both available, you know that multiple records have been found for this name. To scroll through the records one at a time, you can click either button or press PgUp or PgDn at the keyboard. When the program reaches the first or last matching record, either the Previous or Next button is disabled. Figure 7-5 shows the first record for this particular search; as you can see, the Next button is still available, but the Previous button is not.

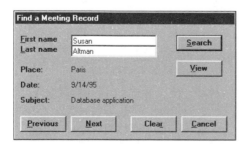

Figure 7-4
Searching for a meeting record.

Figure 7-5

Using the Previous and Next buttons.

Once you've identified a set of meeting records, you may want to view a particular record in its entirety. To do so, you simply click the View button at the right side of the Find a Meeting Record dialog box. In response, the program immediately switches back to the Business Meetings dialog box and shows all the fields of the record you've selected, as in Figure 7-6. At this point, the dialog box is in its read-only mode. You can examine the record, but you can't change it or save it again. (Notice that the Save button is disabled.) Click the Clear button when you've finished reading the information, or click Find to search for yet another record.

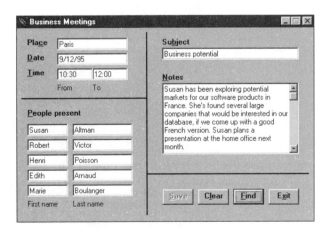

Figure 7-6

Retrieving an entire meeting record.

If you decide that you want to close the Find dialog box without retrieving a record, simply click Cancel or press the Escape key. The program returns to the empty Business Meeting dialog box and prepares to accept a new record entry. Click Exit when you're ready to quit the program. Of course, the Meetings database is retained on disk; you can retrieve and view records from it any time you run the program.

INSIDE THE MEETINGS PROGRAM

The program's code is shown in Listings 7-1 through 7-11. Here's a summary of what you'll find in these listings:

- Listing 7-1 shows the code from the Meetings.Bas module. The general declarations section contains Type statements for the program's two major data structures, and Public declarations for global variables and arrays. In particular, notice the *Meeting* variable, which represents a meeting record that's been read from the database or is about to be written to the file; and the *NameList* array, which stores a special index structure that the program uses to search for records. You'll see a lot of these two structures as you examine the program. The module also contains two short string functions used to standardize names and ensure reliable comparisons.

- Listings 7-2 through 7-6 show the code from the Meetings.Frm module, the startup form. Among these listings you'll find a variety of event procedures, including Form_Load, which initially opens the database file and creates an index; Click procedures that respond to each of the form's command buttons; and the Form_Activate procedure, which displays a selected record from the database when the program returns to this form from the secondary frmMeetFind form.

- Listings 7-7 through 7-11 show the code from the MeetFind.Frm module. Again, you'll find event procedures that carry out the operations corresponding to each of the form's command buttons. You'll also see a variety of general procedures that help in the process of searching for records and displaying them in the dialog box.

The program contains many interesting illustrations of decisions, loops, arrays, and records. It also contains examples of a control structure that is new in Visual Basic 4.0, the With statement. In upcoming sections of this chapter, you'll look in detail at many passages from the program's code as you review the use of control structures and data structures in Visual Basic.

Decisions

Decision statements give your program the power to choose between options available in your code and to react appropriately to situations that occur during a run. For example, a decision may take place when a program responds correctly to a request made from the keyboard or provides relevant information based on a particular condition. The If statement is the most common way to express decisions in Visual Basic programs. At the heart of every If decision is a *condition* — an expression your program evaluates as True or False. If the condition is True, the program follows one course of action; if False, another.

WRITING IF STATEMENTS

Depending on the complexity of the decision, you can use If either as a one-line statement or as a multiline block structure. Both formats make use of the keywords If, Then, and Else:

- *If* introduces the condition on which the decision will be based.
- *Then* identifies the action that will be performed if the condition is True.
- *Else* specifies an alternate action, to be performed if the condition is False.

   A block structure uses some additional keywords:

- *ElseIf* introduces another condition that the program will evaluate if no previous condition has turned out to be True. (ElseIf is an optional clause; it may be included one or more times in a single decision structure.)
- *End If* marks the end of the decision structure.

The one-line If statement is the simplest decision format. It presents a condition and a choice of actions all in a single statement:

```
If condition Then action1 Else action2
```

In this format, *condition* is an expression that Visual Basic evaluates as True or False; and *action1* and *action2* are statements — such as assignments, procedure calls, or any other Visual Basic statement. If *condition* is True, the program performs *action1* and skips *action2*; conversely, if *condition* is False, the program skips *action1* and performs *action2*.

The Else clause is optional in the If statement. If you leave it out, the one-line If statement becomes simply:

```
If condition Then action
```

In this case, the *action* is performed if the *condition* is True. If the *condition* is False, this If statement results in no action at all. For example, the following statement appears in the Form_Load procedure of the frmMeetings module (Listing 7-3):

```
If listLength > 1 Then _
   SortNameList
```

To prepare for retrieving records from the Meetings database, the Form_Load procedure reads through the entire file and copies the names of the people in each record to the index array called *NameList*. When this process is complete, the program needs to alphabetize the name list, but only if the list contains more than one entry. Accordingly, this If statement decides whether alphabetization is necessary. The variable *listLength* represents the number of names in the list. If *listLength* is greater than 1, the program makes a call to the SortNameList procedure to alphabetize the list.

Notice that this If statement is divided into two physical lines by use of the line-continuation character (_). Although this is a convenient and readable way to present an If statement in your code, keep in mind that this particular decision is carried out as a single statement.

Take a look at the condition in this decision. In the expression *listLength > 1*, the > symbol represents *greater than*, one of Visual Basic's *comparison operations*. If *listLength* contains a value that is greater than 1, Visual Basic evaluates this expression as True, and the action of the If statement is carried out. Otherwise, if *listLength* contains a value of 0 or 1, the condition is False, and no action takes place.

To write successful decisions, you need to understand clearly the various operators available for expressing conditions.

CONDITIONAL EXPRESSIONS

You've learned to write arithmetic expressions in Visual Basic, using operations such as multiplication (*), division (/), addition (+), and subtraction (–); an *arithmetic expression* produces a value belonging to one of Visual Basic's numeric data types. By contrast, a *conditional expression* results in a *Boolean* value, also sometimes known as a *logical* value. The *Boolean* data type comprises two values, True and False, which are themselves keywords in Visual Basic 4.0. (This data type is named after the 19th-century English mathematician and logician George Boole. True and False are sometimes known as Boolean values.)

Two special sets of operations are available for conditional expressions. The *comparison* operations perform comparisons between two values. For example, the *equal to* (=) operation is True if two operands have the same value; *less than* (<) is True if the first operand has a smaller value than the second. The *logical* operations combine or modify Boolean expressions to produce results of True or False. The most commonly used among Visual Basic's logical operations are And, Or, and Not.

Understanding the logic of conditional expressions is not hard; the only difficulty is in learning to use the operators themselves. Note the distinction between the terms *operator* and *operation*. An operator is a symbol or keyword that represents an operation. For example, the + symbol is the operator that represents addition; likewise, < represents the comparison operation *less than*. An operand is a value that is the object of an operation. In the expressions *a + b* and *a < b*, the values *a* and *b* are operands.

Relational Operations

There are six comparison operations, represented by the following symbols:

<	less than
<=	less than or equal to
>	greater than
>=	greater than or equal to
=	equal to
<>	not equal to

You use these operators to compare two values in a conditional expression. The expression is True if the comparison is accurate, or False if it is inaccurate. For example, suppose *a* equals 1, *b* equals 2, and *c* equals 3; the following comparisons are all True:

```
a < c
c >= a + b
c - a = b
```

And the following are all False:

```
a > c
b = a * 3
c <= b
```

In an expression that contains both arithmetic and comparison operations, Visual Basic performs the arithmetic first, and then the comparison. For example, in the expression $c >= a + b$, Visual Basic first finds the value of $a + b$ and then compares the sum with the value of *c*. (You'll learn more about the order of operations later in this chapter.)

You'll find many illustrations of comparison operations in the Meetings program. One simple example appears in the Form_Activate procedure of the frmMeetings module (Listing 7-5). This is the event procedure that takes control whenever the program's startup form is activated or reactivated during a run. When the user selects a record in the secondary frmMeetFind form and then clicks the View button, the

program stores the target record number in a public variable named
curRec. The frmMeetings form is then activated, and the program reads
the *curRec* record from the database and displays it in the form. But if
the user clicks the Cancel button on the frmMeetFind form, the program
assigns a value of 0 to *curRec*. This is a signal that the user has not
requested a record search. Accordingly, before reading a record from the
database, the Form_Activate procedure checks the value of *curRec*:

```
If curRec <> 0 Then
```

If *curRec* is not equal to 0, the program opens the database and
retrieves the target record. By contrast, if *curRec* is 0, the program
clears the *frmMeetings* form and stands ready for the user's next action.

Logical Operations

Visual Basic's six logical operations are represented by the keywords
Not, And, Or, Xor, Eqv, and Imp. Five of the logical operators — And,
Or, Xor, Eqv, and Imp — are designed to work with pairs of operands;
you use them to combine two logical values in an expression. By contrast, Not is a *unary* operator; it works on a single value. Each of these
operators produces a logical result. In the following descriptions, assume
that the operands *v1* and *v2* represent values of True or False.

Not produces the reverse value of its operand:

```
Not v1
```

If *v1* is True, Not *v1* results in a value of False; if *v1* is False, Not *v1*
is True.

And results in a value of True only if both of its operands are True:

```
v1 And v2
```

If both *v1* and *v2* are True, the And operation results in a value of True.
If either value is False or if both are False, And results in False.

Or results in a value of True if either or both its operands are True:

```
v1 Or v2
```

If *v1* is True, or *v2* is True, or both are True, the Or operation results in True. Only if *v1* and *v2* are both False does Or result in False.

Xor is True only if its two operands have different values:

```
v1 Xor v2
```

If one of the operands is True and the other is False, Xor results in True. If both *v1* and *v2* are True or if both are False, Xor is False.

Eqv is True if its two operands are the same:

```
v1 Eqv v2
```

If both *v1* and *v2* are True or both are False, Eqv results in True. If one of the operands is True and the other is False, Eqv is False.

Imp is False if its first operand is True and the second is False. Otherwise, Imp is True:

```
v1 Imp v2
```

If *v1* is True and *v2* is False, Imp is False. For all other combinations of values, Imp is True.

The simplest and most commonly used of Visual Basic's six logical operators are And and Or. The Form_KeyDown event procedure (Listing 7-10) contains some interesting examples. While the frmMeetFind form is displayed on the desktop, this procedure captures any keyboard activity and determines whether the user has pressed PgUp or PgDn as an instruction to scroll to a new record. If one of these keys has been pressed *and* the equivalent command button — Previous or Next — is currently enabled, the program makes a call to the appropriate procedure to display a new record:

```
If KeyCode = PgDn _
  And cmdNext.Enabled = True _
    Then cmdNext_Click
```

The resulting action takes place only if both of these conditions are true. If one condition is false or both are false, the action is skipped.

Some conditional expressions may use a combination of two or more logical operators. For example, consider the following assignment statement from the *OKRecord* function (Listing 7-4):

```
temp2 = temp2 Or _
        (Trim(txtFirstName(i).Text) <> "" And _
        Trim(txtLastName(i).Text) <> "")
```

The *OKRecord* function has the job of determining whether a new record entry is complete and therefore suitable for saving to the database. This statement takes place in a loop that examines the five pairs of name text boxes. Using a combination of Or and And operations, the statement examines each name entry and confirms that the user has entered both a first name and a last name. In this case, the result of each condition is assigned to the variable *temp2*, which is declared as a Boolean-type variable.

When you write a condition that contains a combination of two or more operations, you have to be aware of the default order in which Visual Basic will evaluate the operations.

Order of Precedence

In an expression that contains a combination of arithmetic, comparison, and logical operations, Visual Basic performs the operations in this order, by default:

1. All the arithmetic operations first, following the usual order of arithmetic precedence

2. All the comparison operations, from left to right

3. All the logical operations, in this order: Not, And, Or, Xor, Eqv, Imp

Thanks to this preset order, many expressions you write will automatically be evaluated in the way you would expect. For example, in the following expressions, Visual Basic performs the arithmetic operations before the comparison ones:

```
c >= a + b
c - a = b
b = a * 3
```

And in this expression, the comparison operations are evaluated before the logical operation:

```
x >= 5 And x < 32
```

But sometimes the default order of operations gives the wrong answer for a particular application. Just as with arithmetic operations, you can use parentheses to override Visual Basic's default order of precedence. Simply place parentheses around the operation that you want Visual Basic to evaluate first. In addition, you may sometimes decide to use parentheses simply to make an expression more readable.

WRITING DECISION STRUCTURES

A one-line decision statement makes a simple choice between one action or another. By contrast, a decision structure allows your program to choose between two or more *blocks* of code, where a block consists of several Visual Basic statements in sequence. One form of the decision structure can be represented as follows:

```
If condition Then
  ' Block of code to be performed
  ' if the condition is true.
Else
  ' Block of code to be performed
  ' if the condition is false.
End If
```

In this format, the keywords of the decision structure itself serve to define distinct blocks of code. The statements located between the If line and the Else line make up the block that will be performed if the condition is true, and the statements between Else and End If make up the block that the decision will select if the condition is false. Each block may contain any number of statements. For example, here is the complete decision structure in the Form_Activate procedure that determines whether or not to retrieve a record and display it on the frmMeetings form:

```
If curRec <> 0 Then
  Open "\Meetings.DB" For Random As #1 _
    Len = Len(Meeting)
    Get #1, curRec, Meeting
  Close #1
```

```
With Meeting
  txtPlace.Text = .MeetPlace
  txtDate.Text = .MeetDate
  txtTimeFrom.Text = .TimeFrom
  txtTimeTo.Text = .TimeTo
  txtSubject.Text = .Subject
  txtNotes.Text = .Notes

  For i = 0 To 4
    txtFirstName(i).Text = .FirstName(i)
    txtLastName(i).Text = .LastName(i)
  Next i
End With

ReadOnlyStatus True

Else

cmdClear_Click

End If
```

In this passage, the If block contains many statements that carry out the task of opening the database, reading a record, displaying its fields on the form, and switching to the read-only status. By contrast, the Else block contains a single statement that simply clears all information from the form in preparation for the user's next action.

Again, the Else clause is optional. In the following example from the *SortNameList* procedure (Listing 7-4), the If condition compares two string values in the *NameList* array. If the two items are out of alphabetical order, the procedure swaps their positions in the list; otherwise, if they are already in the correct order, no action takes place:

```
If NameList(i).FullName > _
    NameList(j).FullName Then

  temp = NameList(i)
  NameList(i) = NameList(j)
  NameList(j) = temp
End If
```

USING THE *ELSEIF* CLAUSE

Finally, the ElseIf clause gives you the opportunity to write decisions based on multiple conditions. A decision structure may contain any number of ElseIf clauses, each with its own condition and corresponding block of code:

```
If condition1 Then

  ' Block of code to be performed
  ' if condition1 is true.

ElseIf condition2 Then

  ' Block of code to be performed
  ' if condition2 is true.

ElseIf condition3 Then

  ' Block of code to be performed
  ' if condition3 is true.

Else

  ' Block of code to be performed
  ' if none of the conditions is true.

End If
```

In this structure, Visual Basic evaluates each condition in sequence — first the condition in the If statement at the top of the decision, then each of the ElseIf conditions in turn. If any condition is True, the corresponding block of code is performed, and then the remainder of the decision structure is skipped. But if none of the conditions is True, Visual Basic performs the block located between Else and End If, if the structure contains an Else clause.

You can find an example of the ElseIf clause in a function procedure named *SearchForName* (Listing 7-9). When the user enters a name into the frmMeetFind form and clicks the Search button, this procedure searches through the alphabetized name index to see if the target name exists in the database. Rather than look through the entire list from beginning to end, the function carries out an efficient algorithm known as a *binary search*. In this technique, the program divides the alphabetized list into progressively smaller sections in an effort to zero in on the part of the list that will contain the name, if it exists. Along the way, the following If structure determines which of three conditions is true:

```
If findName = NameList(midPos).FullName Then
  posX = midPos
ElseIf findName > NameList(midPos).FullName Then
  pos1 = midPos + 1
Else
  pos2 = midPos - 1
End If
```

If the name has been found, the variable *posX* records its position in the list. Otherwise, the search continues either in a lower portion or a higher portion of the list, depending on a comparison between the target name and the name at the current position. This fairly complex decision is carried out gracefully in the If-Then-ElseIf structure.

THE SELECT CASE STRUCTURE

Visual Basic provides a second decision structure, identified by the keywords Select Case. Like the If structure, Select Case allows you to divide a decision into blocks of code representing different options that the decision can choose among. The Select Case decision bases its choice on a match between a *test expression* and individual Case expressions located at the top of each block of code.

A Select Case decision chooses at most one block of code to perform, among the multiple blocks you include in the structure. Each block of code is marked by a Case clause. The decision works by comparing the value of a test expression with expressions that appear at the top of each Case block. When a match is found, the decision performs the corresponding block of code.

Here is one way to represent the general format of the Select Case structure:

```
Select Case testExpression

Case expression1

    ' Block of code to be performed
    ' if a match is found between
    ' testExpression and expression1

Case expression2

    ' Block of code to be performed
    ' if a match is found between
    ' testExpression and expression2

Case expression3

    ' Block of code to be performed
    ' if a match is found between
    ' testExpression and expression3

' Any number of additional Case
' blocks may be included.

Case Else

    ' Block of code to be performed
    ' if no match is found between
    ' testExpression and any of the
    ' previous Case expressions.

End Select
```

This is how the Select Case decision proceeds:

1. The decision begins by comparing the value of *testExpression* with *expression1* in the first Case clause.

2. If there is a match between the two expressions, Visual Basic performs the first block of code — that is, the statements between the first and second Case clauses.

3. If there is no match, the program goes on to the next Case expression.

4. Whenever a match is found, the corresponding block of code is performed. Then the action of the decision is complete; no further Case expressions are compared.

5. If the decision reaches the final Case clause — identified as Case Else — without having found a match in any of the previous Case clauses, the Case Else block is performed. (But note that the Case Else clause is optional. If it is not present, the decision results in no action if no match is found between *testExpression* and a Case expression.)

UNDERSTANDING CASE EXPRESSIONS

The Case clause can contain a *list* or *range* of values, in any of the following formats:

- A list, where each value is separated from the next by a comma:

```
Case expression1, expression2, ...
```

A match occurs when *testExpression* equals any of the values in the list.

- A range of values, expressed with the keyword To:

```
Case expression1 To expression2
```

A match occurs when *testExpression* equals any value within the range.

- A comparison expression, introduced by the keyword Is, and employing one of Visual Basic's six comparison operators (<, <=, >, >=, =, <>):

```
Case Is relationalOperation expression
```

A match occurs if the value of *testExpression* is correctly described by the relation.

Sometimes Select Case may result in clearer code than an If structure with a long sequence of ElseIf clauses. For example, the decision you've already examined from the *SearchForName* procedure could just as well have been written as a Select Case structure:

III

7

```
Select Case findName
  Case Is = NameList(midPos).FullName
    posX = midPos
  Case Is > NameList(midPos).FullName
    pos1 = midPos + 1
  Case Else
    pos2 = midPos - 1
End Select
```

Your choice between the If and Select Case structures is often a matter of personal preference.

NESTED DECISIONS

Sometimes one decision leads to another. When this happens in a program, you may find yourself organizing your code in a series of *nested* decisions. This means that an "inner" decision is contained within one of the blocks of code belonging to an "outer" decision. If the outer decision selects that particular block for performance, the program will have yet another decision structure to perform. You'll find an examples of nested decisions in the *cmdSave_Click* procedure (Listing 7-3). The outer decision determines whether the current record is complete and therefore suitable for saving to the database:

```
If OKRecord Then
```

Within this structure, one nested decision examines each name entry in the current record and decides whether to add it to the name index. Another nested decision determines whether the index needs to be realphabetized.

As you'll learn in the upcoming sections, decisions are not the only structures that can be nested. You can write nested loops, decisions nested within loops, loops within decisions, and a variety of other powerful combinations.

Loops

Repetition is a central feature of programming. To carry out repetition in a program, you organize a block of code in a loop structure. Whatever the task — processing hundreds of database records, performing scores of calculations, or printing dozens of copies of nearly identical documents — a well-designed loop controls the repetition reliably and efficiently.

A loop has two basic components:

- The block of code that you want the computer to perform repeatedly
- An instruction that controls the duration of the looping

In the design of a loop, your typical goal is to provide the computer with distinct information to work with during each *iteration* of the loop. The code remains the same, but the data changes. This is what makes repetition truly powerful: Each time around the loop, the computer can process the *next* record in a database, perform a calculation on a *different* set of data, or conduct a *new* output operation.

Visual Basic has two major varieties of loops, known by the keywords Do and For.

UNDERSTANDING DO LOOPS

The first requirement of a loop structure is to identify the block of code that will be performed repeatedly during the looping. In a Do loop you meet this requirement by writing specific statements at the beginning and the end of the loop. A Do statement always marks the top of the loop, and a Loop statement marks the bottom. The statements located between Do and Loop make up the body of the loop — that is, the code that will be performed once for each iteration.

The conditional expression that controls the duration of the looping can appear either in the Do statement at the top of the loop or in the Loop statement at the bottom. Furthermore, the condition can appear in either of two clauses, introduced by the keywords While or Until. In the two most commonly used Do loop formats, a While clause appears in the Do statement at the top of the loop, or an Until clause appears in the Loop statement at the bottom. Here is a loop with the condition at the top:

```
Do While condition

    ' The block of statements that the
    ' computer will perform repeatedly
    ' as long as the condition is true.

Loop
```

And here is a loop with the condition located at the bottom:

```
Do

    ' The block of statements that the
    ' computer will perform repeatedly
    ' until the condition is true.

Loop Until condition
```

In both cases, the *condition* is an expression that results in a value of True or False.

Visual Basic evaluates the condition once for each iteration of the loop. A change in the condition's value ultimately causes the loop to stop. In a While clause, the looping continues as long as the condition is True; looping stops when the condition becomes False. In an Until clause, the looping continues as long as the condition is False; looping stops when the condition becomes True.

Just as in decision statements, you can use a variety of operations to build conditions. The comparison operations (represented by <, <=, >, >=, =, <>) and the logical operations (represented by Not, And, Or, Xor, Eqv, and Imp) are all available for use in Do loops.

The placement of the condition at the top or the bottom of a loop can be an important factor in the loop's behavior. With the expression located at the top of the loop, Visual Basic evaluates the condition *before* the first iteration; if the condition has the wrong value — False in a While clause, or True in an Until clause — Visual Basic immediately skips the entire loop without performing a single iteration. By contrast, if the expression is located at the bottom of the loop, Visual Basic always performs the block of code at least one time. *After* the first iteration, Visual Basic evaluates the condition and determines whether to continue the looping.

The actual mechanism for controlling the duration of the loops depends on your choice of a While clause or an Until clause for a Do loop.

Using the While clause

When you want the repetition to continue as long as a condition remains true, use a While clause in your Do loop. With the While clause in the Do statement at the top of the loop, Visual Basic evaluates the condition before the first iteration. For example, the following loop, found in the *cmdSearch_Click* procedure (Listing 7-8) looks to see if the name index contains more than one instance of a target name:

```
Do While inName = _
    NameList(curPos + 1).FullName
  timesCount = timesCount + 1
  curPos = curPos + 1
  If curPos = listLength Then Exit Do
Loop
```

For each iteration of the loop, a counter variable, *timesCount*, is increased by 1. (Notice that this code also illustrates the Exit Do command, which conditionally terminates the Do loop.)

Using the Until clause

An Until clause stops the looping when a condition becomes True. As long as the value of the condition is False, the iterations continue. For example, consider the following hypothetical input operation:

```
prompt = "Enter a value from 1 to 10"

Do
  inValue = InputBox(prompt, "Input Value")
Loop Until inValue >= 1 And inValue <= 10
```

This loop uses Visual Basic's built-in InputBox function to display a prompt on the screen and elicit a numeric input value. Because the required value must be between 1 and 10, the loop iterates until the user enters a number in the appropriate range. As you can see, the Until condition is True only when the user meets the input requirement; a False condition results in another iteration of the loop.

III

7

In short, a Do loop is based on a condition; the looping stops when the value of the condition changes from True to False or from False to True. By contrast, a traditional For loop contains a numeric counter variable that controls the duration of the looping. The loop completes one iteration for each change in the value of this counter variable. When the counter moves beyond a specified range, the looping stops.

UNDERSTANDING FOR LOOPS

For loops are useful in a variety of programming contexts. You should consider using a For loop whenever you can

- Specify in advance the exact number of iterations that the loop should go through.

- Define a variable that represents the correct number of iterations. (The value of this variable can be determined during the program run, so that each performance of a loop may result in a different number of iterations.)

- Write an expression that calculates the appropriate number of iterations. (Again, the number of iterations may vary from one run to the next.)

As in a Do structure, the For loop identifies a block of code that will be performed repeatedly during the looping. Two parts of a For loop serve as markers for the beginning and the end of the code. The For statement always marks the beginning of the loop. This statement also defines the counter variable and specifies the range of values it will go through during the looping. The Next statement marks the end of the loop. The statements between For and Next are performed once for each iteration of the loop.

In many For loops, the counter variable itself becomes a useful data item in the performance of the loop. You can display this counter on the screen, perform calculations with it, or use it as an *index* to access other information. The more you learn about using For loops, the more important this counter variable can become in the design of your program.

In its simplest form, the For loop uses an integer counter that increases by 1 for each iteration. The loop's syntax can be represented as follows:

```
For counter = v1 To v2

    ' The block of statements that the
    ' computer will perform repeatedly
    ' as counter increases from v1 to v2.

Next counter
```

In this format, *counter* is the name of a variable, and *v1* and *v2* specify the range of values that counter will represent during the looping. You can write *v1* and *v2* as literal numeric values, variables, or expressions. Here are the steps Visual Basic goes through to perform a For loop:

1. Assign the value of *v1* to *counter*.

2. Compare the value of *counter* with *v2*. If *counter* is greater than *v2*, terminate the loop and jump down to the statement located after Next. If *counter* is less than or equal to *v2*, perform all the statements located between For and Next once.

3. If the looping hasn't terminated, increase the value of *counter* by 1 and continue again as described in step 2, above.

Consider the following example from the *cmdClear_Click* procedure (Listing 7-6):

```
For i = 0 to 4
    txtFirstName(i).Text = ""
    txtLastName(i).Text = ""
Next i
```

This loop clears any text entries in all five pairs of name text boxes in the *frmMeetings* form. As you may notice, the text boxes themselves — *txtFirstName* and *txtLastName* — are indexed, or numbered sequentially, from 0 to 4. These text boxes are defined as *control arrays* — that is, two groups of controls that have common names. This arrangement considerably simplifies the program's processing of the information in these particular text boxes, as shown in this example. You'll learn more about control arrays in Chapter 9.

Using the Step Clause

Sometimes you'll want to increase the counter variable by a value other than 1 for each iteration of a For loop. In this case, you can use the Step clause in the For statement to indicate the increment amount. Here is a general format for the For loop with a Step clause:

```
For counter = v1 To v2 Step incr

    ' The block of statements that the
    ' computer will perform repeatedly.

Next counter
```

As a result of the Step clause, Visual Basic increases the value of *counter* by *incr* instead of 1 after each iteration. You can express the incrementation amount as a literal value, a variable, or an expression.

The Step clause also allows you to *decrease* the value of the counter variable as the iterations progress. If this is what you want to do, you write the For statement as follows:

```
For counter = v2 To v1 Step decr
```

where *v2* is greater than *v1* and the Step clause provides a *decrement* amount — that is, a negative value.

Under two sets of circumstances, a For loop results in no iterations:

- The starting value you specify for the counter variable is greater than the ending value, and the Step value is positive
- The starting value is less than the ending value and the Step value is negative

Although the use of integer counters is common in For loops, you are free to use counters belonging to any of Visual Basic's numeric data types — including integer, long integer, single-precision, or double-precision variables. Using a noninteger counter allows you to increase or decrease the variable by fractional values as the iterations proceed.

Nested Loops

Like decisions, Do loops and For loops can be nested, resulting in powerful patterns of repetition. When one loop is nested inside another, the inner loop goes through its entire cycle of iterations once for each iteration of the outer loop. Carefully planned, nested loops allow you to accomplish a lot of work in a very compact amount of code.

A simple but classic example of nested loops appears in the procedure SortNameList (Listing 7-4), which alphabetizes the program's name index:

```
For i = 1 To listLength - 1
  For j = i + 1 To listLength
    If NameList(i).FullName > _
      NameList(j).FullName Then
        temp = NameList(i)
        NameList(i) = NameList(j)
        NameList(j) = temp
    End If
  Next j
Next i
```

The outer loop uses the variable *i* as its counter, and the inner loop uses *j*. The outer loop goes through the list of names, from the beginning to the second-to-last element (represented by *listLength - 1*). For each iteration of the outer loop, the inner loop goes through all the elements located *below* the current *i* position. If any two names, represented by the positions *i* and *j*, are found to be out of order, the decision structure swaps their positions. When the looping is complete, the list is alphabetized. (This algorithm is known as the bubble sort. Although it's a rather inefficient way to alphabetize a list, it's one of the easiest sorting algorithms to code and to understand. As an exercise, you might want to try replacing this procedure with a more efficient routine, such as the Shell sort.)

III

7

The *For Each* Loop

Visual Basic 4.0 has a new loop structure known by the keywords For Each. Although you can use a For Each loop to process an array, its ideal application is with a new type of object known as a *collection*. You'll learn about collections and the For Each loop in Chapter 11.

As you now turn your attention to Visual Basic's major data structures, you'll continue to see how control structures are suited for working with arrays and records.

Arrays

An *array* is a list, a table, or another multidimensional arrangement of data items, all represented by a single variable name. The Dim statement (or a related statement such as Private or Public) declares an array and defines its characteristics.

An array has some features in common with a simple variable; both represent values belonging to a consistent data type, and both have a designated *scope* that determines where they are available for use in your program. But an array has some additional characteristics. Most importantly, every array has a specific number of *dimensions*, which determine how the array's data items are organized. Arrays containing one, two, or three dimensions are probably the most commonly used data structures in Visual Basic programs:

- A one-dimensional array represents a list of data.

- A two-dimensional array represents a table of data, arranged in rows and columns.

- A three-dimensional array represents several data tables, each with the same number of rows and columns.

DECLARING ARRAYS

You can use Dim, Private, or Public to declare the characteristics of an array, including its name, scope, data type, and dimensions. For example, you can declare a one-dimensional array as follows:

```
Dim arrayName(length) As dataType
```

Here are the components of this declaration:

- *arrayName* is a name that conforms to Visual Basic's rules for variable names; it must begin with a letter and may contain a combination of letters and digits.
- *length* specifies the number of data items the array can represent. By default, the actual size is *length + 1* because items are numbered from 0 to *length* in the array.
- *dataType* is a keyword representing one of Visual Basic's data types or a user-defined type.

If you omit the As clause, the array belongs to the Variant type by default.

For example, the following Dim statement declares a one-dimensional string array named *MeetingPlace*, and specifies its length as 5:

```
Dim MeetingPlace(5) As String
```

Once you've declared an array, you can use Visual Basic statements to assign values to the *elements* of the array. You identify each element by specifying a subscript in parentheses immediately after the array name. For example, the *MeetingPlace* array has six elements, with subscripts ranging from 0 to 5:

```
MeetingPlace(0)
MeetingPlace(1)
MeetingPlace(2)
MeetingPlace(3)
MeetingPlace(4)
MeetingPlace(5)
```

Although the length of the *MeetingPlace* array is specified as 5, the array contains six elements, because the subscripts begin at 0. The array can therefore store a list of six strings. Of course you're free to use these array elements in any way that suits the data requirements of your program. For example, you might decide to store values only in *MeetingPlace(1)* to *MeetingPlace(5)*, leaving *MeetingPlace(0)* unused.

III

7

As you've already begun to see, the For loop is an extremely convenient structure for handling arrays. The loop's counter variable serves perfectly as the subscript for accessing the elements of an array. For example, in the *SortNameList* procedure, which you examined earlier in this chapter, the counter variables of two loops are used to access pairs of elements from the *NameList* array.

Visual Basic also enables you to establish a custom range of subscripts for an array. In the Dim statement that declares the array, you use the keyword To to specify the range:

```
Dim arrayName(sub1 To sub2)
```

In this format, the elements of the array range from *arrayName(sub1)* to *arrayName(sub2)*. Another way to control the range of indexes for an array is to include an Option Base statement in the general declarations section of a module. This statement can take one of the following two forms:

```
Option Base 0
```

or

```
Option Base 1
```

Depending on the value specified in the Option Base statement, all array indexes start either at 0 or 1.

MULTIDIMENSIONAL ARRAYS

To create an array of more than one dimension, you specify the length of each dimension in a Dim statement. The dimensions appear in parentheses just after the array name. Here is the general format for declaring a two-dimensional array:

```
Dim arrayName2(length1, length2)
```

And here is the format for a three-dimensional array:

```
Dim arrayName3(length1, length2, length3)
```

A pair of nested For loops presents the ideal structure for processing a two-dimensional array. For example, the following pair of loops assigns values to all the elements of a two-dimensional array:

```
Dim test(3, 4)

For i = 0 To 3
  For j = 0 To 4
    test(i, j) = i * j
  Next j
Next i
```

Likewise, a sequence of three loops can efficiently handle the elements of a three-dimensional array.

DYNAMIC ARRAYS

When you use a literal numeric value to declare the length of an array, Visual Basic creates a *static* array by default. For example, *MeetingPlace* is a static array:

```
Dim MeetingPlace(5) As String
```

In this context, *static* means that Visual Basic allocates the memory space required for the array when you first start the program. The allocation remains unchanged throughout the program run.

A static array works fine whenever you know in advance how much data you want to store in the array. But sometimes the size requirements are determined during a program run. In this case, you need to create a *dynamic* array. Visual Basic allocates memory space for a dynamic array during a run. The initial size of the array can therefore be based on information that's not available until the program begins. Furthermore, Visual Basic allows dynamic arrays to be redimensioned any number of times during a program run. The size of the array can change if a program needs to accommodate specific data.

Here is the general approach to creating and working with a dynamic array: Begin by declaring the array (in a Dim, Private, or Public statement) using empty parentheses in place of the array's dimensions:

```
Public arrayName() as dataType
```

At the point when the program is ready to store data in the array, use a ReDim statement to define the array's size:

```
ReDim arrayName(length)
```

To change the array's size later without losing any of the data already stored in the array, use the Preserve keyword in another ReDim statement:

```
ReDim Preserve arrayName(length)
```

The Meetings program contains a good example of a dynamic array. As you know, the program creates an array called *NameList* to store an index of all the people's names that appear in the Meetings database. (The array also stores the record number where each person's name can be found in the database; you'll see exactly how the array is organized in the final section of this chapter.) The program initially creates *NameList* at the very beginning of a performance, by opening the database file and reading the names of all the people stored in each record. But the length of *NameList* may change many times during the performance, as the user adds new meeting records to the database. *NameList* is therefore defined as a dynamic array whose length can be changed at any time.

The array is declared as a Public variable in the general declarations section of the Meetings.Bas module:

```
Public NameList() As IndexEntry
```

As you'll see shortly, *IndexEntry* is a user-defined type. Notice the empty parentheses in the *NameList* declaration; whenever you see these in a variable declaration, you can expect to find one or more ReDim statements to define the array's length.

The Form_Load procedure in the frmMeetings module (Listing 7-2) performs the program's first ReDim statement. The procedure opens the Meetings database file and reads each record from beginning to end.

Because a given meeting record may contain from one to five names of people who attended the meeting, the number of names in the database is unpredictable, even though the number of records can be calculated from the size of the file. The program therefore redimensions the *NameList* array each time a new name is read from the database:

```
listLength = listLength + 1
ReDim Preserve NameList(listLength)
```

The *listLength* variable keeps a running count of the number of names that have been read. For each new name, the count is increased by 1 and then the array is redimensioned to accommodate the new data. Finally, the new name is stored in the array. Thanks to the Preserve keyword, none of the previous names are lost.

The *cmdSave_Click* procedure (Listing 7-3) goes through a similar process each time the user adds a new meeting record to the database. As you've seen, the program sorts the *NameList* array after each increase in its length. Whenever the user requests a particular record from the database, the array serves as a convenient index for locating the target record.

Keep in mind that ReDim works only with dynamic arrays. An attempt to redimension a static array results in an error, as does an attempt to change the *number of dimensions* in a dynamic array. You can change the length of any dimension, but not the number of dimensions.

Now it's time to turn to the final topics of this chapter, user-defined types and record variables.

User-Defined Types

An array contains multiple data values, all belonging to one data type. In a string array all the elements are strings, and in a numeric array all the values are numbers. By contrast, the *user-defined type* allows you to create variables that represent multiple values of different types.

The user-defined type is ideal for use in database applications, as is clearly illustrated in the Meetings program. A database is a collection of records in which information is organized in a consistent way. The individual data items in a record are known as *fields*. For example, the fields of a meeting record include the place, date, time, and subject of the meeting, the list of people who attended, and the notes recorded about the meeting.

Because the user-defined type is so closely associated with database programs, Visual Basic programmers commonly use database terminology to describe the components of the data structure itself. Most programmers refer to a user-defined type as a *record structure*. In this terminology, the *elements* of a user-defined type are known as the *fields* of the record structure. A variable belonging to a user-defined type is simply a *record variable*. An array belonging to a user-defined type is an *array of records*.

Creating a record variable is a two-step process in a Visual Basic program:

1. Use a Type statement to define a record structure. The definition consists of a type name followed by a list of field names. Each field belongs to a specific data type.

2. Write a Dim statement to declare a record variable or an array of records.

DEFINING A RECORD STRUCTURE

The general form of the Type statement is as follows:

```
Type TypeName
   Element1 As dataType
   Element2 As dataType
   Element3 As dataType

     ' ... additional field definitions

End Type
```

In this statement, *TypeName* is the name you devise for the record structure, and *Element1*, *Element2*, *Element3* (and so on) are the names you give to the fields in the structure. You must also identify a data type for each field. The *dataType* may be any of Visual Basic's predefined types. An element may also be defined as an array or as an item belonging to another user-defined type.

A Public Type statement may appear only in the general declarations section of a module. A form module may not declare a public type; if you want a type to be available everywhere in your program, place the Type statement in the general declarations section of a code module. A Private Type statement may appear in the general declarations section of a form or module. In this case, the type is available only in the module where it is defined.

In the Meetings.Bas module of the Meetings program, two user-defined types are declared. The first defines the structure of a meeting record:

```
Type MeetingRec
    MeetPlace As String * 18
    MeetDate As String * 10
    TimeFrom As String * 10
    TimeTo As String * 10
    FirstName(4) As String * 10
    LastName(4) As String * 18
    Subject As String * 35
    Notes As String * 400
End Type
```

The first four elements of the MeetingRec type correspond to the Place, Date, and From Time, and To Time fields of a meeting record. The next two are arrays of strings, *FirstName* and *LastName,* designed to store as many as five names of people who attended a meeting. The last two elements are for the *Subject* and *Notes* fields. Notice that the Notes field is a fixed string of length 400.

The Type statement defines a new data structure, but does not create any new variables belonging to this data type. You use Dim, Public, or Private for this task. For example, here is the general form of a Dim statement for declaring a record variable:

```
Dim RecordVar As TypeName
```

The Meetings program uses Public rather than Dim to declare a variable belonging to the *MeetingRec* type:

```
Public Meeting As MeetingType
```

Given this variable declaration, Visual Basic supplies a special notation for referring to the elements of the Meeting record. This notation is a combination of the record name and an element name, separated by a period, as in the general form *RecordVar.Element*. For example, here are the names of the first four fields in the Meeting record variable:

```
Meeting.MeetPlace
Meeting.MeetDate
Meeting.TimeFrom
Meeting.TimeTo
```

You can use the *RecordVar.Element* notation in assignment statements or any other kind of statement in which you normally include variable names.

THE WITH STATEMENT

Visual Basic 4.0 has a new control structure you can use to simplify any code that refers to the elements of a user-defined type. The With statement enables you to abbreviate the names of any user-defined data elements. Here is the general form of the With structure for use with a variable belonging to a user-defined type:

```
With RecordVar

    ' Statements that may refer to
    ' the elements of RecordVar

End With
```

Inside the With block, you refer to *RecordVar.Element* simply as:

```
.Element
```

The Meeting program uses the With statement frequently to streamline references to elements of the *Meeting* record variable. For example, here is how the cmdSave_Click procedure (Listing 7-3) copies data from text boxes to the corresponding elements of the *Meeting* variable:

```
With Meeting
  .MeetPlace = txtPlace.Text
  .MeetDate = txtDate.Text
  .TimeFrom = txtTimeFrom.Text
  .TimeTo = txtTimeTo.Text
  .Subject = txtSubject.Text
  .Notes = txtNotes.Text
  For i = 0 To 4
    .FirstName(i) = txtFirstName(i).Text
    .LastName(i) = txtLastName(i).Text
  Next i
End With
```

The abbreviated names for the elements of the *Meeting* record appear on the left side of the equal signs in a sequence of assignment statements. Conversely, here is how the Form_Activate procedure (Listing 7-5) displays the elements of a newly retrieved record in the text boxes of the Business Meetings dialog box:

```
With Meeting
  txtPlace.Text = .MeetPlace
  txtDate.Text = .MeetDate
  txtTimeFrom.Text = .TimeFrom
  txtTimeTo.Text = .TimeTo
  txtSubject.Text = .Subject
  txtNotes.Text = .Notes

  For i = 0 To 4
    txtFirstName(i).Text = .FirstName(i)
    txtLastName(i).Text = .LastName(i)
  Next i
End With
```

In this case, the abbreviated names appear on the right side of the equal signs.

CREATING AN ARRAY OF RECORDS

The *Meeting* variable can store only a single record at a time. But it's also possible to declare an array that belongs to a user-defined type, or in other words, an array of records. Here is the general format for declaring such an array:

```
Dim RecordArray(length) As TypeName
```

As you would expect, *length* indicates the number of records that the array can store. (Actually, the array can contain *length + 1* records, because the subscripts of the array begin at 0.) Once this array is declared, your program uses the following notation to identify the fields of a single record in the array:

```
RecordArray(i).FieldName1
RecordArray(i).FieldName2
RecordArray(i).FieldName3
```

where *i* is a subscript for one of the elements of the array.

The Meetings application creates an array of records to represent the name index that the program uses to retrieve individual meeting records from the database. The second user-defined type in the Meetings.Bas module is named *IndexEntry*:

```
Type IndexEntry
   FullName As String
   RecordNum As Long
End Type
```

This is the type on which the *NameList* array is based. The following Public statement declares the array:

```
Public NameList() As IndexEntry
```

As you can see, each element of the array has two fields, which are identified as

```
NameList(i).FullName
NameList(i).RecordNum
```

The *FullName* field contains the name of each person who is added to the *NameList* array, and the *RecordNum* field is the record number where the person's name can be found in the database. When the program locates a name in this array, it can simply look at the *RecordNum* field of the same array element to find out which database record contains the name.

To see how this is accomplished, take a look at the cmdView_Click procedure in Listing 7-11. This procedure takes control when the user chooses a record in the frmMeetFind form and then clicks the View button. Before switching back to the program's original dialog box, this procedure assigns the target record number to the Public variable named *curRec*:

```
curRec = NameList(numInList).RecordNum
```

Back in the *frmMeetings* form, the program retrieves this record directly from the database and displays its fields in the text boxes of the form.

You'll continue exploring data structures and control structures as you turn to the topic of data file programming in Chapter 8.

Listing 7-1
The Meetings.Bas module

```
' The Meetings program
' --------------------


' Module: Meetings.Bas
' --------------------

' This module contains the type definitions
' for the Meetings records and for the index
' list.


' The meeting record type.
Type MeetingRec
  MeetPlace As String * 18
  MeetDate As String * 10
  TimeFrom As String * 10
  TimeTo As String * 10
  FirstName(4) As String * 10
  LastName(4) As String * 18
  Subject As String * 35
  Notes As String * 400
End Type
```

A user-defined type, defined for global use

```
' The global Meeting record variable
' and the global record pointer, curRec.
Public Meeting As MeetingRec
Public curRec As Integer
```

A public variable belonging to the user-defined type

```
' The dynamic NameList array stores the
' list of all names in the database.
Type IndexEntry
  FullName As String
  RecordNum As Long
End Type

Public NameList() As IndexEntry
Public listLength As Long
```

Declaration for a dynamic array

```
Function StrFix(s As String) _
  As String

  ' The StrFix function converts a
  ' string argument to all uppercase
  ' letters and removes any leading
  ' or trailing blanks. This ensures
  ' reliable comparisons between strings
  ' in the program.

  StrFix = UCase(Trim(s))

End Function   ' StrFix

Function FixName(first As String, last As String) _
  As String

  ' The FixName function returns a name string
  ' in the standard format LASTNAME FIRSTNAME.

  FixName = StrFix(last) & " " & StrFix(first)

End Function   ' FixName
```

Listing 7-2
General declarations for Meetings.Frm and the Form_Load procedure

```
' The Meetings program
' --------------------


' Files:
' ------
' Project File: Meetings.Mak
' Form Files:   Meetings.Frm (startup)
'               MeetFind.Frm
' Module File: Meetings.Bas


' This program saves information and notes about
' meetings conducted during business trips.
' The meeting records are saved on disk
' in a database file named \Meetings.DB.
' Each record in the database includes
' the place, date, and time of the
' meeting, the names of the people
' present (as many as five), the subject
' of the meeting, and a text field for
' keeping notes about the meeting.
' The program allows the user to search
' for and view any meeting record, using the
' name of any person who was present at
' the meeting as the key for the search.

Option Explicit   ' Declare all variables.

' End of general declarations for the
' startup form, Meetings.Frm.


Private Sub Form_Load()

   ' The Form_Load procedure opens Meetings.DB
   ' and reads through each record in the
   ' database. It forms the name index by
   ' reading all the nonblank names from each
   ' record. Finally, it calls SortNameList to
   ' sort the index.
```

```
Dim i, j

' Open the database and calculate the
' number of records it currently contains.
Open "\MEETINGS.DB" For Random As #1 _
     Len = Len(Meeting)
   curRec = LOF(1) / Len(Meeting)

  ' Initialize the length of the name
  ' index to zero.
  listLength = 0

  ' Read the records from the database
  ' one at a time.
  For i = 1 To curRec
    Get #1, i, Meeting

    ' For each record, read as many as
    ' five names of people who were
    ' present at a given meeting.
    For j = 0 To 4
      With Meeting

        ' If the FirstName and LastName
        ' fields of a given record are not
        ' blank, increase the length of the
        ' name index by 1 and add the new
        ' name to the list.
        If Trim(.FirstName(j)) <> "" And _
          Trim(.LastName(j)) <> "" Then
          listLength = listLength + 1
          ReDim Preserve NameList(listLength)

        ' Standardize each new name in
        ' the form LASTNAME FIRSTNAME.
        NameList(listLength).FullName = _
          FixName(.FirstName(j), .LastName(j))

        ' The RecordNum field stores the
        ' record number corresponding to each
```

Changing the size of a dynamic array

```
                      ' name in the index. (Note that a given
                      ' name may appear multiple times in
                      ' the index if a person has been present
                      ' at two or more meetings.)
                      NameList(listLength).RecordNum = i


                End If
              End With
          Next j


        Next i
      Close #1

      ' If the index is longer than one element,
      ' sort the NameList array in alphabetical
      ' order by the FullName field.
      If listLength > 1 Then _
        SortNameList


      curRec = 0


    End Sub   ' Form_Load
```

Listing 7-3
The cmdSave_Click procedure

```
    Private Sub cmdSave_Click()

        ' The cmdSave_Click procedure saves the
        ' current record to the database (after
        ' confirming that it is a valid record)
        ' and then updates the index of names.

        Dim i

        ' Call OKRecord to validate the current
        ' record entry, then assign each field to
        ' the appropriate element of the Meeting
        ' structure.
```

```
If OKRecord Then
  With Meeting
    .MeetPlace = txtPlace.Text
    .MeetDate = txtDate.Text
    .TimeFrom = txtTimeFrom.Text
    .TimeTo = txtTimeTo.Text
    .Subject = txtSubject.Text
    .Notes = txtNotes.Text
    For i = 0 To 4
      .FirstName(i) = txtFirstName(i).Text
      .LastName(i) = txtLastName(i).Text
    Next i
  End With
```

Using the With structure to simplify references to the elements of a user-defined type

```
  ' Open the Meetings database and write
  ' the new record to the end of the file.
  Open "\MEETINGS.DB" For Random As #1 _
      Len = Len(Meeting)
    curRec = LOF(1) / Len(Meeting)
    Put #1, curRec + 1, Meeting
  Close #1

  ' Update the name index.
  For i = 0 To 4

    ' Add a name to the index only if
    ' the user has entered both a first
    ' name and a last name.
    If Trim(txtFirstName(i).Text) <> "" And _
      Trim(txtLastName(i).Text) <> "" Then

        ' Increase the length counter by 1,
        ' and then redimension the NameList
        ' array. (The Preserve keyword ensures
        ' that the data in the array will be
        ' retained after the redimensioning.)
        listLength = listLength + 1
        ReDim Preserve NameList(listLength)
```

```
            ' Standardize the name entry in the
            ' form LASTNAME FIRSTNAME, and then
            ' assign it to the final element of
            ' the array.
            NameList(listLength).FullName = _
              FixName(txtFirstName(i).Text, _
                      txtLastName(i).Text)

            ' Save the record number as the
            ' RecordNum element of the entry.
            NameList(listLength).RecordNum = _
              curRec + 1

        End If
      Next i

      ' If the index is longer than 1
      ' entry, sort the list of names
      ' in alphabetical order.
      If listLength > 1 Then _
        SortNameList

      ' Clear the frmMeetings form so the
      ' user can enter a new record.
      cmdClear_Click
    Else

      ' If the current record is not complete,
      ' don't save it to the file. Instead,
      ' display a brief error message.
      MsgBox "Can't save an incomplete record.", _
        , "Save"
    End If

  End Sub  ' cmdSave_Click
```

Listing 7-4

The OKRecord function and the SortNameList procedure

```
Private Function OKRecord() As Boolean

    ' The OKRecord function looks for empty text boxes
    ' in the current meeting record. The function returns
    ' a value of true if the record is OK to save, or
    ' false if it is not. (If the user has left any field
    ' blank, the program will not save the record.

    Dim temp1 As Boolean, temp2 As Boolean
    Dim i

    ' First check all the text boxes except the names.
    temp1 = Trim(txtPlace.Text) <> "" And _
            Trim(txtDate.Text) <> "" And _
            Trim(txtTimeFrom.Text) <> "" And _
            Trim(txtTimeTo.Text) <> "" And _
            Trim(txtSubject.Text) <> "" And _
            Trim(txtNotes.Text) <> ""
```

A compound logical expression

```
    ' Check the two arrays of name text boxes,
    ' txtFirstName and txtLastName.
    temp2 = False
    For i = 0 To 4
        temp2 = temp2 Or _
                (Trim(txtFirstName(i).Text) <> "" And _
                Trim(txtLastName(i).Text) <> "")
    Next i
```

Using relational and logical operations in the same expression

```
    ' OKRecord is true if both temp1 and
    ' temp2 are true.
    OKRecord = temp1 And temp2

End Function    ' OkRecord



Private Sub SortNameList()
```

```
' The SortNameList procedure alphabetizes
' the name index by the entries in the
' FullName field.
Dim i, j
Dim temp As IndexEntry

' Compare each record with each of
' the records below it.
For i = 1 To listLength - 1
  For j = i + 1 To listLength

    ' Check to see whether two records
    ' are currently out of order.
    If NameList(i).FullName > _
        NameList(j).FullName Then

      ' If they are, swap their positions
      ' in the list.
      temp = NameList(i)
      NameList(i) = NameList(j)
      NameList(j) = temp
    End If
  Next j
Next i
```

Nesting of loops and a decision

```
End Sub  ' SortNameList
```

Listing 7-5

The cmdFind_Click, Form_Activate, and ReadOnlyStatus procedures

```
Private Sub cmdFind_Click()

  ' The cmdFind_click procedure
  ' switches forms when the user
  ' clicks the Find button.

  frmMeetings.Hide
  frmMeetFind.Show

End Sub  ' cmdFind_Click
```

III

7

```
Private Sub Form_Activate()

  ' The Form_Activate procedure displays a
  ' complete meeting record in the frmMeetings
  ' form after the user has selected a record and
  ' clicked the View button in the frmMeetFind
  ' form. The public variable curRec indicates
  ' the target record that should be read from
  ' the database. (If curRec is zero, the user has
  ' clicked the Cancel button in frmMeetFind.)

  Dim i

  ' If curRec is not zero, read a record
  ' from the databse file.
  If curRec <> 0 Then
    Open "\Meetings.DB" For Random As #1 _
      Len = Len(Meeting)
      Get #1, curRec, Meeting
    Close #1

    ' Display all the fields of information
    ' from the record in the various text
    ' boxes in the frmMeetings form.
    With Meeting
      txtPlace.Text = .MeetPlace
      txtDate.Text = .MeetDate
      txtTimeFrom.Text = .TimeFrom
      txtTimeTo.Text = .TimeTo
      txtSubject.Text = .Subject
      txtNotes.Text = .Notes

      For i = 0 To 4
        txtFirstName(i).Text = .FirstName(i)
        txtLastName(i).Text = .LastName(i)
      Next i
    End With

    ' Don't allow the user to modify
    ' this record or to save it to disk.
    ReadOnlyStatus True

  Else
```

A call to a procedure that takes a Boolean argument

```
      ' Otherwise, if curRec is zero when
      ' frmMeetings is reactivated, simply
      ' clear all information from the form
      ' and allow the user to enter a new record.
      cmdClear_Click
   End If

End Sub  ' Form_Activate


Private Sub ReadOnlyStatus(onOff As Boolean)

   ' The ReadOnlyStatus procedure switches
   ' the Locked property to either true or
   ' false for all the text boxes in the
   ' frmMeetings form.

   ' (The Form_Activate procedure switches the
   ' read-only status to true in order to
   ' prevent changes in a record that's been
   ' read from the database. By contrast, the
   ' cmdClear_Click procedure switches the status
   ' to false so that the user can enter and save
   ' a new meeting record.)

   Dim i

   ' Set the Locked property for each of
   ' the text boxes in the form. (Note that
   ' this text box property was named ReadOnly
   ' in previous versions of Visual Basic.)
```

```
txtPlace.Locked = onOff
txtDate.Locked = onOff
txtTimeFrom.Locked = onOff
txtTimeTo.Locked = onOff
txtSubject.Locked = onOff
txtNotes.Locked = onOff

For i = 0 To 4
  txtFirstName(i).Locked = onOff
  txtLastName(i).Locked = onOff
Next i
```

Using the Boolean argument to set the Locked property

```
' If the read-only status is true,
' disable the Save button. Conversely,
' if the read-only status is false,
' the Save button is available to the user.
cmdSave.Enabled = Not onOff
```

*Using the
Not operator*

```
End Sub  ' ReadOnlyStatus
```

Listing 7-6
The cmdClear_Click and cmdExit_Click procedures

```
Private Sub cmdClear_Click()

    ' The cmdClear_Click procedure clears
    ' the current record from the frmMeetings
    ' form when the user clicks the Clear
    ' button.

    Dim i

    ' Clear the place, date, and time.
    txtPlace.Text = ""
    txtDate.Text = ""
    txtTimeFrom.Text = ""
    txtTimeTo.Text = ""

    ' Clear the name fields.
    For i = 0 To 4
        txtFirstName(i).Text = ""
        txtLastName(i).Text = ""
    Next i

    ' Clear the subject and the notes.
    txtSubject.Text = ""
    txtNotes.Text = ""

    ' Allow the user to resume entering
    ' and editing fields of information
    ' in the form. (This is relevant only
    ' if the form was previously displaying
    ' a record that the program searched for
```

```
' and read from the database.
ReadOnlyStatus False

' Move the focus to the Place field.
txtPlace.SetFocus

End Sub   ' cmdClear_Click



Private Sub cmdExit_Click()

' The cmdExit_Click procedure ends
' the program's performance when the
' user clicks the Exit button.

End

End Sub   ' cmdExit_Click
```

Listing 7-7

General declarations for MeetFind.Frm and the Form_Activate and cmdClearName_Click procedures

```
' The Meetings program
' --------------------

' Form: frmMeetFind (MeetFind.Frm)

' This form allows the user to search for
' the name of any person in the database
' (that is, anyone who has attended one of
' the meetings recorded in the file). If
' a given name appears in more than one
' record, the user can scroll through the
' target records, viewing the place, date,
' and subject fields for each record. To
' switch to the frmMeetings form and view
' all the fields of a selected record, the
' user simply clicks the View button after
' scrolling to the target record.
```

```
Option Explicit   ' Declare all variables.

' The numInList variable identifies
' index number of the record that is
' currently displayed in the form. Note
' that a given name may appear multiple
' times in the index list.
Dim numInList

' End of general declarations
' for the frmMeetFind form.


Private Sub Form_Activate()

  ' The Form_Activate clears the frmMeetFind
  ' form at the time it is activated.

  cmdClearName_Click

End Sub   ' Form_Activate



Private Sub cmdClearName_Click()

  ' The cmdClearName_Click procecure
  ' clears current record information
  ' from the frmMeetFind form so that
  ' the user can search for a new name.

  ' Clear the name text boxes.
  txtFirst.Text = ""
  txtLast.Text = ""

  ' Clear the labels designated
  ' for displaying the place, date
  ' and subject fields.
  lblPlace.Caption = ""
  lblDate.Caption = ""
  lblSubject.Caption = ""
```

```
' Disable the Previous, Next,
' and View buttons.
cmdPrevious.Enabled = False
cmdNext.Enabled = False
cmdView.Enabled = False

' Move the focus to the first
' of the text boxes in the form.
txtFirst.SetFocus

End Sub    ' cmdClearName_Click
```

Listing 7-8
The cmdSearch_Click procedure

```
Private Sub cmdSearch_Click()

    ' The cmdSearch_Click procedure searches
    ' for the name that the user has entered
    ' into the First Name and Last Name text
    ' boxes. If the name is found in the index,
    ' the procedure reads the corresponding
    ' record from the database and displays the
    ' Place, Date, and Subject fields.

    Dim inName As String
    Dim curPos As Long
    Dim timesCount As Long

    ' Standardize the name that the user
    ' has entered into the form. The standard
    ' name format in the index list is
    ' LASTNAME FIRSTNAME.
    inName = FixName(txtFirst.Text, _
        txtLast.Text)

    ' Search for the name in the list. The
    ' SearchForName function returns the
    ' index number of the first instance of
    ' the name.
```

```
numInList = SearchForName(inName)

' If the name appears in the list at
' least once, check to see if there are
' any additional instances of the same name.
If numInList <> 0 Then
  timesCount = 1
  If numInList <> listLength Then
    curPos = numInList
    Do While inName = _
        NameList(curPos + 1).FullName
      timesCount = timesCount + 1
      curPos = curPos + 1
      If curPos = listLength Then Exit Do
    Loop
  End If
End If
```

Nested decisions and a nested loop

```
' Disable the Previous button,
' because this is the first instance
' of this name in the index.
' If the name appears more than
' once in the index list, then
' activate the Next button so the
' user can scroll through the
' selection of records.
cmdPrevious.Enabled = False
If timesCount > 1 Then _
  cmdNext.Enabled = True

' Display the first record for
' the target name. Notice that
' NameList(numInList).RecordNum
' represents the number of the record
' in which the target name appears.
ShowRecord NameList(numInList).RecordNum

' Enable the View button so the
' user can switch to the Meetings form
' and fiew the entire record.
cmdView.Enabled = True
```

```
  Else

    ' If the name is not found in the index,
    ' display a message on the screen.
    MsgBox txtFirst.Text & " " & txtLast.Text & _
      " is not in the Meetings database.", , _
      "Search"

  End If

End Sub  ' cmdSearch_Click
```

Listing 7-9
The SearchForName function and the ShowRecord procedure

```
Private Function SearchForName(findName As String) _
  As Long

  ' The SearchForName function performs a binary
  ' search on the alphabetized name index and
  ' looks for the first instance of the target
  ' name represented by the argument findName.

  Dim pos1 As Long, pos2 As Long
  Dim posX As Long, midPos As Long

  ' Initialize the markers in the list.
  pos1 = 1
  pos2 = listLength
  posX = 0

  ' Divide the list in half and focus
  ' the search on the half that will contain
  ' the target name if it exists. Continue
  ' this process until the name is found or
  ' the entire list has been searched.
  Do While pos1 <= pos2 And posX = 0
    midPos = (pos1 + pos2) / 2
```

```
If findName = NameList(midPos).FullName Then
   posX = midPos
ElseIf findName > NameList(midPos).FullName Then
   pos1 = midPos + 1
Else
   pos2 = midPos - 1
End If
```

*Using the
ElseIf clause*

```
Loop


' If the name has been found, then
' check to see if there are any other
' instances of the same name higher
' in the list.
If posX > 1 Then
  Do While NameList(posX).FullName _
       = NameList(posX - 1).FullName
    posX = posX - 1
  Loop
End If


' Return the index number of the
' first instance of the name in the list.
SearchForName = posX


End Function   ' SearchForName




Private Sub ShowRecord(which As Long)

  ' The ShowRecord procedure reads a
  ' record from the Meetings database and
  ' displays the Place, Date, and Subject
  ' fields in the frmMeetFind form.

  ' Open the database and read the record.
  Open "\Meetings.DB" For Random As #1 _
      Len = Len(Meeting)
    Get #1, which, Meeting
  Close #1
```

```
' Display the fields as the captions
' of the appropriate labels.
With Meeting
  lblPlace.Caption = .MeetPlace
  lblDate.Caption = .MeetDate
  lblSubject.Caption = .Subject
End With

End Sub   ' ShowRecord
```

Listing 7-10
The cmdNext_Click, cmdPrevious_Click, and Form_KeyDown procedures.

```
Private Sub cmdNext_Click()

    ' The cmdNext_Click procedure displays
    ' the next record that matches the
    ' current name entry.

    ' Increase numInList by 1 and display
    ' the corresponding record.
    numInList = numInList + 1
    ShowRecord NameList(numInList).RecordNum

    ' Enable to Previous button so that
    ' the user can go back to the previous
    ' record.
    cmdPrevious.Enabled = True
    cmdNext.Enabled = False

    ' Check to see if there is another
    ' entry of the same name in the index
    ' list. If there is, enable the Next
    ' button to allow the user to scroll
    ' forward through the database.
    If numInList <> listLength Then _
        If NameList(numInList + 1).FullName = _
            FixName(txtFirst.Text, txtLast.Text) Then _
                cmdNext.Enabled = True

End Sub   ' cmdNext_Click
```

Using the NameList *index to identify a record*

```
Private Sub cmdPrevious_Click()

   ' The cmdPrevious_Click procedure displays
   ' the previous record that matches the
   ' current name entry.

   ' Decrease numInList by 1 and display
   ' the corresponding record.
   numInList = numInList - 1
   ShowRecord NameList(numInList).RecordNum

   ' Enable to Next button so that
   ' the user can go forward to the next
   ' record.
   cmdNext.Enabled = True

   ' Check to see if there is another
   ' entry of the same name earlier in the index
   ' list. If there is not, disable the Previous
   ' button to prevent the user from scrolling
   ' backward through the database.
   If NameList(numInList - 1).FullName <> _
     FixName(txtFirst.Text, txtLast.Text) Then _
       cmdPrevious.Enabled = False

End Sub   ' cmdPrevious_Click




Private Sub Form_KeyDown _
   (KeyCode As Integer, Shift As Integer)

   ' The Form_KeyDown procedure allows the user to
   ' scroll through a sequence of records by pressing
   ' the PgUp or PgDn keys on the keyboard.

   ' *** Note that the form's KeyPreview property
   '        is set to True to make this event possible.
```

```
' Code numbers for the
' PgDn and PgUp keys.
Const PgDn = 34
Const PgUp = 33

' If the user presses PgDn and the Next
' button is currently enabled, force a call
' to the cmdNext_Click event procedure.
If KeyCode = PgDn _
   And cmdNext.Enabled = True _
      Then cmdNext_Click
```

The And operator

```
' If the user presses PgUp and the Previous
' button is currently enabled, force a call
' to the cmdPrevious_Click event procedure.
If KeyCode = PgUp _
   And cmdPrevious.Enabled = True _
      Then cmdPrevious_Click


End Sub   ' Form_KeyDown
```

Listing 7-11
The cmdView_Click and cmdCancel_Click procedures

```
Private Sub cmdView_Click()

   ' The cmdView_Click procedure switches
   ' forms when the user clicks the View
   ' button. The global variable curRec
   ' indicates which record will be displayed
   ' in the Meetings form.

   curRec = NameList(numInList).RecordNum

   frmMeetFind.Hide
   frmMeetings.Show
```

*Hiding and
showing forms*

```
End Sub   ' cmdView_Click
```

III

7

```
Private Sub cmdCancel_Click()

    ' The cmdCancel_Click procedure switches
    ' back to the Meetings form when the user
    ' clicks the Cancel button.

    ' By setting the value of the global
    ' variable curRec to zero, this procedure
    ' notifies the Meetings form that the
    ' user does not currently want to view
    ' a target record.
    curRec = 0
    frmMeetFind.Hide
    frmMeetings.Show

End Sub   ' cmdCancel_Click
```

Data File Programming

*D*ata file management is an essential skill for all programmers. Files on disk serve a variety of purposes in Visual Basic projects:

- Applications often create files as permanent records of the information they generate; data produced during one program run can be retrieved during the next.

- A data file may become a medium for exchanging information between different applications.

- Programs can produce text files designed for *people* to read; these files may contain information that a user can view, modify, incorporate into larger documents, and print.

Every project you've worked with so far in this book has used data files to store or retrieve information. The Travel Guide and Currency Exchange programs (Chapters 1 through 4) are both designed to read a data file containing international currency exchange rates. The programs use this information to provide a variety of currency calculation tools for the business traveler..

The Travel Expense Log program (Chapter 5) creates a text file to record expense records from business trips. The program also creates a readable text file containing a summary of travel expenses.

The Restaurant Review program (Chapter 6) develops a database for storing your comments about restaurants in your city or around the world. The database format makes it easy for the program to retrieve any restaurant record on request.

The Meetings program (Chapter 7) saves information about meetings that you conduct or attend during business trips. Again, the database file is designed for efficient retrieval of any record that you need to review.

These programs illustrate two kinds of files you can create in Visual Basic — text files and random-access files:

■ A text file consists exclusively of ASCII characters. You can therefore read the information yourself if you open the file in a text editor. For use in programming, a text file is arranged for *sequential access*; a program generally reads a text file's data from beginning to end. But text files can also be formatted as reports designed for *people* to read.

■ A random-access file contains individual records in a fixed-length format. Numeric and string data items in a random-access file are stored in special formats that give each item a predictable length. Thanks to this structure, a Visual Basic program can go directly to any record in the file without having to read other records first. The random-access file format is often used in database management applications.

Text files and random-access files require different programming techniques for reading and writing data. You'll study these techniques in this chapter, as you examine a sample project called the Phone Directory program.

The Phone Directory Program

A program in charge of a database typically gives you simple ways to perform several important operations on individual records. Probably the two most basic operations are saving and retrieving records. You'll want be able to add new records at any point during your work with the database, and you'll want the program to find and display records that you request. In addition, you may need to revise records when information changes over time, and scroll through records one by one as a direct means of searching for particular data.

The database managed by the Phone Directory program is a collection of names, phone numbers, and e-mail addresses. The records in the database have fields for a person's name (first and last), three phone numbers (home phone, work phone, and fax number), and an e-mail address. Open the project now from the program disk; the project file is named Phone.VBP. When you press F5 to run the program for the first time, the Phone Directory window appears on the desktop (Figure 8-1). As you can see, the boxes where you enter the fields of a new record are clearly labeled in the window.

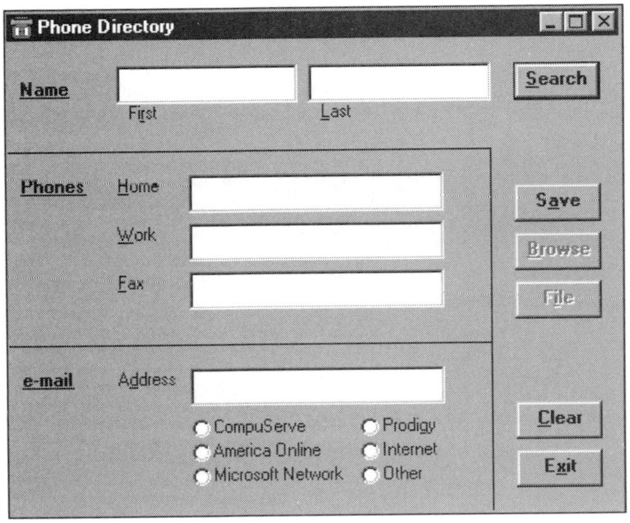

Figure 8-1
The Phone Directory window.

You can use this program on business trips, when your primary tool for communication with the outside world is the telephone, and your laptop computer is never far from reach. The program gives you a quick way to look up people's phone numbers and e-mail addresses whenever you need them. You find a record simply by typing a person's name and clicking the Search button. You can also add phone records to your database at any time, and you can revise any record when necessary. Finally, you may occasionally want to produce a printed directory of all the telephone numbers in your database. To provide this feature, the program creates a text file containing all the records in the database, alphabetized by last names. You can print this file — or incorporate it into a larger document — by loading it into a text editor such as Notepad or WordPad, applications that come with Windows 95.

Simplicity is always the key to an effective database management program. People want fast and easy ways to find information so they can get on with their work. Paradoxically, from your point of view as a programmer, simplicity can be difficult to provide. Although the Phone Directory application is easy to use — allowing the user to add, retrieve, and revise phone records, and to produce a readable directory — the program has many detailed procedures to perform in the background.

Running the Telephone Database Program

When you run this program, your initial task is data entry. To enter a new record you begin by typing the first and last name of a person whose phone numbers you want to save. Then you type the other fields of the record. When you arrive at the e-mail address field, you enter the address and then select one of the online services listed below the address.

The phone number fields are long enough to accommodate area codes, extensions, and international telephone numbers. If you have no number to enter for a particular field, leave the text box blank. (You can fill in a missing number later by revising the record.) When you complete the fields for a given entry, click the Save button at the right side of the Phone Directory window, as shown in Figure 8-2.

Note that the program requires entries for both the first and last name in order to save a new record in the database. If you attempt to enter a record in which one of these fields is missing, the program displays a small message box reminding you to enter both of these fields before trying to save a record. The first and last names are the keys by which the program organizes and retrieves information from the database; for consistency and reliability, the program therefore needs both entries.

To begin another new entry, click the Clear button to remove the previous record from the window, and then begin typing the fields of the next record.

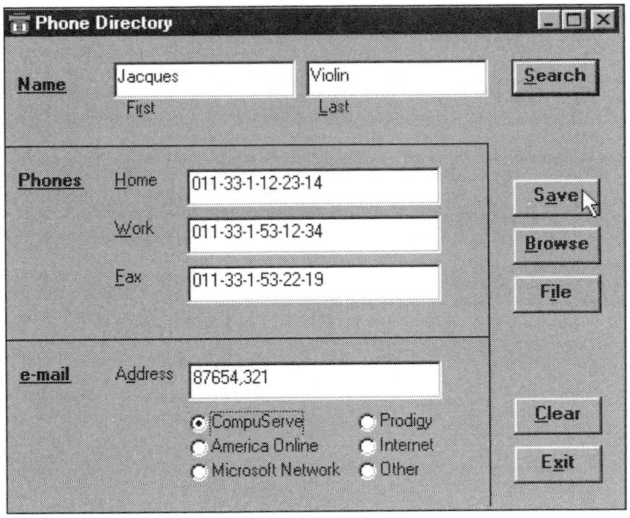

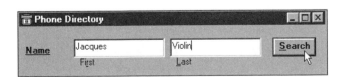

Figure 8-2
Saving a Phone Directory record.

Once your database contains a collection of records, you can begin using the program to look up phone numbers. To do so, you enter the first and last name of the person you want to look up, and click the Search button, as in Figure 8-3. (Alternatively, you can simply press the Enter key after you type the person's name. Because Search is designated as the default command button, its Click procedure is performed automatically in response to the Enter key.) The program immediately searches for the name in the database and, assuming the name is found, displays the complete record in the Phone Directory window. Like other database management programs you've seen in this book, the main dialog box serves both as a location for entering new records and as a window for retrieving and viewing existing records.

Figure 8-3
Searching for a record.

If you misspell a name — or otherwise enter a name that's not in the database — the program displays an error message, as in Figure 8-4.

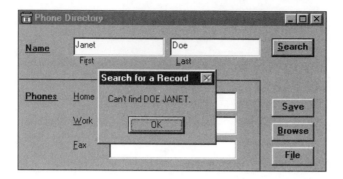

Figure 8-4
Seaching for a name that's not in the database.

When you need to revise a phone number or e-mail address, begin by retrieving the target record, following the steps you've just seen: Enter the person's name and click the Search button. The program retrieves the target record and displays its fields in the Phone Directory window. You can then revise the information in any of the phone, fax, or e-mail boxes, and in the list of network services if necessary.

When you've completed the revisions, click the Save button. The program recognizes that the current name already exists in the database and displays the message box shown in Figure 8-5. If you're sure you want to revise the current record, click the Yes button in response to the prompt. The next time you retrieve this record, you'll see that the revision has been saved. (If you change your mind about making a revision, click No in the Revise a Record dialog box.)

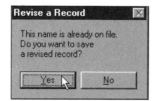

Figure 8-5
Revising a Phone Directory record.

Sometimes you may prefer to select a record by browsing through all the names currently stored in your database. In this case, you can click the Browse button to open a new dialog box entitled Browse through Phone Directory, as shown in Figure 8-6. (By the way, the Browse and File buttons are both disabled until you've entered at least one record in your database.) In the Browse dialog box you can click the Previous and Next buttons to move alphabetically through the names in your database. When you find the name you want to retrieve, click the View button. In response, the program closes the Browse window and displays the record you've requested in the main Phone Directory window (Figure 8-7).

Figure 8-6
Using the Browse window to search for a record.

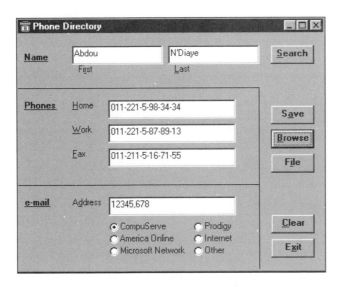

Figure 8-7
The program retrieves a record when you click the View button.

Finally, you can create a readable text listing of all the phone records in your database by clicking the File button. In response the program produces a file named Phones.TXT in the root directory of your hard disk; a message box appears on the desktop to confirm that the file has been created (Figure 8-8). Open this file into any text editor, as shown in Figure 8-9. You can reformat the information it contains, incorporate the list into another document, or simply print the file directory from the text editor.

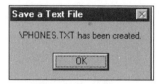

Figure 8-8

Creating the Phones.TXT directory file.

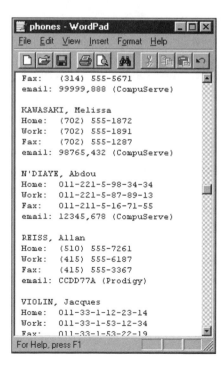

Figure 8-9

Loading the Phones.TXT file into a text editor.

You'll find that the Phone Directory program continues to work effectively and efficiently as your phone database increases in size. Whether you have a few dozen or a few hundred records in the database, the database operations work the same.

The phone database is stored on disk as a random-access file named PhoneVB4.DB. (The name identifies this as a database file that's created by a Visual Basic 4 application.) As you've just seen, the program also creates a text file named Phones.TXT. In the upcoming sections of this chapter, you'll examine the Visual Basic tools for creating and working with both kinds of files, starting with random-access ones.

The program's code appears in Listings 8-1 through 8-13. The Phone.BAS module (Listing 8-1) contains the program's central data type definitions and public declarations for key variables and arrays. The code from the Phone.FRM module (Listings 8-2 through 8-9) includes a variety of event procedures, most notably the Click procedures that respond to command-button clicks. This module also has several important general procedures. *CreateIndex* (Listing 8-5) continually updates and sorts the Index array that the program uses for retrieving records from the database. The *Search* function (Listing 8-4) efficiently searches through the index for a particular name in the database. Finally, the code from the PhonBrow.FRM module (Listings 8-10 through 8-13) controls activities on the program's secondary dialog box, and coordinates the transition back to the main Phone Directory window when the user clicks the View or Cancel button. You'll examine selections from many of these procedures as you continue through this chapter.

Working with Random-Access Files

A random-access file contains individual records of information. Each record is a collection of data items organized in a consistent format. The most important feature of this file type is *access*; after opening a file, a program can go directly to any record and read the information it contains. Data access is efficient and reliable.

To create a random-access file in Visual Basic, you begin by declaring a user-defined record structure. As you learned in Chapter 7, the Type statement defines the name of a structure and provides a list of individual field names and their data types. In a subsequent Dim statement you declare a record variable belonging to the user-defined type. This variable becomes the perfect medium for writing records to — or reading records from — a random-access file. Each write operation stores an entire record, with all its fields of data, in the file; likewise, each read operation retrieves a complete record from the file and gives your program access to the data in the record.

A program refers to records in a random-access file by number, from 1 up to the current number of records. The record number indicates a record's position in the file. Keeping track of the numbers for specific records is one of the challenging problems in a database management program. Programmers devise a variety of ways to solve this problem. In some applications, the record number itself may have special significance to the user — for example, it may be a part number or an invoice number. In this special case, the user's request for a particular record number may correspond precisely to the record's position in the file.

But more typically, the user needs to request records by some item of information other than the record number. For example, in the Phone Directory database, the programming goal is to give the user easy access to any *name* in the file. When the user provides the name of a person to look up in the file, the program retrieves the corresponding record. To achieve this goal, the program has to maintain an index of all the names in the file and their corresponding record numbers. If the user requests the address for Mary Doe, your program looks up "DOE MARY" in the index, finds the record number, and then reads the correct record from the file. You'll see exactly how the index works as you begin exploring the program.

DESIGNING A RANDOM-ACCESS FILE

Visual Basic supplies a variety of tools for working with random-access files; three of the most important are

- Open, to open a file in the Random mode
- Put #, to write a record to the file
- Get #, to read a record from the file

In addition, you use Type and Dim to prepare data structures for the file. Here are the typical programming steps you follow to create and work with a random-access file in Visual Basic:

1. Write a Type statement to define the structure of the records you intend to store in the file.

2. Write a Dim statement to declare a record variable for storing information on its way to or from the file.

3. Use the Open statement to open the file in the Random mode. In this mode a file is available for both writing and reading information.

4. Use the Put # statement to write individual records to the file.

5. Use the Get # statement to read individual records from the file.

In the Phone Directory program, the Phone.BAS module (Listing 8-1) defines the record structure for the database:

```
Type PhoneType
   FirstName As String * 20
   LastName As String * 20
   WorkPhone As String * 25
   HomePhone As String * 25
   FaxNumber As String * 25
   EmailAddress As String * 25
   ServiceType As Byte
End Type
```

The structure has seven fields, including six fixed-length strings and a Byte element. The *FirstName* and *LastName* fields store a person's full name; *WorkPhone*, *HomePhone*, and *FaxNumber* are for the three phone numbers; *EmailAddress* is for the text of an online address; and *ServiceType* is an integer from 0 to 5 representing one of the online services listed in the Phone Directory window. After defining this structure, the program declares a record variable belonging to the user-defined type:

```
Public Phones As PhoneType
```

When a program reads a record from the database file, or prepares to write a record to the file, the following names represent the seven fields of the record:

```
Phones.FirstName
Phones.LastName
Phones.WorkPhone
Phones.HomePhone
Phones.FaxNumber
Phones.EmailAddress
Phones.ServiceType
```

As you'll recall from Chapter 7, these names can be abbreviated within the control of a With structure. For example, here is how the *cmdSave_Click* procedure (Listing 8-3) copies the user's field entries to the elements of the *Phones* record:

```
With Phones
  .FirstName = txtFirstName.Text
  .LastName = txtLastName.Text
  .HomePhone = txtHomePhone.Text
  .WorkPhone = txtWorkPhone.Text
  .FaxNumber = txtFaxNumber.Text
  .EmailAddress = txtEMailAddress.Text

  For i = 0 To 5
    If optService(i).Value Then _
      .ServiceType = i
  Next i
End With
```

The program also uses the *Phones* variable in Open, Put #, and Get # statements, as you'll see in upcoming examples.

OPENING A FILE IN THE RANDOM MODE

An open random-access file is available for both reading and writing. The Visual Basic keyword that represents this file mode is Random. The Open statement for a random-access file normally contains a Len clause that indicates the total length of each record in the file. Keep in mind that access to information in the file is based on the fact that all records have a consistent structure. Thanks to this structure, Visual Basic can determine where a given record begins and ends. Accordingly, the Len clause tells Visual Basic the length of records in the file:

```
Open fileName For Random As #fileNum Len = recordLength
```

In this statement, *fileName* is the name and path of the file on disk, and *fileNum* is an integer that identifies the file in subsequent input and output statements. In the Len clause, *recordLength* is the length, in bytes, of a record in the file.

To supply a *recordLength* value for the Len clause, you can use Visual Basic's Len function. Given a record variable as its argument, Len returns the total length of all the fields in the record. Consequently, you can write the Len clause as follows:

```
Len = Len(recordVariable)
```

The first Len is the keyword for the clause itself; the second refers to Visual Basic's built-in function that supplies the length of a variable.

For example, here's how the Phone Directory program opens the phone database as a random-access file (Listing 8-2):

```
Open PhoneDB For Random As #1 _
   Len = Len(Phones)
```

In this Open statement, the name of the database file is represented by the named constant, *PhoneDB*. Here's how the constant is defined:

```
Const PhoneDB = "\PhoneVB4.DB"
```

Because the record variable *Phones* has already been declared in a Dim statement, and its structure defined in a Type statement, the expression *Len(Phones)* tells Visual Basic the length of records in the PhoneVB4.DB file. Once the file is open, the program is ready to write records to the database or read records from it.

After opening a random-access file, an application typically needs to find out the number of records currently stored in the file. Visual Basic's built-in LOF (length of file) function returns the total length, in bytes, of an open file. LOF takes one argument, the file number assigned to the file in the corresponding Open statement. If you divide the length of the file by the length of a single record in the file, the result is the number of records. For example, here's how the Phone Directory program calculates the current number of records in the database:

```
numPhones = LOF(1) / Len(Phones)
```

Once again notice the use of the expression *Len(Phones)* to find the length of a single record.

A program uses Put # to write records to an open random-access file and Get # to read records from the file.

USING PUT # TO WRITE RECORDS TO A FILE

The Put # statement sends a complete data record to a particular position in an open random-access file. Here is the usual syntax for this statement:

```
Put #fileNum, recordNum, recordVariable
```

In this format, *fileNum* is the integer that identifies the open file; this is the same number assigned to the file in the corresponding Open statement. The next value, *recordNum*, is an integer specifying the position where the record will be stored in the file. Finally, *recordVariable* is the variable containing the record that Put # writes to the file. Before the Put # statement, your program assigns values to the fields of *recordVariable*.

Of the three items you supply in the Put # statement, the second, *recordNum*, is probably the trickiest. Depending on the value of *recordNum*, Put # does one of two things:

- If *recordNum* is a value from 1 up to the current number of records in the file, Put # overwrites an existing record in the file. For example, suppose a file contains 10 records, and you supply a value of 5 as the *recordNum*. Your Put # statement writes a new record to position 5 in the file.

- If *recordNum* is equal to 1 greater than the current number of records in the file, Put # appends a new record to the file. For example, in the file containing 10 records, you would supply a *recordNum* value of 11 to append a new record. As a result of this Put # statement, the length of your file increases by one record.

The Phone Directory program allows the user to append new records to the end of the phone database at any time during a run. As you've seen, the variable *numPhones* specifies the number of records currently in the file. Before writing a new record, the program copies the seven fields of information from the Phone Directory window to the elements of the *Phones* record (as you saw in the With structure listed earlier) and then increases the value of numPhones by 1:

```
numPhones = numPhones + 1
```

Then the following Put # statement appends the record to the end of the database file:

```
Put #1, numPhones, Phones
```

In other words, the next new record number will be 1 greater than the current number of records in the file. In this way, each Put # statement adds a new record to the file. Careful management of the *numPhones* variable prevents the possiblity of inadvertently overwriting any existing records in the database.

Visual Basic allows you to omit the *recordNum* argument in the Put # statement:

```
Put #fileNum, , recordVariable
```

If you write the statement in this way, each succeeding Put # automatically writes a record to the next position in the file. This can be a convenient way to store an initial set of records in a new file. But if your program opens an existing file that already contains records, Visual Basic initially sets the current record number at 1. If you don't specify a new starting record number, a series of Put # statements can therefore overwrite the existing records. To avoid loss of data, you should always make sure you know where Put # will be writing data in your file.

USING GET # TO READ RECORDS FROM A FILE

Get # reads a complete data record from a particular position in an open random-access file. Here is the syntax:

```
Get #fileNum, recordNum, recordVariable
```

Again, *fileNum* is the integer that identifies the open file, and *recordNum* is the position from which the record will be read. In this case, *record-Variable* receives the record from the file. After Get #, your program refers to the individual fields of *recordVariable* to gain access to the information that's been read from the file.

One of the first tasks in the Phone Directory program is to create an index for the phone database. The Form_Load procedure (Listing 8-2) opens the file and calculates the current number of records, *numPhones*. Then, if *numPhones* is greater than 0, the program resizes the Index array appropriately and makes a call to the CreateIndex procedure to develop the index for the first time:

```
If numPhones > 0 Then
   ReDim Index(numPhones)
   CreateIndex
```

The CreateIndex procedure, in turn, uses a For loop to read each record from the beginning to the end of the file:

```
For i = 1 To numPhones
   Get #1, i, Phones
```

During the iterations of this loop, the counter variable *i* represents record numbers from 1 to the last record in the file. The Get # statement therefore reads each record in turn. After each Get #, the fields of the newly accessed record are represented by *Phones.FirstName*, *Phones.LastName*, and so on.

Just as in Put #, the *recordNum* is optional in the Get # statement:

```
Get #fileNum, , recordVariable
```

If you write the statement this way, each succeeding Get # reads the *next* record in the file. In a program that doesn't otherwise need to know the number of records in the file, you can use a Do loop to read the records from beginning to end:

```
Do While Not EOF(1)
  Get #1, , Phones
  ' ...
Loop
```

In this loop, Visual Basic automatically increments the record number after each Get #. When the loop reaches the end of the file (EOF), the built-in EOF(1) function returns a value of True, and the program stops reading records.

USING SEEK # TO SELECT THE CURRENT RECORD NUMBER

In some applications you may want to begin by specifying a particular starting point in your database for subsequent Put # or Get # operations. Visual Basic's Seek # statement allows you to do this. Seek # sets the position for a particular open file:

```
Seek #fileNum, recordNum
```

After Seek #, you can use the Put # statement to write a record to the recordNum position in the database:

```
Put #fileNum, , recordVariable
```

Alternatively, use a Get # statement to read a record from the Seek # position:

```
Get #fileNum, , recordVariable
```

DESIGNING AN INDEX FOR A RANDOM-ACCESS FILE

The order in which records are entered into a database is often random. For example, as you develop your phone database you're unlikely to enter all the records in alphabetical order by people's names. Instead, you'll probably enter a particular record into the database when the information becomes available.

There's nothing unusual about randomly ordered entries in a database. But when you get ready to use the information, you want it to be presented systematically in a planned order. For example, you'll want to print your phone directory in alphabetical order by people's names.

As you know, the task of rearranging records in a particular order is called *sorting*. A practical way to present database records in a sorted order is to create an index for the database and then to sort the index rather than the database itself. This technique enables you to leave a potentially large database file in its original order, and focus on sorting the smaller data set represented by the index.

The Phone Directory program creates an index consisting of all the names in the database and their corresponding record numbers. The program sorts the index in alphabetical order by names, and produces a sorted list of records by retrieving each record from the database in the order represented by the index. The index is stored in memory as an array of records — a smaller array than the one that would have been needed to store the entire database in memory. Here are the steps the program follows to create and manage this index:

1. A Type statement in the Phone.BAS module declares a special structure for the elements of the index array. The structure contains two fields: *FullName* to represent the name in each phone record, and *RecNum* to represent the corresponding record number:

```
Type IndexType
   FullName As String * 41
   RecNum As Integer
End Type
```

2. After defining the record structure, the program declares a dynamic array of *IndexType* records to represent the index:

```
Public Index() As IndexType
```

Before creating or updating the index, the program always resizes this array:

```
ReDim Index(numPhones)
CreateIndex
```

The index thus contains one element for each record in the array.

3. The *CreateIndex* procedure then builds the index by storing the name and record number of each phone record in the database:

```
For i = 1 to numPhones
  Get #1, i, Phones
  temp = MakeName _
    (Phones.FirstName, Phones.LastName)
  Index(i).FullName = temp
  Index(i).RecNum = i
Next i
```

The *MakeName* function creates a standard format for all the names in the index: last name first, all capital letters, and no extraneous spaces.

4. The *CreateIndex* procedure then sorts the index by the *FullName* field:

```
For i = 1 to numPhones - 1
  For j = i + 1 to numPhones
    If Index(i).FullName > Index(j).FullName Then
      indexEntry = Index(i)
      Index(i) = Index(j)
      Index(j) = indexEntry
    End if
  Next j
Next i
```

5. When the user enters a name and clicks the Search button to find a record in the phone directory, the cmdSearch_Click procedure standardizes the name and then calls the *Search* procedure to look for the name in the index:

```
searchName = MakeName(txtFirstName.Text, _
                      txtLastName.Text)

rec = Search(searchName)
```

The variable *rec* represents the element in the index array where the name is located. The corresponding record number is provided by the expression Index(rec).RecNum. In other words, the *RecNum* field in the index array represents the database position from which the program reads the record. Once this record number is known, the program calls the *ShowRecord* procedure to display the phone record on the screen:

```
inFileRec = Index(rec).RecNum
ShowRecord inFileRec
```

In this way the program allows the user to view any record in the database.

USING THE INDEX FOR OTHER DATABASE OPERATIONS

The Phone Directory program also uses the *Index* array in several other important contexts. When the user clicks the Save button to add a record to the database, the cmdSave_Click procedure (Listing 8-3) calls the *Search* function to look for the name in the index:

```
isFound = Search(MakeName(txtFirstName.Text, _
                             txtLastName.Text))
```

If the *Search* function returns a value of 0, the current name does not already exist in the *Index* array. Accordingly, the program can safely add the record to the end of the database:

```
If isFound = 0 Then
  numPhones = numPhones + 1

  ' ...

  Put #1, numPhones, Phones
```

But if *isFound* receives a value other than 0, the *Search* function has located the current name in the *Index* array. In this case, *isFound* represents the position in *Index* where the name was found. The program's first step is to ask the user whether this Save operation is intended as a revision of the record:

```
Else

  answer = MsgBox("This name is already on file." _
    & lf & "Do you want to save " & lf & _
    "a revised record?", 4, "Revise a Record")
```

If the user responds affirmatively (as indicated by a return value of 6 from the MsgBox function), the program writes the record back to its original position, represented by *Index(isFound).RecNum*:

```
If answer = 6 Then
   Put #1, Index(isFound).RecNum, Phones
```

The procedures in the frmBrowse form illustrate another use of the Index array, allowing the user to scroll alphabetically through the database records. Throughout this form's code, the variable *whichRecord* represents the Index number of the name currently displayed in the dialog box. If the user clicks the Next button, the program increases the value of *whichRecord* by 1 (Listing 8-11):

```
whichRecord = whichRecord + 1
```

Conversely, if the user clicks Previous, the value is decreased by 1 (Listing 8-11):

```
whichRecord = whichRecord - 1
```

Whenever the value of *whichRecord* is changed, a call to the *Show-Name* procedure (Listing 8-10) displays the new current record. This procedure reads the target record from the database file and displays the name from the record as the Caption property of a label named lblFullName:

```
Get #1, Index(whichRecord).RecNum, Phones
With Phones
   lblFullName.Caption = Trim(UCase(.LastName)) _
                        & ", " & _
                        Trim(.FirstName)
End With
```

Finally, the cmdFile_Click procedure (Listing 8-8) uses the Index array to create a text file containing an alphabetical listing of the entire phone directory. You'll examine this procedure in upcoming sections of this chapter, as you now turn to the subject of text files.

Working with Text Files

You can use a text file to store individual data items in an order and structure that a Visual Basic program can read conveniently. Alternatively, a text file might contain a table of text and numbers, ready to be printed or incorporated into a larger document for *people* to read. As you'll see, Visual Basic provides two sets of input and output commands for use with a text file, depending on the purpose of the file.

OPENING A TEXT FILE FOR WRITING

You use Visual Basic's Open statement to open a text file for any of three purposes:

- To create a new file
- To append information to an existing file
- To read data from a file

For text files, the Open statement typically appears in the following format:

```
Open fileName For mode As #fileNum
```

This statement supplies three essential items of information. The name of the file on disk is *fileName*. The name is always expressed as a string value in the Open statement — a literal string enclosed in quotation marks, a string variable, or a string expression. The string may include the file's directory path. The file *mode* identifies the kind of operation you intend to perform on the file. For text files, the most common modes are identified by the Visual Basic keywords Output, Append, and Input. The file number, *fileNum*, is an integer that identifies the open file in subsequent input or output statements.

For output to a text file, the Open command can create a new file or open an existing file. This important distinction is represented by the keywords Output and Append:

- The Output mode creates a new file and prepares to write data to the file. If a file by the same name already exists on disk, the Open statement overwrites that file in the Output mode. In other words, the previous file will be deleted and its data lost.

■ The Append mode opens an existing file and prepares to add new
data to the end of the file. Any data already in the file is safely
retained. If the named file does not exist yet, the Append mode is
the same as the Output mode; Open creates the file and prepares to
write the first data to the file.

Your choice between these operations depends on the design of the
program you're creating. For example, the Phone Directory program
opens the Phone.TXT file — represented by the named constant *Phone-
TextFile* — in the Output mode, as you can see in the cmdFile_Click
procedure (Listing 8-8):

```
Open PhoneTextfile For Output As #1
```

This means that the program creates a new alphabetized phone directory
in text format each time the user clicks the File button. Any previous
version of the Phone.TXT file is overwritten. The new file is based on
the entire data set currently stored in the phone database.

By contrast, the Travel Expense Log program presented in Chapter 5
creates a different kind of text file for saving the chronological expense
records that the user enters into the program's dialog box. To ensure
that each new record is added to the end of the file, without destroying
any existing records, the program opens the file in the Append mode
(see Listing 5-2):

```
Open logFileName For Append As #1
```

Once a file is open in the Output or the Append mode, your program
can use either the Write # statement or the Print # statement to begin
sending data to the open file. Write # is ideal for storing raw data in a format that a Visual Basic program can easily read back. By contrast, the
Print # statement gives you the ability to save data in formats that people
can read easily. As you'll see in the upcoming sections of this chapter,
these commands use the # notation to identify by number the file to
which they are sending data.

USING THE WRITE # STATEMENT

Write # sends a line of data items to an open file. This statement automatically supplies important punctuation to separate data items inside the file:

- A string is enclosed in double quotation marks in the file.
- Data items in a given line are separated by commas.
- Each line of data ends with a carriage-return/line-feed sequence (ASCII characters 13 and 10, respectively).

As you'll learn shortly, Visual Basic's Input # statement uses this punctuation to distinguish between one data item and the next as it reads information from a text file.

In the Travel Expense Log program, the cmdSave_Click procedure (Listing 5-2) contains a good example of the Write # statement. After opening the expense log file, the program uses the following statement to write the user's current input to the file:

```
Write #1, txtDate.Text, _
          cboCountry.Text, _
          cboCity.Text, _
          Val(txtAmount.Text), _
          txtDescript.Text, _
          Val(txtRate.Text)
```

The output file is identified in the Write # statement by the notation #1. This is the file number assigned to the open file in the previous Open statement. Each successive Write # statement sends a new line of comma-delimited data to the file. For example, here is how a sequence of records might appear in the file:

```
"09/07/95","France","Strasbourg",665,"Miscellaneous supplies",5.45
"09/07/95","Switzerland","Basel",485,"Dinner with buyers",1.3
"09/08/95","Switzerland","Geneva",185,"l'Hotel du lac, one night",1.3
"09/08/95","Switzerland","Geneva",295,"Lunch with agents",1.3
"09/09/95","Italy","Florence",240000,"English Hotel, one night",1614
"09/10/95","Italy","Florence",210000,"Dinner with buyers",1614
"09/11/95","France","Paris",1850,"Car rental",5.5
```

Each line consists of four string items and two numeric items.

USING THE PRINT # STATEMENT

Print # sends output to an open text file, identified by the # notation. This statement gives you greater control over the format and appearance of the output. Normally you'll use Print # when you're writing a procedure that creates a report.

Each Print # statement sends one or more undelimited text items to the designated file. In the Phone Directory program, the cmdFile_Click procedure (Listing 8-8) contains a long sequence of examples:

```
For i = 1 To numPhones
  Get #1, Index(i).RecNum, Phones
  With Phones
    Print #2, UCase(Trim(.LastName)); ", ";
    Print #2, .FirstName
    Print #2, "Home:   "; .HomePhone
    Print #2, "Work:   "; .WorkPhone
    Print #2, "Fax:    "; .FaxNumber
    Print #2, "email: "; Trim(.EmailAddress);
    Print #2, " (";
    Print #2, optService(.ServiceType).Caption;
    Print #2, ")"
    Print #2,
  End With
Next i
```

As this passage illustrates, Visual Basic allows a program to open multiple files at the same time, each identified with a different *fileNum* value. In this case, the phone database is open as file #1; the procedure reads records from the file one by one from beginning to end. The Phone.TXT file is open as file #2. The sequence of Print #2 statements write phone directory records to the text file, in the following format:

```
KAWASAKI, Melissa
Home:   (702) 555-1872
Work:   (702) 555-1891
Fax:    (702) 555-1287
email: 98765,432 (CompuServe)
```

Notice some of the syntactical elements of the Print # statement. Multiple data items are separated by semicolons (;) in the statement. Normally each Print # statement results in a new line of text in the file, but a semicolon at the end of the statement suppresses the usual carriage-return/line-feed sequence so that additional output can be sent to the same line. For additional examples of output operations using the Print # statement, take another look at the Travel Expense Log program in Chapter 5, specifically the *cmdExpRept* procedure (Listing 5-4).

OPENING A TEXT FILE FOR READING

To read a text file, you open it in the Input mode:

```
Open fileName For Input As #fileNum
```

For example, in the Travel Expense Log program, the cmdRate_Click procedure (Listing 5-3) opens the expense file for input in order to read its records one by one:

```
Open logFileName For Input As #1
```

Using the Input mode presupposes that the file exists on disk. If the file is missing, the Open statement causes a runtime error known as the "File not found" error. In the next section you learn how to avoid an interruption in your program when a text file doesn't exist.

TRAPPING THE "FILE NOT FOUND" RUNTIME ERROR

If Visual Basic cannot find the disk file named in an Open *fileName* For Input statement, the program run is interrupted by default, and the following error message appears in a message box on the screen:

```
File not found
```

This error may occur when a program asks the user to supply a file name interactively from the keyboard. If the user misspells the file name, or otherwise supplies a name that doesn't exist on disk, the "File not found" error takes place and the program run is interrupted.

You can prevent the interruption by creating a special structure known as an *error trap*. An error trap puts Visual Basic on alert for a potential runtime error. If an error occurs that would normally interrupt the program, the error trap instead directs control of the program to a special block of code — an *error routine* — designed to handle the error more gracefully.

You create an error trap by placing an On Error Goto statement above the code where you're anticipating a possible runtime error. On Error Goto refers by name to an error routine located in the same procedure. The routine is identified by a *label*, a name that marks a particular location in the listing. A label ends in a colon, which distinguishes it from other kinds of names that you write in a Visual Basic program.

A good example of the On Error Goto statement — and a corresponding error routine — appears in the Travel Expense Log program in a function named *FileExists* (Listing 5-11). This function is designed specifically to find out whether a given expense file can be found on disk — before the program attempts to read data from the designated file. The function receives a string argument that identifies the target file by name, and returns a Boolean value — True if the file exists or False if it does not. Here is the complete code of the function:

```
Private Function FileExists(fileName As String) _
   As Boolean

   On Error GoTo noFile

      Open fileName For Input As #1
      Close #1

      FileExists = True
      Exit Function

noFile:

   FileExists = False

End Function   ' FileExists
```

The Open statement at the top of the function tries to open the file for reading. If the operation is not successful — that is, if Visual Basic can't find the designated file — the On Error Goto statement redirects control of the program to the routine labeled *noFile*, and the function returns a value of False. On the other hand, if the program finds the file, the error trap is not triggered, and the function returns a value of True. Elsewhere in the program, you'll find several procedures that make calls to the *FileExists* function before attempting to open the expense log file:

```
If FileExists(logFileName) Then
```

Once a program has successfully opened a file for Input, the Input # statement can be used to read individual data items from the file. You learn about this statement next.

USING THE INPUT # STATEMENT

Input # identifies the number of the open file from which it will read data, and provides a list of variables that will receive the input data:

```
Input #fileNum, varName1, varName2, varName3, ...
```

For example, here is an Input # statement from the Travel Expense Log program that reads a line of data from the expense log file:

```
Input #1, expDate, country, city, amount, _
             descript, exchRate
```

As you can see, the statement reads six data items from the file — the date, country, city, amount of the expense, description, and exchange rate. The program can then use these variables to work with this data in any appropriate way.

When the Input # statement reads data from a text file, it recognizes a comma as a delimiter between one data item and the next. In addition, it reads a value enclosed in quotation marks as a string — even if the string contains commas or other punctuation characters that would normally serve as delimiters between data items. The Write # statement is therefore the perfect counterpart to Input #. Write # organizes data in a file in just the way that Input # expects to find it.

USING THE LINE INPUT # STATEMENT

Another way to get information from a text file is to read entire lines at a time, with the Line Input # statement. Line Input # recognizes only the end-of-line markers (ASCII 13 and 10) as delimiters in the text. The statement therefore reads a line of text and stores it in a string variable:

```
Line Input #fileNum, stringVarName
```

Line Input # is perfect for reading text files that contain unpredictable combinations of text and numbers, in tables or in other formats. In this sense, Line Input # is often a good way to read a file that has been created with the Print # statement. You'll find an example in the International Sales program, presented in Chapter 9.

CLOSING A FILE

When your program is finished with a file, you can use the Close statement to close the file:

```
Close #fileNum
```

For example, here is how the Phone Directory program closes the two files that it works with:

```
Close #1
```

and

```
Close #2
```

These Statements also release the file numbers so they can be used for opening a different file.

Alternatively, you can use the Close statement without a file number:

```
Close
```

This statement closes all open files. Likewise, the End statement that terminates a program performance closes any files that remain open.

III

8

You'll find more examples of database management applications and data file programming techniques as you continue through this book. Note that Visual Basic 4.0 also contains important data access features for connecting a project to a database created by an external application such as Microsoft Access or dBASE. You can read about this topic in Part III.

Listing 8-1
The Phone.BAS module

```
' The Phone Directory program.
' ----------------------------

' Module: Phone.Bas
' -----------------

' This module contains the type definitions
' for the phone records and the index array.

' The structure for phone records.
Type PhoneType
   FirstName As String * 20
   LastName As String * 20
   WorkPhone As String * 25
   HomePhone As String * 25
   FaxNumber As String * 25
   EmailAddress As String * 25
   ServiceType As Byte
End Type

Public Phones As PhoneType
```

The Phones
record variable

```
' The structure for the index array.
Type IndexType
   FullName As String * 41
   RecNum As Integer
End Type

' Declare the Index array. (Note that this
' is a dynamic array that is redimensioned
' each time a new record is added to the
```

```
' database.
Public Index() As IndexType
```

The Index *array of* IndexType *records*

```
' The variable numPhones indicates the current
' number of records in the database, and the
' variable whichRecord identifies the record
' that the user has selected for viewing. Both
' variables are available globally.
Public numPhones As Integer
Public whichRecord As Integer


' End of Phone.Bas module.
```

Listing 8-2
General declarations for Phone.FRM, and the Form_Load procedure

```
' The Phone Directory program.
' ----------------------------

' Files:
' Project File:  Phone.VBP
' Form Files:    Phone.FRM (startup)
'                PhonBrow.FRM
' Module File:   Phone.BAS

' This program maintains a phone directory as
' a database file on disk, and allows the user
' to retrieve any record by entering or selecting
' the name of a person who is in the directory.
' Each record may contain phone and fax numbers
' and an e-mail address. In addition to saving
' and retrieving records, the user can browse
' through all the names in the database and create
' a printable directory as a text file on disk.

Option Explicit

' PhoneDB represents the name of the database
' file, and PhoneTextFile represents the name
```

III

8

```
' of the printable text file.
Const PhoneDB = "\PhoneVB4.DB"
Const PhoneTextFile = "\Phones.Txt"

' End of General Declarations, Phone.FRM


Private Sub Form_Load()

  ' The Form_Load procedure opens the database
  ' file and creates the initial version of the
  ' index for the file. (Note that the Index
  ' array allows the program to access the phone
  ' records in alphabetical order by last names,
  ' and to search efficiently for a particular
  ' record in the file.)

  ' Open the database file.
  Open PhoneDB For Random As #1 _
    Len = Len(Phones)

  ' Compute the number of records.
  numPhones = LOF(1) / Len(Phones)

  ' If the file exists and contains one or
  ' more records, create the Index array.
  If numPhones > 0 Then
    ReDim Index(numPhones)
    CreateIndex

  ' Otherwise, disable the Browse and File
  ' buttons. (They have no use until the
  ' database contains at least one record.)
  Else
    cmdBrowse.Enabled = False
    cmdFile.Enabled = False
  End If

End Sub  ' Form_Load
```

Using LOF and Len to calculate the number of records in the file

Redimensioning the Index array

Listing 8-3
The cmdSave_Click procedure

```
Private Sub cmdSave_Click()
  ' The cmdSave_Click procedure stores the current
  ' record entry in the phone database and updates
  ' the index to the database.

  Dim blankFirst As Boolean, blankLast As Boolean
  Dim isFound As Integer
  Dim i, answer As Integer
  Dim lf As String

  lf = Chr(13) & Chr(10)

  ' Check to see if either of the name
  ' fields is blank.
  blankFirst = (Trim(txtFirstName.Text) = "")
  blankLast = (Trim(txtLastName.Text) = "")

  ' If so, prompt the user to enter both
  ' a first and a last name. (These fields
  ' are required for correct indexing of
  ' the database.
  If blankFirst Or blankLast Then
    MsgBox "Enter first and last names.", _
        , "Add a Record"

  ' Otherwise, if the record entry is valid,
  ' begin by searching the database to find
  ' out whether this name is already recorded.
  Else
    isFound = Search(MakeName(txtFirstName.Text, _
                              txtLastName.Text))

    ' Copy the user's record entry to the
    ' fields of the Phones record.
    With Phones
      .FirstName = txtFirstName.Text
      .LastName = txtLastName.Text
      .HomePhone = txtHomePhone.Text
```

Using With to abbreviate field references

III

8

```
                  .WorkPhone = txtWorkPhone.Text
                  .FaxNumber = txtFaxNumber.Text
                  .EmailAddress = txtEMailAddress.Text

                  For i = 0 To 5
                    If optService(i).Value Then _
                      .ServiceType = i
                  Next i
                End With


              ' If the name doesn't already exist
              ' in the database file, add the record
              ' to the file.
              If isFound = 0 Then
                numPhones = numPhones + 1

                ' Enable the Browse and File buttons.
                If numPhones > 0 Then
                  cmdBrowse.Enabled = True
                  cmdFile.Enabled = True
                End If

                ' Write the record to the file
                ' and update the index array.
                Put #1, numPhones, Phones
                ReDim Index(numPhones)
                CreateIndex


              ' If the name already exists in the
              ' database, give the user the opportunity
              ' to write a revised version of the record
              ' (overwriting the record's previous contents).
              Else

                answer = MsgBox("This name is already on file." _
                  & lf & "Do you want to save " & lf & _
                  "a revised record?", 4, "Revise a Record")

                ' If the user answers affirmatively,
                ' write the revised record to its
```

Using Put # to write a record to the database

```
          ' original position in the database.
        If answer = 6 Then _
           Put #1, isFound, Phones
     End If
  End If

End Sub   ' cmdSave_Click
```

Listing 8-4
The Search and MakeName procedures

```
Function Search(findText As String) As Integer

   ' The Search function performs a binary
   ' search to look for a name in the
   ' Index array.

   Dim pos1 As Integer, pos2 As Integer
   Dim posX As Integer, midPos As Integer
   Dim midStr As String

   ' Initialize position markers.
   pos1 = 1
   pos2 = numPhones
   posX = 0

   ' Search for the target string.
   Do While pos1 <= pos2 And posX = 0
     midPos = (pos1 + pos2) \ 2
     midStr = RTrim(Index(midPos).FullName)
     If findText = midStr Then
       posX = midPos
     ElseIf findText > midStr Then
       pos1 = midPos + 1
     Else
       pos2 = midPos - 1
     End If
   Loop
```

A binary search

```
        ' Return the Index subscript where the
        ' name is located, or zero if the name
        ' was not found.
        Search = posX

End Function   ' Search


Function MakeName(f As String, l As String) _
    As String

        ' The MakeName function standardizes the
        ' full name of each phone record, so that
        ' different name entries can be compared
        ' successfully.

        ' Concatinate the first and last name fields
        ' into a standard uppercase and trimmed format.
        MakeName = UCase(Trim(l) + " " + Trim(f))

End Function   ' MakeName
```

Listing 8-5
The CreateIndex procedure

```
Sub CreateIndex()

        ' The CreateIndex procedure develops the
        ' Index array at the beginning of the program
        ' run, and again after each new record is added
        ' to the database.

        Dim indexEntry As IndexType
        Dim i, j
        Dim temp As String

        ' Read each record, from the beginning
        ' to the end of the database.
        For i = 1 To numPhones
            Get #1, i, Phones
```

```
      ' Standardize the name entry in
      ' each record.
      temp = MakeName _
        (Phones.FirstName, Phones.LastName)

      ' Store the full name and the
      ' record number as the two fields
      ' of the index array.
      Index(i).FullName = temp
      Index(i).RecNum = i
    Next i

    ' Sort the index array by the FullName field.
    For i = 1 To numPhones - 1
      For j = i + 1 To numPhones
        If Index(i).FullName > Index(j).FullName Then
          indexEntry = Index(i)
          Index(i) = Index(j)
          Index(j) = indexEntry
        End If
      Next j
    Next i
```

Sorting the Index *array*

```
End Sub   ' CreateIndex
```

Listing 8-6
The cmdSearch_Click and ShowRecord procedures

```
Private Sub cmdSearch_Click()

    ' The cmdSearch_Click procedure searches for
    ' a name in the phone directory, and retrieves
    ' the record if the search is successful.

    Dim searchName As String
    Dim rec As Integer, inFileRec As Integer

    ' Standardize the format of the target name.
    searchName = MakeName(txtFirstName.Text, _
                          txtLastName.Text)
```

```
          ' Search for the name.
          rec = Search(searchName)

          ' If the name is found, display the record.
          If rec > 0 Then
            inFileRec = Index(rec).RecNum
            ShowRecord inFileRec

          ' Otherwise, tell the user that the
          ' search was not successful.
          Else

            MsgBox "Can't find " & searchName & ".", , _
              "Search for a Record"

          End If

      End Sub  ' cmdSearch_Click



      Private Sub ShowRecord(readRecord As Integer)

        ' The ShowRecord procedure retrieves a record
        ' from the database and displays its fields in
        ' the frmPhone form. (Note that this procedure
        ' is called from cmdSearch_Click and from
        ' Form_Activate.)

        ' The variable readRecord represents an actual
        ' record number, not an element of the Index
        ' array.

        ' Read the target record from the database.
        Get #1, readRecord, Phones

        ' Copy the fields of the record to
        ' the controls on the frmPhone form.
        With Phones
          txtFirstName.Text = .FirstName
```

A call to the Search *function to find a name in the database*

```
        txtLastName.Text = .LastName
        txtHomePhone.Text = .HomePhone
        txtWorkPhone.Text = .WorkPhone
        txtFaxNumber.Text = .FaxNumber
        txtEMailAddress.Text = .EmailAddress
        optService(.ServiceType) = True
    End With

End Sub    ' ShowRecord
```

Listing 8-7
The cmdBrowse_Click and Form_Activate procedures

```
Private Sub cmdBrowse_Click()

    ' The cmdBrowse_Click procedure activates
    ' the frmBrowse form.

    ' The global variable whichRecord indicates
    ' which name should be displayed first in
    ' the form. If no record is current, the
    ' program simply displays the first name
    ' in alphabetical order.
    If whichRecord = 0 Then _
        whichRecord = 1

    ' Activate frmBrowse as a modal form. (In other
    ' words, the form retains control until the
    ' user takes a specific action to switch back to
    ' the other form.)
    frmBrowse.Show 1

End Sub    ' cmdBrowse_Click
```

Displaying a modal form

```
Private Sub Form_Activate()

    ' When control returns to the frmPhone form
```

```
' from the frmBrowse form, display the record
' that the user has requested. (Note: If
' whichRecord is zero, the user has clicked
' the Cancel button rather than the View button
' on the frmBrowse form.)

If whichRecord > 0 Then _
    ShowRecord Index(whichRecord).RecNum

End Sub   ' Form_Activate
```

Listing 8-8
The cmdFile_Click procedure

```
Private Sub cmdFile_Click()

    ' The cmdFile_Click procedure creates a
    ' printable text file, containing all the
    ' phone records in the directory arranged
    ' in alphabetical order by last names.

    Dim i

    ' If the file already exists, it is
    ' overwritten by this new version.
    Open PhoneTextFile For Output As #2

    ' Retrieve each record in turn, in
    ' alphabetical order.
    For i = 1 To numPhones

        ' The Index array is the tool for
        ' accessing records in order.
        Get #1, Index(i).RecNum, Phones

        ' Write all the fields of the current
        ' record to the text file.
        With Phones
```

```
        Print #2, UCase(Trim(.LastName)); ", ";
        Print #2, .FirstName
        Print #2, "Home:   "; .HomePhone
        Print #2, "Work:   "; .WorkPhone
        Print #2, "Fax:    "; .FaxNumber
        Print #2, "email: "; Trim(.EmailAddress);
        Print #2, " (";
        Print #2, optService(.ServiceType).Caption;
        Print #2, ")"
        Print #2,
    End With
  Next i


  Close #2


  ' Inform the user that the file
  ' has been created on disk.
  MsgBox UCase(PhoneTextFile) _
    & " has been created.", , _
    "Save a Text File"


End Sub   ' cmdFile_Click
```

Listing 8-9
The cmdClear_Click and cmdExit_Click procedures

```
Private Sub cmdClear_Click()

  ' The cmdClear_Click procedure clears all
  ' the controls on the main dialog box so
  ' that the user can begin entering a new
  ' record.

  Dim i

  ' Blank out all the text boxes.
  txtFirstName.Text = ""
  txtLastName.Text = ""
  txtHomePhone.Text = ""
  txtWorkPhone.Text = ""
```

```
    txtFaxNumber.Text = ""
    txtEMailAddress.Text = ""

    ' Deselect all the option buttons.
    For i = 0 To 5
      optService(i).Value = False
    Next i

    ' Move the focus to the first name text box.
    txtFirstName.SetFocus

End Sub   ' cmdClear_Click




Private Sub cmdExit_Click()

' The cmdExit_Click procedure ends the
' program performance when the user clicks
' the Exit button.

   Close #1
   End

End Sub   ' cmdExit_Click
```

Listing 8-10

General declarations for PhonBrow.FRM and the Form_Activate and ShowName procedures

```
' The Phone Directory program.
' ---------------------------

' Form: frmBrowse (PhonBrow.Frm)
' This form allows the user to browse through
' the names recorded in the phone directory, and
' to view the complete record for any selected
' name.
```

```
Option Explicit

' End of General Declarations, PhonBrow.FRM


Private Sub Form_Activate()

  ' The Form_Activate procedure shows the current
  ' name in the lblFullName label when the form
  ' is first activated.

  ShowName

  ' Enable or disable the Next and Previous
  ' buttons as appropriate.
  If whichRecord > 1 Then
    cmdPrevious.Enabled = True
  Else
    cmdPrevious.Enabled = False
  End If

  If whichRecord < numPhones Then
    cmdNext.Enabled = True
  Else
    cmdNext.Enabled = False
  End If

End Sub   ' Form_Activate


Private Sub ShowName()

  ' The ShowName procedure displays a new name
  ' as the Caption property of the lblFullName
  ' label.

  ' Read the record.
  Get #1, Index(whichRecord).RecNum, Phones
```

Using the Index *array to read records in alphabetical order*

```
' Display the full name in the format
' LASTNAME, Firstname.
With Phones
   lblFullName.Caption = Trim(UCase(.LastName)) _
                         & ", " & _
                         Trim(.FirstName)
End With

End Sub   ' ShowName
```

Listing 8-11
The cmdNext_Click and cmdPrevious_Click procedures

```
Private Sub cmdNext_Click()

   ' The cmdNext_Click procedure displays the
   ' next name in the phone directory index, in
   ' alphabetical order.

   ' The variable whichRecord is used (in ShowName)
   ' to access a particular entry of the Index
   ' array.
   whichRecord = whichRecord + 1
   ShowName
```

Displaying the next record in the alphabetized database

```
   ' Enable and/or disable the Next and Previous
   ' buttons, as appropriate.
   If whichRecord > 1 Then _
      cmdPrevious.Enabled = True

   If whichRecord = numPhones Then _
      cmdNext.Enabled = False

End Sub   ' cmdNext_Click




Private Sub cmdPrevious_Click()
```

```
' The cmdPrevious_Click procedure displays the
' previous name in the phone directory index, in
' reverse alphabetical order.

' The variable whichRecord is used (in ShowName)
' to access a particular entry of the Index
' array.

whichRecord = whichRecord - 1
ShowName

' Enable and/or disable the Next and Previous
' buttons, as appropriate.
If whichRecord < numPhones Then _
   cmdNext.Enabled = True

If whichRecord = 1 Then _
   cmdPrevious.Enabled = False

End Sub  ' cmdPrevious_Click
```

Listing 8-12
The Form_KeyDown procedure

```
Private Sub Form_KeyDown _
   (KeyCode As Integer, Shift As Integer)
```

Trapping a keypress from the Browse dialog box

```
' The Form_KeyDown procedure allows the user to
' scroll through a sequence of records by pressing
' the PgUp or PgDn keys on the keyboard.

' *** Note that the form's KeyPreview property
'        is set to True to make this event possible.

' Code numbers for the
' PgDn and PgUp keys.
Const PgDn = 34
Const PgUp = 33
```

```
' If the user presses PgDn and the Next
' button is currently enabled, force a call
' to the cmdNext_Click event procedure.
If KeyCode = PgDn _
  And cmdNext.Enabled = True _
    Then cmdNext_Click

' If the user presses PgUp and the Previous
' button is currently enabled, force a call
' to the cmdPrevious_Click event procedure.
If KeyCode = PgUp _
  And cmdPrevious.Enabled = True _
    Then cmdPrevious_Click

End Sub   ' Form_KeyDown
```

Listing 8-13

The cmdView_Click and cmdCancel_Click procedures

```
Private Sub cmdView_Click()

  ' The cmdView_Click procedure returns control
  ' to the frmPhone form. (Note that the global
  ' variable whichRecord indicates the index
  ' number that will be displayed in the frmPhone
  ' form. See the Form_Activate procedure in
  ' frmPhone for details.)

  frmBrowse.Hide
```

Removing the Browse dialog box from the screen

```
End Sub   ' cmdView_Click



Private Sub cmdCancel_Click()
```

```
' The cmdCancel_Click procedure switches
' control back to the frmPhone form, without
' requesting a record display.

' A whichRecord value of zero signals to frmPhone
' that the user has clicked Cancel rather than
' the View button.
whichRecord = 0

frmBrowse.Hide

End Sub   ' cmdCancel_Click
```

Input and Output Procedures

*I*nput and output are the defining activities of almost any Visual Basic application. In a well-designed program, input techniques are simple, convenient, reliable, and even self-correcting; and the resulting output is clear, intuitive, useful, and immediate. To achieve these programming goals, you may spend more time on input and output procedures than on any other part of your code.

Input is information that a program receives from an outside source. For example, input operations take place when the user enters values from the keyboard or selects options with the mouse. As a programmer, you always need to think carefully about the problems of getting input from the user:

- What types of information should the user supply, and how will your program prompt the user to enter the data?

- What are the easiest and most reliable ways to accept information and instructions from the keyboard and the mouse?

- How will the program react when the user makes a mistake during data entry? What techniques will your program provide for correcting mistakes?

- Once the user has entered a particular input item, will your program reformat the data in convenient ways so that the user can verify the input?

- How will the user select among the options available in a given application?

These design issues take time to resolve. You may find yourself spending many hours with your code — writing, revising, and fine-tuning — before you're happy with the details of the data-entry process.

Output is the information a program provides to the user. It can be sent to devices such as the display screen, the printer, a disk, or a modem. A program can supply information in various forms, including text, tables of numbers, charts, graphs, or files.

For the user, the output *is* the program. The essence of a program is the information it provides. An important goal in programming is to separate the process from the outcome. A user has no interest in the detailed steps of producing information; only the result matters.

In the graphical interface of a Visual Basic application, input and output sometimes seem to merge into one simultaneous operation. The user's mouse and keyboard activities may produce multiple and instantaneous results on the screen, giving the impression that a keystroke or a mouse click is the *instrument* for creating impressive results from the application.

To help you explore a variety of input and output techniques in Visual Basic, this chapter presents a programming project named the International Sales program. In this application, the user enters a set of sales figures into a small table on the screen. The table is organized into rows of sales regions and columns representing sales periods. As each individual data entry is completed, the program instantly supplies output information in a variety of forms:

- It calculates and displays the regional totals in a column at the right side of the sales table, and the period totals in a row at the bottom.

- It updates the grand total of all the data.

- It draws a chart to represent the sales data pictorially. This display can take the form of a column chart or a pie chart, depending on the user's current selections in a menu of chart options.

The numbers in the sales table are the user's input, and the totals and charts are the program's output. But input and output operations take place simultaneously, providing an instant tool for analyzing sales data.

The International Sales program also illustrates other input and output techniques. For example, the application window contains menus of commands and options that the user can choose with simple mouse or keyboard techniques. The menus include commands to send the sales table to a variety of output destinations; choices between different chart presentations; and options that help the user clarify the meaning of the data table itself. You'll explore these menus as you begin working with the program.

The International Sales Program

The project file is stored on disk as IntSales.VBP. Start Visual Basic now, open the application, and press F5 to begin a first run. The application window initially appears on your screen as shown in Figure 9-1. As you can see, it contains an arrangement of text boxes in which you can enter annual sales totals for five regions. These entries become the sales table.

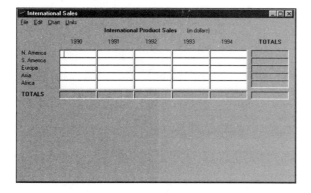

Figure 9-1
The International Sales application window.

Although the program starts out by providing region labels at the left side of the sales table and year labels at the top of the table, you can change these headings to any text that identifies your sales data. You can also give the table a more specific title. For example, in Figure 9-2, the region labels have been changed to the names of countries and the period labels appear as months. A new title identifies a specific product category. To make changes like these, use your mouse to select the text you want to modify, and then enter the new label from the keyboard.

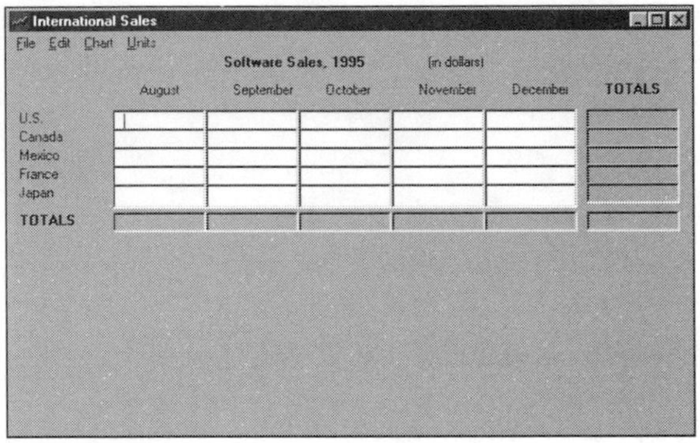

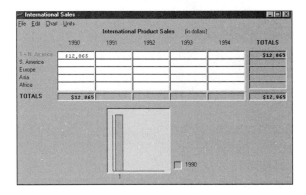

Figure 9-2

Changing the title and the row and column headings.

You can begin entering data anywhere in the sales table. Simply select a text box and begin typing the digits of the entry. To complete the entry you can press an arrow key, the Tab key, or the Enter key to move the focus to another text box in the table. When you do so, you'll see several changes take place at once, as in Figure 9-3.

Figure 9-3

Entering a first sales figure into the table.

First, the program changes your sales entry into a dollar-and-cent format. For example, an entry of 12865 becomes $12,865. If you inadvertently include nonnumeric characters in your entry, the program ignores them. An entry of 12865abc becomes $12,865. (An entry that *begins* with a nonnumeric character, such as a123, is ignored altogether; the text box remains blank. Likewise, the program ignores negative numbers.)

You'll also see three totals appear in the application window. At the right of the sales table, the program displays the total sales for the current row. Below the table, the program shows the total sales for the current column. And at the lower-right corner of the table you'll see the grand total of all the sales figures you've entered up to this point. These totals are for display only, you can't edit them or select the boxes in which they appear.

Finally, in the lower half of the application window, the program begins creating a chart to represent the numeric data you've entered into the table. Initially, the program displays a column chart. When the table contains only one entry (as in Figure 9-3), it is represented as a single column in the chart. But as you continue entering values in a given row of the sales table, the chart displays multicolored stacked columns. Each colored portion of a column represents the periodic sales figure for a given sales region. For example, in Figure 9-4, the column contains proportionally sized stacks representing the annual North American sales figures for 1990, 1991, and 1992.

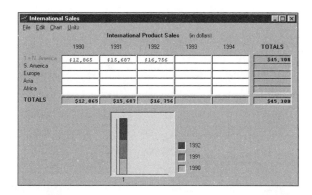

Figure 9-4
Building the stacks of the column chart.

Notice that the program displays a legend at the right side of the chart to identify the stack colors. Just below a given column in the chart, a number identifies the entire column; the same number appears next to one of the labels displayed to the left of the sales table. For example, in Figure 9-5, the first column (identified as *1*) represents North American sales and the second column (*2*) represents South American sales. At the left of the sales table, the program displays the row labels as follows:

```
1 = N. America
2 = S. America
```

In this simple way, the program identifies each column and each stack that appears in the chart.

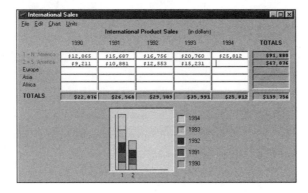

Figure 9-5
Continuing the data entry.

Finish entering a set of sample data values into the sales table now, using the data shown in Figure 9-6. A complete column chart appears in the lower half of the application window. Now pull down the program's Chart menu by clicking Chart with the mouse or by pressing Alt+C at the keyboard. The Chart menu (Figure 9-7) contains four chart options. As you can see, the initial selections are By Years and Column Chart. This means that the program starts out by creating a chart in which each column contains stacks representing annual (or other periodic) sales; an entire column thus represents the total sales for a given region.

International Sales — File Edit Chart Units

International Product Sales (in dollars)					
	1990	1991	1992	1993	1994	TOTALS
1 = N. America	$12,865	$15,687	$16,756	$20,760	$25,812	$91,880
2 = S. America	$9,211	$10,881	$12,553	$15,231	$20,441	$68,317
3 = Europe	$9,335	$13,118	$16,893	$19,814	$23,581	$82,741
4 = Asia	$10,673	$14,789	$15,863	$18,534	$24,131	$83,990
5 = Africa	$7,593	$9,772	$13,121	$15,032	$18,619	$64,137
TOTALS	$49,677	$64,247	$75,186	$89,371	$112,584	$391,065

Legend: 1994, 1993, 1992, 1991, 1990

Figure 9-6

A complete sales table and chart.

Figure 9-7

The Chart menu.

To experiment with the chart, select the By Region entry. In response, the program instantly redraws the chart, producing columns in which the stacks represent individual regions and each column represents the total sales for a given year, as in Figure 9-8. Notice also that the labels displayed in the legend are adjusted accordingly.

The Chart menu also offers another chart type known as the pie chart. Pull down the Chart menu and choose the Pie Chart option to switch to this display type. When you do so, the program redraws the chart as shown in Figure 9-9. In this chart, each wedge represents the total sales for one of the regions and the entire pie represents the total sales for all the regions. To reorient the pie chart, pull down the Chart menu yet again and choose the By Years option. In the resulting chart (Figure 9-10), each wedge represents the total sales for a given year, as indicated by the new labels in the legend. Again, all the wedges together represent total sales for all the years in the sales table.

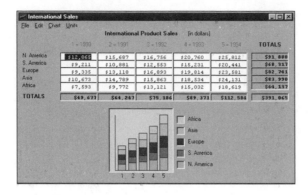

Figure 9-8

Changing the orientation of the chart.

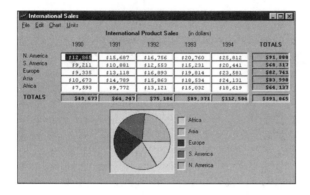

Figure 9-9

The Pie Chart option.

The International sales program offers several techniques for printing the sales table or transferring it to other software environments. If you simply want a printed copy of the entire window, including the numeric sales table and the current sales chart, pull down the File menu and choose the Print Window command or press Ctrl+P from the keyboard (Figure 9-11). In response, the program sends an image of the window to your printer. You can also create a text file of the sales data alone by choosing the Save Report command from the File menu or pressing Ctrl+S.

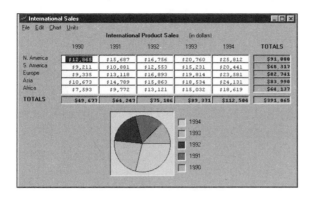

Figure 9-10
Reorienting the pie chart.

Figure 9-11
The Print Window command in the File menu.

Alternatively, to place a copy of the sales table on the Clipboard, pull down the Edit menu and choose Copy or press Ctrl+C (Figure 9-12). You can then paste the sales table into your word processing program or to some other software environment if you want to incorporate the sales data into a larger document. Here's how the table might appear:

International Product Sales
(in dollars)

	1990	1991	1992	1993	1994	Totals
1 = N. America	$12,866	$15,687	$16,756	$20,760	$25,812	$91,881
2 = S. America	$9,211	$10,881	$12,553	$15,231	$20,441	$68,317
3 = Europe	$9,335	$13,118	$16,893	$19,814	$23,581	$82,741
4 = Asia	$10,673	$14,789	$15,863	$18,534	$24,131	$83,990
5 = Africa	$7,593	$9,772	$13,121	$15,032	$18,619	$64,137
Totals	$49,678	$64,247	$75,186	$89,371	$112,584	$391,066

Notice that the Edit menu also contains a Clear command. Choose this command (or press Ctrl+L) when you're ready to clear the current sales table and begin entering a new set of data.

The program offers one additional set of menu commands, under the name Units. The options in this menu enable you to change the units label displayed just to the right of the title at the top of the sales table. When you pull down the Units menu you can choose among three options for this label, as shown in Figure 9-13.

Figure 9-12
The Copy command in the Edit menu.

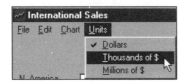

Figure 9-13
The Units menu.

The Units label helps you clarify the meaning of the data you enter into the sales table. Because the individual text boxes in the table are relatively small — and because the sales table doesn't necessarily need to be accurate to the last dollar — the program allows entries up to only six digits long. If you want to represent sales figures of a larger magnitude, you should reduce them by a power of 10, and then choose an appropriate label from the Units menu. For example, rather than entering a sales figure as $9,126,443, you could enter it as $9,126 and change the Units selection to "Thousands of $." In response the program displays the units label as

    (in thousands of $)

Alternatively, enter the value as $9 and change the Units selection to "Millions of $." The units label appears as

```
(in millions of $)
```

Continue experimenting with the International Sales program if you like. When you're ready to quit, pull down the File menu and choose Exit, or press Ctrl+X.

The program's code is contained in a single form, named frmIntSales. You can take a first look at the code in Listings 9-1 through 9-16. Its procedures are designed to manage the input and output techniques that you've seen illustrated in the program run.

Before turning your full attention to the code, you need to explore two important components of the program's interface: the menu bar and the control arrays.

Defining a Menu

As you've seen, the International Sales application has a menu bar containing four main menus, named File, Edit, Chart, and Units. Each of these top-level entries, in turn, represents a list of commands and options. For example, the File menu contains commands for saving and printing sales data and for exiting the program; and the Chart menu contains options for changing the appearance of the sales chart.

Defining a menu system like this one is remarkably easy in Visual Basic. To do so, you use a feature called the Menu Editor. Here are the basic steps for creating a menu:

1. Select and open the form on which you want the menu to appear.

2. Pull down Visual Basic's Tools menu and choose Menu Editor (or simply press Ctrl+E). The Menu Editor dialog box appears on the screen, as shown in Figure 9-14.

3. In the Caption box, type the first main menu entry, just as you want it to appear on the menu bar. Optionally, use the ampersand character (&) to provide keyboard access to the menu. For example, **&File** means that the user will be able to press Alt+F to pull down the File menu. In the menu bar itself, the letter *F* will be underlined.

Figure 9-14
The Menu Editor.

4. In the Name box, enter the name by which this menu entry will be identified in your code. If you normally use standard prefixes to identify different types of controls in a project, consider starting each menu name with the letters *mnu*. For example, the control name for the File menu might be *mnuFile*. (As you'll see shortly, the control name for a menu is used in the same ways as any other control name in a program.)

5. As appropriate, fill in other properties for the current menu entry. In particular, the Shortcut property allows you to select a shortcut key for a particular menu command. For example, you might choose Ctrl+P as the shortcut for a Print command. (You'll learn about other menu properties as you continue in this chapter.)

6. Click the Next button to begin the next menu entry. If you want the new entry to be defined as a command in a pull-down menu list, click the right-arrow button, as illustrated in Figure 9-15. In the large box located in the lower half of the Menu Editor, Visual Basic displays an outline of the menu you're developing. A command within a menu is indented and preceded by four dots.

7. Begin again at step 3, and define the caption, name, and other properties of the new menu entry. Continue this process until you've defined all the main menu entries and their corresponding command lists. After you've developed a list of commands within a menu, click the left-arrow button to define the next caption as a new menu-bar entry.

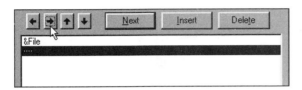

Figure 9-15
Defining top-level menus and their commands.

Figures 9-16 and 9-17 show the complete menu definition for the International Sales project. (You can view the program's menu definition on your screen by opening the IntSales.Frm form in design mode and pressing Ctrl+E to open the Menu Editor.) As you can see, each of the four main menu entries is followed by its own list of indented commands. Notice the use of the ampersand character to define access keys throughout. In addition, the Menu Editor displays the Ctrl key shortcuts that have been defined for particular menu commands (as in Figure 9-16). When you complete a menu definition like this one, you click the OK button to confirm. In response, the current form displays the menu system you've created. You can view the menu both in design mode and in run mode.

Like any other control in a project, menu entries have events and properties that become part of your program's code. For example, the *Click* event for a menu control takes place when the user pulls down a menu and chooses a particular command. Figure 9-18 shows the code window for the frmIntSales form. As you can see, the object list contains the names of all the menu entries defined for the program. To create an event procedure for one of these objects, you simply select its name in the object list, and then select the name of the event procedure you want to develop. As you examine the code of the International Sales program, you'll find event procedures that define the action of all the program's menu commands.

III

9

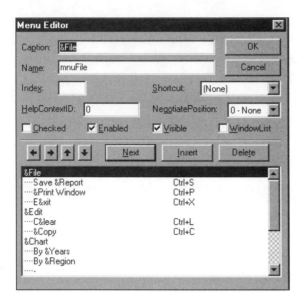

Figure 9-16

The program's menu definition, part 1.

Figure 9-17

The program's menu definition, part 2.

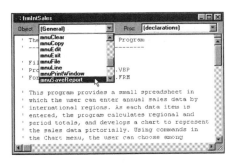

Figure 9-18
The list of menu objects.

You may have noticed that one of the properties available in the Menu Editor is named Index. You can use this property to define an *array* of menu controls. You've seen examples of control arrays in applications presented in previous chapters. Now you'll take a closer look at the techniques for defining and using control arrays in Visual Basic.

Defining Control Arrays

A *control array* is a group of objects that belong to the same type and share a common name. The International Sales application contains several control arrays. For example, the 25 text boxes into which the user enters the sales table form an array named txtAmount.

Like the elements of ordinary data arrays, each object in a control array is identified by a numeric index. As you might guess, the property named Index defines the index of each control in an array. For instance, the txtAmount text boxes have Index values from 0 to 24.

You create a control array in a form simply by assigning the same Name property to two or more controls. When you do so, Visual Basic displays a dialog box asking you to confirm the definition.

For example, suppose you've created a text box and given it the name txtAmount. Then you add a second text box to the same form and once again enter txtAmount as the object's Name property. As soon as you confirm the new Name property, the dialog box shown in Figure 9-19 appears on the desktop, asking you if you want to create a control array. To confirm the definition, you simply click Yes. In response, Visual Basic automatically assigns appropriate Index values to each object in the array; the first text box has an Index property of 0, the second 1, and so on. Each new control you add to the array is assigned the next available Index value.

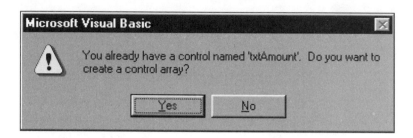

Figure 9-19
Creating a control array.

There are many advantages to creating control arrays for groups of objects that have a common purpose in your project. Because the controls in the array are indexed, you can conveniently use For loops to process all the elements of the array. Here is the general form for identifying the properties of a control array:

```
controlName(Index).propertyName
```

As usual, the control name and property name are separated by a period, but here the control name is followed by an index number enclosed in parentheses.

For example, consider the mnuClear_Click procedure, shown in Listing 9-16. When the user chooses the Clear command from the Edit menu, this procedure is responsible for clearing all the sales data from the *txtAmount* controls. It does so in a simple For loop:

```
For i = 0 to 24
  txtAmount(i).Text = ""
     ' ...
  Next i
```

As the loop increments the value of *i* from 0 to 24, the program assigns an empty string value to the Text property of each control in the *txtAmount* array. When the looping is complete, the entire sales table is blank.

Event procedures for a control array apply to any object in the array. In other words, you can write a single procedure to define an event for the entire array. When the event occurs, Visual Basic supplies the Index value of the control that was the object of the event.

For example, the txtAmount_GotFocus procedure (Listing 9-11) is responsible for highlighting the current contents of a txtAmount text box whenever the user selects a value in the sales table:

```
Private Sub txtAmount_GotFocus(Index As Integer)

  txtAmount(Index).SelStart = 0
  txtAmount(Index).SelLength = _
    Len(txtAmount(Index).Text)

End Sub   ' txtAmount_GotFocus
```

When you create an event procedure for a control array, Visual Basic automatically includes an Index argument as part of the procedure definition. This argument identifies the object of the event. Each time the event is triggered, Visual Basic passes the appropriate Index value to the event procedure. You use Index in your code to specify the control that the code will act upon. In this case, the txtAmount_GotFocus procedure highlights the contents of the control that has just received the focus.

You'll see many more examples of control arrays as you examine the code of the International Sales program. Here is a list of all the control arrays in the frmIntSales form:

- The txtAmount array, with Index values from 0 to 24, provides the text boxes in which the user enters the sales table.

- The txtYear and txtPlace arrays display the column and row headings at the top and left side of the sales table, respectively. Each of these arrays contains five text boxes, indexed from 0 to 4.

- The lblPeriodTotal and lblRegionTotal arrays represent the row of totals at the bottom of the sales table and the column of totals at the right side of the table. Because these are arrays of labels, the user cannot change their contents; the program is responsible for supplying any information that each label displays. The arrays have index values from 0 to 4.

- The lblLegendColor array is a group of labels located just to the right of the chart. (The program draws the chart itself in a picture box control named picSalesChart.) These labels display the colors that identify the stacks of a column chart or the wedges of a pie chart. Just to the right of these labels, the corresponding lblLegendText array displays the regions or sales periods represented by the chart colors. Again, these arrays have indexes from 0 to 4.

- The lblxAxis array displays integers from 1 to 5 along the x-axis, identifying the five columns of a column chart.

- The mnuChartBy and mnuChartType arrays, in the project's menu definition, identify the two sets of charting options. To create a control array in the Menu Editor, you simply assign the same Name property to two or more menu entries and then enter appropriate Index values for each object in the array. In these examples, each array contains two controls, indexed 0 and 1.

- Finally, the mnuUnitType array, also part of the menu definition, identifies the options that the user can select from the Units menu. This array contains three controls, indexed from 0 to 2.

You'll learn how the application uses these various arrays as you now turn to the program's code.

Input Techniques

You've seen how the International Sales program manages the data-entry process in the sales table:

- In any of the txtAmount text boxes, the program accepts positive numeric values up to six digits long. Once the focus moves to another control, the program redisplays the previous input in a dollar–and-cent format, right-aligned within its column.

- Any nonnumeric characters entered in a txtAmount box are ignored. If the nonnumeric characters occur at the end of an entry (such as

1234abc) they are simply truncated from the numeric part of the value. But if an entry *begins* with a nonnumeric character (such as *abc1234*) the entire value is ignored and the program empties the text box when the focus moves to another control.

- The program gives the user a variety of techniques for moving from one text box to another within the sales table. The arrow keys, Enter, or Tab are all available for selecting a text box. Of course, the user can also click any box with the mouse to select it. When the focus moves to a text box that already contains an entry, the program highlights the entry; as a result, any new information typed from the keyboard replaces the current contents of the box.

These details are all handled by the event procedures written for the txtAmount array. Specifically, the txtAmount_LostFocus procedure (Listing 9-3) validates and reformats each new numeric entry when the focus moves to another text box. The txtAmount_KeyDown procedure (Listing 9-11) defines the keyboard techniques for moving from one text box to another. And, as you've already seen, the txtAmount_GotFocus procedure (also Listing 9-11) arranges to highlight the text box that receives the focus. In the upcoming sections you'll learn how each of these procedures works.

VALIDATING AND FORMATTING THE INPUT

For convenience, the program uses several data arrays to keep track of the current contents of the sales table. The Dim statements for all these arrays are located in the general declarations section of the frmIntSales form (Listing 9-1):

```
Dim amounts(24)
Dim amountStr(24) As String
Dim periodTots(4)
Dim periodLabels(4) As String
Dim regionTots(4)
Dim regionLabels(4) As String
```

The *amounts* array records the numeric values that the user has entered into the 25 text boxes of the sales table, and the *amountStr* array records the formatted dollar-and-cent displays. The other four arrays record the sales totals (*periodTots* and *regionTots*) and the row and column of labels (*periodLabels* and *regionLabels*). Throughout the code these arrays help the program manage the content and appearance of the sales table and the corresponding chart.

For example, the txtAmount_LostFocus procedure begins by determining whether the target text box contains a *new* data entry:

```
If amountStr(Index) <> txtAmount(Index).Text Then
```

In other words, if the current entry in the text box is different from the entry recorded in the *amountStr* array, the procedure has a new data item to work with. (Notice the use of the Index argument to identify the specific text box that has lost the focus.)

The procedure assigns the numeric value of this new entry to the appropriate element of the *amounts* array:

```
amounts(Index) = Val(txtAmount(Index).Text)
```

On the surface, this might seem like an unnecessary use of Visual Basic's Val function, which simply converts a string of digits into a numeric value. But Val serves an important purpose here. If the numeric value contains trailing characters that are not numeric, Val ignores them. Furthermore, if the entry *begins* with a nonnumeric character, Val returns a value of 0. This simple tool is therefore a central part of the program's input validation procedure.

The program next checks the numeric range of the input. If the user has entered a negative number or a value that's longer than six digits, the entry is rejected:

```
If amounts(Index) < 0 Or _
    amounts(Index) > 999999 _
    Then amounts(Index) = 0
```

Now if the entry is not 0, the procedure reformats the value for display. There are two parts to this task. First the value is converted to a dollar-and-cent display and then it's right-aligned within the text box. These are accomplished by use of the Format function and the RSet statement, respectively:

```
RSet entryWidth = _
   Format(amounts(Index), AmtFormat)
txtAmount(Index).Text = entryWidth
```

The variable *entryWidth* is assigned a string of eight spaces at the beginning of the procedure; the RSet statement therefore right-aligns the entry within this width. *AmtFormat* is a named constant that contains the formatting string for converting a value to a dollar-and-cent display. The constant is defined in the program's general declarations:

```
Const AmtFormat = "$#,###0"
```

If the entry is 0, the program empties the text box that has lost the focus:

```
Else
   txtAmount(Index).Text = ""
```

Once the formatted value has been displayed in the text box, the string value is recorded in the *amountStr* array:

```
amountStr(Index) = txtAmount(Index).Text
```

In short, the *txtAmount_LostFocus* procedure carries out its input validation and formatting tasks through the use of three built-in tools: the Val function, the RSet statement, and the Format function. You can read more about these tools in Visual Basic's online help.

After confirming and redisplaying each entry, the procedure makes a call to the *CalculateTotals* procedure to update the sales totals, and then a call to the *DrawGraph* procedure to redraw the chart. You'll read about these two procedures later in this chapter.

MOVING THE FOCUS

The *txtAmount_KeyDown* procedure (Listing 9-11) is designed to recognize special keystrokes for moving the focus from one text box to another in the sales table. These keystrokes include the arrow keys (up, down, left, and right) and the Enter key, as defined in the Const statements at the beginning of the procedure:

III

9

```
Const leftKey = 37
Const upKey = 38
Const rightKey = 39
Const downKey = 40
Const enter = 13
```

Visual Basic passes a KeyCode argument to a KeyDown event procedure to identify the key that the user has pressed. In *txtAmount_KeyDown*, a Select Case structure uses this argument to decide which direction to move the focus:

```
Select Case KeyCode
```

For example, if the user has pressed the right-arrow key or the Enter key, the focus is moved to the *next* text box in the txtAmount array:

```
Case rightKey, enter
  If Index <> 24 Then
    txtAmount(Index + 1).SetFocus
  Else
    txtAmount(0).SetFocus
  End If
```

The procedure uses the SetFocus method the make the move. Also notice the one contingency: If the last text box in the txtAmount array currently has the focus, the procedure moves the focus up to the first control in the array in response to the right-arrow or Enter key.

Once a text box receives the focus, the txtAmount_GotFocus procedure (Listing 9-11) arranges to highlight the contents of the control. The SelStart method establishes the starting point of the highlight:

```
txtAmount(Index).SelStart = 0
```

Then the SelLength method defines the length of the highlight:

```
txtAmount(Index).SelLength = _
  Len(txtAmount(Index).Text)
```

The procedure uses Visual Basic's built-in Len function to determine the length of the entry.

The program's menu commands represent another important input technique. In this case, the purpose of the user's input is to issue specific instructions to the program rather than to enter data. You'll look at the menu procedures in the next section.

RESPONDING TO THE USER'S MENU CHOICES

Conveniently, some menu techniques are built into the definition of the menu itself, and therefore require no extra code. For example, the Menu Editor allows you to define shortcut keys for carrying out menu commands directly from the keyboard. In addition, you can use the ampersand character to define Alt keys for pulling down menus and choosing specific commands or options.

But other menu events are controlled by the program itself. Each menu command in the International Sales application is represented by a Click procedure, as you can see in Listings 9-12 through 9-16. These procedures take control when the user pulls down a menu and chooses an option or presses a shortcut key to perform a menu command. You'll be examining several of these procedures later in this chapter.

Two of the program's menus — the Chart menu and the Units menu — contain lists of options rather than commands. As you'll recall, the Chart menu has two pairs of options that allow the user to choose the orientation and format of the chart display. The Units menu contains three options for defining the dollar units represented by the sales figures themselves. When the user selects an option in either of these menus, the new selection is *checked* — that is, a check mark is displayed just to the left of the currently selected option. Appropriately enough, a menu property named Checked determines which option will display a check mark in a given menu list. The property has two settings, True or False.

For example, consider the two chart-type options in the Chart menu. These options are displayed as *Column Chart* and *Pie Chart* in the menu list itself, but in the program they are represented as a control array named mnuChartType. This array contains two elements, with indexes of 0 and 1. When the user pulls down the Chart menu and chooses one of these options, the mnuChartType_Click procedure (Listing 9-12) takes control.

The procedure's first task is to display a check next to the option that the user has selected, and remove the check from the other option. The following If structure accomplishes this task by changing the settings of the Checked properties appropriately:

```
If Index = 0 Then
  mnuChartType(0).Checked = True
  mnuChartType(1).Checked = False
Else
  mnuChartType(0).Checked = False
  mnuChartType(1).Checked = True
End If
```

Once this is finished, the procedure makes a call to the *DrawGraph* routine to redraw the chart itself, following the new instructions the user has issued for the chart's format:

```
If grandTot <> 0 Then DrawGraph
```

Notice that this call is made only if the total of all the sales data (represented by the variable *grandTot*) is not 0. If the sales table is currently empty, the program draws no chart.

You'll find similar steps in other menu procedures. The mnuChartBy_Click procedure (Listing 9-12) changes the selection between the *By Years* and *By Region* selections in the Chart menu; and the mnuUnitType_Click procedure selects one of the three dollar units in the Units menu.

In the mnuUnitType_Click procedure, the control array mnuUnitType represents all three options in the menu, indexed from 0 to 2. Here's how the procedure determines which option should be checked:

```
For i = 0 To 2
  If i = Index Then
    mnuUnitType(i).Checked = True
  Else
    mnuUnitType(i).Checked = False
  End If
Next i
```

A call to the *ShowUnits* procedure then makes the appropriate change in the unit display, represented by the lblUnits label:

```
Select Case True
  Case mnuUnitType(0).Checked
    lblUnits.Caption = "(in dollars)"
  Case mnuUnitType(1).Checked
    lblUnits.Caption = "(in thousands of $)"
  Case mnuUnitType(2).Checked
    lblUnits.Caption = "(in millions of $)"
End Select
```

The program reads the values of the Checked properties in the Units menu to decide which units label to display on the form.

Next you'll look at a variety of output techniques illustrated in the International Sales program.

Output Techniques

Each time the user enters a new figure into the sales table, the International Sales program displays instant output in the controls of the frmIntSales form. The two arrays of labels named lblPeriodTotal and lblRegionTotal receive the updated total sales figures for the current sales period and region. A label named lblGrandTotal displays the total of all the sales. And a picture box control named picSalesChart displays either a column chart or a pie chart representing the current sales data.

In addition, the program's menu commands offer the user several ways to send the data to other destinations:

- The Save Report command in the File menu creates a text file to store the numeric data on disk. The mnuSaveReport_Click procedure (Listing 9-13) performs this output operation.

- The Print Window command in the File menu sends an image of the application window to the printer. The mnuPrintWindow_Click procedure takes care of this step.

- The Copy command in the Edit menu sends a copy of the sales table to the Windows 95 Clipboard. The mnuCopy_Click procedure takes control when the user chooses this command.

You'll examine all of these output procedures in the section ahead.

CALCULATING AND DISPLAYING SALES TOTALS

The txtAmount_LostFocus procedure makes a call to the *CalculateTotals* procedure whenever the user completes a new data entry in the sales table:

```
CalculateTotals Index
```

CalculateTotals (Listing 9-4) needs to recalculate only those totals that are affected by the new entry: the total regional sales in the current row, the total period sales in the current column, and the grand total at the lower-right corner of the table. For this reason, a call to the procedure sends the index number of the current entry as an argument. The procedure receives this value in the variable *amtIndex*:

```
Private Sub CalculateTotals(amtIndex As Integer)
```

As you know, the txtAmount array has index values from 0 to 24, but the two totals arrays (lblPeriodTotal and lblRegionTotal) have index values from 0 to 4. To determine the relevant indexes for the totals arrays, the program uses the Mod and integer division operations:

```
periodIndex = amtIndex Mod 5
regionIndex = amtIndex \ 5
```

Then the procedure needs to calculate the indexes corresponding to the first text boxes in the row and column of the new entry:

```
firstRowIndex = regionIndex * 5
firstColIndex = periodIndex
```

These indexes allow the procedure to loop through all the values in the target row and column to calculate the corresponding totals.

For example, here's how the procedure finds the total of all the sales entries in the target row:

```
totTemp = 0
For i = firstRowIndex To firstRowIndex + 4
  totTemp = totTemp + amounts(i)
Next i
```

Likewise, here is the code for calculating the total of all the sales amounts in the target column:

```
totTemp = 0
For i = firstColIndex To firstColIndex + 20 Step 5
  totTemp = totTemp + amounts(i)
Next i
```

Once these totals are computed, the program formats them and displays them in the appropriate label controls:

```
lblRegionTotal(regionIndex).Caption = _
  Format(totTemp, AmtFormat)
```

and:

```
lblPeriodTotal(periodIndex).Caption = _
  Format(totTemp, AmtFormat)
```

Finally, the procedure calculates the new grand total of all the sales figures:

```
totTemp = 0
For i = 0 To 24
  totTemp = totTemp + amounts(i)
Next i
```

This amount is displayed in the label control named lblGrandTotal:

```
lblGrandTotal.Caption = _
  Format(totTemp, AmtFormat)
```

Along the way, the *CalculateTotals* procedure records the numeric totals in the data arrays *regionTots* and *periodTots*, and in the variable named *grandTot*. As you'll see shortly, the charting procedures make use of these totals to determine the correct proportions for drawing the elements of a column or pie chart.

DRAWING CHARTS

The txtAmount_LostFocus procedure also makes a call to the *Draw-Graph* procedure after confirming each new entry into the sales table. *DrawGraph* has the job of determining which of four charting procedures to call, depending on the current selections in the Chart menu. The procedure uses a Select Case structure to make this decision:

```
Select Case True

    Case mnuChartBy(0).Checked And _
        mnuChartType(0).Checked

        DrawAxes
        ColumnByYears

    Case mnuChartBy(0).Checked And _
        mnuChartType(1).Checked

        PieByYears

    Case mnuChartBy(1).Checked And _
        mnuChartType(0).Checked

        DrawAxes
        ColumnByRegion

    Case mnuChartBy(1).Checked And _
        mnuChartType(1).Checked

        PieByRegion

    End Select
```

As you can see, the decision depends on the specific combination of Chart menu options that the user has selected. A column chart is drawn by either the *ColumnByYears* or *ColumnByRegion* procedure, and a pie chart is drawn by either the *PieByYears* or the *PieByRegion* procedure. In the case of a column chart, the program also makes a call to the *DrawAxes* procedure to draw the horizontal x-axis and the vertical y-axis for the chart.

These procedures make use of properties and methods defined for a picture box control — in this case the picSalesChart object. For example, the Line method draws the rectangular "stack" elements of a column chart, and the Circle method draws the wedges of a pie chart. In addition, the Scale method defines a coordinate system within the picture box, with the goal of making the chart as easy to draw as possible. You'll see how these methods work as you examine the chart procedures.

Drawing a Column Chart

Before the program draws a column chart, a call to the *DrawAxes* procedure accomplishes two tasks. First, the procedure uses the Scale method to establish an appropriate coordinate system. Here is the general format of this method:

```
objectName.Scale (x1, y1)-(x2, y2)
```

where (*x1, y1*) is the coordinate address of the control's upper-left corner, and (*x2, y2*) is the address of the lower-right corner. The *DrawAxes* procedure uses this method to establish the *picSalesChart* coordinates as follows:

```
picSalesChart.Scale (-1, 11)-(11, -0.25)
```

Under this coordinate system, the *origin* of the chart — that is, the point that has the coordinate address (0, 0) — is located slightly above and to the right of the control's lower-left corner. Furthermore, the drawing area is 10 units high and 10 units across, as you can see by the lengths of the two axes:

```
picSalesChart.Line (0, 0)-Step(10, 0)
picSalesChart.Line (0, 0)-Step(0, 10)
```

This means that the maximum height of any column in the chart is 10.

The major arithmetic problem in a column chart is determining the scale factor by which each sales value should be multiplied to calculate the proportional height of the corresponding chart stack. This scale factor is based on the height of the drawing area (which, as you've seen, is 10) and the tallest column that will be drawn within this area. Both the *ColumnByRegion* and *ColumnByYears* procedures must therefore begin their work by determining the largest total value that will be represented in the chart.

For example, here is how the *ColumnByRegion* procedure finds the value of *maxPeriod*, the largest annual sales total:

```
maxPeriod = 0
For i = 0 To 4
  If periodTots(i) > maxPeriod Then _
    maxPeriod = periodtots(i)
Next i
```

Given *maxPeriod*, the following statement calculates the scale factor:

```
scaleFactor = 10 / maxPeriod
```

Multiplying this scale factor by the largest annual total results in a product of 10, the total height of the drawing area.

The *ColumnByRegion* procedure draws the columns of the chart in a pair of For loops, one nested within the other. The outer loop contains the code for drawing each complete column, and the inner loop draws the stacks in a given column. Thanks to the scale factor, the height of each individual stack appropriately represents the corresponding sales value:

```
y2 = scaleFactor * amounts(j)
```

Before drawing a given stack, the program uses the FillColor property to select a color. A convenient built-in function named QBColor identifies colors by numeric arguments from 0 to 15:

```
picSalesChart.FillColor = _
  QBColor(j \ 5 + colorOffset)
```

To draw a rectangle filled with color, the program uses the Line method in the following form:

```
object.Line (x1, y1)-Step(x2, y2), outlineColor, B
```

The keyword Step indicates that $(x2, y2)$ is an offset measurement from the starting point $(x1, y1)$. The *outlineColor* defines the color around the rectangle's perimeter. The letter B is an instruction to draw a box rather than a line. For example, here is how the *ColumnByRegion* procedure draws each stack in a given column:

```
picSalesChart.Line (x, y)-Step(1.5, y2), _
    0, B
```

Notice that the vertical offset is $y2$, the calculated height of the stack. The vertical starting point is y, which is the top coordinate of the *previous* stack. The width of each column is specified as 1.5 units in the coordinate scale. The outline color is 0, which represents black. After drawing each stack, the program increases the value of y by the height of the previous stack:

```
y = y + y2
```

If you take a look at the *ColumnByYears* procedure (Listing 9-6), you'll see that the steps for producing the other chart orientation are about the same, except that the scale factor is based on the regional sales totals rather than the annual sales.

Drawing a Pie Chart

In a pie chart, the angle of a given wedge represents one value in relation to the total of all the values. Here's the general formula for calculating the angle to represent a value, x, which is part of a total, t:

```
360 * (x / t)
```

For example, suppose the sales total for a five-year period is $120,000 and the sales total for the year 1994 is $40,000. Because the 1994 sales are one-third of the overall total, the year is represented by a pie-chart wedge with an angle of 120 degrees, or one-third of a full circle.

In Visual Basic's Circle method, angles are measured in *radians* rather than degrees. A full circle of 360 degrees is equal to a radian measurement of 2π. To draw a wedge, you must supply the starting and ending angles as *negative* radian values in the Circle method:

```
Object.Circle (x, y), radius, outlineColor, -angle1, -angle2
```

In this general format, (*x, y*) represents the circle's center; *radius* is the length of the radius; *outlineColor* is a color selection for the perimeter of the wedge; and *angle1* and *angle2* are the starting and ending angles in radians.

By convention, an angle of 0 is defined as the radius that extends horizontally to the right from the circle's center point. Interestingly, the Circle method has a quirk: Using 0 or 2π as one of the angles of a wedge produces unexpected results. You should therefore substitute values that are slightly offset from 0 or 2π to represent these angles.

The *PieByYears* procedure (Listing 9-8) begins by calculating a value of π using a standard formula that includes a call to Visual Basic's built-in Atn (arctangent) function:

```
pi = 4 * Atn(1)
```

Then the procedure establishes a coordinate scale for the picture box in which the chart will be drawn:

```
picSalesChart.Scale (-1, 1)-(1, -1)
```

Under this coordinate system, the origin of the chart (0, 0), is located at the center of the picture box. This simplifies the use of the Circle method to draw the wedges of the pie chart.

The wedges are drawn in a For structure that loops through the total sales figures for each year in the five-year period. The starting angle of the first wedge is set at a very small nonzero value:

```
a1 = 0.00001
```

Then the ending angle is calculated as a portion of the full 2π sweep of the circle:

```
a2 = a1 + (2 * pi) * _
   (periodTots(i) / grantTot)
```

As you'll recall, the data array *periodTots* contains the total annual sales figures, and the variable *grandTot* contains the grand total of all the sales.

Once the angles have been calculated, the procedure uses the FillColor property to select a color for the wedge:

```
picSalesChart.FillColor = _
   QBColor(i + colorOffset)
```

Then a call to the Circle method draws the wedge itself:

```
picSalesChart.Circle (0, 0), 0.9, _
   0, -a1, -a2 + 0.00001
```

Notice that the center of the circle is (0, 0) and the radius is 0.9, slightly less than half the width of the picture box itself. Also notice that the procedure adds a small nonzero value to *a2* to avoid using an angle of 2π.

When one wedge has been drawn, the starting angle of the next wedge is predefined as the ending angle of the current wedge:

```
a1 = a2
```

You'll find that the *PieByRegion* procedure (Listing 9-9) uses these same techniques to draw its version of the pie chart, except that it bases the wedge calculations on the regional sales totals rather than the annual totals.

PERFORMING OTHER OUTPUT TASKS

The mnuSaveReport_Click procedure (Listing 9-14) responds to the user's selection of the Save Report command in the File menu. The procedure creates a file named IntSales.Txt in the root directory of the current disk:

```
Open "\IntSales.Txt" For Output As #1
```

The procedure then uses a sequence of Print # statements to send the sales table and totals to the file. (Refer back to Chapter 8 for more information about data file commands.) This file can then be printed or incorporated into a larger document.

The mnuPrintWindow_Click procedure (Listing 9-14) makes a call to Visual Basic's PrintForm method to send an image of the International Sales window to the printer. This procedure responds to the user's selection of the Print Window command in the File menu.

Finally, the mnuCopy_Click procedure arranges to send a copy of the sales table to the Clipboard. To do so, it begins by forcing a call to the mnuSaveReport_Click procedure to make sure that the IntSales.Txt file exists in the root directory. Then the procedure opens the file, reads it line by line, and assigns its entire contents to a string variable named *temp:*

```
temp = ""
Open "\IntSales.Txt" For Input As #1
  Do While Not EOF(1)
    Line Input #1, inTemp
    temp = temp + inTemp + Chr(13) + Chr(10)
  Loop
Close #1
```

Notice the use of the Line Input command to read entire lines at a time from the file. Also note that the procedure adds a carriage-return/line-feed combination (Chr(13) and Chr(10)) to each line stored in *temp*.

The procedure uses the SetText method to store this string value in the Clipboard:

```
Clipboard.SetText temp
```

When this operation is complete, the user can paste the sales table to a word processed document or to another software environment.

In summary, the International Sales application illustrates several interesting input and output techniques, including data validation and formatting, menu procedures, numeric and graphical output to the screen, and output to a variety of other destinations. You'll continue to explore these techniques in other programs presented in this book.

Listing 9-1
General declarations for IntSales.FRM

```
' The International Sales Program
' -------------------------------

' Files:
' Project File:  IntSales.VBP
' Form File:     IntSales.FRM

' This program provides a small spreadsheet in
' which the user can enter annual sales data by
' international regions. As each data item is
' entered, the program calculates regional and
' period totals, and develops a chart to represent
' the sales data pictorially. Using commands in
' the Chart menu, the user can choose among
' several graph formats, including two arrangements
' of column charts and pie charts. In addition, the
' File menu contains commands that allow the user
' to print a copy of the program window, or to
' save the sales data as a text file on disk.
' Finally, the Copy command in the Edit menu
' places a copy of the data table on the Windows
' Clipboard; from there, the user can paste the
' data to other software environments.

Option Explicit

' The AmtFormat constant provides the dollar-and-
' cents format for data displayed in the sales
' table. The colorOffset constant determines the
' selection of colors used in the column charts
' and pie charts.
Const AmtFormat = "$#,###0"
Const colorOffset = 7

' For convenience in a variety of operations,
' the program uses six arrays to record the sales
' data currently stored in the table. The arrays
' named amounts and amountStr record the actual
```

```
' data in numeric and string formats. The periodTots
' and regionTots arrays record the current totals.
' The periodLabels and regionLabels record the
' column and row labels for the table, which the
' user can revise if necessary to represent the
' actual content of the table.
Dim amounts(24)
Dim amountStr(24) As String
Dim periodTots(4)
Dim periodLabels(4) As String
Dim regionTots(4)
Dim regionLabels(4) As String

' The IDPrefixes array represents key prefixes that
' are appended to the column or row labels to
' identify the elements of a particular column chart.
Dim IDPrefixes(4) As String

' The grandTot variable represents the grand total
' of all the current sales data.

Dim grandTot

' End of General Declarations, IntSales.FRM
```

Listing 9-2
The Form_Load procedure

```
Private Sub Form_Load()

    ' The Form_Load procedure performs a variety
    ' of initializations at the beginning of the
    ' program's performance.

    Dim i
    Dim tempYear As String

    ' Display the initial column labels and
    ' initialize the arrays that record the
    ' current labels.
```

```
For i = 0 To 4
  tempYear = Year(Date) - (5 - i)
  txtYear(i).Text = tempYear
  periodLabels(i) = txtYear(i).Text
  regionLabels(i) = txtPlace(i).Text
  IDPrefixes(i) = Format((i + 1), "# = ")
Next i

' Display the current dollar unit selection.
' (The user can change this display by making
' a new selection from the Units menu.)
ShowUnits


End Sub   ' Form_Load
```

Listing 9-3
The txtAmount_LostFocus procedure

```
Private Sub txtAmount_LostFocus(Index As Integer)

  ' The txtAmount_LostFocus procedure performs
  ' a variety of important tasks after each new
  ' data item has been entered into the sales
  ' table. (Note that txtAmount is a control
  ' array, with Index values from 0 to 24.) The
  ' procedure validates the data entry, reformats
  ' it for display, recalculates the appropriate
  ' totals, and redraws the current chart.

  ' The entryWidth variable defines the width
  ' within which the program right-justifies
  ' entries into the sales table.
  Dim entryWidth As String
  entryWidth = Space(8)

  ' Compare the entry with the corresponding
  ' value in the amountStr array, to determine
  ' whether the value has changed.
  If amountStr(Index) <> txtAmount(Index).Text Then
```

III

9

```
' If so, record the new numeric value in the
' amounts array. Use the Val function to
' eliminate any nonnumeric characters in the
' entry. (Note that an entry beginning with
' a nonnumeric character becomes zero.)
amounts(Index) = Val(txtAmount(Index).Text)

' Do not allow negative entries or entries
' that are longer than six digits in the
' sales table.
If amounts(Index) < 0 Or _
   amounts(Index) > 999999 _
   Then amounts(Index) = 0

' If the entry is not zero, display the value
' in a right-justified dollar-and-cent format.
If amounts(Index) <> 0 Then
  RSet entryWidth = _
     Format(amounts(Index), AmtFormat)
  txtAmount(Index).Text = entryWidth
Else
  ' Otherwise, if the entry is zero,
  ' display it as a blank entry.
  txtAmount(Index).Text = ""
End If

' Record the formatted value in the
' string array named amountStr.
amountStr(Index) = txtAmount(Index).Text

' Recaculate the totals for the row and
' column where this new entry is located.
CalculateTotals Index

' If the current grand total is not zero,
' redraw the current chart. Otherwise,
' hide the chart controls.
If grandTot <> 0 Then
  DrawGraph
```

Using Val to eliminate nonnumeric characters from the input

```
      Else
        HideGraph
      End If

   End If

End Sub   ' txtAmount_LostFocus
```

Listing 9-4
The CalculateTotals procedure

```
Private Sub CalculateTotals(amtIndex As Integer)

   ' The CalculateTotals procedure updates the
   ' row and column of sales totals each time the
   ' user enters a new value into the sales table.
   ' Note that the totals are displayed in two
   ' arrays of labels, named lblPeriodTotal and
   ' lblRegionTotal. Each array has Index values
   ' from 0 to 4.

   Dim i As Integer
   Dim periodIndex As Integer
   Dim regionIndex As Integer
   Dim firstRowIndex As Integer
   Dim firstColIndex As Integer
   Dim totTemp

   ' Create indexes to identify the
   ' totals that need to be recalculated.
   periodIndex = amtIndex Mod 5
   regionIndex = amtIndex \ 5
   firstRowIndex = regionIndex * 5
   firstColIndex = periodIndex

   ' Find the total sales for the current region.
   totTemp = 0
```

```
For i = firstRowIndex To firstRowIndex + 4
  totTemp = totTemp + amounts(i)
Next i

' Record this numeric value in the
' regionTots array.
regionTots(regionIndex) = totTemp

' Display the formatted value in the
' appropriate lblRegionTotal control.
If totTemp <> 0 Then
  lblRegionTotal(regionIndex).Caption = _
    Format(totTemp, AmtFormat)
Else
  lblRegionTotal(regionIndex).Caption = ""
End If

' Calculate the total sales for the
' current period.
totTemp = 0
For i = firstColIndex To firstColIndex + 20 Step 5
  totTemp = totTemp + amounts(i)
Next i

' Record this numeric value in the
' periodTots array.
periodTots(periodIndex) = totTemp

' Display the formatted value in the
' appropriate lblPeriodTotal control.
If totTemp <> 0 Then
  lblPeriodTotal(periodIndex).Caption = _
    Format(totTemp, AmtFormat)
Else
  lblPeriodTotal(periodIndex).Caption = ""
End If

' Calculate the new grand total.
totTemp = 0
```

Displaying the total as the Caption property of a label control

```
    For i = 0 To 24
      totTemp = totTemp + amounts(i)
    Next i

    ' Record the numeric value in the
    ' grandTot variable.
    grandTot = totTemp

    ' Display the formatted value in the
    ' lblGrandTotal control.
    If totTemp <> 0 Then
      lblGrandTotal.Caption = _
        Format(totTemp, AmtFormat)
    Else
      lblGrandTotal.Caption = ""
    End If

End Sub   ' CalculateTotals
```

Listing 9-5

The DrawGraph and HideGraph procedures

```
Private Sub DrawGraph()

    ' The DrawGraph procedure redraws the chart,
    ' based on the current selections in the
    ' Chart menu.

    ' Display picture box control and
    ' clear its contents.
    picSalesChart.Visible = True
    picSalesChart.Cls

    ' Determine which chart to draw, according
    ' to the current Checked values in the
    ' mnuChartBy and mnuChartType arrays.
    Select Case True

      Case mnuChartBy(0).Checked And _
```

Using a Case structure to respond to the user's Chart menu choices

```
                    mnuChartType(0).Checked

          ' For a column chart, draw the
          ' vertical and horizontal axes first,
          ' then draw the columns of the chart.
          DrawAxes
          ColumnByYears

       Case mnuChartBy(0).Checked And _
             mnuChartType(1).Checked

          ' For a pie chart, no axes are needed.
          PieByYears

       Case mnuChartBy(1).Checked And _
             mnuChartType(0).Checked

          DrawAxes
          ColumnByRegion

       Case mnuChartBy(1).Checked And _
             mnuChartType(1).Checked

          PieByRegion

    End Select

    ' Display the legend for the chart.
    ShowLegend

End Sub   ' DrawGraph



Private Sub HideGraph()

    ' The HideGraph procedure hides the picture box
    ' and other controls related to the chart and
    ' its legend. The program calls this routine
    ' whenever the grand total value is zero.
```

```
Dim i

' Hide the picture box.
picSalesChart.Visible = False

For i = 0 To 4

   ' Hide all of the legend labels.
   lblLegendColor(i).Visible = False
   lblLegendText(i).Caption = ""

   ' Erase the labels arranged beneath
   ' the horizontal axis of a column chart.
   lblxAxis(i).Caption = ""

   ' Restore the original year and region
   ' labels above and to the left of the
   ' sales table.
   txtYear(i).Text = periodLabels(i)
   txtYear(i).Enabled = True
   txtPlace(i).Text = regionLabels(i)
   txtPlace(i).Enabled = True
Next i

End Sub   ' HideGraph
```

Listing 9-6
The ColumnByYears procedure

```
Private Sub ColumnByYears()

   ' The ColumnByYears procedure draws a column
   ' chart if the user has selected the "By Years"
   ' option in the Chart menu.

   Dim i
   Dim x, y, y2
   Dim maxRegion
   Dim scaleFactor
```

```
' Determine the largest region total.
maxRegion = 0
For i = 0 To 4
  If regionTots(i) > maxRegion Then _
    maxRegion = regionTots(i)
Next i

' The scale factor for the chart is based
' on the largest region total. (This value
' will have a height of 10 in the chart.)
scaleFactor = 10 / maxRegion
```

The scale factor for a column chart

```
' Depict each nonzero value in the sales
' table as a "stack" in one of the charts.
For i = 0 To 24

  ' At the beginning of each row of data,
  ' reinitialize the x and y values for a
  ' new column in the chart.
  If i Mod 5 = 0 Then
    x = 0.5 + 2 * (i / 5)
    y = 0
  End If

  ' If an amount is not zero, calculate
  ' the height of the corresponding "stack."
  If amounts(i) <> 0 Then
    y2 = scaleFactor * amounts(i)
```

Using the scale factor to calculate the height of a "stack"

```
    ' Select a color and a fill style.
    picSalesChart.FillColor = _
      QBColor(i Mod 5 + colorOffset)
    picSalesChart.FillStyle = 0

    ' Draw the "stack."
    picSalesChart.Line (x, y)-Step(1.5, y2), _
      0, B
```

Drawing the column chart

```
              ' Increment the value of y by the
              ' height of the previous "stack."
              y = y + y2
          End If
      Next i


  End Sub   ' ColumnByYears
```

Listing 9-7
The ColumnByRegion procedure

```
  Private Sub ColumnByRegion()

      ' The ColumnByRegion procedure draws a column
      ' chart if the user has selected the "By Region"
      ' option in the Chart menu.

      Dim i, j
      Dim x, y, y2
      Dim maxPeriod
      Dim scaleFactor

      ' Determine the largest year total
      ' in the sales table.
      maxPeriod = 0
      For i = 0 To 4
        If periodTots(i) > maxPeriod Then _
          maxPeriod = periodTots(i)
      Next i

      ' The scale factor for the chart is based on
      ' the largest year total. (This value has a
      ' height of 10 in the chart.)
      scaleFactor = 10 / maxPeriod


      For i = 0 To 4

        ' Reinitialize the x and y values for the
        ' beginning of each new column in the chart.
```

```
                    x = 0.5 + 2 * i
                    y = 0

                    ' Draw a "stack" for each numeric entry in
                    ' a given year of the sales table.
                    For j = i To i + 20 Step 5

                        ' If the value is not zero, calculate
                        ' the "stack" height that will represent
                        ' this value in the column chart.
                        If amounts(j) <> 0 Then
                            y2 = scaleFactor * amounts(j)

                            ' Select a color and a fill style.
                            picSalesChart.FillColor = _
                                QBColor(j \ 5 + colorOffset)
                            picSalesChart.FillStyle = 0

                            ' Draw the "stack."
                            picSalesChart.Line (x, y)-Step(1.5, y2), _
                                0, B

                            ' Add the height of the previous
                            ' "stack" to the current value of y.
                            y = y + y2
                        End If
                    Next j
                Next i

            End Sub   ' ColumnByRegion
```

Listing 9-8
The PieByYears procedure

```
    Private Sub PieByYears()

        ' The PieByYears procedure draws a pie chart
        ' if the user has selected the "By Years"
        ' option in the Chart menu.
```

```
Dim i, pi, a1, a2

' Calculate the value of pi.
pi = 4 * Atn(1)
```
A calculation of π

```
' Set the scale for the picture box. The
' "origin" is located in the center of the
' box in this case.
picSalesChart.Scale (-1, 1)-(1, -1)
```
The Scale method for a pie chart

```
' Because of a quirk in the Circle method, the
' starting angle for the first wedge in the chart
' must be a very small nonzero value.
a1 = 0.00001

' Draw a wedge to represent the total sales
' for each year in the sales table.
For i = 0 To 4
  If periodTots(i) <> 0 Then

    ' Calculate the ending angle of the
    ' current wedge.
    a2 = a1 + (2 * pi) * _
      (periodTots(i) / grandTot)

    ' Select a color and a fill style.
    picSalesChart.FillColor = _
      QBColor(i + colorOffset)
    picSalesChart.FillStyle = 0

    ' Draw the wedge.
    If periodTots(i) < grandTot Then
      picSalesChart.Circle (0, 0), 0.9, _
        0, -a1, -a2 + 0.00001
```
Drawing the wedges of the chart

```
    ' But if this sales total is currently
    ' the only annual total availble in the
    ' table, draw a full circle instead.
    Else
      picSalesChart.Circle (0, 0), 0.9, 0
```

III

9

```
        End If

        ' The starting angle for the next wedge
        ' is the ending angle of the current wedge.
        a1 = a2
      End If
    Next i


End Sub   ' PieByYears
```

Listing 9-9
The PieByRegion procedure

```
Private Sub PieByRegion()

    ' The PieByRegion procedure draws a pie chart
    ' if the user has selected the "By Region"
    ' option in the Chart menu.

    Dim i, pi, a1, a2

    ' Calculate the value of pi.
    pi = 4 * Atn(1)

    ' Set the scale of the picture box. The "origin"
    ' is at the center of the box in this case.
    picSalesChart.Scale (-1, 1)-(1, -1)

    ' Because of a quirk in the Circle method, the
    ' starting angle of the first wedge must be a
    ' very small nonzero value.
    a1 = 0.00001

    ' Draw a wedge to represent each regional
    ' sales total.
    For i = 0 To 4

      ' If the current sales total is not zero,
      ' calculate the ending angle of the wedge.
      If regionTots(i) <> 0 Then
```

```
      a2 = a1 + (2 * pi) * _
        (regionTots(i) / grandTot)

      ' Select a color and a fill style.
      picSalesChart.FillColor = _
        QBColor(i + colorOffset)
      picSalesChart.FillStyle = 0

      ' Draw the wedge.
      If regionTots(i) < grandTot Then
        picSalesChart.Circle (0, 0), 0.9, _
          0, -a1, -a2 + 0.00001

      ' But if this total value is currently
      ' the only regional total available in the
      ' sales table, draw a full circle instead.
      Else
        picSalesChart.Circle (0, 0), 0.9, 0
      End If

      ' The starting angle for the next wedge
      ' is the ending angle of the current wedge.
      a1 = a2
    End If
  Next i

End Sub   ' PieByRegion
```

Listing 9-10
The DrawAxes and ShowLegend procedures

```
Private Sub DrawAxes()

  ' The DrawAxes procedure draws the vertical
  ' and horizontal axes for a column chart.

  Dim i

  ' Begin by creating a convenient coordinate
  ' system for the chart. (The "origin" of the
```

```
' chart is located just above and to the right
' of the lower-left corner of the picture box.)
picSalesChart.Scale (-1, 11)-(11, -0.25)

' Then draw the two axes, each starting
' at the "origin" defined by the coordinate
' scale.
picSalesChart.Line (0, 0)-Step(10, 0)
picSalesChart.Line (0, 0)-Step(0, 10)

End Sub   ' DrawAxes



Private Sub ShowLegend()

' The ShowLegend procedure displays the labels
' and colors of the legend for a pie chart or a
' column chart. In addition, the procedure adds
' numeric prefixes to labels above or to the left
' of the sales table, to identify the individual
' columns of a column chart.

Dim i

For i = 0 To 4

  ' If the "By Years" option has been selected
  ' in the Chart menu, display the years as the
  ' legend labels.
  If mnuChartBy(0).Checked Then
    If periodTots(i) <> 0 Then
      lblLegendColor(i).Visible = True
      lblLegendColor(i).BackColor = _
        QBColor(i + colorOffset)
      lblLegendText(i).Caption = periodLabels(i)

    ' But don't display a box or label for
    ' a sales table column that has a
    ' total value of zero.
```

*The Scale method
for a column chart*

```
    Else
      lblLegendColor(i).Visible = False
      lblLegendText(i).Caption = ""
    End If


    ' For a column chart, add a numeric
    ' prefix to the region labels to identify
    ' each column of the chart.
    If mnuChartType(0).Checked And _
        regionTots(i) <> 0 Then
      lblxAxis(i).Caption = i + 1
      txtPlace(i).Text = IDPrefixes(i) + _
        regionLabels(i)
      txtPlace(i).Enabled = False
    Else
      lblxAxis(i).Caption = ""
      txtPlace(i).Text = regionLabels(i)
      txtPlace(i).Enabled = True
    End If

  Else

    ' If the "By Region" option has been
    ' selected in the Chart menu, display
    ' the regions as the legend labels.
    If regionTots(i) <> 0 Then
      lblLegendColor(i).Visible = True
      lblLegendColor(i).BackColor = _
        QBColor(i + colorOffset)
      lblLegendText(i).Caption = regionLabels(i)
    Else
      lblLegendColor(i).Visible = False
      lblLegendText(i).Caption = ""
    End If

    ' For a column chart, add numeric prefixes
    ' to the year labels to identify each
    ' column of the chart.
    If mnuChartType(0).Checked And _
        periodTots(i) <> 0 Then
      lblxAxis(i).Caption = i + 1
```

III

9

```
          txtYear(i).Text = IDPrefixes(i) + _
            periodLabels(i)
          txtYear(i).Enabled = False
        Else
          lblxAxis(i).Caption = ""
          txtYear(i).Text = periodLabels(i)
          txtYear(i).Enabled = True
        End If

    End If
  Next i


End Sub  ' ShowLegend
```

Listing 9-11
The txtAmount_GotFocus and txtAmount_KeyDown procedures

```
Private Sub txtAmount_GotFocus(Index As Integer)

  ' The txtAmount_GotFocus procedure arranges to
  ' highlight the contents of a given txtAmount
  ' box when the control receives the focus. This
  ' effect is achieved through use of the SelStart
  ' and SelLength properties.

  txtAmount(Index).SelStart = 0
  txtAmount(Index).SelLength = _
    Len(txtAmount(Index).Text)
```

Selecting the contents of a text box

```
End Sub   ' txtAmount_GotFocus



Private Sub txtAmount_KeyDown(Index As Integer, _
  KeyCode As Integer, Shift As Integer)

  ' The txtAmount_KeyDown procedure allows the
  ' txtAmount text boxes to respond to the four
  ' arrow keys (left, up, right, and down) and to
  ' the Enter key as techniques for moving the
```

```
' focus from one box to the next. (Note that
' the 25 txtAmount boxes form a control array,
' with Index values from 0 to 24.)

' Define names to represent the code numbers of
' the relevant keys.
Const leftKey = 37
Const upKey = 38
Const rightKey = 39
Const downKey = 40
Const enter = 13
```

Using a Case structure to respond to the user's keystrokes

```
Select Case KeyCode

    ' Move the focus down to the next row,
    ' or from the bottom row to the top.
    Case downKey
      If Index < 20 Then
        txtAmount(Index + 5).SetFocus
      Else
        txtAmount(Index Mod 5).SetFocus
      End If

    ' Move the focus up to the previous row,
    ' or from the top row to the bottom.
    Case upKey
      If Index > 4 Then
        txtAmount(Index - 5).SetFocus
      Else
        txtAmount(Index + 20).SetFocus
      End If

    ' Move the focus to the previous text
    ' box, or from the upper-left corner to
    ' the lower-right corner of the table.
    Case leftKey
      If Index <> 0 Then
        txtAmount(Index - 1).SetFocus
      Else
        txtAmount(24).SetFocus
```

III

9

```
         End If

    ' Move the focus to the next text box,
    ' or from the lower-right corner to the
    ' upper-left corner of the table. (Note
    ' that the right-arrow key and the Enter
    ' key are both available for this action.)
    Case rightKey, enter
      If Index <> 24 Then
        txtAmount(Index + 1).SetFocus
      Else
        txtAmount(0).SetFocus
      End If

  End Select

End Sub    ' txtAmount_KeyDown
```

Listing 9-12

The mnuChartBy_Click and mnuChartType_Click procedures

```
Private Sub mnuChartBy_Click(Index As Integer)

    ' The mnuChartBy_Click procedure responds to
    ' the user's choice of an option in the Chart
    ' menu. The user can choose to chart the data
    ' by region or by time period.

    Dim i

    ' Adjust the selection within the menu itself.
    If Index = 0 Then
      mnuChartBy(0).Checked = True
      mnuChartBy(1).Checked = False
    Else
      mnuChartBy(0).Checked = False
      mnuChartBy(1).Checked = True
    End If
```

Changing the Checked property for an array of menu options

```
' Restore the original column and row
' labels, in preparation for displaying
' new keys for a column chart.
For i = 0 To 4
  txtYear(i).Text = periodLabels(i)
  txtYear(i).Enabled = True
  txtPlace(i).Text = regionLabels(i)
  txtPlace(i).Enabled = True
Next i

' If any sales information has been entered
' into the table, redraw the chart at this point.
If grandTot <> 0 Then DrawGraph

End Sub   ' mnuChartBy_Click



Private Sub mnuChartType_Click(Index As Integer)

  ' The mnuChartType_Click procedure responds to
  ' the user's choice of an option in the Chart
  ' menu. The user can choose to create a column
  ' chart or a pie chart.

  ' Adjust the current selection in the menu.
  If Index = 0 Then
    mnuChartType(0).Checked = True
    mnuChartType(1).Checked = False
  Else
    mnuChartType(0).Checked = False
    mnuChartType(1).Checked = True
  End If

  ' If any sales information has been entered
  ' into the table, redraw the chart at this point.
  If grandTot <> 0 Then DrawGraph

End Sub    ' mnuChartType_Click
```

III

9

Listing 9-13

The mnuCopy_Click, mnuSaveReport_Click, and mnuPrintWindow procedures

```
Private Sub mnuCopy_Click()

    ' The mnuCopy_Click procedure takes control
    ' when the user chooses the Copy command from
    ' the Edit menu. The purpose of the procedure
    ' is to place a copy of the current sales table
    ' on the Windows Clipboard. From there, the
    ' user can paste the data to another software
    ' environment, such as a word processing
    ' program or a spreadsheet.

    Dim temp As String, inTemp As String

    ' Begin by creating a text file on disk for
    ' the current data set.
    mnuSaveReport_Click

    ' Then open the file and read each line it
    ' contains.
    temp = ""
    Open "\IntSales.Txt" For Input As #1
      Do While Not EOF(1)
        Line Input #1, inTemp

        ' Concatenate each line of text to
        ' the string variable temp.
        temp = temp + inTemp + Chr(13) + Chr(10)
      Loop
    Close #1

    ' Finally, place the temp string on
    ' the Clipboard.
    Clipboard.SetText temp

End Sub   ' mnuCopy_Click
```

Writing text to the Clipboard

```
Private Sub mnuSaveReport_Click()

  ' The mnuSaveReport_Click procedure takes control
  ' when the user chooses the Save Report command
  ' from the File menu. The procedure creates a
  ' text file (named \IntSales.Txt) on disk and
  ' stores the numeric data currently displayed in
  ' the program's form.

  Dim i, j
  Dim f As String, b As String

  f = "$#,###0"
  b = "              "

  ' Create the file. (If the file already
  ' exists, overwrite the previous version.)
  Open "\IntSales.Txt" For Output As #1

    ' Write the title and the column labels
    ' to the file.
    Print #1, b; b; txtTitle
    Print #1, b; b; "    "; lblUnits
    Print #1,

    Print #1, b;
    For i = 0 To 4
      RSet b = txtYear(i)
      Print #1, b;
    Next i
    Print #1, "      Totals"
    Print #1,

    ' Write the table of sales data to the file.
    For i = 0 To 4
      LSet b = txtPlace(i).Text
      Print #1, b;
      For j = i * 5 To i * 5 + 4
        RSet b = txtAmount(j).Text
        Print #1, b;
      Next j
```

```
            RSet b = lblRegionTotal(i).Caption
            Print #1, b
         Next i

         ' Write the totals to the file.
         Print #1,
         Print #1, "Totals        ";
         For i = 0 To 4
           RSet b = lblPeriodTotal(i).Caption
           Print #1, b;
         Next i
         RSet b = lblGrandTotal
         Print #1, b

      Close #1

   End Sub   ' mnuSaveReport_Click



   Private Sub mnuPrintWindow_Click()

      ' The mnuPrintWindow_Click procedure takes control
      ' when the user chooses the Print Window command
      ' from the File menu. The procedure sends an
      ' image of the program's form to the printer.

      PrintForm

   End Sub   ' mnuPrintWindow_Click
```

Listing 9-14
The mnuUnitType_Click and ShowUnits procedures

```
   Private Sub mnuUnitType_Click(Index As Integer)

      ' The mnuUnitType_Click procedure takes control
      ' when the user chooses a new option from the
      ' Units menu. (Note that the three options in
```

```
' this menu form a control array with Index
' values from 0 to 2.) The procedure changes
' the selection in the menu and then displays
' the appropriate caption in the lblUnits control.

Dim i

' Determine which option should be checked.
For i = 0 To 2
  If i = Index Then
    mnuUnitType(i).Checked = True
  Else
    mnuUnitType(i).Checked = False
  End If
Next i

' Display the selected units caption.
ShowUnits

End Sub   ' mnuUnitType_Click



Private Sub ShowUnits()

  ' The ShowUnits procedure reads the current
  ' selection in the Units menu and displays
  ' the corresponding units caption in the form.

  Select Case True
    Case mnuUnitType(0).Checked
      lblUnits.Caption = "(in dollars)"
    Case mnuUnitType(1).Checked
      lblUnits.Caption = "(in thousands of $)"
    Case mnuUnitType(2).Checked
      lblUnits.Caption = "(in millions of $)"
  End Select

End Sub   ' ShowUnits
```

III

9

Listing 9-15
The txtPlace_LostFocus and txtYear_LostFocus procedures

```
Private Sub txtPlace_LostFocus(Index As Integer)

   ' The txtPlace_LostFocus procedure is called when
   ' the user completes a change in any one of the
   ' region labels displayed to the left of the
   ' sales chart. The procedure records this change
   ' in the regionLabels array.

   regionLabels(Index) = txtPlace(Index).Text
   If grandTot <> 0 Then ShowLegend

End Sub   ' txtPlace_LostFocus



Private Sub txtYear_LostFocus(Index As Integer)

   ' The txtYear_LostFocus procedure is called when
   ' the user completes a change in any one of the
   ' year labels displayed above the sales chart.
   ' The procedure records this change in the
   ' periodLabels array.

   periodLabels(Index) = txtYear(Index).Text
   If grandTot <> 0 Then ShowLegend

End Sub   ' txtYear_LostFocus
```

Listing 9-16
The mnuClear_Click and mnuExit_Click procedures

```
Private Sub mnuClear_Click()

   ' The mnuClear_Click procedure takes control when
   ' the user chooses the Clear command from the
   ' Edit menu. The procedure clears all data from
```

```
' the sales table, and temporarily hides the
' objects in the chart area of the form.

Dim i

' Reinitialize the text boxes in the sales
' table and the values in the amounts and
' amountStr arrays.
For i = 0 To 24
  txtAmount(i).Text = ""
  amounts(i) = 0
  amountStr(i) = ""
Next i
```

Processing an array of controls

```
' Erase the totals and reinitialize the totals
' arrays. Also restore the original row and
' column labels.
For i = 0 To 4
  lblPeriodTotal(i).Caption = ""
  lblRegionTotal(i).Caption = ""
  periodTots(i) = 0
  regionTots(i) = 0
  txtPlace(i).Text = regionLabels(i)
  txtYear(i).Text = periodLabels(i)
Next i

' Erase the grand total and reinitialize
' the grandTot variable.
lblGrandTotal.Caption = ""
grandTot = 0

' Hide the graph objects.
HideGraph

' Move the focus to the first text box in the
' table, in preparation for new data entries.
txtAmount(0).SetFocus

End Sub   ' mnuClear_Click
```

III

9

```
Private Sub mnuExit_Click()

    ' The mnuExit_Click procedure takes control when
    ' the user chooses the Exit command from the
    ' File menu. The procedure simply terminates the
    ' program performance.

    End

End Sub   ' mnuExit_Click
```

10 Visual Basic Controls

*U*p to this point, you've worked primarily with a small subset of the controls available in Visual Basic. Text boxes, labels, command buttons, check boxes, option buttons, picture boxes, lists — these and a few others are among the most familiar objects in Windows dialog boxes, and are therefore the controls that most Visual Basic programmers learn to use first.

But a number of other significant tools are available. The selection of controls depends on the edition of Visual Basic you have installed on your computer. The Standard Edition provides the familiar Toolbox of controls shown in Figure 10-1. This collection includes all the *intrinsic* controls — that is, the basic controls built into the Visual Basic development system — along with a few *custom controls*, which are supplied as separate files with VBX or OCX extension names.

Custom controls are provided by Microsoft or by other developers who create tools for use in Visual Basic. These controls tend to serve more complex roles — and meet more sophisticated programming requirements — than the intrinsic controls you've worked with up to now. For example, here are brief descriptions of the custom controls included with the Standard Edition of Visual Basic 4.0:

- The Grid control is a rectangular arrangement of cells that you can use to create worksheets of data in an application.

- The Outline control allows you to organize lists of data in outline form in an application. Levels of data can be opened or closed, depending on the portion of the list that the user wants to focus on at any given time.

- The DBList (data-bound list) and DBCombo (data-bound combo) controls provide connections between existing databases on disk and a Visual Basic application. Given a data control and the appropriate property settings, a data-bound list box or combo box can automatically display the information from a specific database field. You'll learn more about this subject in Chapter 14.

- The Common Dialog control gives you access to standard Windows dialog boxes including Save As, Open, Print, Font, and Color. By using this control, you avoid having to recreate these dialog boxes, and you ensure that your application will have the same basic operations as other Windows programs. You'll see how the Common Dialog control works in this chapter.

Figure 10-1
The Toolbox of intrinsic controls and a few of the custom controls available in the Standard Edition.

The Professional and Enterprise Editions of Visual Basic provide much larger collections of custom controls, as you can see in Figure 10-2. In any of the three editions, you can view a list of all the available custom controls by pulling down the Tools menu and choosing Custom Controls. (Alternatively, click the Toolbox with the right mouse button and choose

Custom Controls from the resulting pop-up menu.) The Custom Controls dialog box, shown in Figure 10-3, allows you to add or remove custom controls as you formulate the programming requirements of a particular application. When you do so, the Toolbox itself changes in size and shape to accommodate the controls you've selected for the program you're developing.

Figure 10-2

The expanded Toolbox of controls available in the Professional and Enterprise Editions.

All of the custom controls included in any of the Visual Basic editions are extensively documented in on-line help. You can find information about events, properties, and methods that apply to a selected control, as well as general instructions for using the control. Some custom controls are as easy to use as any of the intrinsic controls; others can be complex and detailed, almost like small programming environments in themselves.

The controls you've used in applications up to this point have all been *interactive* — that is, responsive to specific events that take place as the user makes selections and performs other operations in a program. By contrast, some controls present features that are available for use only in your program's code. These *static* controls are invisible at runtime and have no associated events that trigger automatic procedure calls as the user works in your application.

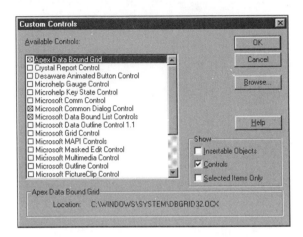

Figure 10-3
The Custom Controls dialog box.

One example of such a static object is the custom tool known as the common dialog control. You'll explore the use of this control in this chapter's application example, the Transportation Planner program. The program is designed to help you record information about the various modes of transportation you might use on a multistop business trip or vacation. For trips by plane, train, bus, or car, the Transportation Planner program helps you keep track of travel reservations and schedules. You can use the program to create any number of itinerary databases on disk. As you'll see shortly, the program's file-handling interface is provided by the common dialog control.

The Transportation Planner Program

The project's name on the disk is TranPlan.VBP. When you open it, you'll see that the application consists of one form, TranPlan.Frm, and one module, TranPlan.Bas. Before you run the program for the first time, open the form in design mode to take a look at the controls it contains.

As in Figure 10-4, you can see an assortment of controls representing the various fields of a single transportation record; you'll examine these controls in detail shortly. For now, take a close look at the small, perhaps unfamiliar, control located at the right side of the form, beneath the check boxes labeled Reserved and Paid. This is the common dialog control. Although it has no associated events and offers no direct interaction with the user, its presence on the form gives the application access to Windows-style dialog boxes for opening and saving files.

Now press F5 or click the Start button on the toolbar to begin a performance of the program. In run mode, the common dialog control disappears completely from the dialog box, as you can see in Figure 10-5. Nonetheless, you'll experience the benefit of its presence as you explore the program's features.

The program's dialog box is designed to accept or display one complete transportation record. The fields of a record include the following:

- The transportation mode, which you indicate by selecting one of the four option buttons at the left side of the form — Air, Train, Bus, or Car. (If you select the Car option, you can also specify whether or not the car is a rental; this option is itself a separate field in the travel record.)

- The name of the airline, train line, bus line, or car rental agency

- The reservation status (reserved or not)

- The payment status (paid or not paid)

- The date of departure

- The time of departure

- The place where your trip begins

- The destination of the trip

- A set of notes, comments, reminders, plans, or ideas that you want to record about this particular segment of the trip

For example, Figure 10-6 shows a first record that has been entered into the application window. In this case, the record describes an airline flight that's been reserved and paid for in advance. Of the application's seven text boxes, six are designed to accept short text entries, but the seventh (at the bottom of the window) is a multiline box in which you can enter as many as 200 characters, or approximately 40 words.

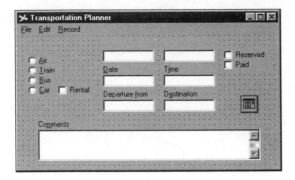

Figure 10-4

The Transportation Planner form in design mode, showing the common dialog control.

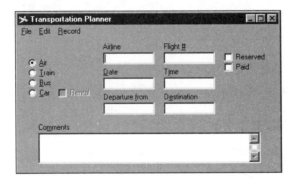

Figure 10-5

The Transportation Planner form in run mode.

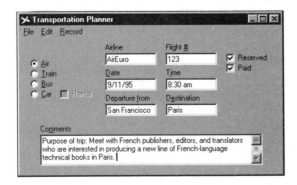

Figure 10-6

Entering a first travel record into the Transportation Planner window.

A transportation file that you create with this program may contain any number of individual travel records like this one. Together these records are meant to describe a complete itinerary — that is, all the segments of an upcoming business trip or vacation that you're planning.

The program allows you to enter one initial travel record for any trip without first specifying a file name under which to save the itinerary database. But to continue your work, you need to save the file to disk. As you might expect in this menu-driven application, the Save As command is located in the File menu. As indicated in Figure 10-7, you can invoke this command either by choosing it directly from the menu list or by pressing Ctrl+A at the keyboard. Either way, the Save As dialog box appears on the screen (Figure 10-8).

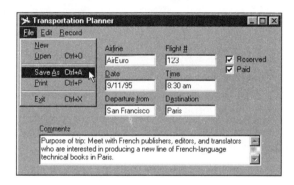

Figure 10-7
Choosing the Save As command from the File menu.

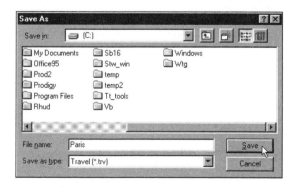

Figure 10-8
The Windows-style Save As dialog box.

Take a moment to examine the features of the Save As window. This dialog box is the same one that appears when you choose the Save As command in any other Windows 95 application. In the center of the window is a large box that shows the folders on your hard disk; when you begin creating travel files, this window will also list them. Above the file list you can see a variety of tools designed for navigating to different directories, creating new folders, or changing the way the file list is displayed. Beneath the file list is a text box in which you'll enter the name for the new file you're about to create. The Save as type box indicates the type of file that the program will create; as you can see, the Transportation Planner application automatically adds a TRV extension to any file name you enter.

There are other features to notice in the Save As dialog box. If you position the mouse pointer over certain objects in the box (in particular, the four buttons located above and to the right of the file list), a small ToolTip box appears, explaining the purpose of the object. For additional help, you can click the **?** button at the right side of the title bar and then click any other object in the window; a help box appears on the screen. All of these features are built-in elements of the Windows 95 Save As dialog box. The Transportation Planner application inherits the benefit of these features automatically through the services of the common dialog control.

To complete the Save operation, enter a name for the travel file you want to create and click the Save button. By default, the program saves TRV files in the root directory of your hard disk. When you complete the Save As operation, the program's dialog box returns to view. But now the title bar displays the name of the file you're creating and the record number of the travel segment currently displayed in the window; for example:

```
Transportation Planner -- C:\Paris.trv, #1
```

Now that you've saved your work as a TRV file, the program allows you to create new records and scroll from one record to the next. At the moment the file contains only the one record that you initially entered into the dialog box, but you can scroll one record further, to the blank record #2. To do so, pull down the Record menu and choose Next, or simply press the PgDn key at the keyboard. As you can see in

Figure 10-9, the program presents a blank set of controls, ready for you to enter the fields of the second travel record. To view the first record again, simply choose the Previous command from the Record menu, or press PgUp at the keyboard.

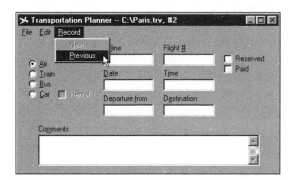

Figure 10-9

Preparing to scroll back to the first record in the file.

Figures 10-10, 10-11, and 10-12 show three additional records that have been entered into a travel file, each illustrating a different mode of transportation. If you examine these figures carefully, you'll see that the program makes a variety of small but important changes in the dialog box itself in response to your selection of a transportation mode. Most obviously, the labels displayed above the first two text boxes are adjusted to represent the travel mode selection. When you choose the Car option (Figure 10-12), the program activates the Rental check box, allowing you to specify whether or not you're planning to rent a car. If you check this box, the Rental Agency and Reservation number text boxes are available to accept your entries; if not, these fields are dimmed.

Each time you enter a new travel record and scroll forward (or backward) in your itinerary database, the program automatically saves the new record to the file on disk. Furthermore, you can scroll to an existing record in the file at any time and make changes in the information that the record contains. Again, when you scroll to a different record, the program automatically saves your revisions to disk. For this reason, the program doesn't provide a Save command for saving individual records. Whenever you create or open a travel file, the program makes sure that any new or revised records are saved to the file.

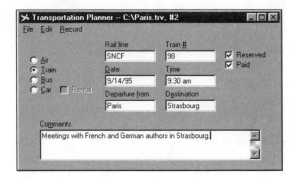

Figure 10-10

Traveling by train.

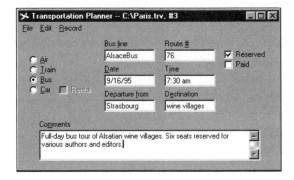

Figure 10-11

Traveling by bus.

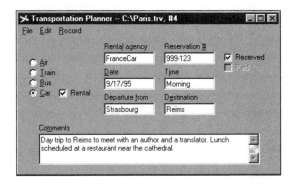

Figure 10-12

Traveling by car.

Over time, you may find yourself creating a number of TRV files to record the details of business trips or vacation travel. When each trip is over, these files remain on disk as a record of your travels. To review any existing file for a past or future trip, you can open the corresponding TRV file from disk and examine its records one by one. Simply pull down the program's File menu and choose the Open command. The Open dialog box appears on the screen, as shown in Figure 10-13. This window provides a list of all the TRV files you've created. (By default the program shows the contents of the root directory of your hard disk.) To open a file, choose its name in the list and click Open. Then, back in the program's main dialog box, choose the Previous command (or press PgUp repeatedly) to scroll back through the existing records in the file you've opened. Of course, you're always free to revise existing records or add new records to the file.

Figure 10-13
The Open dialog box.

Like the Save As window, the Open dialog box is the same as the one used for all standard Windows 95 applications. Thanks to the common dialog control, you don't have to redesign these dialog boxes for each application you create; rather, you can incorporate them automatically into the operations of your program, and take advantage of all their built-in features.

As in many applications, the Save As command has two possible uses. The first, as you've seen, is to create a new file on disk to save a new set of travel records that you're planning to enter. But you can also use Save As to create a *duplicate* file containing the same records as a file you've already created and opened. Consider this scenario: You and a colleague are planning a sales trip to Europe. You're traveling together to France, but then you're planning to split up and proceed in different directions. The first several records in your itinerary files will therefore be identical, but the remaining records will be different. Here are the steps you might take to create the two travel files for yourself and your colleague:

1. Start the Transportation Planner program and enter the first travel record.

2. Choose the Save As command and create a file for your own itinerary records.

3. Continue entering travel records up until the point where your own travel plans diverge from your colleague's.

4. Choose the Save As command again, but this time enter a different file name to create your colleague's travel file, as in Figure 10-14. When you complete the Save operation, there will be two travel files on disk — your file and your colleague's file — containing the same set of travel records.

5. Continue developing each of the travel files independently, entering the remaining records for each trip.

Figure 10-14

Using the Save As command to create a duplicate of an existing travel file.

The Save As dialog box will also enable you to overwrite an existing TRV file. If you do so, the information in the original file will be replaced by the new records you're storing under the existing name. To avoid any inadvertant loss of data, the Save As dialog box displays a warning dialog box on the screen and asks you to confirm that you really want to replace an existing file (Figure 10-15). Again, this warning box is a built-in feature of the Save As dialog box; when you examine the code of the Transportation Planner application, you'll see exactly how this warning is produced.

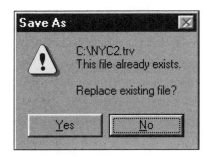

Figure 10-15
A warning box for replacing an existing file.

The menus of the Transportation Planner program contain several other useful commands. For example, you can clear the contents of any record by pulling down the Edit menu and choosing Clear. Alternatively, you can close the current Travel file completely — and then start again with a new file of travel records if you want — by choosing the New command from the File menu. By the way, you might notice a couple of apparent conflicts among the shortcut keys defined for menus and controls in the Transportation Planner window: The File menu and the "Departure from" text box both use Alt+F, and the Edit menu and the Destination text box both use Alt+E. You can work around these conflicts by using Alt,F and Alt,E to pull down the menus (that is, press the Alt key, release it, and then press the shortcut key) and Alt+F and Alt+E to activate the text box controls (press Alt and the shortcut key concurrently).

Finally, you can use the Print command to produce a printed copy of all the records in any travel file. Begin by opening the file you want to print. Turn on your printer and then pull down the File menu and choose Print (Figure 10-16).

III

10

Figure 10-16
Printing the records of a travel file.

The program prints formatted copies of each record in the file, as in the following example:

```
Airline -- AirEuro
     #123

     Date:     9/11/95
     Time:     8:30 am
     From:     San Francisco
     To:       Paris

     Reserved: Yes
     Paid:     Yes

     Comments:
     Purpose of trip: Meet with French
     publishers, editors, and translators
     who are interested in producing a new
     line of French-language technical books
     in Paris.


Train Line -- SNCF
     #98

     Date:     9/14/95
     Time:     9:30 am
     From:     Paris
     To:       Strasbourg
```

```
Reserved: Yes
Paid:     Yes

Comments:
Meetings with French and German authors
in Strasbourg.


Bus Line -- AlsaceBus
    #76

    Date:     9/16/95
    Time:     7:30 am
    From:     Strasbourg
    To:       wine villages

    Reserved: Yes
    Paid:     No

    Comments:
    Full-day bus tour of Alsatian wine
    villages. Six seats reserved for
    various authors and editors.


Car Rental Agency -- FranceCar
    #999-123

    Date:     9/17/95
    Time:     Morning
    From:     Strasbourg
    To:       Reims


    Comments:
    Day trip to Reims to meet with an
    author and a translator. Lunch
    scheduled at a restaurant near the
    cathedral.
```

III

10

```
Airline -- AirEuro
      #234

    Date:      9/18/95
    Time:      11:30 am
    From:      Strasbourg
    To:        London

    Reserved: Yes
    Paid:      Yes

    Comments:
    Stop in London on the way home.
```

As you now turn to the program's code, you'll focus particularly on the use of the common dialog control, and then on the procedures that perform printing operations.

Inside the Transportation Planner Program

The program's code is shown in Listings 10-1 through 10-15 at the end of this chapter. Here is an overview of the code.

The TranPlan.BAS module, shown at the top of Listing 10-1, defines the structure of the travel records that this program works with:

```
Type TranRecType
   TranMode As Integer
   RentalCar As Boolean
   Carrier As String * 30
   TripNumber As String * 30
   ReservedStatus As Boolean
   PaidStatus As Boolean
   TripDate As String * 30
   TripTime As String * 30
   TripFrom As String * 30
   TripTo As String * 30
   Comments As String * 200
End Type
```

In the module's Type statement, you can see field definitions for each of the data items in the application window. Notice that the transportation mode (*TranMode*) is represented as an integer. The three check boxes (*RentalCar, ReservedStatus,* and *PaidStatus*) are Boolean values. The remaining fields are fixed-length strings, including the *Comments* field, which accommodates entries as long as 200 characters.

Listing 10-1 also contains the general declarations section of the program's only form, TranPlan.FRM. This section declares a record variable named *TranRecord*, belonging to the *TranRecType* record type. In addition, the program declares several module-level variables that keep track of essential conditions and data items during a program run:

```
Dim TranRecord As TranRecType
Dim tranFileOpen As Boolean
Dim tranFileName As String
Dim curTranRecord As Integer
Dim titleBarText As String
Dim recordChanged As Boolean
```

The Boolean variables *tranFileOpen* and *recordChanged* are among the most important; the first of these indicates whether a Travel file is currently open, and the second keeps track of whether the current record has been changed. The program uses these variables in many contexts to decide how to respond to the user's actions. In addition, *curTranRecord* is an integer that represents the number of the current record. The variables *tranFileName* and *titleBarText* keep track of the name of the open file and the caption displayed on the progam's title bar, respectively. Several of these variables are initialized in the program's Form_Load procedure, also in Listing 10-1.

Listings 10-2 and 10-3 contain a variety of procedures devoted to the tasks of creating a new travel file or a duplicate of an existing file. First, the mnuSaveAs_Click procedure (Listing 10-2) takes charge when the user chooses the Save As command. This procedure illustrates the essential characteristics of the common dialog control, which is employed here to display the Save As dialog box. Then several related procedures play important roles in the process of saving or copying a travel database. You'll have an opportunity to examine these procedures later in this chapter.

III

10

Conversely, the mnuOpen_Click procedure (Listing 10-4) responds when the user invokes the Open command. Like mnuSaveAs_Click, this event procedure uses the common dialog control and a variety of general procedures (Listing 10-5) to complete its task.

The mnuNext_Click and mnuPrevious_Click routines appear in Listing 10-6. These are the event procedures that allow the user to scroll through the records of an open travel database. In Listing 10-7, the Form_KeyDown procedure (versions of which you've seen in other applications) allows the user to press PgUp or PgDn at the keyboard as an alternative to choosing the Previous or Next command. Once the program has read the next or previous record from the database on disk (a task performed in the mnuNext_Click or mnuPrevious_Click procedure), the *ShowRecord* procedure (Listing 10-8) is called to display the new record in the application window.

When the user chooses the Print command from the File menu, the event procedure named mnuPrint_Click (Listing 10-9) takes charge of printing each record of the current file, from beginning to end. This procedure reads each record in turn and then calls the *PrintRecord* procedure (Listing 10-10) to carry out the printing operation. As you'll see later in this chapter, the *PrintRecord* procedure illustrates the use of Visual Basic's important Printer object. The *PrintComments* procedure (Listing 10-11) carries out the somewhat complex task of dividing the *Comments* field into manageable lines of printed output.

The remaining procedures contain a variety of event procedures, designed to respond to menu commands or to the user's activities in the dialog box itself. For example, the mnuNew_Click procedure (Listing 10-12) closes the current file and prepares the dialog box for the possible creation of a new database. The Click procedures in Listings 10-13 and 10-14 keep track of any changes in the travel mode option buttons or the application's three check boxes. And a sequence of Change event procedures in Listing 10-15 allow the program to keep track of whether the user has modified the current record.

Among the program's most interesting techniques are the two different uses it makes of the common dialog control. You'll learn about this control in the next section.

USING THE COMMON DIALOG CONTROL

To use the common dialog control in an application, you begin by placing an instance of the object on a form. As with any other control, you can accomplish this task by opening the form and double-clicking the appropriate button in the Toolbox.

Because this control isn't visible at runtime, its precise location is unimportant; you can drag it to any out-of-the-way corner of your form. Unlike most controls, the common dialog icon can't be resized, but its presence on your form at design time serves to remind you that the considerable resources of this control are available to your program.

As you'll see shortly, the common dialog control has several important properties. Some of these you'll want to set at design time; others, in your program's code. To ensure that you can identify the control consistently in your code, the first property you should assign is Name. (Select the control, press F4 to open the Properties window, scroll to the Name property, and enter a name for the control.) In the Transportation Planner application, the common dialog control is named cdlFileManager.

The control has several associated methods, each designed to display and activate one of the standard Windows dialog boxes. These methods include ShowPrint, ShowColor, ShowFont, ShowOpen, and ShowSave. (An additional method, ShowHelp, is available to invoke the Windows on-line Help facility.) To open a particular dialog box, you simple make a call to one of these methods in your code. For example, the following call appears in the mnuSaveAs_Click procedure (Listing 10-2):

```
cdlFileManager.ShowSave
```

And this call is in the mnuOpen_Click procedure (Listing 10-4):

```
cdlFileManager.ShowOpen
```

During a program run, these calls give the user access to the Save As and Open dialog boxes, respectively.

III

10

Setting the Properties of the Common Dialog Control

Among the properties available for the common dialog control, certain settings apply specifically to particular Windows dialog boxes. For example, the following five properties have important meanings for the Save As and Open dialog boxes, invoked by the ShowSave and ShowOpen methods:

- The InitDir property designates the directory that will be displayed when the Save As or Open dialog box first appears on the screen. In the Transportation Planner program, this property has a setting of \ so that the dialog boxes will initially show the contents of the root directory on your hard disk.

- The DefaultExt property provides a default extension for file names entered into the Save As dialog box. For example, the setting of *trv* provides the default extension name for files created from the Transportation Planner program.

- The Filter property determines the types of files that will be displayed in the Open and Save As dialog box. A filter setting includes a file-type description and a file name extension, in the form *description* | *extension*. (Notice that the two parts of this definition are separated by the vertical line character, |, sometimes known as the *pipe symbol*.) The Filter property setting in the Transportation Planner program is Travel *(*.trv)* | **.trv*. You can see the results of this setting back in Figures 10-8 and 10-13. The "Files of type" box displays the text *Travel (*.trv),* and the file list (in Figure 10-13) includes only those files that have TRV extensions.

- The CancelError property is a Boolean setting that indicates whether an error will be generated when the user clicks the Cancel button on a Windows dialog box. When you assign a value of True to this property, your program can read the resulting error as a signal that the Cancel button has been clicked; in response, your program should be prepared to skip the subsequent file operation. You'll see exactly how the Transportation Planner program makes use of this property a little later in this chapter.

- The MaxFileSize property is an integer setting that specifies the maximum *name* length, in characters, of a file you can open or save from one of the Windows dialog boxes. (The setting applies to the length of the path name and the file name together.) In the Transportation Planner application, this property has a fairly low setting of 20, allowing the program to display the entire file name and path in the title bar. But this setting may restrict not only the length of the file names you devise, but also the directory locations in which you can save your transportation files. If you don't like these restrictions, enter a larger setting for the MaxFileSize property. (The default setting is 256.)

As always, you can enter settings for these and other properties directly into the Properties window. But Visual Basic provides a convenient alternative for working with the properties of many custom controls, including the common dialog control. When you open the Properties window, an entry identified as "(Custom)" appears near the top of the list, as shown in Figure 10-17. Select this entry and click the small button that appears at the right side of the settings box. In response, Visual Basic displays the Common Dialogs Control Properties box (Figure 10-18). This tabbed dialog box gives you a quick way to set the properties for any of the functional categories of this control.

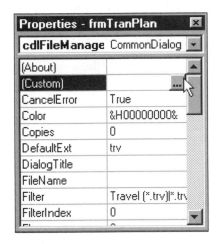

Figure 10-17
The Properties window for the common dialog control.

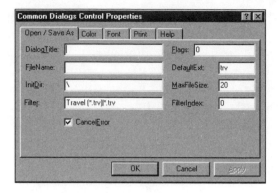

Figure 10-18
A convenient window for setting the common dialog properties.

One additional property, named Flags, is essential for defining the behavior and characteristics of the dialog boxes for a particular application. You'll learn about the Flags property next.

Working with the Common Dialog Control in Code

In both the mnuSaveAs_Click and mnuOpen_Click procedures, the use of the common dialog control requires three main steps:

1. Setting the Flags property to establish the characteristics of the Save As or Open dialog box.

2. Calling the ShowSave or ShowOpen method within the control of an error trap. (If the user clicks the Cancel button on the resulting dialog box, the error trap allows the procedure to avoid any further action.)

3. Reading the value of the FileName property to find out the name of the file that the user has entered or selected in the dialog box.

The Flags property is the key to ensuring that a Windows dialog box will work just the way you want it to in a particular application. For example, in the Transportation Planner program, the Save As dialog box provides a warning message if the user selects an existing file name. Look back at Figure 10-15 to review this feature. The warning is a result of a specific setting of the Flags property.

Visual Basic defines a variety of flags for each Windows dialog box. (To view a list of all the settings available for the Flags property, search for the Flags topic in the Visual Basic Help window.) The setting that produces an *existing file* warning message in the Save As dialog box is a flag named cdlOFNOverwritePrompt. This is one of four flags that the mnuSaveAs_Click procedure uses:

```
cdlFileManager.Flags = cdlOFNOverwritePrompt Or _
                       cdlOFNHideReadOnly Or _
                       cdlOFNNoChangeDir Or _
                       cdlOFNPathMustExist
```

The other three flags specify a variety of characteristics: omitting the Read Only check box (cdlOFNHideReadOnly); ensuring a consistent directory location for the save operation (cdlOFNNoChangeDir); and validating the directory path (cdlOFNPathMustExist).

The mnuOpen_Click procedure uses a slightly different set of flags to specify the behavior of the Open dialog box:

```
cdlFileManager.Flags = cdlOFNFileMustExist Or _
                       cdlOFNHideReadOnly Or _
                       cdlOFNNoChangeDir Or _
                       cdlOFNPathMustExist
```

The first of these flags, cdlOFNFileMustExist, prevents an attempt to open a nonexistent file; if the user enters a file name that can't be found on disk, the Open dialog box displays an error message. The other three flags are the same as those used for the Save As dialog box.

After setting the Flags property, each event procedure is ready to make a call to the appropriate common dialog method, ShowSave or ShowOpen. Thanks to the True setting assigned to the CancelError property, the method generates an error if the user clicks the Cancel button. To recognize this error, each method is called within an error trap. For example, here is how the mnuSaveAs_Click procedure calls the ShowSave method:

```
On Error GoTo userCancel
   cdlFileManager.ShowSave
On Error GoTo 0
```

III

10

If the error occurs — that is, if the user clicks Cancel instead of Save on the dialog box — the On Error GoTo statement arranges to send control to the *userCancel* label, located at the very end of the procedure:

```
userCancel:

End Sub   ' mnuSaveAs_Click
```

In this way, the action of the procedure is skipped completely if the user decides to cancel the Save As operation.

But if the user enters a valid file name and clicks Save, the procedure's next step is to find out the name of the file. As you might expect, a common dialog property named FileName supplies this essential piece of information:

```
newFileName = cdlFileManager.FileName
```

Eliciting this file name from the user is the whole purpose of the Save As or Open dialog box. Once the name is available, the program continues with the file operation, either creating a new travel database on disk or opening an existing database. You can continue exploring the mnuSaveAs_Click and mnuOpen_Click procedures to see exactly how these tasks are carried out.

Common dialog is only one of many custom controls that you might decide to incorporate into the applications you design. Each custom control has specific properties, methods, and events that you need to learn about in detail before you can use the object successfully. In Part IV you'll experiment with some additional examples of custom controls.

The Transportation Planner application illustrates a variety of other programming techniques that are worth exploring. Among these is the use of the Printer object to produce a printed copy of the current travel file. You'll take a look at the printing procedures in the final section of this chapter.

USING THE PRINTER OBJECT

The Printer object represents the system printer in a Visual Basic application. Using the various properties and methods defined for this object, you can prepare a document for printing. Then your program makes a call to a method named EndDoc to release your document to the printer.

In the Transportation Planner application, the mnuPrint_Click procedure (Listing 10-9) is designed to print all the records of the current travel database. Assuming a file is open, the procedure reads each record from the beginning to the end of the file, and calls a procedure named *PrintRecord* to carry out the printing:

```
For i = 1 To FindRecordCount
   Get #1, i, TranRecord
   PrintRecord
Next i
```

The PrintRecord in turn uses the Print method to send individual lines of text to the Printer object, as in the following example:

```
Printer.Print
Printer.Print Tab(t1); "Date:";
Printer.Print Tab(t2); .TripDate
Printer.Print Tab(t1); "Time:";
Printer.Print Tab(t2); .TripTime
Printer.Print Tab(t1); "From:";
Printer.Print Tab(t2); .TripFrom
Printer.Print Tab(t1); "To:";
Printer.Print Tab(t2); .TripTo
Printer.Print
```

Notice the various formats of the Print method. The Tab function allows you to specify where the horizontal position of the line will begin. A semicolon separates one element from the next in the list of values that will be printed. If a call to the Print method ends in a semicolon, the line-feed/carriage-return is suppressed; as a result, the *next* Print method sends information to the same line of text. Finally, a Printer.Print statement by itself results in a blank line.

When all the records have been sent to the Printer object, the mnuPrint_Click procedure makes a call to the EndDoc method to release the document to the printer:

```
Printer.EndDoc
```

The Print and EndDoc methods are only two of a dozen methods associated with the Printer object. Other methods are available for a variety of printing operations, including graphic output and document formatting. You can explore these methods by searching for the Printer Object topic in the Visual Basic Help window and then clicking Methods in the resulting Help page.

In its current version, the Transportation Planner application prints the records of the current travel database just as soon as the user chooses the Print command from the File menu. An intervening Print dialog box would give the user much greater control over the process. As a hands-on programming exercise with this project, you might therefore consider using the common dialog control to display a Print dialog box before the program goes forward with the printing procedure.

Listing 10-1
General declarations for TranPlan.Bas and TranPlan.Frm, along with the Form_Load procedure

```
' The Transportation Planner program.
' -----------------------------------

' Module File:    TranPlan.BAS

' The structure of transportation records.
Type TranRecType
   TranMode As Integer
   RentalCar As Boolean
   Carrier As String * 30
   TripNumber As String * 30
   ReservedStatus As Boolean
   PaidStatus As Boolean
   TripDate As String * 30
   TripTime As String * 30
```

```
      TripFrom As String * 30
      TripTo As String * 30
      Comments As String * 200
   End Type


   ' End of TranPlan.Bas module file.




   ' The Transportation Planner program.
   ' ------------------------------------


   ' Files:
   ' Project File:   TranPlan.VBP
   ' Form File:      TranPlan.FRM
   ' Module File:    TranPlan.BAS


   ' This menu-driven program allows the user to
   ' create itinerary files on disk. Each random-
   ' access file contains records describing the
   ' transportation plans and reservations for an
   ' upcoming business trip or vacation. Files are
   ' stored on disk with TRV extension names. The
   ' user can open any file, browse through records
   ' in the file, revise records, or add new records.


   ' The program illustrates the use of Visual Basic's
   ' Custom Dialog control. This control provides
   ' easy access to standard Windows dialog boxes,
   ' including the Save As and Open dialog boxes, as
   ' shown in this application.
```

The record variable for a transportation record

```
   Option Explicit

   ' Variables for this form.
   Dim TranRecord As TranRecType ' A single record.
   Dim tranFileOpen As Boolean    ' Is a file open?
   Dim tranFileName As String     ' Name of open file.
   Dim curTranRecord As Integer   ' Current record number.
   Dim titleBarText As String     ' Title bar text.
   Dim recordChanged As Boolean   ' Has record changed?
```

```
' End of general declarations for TranPlan.Frm.



Private Sub Form_Load()

    ' The Form_Load procedure initializes a few
    ' of the program's variables and control
    ' properties.

    ' No file is open yet.
    tranFileOpen = False
    recordChanged = False

    ' Set the record pointer to 1.
    curTranRecord = 1

    ' Disable the Next and Previous
    ' commands.
    mnuNext.Enabled = False
    mnuPrevious.Enabled = False

End Sub   ' Form_Load
```

Listing 10-2
The mnuSaveAs_Click and CopyDatabase procedures

```
Private Sub mnuSaveAs_Click()

    ' The mnuSaveAs_Click procedure takes control when
    ' the user clicks the Save As command, and gives
    ' the user the opportunity to create a new file.

    Dim newFileName As String

    ' Set the Flags property of the Save As
    ' dialog box.
```

```
cdlFileManager.Flags = cdlOFNOverwritePrompt Or _
                       cdlOFNHideReadOnly Or _
                       cdlOFNNoChangeDir Or _
                       cdlOFNPathMustExist
```

Setting the flags for the Save As dialog box

```
' If the user clicks Cancel on the Save
' dialog box, the ShowSave method generates
' an error. In this case, exit from this
' procedure.
On Error GoTo userCancel
   cdlFileManager.ShowSave
On Error GoTo 0
```

A call to the ShowSave method to display the Save As dialog box

```
' Record the file name
' that the user has entered.
newFileName = cdlFileManager.filename
```

Reading the user's file request in the FileName property of the Common dialog control

```
' If a file is currently open, save its
' final record and then copy its records
' to the new "save as" file.
If tranFileOpen Then
  If recordChanged Then SaveCurRec
  Close
  CopyDatabase newFileName, tranFileName
Else
' Otherwise, if no file is open, check
' to see if the "save as" file currently
' exists on disk; if it does, delete it.
  tranFileName = newFileName
  On Error Resume Next
    Kill tranFileName
  On Error GoTo 0

  ' Open the new file and save the current
  ' entry as its first record.
  Open tranFileName For Random As #1 _
    Len = Len(TranRecord)
  If recordChanged Then
    SaveCurRec
    mnuNext.Enabled = True
  End If
End If
```

III

10

```
            tranFileOpen = True
            recordChanged = False

            ' Prepare to display a new caption
            ' in the program's title bar.
            titleBarText = _
              "Transportation Planner -- " & _
              tranFileName

            ' Display the file name and record number
            ' on the form's title bar.
            frmTranPlan.Caption = titleBarText & _
              ", #" & curTranRecord

        ' Terminate the procedure if the user
        ' has clicked the Cancel button.
        userCancel:

        End Sub   ' mnuSaveAs_Click



        Private Sub CopyDatabase _
          (toFile As String, fromFile As String)

            ' The CopyDatabase procedure copies the records
            ' of the current transportation file to a new
            ' file, in response to the user's instructions
            ' in the Save As command.

            Dim i As Long

            ' If the destination file already exists,
            ' delete it from disk. (Note that the Save As
            ' dialog box provides a warning if the user
            ' chooses an existing file; the Save As
            ' operation continues only if the user confirms.)
            On Error Resume Next
              Kill toFile
            On Error GoTo 0
```

```
' Open the two files.
Open toFile For Random As #1 _
   Len = Len(TranRecord)
Open fromFile For Random As #2 _
   Len = Len(TranRecord)

' Copy all the records from the source file
' to the destination file.
For i = 1 To LOF(2) / Len(TranRecord)
   Get #2, i, TranRecord
   Put #1, i, TranRecord
Next i

' Close the source file. The destination
' file becomes the current tranporation
' database.
Close #2
tranFileName = toFile

End Sub  ' CopyDatabase
```

Listing 10-3
The SaveCurRec and MakeTranRecord procedures

```
Private Sub SaveCurRec()

   ' The SaveCurRec procedure writes the current
   ' transportation record to its correct position
   ' in the open file.

   ' Copy the user's input to the
   ' TranRecord structure.
MakeTranRecord

   ' Write the record to the file. The variable
   ' curTranRecord keeps track of the current
   ' record position.
Put #1, curTranRecord, TranRecord
recordChanged = False
```

III

10

```
End Sub   ' SaveCurRec



Private Sub MakeTranRecord()

  ' The MakeTranRecord procedure copies the
  ' user's entries for the current transportation
  ' record to the TranRecord structure.
  ' Note that the TranRecType is defined in
  ' the TranPlan.Bas module, and TranRecord
  ' is declared in the general declarations section
  ' of this form.

  Dim i

  With TranRecord


    ' Determine which of the four optMode
    ' buttons is currently selected.
    For i = 0 To 3
      If optMode(i).VALUE Then
        .TranMode = i
      End If
    Next i

    ' If the selection is Car, read the
    ' value of the chkRental check box.
    If .TranMode = 3 Then
      If chkRental.VALUE = 0 Then
        .RentalCar = False
      Else
        .RentalCar = True
      End If
    End If

    ' Read the first two text boxes.
    .Carrier = txtCarrier.TEXT
    .TripNumber = txtTripNumber.TEXT
```

Using a With structure to simplify field references

```
' Read the values of the Reserved
' and Paid check boxes.
If chkReserved.VALUE = 0 Then
  .ReservedStatus = False
Else
  .ReservedStatus = True
End If

If chkPaid.VALUE = 0 Then
  .PaidStatus = False
Else
  .PaidStatus = True
End If

' Read the remaining text boxes.
.TripDate = txtDate.TEXT
.TripTime = txtTime.TEXT
.TripFrom = txtFrom.TEXT
.TripTo = txtTo.TEXT

.Comments = txtNotes.TEXT

End With

End Sub   ' MakeTranRecord
```

Listing 10-4
The mnuOpen_Click procedure

```
Private Sub mnuOpen_Click()

  ' The mnuOpen_Click procedure allows the user
  ' to open an existing TRV file from disk. Once
  ' the file is open, the user can browse through
  ' its records, revise any record, or add new
  ' records.

  ' If a file is already open, begin by saving
  ' the current record to disk if necessary.
```

```
If tranFileOpen And recordChanged Then _
  SaveCurRec
recordChanged = False

' Set the Flags property of the Open dialog box.
cdlFileManager.Flags = cdlOFNFileMustExist Or _
                       cdlOFNHideReadOnly Or _
                       cdlOFNNoChangeDir Or _
                       cdlOFNPathMustExist
```

Setting the flags for the Open dialog box

```
' Use the ShowOpen method to display the Open
' dialog box. An error trap allows for the
' possibility that the user will click the
' Cancel button. In this case, terminate the
' procedure by jumping to the userCancel label.
On Error GoTo userCancel
  cdlFileManager.ShowOpen
On Error GoTo 0
Close
```

A call to the ShowOpen method to display the Open dialog box

```
' Record the file name
' that the user has entered.
tranFileName = cdlFileManager.filename
```

Reading the user's file request in the FileName property

```
' Prepare a new caption for the
' program's title bar.
titleBarText = _
  "Transportation Planner -- " & _
  tranFileName

' Open the file and switch
' tranFileOpen to true.
Open tranFileName For Random As #1 _
  Len = Len(TranRecord)
tranFileOpen = True

' Prepare to append a new record to
' the end of the file.
BlankEOFRecord
```

```
' If the file contains more than one record,
' enable the Previous command so that the user
' can scroll backward throught the records.
If curTranRecord > 1 Then _
   mnuPrevious.Enabled = True

' Display the new caption in the title bar.
frmTranPlan.Caption = titleBarText & _
   ", #" & curTranRecord

' Terminate the procedure if the
' user clicks the Cancel button.
userCancel:

End Sub   ' mnuOpen_Click
```

Listing 10-5
The BlankEOFRecord, FindRecordCount, and mnuClear_Click procedures

```
Private Sub BlankEOFRecord()

   ' This procedure moves the record pointer
   ' one position past the end of the current
   ' file, in preparation for a new record entry.

   curTranRecord = FindRecordCount + 1
   mnuClear_Click
   recordChanged = False

   ' Disable the Next command until the
   ' user makes an entry into this new record.
   mnuNext.Enabled = False

End Sub   ' BlankEOFRecord
```

```
Private Function FindRecordCount()

   ' The FindRecordCount function determines
   ' the number of records in the current
   ' transportation file. Note that this
   ' function is called only if a file is open.

   FindRecordCount = LOF(1) / Len(TranRecord)

End Function   ' FindRecordCount



Private Sub mnuClear_Click()

   ' The mnuClear_Click procedure clears the
   ' entries from all the controls in the
   ' Transportation Planner form, preparing
   ' for a new record entry.

   optMode(0).VALUE = True
   txtCarrier.TEXT = ""
   txtTripNumber.TEXT = ""
   chkReserved.VALUE = 0
   chkPaid.VALUE = 0
   txtDate.TEXT = ""
   txtTime.TEXT = ""
   txtFrom.TEXT = ""
   txtTo.TEXT = ""
   txtNotes.TEXT = ""

   txtCarrier.SetFocus

End Sub   ' mnuClear_Click
```

Listing 10-6
The mnuNext_Click and mnuPrevious_Click procedures

```
Private Sub mnuNext_Click()

    ' The mnuNext_Click procedure scrolls to the
    ' next transportation record in the current file.
    ' (The Next command is disabled if no file is open;
    ' it is also unavailable if the record pointer is
    ' past the end of the file.)

    ' First save the current record
    ' if necessary.
    If recordChanged Then SaveCurRec

    ' If the current record is the end of
    ' the file, prepare to accept a new
    ' record from the user.
    If curTranRecord = FindRecordCount Then
        BlankEOFRecord

    ' Otherwise, read and display the
    ' next record in the file.
    Else
        curTranRecord = curTranRecord + 1
        Get #1, curTranRecord, TranRecord
        ShowRecord
        recordChanged = False
    End If

    ' Display the file name and the record
    ' number in the form's title bar.
    frmTranPlan.Caption = titleBarText & _
        ", #" & curTranRecord

    ' Enable the Previous command, so the user
    ' can now scroll backward through the file.
    mnuPrevious.Enabled = True

End Sub  ' mnuNext_Click
```

Saves the current record before scrolling to a new one

Presents blank fields for a new record if this is the end of the file

III

10

```
Private Sub mnuPrevious_Click()

  ' The mnuPrevious_Click procedure scrolls one
  ' record back in the current file. Note that
  ' the Previous command is disabled until a file
  ' is open and the program determines that the
  ' file contains more than one record.

  ' First save the current record if necessary.
  If recordChanged Then SaveCurRec

  ' Decrease the value of the record pointer
  ' (curTranRecord) by 1, and read the
  ' corresponding record from the file. Then
  ' display the record in the form.
  curTranRecord = curTranRecord - 1
  Get #1, curTranRecord, TranRecord
  ShowRecord
  recordChanged = False

  ' Display the file name and the record number
  ' in the form's title bar.
  frmTranPlan.Caption = titleBarText & _
    ", #" & curTranRecord

  ' Enable the Next command.
  ' If the user has scrolled back to the first
  ' record in the file, disable the Previous command.
  mnuNext.Enabled = True
  If curTranRecord = 1 Then _
    mnuPrevious.Enabled = False

End Sub  ' mnuPrevious_Click
```

Listing 10-7

The Form_KeyDown procedure

```
Private Sub Form_KeyDown(KeyCode As Integer, _
  Shift As Integer)

  ' The Form_KeyDown procedure allows the user
  ' to press PgDn or PgUp to scroll through the
  ' records of an open transportation file.

  ' *** Note that the form's KeyPreview property
  '     is set to True to make this event possible.

  ' Code numbers for the
  ' PgDn and PgUp keys.
  Const PgDn = 34
  Const PgUp = 33

  ' If the user presses PgDn and the Next
  ' command is currently enabled, force a call
  ' to the mnuNext_Click event procedure.
  If KeyCode = PgDn _
    And mnuNext.Enabled = True _
      Then mnuNext_Click

  ' If the user presses PgUp and the Previous
  ' command is currently enabled, force a call
  ' to the mnuPrevious_Click event procedure.
  If KeyCode = PgUp _
    And mnuPrevious.Enabled = True _
      Then mnuPrevious_Click

End Sub   ' Form_KeyDown
```

III

10

Listing 10-8
The ShowRecord procedure

```
Private Sub ShowRecord()

   ' The ShowRecord procedure displays the fields
   ' of the current record in an open file. Before
   ' calling this procedure, the program always
   ' reads a record from the open file into the
   ' TranRecord structure.

   With TranRecord

     ' Set the transportation selection.
     optMode(.TranMode).VALUE = True

     ' If the Car option is selected,
     ' set the value of the Rental check box.
     If .TranMode = 3 Then
       If .RentalCar Then
         chkRental.VALUE = 1
       Else
         chkRental.VALUE = 0
       End If
     End If

     ' Read the remaining fields and
     ' set the corresponding controls
     ' appropriately.
     txtCarrier.TEXT = Trim(.Carrier)
     txtTripNumber.TEXT = Trim(.TripNumber)

     If .ReservedStatus Then
       chkReserved.VALUE = 1
     Else
       chkReserved.VALUE = 0
     End If

     If .PaidStatus Then
       chkPaid.VALUE = 1
```

```
      Else
        chkPaid.VALUE = 0
      End If

      txtDate.TEXT = Trim(.TripDate)
      txtTime.TEXT = Trim(.TripTime)
      txtFrom.TEXT = Trim(.TripFrom)
      txtTo.TEXT = Trim(.TripTo)

      txtNotes.TEXT = Trim(.Comments)

   End With

End Sub   ' ShowRecord
```

Listing 10-9
The mnuPrint_Click procedure

```
Private Sub mnuPrint_Click()

   ' The mnuPrint_Click procedure prints one or
   ' more transportation records when the user
   ' chooses the Print command.

   Dim i As Long

   ' If a file is open, print all the records
   ' in the file, from beginning to end.
   If tranFileOpen Then

      ' Begin by saving the current record to
      ' the file if necessary.
      If recordChanged Then SaveCurRec
      recordChanged = False

      ' Print each record in turn.
      For i = 1 To FindRecordCount
        Get #1, i, TranRecord
        PrintRecord
      Next i
```

Reads each record and sends it to the printer

```
         ' If no file is open, just print the
         ' current contents of the form.
         Else
           MakeTranRecord
           PrintRecord
         End If

         ' Complete the output process.
         Printer.EndDoc

     End Sub   ' mnuPrint_Click
```

Listing 10-10

The PrintRecord procedure

```
     Private Sub PrintRecord()

         ' The PrintRecord procedure uses the
         ' Printer.Print method to send the fields of
         ' the current record to the printer. The current
         ' record is stored in the TranRecord structure.

         Const t1 = 5    ' First tab stop.
         Const t2 = 15   ' Second tab stop.

         With TranRecord

           ' Print the transportation mode.
           Select Case .TranMode
             Case 0
               Printer.Print "Airline -- ";
             Case 1
               Printer.Print "Train Line -- ";

             Case 2
               Printer.Print "Bus Line -- ";

             Case 3
               If .RentalCar Then
```

```
      Printer.Print "Car Rental Agency -- ";
    Else
      Printer.Print "Private Car"
    End If
End Select

' Print the Carrier and TripNumber fields.
If .TranMode < 3 Then
  Printer.Print .Carrier
  Printer.Print Tab(t1); " #"; .TripNumber
Else
  If .RentalCar Then
    Printer.Print .Carrier;
    If .ReservedStatus Then
      Printer.Print Tab(t1); " #"; .TripNumber
    Else
      Printer.Print
    End If
  End If
End If

' Print the date, time, starting point,
' and destination.
Printer.Print
Printer.Print Tab(t1); "Date:";
Printer.Print Tab(t2); .TripDate
Printer.Print Tab(t1); "Time:";
Printer.Print Tab(t2); .TripTime
Printer.Print Tab(t1); "From:";
Printer.Print Tab(t2); .TripFrom
Printer.Print Tab(t1); "To:";
Printer.Print Tab(t2); .TripTo
Printer.Print
```

*Using the
Printer object*

```
' Print the reservation and paid status.
' Note the use of the YesNo function to
' supply a printable value of "Yes" or "No."
```

III

10

```
        If .TranMode < 3 Then
          Printer.Print Tab(t1); "Reserved:";
          Printer.Print Tab(t2); YesNo(.ReservedStatus)
          Printer.Print Tab(t1); "Paid:";
          Printer.Print Tab(t2); YesNo(.PaidStatus)
        End If

        ' Print the comments.
        Printer.Print
        Printer.Print Tab(t1); "Comments:"
        PrintComments (RTrim(.Comments))

        Printer.Print
        Printer.Print


      End With


    End Sub   ' PrintRecord
```

Listing 10-11
The PrintComments procedure and the YesNo function

```
  Private Sub PrintComments(noteStr As String)

    ' The PrintComments procedure arranges to
    ' print the Comments field of any record
    ' in a sequence of approximately 40-character
    ' lines, without breaking any words in the text.

    Const lineLen = 40    ' Line length.
    Const t1 = 5          ' Tab stop.

    Dim curPos As Integer
    Dim curLine As String
    Dim curChar As String
```

```
' Divide the text into 40-character lines.
Do While Len(noteStr) > lineLen
  curPos = lineLen

  ' Break each line after a word.
  Do
    curChar = Mid(noteStr, curPos, 1)
    curPos = curPos - 1
  Loop Until curChar = " "

  ' Print the current line.
  Printer.Print Tab(t1); _
    Left(noteStr, curPos)

  ' Reduce the string by the line
  ' that has just been printed.
  noteStr = Mid(noteStr, curPos + 2)
Loop
```

Divides the Comments field into printable lines of text

```
  ' Print the final line of the text.
  Printer.Print Tab(t1); noteStr

End Sub    ' PrintComments




Private Function YesNo(which As Boolean) As String

  ' The YesNo function converts a Boolean value
  ' into a string value of "Yes" or "No." This
  ' conversion is used in the process of printing
  ' transportation records.

  If which Then
    YesNo = "Yes"
  Else
    YesNo = "No"
  End If

End Function    ' YesNo
```

III

10

Listing 10-12

The mnuNew_Click and mnuExit_Click procedures

```
Private Sub mnuNew_Click()

    ' The mnuNew_Click procedure starts a
    ' new database.

    ' If a file is open, save its current
    ' record if necessary.
    If tranFileOpen And recordChanged Then _
        SaveCurRec

    ' Then close the file.
    Close
    tranFileOpen = False

    ' Clear any entries from the form, and
    ' initialize the recordChanged and
    ' curTranRecord variables.
    mnuClear_Click
    recordChanged = False
    curTranRecord = 1

    ' Disable the Previous and Next commands.
    mnuPrevious.Enabled = False
    mnuNext.Enabled = False

    ' Display a new caption in the title bar.
    titleBarText = "Transportation Planner"
    frmTranPlan.Caption = titleBarText

End Sub    ' mnuNew_Click



Private Sub mnuExit_Click()
```

```
' The mnuExit_Click procedure ends the program
' performance when the user chooses the Exit
' command.

' Save the current record if a file is open.
If tranFileOpen And recordChanged Then _
    SaveCurRec

End

End Sub   ' mnuExit_Click
```

Listing 10-13
The optMode_Click procedure

```
Private Sub optMode_Click(Index As Integer)

    ' The optMode_Click procedure sets the properties
    ' of relevant controls whenever the user changes
    ' the selection in the optMode control array.

    ' Set the default property values for the
    ' program's three check box controls.
    chkRental.Enabled = False
    chkRental.VALUE = 0
    chkReserved.Enabled = True
    chkPaid.Enabled = True

    ' Enable the txtCarrier and txtTripNumber
    ' controls and their associated labels.
    lblTripNumber.Enabled = True
    txtTripNumber.Enabled = True
    txtCarrier.Enabled = True
    lblCarrier.Enabled = True
```

```
                   ' Adjust the label captions according
                   ' to the selected mode of transportion.
                 Select Case Index
                   Case 0
                     lblCarrier.Caption = "Air&line"
                     lblTripNumber.Caption = "Flight &#"

                   Case 1
                     lblCarrier.Caption = "Rail &line"
                     lblTripNumber.Caption = "Train &#"

                   Case 2
                     lblCarrier.Caption = "Bus &line"
                     lblTripNumber.Caption = "Route &#"

                   ' If the user chooses the Car option,
                   ' adjust the appropriate check boxes.
                   Case 3
                     lblCarrier.Caption = "Renta&l agency"
                     lblTripNumber.Caption = "Reservation &#"
                     chkRental.Enabled = True
                     chkRental.VALUE = 1
                     chkReserved_Click
                     chkPaid.Enabled = False
                 End Select
```

Responds to the user's transportation mode selection

```
                   ' Give the focus to the txtCarrier
                   ' text box control.
                   txtCarrier.SetFocus

               End Sub   ' optMode_Click
```

Listing 10-14
The chkReserved_Click, chkPaid_Click, and chkRental_Click procedures

```
     Private Sub chkReserved_Click()

       ' The chkReserved_Click procedure enables or
       ' disables the "Reservation #" text box
```

```
' (txtTripNumber), depending on the value of
' the chkReserved check box. This action
' occurs only if the current transporation
' selection is "Car."

If optMode(3).VALUE Then
  If chkReserved.VALUE = 0 Then
    txtTripNumber.Enabled = False
    lblTripNumber.Enabled = False
  Else
    txtTripNumber.Enabled = True
    lblTripNumber.Enabled = True
  End If
End If

recordChanged = True

End Sub   ' chkReserved_Click




Private Sub chkPaid_Click()

  ' The chkPaid_Click procedure changes the
  ' Boolean value of the recordChanged variable
  ' if the user changes the status of the Paid
  ' check box.

  recordChanged = True

End Sub   ' chkPaid_Click




Private Sub chkRental_Click()

  ' The chkRental_Click procedure adjusts
  ' the Enabled properties of several controls,
  ' depending on the value of the chkRental
```

III

10

```
' check box. (If the car option is selected,
' the Rental box indicates whether the
' car is a rental or a private vehicle.)

' If chkRental is checked, enable the
' text boxes for the rental agency (txtCarrier)
' and the reservation number (txtTripNumber).
' Also enable the chkReserved check box, which
' indicates whether a reservation has been made.

If optMode(3).VALUE Then
  If chkRental.VALUE = 1 Then
    txtCarrier.Enabled = True
    lblCarrier.Enabled = True
    txtTripNumber.Enabled = True
    lblTripNumber.Enabled = True
    chkReserved.Enabled = True
    chkReserved_Click

  ' If chkRental is unchecked, disable
  ' all these controls.
  Else
    txtCarrier.Enabled = False
    lblCarrier.Enabled = False
    txtTripNumber.Enabled = False
    lblTripNumber.Enabled = False
    chkReserved.VALUE = 0
    chkReserved.Enabled = False
  End If

  recordChanged = True
End If

End Sub   ' chkRental_Click
```

Listing 10-15

The Change event procedures for text box controls, and the
ChangedStatus procedure

```
Private Sub txtCarrier_Change()

    ' The txtCarrier_Change procedure sets
    ' recordChanged to True if the user enters
    ' new text into this text box control.

    ChangedStatus

End Sub   ' txtCarrier_Change




Private Sub txtTripNumber_Change()

    ' The txtCarrier_Change procedure sets
    ' recordChanged to True if the user enters
    ' new text into this text box control.

    ChangedStatus

End Sub   ' txtTripNumber_Change




Private Sub txtDate_Change()

    ' The txtDate_Change procedure sets
    ' recordChanged to True if the user enters
    ' new text into this text box control.

    ChangedStatus

End Sub   ' txtDate_Change
```

III

10

```
Private Sub txtTime_Change()

   ' The txtTime_Change procedure sets
   ' recordChanged to True if the user enters
   ' new text into this text box control.

   ChangedStatus

End Sub   ' txtTime_Change




Private Sub txtFrom_Change()

   ' The txtFrom_Change procedure sets
   ' recordChanged to True if the user enters
   ' new text into this text box control.

   ChangedStatus

End Sub   ' txtFrom_Change




Private Sub txtTo_Change()

   ' The txtTo_Change procedure set
   ' recordChanged to True if the user enters
   ' new text into this text box control.

   ChangedStatus

End Sub   ' txtTo_Change
```

```
Private Sub txtNotes_Change()

    ' The txtNotes_Change procedure sets
    ' recordChanged to True if the user enters
    ' new text into this text box control.

    ChangedStatus

End Sub    ' txtNotes_Change




Private Sub ChangedStatus()

    ' The ChangedStatus procedure sets the
    ' recordChanged variable and, if appropriate,
    ' enables the Next command, in response to
    ' a change in the contents of one of the
    ' program's text boxes.

    recordChanged = True
    If tranFileOpen Then _
        mnuNext.Enabled = True

End Sub    ' ChangedStatus
```

III

10

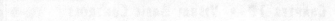

IV Advanced Programming Techniques

*O*nce you've mastered the essentials of Visual Basic programming and project design, there are several interesting new directions to investigate as you continue to expand your understanding of the language. The techniques covered in this final part of the book are four of the most useful ones.

Chapter 11 surveys some of the concepts and terminology of object-oriented programming, and reviews the significance of classes and objects in Visual Basic. You'll learn the techniques for creating class modules in a project, and you'll see how an application creates objects from a class definition. Along the way, you'll learn how and why to develop property procedures as part of a class module, and you'll see examples of Visual Basic's useful new collection object. This chapter's Travel Reminders application illustrates class modules, property procedures, and collections. The program provides check lists to help you keep track of the tasks you need to complete before, during, and after a business trip.

Chapter 12 discusses the use of multiple-document interface forms in a Visual Basic application. With an MDI form, a program can allow the user to open and work with more than one document file at a time. A program creates instances of a child form inside the parent MDI form. This technique is illustrated in an MDI version of the Transportation Planner application, which displays as many as five windows to represent the contents of open itinerary files.

Chapter 13 introduces two topics: object linking and embedding, and OLE automation. You'll see how to use the OLE container control to link an object to or embed an object in a Visual Basic form. Then you'll investigate the use of OLE automation to control the operations of other Windows applications from a Visual Basic program. To illustrate the techniques of OLE automation, this chapter presents an OLE version of the International Sales Program, which transfers sales data to an Excel worksheet and then issues the instructions necessary to generate an Excel chart from the data.

Chapter 14 shows you how to use the data control and bound controls to create a connection between a Visual Basic form and an external database. The source of the database can be any one of several database and spreadsheet programs, including Access, dBASE, or Excel. Remarkably enough, the data control can be used without a single line of code to produce a form in which the user can view, edit, and append records to the attached database. You'll see an example of this approach in the Currency Input program, which you'll develop as a hands-on exercise. Alternatively, you can use programming techniques to work with the records of a connected database, as illustrated in the database version of the Currency Exchange program.

11 Objects, Classes, and Collections

*A*n *object* is a unit of code and data, packaged for convenient use in developing new applications. Objects are the essence of Visual Basic programming.

A *control* is one example of an object. As you work with controls, you quickly develop an intuitive understanding of what objects are about. Each control you place on a form is an object with a consistent and predictable set of characteristics, including:

- The properties that define the object's appearance and behavior in your application
- The methods that your program can call to perform specific actions on the object
- The events that can occur around the object, triggering automatic calls to specific event procedures in your application's code

For example, consider the text box, one of the most common objects in Visual Basic programs. When you place a text box on a form, you know in advance that you'll find a specific list of properties for this control in the Properties window. The list includes Name, Text, Width, Height, Font, Multiline, and other text box properties that you've become familiar with. Although you typically set the *values* of these properties independently for each different text box that you create, every text box control has the same list of properties.

Likewise, Visual Basic defines a set of methods that your program can call to perform specific operations on text boxes; for example, you can use the SetFocus method to move the focus to a specific text box at runtime.

Furthermore, you can expect each text box to react to particular events during a program performance. One such event, named LostFocus, takes place when the user moves the focus away from the target text box. In your program you can write a txtBox_LostFocus event procedure, presenting specific code that will be performed whenever this event occurs.

Finally, a text box has a variety of built-in characteristics that the user quickly learns to depend on. For example, every text box has editing capabilities such as selection control, deletion, insertion, and cut-and-paste. Because these are part of the definition of a text box, you don't need to write any code to supply these features in your application; they are automatically part of every text box.

A *class* is the actual definition of a specific type of object. For example, the TextBox button in the Visual Basic Toolbox represents the class that defines all text boxes. Each time you place a text box on a form, you are creating an *instance* of the TextBox class. All text box controls belong to this same class; they all have a common set of properties, methods, and events defined by the class.

Up to now you've worked with classes of objects that are defined as part of the Visual Basic development environment. In this chapter you'll learn that you can create classes of your own, defining new types of objects for use in applications. You begin defining a class by adding a *class module* to a project. A class module is much like a form module, except that a class has no predefined visual appearance in your application. Inside a class module you write code to create the characteristics of the class itself:

- Public variables in the module represent the properties of the class.

- Special property procedures can define additional class properties. *A property procedure* contains a block of code that is performed whenever the property setting is changed or accessed.

- Other public procedures serve as the methods of your class.

The programming techniques for developing a class are not very different from the steps you've learned for creating the other components of a Visual Basic project.

Once you've defined a class, you can create any number of objects belonging to the class. In your code, you use the New keyword in a Dim statement to create an instance of a class. For convenience, you can declare *object variables* to represent instances of a class. You can also define *collections* of objects belonging to one or more classes. A collection is analogous in some ways to an array; but a collection provides different ways of gathering, handling, identifying, and accessing the objects that it contains.

To help you explore the use of class modules, procedure properties, objects, and collections in Visual Basic, this chapter presents a simple demonstration program named the Travel Reminders application. When you open this project and run it, the program displays three different check lists of travel reminders in separate forms inside a containing window. The lists contain brief descriptions of tasks that you may typically need to complete before you start a business trip, during the trip itself, and after you return home to the office. You can customize these lists to match your own travel habits. In short, the application is designed to help you become a more efficient business traveler.

As you'll learn, this application creates and manages these three lists as instances of a class named ReminderPage, which is defined as a class module in the Reminder project.

The Travel Reminders Application

The project is stored on disk as Reminder.VBP. Open the application now and take a first look at the project window, as shown in Figure 11-1. Three files are listed:

- A form module, Reminder.FRM, with an assigned name of frmReminder. The program uses this form definition to create the three lists.

- A second form, ReminMDI.FRM, with an assigned name of MDIReminder. This is a special type of object known as a *multiple-document interface* (or MDI) form. It's designed as a container form for displaying and managing any number of document windows at runtime. You'll learn much more about MDI applications in Chapter 12. For now, you should note that an application may contain only one MDI form. In this program, MDIReminder is the startup form; the MDIForm_Load procedure contains the code that is performed first when the program begins.

■ A class module, Reminder.CLS, with an assigned name of ReminderPage. This module, along with the associated frmReminder form, is a self-contained defintion for a new class of objects. Once an instance of the ReminderPage class is created at runtime, the module's code is designed to display a list window at a specified location on the screen, to read the list itself from a text file on disk, and to provide a set of basic operations for managing the list. You'll examine the details of this class module later in this chapter.

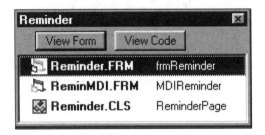

Figure 11-1
The project window of the Travel Reminders application.

Before running the program for the first time, select the frmReminder form, the first entry in the project window, and click the View Form button. As you can see in Figure 11-2, the form contains a vertically-arranged array of command buttons and a corresponding array of check box controls. The check boxes will eventually display the list of travel reminders in each ReminderPage object that the program places on the screen. The command buttons give the user the opportunity to change the text of any reminder in the list.

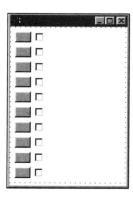

Figure 11-2
The frmReminder form at design time.

ADDING AN MDI FORM AND A CLASS MODULE TO A PROJECT

This project contains two types of files that you haven't worked with before — the MDI form and the class module. Visual Basic's Insert menu (Figure 11-3) contains the commands for inserting both of these into a new application that you're developing.

Figure 11-3
The MDI Form and Class Module commands in Visual Basic's Insert menu.

To add an MDI form to a project, pull down the Insert menu and choose MDI Form. Because a project may have only one such form, the MDI Form command is dimmed after you've chosen it for the current project. Like any form, an MDI form is saved on disk with an FRM extension. But the MDI form is a different class from an ordinary form; it has its own list of properties and events. If you open the code window for an MDI form, you'll discover that the form's event procedures are all preceded by the name MDIForm. For example, the MDI form in the Travel Reminders project contains event procedures named MDIForm_Load, MDIForm_DblClick, and MDIForm_QueryUnload.

To add a class module to a project, pull down the Insert menu and choose Class Module. As you've seen, Visual Basic saves a class module with a CLS extension. A project may include one or more class modules. At design time, a class module is represented as a code window in which you develop the declarations, general procedures, and event procedures that define the class. If you open the class module and press F4 to view the Properties window, you'll see that the module has only a short list of properties. Among these, the Name property defines the name of the class.

Visual Basic recognizes two events for a class:

- The Class_Initialize event takes place whenever a program creates a new instance of the class.

- The Class_Terminate event takes place when an instance of a class is released from memory.

In the ReminderPage class, the Class_Terminate event is used to perform some important final operations before a given list window is closed. You'll learn more about this event when you examine the program's code.

RUNNING THE TRAVEL REMINDERS PROGRAM

Now press F5 to start a first run of the application. A maximized window named Travel Reminders appears on the screen; within this window, the program displays three smaller windows labeled "Before Trip," "During Trip," and "After Trip." (As you'll discover later, each of these is produced by an instance of the ReminderPage class.) At the outset, the reminder lists are all empty, and all the check boxes are unchecked (Figure 11-4).

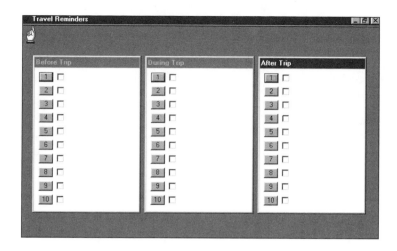

Figure 11-4

The three reminder pages.

To begin developing your reminder lists, follow these steps:

1. Activate any one of the three windows. You can activate a list window by clicking its title bar with the mouse, or by pressing Ctrl+Tab repeatedly until the target window is active.

2. Click one of the numbered command buttons (or press Tab repeatedly until the target button is active, and press the Spacebar to "click" it). When you do, the program displays an input box on the screen, prompting you to enter the text of a new reminder.

3. Type the reminder into the text box (Figure 11-5) and then click OK.

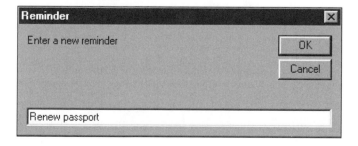

Figure 11-5

The input box for a new reminder.

As you can see in Figure 11-6, the reminder you've just created now appears in the list. If the text you've entered turns out to be too long to display on a single line within the width of the reminder window, try reentering the reminder text in a shorter version.

Figure 11-6
The text of a new reminder appears in the list.

You can complete a list by performing these steps once for each numbered command button in a given window. When you finish developing all three lists, the windows might appear as shown in Figure 11-7. Creating these lists is a one-time task that you perform during your first run of the program. Subsequently, the program records your lists on disk in text files named Before.TXT, During.TXT, and After.TXT, all stored in the root directory of your hard disk. (In fact, if you want to use the lists shown in Figure 11-7, you can copy these three files to your hard disk from the program disk supplied with this book, and then run the program.) Of course, you're free to revise your reminder lists at any time during a program run. Just click a numbered command button and enter the new reminder in the resulting text box.

You can now begin using the lists to keep track of the activities surrounding a business trip. Once you complete one of the tasks described in a list, click the corresponding check box in the appropriate window. A check appears, indicating that the job has been accomplished (Figure 11-8).

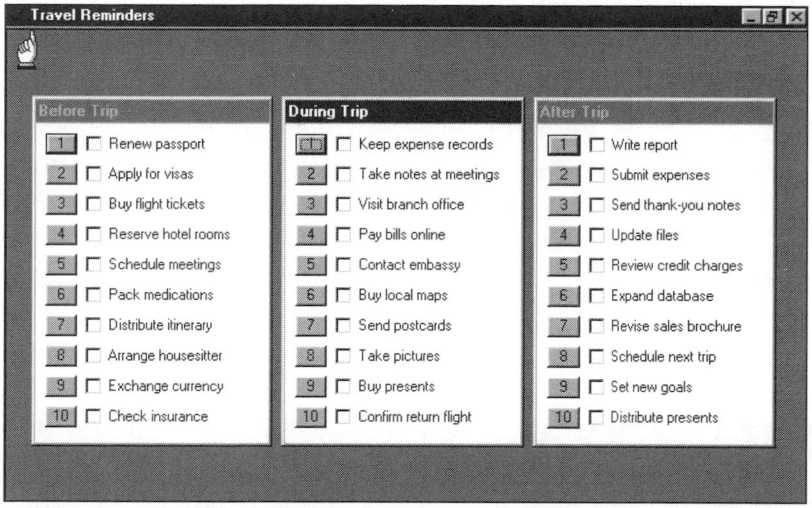

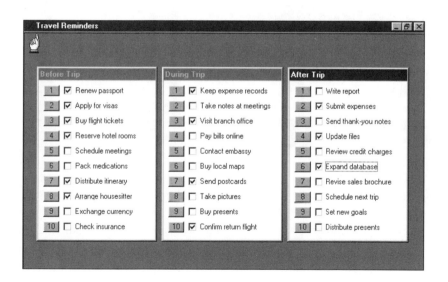

Figure 11-7
Developing the reminder lists.

Figure 11-8
Using the reminder lists to keep track of business trip activities.

For convenience, the program allows you to change the order in which the reminders appear in the lists. At the upper-left corner of the Travel Reminders window, a pointing-hand icon represents this feature. To alphabetize the list in any one of the three windows, double-click the pointing hand or, in fact, double-click the mouse pointer anywhere in the background of the Travel Reminders window. In response, the program immediately changes the order of all three reminder lists, as shown in Figure 11-9. (If any of the lists have fewer than ten reminders, the blank reminder items "float" to the top of the list window as a result of the sort.)

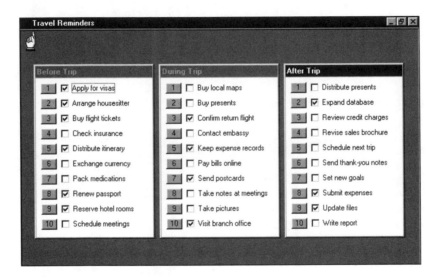

Figure 11-9
Alphabetizing a reminder list.

If you want to restore the original order of the lists, double-click the pointing-hand icon again. The program assumes that the unalphabetized order might be significant to you — for example, you might have originally entered the tasks in their order of importance or in chronological order. Accordingly, the program keeps track of the sequence as you first entered it, and is always prepared to restore this order.

When you eventually quit the program — by clicking the Close button at the upper-right corner of the Travel Reminders window, or by pulling down the window's control menu and choosing Close — the reminders and the current check box values (checked or not checked) are all saved together in the three text files associated with this program. For example, Figure 11-10 shows the contents of the After.TXT file. As you can see, each line in the file contains the text of a reminder, followed by a value of 0 (for unchecked) or 1 (for checked), representing the current value of the corresponding check box. (Because this is a text file, you can view and revise it in a text editor such as the Windows Notepad program.) The next time you run the Travel Reminders application, the program displays the contents of these files in the three reminder lists.

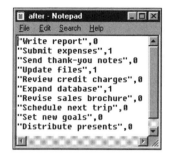

Figure 11-10
The contents of a reminder list text file.

EXAMINING THE PROGRAM'S CODE

The code for the Travel Reminders application appears in Listings 11-1 through 11-13 at the end of this chapter. These listings are organized as follows:

- The code from ReminMDI.FRM, the startup form, is in Listings 11-1 through 11-4. In particular, Listing 11-2 shows MDIForm_Load, the code performed at the beginning of each run.

- Listings 11-5 through 11-12 show the code from the class module, Reminder.CLS. These procedures define the properties, methods, and events of the ReminderPage class.

- Finally, Listing 11-13 shows the single event procedure contained in the frmReminder form module.

You might want to use Visual Basic's Object Browser to examine the contents of this project. Pull down the View menu and choose Object Browser to open this window. (Alternatively, click the Object Browser button on the Visual Basic toolbar or simply press F2 at the keyboard.) As you can see in Figure 11-11, the Object Browser lists the contents of the current project. The list on the left shows the names of the modules and classes in the project. When you select one of these modules, the list on the right displays the procedures it contains.

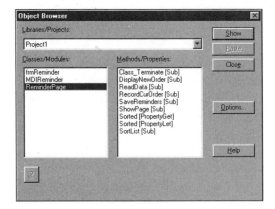

Figure 11-11
The Object Browser shows the contents of the current project.

The Object Browser is a useful tool for making your way around the code of a detailed project. For example, when you double-click the name of any procedure listed in the Methods/Properties list, Visual Basic opens a code window and displays the procedure you've selected. You'll see an even larger purpose for the Object Browser in Chapter 13, when you examine the techniques of OLE animation.

Developing Classes and Collections

The code of the Travel Reminders application introduces several important programming techniques related to objects, collections, classes, and property procedures. Specifically, as you examine the listings, you'll learn how to

- Develop the code inside a class module
- Create instances of a class you've defined
- Organize a group of class objects as a collection
- Loop through the objects in a collection
- Create instances of a form
- Develop methods and property procedures in a class module
- Make calls to property procedures by setting or accessing property values
- Make use of the events that Visual Basic defines for classes
- Release a class object from memory when your program is finished with it

Before you begin exploring these techniques in detail, here's an overview of how the program works. As you know, the MDIForm_Load procedure in the MDIReminder module is the first code to be performed. This procedure creates three instances of the ReminderPage class and then organizes these three objects as a collection. This collection object, represented as *colReminderPages*, provides access to the three ReminderPage objects throughout the program.

Each ReminderPage object in its turn creates an instance of the frmReminder form. You may be surprised to learn that Visual Basic recognizes each form that you add to a project as a class. You can therefore create new form objects from any standard form (but not from an MDI form). Each instance of a form contains all the characteristics defined in the original form class, including properties, controls, and code.

The ReminderPage class contains a method (that is, a public procedure) named *ShowPage*, which is designed to display the current instance of the frmReminder form on the screen. The MDIForm_Load procedure calls this method once for each instance of the ReminderPage class, thus displaying all three reminder pages on the screen. But before calling the *ShowPage* method, the program sets the relevant properties of the new ReminderPage object. These include *TitleBar*, which specifies the title bar caption; *ListFileName*, which provides the name of the text file that contains the list of reminders; and *XPos* and *YPos*, two integer arguments that give the position coordinates of the window.

Once the three reminder pages are displayed, event procedures respond to the user's subsequent actions. For example, the procedure cmdChange_Click in the frmReminder form displays an input box on the screen — with the prompt "Enter a new reminder" — when the user clicks any one of the numbered command buttons. The procedure MDIForm_DblClick takes control when the user double-clicks inside the MDI form. This procedure changes a property named *Sorted* on all three ReminderPage objects. The property change itself results in a call to a property procedure in the class module, which in turn performs the sort.

Finally, when the user closes the application window, the program initiates the process of releasing all three ReminderPage objects from memory. This event triggers a call to a procedure named Class_Terminate in each object. To complete the program's action appropriately, the event procedure writes the current reminder lists back to disk, saving any changes that may have been made during the current run.

You'll begin learning how the program uses the ReminderPage class in the next section.

WORKING WITH A CLASS

Each ReminderPage object — along with the form object that it creates — is a self-contained unit of code, data, and displayable objects. Part of the design of a class is that it should be easy to transport for use in any application. Accordingly, you can add the Reminder.CLS and Reminder.FRM files to any project that contains an MDI form, and successfully create instances of the ReminderPage class. To use a ReminderPage object, you perform the following tasks in your code:

1. Create an instance of the ReminderPage class.

2. Assign values to the properties of the object you've created.

3. Call the appropriate method to display the object on the screen.

4. Prepare for the events that are designed to occur while the object is active.

Thanks to the ReminderPage class, you can manage all these tasks economically, with a very few lines of code. Once the class itself is available, you don't need to concern yourself with the details of its implementation. All you need to know is how to use the properties, methods, and events that the class defines.

Creating a Class Object

The first step for your code is to create an instance of the class. This is accomplished with the Dim statement and the New keyword:

```
Dim objectVariable As New ClassName
```

This statement does two things. First, it creates a new object belonging to the class identified as *ClassName*. (This is analogous to the step you take when you double-click a button on the Toolbox to place a new control on a form; the result is a new object belonging to a particular class of controls.) Second, the Dim statement declares a variable name, *objectVariable*, to represent the new object in your program. (This second task is parallel to the task of assigning a value to the Name property for a control in a form; the name represents the object in your program's code.)

Consider an example from the MDIForm_Load procedure (Listing 11-2). The following statement creates an instance of the ReminderPage class:

```
Dim Before as New ReminderPage
```

The variable named *Before* represents a new ReminderPage object. Once your program has created this object and given it a name, *Before* can be used in several familiar ways. Given the list of properties defined in the ReminderPage class, you can assign specific settings to the *Before* object. For example, the following statement assigns a string value to the object's *TitleBar* property:

```
Before.TitleBar = "Before Trip"
```

Likewise you can make calls to any method defined in the class. This statement calls the *ShowPage* method, displaying a reminder list on the screen:

```
Before.ShowPage
```

You can also use Visual Basic's With structure to simplify references to the properties and methods of the *Before* object. Taking advantage of With, here is how the MDIForm_Load procedure assigns property values to the *Before* object and displays the resulting reminder page on the screen:

```
Dim Before As New ReminderPage
  With Before
    .TitleBar = "Before Trip"
    .ListFileName = "\Before.TXT"
    .XPos = 300
    .YPos = 800
    .ShowPage
  End With
```

As previewed earlier in this chapter, the properties of a Reminder-Page object include the *TitleBar* caption, the *ListFileName* text file, and the *XPos* and *YPos* coordinates. Once these properties have been set, the *ShowPage* method displays the list in the application window. (The fifth property, *Sorted*, isn't used until a list is already displayed on the screen.)

The MDIForm_Load procedure uses similar sequences of code to create the other two ReminderPage objects, first *During*:

```
Dim During As New ReminderPage
  With During
    .TitleBar = "During Trip"
    .ListFileName = "\During.TXT"
    .XPos = 3300
    .YPos = 800
    .ShowPage
  End With
```

and then *After*:

```
Dim After As New ReminderPage
  With After
    .TitleBar = "After Trip"
    .ListFileName = "\After.TXT"
    .XPos = 6300
    .YPos = 800
    .ShowPage
  End With
```

Declaring Object Variables

Sometimes you may want a way to declare an object variable without creating a new object. Perhaps the object itself already exists, and you simply need a new variable to represent it. Or you may want to organize your code in a particular way, declaring the object variable before creating the object that the variable will eventually represent.

To create an object variable belonging to a certain class, use the following familiar format of the Dim statement:

```
Dim objectVariable as ClassName
```

Without the New keyword, this statement only declares a variable; it does not create a new instance of *ClassName*. At this point, the value of the object variable is represented by the keyword Nothing; the variable does not yet refer to any object.

To assign the variable a reference to a specific object, you use Visual Basic's Set statement:

```
Set objectVariable = objectName
```

This statement assumes that an object called *objectName* already exists as an instance of *ClassName*. For example, suppose your program creates a ReminderPage object named *Sometime*:

```
Dim Sometime As New ReminderPage
```

Later in the program you want to refer to this same object as *Before* rather than *Sometime*. The following statements create *Before* as a ReminderPage variable and then assign the variable a reference to the *Sometime* object:

```
Dim Before As ReminderPage
Set Before = Sometime
```

You can also use the Set statement to *create* a new object, in the following format:

```
Dim objectVariable As ClassName
Set objectVariable = New ClassName
```

Finally, you can use Set to disassociate the variable from the object it currently refers to:

```
Set objectVariable = Nothing
```

After this statement, *objectVariable* no longer refers to any object. Furthermore, if *objectVariable* was previously the only existing variable referring to this object, assigning Nothing to the variable is a way to release the object itself from memory. You'll see an example of this in the Travel Reminders program.

When the MDIForm_Load procedure is finished, the three reminder lists are displayed on the screen, as shown in Figure 11-4 (if the \Before.TXT, \During.TXT, and \After.TXT files have not yet been created) or in Figure 11-7 (if the three files exist). At this point, the application is ready for the user to begin interacting with the objects on the screen — developing or revising the reminder lists, checking or unchecking individual tasks in the lists, changing the sort order, and eventually ending the program performance so that the lists can be recorded again on disk.

Creating and Using a Collection of Objects

In some applications, a *collection* proves to be a convenient way to refer to a group of objects and to gain access to individual objects in the group. A collection is itself an object, which you can create using the Dim statement and the New keyword:

```
Dim collectionName As New Collection
```

For example, a collection object named *colReminderPages* is created in the general declarations section of the MDIReminder form:

```
Dim colReminderPages As New Collection
```

Because this object has a module-level scope, it is available to respresent a group of objects throughout the life of the MDI form, which is to say during the entire program run. In general, the objects in a collection need not all belong to the same class; you can use a collection to represent any assortment of related objects in your application. But the *colReminderPages* collection — as its name implies — is created to represent a set of objects that all belong to a single class, ReminderPage.

Once a collection exists, you can add any number of members, using a method named Add. Here is the syntax of the Add method in its simplest form:

```
collectionName.Add objectName
```

The MDIForm_Load procedure uses this format to add the three ReminderPage objects — *Before*, *During*, and *After* — to the *colReminderPages* collection:

```
colReminderPages.Add Before
colReminderPages.Add During
colReminderPages.Add After
```

(See the sidebar named "Organizing a Collection" for more information about the Add method.)

Significantly, the *Before*, *During*, and *After* object variables are declared locally in the MDIForm_Load procedure. When the procedure relinquishes control, these three variables go out of scope, and are no longer available as references to ReminderPage objects. But the *colReminderPages* collection is declared at the module level of the MDIReminder form. For the remainder of the program, this collection is therefore the only way to refer to the set of three ReminderPage objects.

Visual Basic 4 provides an important new variation on the For loop that is ideal for working with a collection. Here is a general format of the For Each loop:

```
For Each objectVariable In collectionName

    ' Inside the loop, use objectVariable to refer
    ' to each successive member of the collection.

Next objectVariable
```

This loop provides ordered access to each member of the collection. For each new iteration of the loop, *objectVariable* is assigned a reference to the next member in the collection.

For example, the MDIForm_DblClick procedure (Listing 11-3) uses a For Next loop to change the Sorted property of each object in the *colReminderPages* collection:

```
Dim Reminder As Object
For Each Reminder In colReminderPages
  With Reminder
    .Sorted = Not .Sorted
  End With
Next Reminder
```

Notice the use of a *generic* object variable — *Reminder* — to serve as the reference to objects in the collection. Because collections may contain objects of diverse classes, it's always a good idea to use a generic object variable in the For Each loop. Of course, in this particular application, the *colReminderPages* collection contains only objects that belong to the ReminderPage class. In this special case, *Reminder* could therefore have been declared as a ReminderPage variable:

```
Dim Reminder as ReminderPage
```

The MDIReminder module illustrates one more convenient use of the *colReminderPages* collection. When the user clicks the Close button to close the Travel Reminders window, the MDIForm_QueryUnload event procedure (Listing 11-4) is performed. (The QueryUnload event takes place just *before* the actual closing of a form, and thus gives an application the opportunity to perform final operations while the form is still open.) This procedure contains a single statement:

```
Set colReminderPages = Nothing
```

Because *colReminderPages* is the only module-level reference to the program's three ReminderPage objects, this statement has the effect of releasing all three objects from memory. But before they are released, a Class_Terminate event procedure is triggered for each instance of the class. As you'll see shortly, this event procedure completes the action of the program by making appropriate arrangements for saving the three reminder lists.

INSIDE THE CLASS MODULE

You've seen how the MDIReminder form makes use of the ReminderPage class — creating instances of the class, setting properties, calling the ShowPage method, and carrying out other operations that trigger events. Now it's time to look inside the class module itself to see how all these class-related resources are defined.

Organizing a Collection

A collection is an *ordered* group of objects. Each time you add an object to a collection, the object is assigned an index value from 1 to the number of objects in the collection. You can use this index number to access a particular member in the collection. You can also use a traditional For loop to go through all the members of the collection. For example, the loop in MDIForm_DblClick could be redesigned as follows:

```
Dim i
For i = 1 to colReminderPages.Count
   With colReminderPages(i)
      .Sorted = Not .Sorted
   End With
Next i
```

Notice the use of the Count property at the top of the For loop. This property indicates the current number of members in a collection.

Another way to identify the members of a collection is to assign a key string to each object at the time the object is added to the collection. Use the following format of the Add method to accomplish this:

collectionName.Add *objectName, keyString*

You can subsequently refer to a collection member using the key string

collectionName(keyString)

For example, suppose you were to use the following statement to add the *Before* object to the *colReminderPages* collection:

```
colReminderPages.Add Before, "BeforeTrip"
```

Later in the program you can refer to this member of the collection as:

```
colReminderPages("BeforeTrip")
```

This format can be a convenient and important alternative to the use of numeric indexes for accessing members in the collection.

The general declarations for the ReminderPage class module appear in Listing 11-5. The first thing to keep in mind about this module is that it uses the frmReminder form as its own visual component. In fact, each instance of the ReminderPage class creates a new instance of the frmReminder form. In this sense, the ReminderPage class and the frmReminder form are two parts of the same package. If you want to use this class in another program, you have to make sure to add both the Reminder.FRM and Reminder.CLS files to the project.

Near the top of the general declarations, you'll find the following Dim statement:

```
Dim newPage As New frmReminder
```

As this statement demonstrates, Visual Basic regards each form in a project as a class definition, and therefore allows the application to create multiple instances of the form. Each instance contains all of the form's controls and all of its code. If the form is designed to present a certain dialog box on the screen and react to particular events, each instance of the form will behave in the same way.

In the Reminder.CLS module, *newPage* is a module-level object variable that retains its scope throughout the life of a given ReminderPage object. The object and its associated *newPage* form are designed to work together to provide the visual interface for each instance of the ReminderPage class. You'll find references to *newPage* throughout the class module.

Several interesting techniques are worth investigating in the code of a class module. How does the module define the properties of the class? How are the methods designed? And what is the role of event procedures in the behavior of class objects? These are the questions you'll explore in the upcoming sections of this chapter.

Defining the Properties of the Class

There are two ways to define properties inside a class module. The easy way is to create one or more public variables in the module's general declarations section. The more difficult — but also more powerful — approach is to write property procedures. A property procedure is automatically called every time a particular property setting is changed or accessed.

The ReminderPage class contains examples of both these approaches. Four of the class properties are defined as public variables in the general declarations section of the class module:

```
Public TitleBar As String       ' The window title.
Public ListFileName As String   ' The text file name.
Public XPos As Integer          ' The position
Public YPos As Integer          '     coordinates.
```

As you've seen, the Travel Reminders program assigns values to these properties immediately after creating an instance of the Reminder-Page class, but before making a call to the ShowPage method:

```
Dim During As New ReminderPage
  With During
    .TitleBar = "During Trip"
    .ListFileName = "\During.TXT"
    .XPos = 3300
    .YPos = 800

    .ShowPage
  End With
```

In short, the values of these properties determine the appearance and content of each new reminder list: *TitleBar* is the caption, *ListFileName* identifies the text file that contains the reminder list itself, and *XPos* and *YPos* specify the position of the window.

Developing Property Procedures

But the ReminderPage class has a fifth property, named *Sorted*. Unlike the other four properties, this property is meant to be used *after* a given list is already displayed on the screen. As you've seen, the MDIForm_DblClick procedure changes the value of the *Sorted* property each time the user double-clicks the mouse in the background of the form. The ReminderPage class takes any change in the value of this property as a signal to sort the list displayed in a particular instance of the class. The *Sorted* property procedures, shown in Listing 11-8, make this possible.

As you'll see, *two* property procedures are related to the *Sorted* property. The first, Property Let Sorted, is called in response to any statement that changes the current value of the property:

```
Property Let Sorted(alphabetic As Boolean)
```

The second, named Property Get Sorted, is called in response to any statement that *reads* the value of the Sorted property:

```
Property Get Sorted() As Boolean
```

The Property Let Sorted procedure receives as its argument the new value that is assigned to the property. For example, consider this hypothetical statement:

```
During.Sorted = False
```

In response to this statement, the Property Let Sorted procedure is called and a value of False is sent to its *alphabetic* argument.

By contrast, the role of the Property Get Sorted procedure is to supply the current value of the *Sorted* property. In response to a statement that reads the value of *Sorted*, the Property Get Sorted procedure is called and returns the current value of the *Sorted* property. For example, the following statement results in a call to Property Get Sorted; the property value is then assigned to the variable *isAlpha*:

```
isAlpha = During.Sorted
```

Take a quick look at the design of these two property procedures in the class module. The Property Let Sorted procedure uses its *alphabetic* argument to determine whether the target list should be alphabetized or returned to its original order. To accomplish either of these tasks, the routine makes three procedure calls of its own:

```
Property Let Sorted(alphabetic As Boolean)

   RecordCurOrder alphabetic
   SortList alphabetic
```

```
DisplayNewOrder
isSorted = alphabetic

End Property  ' Sorted (PropertyLet)
```

The *RecordCurOrder* procedure (Listing 11-10) makes a copy of the current list in an array named *curList*. This procedure also keeps track of the original order of the list so that this order can be restored if the *Sorted* property is changed to False again. The *SortList* procedure (Listing 11-9) performs the sort, either alphabetizing the text entries of the reminder list if the program has requested an alphabetical sort, or sorting the *originalOrder* field if the program has requested a return to the original order of the list. Finally, the *DisplayNewOrder* procedure (Listing 11-10) redisplays the list in its newly sorted order.

After these three procedure calls, the Property Let Sorted procedure changes the value of a module-level variable named *isSorted*. The Property Get Sorted procedure simply returns the value of this variable, supplying the current value of the *Sorted* property itself:

```
Property Get Sorted() As Boolean

  Sorted = isSorted

End Property  ' Property Get Sorted
```

You may want to spend some time studying these two property procedures — and the three procedures called by the Property Get Sorted routine — to learn exactly how the sort operations are carried out in a ReminderPage object.

Designing a Method for the Class

Looking through all the procedures in the Reminder.ClS module, you'll find that all but three of them are labeled Private. By design, the bulk of the code inside the module is invisible to a program that creates instances of the class.

Of the three procedures available for use outside the class module itself, two are the property procedures that you've just looked at, Property Let Sorted and Property Get Sorted. The third is the *ShowPage* procedure (Listing 11-6), the one method defined for this class. After creating a

ReminderPage object and assigning values to its properties, a program uses the *ShowPage* method to display the reminder list on the screen. As you've seen, a call to this method looks like this:

```
During.ShowPage
```

The *ShowPage* procedure itself is surprisingly simple:

```
Sub ShowPage()

  ReadData ListFileName

  newPage.Caption = TitleBar
  newPage.TOP = YPos
  newPage.Left = XPos

  newPage.Show

End Sub   ' ShowPage
```

The procedure begins by making a call to the *ReadData* procedure (Listing 11-7), which has the task of opening the appropriate text file on disk and copying its contents to the control arrays on the *newPage* form. (If this procedure doesn't find the target file on disk, the check box captions remain blank.) Then *ShowPage* sets the caption and position properties of the *newPage* form. Finally, a call to the Show method displays the form on the screen.

Responding to Events around the ReminderPage Objects

Once the reminder lists are displayed, three kinds of events can take place:

- The user can click one of the numbered command buttons located at the left side of all three lists (see Figure 11-4). In response, the program elicits a new text entry for the current reminder (Figure 11-5) and then displays this new value as part of the list. This particular event is handled by a procedure contained in the frmReminder form itself. The cmdChange_Click procedure (Listing 11-13) uses Visual Basic's InputBox function to display the prompt, and then assigns the input to the appropriate chkReminder control:

```
Private Sub cmdChange_Click(Index As Integer)

  Dim newStr As String

  newStr = InputBox("Enter a new reminder")
  If Trim(newStr) <> "" Then _
    chkReminder(Index).Caption = newStr

End Sub   ' cmdChange_Click
```

- The user can double-click inside the MDI form to request a change in the sort order. As you've seen, the MDIForm_DblClick procedure responds to this event by changing the value of the *Sorted* property for all three ReminderPage objects. In response, the property procedures in the Reminder.ClS module are called.

- The user can click the close button at the upper-right corner of the MDI form, a signal to terminate the program. In response, the MDIForm_QueryUnload procedure (Listing 11-4) assigns a value of Nothing to the *colReminderPages* collection, releasing all three of the ReminderPage objects from memory. But before the objects can be released, this assignment triggers a call to the Class_Terminate procedure in the class module (Listing 11-11).

The Class_Terminate procedure has two tasks to perform before releasing an object from memory. If the current list is in alphabetical order, this procedure restores it to its original order before writing the list back to disk:

```
If Me.Sorted then Me.Sorted = False
```

Notice the use of the keyword Me. Me can be used anywhere inside a class module to refer to the current instance of the class. Because a program may create many objects from a given class defintion, Me is an easy way to refer to the instance that is currently the target of operations.

Finally, the Class_Terminate procedure saves the current reminder list back to its text file on disk. A call to the SaveReminders procedure (Listing 11-12) accomplishes this task:

```
SaveReminders
```

The procedure saves not only the text of the current reminder list, but also the checked or unchecked settings of each check box. This ensures that the user will see the same list at the beginning of the next program run.

Objects, classes, collections, methods, property procedures, and class events — all of these features give you powerful new ways to organize your Visual Basic programming projects. You'll continue to learn more about these techniques in the remaining chapters of this book.

Listing 11-1
General declarations for ReminMDI.FRM

```
' The Travel Reminders Program.
' ----------------------------

' Files:
' ------
' Project File:    Reminder.VBP
' MDI Form File:   ReminMDI.FRM
' Class File:      Reminder.CLS

' This program illustrates the use of classes,
' collections, property procedures, and other
' object-related features available in Visual
' Basic 4. The program creates three instances
' of the ReminderPage class, which in turn display
' three instances of the frmReminder form inside
' a containing MDI form. Each of these "pages"
' displays a check list of travel reminders--
' tasks that need to be accomplished before,
' during, and after a business trip. The text
' of these lists, and the current check-box
' settings, are stored in three text files,
' \Before.TXT, During.TXT, and \After.TXT.
' The user can change the text of any reminder
' in a list at any time, and can click the
' reminder itself to change the check-box status.
' The user can also choose to sort the reminder
```

```
' lists in alphabetical order, or to restore
' the lists to their original orders. (Double-
' click the up-pointing hand icon to toggle
' between these two sort-order options.) Upon
' termination, the program saves the current
' lists back to disk in the same three text files.

Option Explicit

' Create a new collection object to represent
' the three "pages" of reminder lists.
Dim colReminderPages As New Collection
'
' End of general declarations, MDIReminder.
```

Creating a collection object

Listing 11-2
The MDIForm_Load procedure

```
Private Sub MDIForm_Load()

    ' The MDIForm_Load procedure is the
    ' startup routine for this program. It
    ' creates an instance of the ReminderPage
    ' class for each of the three lists.

    ' Create the Before object, and assign
    ' values to its properties.
    Dim Before As New ReminderPage
        With Before
            .TitleBar = "Before Trip"
            .ListFileName = "\Before.TXT"
            .XPos = 300
            .YPos = 800
```

Creating an instance of the ReminderPage class, and assigning properties to the new object

```
            ' Call the ShowPage method for the
            ' Before object.
            .ShowPage
        End With
```

Calling a method of the ReminderPage object

```
' Add the Before object to the
' colReminderPages collection.
colReminderPages.Add Before

' Create the During object and assign
' values to its properties.
Dim During As New ReminderPage
   With During
      .TitleBar = "During Trip"
      .ListFileName = "\During.TXT"
      .XPos = 3300
      .YPos = 800

      ' Call the ShowPage method for the
      ' During object.
      .ShowPage
   End With

' Add the During object to the
' colReminderPages collection.
colReminderPages.Add During

' Create the After object and assign
' values to its properties.
Dim After As New ReminderPage
   With After
      .TitleBar = "After Trip"
      .ListFileName = "\After.TXT"
      .XPos = 6300
      .YPos = 800

      ' Call the ShowPage method for
      ' the After object.
      .ShowPage
   End With

' Add the After object to the
' colReminderPages collection.
colReminderPages.Add After

End Sub   ' MDIForm_Load
```

Adding the object to a collection

Listing 11-3
The MDIForm_DblClick procedure

```
Private Sub MDIForm_DblClick()

    ' The MDIForm_DblClick procedure responds to a
    ' double-click on the pointing-hand icon, or
    ' elsewhere inside the MDI form. This is the
    ' signal for changing the sort order of the
    ' reminder lists -- from the original order to
    ' alphabetical order, or from alphabetical back
    ' to the original order.

    ' Create a generic object variable.
    Dim Reminder As Object

    ' Loop through the ReminderPage objects in
    ' the colReminderPages collection.
    For Each Reminder In colReminderPages

        ' For each object in the collection,
        ' switch the Sorted property to its
        ' opposite value.
        With Reminder

            ' This change in the Sorted property
            ' triggers calls to both the Get Sorted
            ' and Let Sorted property procedures in
            ' each ReminderPage class object.
            .Sorted = Not .Sorted
        End With
    Next Reminder

End Sub  ' MDIForm_DblClick
```

Looping through the objects in the collection

Changing the value of the Sorted property

Listing 11-4

The MDIForm_QueryUnload procedure

```
Private Sub MDIForm_QueryUnload(Cancel As Integer, _
   UnloadMode As Integer)

   ' The MDIForm_QueryUnload procedure
   ' releases the colReminderPages collection
   ' from memory, triggering a call to the
   ' Class_Terminate event procedure on each
   ' of the instances of the ReminderPage class.

   ' Note: The QueryUnload procedure is used
   ' (instead of Unload) to perform this
   ' termination task before the forms are
   ' actually closed. The program performance
   ' ends after the MDI form is closed.

   Set colReminderPages = Nothing

End Sub    ' MDIForm_QueryUnload
```

Releasing the members of the collection from memory

Listing 11-5

General declarations for the Reminder.CLS class module

```
' The Travel Reminders Program.
' -----------------------------
'
' Class Module:   Reminder.CLS
'
' This class module contains the methods and
' properties associated with a reminder page.
' A program can create instances of this class
' and assign appropriate property values to
' each instance. Each class object in turn creates
```

```
' an instance of the frmReminder form. A call to
' the ShowPage method displays each reminder
' list on the screen.

Option Explicit

' Create a new instance of the frmReminder form.
Dim newPage As New frmReminder

' Declare the public variables that will
' represent the properties of this class.

Public TitleBar As String       ' The window title.
Public ListFileName As String   ' The text file name.
Public XPos As Integer          ' The position
Public YPos As Integer          '       coordinates.

Dim isSorted As Boolean

' Define a record type to represent individual
' reminder items, with fields for the text of
' the reminder, the status (checked or not checked)
' and the original position of the item in the
' list. The originalOrder field allows the program
' to restore the original order of a list after
' a sort operation. Notice that this is a Private
' Type declaration, available only inside the
' class module. (Public Type definitions may
' appear only in BAS modules in Visual Basic.)
Private Type curItemType
   remindText As String
   remindStatus As Byte
   originalOrder As Byte
End Type

' Declare an array of curItemType records, to
' store the entire list of reminders.
Dim curList(9) As curItemType
'
' End of general declarations, the
' ReminderPage class module.
```

*Properties
of the class*

Listing 11-6
The ShowPage procedure

```
Sub ShowPage()

    ' The ShowPage procedure prepares a page of
    ' reminders and displays the corresponding
    ' window on the screen.

    ' Read the text file and copy its contents
    ' to the array of check boxes on the newPage
    ' form.
    ReadData ListFileName

    ' Display the title as the caption on the
    ' form's title bar.
    newPage.Caption = TitleBar

    ' Assign the position properties.
    newPage.TOP = YPos
    newPage.Left = XPos

    ' Display the form object on the screen.
    newPage.Show

End Sub    ' ShowPage
```

Listing 11-7
The ReadData procedure

```
Private Sub ReadData(inFile As String)

    ' The ReadData procedure reads the original
    ' reminder list from a TXT file on disk.
    ' The name of each TXT file is passed to the
    ' ReminderPage object as the value of the
    ' ListFileName property.
```

```
Dim i
Dim reminderTxt As String
Dim checkStatus As Byte

' Open and read the file under the control of
' an error trap. If the file doesn't exist, or
' if its format is inappropriate, this On Error
' statement sends control to the end of the
' ReadData procedure.
On Error GoTo fileProblem

Open inFile For Input As #1

  ' Read the file line by line, and assign
  ' each text value to the Caption property
  ' of the corresponding check box. Assign
  ' the checkStatus value (0 or 1) to the
  ' Value property of the check box.
  For i = 0 To 9
    Input #1, reminderTxt, checkStatus
    With newPage.chkReminder(i)
      .Caption = reminderTxt
      .VALUE = checkStatus
    End With
  Next i

  On Error GoTo 0

' In the event of a file error, the On Error
' Goto statement sends control to this label.
fileProblem:

  Close #1
  For i = 0 To 9
    ' Display an integer value on
    ' each cmdChange command
    ' button.
    newPage.cmdChange(i).Caption = i + 1
  Next i

End Sub   ' ReadData
```

Listing 11-8

The Let Sorted and Get Sorted property procedures

```
Property Let Sorted(alphabetic As Boolean)

  ' The Let Sorted property procedure rearranges
  ' a reminder list. This procedure is called in
  ' response to a change in the value of the
  ' Sorted property.

  ' The alphabetic argument indicates whether
  ' the reminder list is to be alphabetized (True)
  ' or restored to its original order (False).
  RecordCurOrder alphabetic
  SortList alphabetic

  ' After the sort, copy the array of reminders
  ' back to the array of check boxes.
  DisplayNewOrder
  isSorted = alphabetic

End Property   ' Sorted (PropertyLet)


Property Get Sorted() As Boolean

  ' The Property Get Sorted procedure returns
  ' the current value of the Sorted property.

  Sorted = isSorted

End Property   ' Property Get Sorted
```

Property procedures

Property procedures

Listing 11-9

The SortList procedure

```
Private Sub SortList(byReminders As Boolean)

    ' The SortList procedure rearranges a list of
    ' reminders. If the byReminders argument is
    ' true, the procedure alphabetizes the list; if
    ' false, the list is restored to its original
    ' order, as represented by the originalOrder
    ' field of the curList array.

    Dim i, j
    Dim tempItem As curItemType

    ' Use a bubble sort to rearrange the list.
    For i = 0 To 8
      For j = i + 1 To 9

        ' Sort the list alphabetically.
        If byReminders Then
          If curList(i).remindText > _
            curList(j).remindText Then
              tempItem = curList(i)
              curList(i) = curList(j)
              curList(j) = tempItem
          End If

        ' Or restore the original order.
        Else
          If curList(i).originalOrder > _
            curList(j).originalOrder Then
              tempItem = curList(i)
              curList(i) = curList(j)
              curList(j) = tempItem
          End If
        End If
      Next j
    Next i

End Sub   ' SortList
```

Listing 11-10

The RecordCurOrder and DisplayNewOrder procedures

```
Private Sub RecordCurOrder(saveOrderField)

    ' The RecordCurOrder procedure is called just
    ' before the program sorts a list of reminders.
    ' This procedure records the previous order so
    ' that this order can be restored if the user
    ' requests. If the list is currently in
    ' alphabetical order, this procedure should not
    ' change the values of the originalOrder field.
    ' The program therefore sends a value of False
    ' to the saveOrderField argument to signal
    ' that this is the case.

    Dim i

    ' Assign the current values of the Caption
    ' and Value properties to the remindText and
    ' remindStatus fields of the curList array.
    For i = 0 To 9
      With newPage.chkReminder(i)
        curList(i).remindText = .Caption
        curList(i).remindStatus = .VALUE
      End With

        ' If the list is currently in its original
        ' order (saveOrderField is True), assign
        ' the ordinal values to the originalOrder
        ' field in the curList array.
        If saveOrderField Then _
          curList(i).originalOrder = i
      Next i

    End Sub   ' RecordCurOrder




    Private Sub DisplayNewOrder()
```

```
' The DisplayNewOrder procedure redisplays
' the list of reminders after the curList
' array has been sorted, either alphabetically
' or by the originalOrder field.

Dim i

For i = 0 To 9
  With newPage.chkReminder(i)

    ' Assign the fields of the curList
    ' array to the Caption and Value
    ' properties of each check box.
    .Caption = curList(i).remindText
    .VALUE = curList(i).remindStatus
  End With
Next i


End Sub   ' DisplayNewOrder
```

Listing 11-11

The Class_Terminate event procedure

```
Private Sub Class_Terminate()

  ' The Class_Terminate event procedure takes
  ' place just before the class object is released
  ' from memory.

  ' Always save the reminder lists in their
  ' original (not alphabetized) orders. If
  ' a list is currently alphabetized, restore
  ' its order before terminating.
  If Me.Sorted Then Me.Sorted = False

  ' Save the current text and status of each
  ' reminder list back to disk. This is the
  ' program's final action.
  SaveReminders

End Sub   ' Class_Terminate
```

Using Me to refer to the current instance of the class

Listing 11-12
The SaveReminders procedure

```
Private Sub SaveReminders()

    ' The SaveReminders procedure saves the current
    ' reminder list as a TXT file on disk. This
    ' action takes place once for each list, at
    ' the end of a program run.

    Dim i

    With newPage

        ' The correct file name for each list is
        ' passed to the ReminderPage object as the
        ' value of the ListFileName property.
        Open ListFileName For Output As #1
          For i = 0 To 9

            ' Save the text of the reminder
            ' and the current check-box status
            ' (checked or not checked).
            Write #1, _
              .chkReminder(i).Caption; _
              .chkReminder(i).VALUE
        Next i
      Close #1
    End With

End Sub   ' SaveReminders
```

Listing 11-13

*The beginning of the Reminder.FRM code, and the cmdChange_Click
procedure*

```
' The Travel Reminders Program.
' ----------------------------
'
' Form File:  Reminder.FRM
'
' Note: An instance of this form is created as
' part of each instance of the ReminderPage
' class. The form contains one event procedure
' Each instance of the form contains this procedure.



Private Sub cmdChange_Click(Index As Integer)

    ' The cmdChange_Click procedure is called when
    ' the user clicks any of the array of command
    ' buttons displayed just to the left of the
    ' reminder check boxes. This procedure gives
    ' the user the opportunity to change the text
    ' of any reminder in the list.

    Dim newStr As String

    ' Elicit a new text entry for the current
    ' reminder.
    newStr = InputBox("Enter a new reminder")

    ' If the user's input is not blank, assign
    ' the new string entry to the Caption
    ' property of the current check box. (Note
    ' that a click of the Cancel button on the
    ' input box results in a empty string; in
    ' this case, the program does not change
    ' the Caption property.)
    If Trim(newStr) <> "" Then _
        chkReminder(Index).Caption = newStr

End Sub   ' cmdChange_Click
```

12 Multiple-Document Interface

*M*any Windows applications are designed to let you work with more than one file at a time. For example, major word processing programs enable you to open multiple documents concurrently. This gives you a convenient way to compare the information contained in different documents and to move or copy text from one file to another.

Similarly, you can create Visual Basic programs that permit the user to open multiple instances of a given form inside an appropriately designed application window. This feature is known as *multiple-document interface*, or simply MDI. A Visual Basic application may contain one MDI form, along with any number of standard forms from which the program can create instances. The MDI form is known as the *parent* and the windows displayed inside it are known as *child* forms.

An MDI form can provide familiar tools designed to help the user open and work with documents:

- A set of menu commands often appears at the top of the MDI form. These commands generally apply to the child document that is active at a given moment during a program run.

- The MDI form may also display a toolbar, containing single-click shortcuts for carrying out the most common menu commands.

- A Window menu on the MDI form typically lists the names of all the open windows inside the form, and provides an easy way to select and activate a given document.

- The Window menu may also contain commands designed to rearrange the open documents within the MDI form. For example, the Cascade command places the open windows in an overlapping stack, and the Tile command arranges them side-by-side.

- The programming resources of the MDI environment allow you to write code that carries out common operations on all open files. For instance, before the end of a performance, your program can ensure that all changes will be saved to disk from open documents.

In Chapter 11 you saw a simple example of an MDI application, called the Travel Reminders program. That program presents three check lists of typical travel-related activities — tasks that you need to accomplish before, during, and after a business trip. The windows for these lists are created as three instances of the same form definition, all displayed inside an MDI form.

In this chapter you'll work with a somewhat more elaborate application example, an MDI version of the Transportation Planner application. First presented in Chapter 10, the Transportation Planner is designed to create files describing the travel arrangements for a multi-stop business trip. The files are saved on disk as random-access databases with TRV extensions; each record in a file contains information about one leg of a trip. In the fields of a record you specify the mode of transportation, the reservation status and number, the date and time of departure, the origin and destination of the trip, and any brief notes that you want to keep about the trip.

The original version of the program consists of a single form in which you can enter or review a record. Using this one form, you can open any TRV file and scroll through its existing records; and you can save new TRV files to disk. By contrast, the MDI version presented in this chapter enables you to open several travel files at once in a convenient working environment. In this case, the "documents" of the MDI application are travel databases; each window that you open in the program becomes a scrollable display of a particular TRV file that you're creating or reviewing. This program illustrates the full potential of MDI in Visual Basic applications.

The Transportation Planner, MDI Version

The program is stored on disk as TranMDI.VBP. (Don't confuse its component files with the original version of the program, which is stored as TranPlan.VBP.) Open the program now and take a look at its project window. As you can see in Figure 12-1, the program contains two form files. The MDI parent form is saved as TranMDIp.FRM and is named frmTranParent. The child form is saved as TranMDIc.FRM and named frmTranPlan.

Figure 12-1
The project window for the Transportation Planner program, MDI version.

Both forms contain important quantities of code. In general, the code in the parent form deals with MDI events and processing tasks that apply to all child windows. By contrast, the code in the child form focuses on operations for an open travel file. As you know, each instance of a child form contains its own copy of the code from the form definition, and keeps track of its own data. In other words, each new instance of the frmTranPlan form operates as an independent window for a particular open travel file. You'll see exactly how this works as you run the program for the first time.

RUNNING THE PROGRAM

Press F5 or click the Start button on the Visual Basic toolbar to begin the program. When you do, you'll see the Transportation Planner window take over the screen, as shown in Figure 12-2. The MDI window starts out in a maximized state and initially displays one instance of the child form with the generic name Trip1; at this point, no file is open. Like the original version of the program, this form displays an assortment of option buttons, text boxes, and check boxes representing the fields of a transportation record.

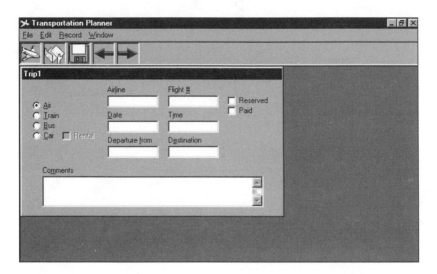

Figure 12-2
The Transportation Planner program at the beginning of a run.

Examining the elements of the application, you'll find that the program's menu bar is displayed at the top of the application window, not inside the Trip window. The menu bar identifies four lists of commands: The File menu contains commands for creating new Trip windows, opening travel files, saving a file to disk, printing the records of an open travel file, and exiting from the program. The Edit menu has a Clear command that erases the information from the current record. The Record menu contains Next and Previous commands for scrolling through the records of a travel file. The Window menu, as discussed earlier, presents a list of all the open windows, and provides commands for rearranging Trip windows within the application window.

Just below the menu line you can see the toolbar (Figure 12-3), which in this application contains a row of five buttons representing specific menu operations:

- The first button, showing an image of an airplane, is the New button. Clicking it adds a new Trip window to the group of open windows.

- The second is the Open button. It displays the Open dialog box on the screen so that you can open an existing travel file in the active Trip window.

- The third is the Save As button. It displays the Save As dialog box so you can save the contents of the active Trip window as a new travel file on disk.

- The fourth and fifth buttons are for scrolling through the records of an open travel file. The Previous button takes you one record back in the file, and the Next button displays the next record forward.

You'll have a chance to experiment with the program's menu commands and toolbar buttons in the upcoming exercises.

Figure 12-3
The toolbar of the Transportation Planner program, MDI version.

ADDING TRIP WINDOWS AND OPENING FILES

You can open additional Trip windows either by clicking the New button on the toolbar or by choosing the New command from the File menu (Figure 12-4). The program gives each new window a generic name (Trip2, Trip3, and so on), and initially displays the windows in a cascade arrangement. In its current version, the program enables you to open as many as five Trip windows. When you reach that maximum, as in Figure 12-5, the New command is dimmed in the File menu, and the New button is removed from the toolbar.

The five-window maximum is an arbitrary limitation. Later in this chapter you'll find out how to adjust the program's code if you want to increase the number of files that can be opened at one time.

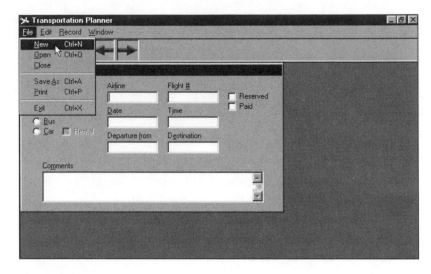

Figure 12-4

Choosing the New command to open an additional Trip window.

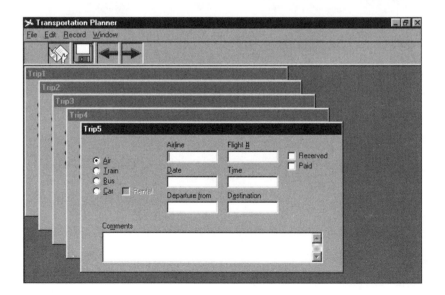

Figure 12-5

Opening the maximum number of windows.

Initially, each new Trip window contains no data and displays no open file. To open an existing TRV file from disk, you follow these steps:

1. Click the title bar of the Trip window in which you want to open the file. This becomes the *active* window.

2. Pull down the File menu and choose the Open command or click the Open button on the toolbar. The Open dialog box appears on the screen, as shown in Figure 12-6.

3. Choose the name of the file that you want to open, or type the name into the File name text box. Then click Open.

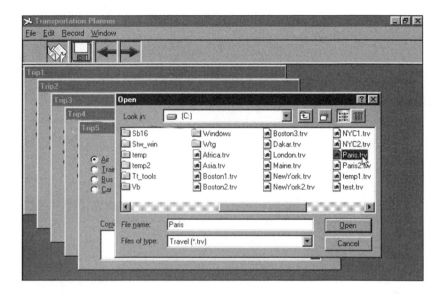

Figure 12-6
Opening a travel file.

In response, the program opens the file you've selected and displays its path and file name in the title bar of the active Trip window. (Initially the trip window displays a blank form in which you can enter the fields of a new record to be stored in the file; to scroll backward through existing records, click the Previous button on the toolbar.) If you want to open files in other Trip windows, repeat these three steps, activating a different window each time. For example, Figure 12-7 shows the five Trip windows at a moment when each one contains an open travel file. Notice that the title bar of each window displays not only the file name, but the number of the current record that's displayed in the window.

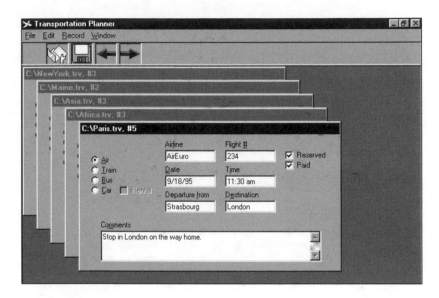

Figure 12-7
Opening a different file in each of the five Trip windows.

By the way, the program prevents you from opening the same file twice in two different Trip windows. If you choose the Open command and select the name of a file that's already open, the program simply skips the operation.

Whether a Trip window contains a single new record that you've just entered or a file that you've opened, you can use the Save As operation to save the information in the window under a new file name. Here are the steps:

1. Click the title bar of the target Trip window. This becomes the active window.

2. Pull down the File menu and choose Save As, or click the Save As button on the toolbar. The Save As dialog box appears on the screen, as shown in Figure 12-8.

3. Enter the name of the file you want to create. Alternatively, select the name of an existing file that you want to overwrite. In this case, the program displays a warning ("This file already exists") and asks you to confirm that you want to replace the existing file; click Yes if you do. Then click Save to complete the operation.

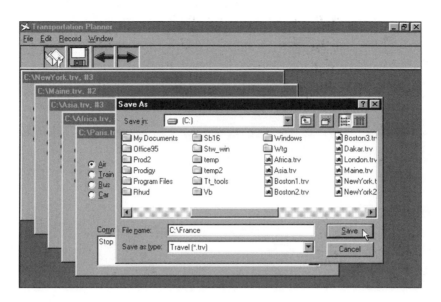

Figure 12-8
Saving a travel file under a new name on disk.

After these steps, the program displays the name of the new file in the title bar of the active Trip window. There are actually three ways to scroll through the records of an open file. You can press the PgUp or PgDn key to scroll backward or forward through the file; you can choose the Previous or Next command from the Record menu; or you can click the Previous or Next button on the toolbar.

USING THE WINDOW MENU

The Window menu gives you an easy way to activate any of the open Trip windows using the keyboard or the mouse. You can pull down the menu either by clicking Window with the mouse or by pressing Alt,W from the keyboard. As shown in Figure 12-9, the menu displays a list of all the open windows. For each window that contains an open file, the list displays the file name — that is, the full text from the window's title bar. For a window that does not contain an open file, the list displays a generic name such as Trip1 or Trip2. To activate a window, click any name in the list or press the corresponding number (from 1 to 5) at the keyboard.

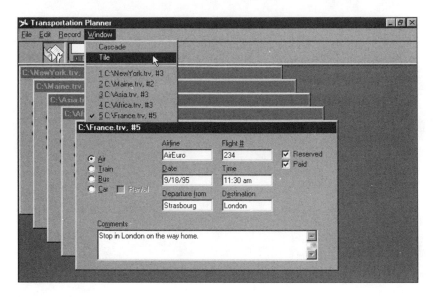

Figure 12-9
The Window menu.

For example, suppose you want to close the file displayed in a particular Trip window so you can begin recording a new itinerary. Here's how you can use the Window menu to select the window, and then the Close command to close the file:

1. Using the mouse or the keyboard, pull down the Window menu and select the name of the file you want to close. The Trip window containing this file becomes the active form.

2. Pull down the File menu and choose Close. The program saves the current record if it has been revised in any way, and then closes the file. The active window returns to its generic title, such as Trip1 or Trip2.

3. Now you can begin entering the first record of a new travel file. Choose Save As when you're ready to create the file on disk.

At the top of the Window menu you can see two additional entries, the Cascade and Tile commands. As you know, Cascade is the program's default arrangement for new Trip windows that you open. To change this arrangement, choose Tile from the Window menu. The program rearranges the open windows in a side-by-side format, as shown in Figure 12-10. Note that you can also move any window to a new position inside the MDI form simply by dragging the target window by its title bar. To return to the original cascade arrangement, pull down the Window menu again and choose Cascade.

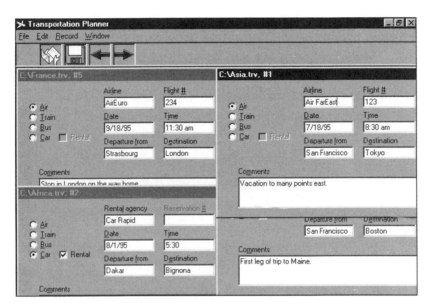

Figure 12-10

Arranging the open windows side-by-side using the Tile option.

When you've finished working with travel files, you can end the program performance by choosing Exit from the File menu or by clicking the close button at the upper-right corner of the Transportation Planner window. Either way, the program ensures that any unsaved records are written to their respective files before the performance ends.

Inside the MDI Application

In the steps for developing a successful MDI application, you begin by setting form properties, defining menus, and designing a toolbar. Then you write the code to manage specific operations in the multiple-document environment.

At the outset, you need to understand several important points about an MDI form:

- An MDI form may contain its own menu definition. But whenever a child form is active within the MDI form, the child's menu is displayed at the top of the application window, completely taking the place of the MDI parent menu. Only when no child form is open does the parent menu appear. This arrangement allows an application to adjust its menus according to the context of particular runtime events. In the Transportation Planner program, at least one child form is always open; the menu bar therefore derives from the menu definition of the child form, frmTranPlan. The MDI form in this program contains no menu definition.

- To create a Window menu — displaying the names of all open child forms in the MDI form — you simply check the WindowList property in the Menu Editor at design time. At runtime, Visual Basic automatically builds and updates the window list as changes occur in the number of open windows. Figure 12-11 shows the menu definition for the child form, frmTranPlan, in the Transportation Planner application. The WindowList property is checked for the Window menu. You can review the result of this setting by looking again at Figure 12-9.

- An MDI form cannot contain the same variety of controls that are available for a standard form. In fact the only intrinsic control that you can place on an MDI form is the picture box. This control's Align property specifies where the box will be displayed within the form. The default Align setting for a picture box in an MDI form is 1-Top. A picture box works ideally as the container for a toolbar. Inside the picture box you can add an assortment of command buttons or image controls, as you'll learn a little later in this chapter.

- You define a child form by assigning a setting of True to the property named MDIChild on a standard form in your application. If a child form is designated as the startup form in an MDI application, Visual Basic displays the child form inside the MDI form at the beginning of a program run. But if the MDI form is the startup, no child form is automatically loaded into the parent. In the Transportation Planner, the MDI form is the startup. An MDIChild setting of True designates the frmTranPlan form as the child, as shown in Figure 12-12. The MDIForm_Load procedure arranges to display the first instance of frmTranPlan in the application window. You'll see how this works when you examine the program's code.

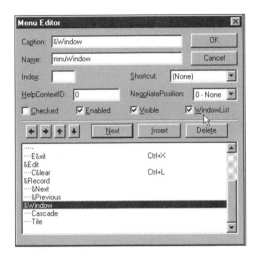

Figure 12-11
Setting the WindowList property for the Window menu.

Figure 12-12
Using the MDIChild property to designate a child form in an MDI application.

CREATING A TOOLBAR ON THE MDI FORM

To prepare a toolbar for an MDI form, you begin by placing a picture box on the form. Then you can add any number of image controls or command button controls to the containing picture box. (Keep in mind that the image and command button controls may not be placed directly on the MDI form, only inside the picture box control.) Here's an outline of the steps for creating a toolbar like the one that appears in the Transportation Planner:

1. Open your project's MDI form at design time, and double-click the PictureBox button in the Toolbox. The picture box control automatically appears just beneath the title bar of the MDI form, in the typical position of a toolbar.

2. Select the Image control in the Toolbox. Carefully draw a row of image controls inside the picture box. Each control you draw will become a button in the toolbar.

3. Select the first image control and press F4 to open the Properties window. Select the Picture property and click the small button displayed at the right side of the property setting. In the Load Picture dialog box, navigate to the Icons directory and select a subdirectory that contains the icon you want to display on the image control. Select the icon file and click Open. The image you've selected appears on the face of the control. Repeat this step for each of the other image controls you've placed inside the picture box.

4. Set other properties of each individual image control. Begin by selecting the Name property and entering a meaningful name for each control. Then experiment with the BorderStyle property to modify the appearance of each image; the Stretch property to adjust the size of the icon displayed on each button; and, if necessary, the Left, Top, Height, and Width properties to correct the position and dimensions of each control within the picture box.

5. Finally, write a Click event procedure for each button in the toolbar you've created. Typically these procedures make calls to corresponding menu procedures; as a result, the toolbar buttons perform the

same operations as the menu commands that they represent. For example, in the Transportation Planner, the imgOpen_Click procedure — the Click event for the Open button on the toolbar — simply calls the mnuOpen_Click procedure for the active Trip window.

You'll learn more about the event procedures for toolbar buttons as you now turn to the code of the Transportation Planner MDI application.

Other Ways to Create a Toolbar

You've probably noticed an interesting anomaly in the use of image controls for the buttons of a toolbar. When the user clicks an image control with the mouse, the object doesn't behave quite like a typical Windows button. The satisfying push-button effect — the action that normally takes place on the screen when a button is clicked — doesn't happen with an image control.

One way to solve this problem is to fill the picture box with a row of command buttons rather than image controls. As you know, a command button control provides the usual push-button behavior in response to a click at runtime. Unfortunately, a command button can display only text, the setting of the control's Caption property. The control has no Picture property that could enable you to display a graphics image on the face of the button. A toolbar made up of command buttons would therefore display a row of text captions, not icons, to represent the common operations of the application.

A more sophisticated approach for creating a toolbar is to use the Toolbar custom control, which is supplied with the Professional and Enterprise editions of Visual Basic. (This feature is not available in the Standard edition.) The Toolbar control and its associated ImageList control enable you to create the visual elements of a Windows-style toolbar in an application. To use the Toolbar control, you place an instance of it on a form. Then click the control with the right mouse button and choose Properties from the resulting pop-up menu list. In the Toolbar Control Properties dialog box, you can add a collection of Button objects to the Toolbar control and set other important properties of the control.

For more information about this custom control, select the Toolbar button in Visual Basic's Toolbox, and press F1 to open the Help facility. In the Custom Control Reference help index, enter the words "Toolbar control" and press Enter. The resulting help topic provides the details about this control and the related ImageList control.

EXPLORING THE PROGRAM'S CODE

The code appears in Listings 12-1 through 12-20 at the end of this chapter. The declarations, event procedures, and general procedures of the MDI parent form, frmTranParent, are in Listings 12-1 through 12-5; these will be the main focus of your attention in this chapter.

The remaining listings (12-6 through 12-20) contain the declarations and procedures of the child form, frmTranPlan. Although these procedures are similar to the code of the original program, as presented in Chapter 10, there are several significant revisions. (Notice again that the child form for the MDI program is saved as TranMDIc.FRM; the corresponding form in the original program is TranPlan.FRM.) Here are some of the differences that you should keep in mind as you examine the code of the MDI program:

- The child form now has a public variable named *fileNumber*, which represents the number that the program assigns to the travel file that is open in a particular Trip window. The variable is declared in the general declarations section of the child form (Listing 12-6):

```
Public fileNumber As Integer
```

After creating an instance of the child form, the program assigns a unique integer value from 1 to 5 to the new form's *fileNumber* property. This avoids any conflicts among the multiple files that may be open at one time. Procedures that work with an open file in the child form use this variable to identify the file; for example, here is how a file is opened in the mnuOpen_Click procedure (Listing 12-8):

```
Open tranFileName For Random As #fileNumber _
   Len = Len(TranRecord)
```

And here is how individual records are read from an open file (Listing 12-14):

```
Get #fileNumber, curTranRecord, TranRecord
```

- Three other key variables are declared publicly in the child form so that the parent form can read the data they contain for each instance of the child. Specifically, the variable *tranFileOpen* indicates whether a file is open in a given child form; *tranFileName* is the name of the open file; and *recordChanged* indicates whether the current record has been revised, and therefore needs to be saved to disk:

```
Public tranFileOpen As Boolean
Public tranFileName As String
Public recordChanged as Boolean
```

- Likewise, several key routines in the child form are defined as Public procedures. This allows the parent form to call procedures as methods of a particular instance of the child form. In particular, several major menu procedures in the child form are declared publicly; when the user clicks a button on the toolbar, the parent form makes a call to the appropriate menu procedure on the child form.

- Finally, several new menu procedures are included in the code of the child form. Keep in mind that the application's menu is defined on the child form, not the parent form. As a result, each instance of the child form displays and responds to its own menu commands. The new menu procedures include mnuClose_Click (Listing 12-13) — which closes the current travel file for the active instance of the child form and restores the form's generic Trip title — and the two event procedures for Window commands, mnuCascade_Click and mnuTile_Click, which rearrange the open windows within the parent form. These two procedures use Visual Basic's Arrange method to rearrange the windows. For example, this statement produces a cascade arrangement:

```
frmTranParent.Arrange 0
```

And this statement creates a tiled arrangement:

```
frmTranParent.Arrange 2
```

The parent form contains procedures designed to carry out the general operations of the multiple-document application. These operations include creating and displaying new instances of the child form (the NewTranChild procedure, in Listing 12-2); responding to clicks on the toolbar buttons (Click event procedures in Listing 12-3); checking to see whether a requested file is already open in an existing child form (the IsAlreadyOpen function in Listing 12-4); and ensuring that all records are saved to their respective files on disk before the program performance ends (the MDIForm_QueryUnload procedure, in Listing 12-5). You'll examine each of these MDI techniques in the sections ahead.

CREATING NEW INSTANCES OF THE CHILD FORM

The public *NewTranChild* procedure (Listing 12-2) is responsible for creating each new instance of the frmTranPlan form and displaying it inside the parent form as a Trip window. This procedure is called once at the beginning of the program by the MDIForm_Load procedure (Listing 12-1), and again from the mnuNew_Click procedure (Listing 12-13) each time the user chooses the New command from the File menu. Because mnuNew_Click is located in the child form, the call requires a reference to the parent form:

```
frmTranParent.NewTranChild
```

The procedure uses a module-level variable named *tripNum* to keep track of the current number of open Trip windows. At the same time, a constant named *MaxTrips* represents the maximum number of Trip windows that the program allows. If *tripNum* is less than or equal to *MaxTrips* at the time *NewTranChild* is called, the procedure's first action is to create a new instance of the frmTranPlan form:

```
If tripNum <= MaxTrips Then
   Dim newTranPlan As New frmTranPlan
```

As you can see, the object variable *newTranPlan* represents the form for the procedure's remaining operations.

The first task is to assign values to the properties of the new form. The procedure concatenates the current value of *tripNum* to the word "Trip" to create a generic title for the form, such as Trip1, Trip2, and so on:

```
newTranPlan.Caption = "Trip" & tripNum
newTranPlan.Tag = newTranPlan.Caption
```

This value is assigned first to the Caption property so that it will appear on the form's title bar. But in addition, a copy of the generic title is stored in the form's Tag property, where it will be available when the program needs to restore the original title to the form. Specifically, this happens in the mnuClose_Click procedure (Listing 12-13), after the program closes the file currently displayed in a given Trip window. On the title bar, the program replaces the name of the newly closed file with the generic Trip title:

```
Caption = Tag
```

As you've seen in previous programs, the Tag property is a useful place to store items of information that are related to a particular form or control.

The *NewTranChild* procedure's next task is to assign a file number to the newly created instance of the child form:

```
newTranPlan.fileNumber = tripNum
```

As you've seen already, each child form uses *fileNumber* to identify an open file; it's therefore essential that each child possess a unique value for this variable. Assigning the value of *tripNum* to *fileNumber* is a simple way to meet this requirement.

Next the procedure displays the new form inside the parent form, and increments the value of *tripNum*:

```
newTranPlan.Show
tripNum = tripNum + 1
```

When *tripNum* goes past the value of *MaxTrips* — that is, when the user has opened the maximum number of Trip windows that the application allows — the procedure disables the New command in the File menu and removes the New button from the toolbar:

```
If tripNum > MaxTrips Then
  For i = 1 To Forms.Count - 1
    Forms(i).mnuNew.Enabled = False
  Next i
  imgNew.Visible = False
End If
```

Keep in mind that the menu definition belongs to the child form, not the parent form. In fact, each child form has its own menu, which is displayed when the child is active. Because all the child forms are designed to behave identically, this is not an obvious issue until the program needs to make a change in the menu. But to disable the New command, the program has to loop through all the open child forms and disable the command on each form. It uses Visual Basic's built-in Forms collection to do the job. A reference to Forms(i).mnuNew identifies the target menu command for each open form. By contrast, the toolbar is defined on the MDI parent form. A simple reference to imgNew.Visible identifies the button property that the procedure needs to switch to False in order to remove the button from the toolbar.

By the way, you can change the program's maximum number of Trip windows by assigning new values to two important constants. In the general declarations section of the MDI parent form, frmTranParent, change the value assigned to *MaxTrips*:

```
Const MaxTrips = 5
```

Then, in the general declarations of the child form, frmTranPlan, change the value of a constant named *CopyFileNum*:

```
Const CopyFileNum = 6
```

The constant *CopyFileNum* represents an extra file number that's available for the Save As operation. *CopyFileNum* needs a value that is 1 greater than *MaxTrips*. So, for example, if you change the value of *MaxTrips* to 10, change *CopyFileNum* to 11; these changes would allow a maximum of 10 open Trip windows during a program run.

RESPONDING TO CLICKS ON THE TOOLBAR BUTTONS

Listing 12-3 shows the five Click event procedures that handle toolbar operations. The first, imgNew_Click, makes a call to the *NewTranChild* procedure when the user clicks the New menu. As you've just seen, the program removes the New button from the toolbar when the user has opened the maximum number of Trip windows, so this Click procedure cannot be called again after that point.

The imgOpen_Click and imgSaveAs_Click procedures both make calls to menu commands on the active child form. To identify the Trip window that's active when the user clicks the Open or Save As button, the program uses Visual Basic's ActiveForm property. Using this important keyword, the following statements make calls to the menu commands belonging to the active child form:

```
ActiveForm.mnuOpen_Click
ActiveForm.mnuSaveAs_Click
```

Likewise, the imgPrevious_Click and imgNext_Click procedures need to make calls to menu procedures for the active form. But here there is an added complication. As you might recall from Chapter 10, the program is careful to disable the Previous and Next commands in the Record menu whenever their use is not appropriate. For example, if the active Trip window is already displaying the first record in an open file, the Previous command is disabled.

Accordingly, the Click procedures for the Previous and Next toolbar buttons need to avoid making calls to the mnuPrevious_Click or mnuNext_Click procedures if the corresponding menu command has been disabled. To conform to this requirement, the event procedures for the toolbar buttons read the Enabled property of the appropriate menu command, and use this Boolean value as the condition in a decision statement. For example, here is how the imgPrevious_Click procedure decides whether or not to make a call to the mnuPrevious_Click procedure:

```
If ActiveForm.mnuPrevious.Enabled Then _
   ActiveForm.mnuPrevious_Click
```

Once again notice the use of the ActiveForm property to identify the form to which this operation applies.

FINDING OUT WHETHER A FILE IS ALREADY OPEN

The program does not permit the user to open the same file in more than one Trip window. To enforce this rule, the program has to examine the files that are open whenever the user chooses a file from the Open or Save As dialog box. If the selected file name matches the name of a file that is already displayed in one of the Trip windows, the file operation is denied.

A function named *IsAlreadyOpen* (Listing 12-4) is responsible for carrying out this check. The function receives, as its single argument, the name of the file that the user has requested:

```
Function IsAlreadyOpen(testFileName As String) _
    As Boolean
```

The function returns a Boolean value of True if the file is already open, or False if not.

On each child form, the public variable *tranFileName* represents the name of the current file. (If no file is open, *tranFileName* contains an empty string.) To see whether or not a given file is open, the *IsAlreadyOpen* function loops through the Forms collection and examines the value of *tranFileName* on each child form:

```
IsAlreadyOpen = False
For i = 1 To Forms.Count - 1
  With Forms(i)
    If Trim(.tranFileName) = Trim(testFileName) _
       Then IsAlreadyOpen = True
  End With
Next i
```

If the comparison between Forms(i).tranFileName and the *testFileName* argument produces a match for any form in the collection, the function returns a value of True.

In the child form, *IsAlreadyOpen* is called from two menu procedures, mnuOpen_Click and mnuSaveAs_Click. The call takes place just after the Open or Save As dialog box disappears from the screen. The file name provided by the common dialog control, cdlFileManager, is passed as an argument to *IsAlreadyOpen*:

```
If frmTranParent.IsAlreadyOpen _
  (cdlFileManager.FileName) Then Exit Sub
```

If *IsAlreadyOpen* returns a value of True, this statement simply terminates the current procedure, skipping the Open or Save As operation.

SAVING ALL FILES BEFORE THE END OF A RUN

Finally, the MDI parent form is responsible for making sure that all open
travel files are saved properly to disk before the end of a program performance. If the user has revised the current records in any of the Trip
windows, those records must be written to their corresponding files
before the windows are closed. To arrange this, the program uses the
MDIForm_QueryUnload procedure (Listing 12-5), which is triggered
when the user clicks the close button at the upper-right corner of the
application window.

The QueryUnload event gives the program the opportunity to perform final operations on any open child forms before the MDI form is
actually closed. In this program, the event procedure makes a call to a
general procedure named SaveAllFiles (also in Figure 12-5). This procedure in turn loops through all the open Trip windows and checks to see
whether the current record has changed in each case; if so, a call is
made to the *SaveCurRec* procedure in the child form to save the current
record to disk:

```
For i = 1 To Forms.Count - 1
  With Forms(i)
    If .tranFileOpen And .recordChanged Then _
      .SaveCurRec
  End With
Next i
```

Once again, the program uses Visual Basic's built-in Forms collection
to address each open child form in turn. As you'll recall, the *tranFileOpen*
and *recordChanged* variables are declared as public variables on the child
form. If both of these Boolean variables have values of True, the current
record has been changed and must be saved before the Trip window
is closed.

IV

12

The mnuExit_Click procedure in the child form (Listing 12-20) also makes a call to the *SaveAllFiles* procedure on the parent form:

```
frmTranParent.SaveAllFiles
```

This ensures that the final save operation will be performed no matter what technique the user chooses to terminate the program performance.

As a programming exercise, you might want to try developing a new MDI application from another project presented earlier in this book. For example:

- An MDI version of the International Travel Expense Log program (Chapter 5) could enable the user to open expense files from several different business trips at once.

- Similarly, an MDI version of the International Sales program (Chapter 9) could give the user the opportunity to compare sales data for different products, time periods, or geographical regions.

MDI is clearly an important feature that adds a new level of value to your Visual Basic applications.

Listing 12-1

General declarations and the MDIForm_Load procedure from the MDI parent form

```
' The Transportation Planner, MDI version.
' ---------------------------------------

' Files:
' ------
' Project File:     TranMDI.VBP
' MDI Parent Form:  TranMDIp.FRM (this file)
' MDI Child Form:   TranMDIc.FRM

' This MDI version of the Transportation Planner
' program allows the user to open as many as five
' itinerary files at once, and view them within
' the environment of a contining window. The MDI
' window includes a menu bar and a Toolbar designed
```

```
' to simplify the program's various operations.
' There is also a Windows menu that lists the
' names of the open files and offers the
' opportunity of displaying them in cascade or
' tiled arrangements.

Option Explicit

' The maximum number of open files.
Const MaxTrips = 5

' The number of the active file.
Dim tripNum As Integer
'
' End of general declarations, TranMDIp.FRM.




Private Sub MDIForm_Load()

    ' The MDIForm_Load procedure initializes the
    ' tripNum variable to 1 (the first travel file
    ' to be created), and then makes a call to the
    ' NewTranChild procedure to open the first
    ' travel form.

    tripNum = 1
    NewTranChild

End Sub    ' MDIForm_Load
```

Listing 12-2
The NewTranChild procedure

```
Sub NewTranChild()

    ' The NewTranChild procedure creates a new
    ' instance of the frmTranPlan form, sets its
    ' properties, and displays it inside the
    ' containing MDI form.
```

```
Dim i

If tripNum <= MaxTrips Then

  ' Create the new instance of the form.
  Dim newTranPlan As New frmTranPlan

  ' Display a generic title on the form's
  ' title bar, and keep a record of this
  ' first title in the Tag property.
  newTranPlan.Caption = "Trip" & tripNum
  newTranPlan.Tag = newTranPlan.Caption

  ' Assign a unique file number to each
  ' instance of the form, ensuring that
  ' there will be no conflicts among open
  ' files.
  newTranPlan.fileNumber = tripNum

  ' Display the form and increment the
  ' tripNum counter.
  newTranPlan.Show
  tripNum = tripNum + 1

  ' If tripNum now exceeds the maximum
  ' number of open files, disable the New
  ' menu command and the New button on
  ' the toolbar.
  If tripNum > MaxTrips Then
    For i = 1 To Forms.Count - 1
      Forms(i).mnuNew.Enabled = False
    Next i
    imgNew.Visible = False
  End If
End If

End Sub    ' NewTranChild
```

A new instance of frmTranPlan

Disabling the New Command in the menus of all the child forms

Listing 12-3
The Click procedures for the toolbar buttons

```
Private Sub imgNew_Click()

    ' The imgNew_Click procedure responds to a
    ' click of the New button on the program's
    ' toolbar. The procedure makes a call to
    ' NewTranChild to create a new instance of
    ' the frmTranPlan form. Note that the
    ' imgNew button is removed from the toolbar
    ' once the maximum number of forms has been
    ' created.

    NewTranChild

End Sub   ' imgNew_Click


Private Sub imgOpen_Click()

    ' The imgOpen_Click procedure makes a call to
    ' the mnuOpen_Click procedure on the active
    ' form, allowing the user to open a new
    ' travel file.

    ActiveForm.mnuOpen_Click

End Sub   ' imgOpen_Click


Private Sub imgSaveAs_Click()

    ' The imgSaveAs_Click procedure makes a call to
    ' the mnuSaveAs_Click procedure on the active
    ' form, allowing the user to save the current
    ' travel file under a new name.

    ActiveForm.mnuSaveAs_Click

End Sub   ' imgSaveAs_Click
```

```
Private Sub imgPrevious_Click()

    ' The imgPrevious_Click procedure responds to a
    ' click of the Previous button on the program's
    ' toolbar. The program uses the ActiveForm
    ' property to identify the current form, and
    ' makes a call to the form's mnuPrevious_Click
    ' procedure if the menu command is currently
    ' available.

    If ActiveForm.mnuPrevious.Enabled Then _
        ActiveForm.mnuPrevious_Click

End Sub    ' imgPrevious_Click
```

Using Active Form to identify the current form

```
Private Sub imgNext_Click()

    ' The imgNext_Click procedure responds to a
    ' click of the Next button on the program's
    ' toolbar. The program uses the ActiveForm
    ' property to identify the current form, and
    ' makes a call to the form's mnuNext_Click
    ' procedure if the menu command is currently
    ' available.

    If ActiveForm.mnuNext.Enabled Then _
        ActiveForm.mnuNext_Click

End Sub    ' imgNext_Click
```

```
Private Sub picToolbar_Click()

    ' The picToolbar_Click procedure returns the
    ' focus to the active child form if the user
    ' clicks a background area of the toolbar.

    ActiveForm.SetFocus

End Sub    ' picToolbar_Click
```

Listing 12-4

The IsAlreadyOpen function

```
Function IsAlreadyOpen(testFileName As String) _
    As Boolean

  ' The IsAlreadyOpen function determines whether
  ' a file that the user has requested is already
  ' open. (If it is, the program avoids the attempt
  ' to open it a second time.)

  Dim i

  ' Start out assuming the file is not open.
  IsAlreadyOpen = False

  ' Loop through the open forms, not including
  ' the MDI parent form. Use Visual Basic's
  ' Forms collection to identify each form in
  ' turn. (The Count property tells how many
  ' forms are currently open.)
  For i = 1 To Forms.Count - 1                 Looping through the
    With Forms(i)                              forms collection

      ' If the user has entered a file name
      ' that matches one of the open files,
      ' the function returns a value of True.
      If Trim(.tranFileName) = Trim(testFileName) _
        Then IsAlreadyOpen = True
    End With
  Next i

End Function   ' IsAlreadyOpen
```

IV

12

Listing 12-5
The MDIForm_QueryUnload and SaveAllFiles procedures

```
Private Sub MDIForm_QueryUnload(Cancel As Integer, _
  UnloadMode As Integer)

    ' The MDIForm_QueryUnload procedure ensures
    ' that all unsaved records are written to
    ' their respective disk files before the program
    ' run is terminated. This event procedure is
    ' triggered if the user ends the program by
    ' clicking the close button at the upper-right
    ' corner of the MDI form.

    SaveAllFiles

End Sub   ' MDIForm_QueryUnload


Public Sub SaveAllFiles()

    ' The SaveAllFiles procedure is called just
    ' before the end of the program performance
    ' to ensure that any unsaved travel records
    ' are written to disk before the forms are
    ' closed.

    Dim i

    ' Loop through the open forms (except the
    ' MDI parent form), using the Forms collection.
    For i = 1 To Forms.Count - 1
      With Forms(i)

        ' If a given form displays an open file
        ' and if the current record has changed
        ' then the record needs to be written to
        ' disk before the program ends.
        If .tranFileOpen And .recordChanged Then _
          .SaveCurRec
      End With
```

The QueryUnload event proceedure

```
Next i

' Terminate the program performance only
' after making sure all records have been
' saved.
End


End Sub   ' SaveAllFiles
```

Listing 12-6
General declarations from the child form, frmTranPlan

```
' The Transportation Planner, MDI version.
' ----------------------------------------


' Files:
' ------
' Project File:      TranMDI.VBP
' MDI Parent Form:   TranMDIp.FRM
' MDI Child Form:    TranMDIc.FRM (this file)

' This menu-driven program allows the user to
' create itinerary files on disk. Each random-
' access file contains records describing the
' transportation plans and reservations for an
' upcoming business trip or vacation. Files are
' stored on disk with TRV extension names. The
' user can open any file, browse through records
' in the file, revise records, or add new records.

' The program illustrates the use of Visual Basic's
' Custom Dialog control. This control provides
' easy access to standard Windows dialog boxes,
' including the Save As and Open dialog boxes, as
' shown in this application.

Option Explicit
```

```
' A temporary file number for performing
' the Save As command.
Const CopyFileNum = 6

' The structure of transportation records,
' defined as a private type in this module.
Private Type TranRecType
  TranMode As Integer
  RentalCar As Boolean
  Carrier As String * 30
  TripNumber As String * 30
  ReservedStatus As Boolean
  PaidStatus As Boolean
  TripDate As String * 30
  TripTime As String * 30
  TripFrom As String * 30
  TripTo As String * 30
  Comments As String * 200
End Type

' The file number for this instance of the form.
' This number is assigned by the parent form
' at the time the instance of the child form
' is created.
Public fileNumber As Integer
```

The file number for this instance of the form

```
' Variables for this form.
Dim TranRecord As TranRecType ' A single record.
Dim curTranRecord As Integer  ' Current record number.

' Public variables for this form.
' (The parent form needs access to these.)
Public tranFileOpen As Boolean   ' Is a file open?
Public tranFileName As String    ' Name of open file.
Public recordChanged As Boolean  ' Has record changed?
'
' End of general declarations, frmTranPlan.
```

Other public variables for the form

Listing 12-7
The Form_Load and Form_KeyDown procedures

```
Private Sub Form_Load()

    ' The Form_Load procedure initializes a few
    ' of the program's variables and control
    ' properties.

    ' No file is open yet.
    tranFileOpen = False
    recordChanged = False

    ' Set the record pointer to 1.
    curTranRecord = 1

    ' Disable the Next and Previous
    ' commands.
    mnuNext.Enabled = False
    mnuPrevious.Enabled = False

End Sub   ' Form_Load



Private Sub Form_KeyDown(KeyCode As Integer, _
    Shift As Integer)

    ' The Form_KeyDown procedure allows the user
    ' to press PgDn or PgUp to scroll through the
    ' records of an open transportation file.

    ' *** Note that the child form's KeyPreview
    '       property is set to True to make this
    '       event possible.

    ' Code numbers for the
    ' PgDn and PgUp keys.
    Const PgDn = 34
    Const PgUp = 33
```

```
            ' If the user presses PgDn and the Next
            ' command is currently enabled, force a call
            ' to the mnuNext_Click event procedure.
            If KeyCode = PgDn _
              And mnuNext.Enabled = True _
                Then mnuNext_Click

            ' If the user presses PgUp and the Previous
            ' command is currently enabled, force a call
            ' to the mnuPrevious_Click event procedure.
            If KeyCode = PgUp _
              And mnuPrevious.Enabled = True _
                Then mnuPrevious_Click


        End Sub   ' Form_KeyDown
```

Listing 12-8
The mnuOpen_Click procedure

```
        Public Sub mnuOpen_Click()

            ' The mnuOpen_Click procedure allows the user
            ' to open an existing TRV file from disk. Once
            ' the file is open, the user can browse through
            ' its records, revise any record, or add new
            ' records in the active child form.

            ' If a file is already open in the active form,
            ' begin by saving the current record to disk
            ' if necessary.
            If tranFileOpen And recordChanged Then _
              SaveCurRec
            recordChanged = False

            ' Set the Flags property of the Open dialog box.
            cdlFileManager.Flags = cdlOFNFileMustExist Or _
                                   cdlOFNHideReadOnly Or _
                                   cdlOFNNoChangeDir Or _
                                   cdlOFNPathMustExist
```

```
' Use the ShowOpen method to display the Open
' dialog box. An error trap allows for the
' possibility that the user will click the
' Cancel button. In this case, terminate the
' procedure by jumping to the userCancel label.
On Error GoTo userCancel
  cdlFileManager.ShowOpen
On Error GoTo 0

' Check to see if the requested file is already
' open in another child form. (The IsAlreadyOpen
' function on the parent form returns a value of
' True if this is the case.) If so, ignore the
' user's request and exit from this procedure.
If frmTranParent.IsAlreadyOpen _
  (cdlFileManager.filename) Then Exit Sub

' If a file is currently open in this
' child form, close it. Then record the
' requested file name as tranFileName.
If tranFileOpen Then Close #fileNumber
tranFileName = cdlFileManager.filename

' Open the file and switch
' tranFileOpen to true.
Open tranFileName For Random As #fileNumber _
  Len = Len(TranRecord)
tranFileOpen = True

' Prepare to append a new record to
' the end of the file.
BlankEOFRecord

' If the file contains more than one record,
' enable the Previous command so that the user
' can scroll backward through the records.
If curTranRecord > 1 Then _
  mnuPrevious.Enabled = True
```

```
    ' Display the new caption in the title bar.
    Caption = tranFileName & _
      ", #" & curTranRecord

  ' Terminate the procedure if the
  ' user clicks the Cancel button.
  userCancel:

  End Sub   ' mnuOpen_Click
```

Listing 12-9
The SaveCurRec and MakeTranRecord procedures

```
Public Sub SaveCurRec()

    ' The SaveCurRec procedure writes the current
    ' transportation record to its correct position
    ' in the open file of the active child form.

    ' Copy the user's input to the
    ' TranRecord structure.
    MakeTranRecord

    ' Write the record to the file. The variable
    ' curTranRecord keeps track of the current
    ' record position. The variable fileNumber
    ' represents the open file for the active
    ' child form.
    Put #fileNumber, curTranRecord, TranRecord
    recordChanged = False

  End Sub   ' SaveCurRec



Private Sub MakeTranRecord()

    ' The MakeTranRecord procedure copies the
    ' user's entries for the current transportation
    ' record to the TranRecord structure.
```

```
' Note that the TranRecType and the TranRecord
' variable are declared in the general
' declarations section of this form.

Dim i

With TranRecord

  ' Determine which of the four optMode
  ' buttons is currently selected.
  For i = 0 To 3
    If optMode(i).VALUE Then
      .TranMode = i
    End If
  Next i

  ' If the selection is Car, read the
  ' value of the chkRental check box.
  If .TranMode = 3 Then
    If chkRental.VALUE = 0 Then
      .RentalCar = False
    Else
      .RentalCar = True
    End If
  End If

  ' Read the first two text boxes.
  .Carrier = txtCarrier.TEXT
  .TripNumber = txtTripNumber.TEXT

  ' Read the values of the Reserved
  ' and Paid check boxes.
  If chkReserved.VALUE = 0 Then
    .ReservedStatus = False
  Else
    .ReservedStatus = True
  End If

  If chkPaid.VALUE = 0 Then
    .PaidStatus = False
```

```
      Else
        .PaidStatus = True
      End If

      ' Read the remaining text boxes.
      .TripDate = txtDate.TEXT
      .TripTime = txtTime.TEXT
      .TripFrom = txtFrom.TEXT
      .TripTo = txtTo.TEXT

      .Comments = txtNotes.TEXT

   End With

End Sub   ' MakeTranRecord
```

Listing 12-10
The BlankEOFRecord procedure and the FindRecordCount function

```
Private Sub BlankEOFRecord()

   ' This procedure moves the record pointer
   ' one position past the end of the current
   ' file, in preparation for a new record entry.

   curTranRecord = FindRecordCount + 1
   mnuClear_Click
   recordChanged = False

   ' Disable the Next command until the
   ' user makes an entry into this new record.
   mnuNext.Enabled = False

End Sub   ' BlankEOFRecord




Private Function FindRecordCount()
```

```
' The FindRecordCount function determines
' the number of records in the current
' transportation file. Note that this
' function is called only if a file is open.

' The variable fileNumber represents the
' open file in the active child form.
FindRecordCount = LOF(fileNumber) / _
   Len(TranRecord)

End Function   ' FindRecordCount
```

Listing 12-11
The mnuSaveAs_Click procedure

```
Public Sub mnuSaveAs_Click()

   ' The mnuSave_Click procedure takes control when
   ' the user clicks the Save As command, and gives
   ' the user the opportunity to create a new file.

   Dim newFileName As String

   ' Set the Flags property of the Save As
   ' dialog box.
   cdlFileManager.Flags = cdlOFNOverwritePrompt Or _
                          cdlOFNHideReadOnly Or _
                          cdlOFNNoChangeDir Or _
                          cdlOFNPathMustExist

   ' If the user clicks Cancel on the Save
   ' dialog box, the ShowSave method generates
   ' an error. In this case, exit from this
   ' procedure.
   On Error GoTo userCancel
      cdlFileManager.ShowSave
   On Error GoTo 0
```

```
' Check to see if the requested file is already
' open in another child form. (The IsAlreadyOpen
' function on the parent form returns a value of
' True if this is the case.) If so, ignore the
' user's request and exit from this procedure.
If frmTranParent.IsAlreadyOpen _
  (cdlFileManager.filename) Then Exit Sub


' Record the file name
' that the user has entered.
newFileName = cdlFileManager.filename


' If a file is currently open, save its
' final record and then copy its records
' to the new "save as" file. The variable
' fileNumber represents the open file in
' the active child form.
If tranFileOpen Then
  If recordChanged Then SaveCurRec
  Close #fileNumber
  CopyDatabase newFileName, tranFileName
Else
' Otherwise, if no file is open, check
' to see if the "save as" file currently
' exists on disk; if it does, delete it.
  tranFileName = newFileName
  On Error Resume Next
    Kill tranFileName
  On Error GoTo 0

  ' Open the new file and save the current
  ' entry as its first record.
  Open tranFileName For Random As #fileNumber _
    Len = Len(TranRecord)
  If recordChanged Then
    SaveCurRec
    mnuNext.Enabled = True
  End If
End If
```

```
    tranFileOpen = True
    recordChanged = False

    ' Display the file name and record number
    ' on the form's title bar.
    Caption = tranFileName & _
      ", #" & curTranRecord

' Terminate the procedure if the user
' has clicked the Cancel button.
userCancel:

End Sub   ' mnuSaveAs_Click
```

Listing 12-12
The CopyDatabase procedure

```
Private Sub CopyDatabase _
  (toFile As String, fromFile As String)

    ' The CopyDatabase procedure copies the records
    ' of the current transportation file to a new
    ' file, in response to the user's instructions
    ' in the Save As command.

    Dim i As Long

    ' If the destination file already exists,
    ' delete it from disk. (Note that the Save As
    ' dialog box provides a warning if the user
    ' chooses an existing file; the Save As
    ' operation continues only if the user confirms.)
    On Error Resume Next
      Kill toFile
    On Error GoTo 0

    ' Open the two files, using the assigned
    ' file number for the current instance of the
```

```
            ' child form (fileNumber) and the temporary
            ' file number defined for this operation
            ' (CopyFileNum).
            Open toFile For Random As #fileNumber _
              Len = Len(TranRecord)
            Open fromFile For Random As #CopyFileNum _
              Len = Len(TranRecord)

            ' Copy all the records from the source file
            ' to the destination file.
            For i = 1 To LOF(CopyFileNum) / Len(TranRecord)
              Get #CopyFileNum, i, TranRecord
              Put #fileNumber, i, TranRecord
            Next i

            ' Close the source file. The destination
            ' file becomes the current transportation
            ' database.
            Close #CopyFileNum
            tranFileName = toFile

        End Sub   ' CopyDatabase
```

Listing 12-13
The mnuNew_Click, mnuClose_Click, and mnuClear_Click procedures

```
        Private Sub mnuNew_Click()

            ' The mnuNew_Click procedure makes a call
            ' to the NewTranChild procedure in the parent
            ' form when the user chooses the New command
            ' from the File menu.

            frmTranParent.NewTranChild

        End Sub   ' mnuNew_Click
```

```
Private Sub mnuClose_Click()

    ' The mnuClose_Click procedure closes the
    ' travel file in the current child form when
    ' the user chooses the Close command from
    ' the File menu. Note that this procedure
    ' does not close the child form itself, but
    ' simply restores its generic name on
    ' the title bar.

    ' If a file is open, save its current
    ' record if necessary.
    If tranFileOpen And recordChanged Then _
        SaveCurRec

    ' Then close the file.
    If tranFileOpen Then Close #fileNumber

    ' Reinitialize the tranFileName and
    ' tranFileOpen variables. (The parent form
    ' uses both of these to learn the current
    ' status of the child form.)
    tranFileName = ""
    tranFileOpen = False

    ' Clear any entries from the form, and
    ' initialize the recordChanged and
    ' curTranRecord variables.
    mnuClear_Click
    recordChanged = False
    curTranRecord = 1

    ' Disable the Previous and Next commands.
    mnuPrevious.Enabled = False
    mnuNext.Enabled = False

    ' Display a new caption in the title bar.
    ' (Note that the parent form stores the
    ' generic title for the form in the
    ' Tag property at the time the child form
```

```
   ' is first created.)
   Caption = Tag

End Sub   ' mnuClose_Click


Private Sub mnuClear_Click()

   ' The mnuClear_Click procedure clears the
   ' entries from all the controls in the
   ' Transportation Planner form, preparing
   ' for a new record entry.

   optMode(0).VALUE = True
   txtCarrier.TEXT = ""
   txtTripNumber.TEXT = ""
   chkReserved.VALUE = 0
   chkPaid.VALUE = 0
   txtDate.TEXT = ""
   txtTime.TEXT = ""
   txtFrom.TEXT = ""
   txtTo.TEXT = ""
   txtNotes.TEXT = ""

   txtCarrier.SetFocus

End Sub   ' mnuClear_Click
```

Listing 12-14

The mnuPrevious_Click and mnuNext_Click procedures

```
Public Sub mnuPrevious_Click()
```

Public event procedure, available to the MDI form

```
   ' The mnuPrevious_Click procedure scrolls one
   ' record back in the current file. Note that
   ' the Previous command is disabled until a file
   ' is open and the program determines that the
   ' file contains more than one record.
```

```
' First save the current record if necessary.
If recordChanged Then SaveCurRec

' Decrease the value of the record pointer
' (curTranRecord) by 1, and read the
' corresponding record from the file. Then
' display the record in the form. The variable
' fileNumber represents the open file in the
' active child form.
curTranRecord = curTranRecord - 1
Get #fileNumber, curTranRecord, TranRecord
ShowRecord
recordChanged = False

' Display the file name and the record number
' in the form's title bar.
Caption = tranFileName & _
  ", #" & curTranRecord

' Enable the Next command. If the user has
' scrolled back to the first record in the
' file, disable the Previous command.
mnuNext.Enabled = True
If curTranRecord = 1 Then _
  mnuPrevious.Enabled = False

End Sub   ' mnuPrevious_Click
```

*Public event
procedure*

```
Public Sub mnuNext_Click()
```

```
' The mnuNext_Click procedure scrolls to the
' next transportation record in the current file.
' (The Next command is disabled if no file is open;
' it is also unavailable if the record pointer is
' past the end of the file.)
```

```
     ' First save the current record
     ' if necessary.
     If recordChanged Then SaveCurRec

     ' If the current record is the end of
     ' the file, prepare to accept a new
     ' record from the user.
     If curTranRecord = FindRecordCount Then
       BlankEOFRecord

     ' Otherwise, read and display the
     ' next record in the file. The variable
     ' fileNumber represents the open file
     ' on the current child form.
     Else
       curTranRecord = curTranRecord + 1
       Get #fileNumber, curTranRecord, TranRecord
       ShowRecord
       recordChanged = False
     End If

      ' Display the file name and the record
      ' number in the child form's title bar.
     Caption = tranFileName & ", #" _
        & curTranRecord

     ' Enable the Previous command, so the user
     ' can now scroll backward through the file.
     mnuPrevious.Enabled = True

   End Sub  ' mnuNext_Click
```

Listing 12-15
The ShowRecord procedure

```
Private Sub ShowRecord()

  ' The ShowRecord procedure displays the fields
  ' of the current record in an open file. Before
  ' calling this procedure, the program always
  ' reads a record from the open file into the
  ' TranRecord structure.

  With TranRecord

    ' Set the transportation selection.
    optMode(.TranMode).VALUE = True

    ' If the Car option is selected,
    ' set the value of the Rental check box.
    If .TranMode = 3 Then
      If .RentalCar Then
        chkRental.VALUE = 1
      Else
        chkRental.VALUE = 0
      End If
    End If

    ' Read the remaining fields and
    ' set the corresponding controls
    ' appropriately.
    txtCarrier.TEXT = Trim(.Carrier)
    txtTripNumber.TEXT = Trim(.TripNumber)

    If .ReservedStatus Then
      chkReserved.VALUE = 1
    Else
      chkReserved.VALUE = 0
    End If

    If .PaidStatus Then
      chkPaid.VALUE = 1
    Else
```

IV

12

```
            chkPaid.VALUE = 0
        End If

        txtDate.TEXT = Trim(.TripDate)
        txtTime.TEXT = Trim(.TripTime)
        txtFrom.TEXT = Trim(.TripFrom)
        txtTo.TEXT = Trim(.TripTo)

        txtNotes.TEXT = Trim(.Comments)

    End With

End Sub    ' ShowRecord
```

Listing 12-16
The mnuPrint_Click and PrintRecord procedures

```
Private Sub mnuPrint_Click()

    ' The mnuPrint_Click procedure prints one or
    ' more transportation records when the user
    ' chooses the Print command.

    Dim i As Long

    ' If a file is open, print all the records
    ' in the file, from beginning to end.
    If tranFileOpen Then

        ' Begin by saving the current record to
        ' the file if necessary.
        If recordChanged Then SaveCurRec
        recordChanged = False

        ' Print each record in turn. The variable
        ' fileNumber identifies the open file
        ' in the active child form.
```

```
    For i = 1 To FindRecordCount
      Get #fileNumber, i, TranRecord
      PrintRecord
    Next i

  ' If no file is open, just print the
  ' current contents of the form.
  Else
    MakeTranRecord
    PrintRecord
  End If

  ' Complete the output process.
  Printer.EndDoc

End Sub   ' mnuPrint_Click



Private Sub PrintRecord()

  ' The PrintRecord procedure uses the
  ' Printer.Print method to send the fields of
  ' the current record to the printer. The current
  ' record is stored in the TranRecord structure.

  Const t1 = 5    ' First tab stop.
  Const t2 = 15   ' Second tab stop.

  With TranRecord

    ' Print the transportation mode.
    Select Case .TranMode
      Case 0
        Printer.Print "Airline -- ";
      Case 1
        Printer.Print "Train Line -- ";
```

```
      Case 2
        Printer.Print "Bus Line -- ";

      Case 3
        If .RentalCar Then
          Printer.Print "Car Rental Agency -- ";
        Else
          Printer.Print "Private Car"
        End If
End Select

' Print the Carrier and TripNumber fields.
If .TranMode < 3 Then
  Printer.Print .Carrier
  Printer.Print Tab(t1); " #"; .TripNumber
Else
  If .RentalCar Then
    Printer.Print .Carrier;
    If .ReservedStatus Then
      Printer.Print Tab(t1); " #"; .TripNumber
    Else
      Printer.Print
    End If
  End If
End If

' Print the date, time, starting point,
' and destination.
Printer.Print
Printer.Print Tab(t1); "Date:";
Printer.Print Tab(t2); .TripDate
Printer.Print Tab(t1); "Time:";
Printer.Print Tab(t2); .TripTime
Printer.Print Tab(t1); "From:";
Printer.Print Tab(t2); .TripFrom
Printer.Print Tab(t1); "To:";
Printer.Print Tab(t2); .TripTo
Printer.Print
```

```
' Print the reservation and paid status.
' Note the use of the YesNo function to
' supply a printable value of "Yes" or "No."
If .TranMode < 3 Then
  Printer.Print Tab(t1); "Reserved:";
  Printer.Print Tab(t2); YesNo(.ReservedStatus)
  Printer.Print Tab(t1); "Paid:";
  Printer.Print Tab(t2); YesNo(.PaidStatus)
End If

' Print the comments.
Printer.Print
Printer.Print Tab(t1); "Comments:"
PrintComments (RTrim(.Comments))

Printer.Print
Printer.Print

End With

End Sub   ' PrintRecord
```

Listing 12-17
The PrintComments procedure and the YesNo function

```
Private Sub PrintComments(noteStr As String)

  ' The PrintComments procedure arranges to
  ' print the Comments field of any record
  ' in a sequence of approximately 40-character
  ' lines, without breaking any words in the text.

  Const lineLen = 40   ' Line length.
  Const t1 = 5         ' Tab stop.

  Dim curPos As Integer
  Dim curLine As String
  Dim curChar As String
```

```
                ' Divide the text into 40-character lines.
                Do While Len(noteStr) > lineLen
                    curPos = lineLen

                    ' Break each line after a word.
                    Do
                        curChar = Mid(noteStr, curPos, 1)
                        curPos = curPos - 1
                    Loop Until curChar = " "

                    ' Print the current line.
                    Printer.Print Tab(t1); _
                        Left(noteStr, curPos)

                    ' Reduce the string by the line
                    ' that has just been printed.
                    noteStr = Mid(noteStr, curPos + 2)
                Loop

                ' Print the final line of the text.
                Printer.Print Tab(t1); noteStr

        End Sub    ' PrintComments



        Private Function YesNo(which As Boolean) As String

            ' The YesNo function converts a Boolean value
            ' into a string value of "Yes" or "No." This
            ' conversion is used in the process of printing
            ' transportation records.

            If which Then
                YesNo = "Yes"
            Else
                YesNo = "No"
            End If

        End Function    ' YesNo
```

Listing 12-18
Click event procedures for option buttons and check boxes

```
Private Sub optMode_Click(Index As Integer)

  ' The optMode_Click procedure sets the properties
  ' of relevant controls whenever the user changes
  ' the selection in the optMode control array.

  ' Set the default property values for the
  ' program's three check box controls.
  chkRental.Enabled = False
  chkRental.VALUE = 0
  chkReserved.Enabled = True
  chkPaid.Enabled = True

  ' Enable the txtCarrier and txtTripNumber
  ' controls and their associated labels.
  lblTripNumber.Enabled = True
  txtTripNumber.Enabled = True
  txtCarrier.Enabled = True
  lblCarrier.Enabled = True

  ' Adjust the label captions according
  ' to the selected mode of transportion.
  Select Case Index
    Case 0
      lblCarrier.Caption = "Air&line"
      lblTripNumber.Caption = "Flight &#"

    Case 1
      lblCarrier.Caption = "Rail &line"
      lblTripNumber.Caption = "Train &#"

    Case 2
      lblCarrier.Caption = "Bus &line"
      lblTripNumber.Caption = "Route &#"

    ' If the user chooses the Car option,
    ' adjust the appropriate check boxes.
    Case 3
```

```
            lblCarrier.Caption = "Renta&l agency"
            lblTripNumber.Caption = "Reservation &#"
            chkRental.Enabled = True
            chkRental.VALUE = 1
            chkReserved_Click
            chkPaid.Enabled = False
      End Select

      ' Give the focus to the txtCarrier
      ' text box control.
      txtCarrier.SetFocus

End Sub   ' optMode_Click




Private Sub chkPaid_Click()

    ' The chkPaid_Click procedure changes the
    ' Boolean value of the recordChanged variable
    ' if the user changes the status of the Paid
    ' check box.

    recordChanged = True

End Sub   ' chkPaid_Click




Private Sub chkRental_Click()

    ' The chkRental_Click procedure adjusts
    ' the Enabled properties of several controls,
    ' depending on the value of the chkRental
    ' check box. (If the car option is selected,
    ' the Rental box indicates whether the
    ' car is a rental or a private vehicle.)

    ' If chkRental is checked, enable the
    ' text boxes for the rental agency (txtCarrier)
```

```
' and the reservation number (txtTripNumber).
' Also enable the chkReserved check box, which
' indicates whether a reservation has been made.

If optMode(3).VALUE Then
  If chkRental.VALUE = 1 Then
    txtCarrier.Enabled = True
    lblCarrier.Enabled = True
    txtTripNumber.Enabled = True
    lblTripNumber.Enabled = True
    chkReserved.Enabled = True
    chkReserved_Click

    ' If chkRental is unchecked, disable
    ' all these controls.
  Else
    txtCarrier.Enabled = False
    lblCarrier.Enabled = False
    txtTripNumber.Enabled = False
    lblTripNumber.Enabled = False
    chkReserved.VALUE = 0
    chkReserved.Enabled = False
  End If

  recordChanged = True
  End If

End Sub   ' chkRental_Click




Private Sub chkReserved_Click()

  ' The chkReserved_Click procedure enables or
  ' disables the "Reservation #" text box
  ' (txtTripNumber), depending on the value of
  ' the chkReserved check box. This action
  ' occurs only if the current transporation
  ' selection is "Car."

  If optMode(3).VALUE Then
```

```
      If chkReserved.VALUE = 0 Then
        txtTripNumber.Enabled = False
        lblTripNumber.Enabled = False
      Else
        txtTripNumber.Enabled = True
        lblTripNumber.Enabled = True
      End If
    End If

    recordChanged = True

  End Sub   ' chkReserved_Click
```

Listing 12-19
Change event procedures for text boxes and the ChangedStatus procedure

```
  Private Sub txtCarrier_Change()

    ' The txtCarrier_Change procedure sets
    ' recordChanged to True if the user enters
    ' new text into this text box control.

    ChangedStatus

  End Sub   ' txtCarrier_Change


  Private Sub txtTripNumber_Change()

    ' The txtCarrier_Change procedure sets
    ' recordChanged to True if the user enters
    ' new text into this text box control.

    ChangedStatus

  End Sub   ' txtTripNumber_Change
```

```
Private Sub txtDate_Change()

   ' The txtDate_Change procedure sets
   ' recordChanged to True if the user enters
   ' new text into this text box control.

   ChangedStatus

End Sub   ' txtDate_Change


Private Sub txtTime_Change()

   ' The txtTime_Change procedure sets
   ' recordChanged to True if the user enters
   ' new text into this text box control.

   ChangedStatus

End Sub   ' txtTime_Change


Private Sub txtFrom_Change()

   ' The txtFrom_Change procedure sets
   ' recordChanged to True if the user enters
   ' new text into this text box control.

   ChangedStatus

End Sub   ' txtFrom_Change


Private Sub txtTo_Change()

   ' The txtTo_Change procedure set
   ' recordChanged to True if the user enters
   ' new text into this text box control.

   ChangedStatus
```

```
End Sub   ' txtTo_Change


Private Sub txtNotes_Change()

   ' The txtNotes_Change procedure sets
   ' recordChanged to True if the user enters
   ' new text into this text box control.

   ChangedStatus

End Sub   ' txtNotes_Change


Private Sub ChangedStatus()

   ' The ChangedStatus procedure sets the
   ' recordChanged variable and, if appropriate,
   ' enables the Next command, in response to
   ' a change in the contents of one of the
   ' program's text boxes.

   recordChanged = True
   If tranFileOpen Then mnuNext.Enabled = True

End Sub   ' ChangedStatus
```

Listing 12-20
The mnuCascade_Click, mnuTile_Click, and mnuExit_Click procedures

```
Private Sub mnuCascade_Click()

   ' The mnuCascade_Click procedure rearranges
   ' the open child forms on the MDI form when
   ' the user chooses the Cascade command in
   ' the Window menu.

   frmTranParent.Arrange 0
```

Using the Arrange method to display forms in a cascade

```
End Sub   ' mnuCascade_Click



Private Sub mnuTile_Click()

    ' The mnuTile_Click procedure rearranges the
    ' child forms in the MDI form when the user
    ' chooses the Tile command from the Window menu.

    frmTranParent.Arrange 2

End Sub   ' mnuTile_Click
```

IV

12

Using the Arrange method to display forms in a tiled arrangement

```
Private Sub mnuExit_Click()

    ' The mnuExit_Click procedure makes a call
    ' to the SaveAllFiles procedure in the parent
    ' form when the user chooses the Exit command
    ' from the File menu. SaveAllFiles ensures
    ' that all unsaved records are written to
    ' their respective files before the program
    ' run is terminated.

    frmTranParent.SaveAllFiles

End Sub   ' mnuExit_Click
```

13 Object Linking and Embedding

O bject linking and embedding, commonly known as OLE, enables you to create complex documents by employing the resources of two or more Windows applications. OLE provides convenient techniques for combining text with numeric tables, graphics, and other types of data originating from a variety of programs.

OLE defines two basic ways of attaching objects to a host document, embedding and linking:

- An *embedded object* is contained in the host document. When you want to develop or edit the data of an embedded object, you can activate the source application without leaving the document. The resulting object is saved in the host document, not in a separate file. For example, suppose you're creating a word processed document that contains an embedded Excel worksheet. To perform operations on the worksheet, you start Excel inside the document. When you save the word processed file, you also save the data of the embedded worksheet.

- By contrast, a *linked object* is stored in an external file. The host document contains a reference to the data and an image of the linked object, but does not store the data. When you revise the object's data, the changes are *displayed* in the host document but *saved* in the external file. For example, a word processed document containing a linked Excel worksheet gives you complete access to the resources of Excel for editing the worksheet data. The document contains a reference to the separate worksheet file. If the worksheet happens to be linked to any additional documents, the data can be edited from any of its hosts. Windows *updates* the link — providing each host document with the latest version of the data — whenever necessary.

In a Visual Basic application, there are several interesting ways to take advantage of OLE. Using the OLE container control (shown in Figure 13-1), you can link or embed objects inside a form. At runtime, the user can view and edit the object's data, using the resources of the source application.

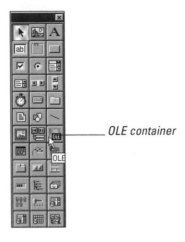 ——— *OLE container*

Figure 13-1
The OLE container control.

Alternatively, you can use the Custom Controls dialog box to add specific application objects to the Visual Basic Toolbox — for example, buttons representing Excel worksheets and charts, Paint drawings, or WordPad documents. These Toolbox buttons are then available as insertable application objects for any Visual Basic project you develop.

A more sophisticated programming technique is known as OLE *automation*. In this approach, certain Windows applications are designated as OLE servers. A *server* is designed to provide its own objects, methods, and properties as programmable components, which are available to other applications. A program that uses the server's objects is known as a *client*. (In the terminology of OLE, a server is said to *expose* its objects to the client.) Using OLE automation, a Visual Basic client application can take complete control over operations in a server application. For example, in this chapter you'll examine a program that creates an Excel worksheet object and then manages a detailed sequence of operations inside the worksheet.

But before you turn to the subject of OLE automation, you'll begin your work in this chapter with a brief look at the OLE container control and the steps for using it in a project.

The OLE Container Control

The OLE control is available in all three editions of Visual Basic. Its provides a tool for embedding or linking application objects in a form. When you add an OLE control to a form at design time, Visual Basic immediately displays the Insert Object dialog box on the screen, giving you the opportunity to select the object that the control will contain. In the process, you can choose between embedding or linking the object.

Here are the steps for placing an OLE control on a form and then choosing the object that the control will contain:

1. Open the form and double-click the OLE container control in the Toolbox. A box representing the control appears in the center of your form, and the Insert Object dialog box opens onto the desktop (Figure 13-2).

2. In the Object Type list, select the application object that you want your OLE control to display. Notice that a single application might provide two or more types of objects in the Object Type list; for example, Excel provides worksheet objects and chart objects.

3. If you want the object to show the data from an existing file, choose the Create from File option at the left side of the Insert Object dialog box. As you can see in Figure 13-3, the dialog box displays a File text box in which you can enter the complete path and name of the file you want to attach. (If you don't know the file's exact location, click the Browse button; in the resulting Browse dialog box, you can select the appropriate folder and look for the file.)

4. By default, the Insert Object dialog box assumes you want to attach the file as an embedded object in your form. Notice that the Result box at the bottom of Figure 13-3 provides a brief description of an embedded object. If you instead want to link the object to your file,

click the Link option. A check appears in the adjacent box, and a general description of a linked object appears in the Result box, as shown in Figure 13-4.

5. Click OK to complete the process. Back on your form, the object appears inside the OLE container control.

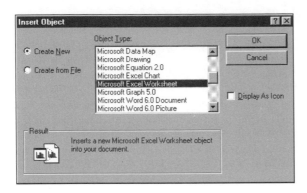

Figure 13-2

The Insert Object dialog box appears when you add an OLE container control to any form in your project.

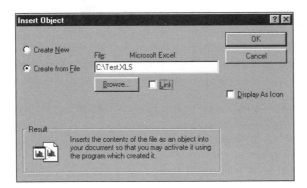

Figure 13-3

To attach the data from an existing file, select the Create from File option.

For example, the Visual Basic application in Figure 13-5 illustrates the use of the OLE control to display a linked object. The object is an Excel worksheet, displayed inside the large box at the bottom of the form. In addition to the OLE container, the form contains a multiline

text box control and command buttons representing operations that
the program provides for working with the linked object.

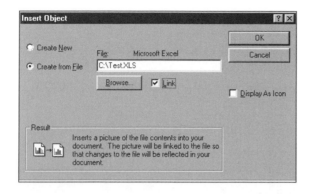

Figure 13-4

To link the object to your form, select the Link option.

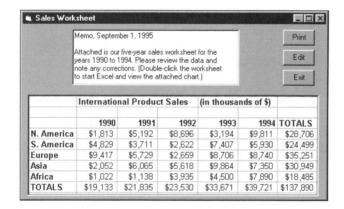

Figure 13-5

*A program illustrating the use of the OLE container control to display a
linked object.*

At runtime the user can double-click inside the OLE container control to start Excel. In response, the Excel application appears in a window of its own and displays the complete source worksheet. The user
then has the opportunity to scroll through all the data and make necessary changes. When the user exits from Excel and returns to the Visual
Basic application, any changes in the linked data are displayed in the
OLE container control.

Another way to provide access to Windows applications in a Visual Basic program is to add specific application objects to the Toolbox; then you can insert these objects in a form directly from the Toolbox. Here are the steps:

1. Pull down the Tools menu and choose Custom Controls to open the Custom Controls dialog box. (Alternatively, press Ctrl+T, or click the Toolbox with the right mouse button and choose Custom Controls from the pop-up menu.)

2. In the Available Controls list, select the application objects that you want to include in your Toolbox. An X appears next to each selected object in the list. Click OK when you've completed your selection.

3. The Toolbox now displays buttons for each of the application objects you've added. For example, the buttons in the bottom row of the Toolbox in Figure 13-6 represent a WordPad document, a Paint drawing, an Excel chart, and an Excel worksheet. To place an instance of any of these objects in the current project, open a form and double-click the target object in the Toolbox.

Figure 13-6
Adding application objects to the Visual Basic Toolbox.

Using the OLE container control or individual application controls, you can quickly build a project that provides access to other Windows applications. But to exert direct programming control over the features of an application, you employ the techniques of OLE automation.

OLE Automation

In OLE automation, the server provides *programmable objects* — that is, objects whose methods and properties can be used in the client program's code. The client creates new instances of these objects at runtime and makes calls to the methods and properties, thereby controlling the server's operations. Note that an OLE automation object is *not* linked or embedded in the client application at design time.

In this chapter you'll learn how to build a Visual Basic project that works as a client, also known as an *OLE automation controller*. Only certain Windows programs are designed to act as OLE automation servers. As you've seen other applications may be linked or embedded in a Visual Basic form; but if an application is not designed as a server, its objects, methods, and properties are not available for programming.

CREATING A REFERENCE TO AN OBJECT LIBRARY

In many cases, an OLE server has an associated *object library*, providing complete information about the server's programmable objects. To develop a Visual Basic program that works as a client, you begin by creating a reference to the appropriate object library in your project. The object library helps you develop your application, as you'll see in the following steps:

1. Pull down the Tools menu and choose the References command. The references dialog box (shown in Figure 13-7) provides a list of available object library files.

2. To add a reference to a particular library for use in the project you're currently developing, select the library's name in the list. An X appears next to each object library that is available to your current project. For example, if you're planning to write a program that works with Excel objects, you should select the Microsoft Excel Object Library entry in the list. Click OK to confirm the new reference.

3. Once a given library is referenced in your project, you can view lists of its objects, methods, and properties in Visual Basic's Object Browser. Press F2 to open the Object Browser, and then select the

appropriate library in the Libraries/Projects list. The Classes/Modules and Methods/Properties lists show the contents of the library, as in Figure 13-8.

4. To learn how to use a particular method or property in the object library, select the object to which it applies and then select the item itself in the Methods/Properties list. The syntax of the method or property appears at the bottom of the Object Browser dialog box.

5. For more information, click the question-mark button just to the left of the syntax. A help window appears on the desktop, displaying the topic you've requested. For example, Figure 13-9 shows the Excel help window for a method named Range.

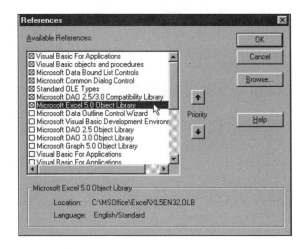

Figure 13-7
The References dialog box with its list of object libraries.

To illustrate the power of OLE automation, this chapter presents an expanded new version of the International Sales program, first presented in Chapter 9. Like the original project, this new program provides an arrangement of text boxes in which you create a table of sales data. As you enter each row and column of figures, the program calculates totals and develops a graph depicting the data. You can choose between a column chart or a pie chart, oriented to depict rows of regional data or columns of periodic data.

Figure 13-8

The Object Browser dialog box, displaying the objects, methods, and properties of a selected object library.

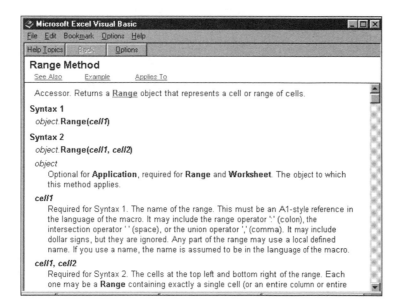

Figure 13-9

A help topic for a particular method in the Microsoft Excel object library.

Think of this chapter's program as the OLE version of the International Sales application. Its main new feature is a technique for copying the sales data to a new software environment, Microsoft Excel. Once you've developed a sales table and chart, you can choose a single menu command to copy the entire data set to an Excel worksheet. In response, the program takes steps to perform the following tasks:

- Create and display a new worksheet
- Copy all the sales data to the sheet, along with titles and headings
- Enter formulas for calculating row and column totals on the worksheet
- Instruct Excel to create a chart, equivalent to the one currently displayed in the International Sales application window

When all these tasks are complete, you can save a copy of the worksheet object to disk as a file that you can later use directly in Excel.

Take a moment now to run the program and experiment with its new features.

RUNNING THE SALES PROGRAM, OLE VERSION

The project is stored on disk as SalesOLE.VBP. Open the application now and take a look at the Project window. It contains a single form named frmIntSales, which is saved as SalesOLE.FRM.

If your computer includes an installation of Excel, press F5 now to run the new version of the International Sales program. (If you don't have Excel, see the sidebar titled "Can You Run This Program?") Initially the application window seems unchanged from the original version. To see the new features, take a look at the File and Edit menus:

- In the File menu, the Save Report and Print Window commands have been replaced by the Transfer to Excel command.
- The Edit menu contains a new command called Random Data, which fills the sales table with random four-digit figures. (This feature gives you a quick way to generate data so you can explore the Transfer to Excel command.)

Can You Run This Program?

Here's a brief note of caution before you try running the OLE version of the International Sales program. The application is designed to run on a system that contains an installation of Microsoft Excel, Version 5 or higher. If your computer *doesn't* have Excel, you won't be able to use the program's OLE automation features. Furthermore, you'll need to delete the project's reference to the Excel object library before you try running the program, as follows:

1. After you've loaded the SalesOLE.VBP project from disk, pull down the Tools menu and choose the References command.

2. Find the reference to the Excel object library in the list. The word MISSING appears just before the name of the library, indicating that there is no installation of Excel on your system.

3. Click the Excel object library entry to remove the X from the corresponding check box. Then click OK to confirm the change.

4. On the Visual Basic toolbar, click the Save Project button to save the International Sales program without its reference to the missing Excel object library.

Now you can run the program on your computer, although it won't perform the OLE automation features described in this chapter. When you choose the Transfer to Excel command from the File menu, the program doesn't take any action.

Pull down the Edit menu now and choose Random Data. The program provides an experimental data set. You can use these data values as they are, or you can revise them selectively to make the data seem more realistic. Either way, you are ready to begin trying out the main new feature of this program, the Transfer to Excel command. Pull down the File menu and choose the command, as show in Figure 13-10.

When you do so, the program immediately starts Microsoft Excel and begins creating a new worksheet. The entire sales table is copied to the worksheet. Summation formulas produce the totals in the last column and the bottom row. Finally, the program generates an Excel chart and arranges it below the worksheet data. All this activity takes a few seconds; when the action is complete, the Excel worksheet and chart appear as shown in Figure 13-11. Notice that the chart is similar to the format of the chart in the original program window.

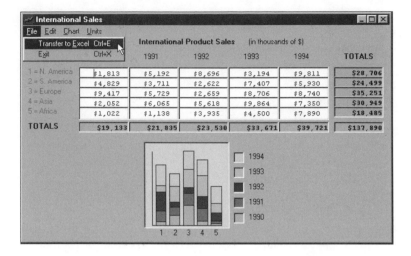

Figure 13-10

Filling the sales table with random data and choosing the Transfer to Excel command.

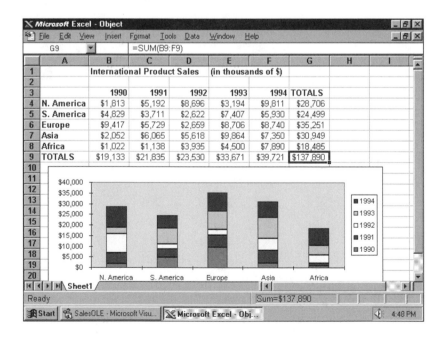

Figure 13-11

An Excel worksheet showing the sales data and the initial column chart.

Significantly, this worksheet is now a self-contained object with its own data, formulas, and charting methods. As you'll learn shortly, you can save this worksheet — or a different version of it — to disk for future work in Excel. But for now, suppose you've finished looking at the worksheet and you want to return to the International Sales program. Follow these steps:

1. Click the SalesOLE button on the Windows 95 Taskbar at the bottom of the screen. This brings the International Sales program to the front of the desktop. At this point you can still see the Excel worksheet in the background.

2. In front of the program window a small message box displays the word "Continue . . ." along with an OK button. Click the button with your mouse. When you do so, the International Sales program closes the Excel application. The original sales data from which the worksheet was generated remains in the application window.

3. Now pull down the program's Chart menu and choose the By Region option. This selection changes the orientation of the column chart. As shown in Figure 13-12, the legend at the right side of the chart now displays the names of the sales regions, and each column represents the sales for a particular year.

4. Pull down the File menu and choose the Transfer to Excel command again. The program generates a new Excel worksheet and chart to represent the sales data. But this time the Excel chart is oriented differently. As you can see in Figure 13-13, the new chart corresponds to the By Region chart option you selected in the International Sales window.

When you've finished examining the worksheet, click the SalesOLE button on the Windows Taskbar to return to the International Sales program. Click OK on the "Continue . . ." message box, and Excel disappears again.

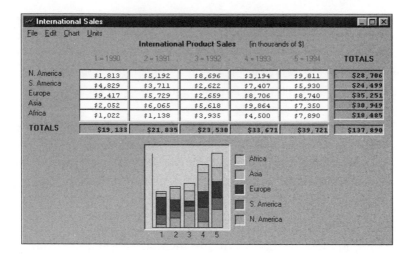

Figure 13-12

Changing the chart orientation in the International Sales window.

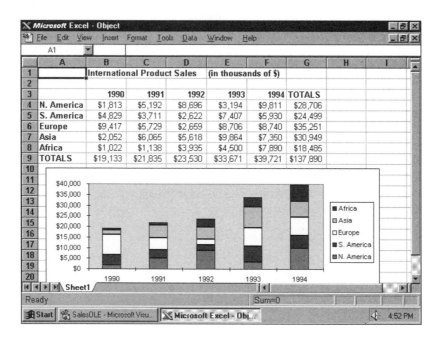

Figure 13-13

Generating an equivalent chart in the Excel sales worksheet.

You may want to continue experimenting with the program now by choosing the Pie Chart option in the application's Chart menu, and then choosing the Transfer to Excel command to view the resulting worksheet. In Figures 13-14 and 13-15 you can see how the pie chart looks when the By Years option is selected. Figures 13-16 and 13-17 show the pie chart when the By Region option is selected. Notice that Excel has its own approach to building a pie chart; you can see differences in the order of the legend entries and the starting angle for the first wedge in the pie. But a close examination confirms that the two pairs of pie charts represent the same sales data. Later in this chapter you'll examine the code that creates a particular chart type in the Excel worksheet, depending on the current settings in the Chart menu of the International Sales window.

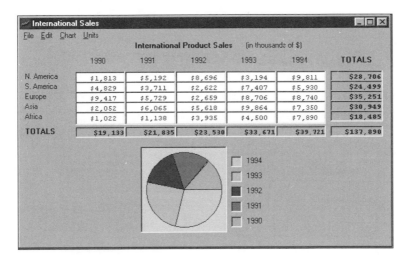

Figure 13-14

The International Sales pie chart, illustrating the By Years option.

As you noticed at the beginning of your work, the OLE version of this program is missing two of the File commands that were available in the original International Sales application: The Save Report command was designed to create a text file containing the sales data, and the Print Window command sent an image of the entire application window to the printer. Why are these two commands both replaced by the Transfer to Excel command in the OLE version? Because Excel provides good alternatives for printing and saving the sales data.

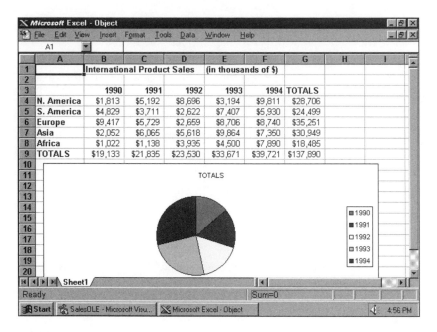

Figure 13-15

The Excel pie chart, illustrating the By Years option.

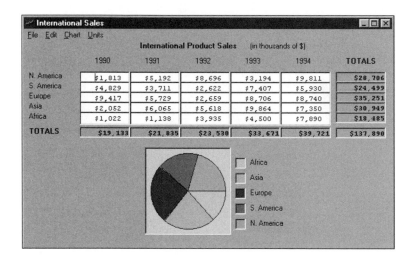

Figure 13-16

The International Sales pie chart, illustrating the By Region option.

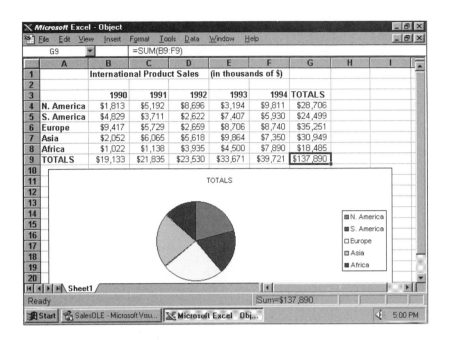

Figure 13-17
The Excel pie chart, illustrating the By Region option.

As a final exercise with this program, generate a new set of sales data by entering individual sales figures yourself or by choosing the Random Data command from the Edit menu. Then choose Transfer to Excel one last time to create a worksheet and chart from the data. When the worksheet is complete, pull down the File menu from the Excel menu bar and look at the available commands, as shown in Figure 13-18.

You can choose the Print command to send a copy of the worksheet data and the chart to your printer. Alternatively, choose the Save Copy As command to create an XLS file on disk. When you do so, the Save As dialog box (Figure 13-19) allows you to select a folder location for the file and enter a file name. Furthermore, you can use tools in the dialog box to navigate through the folder hierarchy on your hard disk; and you can click the Options button to set the properties of the file you're about to create. When you save the worksheet, it becomes an independent record of the sales data. You can later start Excel, open the worksheet, and work with the data in any way you want.

Figure 13-18

Excel's File menu, providing Save and Print commands for the worksheet.

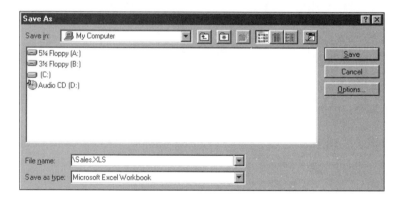

Figure 13-19

Creating a new XLS file, using Excel's Save As dialog box.

In summary, this Visual Basic client program uses Excel as a server application to produce a worksheet object and a chart object for the current sales data. The program copies the sales table to the worksheet and generates formulas for the totals. Significantly, the chart type and chart orientation in the International Sales window are duplicated in the resulting Excel chart.

Although the OLE version of the program makes several changes in the original design of the International Sales Application the frmIntSales form does not contain a linked or embedded Excel object; rather the program creates new worksheet objects at runtime. As you now turn to the program's code, you'll learn how a Visual Basic program works with the objects of a server application.

Inside the SalesOLE program

The program's code appears in Listings 13-1 through 13-16 at the end of this chapter. Your main focus here will be on the declarations and procedures related to OLE automation:

- The program includes a module-level declaration for an object variable that will represent the worksheet (Listing 13-1).

- The mnuExcel_Click event procedure (Listing 13-2) creates the worksheet and then makes calls to procedures that copy the data and generate the chart.

- The *CopyToExcel* procedure (Listing 13-3) takes care of formatting the worksheet appropriately; copying the data, titles, and headings; and creating formulas for the sales totals.

- The *DrawExcelChart* procedure (Listing 13-4) creates a chart object and uses a method named ChartWizard to draw the chart. The properties of the Excel chart depend on the current settings of the mnuChartBy and mnuChartType menus in the International Sales windows.

In the upcoming sections you'll examine the code from each of these listings.

DECLARING AN OBJECT VARIABLE FOR THE WORKSHEET

The following Dim statement creates *ExcelSheet* as an object-type variable to represent the Worksheet object in this program:

```
Dim ExcelSheet As Object
```

Because this statement appears in the general declarations of the frmIntSales form (Listing 13-1), the variable *ExcelSheet* is available any-where in the program. As you'll see shortly, the mnuExcel_Click proce-dure creates a new Worksheet object and stores a reference to this object in *ExcelSheet*. The variable subsequently represents the worksheet in all three of the procedures that perform OLE automation operations.

As an OLE server, Microsoft Excel provides a *hierarchy* of programma-ble objects and collections for the client application to work with. At the top of the hierarchy is the Application object, which represents the Excel application itself. Next in line is the Workbooks collection and the Work-book object; and then the Worksheets collection and Worksheet object.

Even though it is not at the top of the hierarchy, the Worksheet object is *externally creatable*; in other words, a client application can create new instances of it. Certain other objects in the hierarchy are *dependent* on the Worksheet; for example:

- A Range object represents a range of cells on a worksheet.
- A ChartObject object is a container for a chart, embedded on a sheet.
- A Chart object represents the chart displayed inside a ChartObject.

These dependent objects can be referenced indirectly, using the methods and properties of an existing Worksheet object.

As you examine more of this program's code, you'll see examples of dependent objects and you'll gain a clearer understanding of Excel's object hierarchy.

CREATING AND MANAGING THE WORKSHEET OBJECT

The mnuExcel_Click event procedure (Listing 13-2) takes charge when the user chooses the Transfer to Excel command from the File menu. The procedure begins by creating a new Worksheet object:

```
Set ExcelSheet = CreateObject("Excel.Sheet")
```

The CreateObject function creates an OLE animation object belonging to a specified class. In this case, the class is identified as Excel.Sheet. CreateObject returns a reference to the newly created Worksheet object. The Set statement stores the reference in *ExcelSheet*.

At this point, the Worksheet object has been created, but no new application has yet appeared on the desktop. To display Excel, the following statement changes the application's Visible property to True:

```
ExcelSheet.Application.Visible = True
```

The Application property returns a reference to the Excel Application object. The Visible property therefore applies to the application itself.

Next the mnuExcel_Click procedure makes calls to the two general procedures that create the data and the chart on the new worksheet object:

```
CopyToExcel
DrawExcelChart
```

As you'll see shortly, the first of these copies all the sales data to the worksheet, and the second makes calls to an Excel method that draws charts.

Next a MsgBox statement creates a pause in the program, giving the user a chance to examine the contents of the worksheet — and optionally, to print or save the data. When the user eventually clicks the OK button on the message box, the program calls the Quit method to exit from Excel, and then assigns Nothing to *ExcelSheet*, releasing the object reference from memory:

```
MsgBox "Continue...", , "International Sales"
ExcelSheet.Application.Quit
Set ExcelSheet = Nothing
```

As you've seen, the program performance continues; at this juncture the user is free to enter new data into the International Sales window and then transfer the data to Excel again.

Notice that all the action of the mnuExcel_Click procedure takes place under the watch of an error trap:

```
On Error GoTo OLEProblem
```

This trap is triggered if an OLE automation operation fails; control then jumps down to the end of the procedure, to the *OLEProblem* label. For example, an error occurs if Excel is not available on the current system, or if Excel is already running on the Windows desktop. In either of these cases, the program gives no response to the Transfer to Excel command.

COPYING DATA TO THE WORKSHEET

The *CopyToExcel* procedure (Listing 13-3) formats the worksheet, copies the sales data, and creates summation formulas. To refer to Range objects, this procedure uses three Worksheet methods:

- The Columns method returns a Range object consisting of one or more columns.
- The Cells method returns a Range object consisting of a single cell.
- The Range method returns a Range object consisting of a specific range on the worksheet.

Keep in mind that Range is a dependent object that can be referenced only indirectly. These three methods are convenient ways of identifying specific ranges on the active worksheet.

For example, the procedure begins with two formatting operations. First, the following statement applies the bold type style to multiple ranges on the sheet:

```
ExcelSheet.Range("$A$1:$G$3,$A$3:$A$9").Font.Bold _
   = True
```

In this statement, the Range method returns a reference to a specific Range object. The Font method returns a reference to the corresponding Font object. Bold is a property of the Font object.

The next formatting task is to increase the width of column A. In the following statement, the Columns method returns a reference to a Range object that represents a single column:

```
ExcelSheet.Columns("A").ColumnWidth = 10.29
```

The ColumnWidth property applies to a Range object.

To copy the sales data, the program uses the Cells method to identify individual cells in the worksheet. (Or, more precisely, the Cells method returns a reference to a Range object that consists of a single cell.) The Value property, when applied to a Range object, represents the value stored in a cell. For example, the following statements begin by copying the title and the dollar units from the International Sales window to the worksheet:

```
ExcelSheet.Cells(1, 2).VALUE = _
  txtTitle.TEXT
ExcelSheet.Cells(1, 5).VALUE = _
  lblUnits.Caption
```

Then the following loop copies the sales figures from the application window to the worksheet:

```
For i = 0 To 24
  y = i Mod 5 + 2
  x = i \ 5 + 4
  ExcelSheet.Cells(x, y).VALUE = _
    txtAmount(i).TEXT
Next i
```

Inside the loop, the program calculates the location of each individual worksheet cell and then assigns the txtAmount(i).Text setting to the Value property of the resulting Range object.

The Formula property of a Range object allows the program to store a formula in a particular cell or range of cells. For example, this loop enters the summation formulas into the last column and bottom row of the sales table in the worksheet:

```
For i = 0 To 4
  With ExcelSheet
    ' ...
    .Cells(9, i + 2).Formula = _
      "=Sum(R[-5]C:R[-1]C)"
    .Cells(i + 4, 7).Formula = _
      "=Sum(RC[-5]:RC[-1])"
  End With
Next i
```

Notice the use of Visual Basic's With structure to simplify the references to the Cells method in this loop.

When the work of the *CopyToExcel* procedure is complete, all the data, formulas, titles, and labels have been entered into the worksheet, and the program is ready to generate the chart.

CREATING AN EMBEDDED CHART ON THE WORKSHEET

The *DrawExcelChart* procedure (Listing 13-4) works with references to
two new objects. ChartObject is a container object for a chart that's
embedded on a worksheet. (The ChartObjects collection represents all
the embedded charts on a Worksheet object.) The Chart object represents
the chart drawn within a ChartObject object. The procedure declares
object variables to represent references to each of these objects:

```
Dim newChartObj As ChartObject
Dim newChart As Chart
```

To create a new ChartObject, the program uses the Add method to
add a member to the ChartObjects collection on the current worksheet:

```
Set newChartObj =
   ExcelSheet.ChartObjects.Add(10, 120, 400, 150)
```

In this statement, the ChartObjects method returns a reference to the
ChartObjects collection for the ExcelSheet object. The Add method creates a new object in the collection and displays the chart container at
specified coordinates and in a specified size. (The numeric arguments of
the Add method represent the Left, Top, Width, and Height properties of
the ChartObject.) Finally, the Add method returns a reference to the new
ChartObject; this reference is stored in the variable *newChartObj*.

The Chart property represents the Chart object contained within a
ChartObject. The program uses this property to assign a reference to
newChart:

```
Set newChart =
   newChartObj.Chart
```

As a result of this statement, *newChart* contains a reference to the Chart
object inside *newChartObj*. The procedure's final task is to assign appropriate properties to this Chart object, resulting in the display of a chart.

The ChartWizard method is a shortcut technique for assigning properties to a Chart object, in effect defining the chart that the object displays.
ChartWizard takes a long list of arguments, including:

- A reference to the range containing the source data for the chart
- A value identifying the chart type
- A numeric value identifying the chart format
- A value specifying the row or column orientation of the chart
- Two integers specifying the number of rows and columns of labels that are included in the source data
- A Boolean value specifying whether the chart should include a legend

You can see examples of all these arguments in the following call to the ChartWizard method:

```
newChart.ChartWizard _
  ExcelSheet.Range("$A$3:$F$8"), _
  xlColumn, 3, _
  xlColumns, 1, 1, _
  True
```

This particular statement creates a stacked column chart in which each column represents the total sales for a given region (as you can see back in Figure 13-11).

To decide what kind of chart to draw, the *DrawExcelChart* procedure uses a Select Case structure. Each Case statement inside the structure examines the current Checked settings of the mnuChartBy and mnuChartType menu options. The Select structure chooses the Case in which both Checked settings are true; for example:

```
Select Case True

    Case mnuChartBy(0).Checked And _
      mnuChartType(0).Checked
```

As you examine this Select Case structure, look again at Figures 13-10 through 13-17; they demonstrate the relationship between the Checked settings in the International Sales window and the chart type drawn in the Excel worksheet.

For a final programming exercise with this program, consider the following scenario: Suppose the user makes changes in the sales data displayed inside the Excel worksheet and wants these changes to be transferred *back* to the original application window. Write a loop in the mnuExcel_Click procedure (just before the call to the Quit method) to copy a revised sales table from the worksheet back to the International Sales window. This new code completes the connection between the Visual Basic form and the Excel worksheet.

Listing 13-1
The general declarations of the frmIntSales form and the Form_Load procedure

```
' The International Sales Program, OLE Version
' -------------------------------------------

' Files:
' Project File:  IntSales.VBP
' Form File:     IntSales.FRM

' This program provides a small spreadsheet in
' which the user can enter annual sales data by
' international regions. As each data item is
' entered, the program calculates regional and
' period totals, and develops a chart to represent
' the sales data pictorially. Using commands in
' the Chart menu, the user can choose among
' several graph formats, including two arrangements of
' column charts and pie charts. In addition, the
' File menu contains a command that allows the user
' to transfer the current data to an Excel
' worksheet (assuming Excel is installed).
' Finally, the Copy command in the Edit menu
' places a copy of the data table on the Windows
' Clipboard; from there, the user can paste the
' data to other software environments.

Option Explicit

' The AmtFormat constant provides the dollar-and-
' cents format for data displayed in the sales
' table. The colorOffset constant determines the
' selection of colors used in the column charts
```

```
' and pie charts.
Const AmtFormat = "$#,###0"
Const colorOffset = 7


' The ExcelSheet object is used in the
' mnuExcel_Click procedure as a reference to
' an Excel worksheet.
Dim ExcelSheet As Object
```

An object variable to represent the worksheet object

```

' For convenience in a variety of operations,
' the program uses six arrays to record the sales
' data currently stored in the table. The arrays
' named amounts and amountStr record the actual
' data in numeric and string formats. The periodTots
' and regionTots arrays record the current totals.
' The periodLabels and regionLabels record the
' column and row labels for the table, which the
' user can revise if necessary to represent the
' actual content of the table.
Dim amounts(24)
Dim amountStr(24) As String
Dim periodTots(4)
Dim periodLabels(4) As String
Dim regionTots(4)
Dim regionLabels(4) As String


' The IDPrefixes array represents key prefixes that
' are appended to the column or row labels to
' identify the elements of a particular column chart.
Dim IDPrefixes(4) As String


' The grandTot variable represents the grand total
' of all the current sales data.

Dim grandTot    ' End of General Declarations.




Private Sub Form_Load()
```

IV

13

```
' The Form_Load procedure performs a variety
' of initializations at the beginning of the
' program's performance.

Dim i
Dim tempYear As String

' Display the initial column labels and
' initialize the arrays that record the
' current labels.
For i = 0 To 4
  tempYear = Year(Date) - (5 - i)
  txtYear(i).TEXT = tempYear
  periodLabels(i) = txtYear(i).TEXT
  regionLabels(i) = txtPlace(i).TEXT
  IDPrefixes(i) = Format((i + 1), "# = ")
Next i

' Display the current dollar unit selection.
' (The user can change this display by making
' a new selection from the Units menu.)
ShowUnits

End Sub   ' Form_Load
```

Listing 13-2
The mnuExcel_Click procedure

```
Private Sub mnuExcel_Click()

  ' The mnuExcel_Click procedure takes control
  ' when the user chooses the Transfer to Excel
  ' command from the File menu. This procedure
  ' creates and displays a new Excel worksheet
  ' object, copies all the sales data to the new
  ' worksheet, and draws a chart that is
  ' equivalent to the one currently displayed
  ' in the International Sales window.
```

```
Dim i, x, y

' If an error occurs in the attempt to create
' a worksheet object, skip to the end of
' this procedure. Note that errors occur if
' Excel is not installed on the current system,
' or if Excel is already running.
On Error GoTo OLEProblem

' Create the new worksheet object, and
' display the Excel application.
Set ExcelSheet = CreateObject("Excel.Sheet")
ExcelSheet.Application.Visible = True
```

Creating the worksheet object and displaying the Excel application

```
' Copy all the sales data and
' draw the corresponding chart.
CopyToExcel
DrawExcelChart

' Pause to give the user the opportunity to
' examine the worksheet and, optionally, to
' save it to disk.
MsgBox "Continue...", , "International Sales"

' Exit from the Excel application.
ExcelSheet.Application.Quit
```

A call to the Quit method

```
OLEProblem:
    ' Release the reference to the worksheet
    ' object from memory.
    Set ExcelSheet = Nothing
```

Releasing the object method from memory

```
End Sub   ' mnuExcel_Click
```

Listing 13-3
The CopyToExcel procedure

```
Private Sub CopyToExcel()

    ' The CopyToExcel procedure is called by
    ' mnuExcel_Click when the user chooses the
    ' Transfer to Excel command from the File
    ' menu. This procedure copies all the sales
    ' data currently displayed in the International
    ' Sales window to a new Excel sheet object.
    ' It also copies titles and labels, and
    ' enters summation formulas into the bottom
    ' row and last column of the data area.

    Dim i, x, y

    ' Apply the boldface style to the cells
    ' that will display titles and labels.
    ExcelSheet.Range("$A$1:$G$3,$A$3:$A$9").Font.Bold _
        = True

' Adjust the width of column A.
    ExcelSheet.Columns("A").ColumnWidth = 10.29

    ' Copy the title and the units
    ' to the worksheet.
    ExcelSheet.Cells(1, 2).VALUE = _
        txtTitle.TEXT
    ExcelSheet.Cells(1, 5).VALUE = _
        lblUnits.Caption

' Copy the entire table of numeric data.
    For i = 0 To 24
        y = i Mod 5 + 2
        x = i \ 5 + 4
        ExcelSheet.Cells(x, y).VALUE = _
            txtAmount(i).TEXT
    Next i
```

Formatting a range on the worksheet

Copying data from the Visual Basic form to the worksheet

```
' Copy the labels.
For i = 0 To 4
  With ExcelSheet
    .Cells(3, i + 2).VALUE = _
      periodLabels(i)
    .Cells(i + 4, 1).VALUE = _
      regionLabels(i)

    ' Enter the summation formulas.
    .Cells(9, i + 2).Formula = _
      "=Sum(R[-5]C:R[-1]C)"
    .Cells(i + 4, 7).Formula = _
      "=Sum(RC[-5]:RC[-1])"
  End With
Next i

' Enter the "TOTALS" labels and
' a formula for the grand total
' of all the sales data.
With ExcelSheet
  .Cells(9, 1).VALUE = "TOTALS"
  .Cells(3, 7).VALUE = "TOTALS"
  .Cells(9, 7).Formula = _
    "=Sum(RC[-5]:RC[-1])"
End With

End Sub   ' CopyToExcel
```

*Entering formulas
into worksheet cells*

Listing 13-4
The DrawExcelChart procedure

```
Private Sub DrawExcelChart()

  ' The DrawExcelChart procedure is called by
  ' mnuExcel_Click when the user chooses the
  ' Transfer to Excel command from the File menu.
  ' This procedure reads the current settings of
  ' the mnuChartBy and mnuChartType menu options
  ' and uses Excel's ChartWizard method to create
```

```
' an equivalent chart in the new worksheet
' object. Note that a ChartObject is a member
' of the ChartObjects collection for a given
' sheet object. A ChartObject is a container
' for a chart. The Chart object represents the
' actual chart drawn inside the container. The
' ChartWizard method applies to a Chart object.

' Declare variables for a ChartObject
' and a Chart.
Dim newChartObj As ChartObject
Dim newChart As Chart
```

Variables for the ChartObject and Chart objects

```
' Add a new ChartObject to the ChartObjects
' collection for the Sheet object.
Set newChartObj = _
    ExcelSheet.ChartObjects.Add(10, 120, 400, 150)
```

Creating a new ChartObject object

```
' The newChart variable represents the Chart
' contained by the newChartObj object.
Set newChart = _
  newChartObj.Chart

' Read the Checked settings of the
' mnuChartBy and mnuChartType menu options
' to decide what kind of chart to draw.
Select Case True

  ' A column chart in which the legend
  ' lists the time periods.
  Case mnuChartBy(0).Checked And _
    mnuChartType(0).Checked
```

Assigning properties to the chart object for a column chart

```
    newChart.ChartWizard _
      ExcelSheet.Range("$A$3:$F$8"), _
      xlColumn, 3, _
      xlColumns, 1, 1, _
      True
```

```
' A column chart in which the legend
' lists the sales regions.
Case mnuChartBy(1).Checked And _
    mnuChartType(0).Checked
```

The alternative Column Chart

```
newChart.ChartWizard _
    ExcelSheet.Range("$A$3:$F$8"), _
    xlColumn, 3, _
    xlRows, 1, 1, _
    True
```

```
' A pie chart in which the legend lists
' the time periods.
Case mnuChartBy(0).Checked And _
    mnuChartType(1).Checked
```

```
newChart.ChartWizard _
    ExcelSheet.Range("$A$3:$F$3,$A$9:$F$9"), _
    xlPie, 1, _
    xlRows, 1, 1, _
    True
```

```
' A pie chart in which the legend lists
' the sales regions.
Case mnuChartBy(1).Checked And _
    mnuChartType(1).Checked
```

Pie chart options

```
newChart.ChartWizard _
    ExcelSheet.Range("$A$3:$A$8,$G$3:$G$8"), _
    xlPie, 1, _
    xlColumns, 1, 1, _
    True
```

```
    End Select

End Sub    ' DrawExcelChart
```

Listing 13-5
The mnuRandomData_Click procedure

```
Private Sub mnuRandomData_Click()

    ' The mnuRandomData_Click procedure creates
    ' a sales table of randomly-generated data
    ' items; this procedure allows the user to
    ' experiment with the OLE features of this
    ' program without having to enter a real
    ' data set.

    Dim i
    Randomize

    ' Enter random values, and call the
    ' LostFocus event procedure to process
    ' each data entry.
    For i = 0 To 24
        txtAmount(i).TEXT = Int(Rnd * 9000) + 1000
        txtAmount_LostFocus (i)
    Next i

End Sub   ' mnuRandomData_Click
```

Using the Rnd function to generate random data

Listing 13-6
The txtAmount_LostFocus procedure

```
Private Sub txtAmount_LostFocus(Index As Integer)

    ' The txtAmount_LostFocus procedure performs
    ' a variety of important tasks after each new
    ' data item has been entered into the sales
    ' table. (Note that txtAmount is a control
    ' array, with Index values from 0 to 24.) The
    ' procedure validates the data entry, reformats
    ' it for display, recalculates the appropriate
    ' totals, and redraws the current chart.
```

```
' The entryWidth variable defines the width
' within which the program right-justifies
' entries into the sales table.
Dim entryWidth As String
entryWidth = Space(8)

' Compare the entry with the corresponding
' value in the amountStr array, to determine
' whether the value has changed.
If amountStr(Index) <> txtAmount(Index).TEXT Then

  ' If so, record the new numeric value in the
  ' amounts array. Use the Val function to
  ' eliminate any nonnumeric characters in the
  ' entry. (Note that an entry beginning with
  ' a nonnumeric character becomes zero.)
  amounts(Index) = Val(txtAmount(Index).TEXT)

  ' Do not allow negative entries or entries
  ' that are longer than six digits in the
  ' sales table.
  If amounts(Index) < 0 Or _
    amounts(Index) > 999999 _
    Then amounts(Index) = 0

  ' If the entry is not zero, display the value
  ' in a right-justified dollar-and-cent format.
  If amounts(Index) <> 0 Then
    RSet entryWidth = _
      Format(amounts(Index), AmtFormat)
    txtAmount(Index).TEXT = entryWidth
  Else
    ' Otherwise, if the entry is zero,
    ' display it as a blank entry.
    txtAmount(Index).TEXT = ""
  End If

  ' Record the formatted value in the
  ' string array named amountStr.
  amountStr(Index) = txtAmount(Index).TEXT
```

```
    ' Recaculate the totals for the row and
    ' column where this new entry is located.
    CalculateTotals Index

    ' If the current grand total is not zero,
    ' redraw the current chart. Otherwise,
    ' hide the chart controls.
    If grandTot <> 0 Then
      DrawGraph
    Else
      HideGraph
    End If

  End If

End Sub   ' txtAmount_LostFocus
```

Listing 13-7
The txtAmount_GotFocus and txtAmount_KeyDown procedures

```
Private Sub txtAmount_GotFocus(Index As Integer)

  ' The txtAmount_GotFocus procedure arranges to
  ' highlight the contents of a given txtAmount
  ' box when the control receives the focus. This
  ' effect is achieved through use of the SelStart
  ' and SelLength properties.

  txtAmount(Index).SelStart = 0
  txtAmount(Index).SelLength = _
    Len(txtAmount(Index).TEXT)

End Sub   ' txtAmount_GotFocus



Private Sub txtAmount_KeyDown(Index As Integer, _
  KeyCode As Integer, Shift As Integer)
```

```
' The txtAmount_KeyDown procedure allows the
' txtAmount text boxes to respond to the four
' arrow keys (left, up, right, and down) and to
' the Enter key as techniques for moving the
' focus from one box to the next. (Note that
' the 25 txtAmount boxes form a control array,
' with Index values from 0 to 24.)

' Define names to represent the code numbers of
' the relevant keys.
Const leftKey = 37
Const upKey = 38
Const rightKey = 39
Const downKey = 40
Const enter = 13

Select Case KeyCode

  ' Move the focus down to the next row,
  ' or from the bottom row to the top.
  Case downKey
    If Index < 20 Then
      txtAmount(Index + 5).SetFocus
    Else
      txtAmount(Index Mod 5).SetFocus
    End If

  ' Move the focus up to the previous row,
  ' or from the top row to the bottom.
  Case upKey
    If Index > 4 Then
      txtAmount(Index - 5).SetFocus
    Else
      txtAmount(Index + 20).SetFocus
    End If

  ' Move the focus to the previous text
  ' box, or from the upper-left corner to
  ' the lower-right corner of the table.
  Case leftKey
```

```
      If Index <> 0 Then
        txtAmount(Index - 1).SetFocus
      Else
        txtAmount(24).SetFocus
      End If

  ' Move the focus to the next text box,
  ' or from the lower-right corner to the
  ' upper-left corner of the table. (Note
  ' that the right-arrow key and the Enter
  ' key are both available for this action.)
  Case rightKey, enter
      If Index <> 24 Then
        txtAmount(Index + 1).SetFocus
      Else
        txtAmount(0).SetFocus
      End If

  End Select

End Sub   ' txtAmount_KeyDown
```

Listing 13-8
The CalculateTotals procedure

```
Private Sub CalculateTotals(amtIndex As Integer)

  ' The CalculateTotals procedure updates the
  ' row and column of sales totals each time the
  ' user enters a new value into the sales table.
  ' Note that the totals are displayed in two
  ' arrays of labels, named lblPeriodTotal and
  ' lblRegionTotal. Each array has Index values
  ' from 0 to 4.

  Dim i As Integer
  Dim periodIndex As Integer
  Dim regionIndex As Integer
  Dim firstRowIndex As Integer
```

```
Dim firstColIndex As Integer
Dim totTemp

' Create indexes to identify the
' totals that need to be recalculated.
periodIndex = amtIndex Mod 5
regionIndex = amtIndex \ 5
firstRowIndex = regionIndex * 5
firstColIndex = periodIndex

' Find the total sales for the current region.
totTemp = 0
For i = firstRowIndex To firstRowIndex + 4
  totTemp = totTemp + amounts(i)
Next i

' Record this numeric value in the
' regionTots array.
regionTots(regionIndex) = totTemp

' Display the formatted value in the
' appropriate lblRegionTotal control.
If totTemp <> 0 Then
  lblRegionTotal(regionIndex).Caption = _
    Format(totTemp, AmtFormat)
Else
  lblRegionTotal(regionIndex).Caption = ""
End If

' Calculate the total sales for the
' current period.
totTemp = 0
For i = firstColIndex To firstColIndex + 20 Step 5
  totTemp = totTemp + amounts(i)
Next i

' Record this numeric value in the
' periodTots array.
periodTots(periodIndex) = totTemp
```

```
' Display the formatted value in the
' appropriate lblPeriodTotal control.
If totTemp <> 0 Then
  lblPeriodTotal(periodIndex).Caption = _
    Format(totTemp, AmtFormat)
Else
  lblPeriodTotal(periodIndex).Caption = ""
End If

' Calculate the new grand total.
totTemp = 0
For i = 0 To 24
  totTemp = totTemp + amounts(i)
Next i

' Record the numeric value in the
' grandTot variable.
grandTot = totTemp

' Display the formatted value in the
' lblGrandTotal control.
If totTemp <> 0 Then
  lblGrandTotal.Caption = _
    Format(totTemp, AmtFormat)
Else
  lblGrandTotal.Caption = ""
End If

End Sub   ' CalculateTotals
```

Listing 13-9
The DrawGraph procedure

```
Private Sub DrawGraph()

  ' The DrawGraph procedure redraws the chart,
  ' based on the current selections in the
  ' Chart menu.

  ' Display and picture box control and
```

```
' clear its contents.
picSalesChart.Visible = True
picSalesChart.Cls

' Determine which chart to draw, according
' to the current Checked values in the
' mnuChartBy and mnuChartType arrays.
Select Case True

   Case mnuChartBy(0).Checked And _
        mnuChartType(0).Checked

      ' For a column chart, draw the
      ' vertical and horizontal axes first,
      ' then draw the columns of the chart.
      DrawAxes
      ColumnByYears

   Case mnuChartBy(0).Checked And _
        mnuChartType(1).Checked

      ' For a pie chart, no axes are needed.
      PieByYears

   Case mnuChartBy(1).Checked And _
        mnuChartType(0).Checked

      DrawAxes
      ColumnByRegion

   Case mnuChartBy(1).Checked And _
        mnuChartType(1).Checked

      PieByRegion

End Select

' Display the legend for the chart.
ShowLegend

End Sub   ' DrawGraph
```

Listing 13-10
The DrawAxes and ShowLegend procedures

```
Private Sub DrawAxes()

    ' The DrawAxes procedure draws the vertical
    ' and horizontal axes for a column chart.

    Dim i

    ' Begin by creating a convenient coordinate
    ' system for the chart. (The "origin" of the
    ' chart is located just above and to the right
    ' of the lower-left corner of the picture box.)
    picSalesChart.Scale (-1, 11)-(11, -0.25)

    ' Then draw the two axes, each starting
    ' at the "origin" defined by the coordinate
    ' scale.
    picSalesChart.Line (0, 0)-Step(10, 0)
    picSalesChart.Line (0, 0)-Step(0, 10)

End Sub   ' DrawAxes




Private Sub ShowLegend()

    ' The ShowLegend procedure displays the labels
    ' and colors of the legend for a pie chart or a
    ' column chart. In addition, the procedure adds
    ' numeric prefixes to labels above or to the left
    ' of the sales table, to identify the individual
    ' columns of a column chart.

    Dim i

    For i = 0 To 4

        ' If the "By Years" option has been selected
        ' in the Chart menu, display the years as the
```

```
' legend labels.
If mnuChartBy(0).Checked Then
  If periodTots(i) <> 0 Then
    lblLegendColor(i).Visible = True
    lblLegendColor(i).BackColor = _
      QBColor(i + colorOffset)
    lblLegendText(i).Caption = periodLabels(i)

  ' But don't display a box or label for
  ' a sales table column that has a
  ' total value of zero.
  Else
    lblLegendColor(i).Visible = False
    lblLegendText(i).Caption = ""
  End If

  ' For a column chart, add a numeric
  ' prefix to the region labels to identify
  ' each column of the chart.
  If mnuChartType(0).Checked And _
      regionTots(i) <> 0 Then
    lblxAxis(i).Caption = i + 1
    txtPlace(i).TEXT = IDPrefixes(i) + _
      regionLabels(i)
    txtPlace(i).Enabled = False
  Else
    lblxAxis(i).Caption = ""
    txtPlace(i).TEXT = regionLabels(i)
    txtPlace(i).Enabled = True
  End If

Else

  ' If the "By Region" option has been
  ' selected in the Chart menu, display
  ' the regions as the legend labels.
  If regionTots(i) <> 0 Then
    lblLegendColor(i).Visible = True
    lblLegendColor(i).BackColor = _
      QBColor(i + colorOffset)
```

```
      lblLegendText(i).Caption = regionLabels(i)
    Else
      lblLegendColor(i).Visible = False
      lblLegendText(i).Caption = ""
    End If


    ' For a column chart, add numeric prefixes
    ' to the year labels to identify each
    ' column of the chart.
    If mnuChartType(0).Checked And _
        periodTots(i) <> 0 Then
      lblxAxis(i).Caption = i + 1
      txtYear(i).TEXT = IDPrefixes(i) + _
        periodLabels(i)
      txtYear(i).Enabled = False
    Else
      lblxAxis(i).Caption = ""
      txtYear(i).TEXT = periodLabels(i)
      txtYear(i).Enabled = True
    End If

  End If
Next i


End Sub    ' ShowLegend
```

Listing 13-11
The ColumnByYears and ColumnByRegion procedures

```
Private Sub ColumnByYears()

    ' The ColumnByYears procedure draws a column
    ' chart if the user has selected the "By Years"
    ' option in the Chart menu.

    Dim i
    Dim x, y, y2
    Dim maxRegion
    Dim scaleFactor
```

```
' Determine the largest region total.
maxRegion = 0
For i = 0 To 4
  If regionTots(i) > maxRegion Then _
    maxRegion = regionTots(i)
Next i

' The scale factor for the chart is based
' on the largest region total. (This value
' will have a height of 10 in the chart.)
scaleFactor = 10 / maxRegion

' Depict each nonzero value in the sales
' table as a "stack" in one of the charts.
For i = 0 To 24

  ' At the beginning of each row of data,
  ' reinitialize the x and y values for a
  ' new column in the chart.
  If i Mod 5 = 0 Then
    x = 0.5 + 2 * (i / 5)
    y = 0
  End If

  ' If an amount is not zero, calculate
  ' the height of the corresponding "stack."
  If amounts(i) <> 0 Then
    y2 = scaleFactor * amounts(i)

    ' Select a color and a fill style.
    picSalesChart.FillColor = _
      QBColor(i Mod 5 + colorOffset)
    picSalesChart.FillStyle = 0

    ' Draw the "stack."
    picSalesChart.Line (x, y)-Step(1.5, y2), _
      0, B

    ' Increment the value of y by the
    ' height of the previous "stack."
```

```
        y = y + y2
      End If
   Next i

End Sub   ' ColumnByYears



Private Sub ColumnByRegion()

   ' The ColumnByRegion procedure draws a column
   ' chart if the user has selected the "By Region"
   ' option in the Chart menu.

   Dim i, j
   Dim x, y, y2
   Dim maxPeriod
   Dim scaleFactor

   ' Determine the largest year total
   ' in the sales table.
   maxPeriod = 0
   For i = 0 To 4
     If periodTots(i) > maxPeriod Then _
        maxPeriod = periodTots(i)
   Next i

   ' The scale factor for the chart is based on
   ' the largest year total. (This value has a
   ' height of 10 in the chart.)
   scaleFactor = 10 / maxPeriod


   For i = 0 To 4

      ' Reinitialize the x and y values for the
      ' beginning of each new column in the chart.
      x = 0.5 + 2 * i
      y = 0
```

```
' Draw a "stack" for each numeric entry in
' a given year of the sales table.
For j = i To i + 20 Step 5

  ' If the value is not zero, calculate
  ' the "stack" height that will represent
  ' this value in the column chart.
  If amounts(j) <> 0 Then
    y2 = scaleFactor * amounts(j)

    ' Select a color and a fill style.
    picSalesChart.FillColor = _
      QBColor(j \ 5 + colorOffset)
    picSalesChart.FillStyle = 0

    ' Draw the "stack."
    picSalesChart.Line (x, y)-Step(1.5, y2), _
      0, B

    ' Add the height of the previous
    ' "stack" to the current value of y.
    y = y + y2
  End If
Next j
Next i

End Sub   ' ColumnByRegion
```

Listing 13-12
The PieByYears and PieByRegion procedures

```
Private Sub PieByYears()

  ' The PieByYears procedure draws a pie chart
  ' if the user has selected the "By Years"
  ' option in the Chart menu.

  Dim i, pi, a1, a2
```

```
' Calculate the value of pi.
pi = 4 * Atn(1)

' Set the scale for the picture box. The
' "origin" is located in the center of the
' box in this case.
picSalesChart.Scale (-1, 1)-(1, -1)

' Because of a quirk in the Circle method, the
' starting angle for the first wedge in the chart
' must be a very small nonzero value.
a1 = 0.00001

' Draw a wedge to represent the total sales
' for each year in the sales table.
For i = 0 To 4
  If periodTots(i) <> 0 Then

    ' Calculate the ending angle of the
    ' current wedge.
    a2 = a1 + (2 * pi) * _
      (periodTots(i) / grandTot)

    ' Select a color and a fill style.
    picSalesChart.FillColor = _
      QBColor(i + colorOffset)
    picSalesChart.FillStyle = 0

    ' Draw the wedge.
    If periodTots(i) < grandTot Then
      picSalesChart.Circle (0, 0), 0.9, _
        0, -a1, -a2 + 0.00001

    ' But if this sales total is currently
    ' the only annual total availble in the
    ' table, draw a full circle instead.
    Else
      picSalesChart.Circle (0, 0), 0.9, 0
    End If
```

```
            ' The starting angle for the next wedge
            ' is the ending angle of the current wedge.
            a1 = a2
        End If
    Next i

End Sub   ' PieByYears



Private Sub PieByRegion()

    ' The PieByRegion procedure draws a pie chart
    ' if the user has selected the "By Region"
    ' option in the Chart menu.

    Dim i, pi, a1, a2

    ' Calculate the value of pi.
    pi = 4 * Atn(1)

    ' Set the scale of the picture box. The "origin"
    ' is at the center of the box in this case.
    picSalesChart.Scale (-1, 1)-(1, -1)

    ' Because of a quirk in the Circle method, the
    ' starting angle of the first wedge must be a
    ' very small nonzero value.
    a1 = 0.00001

    ' Draw a wedge to represent each regional
    ' sales total.
    For i = 0 To 4

        ' If the current sales total is not zero,
        ' calculate the ending angle of the wedge.
        If regionTots(i) <> 0 Then
            a2 = a1 + (2 * pi) * _
                (regionTots(i) / grandTot)
```

```
                ' Select a color and a fill style.
                picSalesChart.FillColor = _
                  QBColor(i + colorOffset)
                picSalesChart.FillStyle = 0

                ' Draw the wedge.
                If regionTots(i) < grandTot Then
                  picSalesChart.Circle (0, 0), 0.9, _
                    0, -a1, -a2 + 0.00001

                ' But if this total value is currently
                ' the only regional total available in the
                ' sales table, draw a full circle instead.
                Else
                  picSalesChart.Circle (0, 0), 0.9, 0
                End If

                ' The starting angle for the next wedge
                ' is the ending angle of the current wedge.
                a1 = a2
            End If
        Next i

    End Sub    ' PieByRegion
```

Listing 13-13
The mnuClear_Click, HideGraph, mnuCopy_Click, and SaveReport procedures

```
    Private Sub mnuClear_Click()

        ' The mnuClear_Click procedure takes control when
        ' the user chooses the Clear command from the
        ' Edit menu. The procedure clears all data from
        ' the sales table, and temporarily hides the
        ' objects in the chart area of the form.

        Dim i
```

```
' Reinitialize the text boxes in the sales
' table and the values in the amounts and
' amountStr arrays.
For i = 0 To 24
  txtAmount(i).TEXT = ""
  amounts(i) = 0
  amountStr(i) = ""
Next i

' Erase the totals and reinitialize the totals
' arrays. Also restore the original row and
' column labels.
For i = 0 To 4
  lblPeriodTotal(i).Caption = ""
  lblRegionTotal(i).Caption = ""
  periodTots(i) = 0
  regionTots(i) = 0
  txtPlace(i).TEXT = regionLabels(i)
  txtYear(i).TEXT = periodLabels(i)
Next i

' Erase the grand total and reinitialize
' the grandTot variable.
lblGrandTotal.Caption = ""
grandTot = 0

' Hide the graph objects.
HideGraph

' Move the focus to the first text box in the
' table, in preparation for new data entries.
txtAmount(0).SetFocus

End Sub   ' mnuClear_Click



Private Sub HideGraph()
```

```
' The HideGraph procedure hides the picture box
' and other controls related to the chart and
' its legend. The program calls this routine
' whenever the grand total value is zero.

Dim i

' Hide the picture box.
picSalesChart.Visible = False

For i = 0 To 4

    ' Hide all of the legend labels.
    lblLegendColor(i).Visible = False
    lblLegendText(i).Caption = ""

    ' Erase the labels arranged beneath
    ' the horizontal axis of a column chart.
    lblxAxis(i).Caption = ""

    ' Restore the original year and region
    ' labels above and to the left of the
    ' sales table.
    txtYear(i).TEXT = periodLabels(i)
    txtYear(i).Enabled = True
    txtPlace(i).TEXT = regionLabels(i)
    txtPlace(i).Enabled = True
  Next i

End Sub  ' HideGraph



Private Sub mnuCopy_Click()

    ' The mnuCopy_Click procedure takes control
    ' when the user chooses the Copy command from
    ' the Edit menu. The purpose of the procedure
    ' is to place a copy of the current sales table
    ' on the Windows Clipboard. From there, the
```

```
' user can paste the data to another software
' environment, such as a word processing
' program or a spreadsheet.

Dim temp As String, inTemp As String

' Begin by creating a text file on disk for
' the current data set.
SaveReport

' Then open the file and read each line it
' contains.
temp = ""
Open "\IntSales.Txt" For Input As #1
  Do While Not EOF(1)
    Line Input #1, inTemp

    ' Concatenate each line of text to
    ' the string variable temp.
    temp = temp + inTemp + Chr(13) + Chr(10)
  Loop
Close #1

  ' Finally, place the temp string on
  ' the Clipboard.
  Clipboard.SetText temp

End Sub   ' mnuCopy_Click




Private Sub SaveReport()

  ' The SaveReport procedure creates a
  ' text file (named \IntSales.Txt) on disk and
  ' stores the numeric data currently displayed in
  ' the program's form.

  Dim i, j
  Dim f As String, b As String
```

```
f = "$#,####0"
b = "              "

' Create the file. (If the file already
' exists, overwrite the previous version.)
Open "\IntSales.Txt" For Output As #1

  ' Write the title and the column labels
  ' to the file.
  Print #1, b; b; txtTitle
  Print #1, b; b; "    "; lblUnits
  Print #1,

  Print #1, b;
  For i = 0 To 4
    RSet b = txtYear(i)
    Print #1, b;
  Next i
  Print #1, "        Totals"
  Print #1,

  ' Write the table of sales data to the file.
  For i = 0 To 4
    LSet b = txtPlace(i).TEXT
    Print #1, b;
    For j = i * 5 To i * 5 + 4
      RSet b = txtAmount(j).TEXT
      Print #1, b;
    Next j
    RSet b = lblRegionTotal(i).Caption
    Print #1, b
  Next i

  ' Write the totals to the file.
  Print #1,
  Print #1, "Totals        ";
  For i = 0 To 4
    RSet b = lblPeriodTotal(i).Caption
    Print #1, b;
```

```
      Next i
      RSet b = lblGrandTotal
      Print #1, b

   Close #1

End Sub  ' SaveReport
```

Listing 13-14
The mnuChartBy_Click and mnuChartType_Click procedures

```
Private Sub mnuChartBy_Click(Index As Integer)

   ' The mnuChartBy_Click procedure responds to
   ' the user's choice of an option in the Chart
   ' menu. The user can choose to chart the data
   ' by region or by time period.

   Dim i

   ' Adjust the selection within the menu itself.
   If Index = 0 Then
     mnuChartBy(0).Checked = True
     mnuChartBy(1).Checked = False
   Else
     mnuChartBy(0).Checked = False
     mnuChartBy(1).Checked = True
   End If

   ' Restore the original column and row
   ' labels, in preparation for displaying
   ' new keys for a column chart.
   For i = 0 To 4
     txtYear(i).TEXT = periodLabels(i)
     txtYear(i).Enabled = True
     txtPlace(i).TEXT = regionLabels(i)
     txtPlace(i).Enabled = True
   Next i
```

```
        ' If any sales information has been entered
        ' into the table, redraw the chart at this point.
        If grandTot <> 0 Then DrawGraph

End Sub   ' mnuChartBy_Click



Private Sub mnuChartType_Click(Index As Integer)

   ' The mnuChartType_Click procedure responds to
   ' the user's choice of an option in the Chart
   ' menu. The user can choose to create a column
   ' chart or a pie chart.

   ' Adjust the current selection in the menu.
   If Index = 0 Then
     mnuChartType(0).Checked = True
     mnuChartType(1).Checked = False
   Else
     mnuChartType(0).Checked = False
     mnuChartType(1).Checked = True
   End If

   ' If any sales information has been entered
   ' into the table, redraw the chart at this point.
   If grandTot <> 0 Then DrawGraph

   End Sub   ' mnuChartType_Click
```

Listing 13-15
The mnuUnitType_Click and ShowUnits procedures

```
     Private Sub mnuUnitType_Click(Index As Integer)

        ' The mnuUnitType_Click procedure takes control
        ' when the user chooses a new option from the
        ' Units menu. (Note that the three options in
        ' this menu form a control array with Index
```

```
' values from 0 to 2.) The procedure changes
' the selection in the menu and then displays
' the appropriate caption in the lblUnits control.

Dim i

' Determine which option should be checked.
For i = 0 To 2
  If i = Index Then
    mnuUnitType(i).Checked = True
  Else
    mnuUnitType(i).Checked = False
  End If
Next i

' Display the selected units caption.
ShowUnits

End Sub   ' mnuUnitType_Click




Private Sub ShowUnits()

  ' The ShowUnits procedure reads the current
  ' selection in the Units menu and displays
  ' the corresponding units caption in the form.

  Select Case True
    Case mnuUnitType(0).Checked
      lblUnits.Caption = "(in dollars)"
    Case mnuUnitType(1).Checked
      lblUnits.Caption = "(in thousands of $)"
    Case mnuUnitType(2).Checked
      lblUnits.Caption = "(in millions of $)"
  End Select

End Sub   ' ShowUnits
```

IV

13

Listing 13-16
Two miscellaneous LostFocus procedures and the mnuExit_Click procedure

```
Private Sub txtYear_LostFocus(Index As Integer)

   ' The txtYear_LostFocus procedure is called when
   ' the user completes a change in any one of the
   ' year labels displayed above the sales chart.
   ' The procedure records this change in the
   ' periodLabels array.

   periodLabels(Index) = txtYear(Index).TEXT
   If grandTot <> 0 Then ShowLegend

End Sub   ' txtYear_LostFocus



Private Sub txtPlace_LostFocus(Index As Integer)

   ' The txtPlace_LostFocus procedure is called when
   ' the user completes a change in any one of the
   ' region labels displayed to the left of the
   ' sales chart. The procedure records this change
   ' in the regionLabels array.

   regionLabels(Index) = txtPlace(Index).TEXT
   If grandTot <> 0 Then ShowLegend

End Sub   ' txtPlace_LostFocus



Private Sub mnuExit_Click()

   ' The mnuExit_Click procedure takes control when
   ' the user chooses the Exit command from the
   ' File menu. The procedure simply terminates the
   ' program performance.

   End

End Sub   ' mnuExit_Click
```

14 Database Connections

*Y*ou've seen several Visual Basic applications that create database files on disk for storing and retrieving information. These programs illustrate the traditional Basic-language techniques for working with databases:

- The Open statement creates a data file or opens an existing file in one of several modes. In particular, the Random mode provides direct access to structured records in a database file.

- The user-defined data type gives you a clear way to represent the record structure for a random-access file. In a Type statement you list the fields and their types; then in a Dim statement you declare a record variable to serve as the medium for reading records from an open file or for writing new records to the file.

- The Get# statement reads an entire record from a random access file, and the Put# statement writes a record to the file.

- An array of records, appropriately designed and managed, serves as an effective index for a random-access file, allowing a program to locate records by specific key fields.

- A variety of other tools are available to help you work with the file, including the end-of-file function, EOF; the length-of-file function, LOF; and the Len function, which can be used to measure the size of a record variable. Using LOF and Len together, your program can calculate the number of records in an open file.

These techniques produce a database file in a specific random-access format. Any program that uses the same techniques can read or revise the file. A database on disk thereby becomes a medium for exchanging infor-mation between programs.

This final chapter introduces a dramatically different approach to database management. Visual Basic has a special tool called the *data control* that is designed to provide access to files created by major data-base applications such as Microsoft Access, dBASE, and Paradox and spreadsheet programs such as Lotus 1-2-3 and Microsoft Excel. This control is the central topic of this chapter.

The data control is available in all three editions of Visual Basic 4.0. Figure 14-1 shows how it appears in the Toolbox of the Standard Edition. One of the control's most interesting features is its versatility as a program-ming tool. Using this control, you can develop database programs *with or without* writing code. To be sure, the data control has an important group of methods and properties that you can use in a program's code to con-duct sophisticated database-related activities. But this control is intrinsically so powerful that its presence on a form is enough to define a usable connection to an existing database.

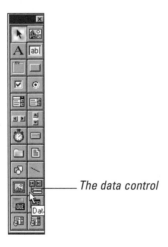 —— *The data control*

Figure 14-1
The data control as it appears in the Toolbox of the Standard Edition.

The data control represents a database technology known as the Microsoft Jet database engine. Also the basis for Microsoft Access, this technology provides database techniques for a variety of application-specific formats.

You'll explore the features of the data control in two Visual Basic projects presented in this chapter. Both programs are designed to improve upon an application that first appeared in Chapter 4: The Currency Exchange program is a simple calculation tool for converting between U.S. dollars and the currencies of other countries. The original version of the program (CurrExch.VBP) gets its data from a text file (Currency.TXT) that contains a list of countries, currencies, and exchange rates.

The two projects in this chapter together produce a broader version of this application:

- The Currency Input project is a convenient data-entry program for creating and updating the records of a currency exchange file. The program works with an Access database named Currency.MDB, which in turn contains a table named Exchange. The Exchange table has fields for country names, currencies, and exchange rates. You'll develop this program, along with the associated database definition, in an extended hands-on exercise presented near the beginning of this chapter. This program is an example of a database application that requires no code of its own.

- The database version of the Currency Exchange application appears to be nearly identical to the first version of the program presented in Chapter 4. It provides a drop-down list of countries to choose from, and a simple way to calculate exchange equivalents for specific currencies. The significant difference is that the program uses the Currency.MDB database file as its source for currency exchange information. This program's code introduces several of the important methods and properties associated with the data control.

If Microsoft Access is installed on your computer, you can use it to develop the Currency.MDB database for this chapter's programming exercises. If not, Visual Basic supplies a smaller-scale program called the Data Manager, which is available for defining databases in the Access format. As you work through the steps of creating a database file with the Data Manager, you'll have the opportunity to review a number of general database concepts.

Using the Data Manager Program

You'll find the Data Manager program in the Visual Basic directory, stored as DatMan32.EXE. You may want to create a shortcut icon for it on the Windows 95 desktop. Open the Visual Basic directory (\VB by default) in the My Computer window, and look for the Data Manager file. Holding down the right mouse button, drag a copy of the file to the desktop, and then choose the Create Shortcut(s) Here option from the resulting pop-up menu. The Data Manager icon appears on the desktop as in Figure 14-2. (You can use this same sequence of steps to create a shortcut for Visual Basic itself, also illustrated in Figure 14-2. To change the name of a shortcut, select the icon, click the name, and type a new name of your choice.)

Figure 14-2
The Data Manager and Visual Basic icons on the Windows 95 desktop.

To start the Data Manager, simply double-click the shortcut icon you've created. When you do so, an empty application window appears on the desktop, as shown in Figure 14-3. The program's File menu contains commands for creating or opening a database. The Help menu provides several entry points into the program's help system. For example, pull down the Help menu and choose Contents for an introduction to the Data Manager.

REVIEWING DATABASE TERMINOLOGY

Take this opportunity to review some of the basic terminology of database management. In a *relational database*, information is organized in rows and columns; a row contains a complete record, and a column represents a particular field of information. A group of records arranged in this way is called a *table*. An Access database may contain many related tables. To retrieve information efficiently from multiple tables, you define *relationships* between key fields; Access uses the relationships to correlate records and to combine information from the two tables in a useful way.

Figure 14-3
The Data Manager window.

Access databases are identified on disk with an extension name of MDB (for Microsoft Database). The database you're about to create, Currency.MDB, will contain a single table, named Exchange, with three fields, Country, Currency, and InDollars. Each record you enter into the table will provide the dollar exchange rate for the currency of a particular country. You can use the Data Manager program to define the field structure for a database table, and then to begin entering records into the table. In the upcoming exercise you'll enter only one record into the table. Then you'll return to Visual Basic, where you'll develop the Currency Input program as a more convenient tool for data entry into the Currency.MDB database.

CREATING THE CURRENCY.MDB DATABASE

With the Data Manager window still open on the desktop, you can create a new MDB file, add a table to the database, and define the record structure of the table. Here are the steps:

1. Pull down the File menu and choose New Database. The New Database dialog box appears on the screen. Click the Up One Level button near the top-right corner of the dialog box to navigate up to the root directory of your hard disk.

2. In the File name text box, near the bottom of the dialog box, enter **Currency** as the name of the new database file you'll be creating (Figure 14-4). The Data Manager automatically adds an extension of MDB to the file name, indicating that the file will be stored in the Microsoft Access database format. Click Save to create the database file.

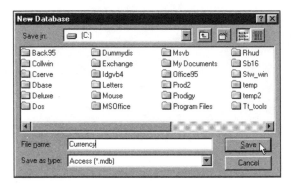

Figure 14-4

Entering a database name into the New Database dialog box.

3. A new Database window appears inside the Data Manager application, as shown in Figure 14-5. Click the New button to add a table to the database. The Add Table dialog box appears on the screen.

4. In the Name text box at the top of the dialog box, enter **Exchange** as the name for the new table (Figure 14-6). Then press the Tab key to activate the Field Name text box. Your next task is to begin defining the fields of the table.

5. Enter **Country** as the first field name. Press Tab again to activate the Data Type box, and then press the T key. The word Text appears as the data type of the first field. (You can also select a data type from the drop-down list attached to this box.)

Figure 14-5
Preparing to add a first table to the Database window.

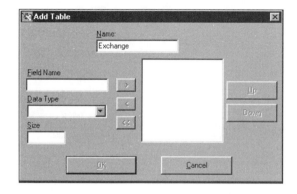

Figure 14-6
Using the Add Table dialog box.

6. Press Tab again to activate the Size box, and enter **15** as the length of the Country field. Then click the > button (located just to the right of the Field Name box) to complete the first field definition. The field name appears in the list box to the right.

7. Define two other fields: Currency, a Text field with a size of 15; and InDollars, a Single-precision numeric field. (No Size entry is needed for numeric fields.) When you've completed the three field definitions, the Add Table dialog box looks like Figure 14-7. Click OK to complete the Table definition.

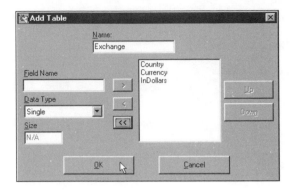

Figure 14-7
Creating the three fields of the Exchange table.

8. Back in the Database window, Exchange appears as the name of the first table. Select the name and then click Open (Figure 14-8). A window named "Table: Exchange" opens inside the Data Manager workspace. In this window you can begin entering records into the table.

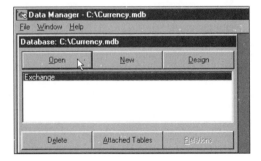

Figure 14-8
The table list in the Database window.

9. Click the Add button to add a blank record to the database. Then begin entering the fields of this first record: **England** in the Country field; **pound** in the Currency field; and **1.5945** as a sample exchange rate in the InDollars field.

10. The "Table: Exchange" window now appears as shown in Figure 14-9. Click the Update button to confirm the entry of the first record into the database table.

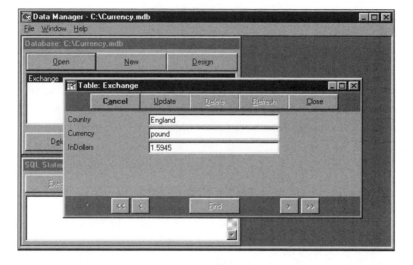

Figure 14-9
Adding a record to the Exchange table.

You could continue adding records to the table; but instead you'll now return to Visual Basic to create the Currency Input program. Close the File Manager window by pulling down the File menu and choosing Exit. The Currency.MDB database file, containing one table named Exchange, is now saved in the root directory of your hard disk.

The Data Control and Bound Controls

To use the data control in a Visual Basic program, you add an instance of the control to a form and then set three essential properties that define a specific database connection:

- The Connect property indicates the type of database you'll attach to the program; Access is the default.

- The DatabaseName property is the file name of the database on disk.

- The RecordSource property is the name of a table in the database.

IV

14

Other properties are also related to the database connection. For example, the EOFAction property determines whether you will be able to use your Visual Basic program to append new records to the end of the database. You'll learn more about this property later.

Once you've defined the properties of the data control, you next begin adding *bound* controls to the same form. Each bound control is designated to represent a field from the table you've selected as the RecordSource property of the data control. For example, you can add bound labels to display field data, or bound text boxes to allow editing of fields. Two important properties define a bound control:

- The DataSource property is the name of the data control to which the control will be bound. In other words, the bound control will display a field from the data control's RecordSource table.

- The DataField property is the name of the field that the bound control will represent.

A variety of intrinsic Visual Basic controls can serve as bound controls in a program. In addition to the label and text box, you can use the list box, combo box, picture box, image, and check box as bound controls. Visual Basic also provides three custom controls, called DBCombo, DBList, and DBGrid, that have special data-bound capabilities in connection with the data control.

Once you've designed a form that contains a data control and one or more bound controls, your program is ready to run. When you start the program, the bound controls display field information from the first record in the designated table. The data control provides buttons for scrolling from one record to the next in the database. The operations you can perform on the database depend on the types of bound controls you've added to your form. Some bound controls, such as labels, simply display field data; others, such as text boxes, provide both read and write capabilities.

In the following exercise you'll use this approach to create the Currency Input program as a tool for entering and revising records in the Exchange table of the Currency.MDB database. As you'll see, the program consists of a form containing a data control, three bound text boxes, and three labels. The program contains no code. To develop the project, you simply add the controls to a form and set the appropriate properties:

1. Start a new project in Visual Basic. Change the dimensions of the project's Form1 to 2910x2820, and move the form to the approximate center of the desktop.

2. Press F4 to activate the Properties window. Change the form's Caption setting to Currency Exchange.

3. Pull down the File menu and choose Save File As. Enter **CurrInDB** as the file name for the form, and click Save; as usual, Visual Basic adds FRM as the extension. Then pull down the File menu again and choose Save Project As. Enter **CurrInDB** as the name for the project, and click Save; Visual Basic adds VBP as the extension.

4. Double-click the data control in the Toolbox. An instance of the data control appears on the form. Drag the control to a position near the top of the form and increase the length of the control to 2295.

5. Without deselecting the control, press F4 and enter **Currency.MDB** as the control's Caption property. The form now appears as shown in Figure 14-10. Notice the visual features of the data control. It contains four buttons designed for scrolling through the records of a database. At the far left and right sides of the control are buttons for jumping to the first and last record. Next to these are buttons for scrolling one record at a time to the previous or next record. The data control's Caption property is displayed in the space between these buttons.

6. Still in the Properties window, notice that the default setting of the Connect property is Access; you'll leave this setting unchanged. Select the DatabaseName property for the data control, and click the small button displayed at the right side of the property setting. The DatabaseName dialog box appears, giving you the opportunity to select an Access database file to connect to your program. Navigate to the root directory of your hard disk, and select the Currency file (or enter \Currency in the file name text box). The DatabaseName dialog box appears as shown in Figure 14-11. Click the Open button to complete your database selection. Visual Basic copies the name of the file to the DatabaseName property in the Properties window.

7. Now scroll down to the EOFAction property. Pull down the list of property settings, and choose 2 – Add New. This setting allows you to use the program to append new records to the database table.

Figure 14-10
Adding a data control to a form.

Figure 14-11
The DatabaseName window.

8. Select the Name property and enter **dbCurrency** as the name of the data control. You'll later use references to this name to define the program's three bound controls.

9. Scroll to the RecordSource property. Once you've set the DatabaseName, the RecordSource property provides a list of all the tables contained in the database. Click the down-arrow button at the right side of the property setting to view the list. In this case, the list contains the name of only one table, Exchange (Figure 14-12). As you know, this is the only table defined in the Currency.MDB database. Select this table name as the setting for the RecordSource property. You've now set all the properties needed to define the database connection.

Figure 14-12
Selecting a setting for the RecordSource property of a data control.

10. Add three labels and three text boxes to the form. Arrange these six new controls as shown in Figure 14-13. Change the Caption properties of the three labels to Country, Currency, and Value in Dollars, respectively. Delete the Text property settings for the three text boxes.

Figure 14-13
Adding controls to the Currency Exchange Input program.

11. Select the first of the three text boxes in the form and press F4 to activate the Properties window. Scroll up to the DataSource property, and click the down-arrow button to view the attached list. The list contains the name of the data control you've added to this form, dbCurrency. Select this name as the setting for the DataSource property.

12. Select the DataField property, and pull down its attached list. As you can see in Figure 14-14, this list displays the names of the three fields in the Exchange table — Country, Currency, and InDollars. Select Country as the DataField setting for the first text box.

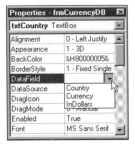

Figure 14-14
Selecting a setting for the DataField property of a bound control.

13. Repeat steps 11 and 12 to set the DataSource and DataField properties for the other two text boxes. Choose Currency as the DataField property for the second text box and InDollars as the DataField for the third box.

14. Your program is complete. Click the Save Project button on the toolbar to save the final version to disk.

Now you're ready to run the program and use it to append records to the Exchange table of the Currency.MDB database. Press F5 or click the Start button on the toolbar. The program connects to the database and, as you can see in Figure 14-15, displays the record that you've already entered into the table. To add a new record, click the Next Record button, the right-pointing arrowhead on the data control. The program presents a set of blank fields in which you can enter the information for a new record.

Figure 14-15
Running the Currency Exchange Input program.

Spend a few moments appending a set of new records to the database table. Look up today's actual currency exchange rates and enter those values, or if you prefer, use the following data instead:

Canada	dollar	.7287
Japan	yen	.0118
Germany	mark	.7236
France	franc	.2066
Italy	lira	.000613
Holland	guilder	.6461
Switzerland	franc	.8707
Mexico	peso	.1603

When you finish entering the last record, click the Close button (X) at the upper-right corner of the window to end the program performance.

Now you may want to open the database table in the Data Manager application to confirm that the records have been saved in the database file. Start the application, and choose Open from the File menu. Open the Currency.MDB file from the root directory of your hard disk. Select the Exchange table in the resulting window, and click the Open button. In the "Table: Exchange" window you can scroll through the records that you've just appended and confirm that each of them has been saved in the table (Figure 14-16). Exit from the Data Manager when you've finished examining the table.

Now the Currency Exchange Input program will serve as a convenient tool for daily updates of your currency database. Keep in mind that you can use the program to view or revise the existing records, or to append new records to the Exchange table.

The database version of the International Currency Exchange program, presented next in this chapter, uses Currency.MDB as its data source. As you'll see, this program contains a data control to connect it to the database. But unlike the Input program that you've just developed, this new program contains no bound controls. Instead, it uses the methods and properties of the data control to carry out specific database operations.

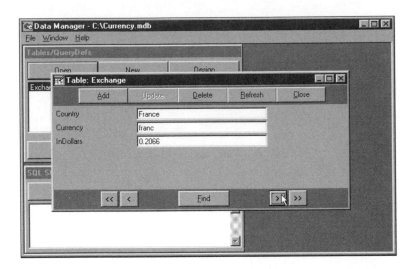

Figure 14-16
Scrolling through the Exchange table in the Data Manager program.

Programming with the Data Control

During runtime, a data control is associated with a Recordset object, which
represents all the records in the corresponding database table. In code, you
use the data control's Recordset property to refer to this object:

```
Data1.Recordset
```

The Recordset object has properties and methods that your program can
use to scroll through the table, to locate specific records, and to read
fields of information:

- The Move methods (MoveNext, MovePrevious, MoveFirst, MoveLast)
  change the *current record* in the database.
- The Find methods (FindNext, FindPrevious, FindFirst, FindLast)
  look for a record that matches a particular search criterion. When
  a matching record is found, it becomes the current record.

- The EOF property indicates whether the program has moved past the last record in the database table.

- The Fields property represents the collection of all the fields in the table. You can use the Fields("fieldName") notation to identify a specific field. The Value property of a field provides access to a data item stored in the current record.

You'll see examples of all these tools in this chapter's version of the International Currency Exchange program. But before examining the program's code, take a moment to run the program and review its operations.

RUNNING THE DATABASE VERSION OF THE CURRENCY EXCHANGE PROGRAM

The new version of the program is saved on disk as CurrExDB.VBP. Open it now and take a look at the project window. The program contains one form, named frmCurrExch (saved on disk as CurrExDB.FRM). Click the View Form button to open the form onto the desktop. As you can see in Figure 14-17, there is a data control at the upper-right corner of the form. This control's Visible property is set to False, so it does not appear on the form at all during runtime. But other properties of this control define the program's connection to the Currency.MDB database. Specifically, the DatabaseName setting is \Currency.MDB and the RecordSource setting is Exchange.

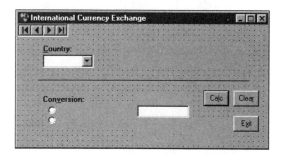

Figure 14-17
The data control appears on the frmCurrExch at design time.

Press F5 or click the Start button on the toolbar to run the program. The program window appears on the desktop (Figure 14-18). Notice that the data control is no longer visible. Also note that the program displays the database name just after the application name on the title bar. This serves as a reminder that this program gets its data from an Access database.

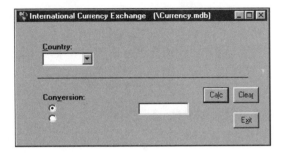

Figure 14-18
The data control disappears at runtime.

Click the down-arrow button at the right side of the Country list to view the list of country names. As you can see in Figure 14-19, the list contains all the names you've entered into the Country field in the Exchange table. Try selecting a country from the list. When you do so, the program finds the corresponding record in the database, reads the fields of the record, and displays the information in various formats inside the program window. For example, just to the right of the Country list you can see the basic exchange-rate data for converting from dollars to the selected currency, or from the currency to dollars (Figure 14-20).

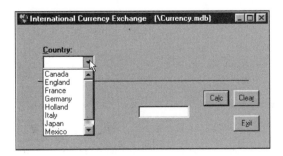

Figure 14-19
The list of countries, read from the Country field of the Exchange table.

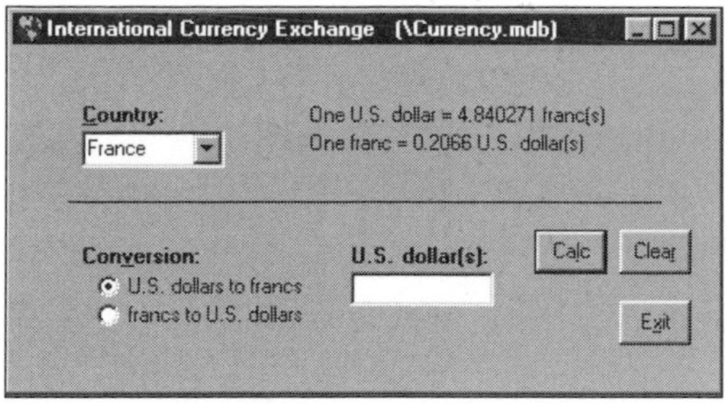

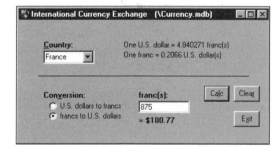

Figure 14-20
The program displays field items from the current record in the table.

The calculation feature works the same in this program as it did in the original version. To find the equivalent of a particular monetary amount, begin by choosing a Conversion option, and then enter an amount in the adjacent text box. Click the Calc button (or press Enter), and the program displays the calculated exchange amount. For example, Figure 14-21 shows a conversion from French francs to dollars.

IV
14

Figure 14-21
Converting from a selected currency to dollars.

Continue experimenting with the program if you like. To terminate the run, click the Exit button or press Escape. Next you'll turn your attention to the program's code and to the methods and properties of the data control.

INSIDE THE DATABASE VERSION OF THE CURRENCY EXCHANGE PROGRAM

The code is displayed in Listings 14-1 to 14-6 at the end of this chapter. Here's a summary of the program's activities:

- The Form_Load procedure (Listing 14-2) activates the database connection and then reads through all the records in the Exchange table, from beginning to end. It copies the Country field from each record to the program's Country list.

- The cboCountry_Click procedure (Listing 14-3) takes control when the user pulls down the Country list and chooses an entry. The procedure begins by searching for the record that contains the selected country; this becomes the current record. Then the procedure reads all three fields — Country, Currency, and InDollars — from the record, and uses these data items to fill in the various labels and captions on the application window.

- The remaining procedures respond to the user's button clicks and option selections. The cmdCalc_Click procedure (Listing 14-4) performs the calculation for a currency conversion if the user has entered a valid monetary amount. The optCurrTo_Click and optDollarsTo_Click procedures (Listing 14-5) make changes in label captions and text box contents when the user switches from one Conversion option to the other. And the cmdClear_Click and cmdExit_Click procedures (Listing 4-6) respond to clicks of the Clear and Exit buttons.

The name of the data control in this program is dbCurrency. The Recordset object associated with this control is therefore referenced as

```
dbCurrency.Recordset
```

As you've already learned, certain methods of the Recordset object have the effect of changing the current record — or, in other words, moving the "record pointer" to a new record. Any field value that the program reads from the database table always comes from the current record. Note that there is no current record when the EOF property is True; consequently, the program has to avoid trying to read a record when the record pointer is beyond the last record of the file. You'll learn more about the *current record* concept as you examine the program's code.

Stepping through the Database Records

The Form_Load procedure (Listing 14-2) begins its work by adding the database name to the title bar of the application window:

```
frmCurrExch.Caption = frmCurrExch.Caption & _
    "   (" & dbCurrency.DatabaseName & ")"
```

The data control's DatabaseName property supplies the file name. The program then calls a data control method named Refresh:

```
dbCurrency.Refresh
```

The Refresh method builds the Recordset object associated with the data control.

The main task of the Form_Load procedure is to read the Country field from each record of the Recordset and to copy the field to the drop-down list of the cboCountry combo box. This takes place in a Do loop that steps through the database table from the first record to the last:

```
With dbCurrency.Recordset

    Do While Not .EOF
        cboCountry.AddItem .Fields("Country").VALUE
        ' ...
        .MoveNext
    Loop

End With
```

The While loop continues reading records as long as the Recordset's EOF property is False. Notice the use of the With structure to simplify references to the Recordset object.

The Fields("Country").Value notation supplies the data item stored in the Country field of the current record. There are actually several ways to refer to this value. The complete reference is

```
dbCurrency.Recordset.Fields("Country").VALUE
```

But you can abbreviate this reference in the following ways:

```
dbCurrency.Recordset.Fields("Country")
```

or

```
dbCurrency.Recordset("Country")
```

Fields and Value are default properties in this expression, so they can be omitted. Another alternative is to refer to the field itself by index number rather than by name.

The procedure uses the AddItem method of the combo box control to add each country name to the drop-down list:

```
cboCountry.AddItem .Fields("Country").VALUE
```

Then the record pointer needs to be moved down to the next record in the database table. A call to the MoveNext method performs this task:

```
.MoveNext
```

Thanks to this method, each succeeding iteration of the loop reads the next record in the table. When the MoveNext method moves the record pointer to a position past the end of the last record, the Recordset.EOF property becomes True, and the looping stops. Consequently, there is no current record when Form_Load finishes its work. Other procedures in the program will have to allow for this condition, as you'll see shortly.

A variety of circumstances could potentially cause runtime errors during the program's work with the currency database. For example, suppose one of these conditions is true:

- The program can't find the Currency.MDB database file on disk.
- The database is found, but it doesn't contain an Exchange table.
- The Exchange table exists, but it doesn't have the three anticipated fields — Country, Currency, and InDollars.

Any one of these problems results in an error that prevents the program from continuing. To handle such an error gracefully, the Form_Load procedure sets up an error trap just before the call to the Refresh method:

```
On Error GoTo databaseProblem
```

If an error occurs, control of the procedure jumps down to the *databaseProblem* label. A MsgBox statement displays an error message on the screen (Figure 14-22), and then the program is terminated.

Figure 14-22

The error message for a database problem.

IV

14

Custom Data-Bound Controls

DBList, DBCombo, and DBGrid are custom data-bound controls for use in database applications. The DBList and DBCombo controls have the following special features:

- Their lists can be filled automatically with data from a specified field. (Your program doesn't have to use the AddItem method to fill the list.)

- They can be used to coordinate activities between two different database tables. Data from one table can be used to update a field on another table.

Despite these extra features, you might still favor the more familiar controls, ListBox and ComboBox, over the custom ones, especially in a simple database application like the one presented in this chapter.

To find out more about the custom data-bound controls, search for DBList, DBCombo, or DBGrid in the Visual Basic Help window. You'll find complete lists of properties and methods, along with examples.

Searching for a Database Record

When the user pulls down the Country list and chooses the name of a country, the event procedure named cboCountry_Click (Listing 14-3) takes control. This procedure's first job is to find the record corresponding to the user's selection from the list. Then it reads the three fields of that record, and uses the field data to display specific information in the application window.

The procedure calls the Recordset.FindFirst method to perform the search. FindFirst steps through a database table, starting from the first record, and searches for a record that meets a specific search criterion. In this case, the criterion is simple. The Country field of the target record should have the same value as cboCountry.Text — that is, the country that the user has selected from the list.

Here is how the procedure expresses this search criterion in the call to the FindFirst method:

```
dbCurrency.Recordset.FindFirst "Country='" & _
   cboCountry.TEXT & "'"
```

The search criterion in this example is a concatenation of three strings, making the expression a little difficult to understand at first glance. The criterion is actually a simple equality. For example, suppose the user pulls down the Country list and chooses France from the list; in effect, the FindFirst method works like this:

```
dbCurrency.Recordset.FindFirst "Country='France'"
```

The record that meets the criterion becomes the current record in the database table. Subsequent statements in the cboCountry_Click procedure refer to the fields of this current record.

Specifically, the procedure goes on to read the data from all three fields of the target record, and to assign the data to variables:

```
With dbCurrency.Recordset
   countryField = .Fields("Country").VALUE
   currencyField = .Fields("Currency").VALUE
   inDollarsField = .Fields("InDollars").VALUE
End With
```

Once again, the Fields notation identifies a field by name, and the Value property supplies the data item stored in that field. These variables represent the field data throughout the procedure. For example, here is how the procedure displays the dollar-to-currency exchange rate in the lblDollar label:

```
lblDollar.Caption = "One U.S. dollar = " & _
    1 / inDollarsField & " " & _
    currencyField & "(s)"
```

Notice that the exchange rate in this case is calculated as the inverse of the currency-to-dollar rate.

Using SQL

SQL (Structured Query Language) is a common idiom for working with relational databases. If you're familiar with SQL, you can use it in the code of a Visual Basic database application. For example, queries in SQL are performed with the Select statement. Here is how you might use SQL in the cboCountry_Click procedure instead of the call to the FindFirst method:

```
SqlStr = "Select * from Exchange Where " _
            & "Country = '" & cboCountry.TEXT & "'"
dbCurrency.RecordSource = SqlStr
dbCurrency.Refresh
```

This code uses a Select statement to change the setting of the RecordSource property. Then a call to the Refresh method rebuilds the Recordset. (If you want to try this approach, include a Dim statement at the top of the procedure to declare the string variable named SqlStr. Also, don't forget to delete the call to the FindFirst method, which these lines replace.)

For more information, search for SQL in the Visual Basic Help window.

Reading the EOF Property

Once the user chooses an entry from the Country list, the Recordset.EOF property is False for the rest of the program performance. But before the first selection from the list, the EOF condition is True, thanks to the action of the While loop in the Form_Load procedure. If the user happens to select a new Conversion option or click the Calc button before making a country selection, the corresponding event procedures need to avoid any action. Because there is no current record, a reference to Recordset.Fields would result in a runtime error.

When the user enters a specific currency amount into the text box at the bottom of the application window and clicks Calc, the cmdCalc_Click procedure (Listing 14-4) normally performs the currency calculation that the user has requested. The procedure begins by reading the Currency and InDollars fields from the current record in the database table:

```
With dbCurrency.Recordset
  currencyField = .Fields("Currency").VALUE
  inDollarsField = .Fields("InDollars").VALUE
End With
```

Then it performs either a dollar-to-currency conversion:

```
If optDollarsTo.VALUE Then
  lblConvText.Caption = "= " & _
    Format(txtConvAmount.TEXT / _
    inDollarsField, "###,###.00") & _
    " " & currencyField & "(s)"
```

or a currency-to-dollar calculation:

```
lblConvText.Caption = "= " & _
  Format(txtConvAmount.TEXT * _
  inDollarsField, "$###,###.00")
```

But under some conditions, the cmdClick_Calc procedure skips the calculation:

- If the user has entered a nonnumeric value into the text box, the program uses the Val function to convert the Text value to zero, and no calculation is performed.

- If the user has not yet selected a name from the Country list, the Recordset.EOF property is still True. Because there is no current record, the currency calculation cannot take place.

The following If statement examines both of these conditions:

```
If txtConvAmount.TEXT = 0 Or _
   dbCurrency.Recordset.EOF Then
   cmdClear_Click
```

If either condition is True, the procedure simply clears the text box and performs no further action.

Similarly, the optCurrTo_Click and optDollarsTo_Click procedures (Listing 14-5) avoid responding to a change in the option button selection if Recordset.EOF is still True. For example, the optCurrTo_Click procedure checks the value of EOF before changing the label caption displayed above the text box:

```
With dbCurrency.Recordset
   If Not .EOF Then _
      lblConvCurr = _
         .Fields("Currency").VALUE & "(s):"
End With
```

This precaution averts the runtime error that would occur if the program were to try reading a field value at a time when there is no current record.

Other Database Exercises

As you've seen, the data control — and the external database connection that it represents — requires programming techniques that are very different from the traditional Basic-language approach to database management. If you want to experiment further with the data control and its associated methods and properties, you might consider converting one of the other programs in this book to a database application using a data control.

One good candidate for this kind of exercise is the Restaurant Review program, presented in Chapter 6. Try using the Data Manager program to create an Access-format version of the RestRevu database. Then redesign the application to take advantage of this new format.

IV

14

Listing 14-1

The general declarations section of the Currency Exchange program, database version

```
' Currency Exchange Program, database version
' -------------------------------------------
'
' Files:
' ------
' Project File:    CurrExDB.VBP
' Form File:       CurrExDB.FRM  (this file)
'
' This program converts between dollars and
' the currencies of other countries.
' The daily exchange rates are stored in
' an Access database file named Currency.MDB.
' Within the database, the table that contains
' the currency data is called Exchange. This
' program illustrates the use of the Data control
' (and its associated methods and properties) in
' working successfully with an Access database in
' a Visual Basic program.

' Note that this program contains a Data control
' named dbCurrency. Here are some of the key
' design-time property settings of this control:

' Property       Setting            Explanation
' --------       -------            -----------
' Connect        Access             MS Access database.
' DatabaseName   C:\Currency.MDB    The file name.
' RecordSource   Exchange           The table name.
' Visible        False              Not displayed.

' To work properly, the program needs to find
' the Currency.MDB file in the root directory
' of the current hard disk. The MDB file must
' contain a table named Exchange, which in turn
' has three fields:
```

```
' Country    -- The name of a country.
' Currency   -- The name of the country's currency.
' InDollars  -- The dollar-to-currency exchange rate.

Option Explicit
'
' End of general declarations, CurrExDB.FRM.
```

Listing 14-2
The Form_Load procedure of CurrExDB.FRM

```
Private Sub Form_Load()

    ' The Form_Load procedure reads the country
    ' list from the database table and adds each
    ' country name to the cboCountry combo box list.

    Dim temp1 As String
    Dim temp2 As Single

    ' Begin by adding the database file name to
    ' the title bar of the application window.
    frmCurrExch.Caption = frmCurrExch.Caption & _
        "   (" & dbCurrency.DatabaseName & ")"

    ' Set up an error trap. If the program
    ' can't find the database, or if the Exchange
    ' table is not organized as expected, the
    ' program displays an error message and
    ' the performance ends.
    On Error GoTo databaseProblem

    ' Use the Refresh method to rebuild the
    ' RecordSet object and prepare the database
    ' table for reading.
    dbCurrency.Refresh
```

Error trap for database connection problems

Rebuilds the Recordset

IV

14

```
With dbCurrency.Recordset

    ' Step through all the records of the
    ' database, from beginning to end.
    Do While Not .EOF

        ' Read the country field from the
        ' current record and add the country
        ' name to the combo box list.
        cboCountry.AddItem .Fields("Country").VALUE

        ' Read the other two fields, just to
        ' confirm that the Exchange table is
        ' organized as expected.
        temp1 = .Fields("Currency").VALUE
        temp2 = .Fields("InDollars").VALUE

        ' Move down to the next record
        ' in the database.
        .MoveNext

    Loop

End With

Exit Sub

databaseProblem:
    ' Display an error message if the program
    ' has had a problem using the database. Then
    ' terminate the program performance.
    MsgBox "Problem opening or using the " & _
        dbCurrency.DatabaseName & " database.", , _
        "International Currency Exchange"
    End

End Sub   ' Form_Load
```

Reads the Country field of each record

Skips to the next record

Listing 14-3
The cboCountry_Click procedure

```
Private Sub cboCountry_Click()

    ' The cboCountry_Click procedure responds to
    ' the user's new selection in the cboCountry
    ' combo box list. Given a country selection,
    ' the procedure begins by finding the
    ' corresponding record in the database table.
    ' This becomes the current record. Then the
    ' procedure reads the fields in the record
    ' and uses them to produce several label
    ' captions in the International Currency
    ' Exchange window.

    Dim countryField As String
    Dim currencyField As String
    Dim inDollarsField As Single

    ' Use the FindFirst method to locate the
    ' record corresponding to the user's country
    ' choice. This becomes the current record.
    dbCurrency.Recordset.FindFirst "Country='" & _
        cboCountry.TEXT & "'"

    ' Read the country name, the currency name,
    ' and the exchange rate from the fields of
    ' the current record.
    With dbCurrency.Recordset
        countryField = .Fields("Country").VALUE
        currencyField = .Fields("Currency").VALUE
        inDollarsField = .Fields("InDollars").VALUE
    End With

    ' Display the dollar-to-currency exchange rate.
    lblDollar.Caption = "One U.S. dollar = " & _
        1 / inDollarsField & " " & _
        currencyField & "(s)"
```

Finds the record that matches the user's selection

Reads the field values of the current record

IV

14

```
                    ' Display the currency-to-dollar exchange rate.
                    lblCurrency.Caption = "One " & _
                      currencyField & " = " & _
                      inDollarsField & " U.S. dollar(s)"

                    ' Display the captions for the two currency
                    ' exchange option buttons.
                    optDollarsTo.Caption = "U.S. dollars to " _
                      & currencyField & "s"
                    optCurrTo.Caption = _
                      currencyField & "s to U.S. dollars"

                    ' Display the caption for the currency
                    ' calculation box.
                    lblConvCurr.Caption = "U.S. dollar(s):"

                    optDollarsTo.VALUE = True
                    cmdClear_Click

                End Sub   ' cboCountry_Click
```

Listing 14-4
The cmdCalc_Click procedure

```
                Private Sub cmdCalc_Click()

                    ' Perform the currency exchange calculation
                    ' that the user requests.

                    Dim currencyField As String
                    Dim inDollarsField As Single

                    ' First make sure that the user has entered
                    ' a numeric value (greater than zero) in the
                    ' txtConvAmount text box.
                    txtConvAmount.TEXT = Val(txtConvAmount.TEXT)

                    ' If not, clear the text box and skip
                    ' the rest of this procedure.
```

```
If txtConvAmount.TEXT = 0 Or _
  dbCurrency.Recordset.EOF Then
  cmdClear_Click
```

Makes sure there is
a current record

```
Else
' If the entry is valid, the calculation
' is based on the user's choice of
' conversion options.

  ' Read the Currency and InDollars fields
  ' from the current record in the database
  ' table.
  With dbCurrency.Recordset
    currencyField = .Fields("Currency").VALUE
    inDollarsField = .Fields("InDollars").VALUE
  End With


  ' Perform a dollars-to-currency calculation.
  If optDollarsTo.VALUE Then
    lblConvText.Caption = "= " & _
      Format(txtConvAmount.TEXT / _
      inDollarsField, "###,###.00") & _
      " " & currencyField & "(s)"

  Else

    ' Perform a currency-to-dollars calculation.
    lblConvText.Caption = "= " & _
      Format(txtConvAmount.TEXT * _
      inDollarsField, "$###,###.00")
  End If

  End If

End Sub   ' cmdCalc_Click
```

IV

14

Listing 14-5
Click procedures for the option buttons

```
Private Sub optCurrTo_Click()

  ' The optCurrTo_Click procedure
  ' changes the conversion option:
  ' foreign currency to U.S. dollars.

  ' Read the currency name from the Currency
  ' field of the current record in the
  ' database table.
  With dbCurrency.Recordset
    If Not .EOF Then _
      lblConvCurr = _
        .Fields("Currency").VALUE & "(s):"
  End With

  ' Clear the calculation text box.
  cmdClear_Click

End Sub   ' optCurrTo_Click




Private Sub optDollarsTo_Click()

  ' The optDollarsTo_Click procedure
  ' changes the currency option:
  ' U.S. dollars to foreign currency.

  If Not dbCurrency.Recordset.EOF Then _
    lblConvCurr = "U.S. dollar(s):"

  ' Clear the calculation text box.
  cmdClear_Click

End Sub   ' optDollarsTo_Click
```

Makes sure EOF is not true

Listing 14-6
Click procedures for the Clear and Exit buttons

```
Private Sub cmdClear_Click()

    ' The cmdClear_Click procedure clears
    ' the previous conversion calculation.

    txtConvAmount.TEXT = ""
    lblConvText.Caption = ""

    ' Return the focus to the
    ' txtConvAmount text box.
    txtConvAmount.SetFocus

End Sub   ' cmdClear_Click



Private Sub cmdExit_Click()

    ' The cmdExit_Click procedure terminates
    ' the program when the user clicks the
    ' Exit button.

    End

End Sub   ' cmdExit_Click
```

Debugging a Program's Code

While you're developing a project, Visual Basic helps you find and correct errors in a variety of important ways. Three categories of errors typically occur during application development:

- *Your code contains syntactical or structural errors that prevent the program from running.* In some cases, Visual Basic displays an error message as soon as you enter a syntactically flawed statement into the editor. For example, suppose you type the keyword "With" onto a line of the Code window and then press Enter. As shown in Figure A-1, Visual Basic immediately displays an error message to let you know that you've forgotten the expression that should follow With. (By the way, you can turn syntax checking on or off by choosing the Options command from the Tools menu, and then selecting the Auto Syntax Check option in the Environment tab.) In other cases an error message appears when you attempt to run the program. For example, if you enter a With statement in your code, but forget to place an End With statement at the end of the structure, an error message appears when you first try to run the program (Figure A-2). These are known as *compile* errors, because they take place at the time when Visual Basic is attempting to translate your source code into executable code.

- *An error condition causes your program to fail at a certain point during a performance.* One example is an attempt to open a file for reading when the file doesn't exist on disk. In response to this error, Visual Basic interrupts your program run and displays the error message shown in Figure A-3. Another common example is division by zero. Problems like these are known as runtime errors.

- *Your program runs without interruption, but it doesn't work as expected.* For example, the program might produce incorrect output, or it might respond inappropriately to an event. These are known as logical errors, and they can be the most difficult kinds of problems to correct.

Figure A-1

An error message that appears when you first enter an incorrect statement into the editor.

Figure A-2

An error message that appears when you attempt to run a program that contains an incorrect structure.

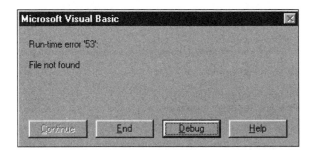

Figure A-3

The error message the appears when your program attempts to open a file that doesn't exist.

Visual Basic's debugging tools are designed to help you find and correct logical errors and runtime errors. Some of these tools are represented by the last five buttons on the toolbar (Figure A-4):

- The Toggle Breakpoint button enables you to specify a line of code where your program's performance will pause so that you can investigate the conditions of the run.

- The Instant Watch button gives you a way to view the current value of a variable or an expression during a break in the program.

- The Calls button displays the list of procedure calls that have led to the current procedure.

- The Step Into button enables you to perform lines of code one at a time during a break in the program run. If a statement makes a call to a procedure, you can use this button to step through the lines of the procedure itself one at a time.

- The Step Over button also performs lines of code one at a time, but treats a procedure call as a single statement. In other words, you use this button if you don't want to step through the lines of the procedure.

Figure A-4
The five debugging buttons on Visual Basic's toolbar.

The debugging activities represented by these buttons take place during *break mode*. Break mode occurs when your program run is interrupted due to an error, or when you intentionally initiate a break yourself. As you can see in Figure A-5, the Visual Basic title bar displays *[break]* when you are in this mode. One way to interrupt a program run intentionally is to click the Break button, located between the Start and End buttons on the toolbar. Another way is to specify a breakpoint in your code. In the break mode, you can use Visual Basic's Debug window to investigate the values of variables and to carry out other debugging activities.

Figure A-5
Visual Basic's title bar during break mode.

To explore some of these debugging tools, you'll work with a project named Bug.VBP in the upcoming exercise. This program is a shortened and modified version of the International Sales application, first presented in Chapter 9. As its name suggests, the Bug program contains errors that you'll have to search for and correct. You'll focus your attention on the procedure named *ColumnByYears*, shown in Listing A-1 at the end of this appendix.

A Debugging Exercise

Open Bug.VBP and take a look at the project window (Figure A-6). The program contains one form, which is saved on disk as Bug.FRM. Press F5 or click the Start button on the toolbar to start a performance. When you do so, the familiar International Sales window appears on the screen (Figure A-7). It contains a small worksheet for entering a table of sales figures, and a space below the worksheet for a chart.

Figure A-6
The Bug project.

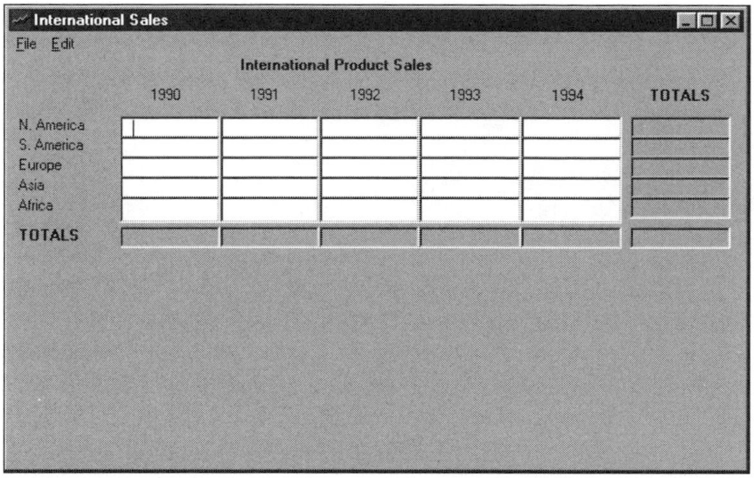

Figure A-7
A modified version of the International Sales window.

In this abbreviated version of the program, only two menus appear. The File menu has an Exit command, for quitting the program. The Edit menu has two commands: Clear, for erasing the current sales data; and Random Data, for entering a set of randomly generated numbers into the sales worksheet. In response to the random data, the program is designed to build a column chart, just as if you had entered real data yourself from the keyboard. As you work with this program, you'll discover two problems: a runtime error that almost immediately interrupts the performance and a logical error that impairs the charting procedure:

1. Pull down the program's Edit menu and choose Random Data, or press Ctrl+R from the keyboard. The program enters the first numeric value into the sales worksheet and attempts to begin drawing the column chart. But something goes wrong. A runtime error interrupts the program, and Visual Basic displays the message shown in Figure A-8. As you may know from experience, the "Subscript out of range" message refers to an error in handling an array. The program has tried to access an element that is beyond the range declared for the array.

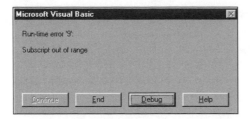

Figure A-8

A runtime error interrupts the program.

2. Click the Debug button in the error message box. In response, Visual Basic switches into break mode, opens the Code window, scrolls to the procedure in which the error occurred (the *Column-ByYears* procedure), and displays a rectangle around the line that caused the error. As you can see in Figure A-9, the offending line contains a reference to an array named *regionTots*. This runtime error illustrates an important point: The statement that causes the error is not always the line that you need to correct.

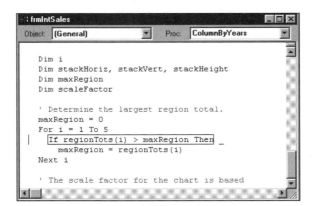

Figure A-9

Visual Basic shows you the location of the error.

3. Like many runtime errors, this one is not hard to correct once Visual Basic shows you its location. If you look in the program's general declarations section, you'll see that the *regionTots* array is declared as follows:

```
Dim regionTots(4)
```

Given this declaration, the array's legal subscripts range from 0 to 4. But the For loop in the *ColumnByYears* procedure defines an index, *i*, that ranges from 1 to 5. This is the problem.

4. Sometimes Visual Basic allows you to correct a runtime error in break mode and then immediately resume the program performance, but not in this case. Click the End button on the toolbar to stop the performance before you correct the code. In the code window, revise the starting and ending values of the For loop as follows:

```
For i = 0 to 4
```

5. Press F5 or click the Start button to restart the program. Once again pull down the Edit menu and choose Random Data. This time the program successfully fills the sales table with randomly generated numeric data and attempts to draw the corresponding chart. But as shown in Figure A-10, there's something very wrong with the chart. Instead of drawing five solid columns to represent the varying levels of regional sales data, the program creates columns that float whimsically up the height of the chart box. This may be an interesting visual effect, but not the result you were hoping for.

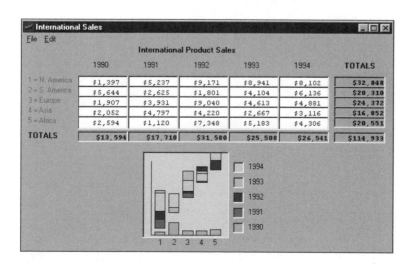

Figure A-10
The program runs now, but doesn't give the expected results.

6. Click the Break button on the toolbar to create a pause in the program run. Then press F7 to view the Code window. Examining the *ColumnByYears* procedure, you can see that the program defines the *stackVert* variable to represent the vertical starting position of each colored stack portion in a column, and *stackHeight* to represent the height of a stack. (The height of each stack is drawn in proportion to the numeric sales value that the stack depicts. In the scale of this chart, the tallest column has a height of 10 units.) The *stackVert* and *stackHeight* variables are obviously the values you need to investigate.

7. Pull down Visual Basic's Tools menu and choose the Add Watch command. The resulting Add Watch dialog box allows you to specify variables or expressions whose values you want to monitor. As you'll see shortly, these watch values are conveniently displayed in the Debug window.

8. Enter **stackVert** in the Expression box. Make sure the Context box displays *ColumnByYears* as the procedure in which this variable is defined, as in Figure A-11. (If not, select *frmIntSales* from the Module list and then select *ColumnByYears* from the Procedure list.) Click OK to confirm the watch expression.

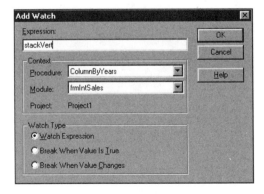

Figure A-11
Defining a watch expression in the Add Watch window.

9. Repeat steps 7 and 8 to define the *stackHeight* variable as a second watch expression.

10. Press F7, if necessary, to activate the code window. In the Column-ByYears procedure, scroll down to the statement that draws each portion of the column chart, a call to the picSalesChart.Line method. You can see that *stackVert* and *stackHeight* provide essential information for this statement. Move the flashing cursor to the beginning of this line and click the Toggle Breakpoint button on the toolbar (or press F9) to designate the line as a breakpoint. Visual Basic highlights the line, as shown in Figure A-12.

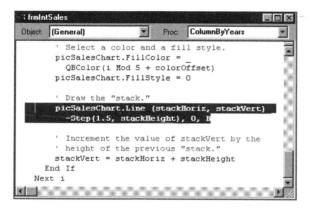

Figure A-12
Using the Toggle Breakpoint button to designate a breakpoint in the code.

11. Now press Ctrl+G to view the Debug window. In the upper pane of the window you can see the two watch expressions you've defined; they currently display no values, because the *ColumnByYears* procedure was not running at the time you interrupted the program. Activate the lower pane in the Debug window and type **ColumnByYears** (Figure A-13), then press Enter. This is one way to make a call to a specific procedure, thereby resuming the program performance. In response, Visual Basic performs the lines of the procedure up to the breakpoint that you've designated, and then stops the program again.

12. Press Ctrl+G to view the Debug window again. Now you can see the values of the two watch expressions for the first stack that the procedure draws. The *stackVert* variable has an initial value of zero, so that the first stack will appear at the bottom of the chart; *stackHeight* contains a calculated value representing the height of the first stack.

(Because the calculation is based on randomly generated data, you'll see a different value for *stackHeight* on your computer.) To prepare for drawing the next stack, the program is supposed to add *stack-Height* to the current value of *stackVert*, ensuring that the next stack will begin where the previous one left off. Accordingly, you'd like to see the value of the expression *stackVert* + *stackHeight* after each stack is drawn. Enter the following statement into the lower pane of the Debug window, just beneath the call to the *ColumnByYears* procedure (Figure A-14):

```
? stackVert + stackHeight
```

Inside the Debug window, the question mark is a command to display the value of an expression. As you can see, Visual Basic displays the sum of the two variables. According to the program's design, this sum should be the next value of the *stackVert* variable.

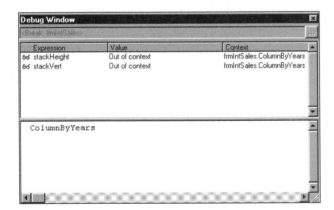

Figure A-13
Using the Debug window to make a call to one of the program's procedures.

13. Press F5 to resume the program. Once again the performance stops at the breakpoint. Press Ctrl+G to view the Debug window. The next values of *stackHeight* and *stackVert* appear in the upper pane. Comparing the new value of *stackVert* with the sum you generated in the lower pane, you can see that the program is clearly not calculating the value of *stackVert* correctly (Figure A-15).

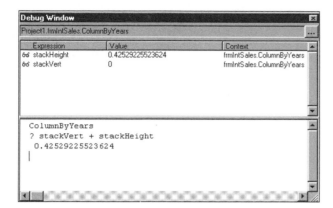

Figure A-14

Viewing the watch expressions in the upper pane and displaying a new expression in the lower pane.

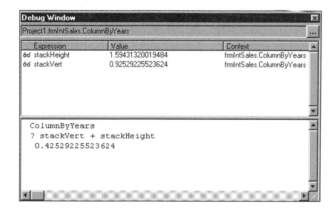

Figure A-15

The new value of stackVert doesn't match the sum displayed in the lower pane.

You can continue this investigation by repeating the same pattern of steps: In the lower pane of the Debug window, place the cursor after the summation expression (*stackVert + stackHeight*) and press Enter. In response, the Debug window displays the new sum of the two variables. Then press F5 to resume the program, and Ctrl+G when the program stops again. Each time you go through these steps, you'll confirm that the program is calculating the wrong value for *stackVert*. This is the source of the program's charting problem.

The discovery will lead you to reexamine the code of the *Column-ByYears* procedure. Just beneath the call to the Line method (where you've established the breakpoint), the following statement is supposed to increment the value of *stackVert* for each new stack of a given column:

```
stackVert = stackHoriz + stackHeight
```

Here is the error. The sum operation at the right side of the equal sign adds *stackHeight* to the wrong variable. The statement should appear as follows:

```
stackVert = stackVert + stackHeight
```

Revise the statement as shown. Then move the cursor back up to the previous statement, and click the Toggle Breakpoint button to deactivate the breakpoint. Click the Stop button to terminate the current performance. Then click the Start button to begin again. When the International Sales window appears on the screen, pull down the Edit menu and choose Random Data. The program now works as it's supposed to (Figure A-16).

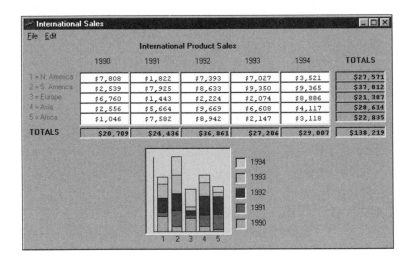

Figure A-16

The program is finally working correctly.

As you've seen in this exercise, the process of tracking down a logical error can require diligence and patience. But Visual Basic's Debug window and other debugging tools provide solid help along the way.

The Sample Program

Listing A-1
The ColumnByYears procedure, with errors

```
Private Sub ColumnByYears()

    ' The ColumnByYears procedure draws
    ' a column chart.

    ' ************************
    ' This procedure has bugs.
    ' ************************

    Dim i
    Dim stackHoriz, stackVert, stackHeight
    Dim maxRegion
    Dim scaleFactor

    ' Determine the largest region total.
    maxRegion = 0
    For i = 1 To 5
      If regionTots(i) > maxRegion Then _
        maxRegion = regionTots(i)
    Next i

    ' The scale factor for the chart is based
    ' on the largest region total. (This value
    ' will have a height of 10 in the chart.)
    scaleFactor = 10 / maxRegion

    ' Depict each nonzero value in the sales
    ' table as a "stack" in one of the charts.
    For i = 0 To 24

      ' At the beginning of each row of data,
      ' reinitialize the stackHoriz and stackVert
      ' values for a new column in the chart.
```

```
        If i Mod 5 = 0 Then
          stackHoriz = 0.5 + 2 * (i / 5)
          stackVert = 0
        End If

        ' If an amount is not zero, calculate
        ' the height of the corresponding "stack."
        If amounts(i) <> 0 Then
          stackHeight = scaleFactor * amounts(i)

          ' Select a color and a fill style.
          picSalesChart.FillColor = _
            QBColor(i Mod 5 + colorOffset)
          picSalesChart.FillStyle = 0

          ' Draw the "stack."
          picSalesChart.Line (stackHoriz, stackVert) _
            -Step(1.5, stackHeight), 0, B

          ' Increment the value of stackVert by the
          ' height of the previous "stack."
          stackVert = stackHoriz + stackHeight
        End If
      Next i

  End Sub   ' ColumnByYears
```

B

Producing an Executable Program File

*A*fter you've developed, tested, and debugged a Visual Basic application, your final task is to create an executable program file that can be run directly on the Windows 95 desktop. To do so, you use the Make EXE File command from Visual Basic's File menu. The steps are simple:

1. Start Visual Basic, and open the project that you want to work with. (The figures in this appendix show the steps for creating an EXE file from the International Sales program, which is saved on disk as IntSales.VBP.)

2. Pull down the File menu and choose Make EXE File. The Make EXE File dialog box appears on the screen, as shown in Figure B-1. In the File name text box, Visual Basic suggests a name for the EXE file; you can accept this suggestion or enter a different name of your choice. You can also use this dialog box to select the directory in which you want to store the EXE file.

3. Click the Options button at the lower-right corner of the Make EXE File dialog box. The EXE Options dialog box appears on the screen (Figure B-2). This box gives you options for identifying the version number of your program, changing the title and the icon, and entering a variety of other items to describe your program.

4. In the Version Information box select a Type item and then enter the corresponding text in the Value box. For example, you can enter copyright information, a general description of your program, and any notes you want to include with the file. (As you'll see shortly, this information will be available directly from the EXE file you're creating.)

5. Click OK on the EXE Options and Make EXE File dialog boxes. Visual Basic creates the EXE file and saves it in the directory you selected in the Make EXE File dialog box. You can now exit from the Visual Basic environment.

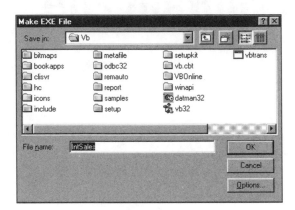

Figure B-1

Using the Make EXE File command to create an executable program file.

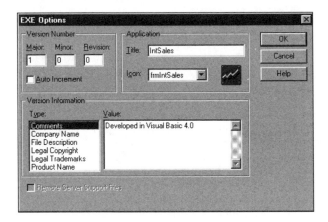

Figure B-2

Entering information about your program in the EXE Options dialog box.

To view the icon for the new EXE file, use the My Computer icon on the Windows 95 desktop to open the directory in which you saved the file. By scrolling through the folder, you'll find the icon for the file. For example, Figure B-3 shows the icon for IntSales.EXE. If you want to try running the program, simply double-click the icon.

Figure B-3

Locating the icon for a new EXE file.

You can also examine the descriptive information that you saved with the file. To do so, click the icon with the right mouse button, and choose Properties from the resulting drop-down menu, as in Figure B-4. A Properties dialog box appears on the screen for the program you've selected. The dialog box has two tabs, named General and Version. In the General tab you can see information about the type, location, size, usage history, and attributes of the EXE file you've created.

Figure B-4

Opening the Properties window for the EXE file you've created.

Click the Version tab to view other information. As shown in Figure B-5, the Properties window displays the information you entered into the EXE Options dialog box. At the top of the Version tab you see the version number, description, and copyright information. At the lower half of the tab, you can select entries in the Item name list and read the corresponding text in the Value box. As you can see, these items give you a useful way to document the software product you've developed.

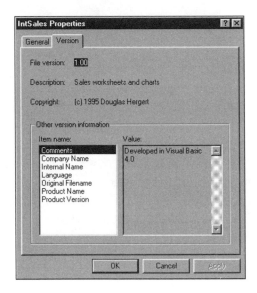

Figure B-5
Reading the Version properties of an EXE file.

Finally, you may want to create a shortcut for your new EXE file on the Windows 95 desktop. There are two simple ways to do so. Begin by opening the folder in which the EXE file is saved. Using the right mouse button, drag the icon for the file to the desktop and choose Create Shortcut(s) Here from the resulting menu. Or drag the icon to the desktop with the left mouse button to create a shortcut directly. The shortcut icon takes its place on the desktop along with any other icons you've already placed there, as in Figure B-6. (If you want, you can change the name of the shortcut. Select the icon by clicking it once. Then click the name displayed beneath the icon, type a new name from the keyboard, and press Enter to confirm.)

Figure B-6

Creating a shortcut icon for an EXE file.

Now to run your application, simply double-click its shortcut icon on the desktop.

APPENDIX

C

The VBASIC Library

*I*n addition to containing all the source code used in *Foundations of Visual Basic 4 for Windows 95 Programming*, the CD-ROM accompanying this book features the VBASIC Library from EMS Professional Shareware of Olney, Md.

The following Appendix tabulates the more than 1,400 programs that make up the VBASIC Library. These Visual Basic programs include shareware, freeware, public domain software, and demos. A corresponding (and more detailed) database resides on the CD. To access it, see the README file.

Most of these programs will run under Visual Basic 4.0; those that won't will presently be upgraded to do so. For more information in this regard, look for the discount upgrade coupon at the back of the book.

SW = Shareware
CR=Contribution requested

Name	Type	Price	Vendor	Phone/E-mail
$20 Help Authoring Tools 2.0	Help	$20	Synergystic Productions	CIS:72322,765
23 Pickup V2.1	Game	$5 SW	Persky, Jonathan D.	Internet:jonpersky@aol.com
256 Colors Control	DLL - Graphics	Free	Rpb	
3-D 1.1	DLL - General	Free	Biggins, Aidan	CIS:100010,1257
3-D Gauge Bar	Custom Control	Free	Polowood, Felipe	
3-D How To	Buttons	Free	Wisecarver, Mike	
3D CTL3DV2.DLL Sample	DLL - General	Free	McGregor, Rob	
3D Effects	Form	Free	Reynaert, John	CIS:76570,2275
3D Effects Demo	Graphics	Free	Stewart, David	CIS:72122,3562
3D Frames Panels And Controls	Form	Free	DeBacker, Greg	CIS:71042,36
3D Look Source Code	Graphics	Free	Sorrentino, Silvio	CIS:100265,1725
3D Look Using CTL3D.DLL	Form	Free	Randriambololona, Roland H.	CIS:100331,2516
3D Map Graphics Example	Graphics	Free	Rogers, Kerry	CIS:71514,735
3D Meter Plug-In	Graphics	$10	Anno Domini, Inc.	
3D Perpetual Calendar	Calendar	Free	Renard, Michael	CIS:100042,3646
3D Picture Button	Custom Control	Free	Gamber, Mark	CIS:76450,2754
3D Routines	Form	Free	Benito, Daniel	CIS:100022,141
3D Routines With Splitter Bars	Form	Free	Benito, Daniel	CIS:100022,141
3D Tabs	Form	Free		
3D Widgets DEMO	Custom Control	Unknown	Sheridan Software Systems	516-753-0985x193
3D Widgets Demo Diskette	Custom Control	Free	Sheridan Software Systems	516-753-0985x193
3D-VB Input 3.0c	Custom Control	$22 SW	Opaque Software	CIS:70621,3034; CIS:74777,3227
3D4VB	Program Control	$10 SW	LAN Services	609-428-3633
3DDEM	Program Control	$10 SW	LAN Services	609-428-3633
3DfxPlus	DLL - General	$10 SW	Digital PowerTOOLS	610-932-5931; CIS:74547,23
5 Pak Custom Controls 3.6	Custom Control	$45 SW	Weimar Software	408-268-6638
AA-ARRAY.DLL Extended Arrays	DLL - General	$30	AA-Software International	33-93-77-50-47; CIS:100343,2570

Name	Type	Price	Vendor	Phone/E-mail
Aarons; Color Mixer	Graphics	Free	Emke, Aaron	CIS:76065,3376
AAVBSORT.DLL	Programming	$35 SW	Willy, C. Scott	33-93-77-50-47; CIS:100343,2570
AAVBSORT.Dll - Sorts VB Arrays	Custom Control	$35 SW	AA-Software International	33-93-77-50-47; CIS:100343,2570
ABC Slots	Game	Free	BMB Production	
Abort Printer	Printer	Free		
About	Program Control	Free	Marino, Lou	609-243-4979
About Box Demo	Form	Free	Gotz, Steven	CIS:70563,207
About DDF Files	Database	Free	Sunil	
About Magic 1.0	Custom Control	$15 SW	Bits & Bytes Solutions	206-328-1523; CIS:72603,1774
About Your Application	Programming	Free		
AboutWin	Form	Free	Stefano, David	CIS:72202,3046
Access 2 Error Msg DLL	DLL Interface	CR	Lynn F. Solon Foundation	
Access 2.0/VB 3.0 Compatibilit	Database	Free	Microsoft	206-882-8080; 800-992-3675
Access 3DCTL.DLL From VB	DLL - Graphics	Free	Bonner, Paul	CIS:76000,13
Access Import Spec Converter	Database	Free	Ferguson, Jim	919-799-4396; CIS:71477,2345
Access Jet 2.0 Reserved Errors	Database	Free		
Access Jet Expression Evaluato	Calculator	Free		
Access Table Design Printing	Printer	Free		
Access Windows Registration DB	System Utility	Free	Pleas, Keith R.	CIS:72331,2150
Access-Style Adding To Tables	Database	Free	Snyder, James Wj	CIS:75141,3549; AOL: JamesWJS
Accordian Solitaire	Game	Free		
Add Help	Help	Unknown	Microsoft (Modified by Unknown	
Add Item	Listbox	Free		
Add-In Potato	Program Utility	Free	Stewart, David	CIS:72122,3562
Adding 3D Effects To Controls	Text	Free	Microsoft	206-882-8080; 800-992-3675; 800-277
AddNew - Multiple Relationship	Database	Free	Snyder, James Wj	CIS:75141,3544; AOL: JamesWJS
Address Application For FoxPro	Database	Free	Anderson, Tim	CIS:100023,3154
Address Book	Productivity	Unknown	Knowledge Works, Inc.	619-528-1026; CIS:72220,2466
Address Database	Database	Free	Murphy, Michael J.	702-633-0792; CIS:71160,1275

Name	Type	Price	Vendor	Phone/E-mail
Adialer	Programming	Free	Lamson, George	
Advanced Control Library VBX	Custom Control	$35 SW	Advanced Applications	704-597-3948; CIS:72713,2106
Advanced Disk Library 3.11	DLL - General	$35 SW	Advanced Applications	704-597-3948; CIS:72713,2106
AFD Postcode	Data Access	$200	AFD Software Ltd.	01294-823221
Affirmations	Inspiration	$25 CR	Troy, Hailaeos	702-256-6447
AIGZIT - Exit Windows Fast	System Utility	Free	Heydman, Matthew	AOL:TheBigShoe
Aircraft Instrument Cont. 2.0	Custom Control	$40	Global Majik Software	CIS:73261,3642
ALARM Custom Control 1.4	Custom Control	$10 SW	Mabry Software	206-634-1443; CIS:71231,2066
Alex's Rocket Programmer	Game	Free		
Alignment For Windows	Program Utility	$15	Graphical Bytes	516-283-4473
All The Time 3.4	Clock	Free	Smith, Wilson, And C.Rogers	CIS:70741,422
Allocating Protected Memory	Programming	Free	Langley, Brent K.	CIS:70312,2142
Alpha-Pager VBX 1.5	Communications	$50 SW	Significa Software	800-214-0504
ALT-PAD Entry Test	System Utility	Free		
Amaza Messagebox Creator	Programming	Free	Joyce, Ben	CIS:100101,36
Analyzer	System Utility	Free	Brody, Evan	
Animated Xerox Copy Button	Buttons	Free		
Animation Code	Graphics	Free	Franklin, Carl	
Another About Box Demo	Form	Unknown	Gotz, Steven	CIS:70563,207
Another Button Bar	Buttons	Free	Koffley, Tim	CIS:70334,16; AOL: TimServo
API Function Spy	Program Utility	Free	Gamber, Mark	CIS:76450,2754
API Helper 3.0	Programming	Free	Bostwick, Marshall	216-864-1778; CIS:76646,2552
API Helper 3.0 New Data	Programming	Free	Bostwick, Marshall	216-864-1778; CIS:76646,2552
API Reference	Reference	Free	User Friendly, Inc.	202-387-1949; CIS:76702,1605
API Servant	Program Utility	$15	Hanson, Mark	CIS:72773,71
APIX	Reference	Free	Simms, Jeff	301-593-6067; CIS:72200,3173
APM-Metafile Support Library	Graphics	Free	Reisewitz, U.	CIS:100042,47
App Shell	Programming	Free	Presley, Jim	
App-Link Form Communications	Form	$100	Synergy Software Technologies	802-878-8514

Name	Type	Price	Vendor	Phone/E-mail
Application Title Spy	Program Utility	Free	Aziz, Atif	41-22-3468028; CIS:72644,3306
Applications Data Server DEMO	Data Access	$99	International Technology Devel	32-2-353-17-12; CIS:100427,400
Appointment Book	Programming	Free	Visual Basic Programmer's Jrnl	800-848-5523; 415-917-7650
Areacode	Programming	Free	McGuiness, Charles	CIS:76701,11
Arrange Icons	Programming	Free	Brown, Martin	CIS:100014,1354
ASC2MDB Ascii To MDB Utility	Database	Free	Curzon, Richard	CIS:71371,2521
Asgard Interface	Form	$30 SW	Asgard Software	44-865-772160; CIS:100113,431
Assoc	System Utility	Free	SP Services	44-703-550037; CIS:100016,1625
Assoc Custom Control	Custom Control	Free	Axiomatic Software	44-21-477-9913; CIS:100273-1543
Asynchronous/Synchronous Shell	Programming	Free	Barber, Jim	CIS:75230,3644; Internet:Jlbarber
Audio Video Demo	Graphics	Free	Turpin, Jerry	800-456-7775; 703-586-8067
Auto Maintenance	Business	Unknown	Schoeffel, Dave	
Autoexec For Windows	Program Utility	$1 SW	Kostelecky Will	
Autoload For Visual Basic	Program Utility	$5	Robar, R.	CIS:100030,10
Automated Questionnaire	Programming Demo	Free	Houtari, Scott	Internet:scotth@wagged.com
Autonum 1.02	Special	Free		
AutoSaveIt	Program Utility	$15	Gatti, Alessandro	415-567-6659
Autosize	Form	Free	Scherer, Bob	CIS:76237,514
AVI Files In Window	Special	Free	Mathison, Rolf	CIS:76376,3224
AVI Viewer	Special	Free		
Backmeup	Program Utility	Unknown	Embrey, Leland E.	408-595-6353; CIS:73131,50
Backup Utility	Program Utility	Free	Fehr, Andreas	CIS:100042,2070; Internet: afehr@itr.ch
Balloon Help Text 3.8	Help	$18 SW	Weimar Software	408-268-6638
Balloon Popup Labels	Help	Unknown	Bencivengo, Nicholas Jr.	CIS:71344,2415
BARCOD 1.5 - Custom Control	Graphics	$15	Mabry Software	206-634-1443; CIS:71231,2066
Barcode/VBX	Printer	$35 SW	Gottschalk, Jeff	CIS:72322,1741
Bars	Programming	$25	Eclipse Software Programming	
BaseConverter	Programming	Free	Huss, Dennis L.	
Basic Code Cache	Programming	$24/1yr	Basic Code Cache	

Name	Type	Price	Vendor	Phone/E-mail
Basically Visual Magazine #2	Programming	$20 yr	Basically Visual Magazine	
BasicBasic For Windows	Programming	$30	Davidsaver, Mark	
BatchEditor 1.2	Form	Free	Liebowitz, Jay	CIS:72733,1601
BEST0894 Program Listings	Programming	Free	Digital PowerTOOLS	609-932-5931; CIS:74547,23
Big Disk Array Demo Of TIME2WI	DLL - General	Free	Renard, Michael	CIS:100042,3646
Big Mak 1.0	Program Utility	$20	Kilgore, Tim	314-442-5776; CIS:72760,1022
Binary Large Object Demo	Database	Free	Rohn, Gary W.	CIS:76050,1012
Biobears Bioryhthm	Graphics	Free		
Bitmap	Programming	Free	Young, Ted	CIS:76703,4343
Bitmap Catalog	Graphics	Free	Bishop, Shawn	606-439-0609
Bitmap Maze Demo	Game	$25	Krystal Cat Software	Internet:KrysCat@Aol.Com
Bitmap Patternbrush	Graphics	Free	Bytes & Letters	49-6831-506534; CIS:100275,3554
BITS.DLL	DLL - General	Free	Peters, Constantine	BBS:301-460-9134
BLFX 1.0	Custom Control	Unknown	Bytes & Letters	49-6831-506534; CIS:100275,3554
BLINC	Mail List	$235	Eastern Digital Resources	766-855-2397; Internet: JohnR238@aol.com
Blind Data Input	Input Routines	$10	Woodward, Kirk	800-553-5883; CIS:70146,51
BMP Kit	Programming	Free	Campbell, George	71571,222; BBS: 805-528-3753
BndRead - Data Control	Listbox	Free		
Bobber And Sinker	Language Extension	Free	Stewart, David	CIS:72122,3562
Books	Special	Free	Book Stacks BBS	BBS:216-861-0469
Borland Visual Controls Info	Reference	Free	Borland	408-431-1000; 800-331-0577
Brand An EXE File	Program Utility	Free	Teter, C. Mark, M.D.	CIS:72530,626
Browse Bound Control VB3/Acc.	Custom Control	$20	Delta Soft Inc.	416-619-2018; CIS:70404,655
Browse Custom Control	Custom Control	$20	Delta Soft Inc.	416-619-2018; CIS:70404,655
Btrieve Create	Database	Free	Highsmith, J	404-412-0827
Btrieve For Windows Test Prog	Database	Free	Meyer, David	
Btrieve ISAM Driver Update	Data Access	Free	Microsoft	206-882-8080; 800-992-3675
Bubble Help	Help	Free	Neese, Al	
Bubble Help Window System	Help	Free	Gamber, Mark	CIS:76450,2714

Name	Type	Price	Vendor	Phone/E-mail
Build MDB Create Code 1.1	Database	Free	JB & Associates	713-647-6539
Build-A-Box MsgBox Generator	Form	$10	Chameleon Group	CIS:71571,222; BBS:805-528-3753
Burglar & Animate	Form	Free	Campbell, George	CIS:100111,2330
Buster	Program Utility	$40	Biney, Dr. B	601-932-5931; CIS:74547,23
Button Picture 1.75	Buttons	$10 SW	Digital PowerTOOLS	301-670-0818
ButtonBar Plus	Program Utility	$18	DiBiasio, Mark	CIS:100552,1570
Buttonmaker VB	Buttons	$12	Naumann, Christian	
Buttons	Programming	Free		CIS:70642,673
Buttons By Freel	Buttons	Free	Freel, Fred	713-726-0396; 800-845-0386
ButtonTool Demo	Programming Demo	$49.95	OutRider Systems	
Calculator	Calculator	Free		CIS:75462-3157; AOL: Mark Main
Calculator In 3D	Calculator	Free	Main, Mark	
Calendar	Calendar	Free	Meadows, Al	
Calendar [Sic]	Calendar	Free	Mower, Chris	407-998-2377; CIS:74032,2412
Calendar 3-D	Calendar	Free		
Calendar Control	Calendar	$50 SW	Software FX Inc.	CIS:71662,47
Calendar Demo	Calendar	Free	Silverman, Glenn	
Calendar Input Form	Calendar	Free	Eisenberg, David F.	619-941-2893
Calendar Program/Add-In	Calendar	$10 SW	IntegrationWare, Inc.	CIS:73322,702
Call Btrieve	Database	Free	Kubelka, Bob	415-737-0870; CIS:71662,205
Call InterruptX In VBWin	DLL - General	Free	Esterling, Rick	CIS:71630,1265
Calling CTL3DV2.DLL	Form	Free	Bridge, Inc	CIS:73051,1761
Calllist	Program Utility	Free	Denenberg, Steve	
CalVBX11	Calendar	$10 SW	Guttilla, Brad	
Cancel Button For Long Process	Buttons	Free		206-820-6107; CIS:75260,732
Canimate Animation VBX	Custom Control	$39	Componere Software	CIS:73261,3642
CANZ Demo - Linked Lists/Trees	Programming	$295	Cz Software Corporation	CIS:70274,103
Car Gauge Control 2.0	Custom Control	$40 SW	Global Majik Software	
Card10	Programming	Free	Sands, Richard R.	

Name	Type	Price	Vendor	Phone/E-mail
CBoxList	Custom Control	Free	OPen Software	
CD Player Utility	Device Control	Free		
CD Volume Control	Device Control	Free	Snyder, James Wj	CIS:75141,3544; AOL: JamesWJS
CdSelect 1.01	Custom Control	Free	Serpoul, Jean Jacques	19-33-40-26-46; CIS:100350,1340
CFGTEXT	Programming	Free	McClure, Jim	CIS:76666,1303
Change Name To Initials	Input Routines	Free	Covell, Stephen E.	CIS:75010,3700
Charlie Data Dictionary Manage	Data Access	$20	Monte Carlo Software	33-9480-3940; CIS:100116,2550
Chess - The Queen's Problem	Graphics	Free		
Chief's Install Pro	Program Utility	$29 SW	Olowofoyeku, Dr. Abimbola	Internet:Laa1@Keele.Ac.Uk
Choyce	Desktop	$10 SW	Amans, Robert L.	313-373-7904; CIS:72716,1522
Classic Timepieces HC	Graphics	$20 SW	Brown, Richard	CIS:70674,1227
Cleanup VBX Clears Screen	Custom Control	$15	Syncom, Inc.	800-457-7884; CIS:72632,345
Clear VB Debug Window	Program Utility	Free	Blaylock, Don	CIS:73132,1073
Clicking With Right Mouse Butt	Menu	Free		
Clip Calendar	Database	Free	Opalko, John	Internet:Johnopalko@Aol.Com
Clip Watch	Program Utility	$10	Owens, Mike	404-472-9017; CIS:75037,2625
Clipboard Spy	Program Utility	Free		
Clipprint	Printer	Free	McIntosh, Rob	CIS:100413,1342
ClipSibling	Program Control	Free	Funk, Keith B.	CIS:72240,2020
Cliptest	Text	Free		
Clock	Clock	Free	BMP Production	
ClockFrame	Programming	$7	Braeuchi, Jakob	31-3331254; CIS:100014,567
ClocVBX	Clock	$10 SW	Guttilla, Brad	CIS:73051,1761
Cloning VB Projects	Program Utility	Free	Big Dog Software	908-885-1513; CIS:70744,1624
CLVB Digest April 1995	Reference	Free	Faarvang, Jakob	Internet:clbv-digest-editor@apexsc.com
CLVB Digest February 1995	Reference	Free	Faarvang, Jakob	Internet:clbv-digest-editor@apexsc.com
CLVB Digest March 1995	Reference	Free	Faarvang, Jakob	Internet:clbv-digest-editor@apexsc.com
CLVB Digest May 1995	Reference	Free	Faarvang, Jakob	Internet:clbv-digest-editor@apexsc.com
Co-Pilot For Visual Basic	Program Utility	Free	ABC Software	01-934-516714; CIS:100342,1207

Name	Type	Price	Vendor	Phone/E-mail
Code Arranger 1.03	Program Utility	$20 SW	Cactus Deve opment Company Inc	800-336-9444; 512-453-2244
Code Browser Using VBAWK	Custom Control	$45	VideoSoft	510-704-8200; 800-547-7295
Code Calendar Demo	Calendar	$15 SW	Hocker, Paul	CIS:73521,2055
Code Keeper 1.2	Program Utility	$10 SW	Princeton Computer Consulting	Internet:bmurray@pluto.njcc.com
Code Librarian	Program Utility	SEE PROG	Infobase	49-251-3111; CIS:100034,3527
Code Librarian 1.03	Program Utility	$10 SW	McMullen, Leigh C.	Internet:Xmcmullen@Dsm1.Dsmnet.Com
Code Librarian For VB 1.1	Program Utility	$15 SW	Okapi (Pat Hayes)	805-257-3377; CIS:74437,134
Code Master Lite	Program Utility	$129	Teletech Systems	CIS:72260,2217
Code Master Macro Pack #1	DDE	Free	Teletech Systems	CIS:72260,2217
Code To Word 6.0	Program Utility	$15 SW	Jacques, Robert R.	CIS:71610,1255
Code-A-Line 1.1	Program Utility	$35 SW	Optimax Corporation	312-561-6363; CIS:75020,3617
Code.Print For VB 2.3	Program Utility	$42 SW	Caladonia Systems, Inc.	206-759-2325; 70711,3300
CodeWiz 1.0	Program Utility	$15	Rhind, Jeff	AOL:Jarhind
Coerce	Language Extension	Free	Aaron, Bud	
Colorgam	Game	Free	Sandell, David	CIS:75366,235
Colors	Programming	Free	Evers, Dave	217-224-3615
Colors.TXT	Form	Free		
Combo List Box Incremental Sea	Listbox	Free		
Comm	Communications	Free		
Common Dialogs Made In VB	Programming	Free	Kitsos, Costas	CIS:73667,1755
Communications Control	Communications	Free	Gamber, Mark	CIS:76450,2754
Communications Control 2.0	Communications	Free	Gamber, Mark	CIS:76450,2754
Communications Demo	Communications	Unknown	MicroHelp, Inc.	800-922-3383; 404-516-0899
Communications Tool Kit INFO	Communications	$299	SilverWare Inc.	214-247-0131; BBS: 214-247-2177
Companion Products Text	Reference	Free	Microsoft	206-882-8080; 800-992-3675
Compare!	Language Extension	Free	Wonderful Computer Services	CIS:100026,506
Component Toolbox Demo 2.0	Custom Control	$95	Gamesman Inc.	204-475-7903; 800-670-8045
Component Toolbox Sampler	Custom Control	$30	Gamesman Inc.	204-475-7903; 800-670-8045
Compress Bucket 1.0	File Management	Free		

APPENDIX

C

Name	Type	Price	Vendor	Phone/E-mail
Compress Wizard	Setup	$12	Simmons, Paul	Internet:3674057@Mcimail.Com
Compress-It	Program Utility	Free	Whiplash Software	CIS:74364,3406
ContACT - Access DBase In ACT!	Data Access	Free	Barlow, Chris	CIS:76440,1370
Contacts Manager	Productivity	$20 SW	Hardaker, Mike	
Control Probe 1.1	Custom Control	$15	Mabry Software	206-634-1443; CIS:71231,2066
Convert MBF Format Numbers	Special	Free	Carr, J. Frank	404-880-5762; CIS:75120,2420
Copy Database Structure	Database	Free	Hernandez, J. M.	CIS:70323,1772
Copy/Move Project Files	Program Utility	Free	Lundberg, Thomas	CIS:74447,1267
Copycode 4.6	Program Utility	$15 SW	Koot, Andre	CIS:100120,2360
Create DBF	Database	$20	Zero-1 Software	64-3-352-6481; CIS:100032,40
CreateHelp V2.02	Help	$40	Barnes, Nic	44-81-694-0110; CIS:100111,3452
Creating DDF Files	Data Access	Free		
Creating Program Group	Program Utility	Free	Decker, Mike	CIS:70651,50
Creating Program Group Workaro	Programming	Free	Hardin, Todd	
Creating Toolbars In VB	Desktop	Free	Murphy, Stephen	CIS:70661,2461
Creating Windows Help Files	Help	Free	Kahn, Theodore	510-562-9900; CIS:70353,203
Crispy Solitaire	Game	Free	Pando, Chris	
Crystal Reports 3.0 Announceme	Text	Free	Crystal Services	604-681-3435; 604-681-2934
Crystal Reports And Bound Repo	Reference	Free	Crystal Services	604-681-3435; 604-681-2934
Crystal Reports DLL Update	Printer	Free	Crystal Services	604-681-3435; 604-681-2934
Crystal Reports Pro License	Reference	Free	Crystal Services	604-681-3435; 604-681-2934
Crystal Reports Runtime Doc	Reference	Free	Crystal Services	604-681-3435; 604-681-2934
Crystal Reports Sample Applica	Printer	Free	Crystal Services	604-681-3435; 604-681-2934
Crystal Reports Technical Docs	Reference	Free	Crystal Services	604-681-3435; 604-681-2934
Crystal Reports/MS Access Time	Data Access	Free	Becker, Thomas	CIS:73473,1363
CsrPlus	DLL - General	$10 SW	Digital PowerTOOLS	601-932-5931; CIS:74547,23
CtDATE Custom Control	Custom Control	$35 SW	Gamesman Inc.	204-475-7903; 800-670-8045
CtFOLD Custom Control	Custom Control	$35 SW	Gamesman Inc.	204-475-7903; 800-670-8045
CTGauge	Custom Control	$25	Gamesman Inc.	204-475-7903; 800-670-8045

Name	Type	Price	Vendor	Phone/E-mail
CTL3D Demo	Form	Unknown	Rodriguez, M. John	CIS:100321,620; Internet:Jrodrigu
CTL3D.DLL Example	Form	Free	Cre8tive Concepts	
Ctlwhnd.Dll	Language Extension	Unknown	User Friendly, Inc.	202-387-1949; CIS:76702,1605
Ctrl-Alt-Del Disable VBX	Security	$20 SW	Bowker, Bob	213-851-5298; CIS:70250,306
CtSplit Split Window VBX	Custom Control	$25	Gamesman Inc.	204-475-7903; 800-670-8045
CtTips Help Tips VBX	Custom Control	$25	Gamesman Inc.	204-475-7903; 800-670-8045
CUA Controls Demonstration	Custom Control	$45	Stingsoft	CIS:100662,3013
CurrencyFix VB	Language Extension	Free	Mack, Jim	CIS:76630,2012
Cursor Libraries Manipulations	Custom Control	$15 SW	Fillion, Pierre	CIS:71162,51
Cursor Manipulation Control	Custom Control	$15 SW	Fillion, Pierre	CIS:71162,51
Cursor Position	Desktop	Free	Joyce, Ben	CIS:100101,36
Cursor Position Example	General	Free	Wisecarver, Mike	
CUSGEN 1.2	Program Utility	$10	RMJ Software	805-267-0217
Custom 3-D Buttons	Custom Control	Free	Gamber, Mark	CIS:76450,2754
Custom Control Code Example	Custom Control	Free	Big Dog Software	908-885-1513; CIS:70744,1624
Custom Control Factory Demo	Program Control	$48	Desaware	408-377-4770; CIS:74431,3534
Custom Cursor Demo	Graphics	Free	Fillion, Pierre	CIS:71162,51
Custom Cursors (Updated)	Graphics	Free	Stanley, Mike	CIS:74632,2227; AOL:MikeStanly
Custom Cursors Over Buttons	DLL - General	Free	Swift, W	
Custom Gauge VBX 2.0	Custom Control	$40	Global Majik Software	CIS:73261,3642
Custom Group Box	Custom Control	Free	Gamber, Mark	CIS:76450,2754
CX Data Compression Library	DLL - General	$45	Nelson, Eugene	CIS:70662,2501
CyberSpace Cruiser	Game	Free	Ivory Tower Software	310-370-7045; CIS:76427,2611
D&DSERVE.DLL	Programming	Free	Zuck, Jonathan	
Data Demo	Database	Free	Fulton, Bruce	
Data Manager Source Code	Data Access	Free	Microsoft	206-882-8080; 800-992-3675
Data Widgets Demo	Database	$129	Sheridan Software Systems	516-753-0985x193
Database Maintenance	Database	$15 SW	Moss, Kevin	CIS:75310,3415
Database Table Structure Print	Database	Free	Gallo, Charles	

Name	Type	Price	Vendor	Phone/E-mail
Datafile Controls Demo FoxPro	Data Access	Free	Tucker, Barry G.	CIS:70324,2404
DataInformatter	Database	Free	Roussos, D.	
DataTable Custom Control	Database	$50	DB Technologies	813-378-3760; CIS:72123,3661
Dataworks	DLL - Database	$50	VXBase Systems	403-488-8100; 800-992-0616
Date And Time Stamp	File Management	Free		
Date Tracker	Calendar	Free	Barrett, David	CIS:100010,2171
Date/Time Custom Control	Custom Control	Unknown	Mitromar, Inc.	407-276-2091
Date/Time Edit Control	Custom Control	Unknown	Jeffery, John	CIS:100237,300
Date/Time Entry Form	Input Routines	Free	Rogers, Kerry	CIS:71514,735
DateComp Function	Calendar	Free	Wray, Richard	
DateTime	Calendar	PD	Michna, Hans-Georg	49-89-C302; CIS:74776,2361
DB-XL Database To Excel	Programming	Free		
Db2db	Database	Free	BillT121	AOL:BillT121
DBA VB Error Handler	Program Control	Free	Murdoch, John	CIS:71507,1212
DBase III File And Index Read	Database	Free	Schulze, Peter	CIS:72253,2602
DBDocumenter 1.1	Database	$8	Dilley, John J., CCP	
DBEngine Custom Control	Custom Control	$75 SW	DB Technologies	813-378-3760; CIS:72123,3661
DBEngine Custom Control Source	Custom Control	$75 SW	DB Technologies	813-378-3760; CIS:72123,3661
DBT Grid Working Model	Data Access	$40	DB Technologies	813-378-3760; CIS:72123,3661
DBTTip 1.21	Custom Control	Free	Skoog, Bengt-Arne	CIS:74362,1256
DDD Professional Toolkit 1.2	Programming	$17	Anno Domini, Inc.	
DDE Control Centre	Communications	$45	O'Neill Software	CIS:100242,2203
DDE In Visual Basic	DDE	Free	Pleas, Keith R.	CIS:72331,2150
DDESHR	Communications	Free	Garrison, Gary P.	612-541-0144; CIS:76400,3555
DDL Manager 1.1	Data Access	$30 SW	MM Technology	201-612-8222; CIS:71155,1010
DDRV Print Preview	Printer	$25	Dickinson, Don	CIS:72762,645
Delayed Drag Demo	Programming	Free	Simms, Jeff	301-593-6067; CIS:72200,3173
Desaware API Declarations	Reference	Free	Desaware	408-377-4770; CIS:74431,3534
Design-Mode Custom Controls	Program Control	Free	Jiang, Jeng Long	

Name	Type	Price	Vendor	Phone/E-mail
Desktop Changer	Form	Free		
Detecting End Of Drag'n'drop	Text	Free	Strathman, Michael D.	408-238-6351; CIS:75663,520
Detour 1.2	System Utility	Free	Bolin, Christopher	
Device Tester	Printer	Free		
DG Status	System Utility	Free		
Dialog Box Generator	Misc.	Free	Goldfarb, David	33-1-43205108; CIS:100412,2653
Dialog Box Wizard	Form	Unknown	Tisoft S.A.	
Dialog Builder Cc	Custom Control	Free	Beekes, Bernd	CIS:100031,2063; 49-2261-55369
Diamond Arrow Pad	Custom Control	Free	Gamber, Mark	CIS:76450,2754
Directory Structure Scan	Programming	Free	Rose, Joel	
Directory To DBF File	File Management	Free	Fabian, Imre	
Disk And File Info CC 2.3	Custom Control	$15 SW	Mabry Software	206-634-1443; CIS:71231,2066
Disk Space DLL Demo	General	Free	Castravet, John	
DiskStat	System Utility	Free	Wykes, Harry	CIS:100014,2573
DiskTrack	File Management	$40 SW	Peninsula Software	310-377-6620; CIS:72356,556
Display Info Message On Form	Form	Free	Cath, Jeremy E.	44-628-789229; CIS:100315,521
DLL - Load Bitmaps And Strings	DLL - Graphics	Free	Lyk, Edward	I:Edlyk@Delphi.Com
DLL Extractor DEMO	Program Utility	$10	E & B Systems	Internet:Mikepark@Ix.Netcom.Com
DLL Investigator	Program Utility	Free	Press, Barry	CIS:72467,2353
DLLManager	Programming	Free	Woodhouse, Mike	CIS:100023,604; CIS:73503,2522
Document Visual Basic	Program Utility	$10	McPhail, G. E.	CIS:72610,10
DoDos	Program Control	Free	Dickson, David	CIS:73477,221
DOS Shell Launcher	Programming	Free	Meredith, Chazz	
DosButton	System Utility	Free		
Drag 'n Drop Using TList	Custom Control	Free	Bennet-Tec Information Serv.	516-433-6283; CIS:71201,1075
Drag And Drop	File Management	Unknown	Bonner, Paul	CIS:76000,13
Drag And Drop Calculator Demo	Calendar	$15	Owens, Mike	404-472-9017; CIS:75037,2625
Drag And Drop From Outline Con	Form	Free		
Drag Form	Programming	Free	Simms, Jeff	301-593-6067; CIS:72200,3173

Name	Type	Price	Vendor	Phone/E-mail
Drag/Drop Items Within Outline	Form	Free	Van Der Sar, D.	CIS:100103,3121
Draw On Iconized Form	Graphics	Free	Young, Ted	CIS:76703,4343
DrawScript 0.8	Printer	Free	McClure, Jim	CIS:76666,1303
Drive Utilities DLL	Disk Utility	$20 SW	TANSTAAFL Software	303-989-7389; CIS:73700,3053
Dropdown Box	Programming	Free		
DrvPlus	DLL - General	$10 SW	Digital PowerTOOLS	601-932-5931; CIS:74547,23
Dynamic Data Exchange Monger	Communications	$10	Averbuch, Michael	
Early Morning Editor Control	Text	$30 SW	Early Morning Software	312-925-1628; CIS:74454,1002
Easter Calculator	Calendar	Free		
Easynet Custom Control 1.70	Custom Control	$125 SW	Lassalle, Patrick	33-1-46-034220; CIS:100325,725
Ed VB Editor Interface 1.0	Desktop	Free	Neal, Randy	CIS:72315,16
Edit Batch Files	Data Access	Free	Davis, Mike	CIS:73122,1474; AOL:VDG Mike
Edit Button For Database	Buttons	Free	Riley, Barth	CIS:72677,3172
Edit Demo - Input Routines	Input Routines	Free	Milligan, Keith	205-291-9712; CIS:70645,520
EditDemo	Form	Free	Campbell, George	CIS:71571,222; BBS:805-528-3753
EditTool Demo	Custom Control	Free	BitRider Inc.	
Elasticman	Form	Free	Stewart, Robert W.	CIS:72632,3004
Electrified Visual Basic #1	Programming	$3.50	Pro-Data / EVB Magazine	BBS:602-942-9405
Electrified Visual Basic #2	Programming	$3.50	Pro-Data / EVB Magazine	BBS:602-942-9405
Electrified Visual Basic #3	Programming	$3.50	Pro-Data / EVB Magazine	BBS:602-942-9405
Electrified Visual Basic #4	Programming	$3.50	Pro-Data / EVB Magazine	BBS:602-942-9405
Encrypt/Decrypt	Special	Free		
End Task DLL	DLL - General	Free	Simms, Jeff	301-593-6067; CIS:72200,3173
Endprn	Programming	Free		
Engine Estimator	Game	Free	O"Massey, Michael	
Enhance Spin Source Code	Programming	Free	Deutch, Jim	CIS:73313,2327
EnumFont	Language Extension	Free	WinWay Corporation	916-332-2671; CIS:70523,2574
Envelogo 1.1	Envelopes	Unknown	Pedersen, John	CIS:76547,357
Envelope Printer 2.0	Envelopes	Free	Federal Hill Software	800-846-4319; 410-356-5592; CIS:716

Name	Type	Price	Vendor	Phone/E-mail
EOF/BOF	Database	Free	Willits, Don	Withheld by request
Eschalon Setup Trial Edition	Setup	$100	Eschalon Development, Inc.	604-945-3198; CIS:76625,1320
Example DLL Programming	Programming	Free	John	
Exitman - Exit Windows	Program Utility	$10 SW	McNeill Consulting Services	CIS:71043,1226
ExitWin - Exit Windows	System Utility	Free	Moyle, Greg	BBS:702-329-5610
Exploding Windows Example	Form	Free		
Expression Evaluator	Programming	Free	Big Dog Software	908-885-1513; CIS:70744,1624
Extended Arrays	Language Extension	$30	Willy, C. Scott	33-93-77-50-47; CIS:100343,2570
Extending VB With Windows DLLs	DLL - General	Unknown	Microsoft	206-882-8080; 800-992-3675
EZ-Tab Tabbed Dialogs DEMO	Custom Control	$28 SW	Beekes, Bernd	CIS:100031,2063; 49-2261-55369
EZAccess 2.5c For VB	Database	$10 SW	Robichaux, Roy J.	CIS:74031,1652
EZBanner 1.1	Fonts	$10 SW	Robichaux, Roy J.	CIS:74031,1652
EZDATA Database Creator	Database	$12	Blessing, John	CIS:100444,623
EZDisk DLL Demo	Disk Utility	Unknown	CMC Systems	CIS:73577,1416
EZFace MDI Template	Form	$11	CMC Systems	CIS:73577,1416
EZHelp Simple Help System	Help	Free	Campbell, George	CIS:71571,222; BBS:805-528-3753
Fade To Black	Form	Free	Stine, Brian D.	CIS:73617,323
Fadeform 1.0	Form	Free	Jwpc, Inc.	Internet:JwpcEMail@Aol.Com
FAQ 04/95	Text	Free	Haugland, Jan Steiner	Internet:Jan.Haugland@Uib.No
FAQ 11/94	Text	Free	Haugland, Jan Steiner	Internet:Jan.Haugland@Uib.No
FAQ 12/94	Text	Free	Haugland, Jan Steiner	Internet:Jan.Haugland@Uib.No
Fast Track Disk	Reference	$29	Wildcat Software	303-733-3924
FastGraph Custom Control 0.9	Graphics	Free	Pienaar, Marc	CIS:70750,1776
Favorite	Programming	Free		
FBIFile WAV Player Demo	Sound	Free	Davis, Mike	CIS:73122,1474; AOL:VDG Mike
FCC File Access Library	File Management	$95 SW	Four Lakes Computing	608-256-3382; CIS:70662,2501
FieldPack 1.2	Custom Control	$39	Software Source	510-623-7854
FieldPack Demo (Gregg Irwin)	Data Access	Free	Irwin, Gregg	CIS:72450,676
File Mgr Drag And Drop CC 1.2	Custom Control	$15 SW	Mabry Software	206-634-1443; CIS:71231,2066

Name	Type	Price	Vendor	Phone/E-mail
File Search Utility	Disk Utility	Free	Malik Information Services	CIS:76055,2722
File Stamper	Program Utility	Free	Irwin, Gregg	CIS:72450,676
File Wizard VBX	Custom Control	$10 SW	Jantzi, Steve	519-655-2242
Filebox	Programming	Free	Kiehl, Thomas	CIS:73215,427
Fileboy's Runway 1.2c	Programming	$5.00	Homegrown Software	CIS:76646,2552
FileMaster	System Utility	Free	VisualSoft	415-565-449
FileOpen	Programming	Free		
FilePak! DEMO	Program Utility	$44	Inspired MultiMedia Inc.	408-281-0996; CIS:73523,752
FileView 1.0	Program Utility	Free	Praxis Software Developments	CIS:100265,1064
Financial Func's From Excel 4	Finance	Free	Scofield, M.L. "Sco"	CIS:71063,157
Find File	Disk Utility	Free	Radford, Andrew	CIS:74151,2317
Find Program Manager Groups	Programming	Free	Germelmann, Christian	49-6421-45457; CIS:100520,2644
Find Screen Saver Password	Programming	Free	Hayward, John	CIS:100034,320
Find Window	Programming	Free	Irwin, Gregg	CIS:72450,676
Find/Sort Window	Misc.	SW	Lee, Joseph	CIS:74013,3316
FindPrt	Programming	Free		
FindVBID	Programming	Free	Kitsos, Costas	CIS:73667,1755
Floating Toolbar Example	Graphics	Free		
Floating Toolbox Demo	Desktop	Free	Dexter, Matthew	Internet:dexter@chem.surrey.ac.uk
Flyhelp Balloon Help DEMO	Help	$5 SW	Streu, Randy	CIS:73512,273
Flyout Menus	Menu	Free	Koch, Peter	714-666-8250; CIS:74007,2450
Focus U-Turn Test Program	Programming	Free	ETN Corporation	717-435-2202
Focus U-Turn Test Program #2	Programming	Free	ETN Corporation	717-435-2202
FocusPrb: Keeping Control	Form	Free		
Folder Custom Control	Custom Control	$30	Mullins, Robert	
Folders	Form	Free	Parr, James	CIS:73312,3615
Folders-II	Graphics	Free	Cordero, Antonio	
Font Central 0.9	Fonts	$15 SW	American Computer Consultants	708-295-8490
Font Rotate	Programming	Free		

Name	Type	Price	Vendor	Phone/E-mail
Font Viewer For Windows	Fonts	$15 SW	Smart Typesetting	CIS:71571,222; BBS:805-528-3753
Fonter 6.0 For Windows	Fonts	$15 SW	Campbell, George	CIS:76044,747
FontShow 1.3	Fonts	$10 SW	Alcott, Glenn	
FontShow For Windows 5.0, 1of2	Fonts	$15 SW	Kaye, Harvey J.	
FontShow For Windows 5.0, 2of2	Fonts	$15 SW	Kaye, Harvey J.	
FontView	Printer	Free	Snider, Charles K.	CIS:73730,1315
FontViewer	Fonts	Free	Freeland, Frederick F. Jr.	
Force Upper Or Lower Case	Text	Free	Bridge, Inc.	415-737-0870; CIS:71662,205
Form On Top	Form	Free		
Form Refresh Workaround	Form	Free	Trahan, Jeff	CIS:72737,2154
Form Scroll 200	Programming	Free	MicroHelp, Inc.	800-922-3383; 404-516-0899
Form Wizard	Form	Free	Bacon, Royce D.	414-462-3418; CIS:70042,1001
Form Wizard 1.0	Form	Free	J&J Software	CIS:73474,3000
Formatted Edit Custom Control	Custom Control	$159	Computer Mindware Corp.	201-884-1123; CIS:76615,2564
Formatted Label Custom Control	Custom Control	$20	Mabry Software	206-634-1443; CIS:71231,2066
Forms Dispatcher	Form	Free	Mangold, Oliver	49-7333-6007; CIS:100277,511
FormTrak 1.2	Program Utility	$20 SW	Margraff, Tom	909-980-7344; CIS:71165,2623
Fortran DLL To VB Demo	DLL Interface	Free	Lewis, Tony	CIS:73357,1730
FPrint 1.53	Printer	Free	Kapune, Albert	CIS:100010,2067
FreeVBX	Language Extension	Free	MicroHelp, Inc.	800-922-3383; 404-516-0899
Frequently Asked Questions	Text	Free	Willits, Don	Withheld by request
FXLaunch	Menu	Free	Snider, Charles K.	CIS:73730,1315
FXTools/VB 1.3 Demo	Graphics	$129	ImageFX	716-272-8030; 800-229-8030
FXTools/VB Pro 2.0 DEMO	Graphics	$349	ImageFX	716-272-8030; 800-229-8030
Gadgets For Windows 1.1 Demo	Custom Control	$40	Universal Dynamics Inc.	602-979-2800
GBLIB 1.1c	DLL - General	Free	Bamber, Gordon	CIS:74437,672
GBLIB2 - Brands VB EXE Files	Program Utility	Unknown	Bamber, Gordon	CIS:74437,672
GCP++ TCP/IP Custom C. Eval.	Communications	$298	Dart Communications	315-841-8106; Internet:sales@dart.com
GeeWiz	Programming	$69	Resolutions Now	312-994-6450

Name	Type	Price	Vendor	Phone/E-mail
Generic DDE In Visual Basic	Communications	Free	Microsoft	206-882-8080; 800-992-3675
GENERIC Sample Files	Programming	Free	McLaughlin, Thomas	AOL:TIMMY12952
Generic Screen Saver	Graphics	Free	Unger, Guinn	713-498-8517; CIS:71053,2232
GENPRINT Generalized Printer	Printer	$20 SW		
Gentypes	Database	Free		
Geometry DLL	DLL - Graphics	Free	Sirabella, John	
Get And Put Disk Volume Labels	Disk Utility	Free	Guimond, Stephen C.	CIS:70253,502
Get Network Login	Data Access	Free	Healy, Joe	CIS:expired
GetAPI 2.0	Program Utility	$20	Velazquez, Chris	CIS:74073,1566
GetHelp	Help	Free	Lorenzini, Greg	CIS:76507,2166
GetHelp	Help	Free	Freel, Fred	CIS:70642,673
GetIdleTime	DLL - General	Free	Malik Information Services	CIS:76055,2722
GIF To BMP DLL	DLL - Graphics	Free	Cramp, Stephen	905-838-2896; CIS:70471,137
Glossary How To	Help	Free	CNS - Companhia Nacional De Se	
Goliath 1.0	Program Utility	Free	Koot, Andre	CIS:100120,2360
GPF General Protection Maker	Prog. - Sys. Util.	Free		
GrabClip	Program Utility	Free	Infocomm(UK) Ltd.	
Graphic Viewer	Graphics	Free	Nordan, Matthew M.	CIS:76535,1421; BBS:704-782-8921
Graphic Viewer 2.0	Graphics	$5 SW	Cramp, Stephen	905-838-2896; CIS:70471,137
Graphical Calendar	Calendar	Free	Marlow, James	CIS:72732,407
Graphical Calendar Variation	Calendar	Free	Eka	CIS:72560,1630
Graphics Viewer DLL	DLL - Graphics	Free	Oliphant, Joe	CIS:71742,1451
Grid 2	Program Control	Unknown	User Friendly, Inc.	202-387-1949 CIS:76702,1605
Grid 3	Custom Control	Free		
Grid Print 1.0	Printer	Free	Overstreet, Mark	CIS:102227,3510
Grid Routines	Programming	Free	Ford, Nelson	CIS:71355,470
Grid Test	Program Control	Free	Microsoft	206-882-8080; 800-992-3675
Grid VBX With SQL Querybuilder	Custom Control	ROYALTY	Marasco Newton Group Ltd.	703-516-9100
Grids 4 Kids	Game	$15 SW	Pritchett, Glenn	

Name	Type	Price	Vendor	Phone/E-mail
GS Help Files	Custom Control	$85	GC Consulting Services Ltd.	44-335-370562; CIS:100113,2774
GSS Tools Custom Controls	Custom Control	$35	Guttilia, Brad	CIS:73051,1761
GSS Wallpaper VBX	Custom Control	$12	Guttilia, Brad	CIS:73051,1761
GSScalc	Calculator	$10	Guttilia, Brad	CIS:73051,1761
GsSetPageOrientation DLL	Printer	$50 SW	Hopkins, Geoff	CIS:100064,3722
GSSgrad Gradient VBX	Custom Control	$10	Guttilia, Brad	CIS:73051,1761
GT Tabbed List Box CC 2.0	Custom Control	$15 SW	Torralba, George R.	206-781-7622
GT Toolbar Kit 1.0	Custom Control	$15 SW	Torralba, George R.	206-781-7622
GTIcon - DLL For Icons	DLL - Graphics	Free	Torralba, George R.	206-781-7622
Handyman	Program Utility	$20 SW	Whittlesley, Scott	
Hardware Control VBX	Custom Control	$45	Vermont Peripherals	CIS:74514,2615
HDC Function Library	Program Utility	$50	HDC Computer Corporation	206-885-5550
HDC Power Toolbox	Program Utility	$50	HDC Computer Corporation	206-885-5550
HelIp! Help Authoring Tool	Help	$30 SW	Guy, Edward	604-926-1370
Help Compiler 3.10.505	Help	Free	Microsoft	206-882-8080; 800-992-3675
Help Compiler Shell	Help	Free	Brown, Tim	CIS:73557,3461
Help File To WinWord	Help	Free	Beyer, Wolfgang	l:Beyer@Lrz-Muenchen.De
Help Project Editor 1.0a	Help	$50	Fletcher, David	
Help S12923	Help	Free	Microsoft	206-882-8080; 800-992-3675
Help Writer's Assistant 2.0	Help	$65	Olson, Stephan	64-6-359-1408; ; CIS:100352,1315
Help Writing Help	Help	$32	TechnoTrends	
HelpBreeze 1.6 Demo	Help	$279	Solutionsoft	408-736-1431; CIS:75210,2214
HelpNavp Plus 3.2	Help	$10 SW	Arnote, Paul	Internet:Aerosolman@Aol.Com
HelpScre	Help	Free	Crygier, Ed	
HelpScrn	Help	Free	Crygier, Ed	
Hex Dump Utility	Program Utility	Free	Main, Mark	CIS:75462,3157; AOL:Mark Main
Hierarchy Listbox 1.1	Custom Control	$55 SW	Krausse, Ralph	CIS:71043,2434
High Resolution Timer VBX	Timer	$20 SW	Mabry Software	206-634-1443; CIS:71231,2066
HighEdit 3.0 DEMO	Text	$299	Pinnacle Publishing	206-251-1900; 800-231-1293

Name	Type	Price	Vendor	Phone/E-mail
HLPKEY.DLL	Programming	Free	Simms, Jeff	301-593-6067; CIS:72200,3173
Holiday Calendar Demo	Calendar	$20 SW	Bridge, Inc.	415-737-0870; CIS:71662,205
Holiday.Bas	Calendar	Free		
Hotkey	System Utility		User Friendly, Inc.	202-387-1949; CIS:76702,1605
Hotkey Gosub	Language Extension	Free		
HotMap Custom Control 1.5	Custom Control	$60	SoftLand Inc.	215-741-2030; CIS:73321,1525
How To Add Print Preview	Printer	Free		
How To Correct ISAM Error	Data Access	Free	Carr, J. Frank	404-880-5762; CIS:75120,2420
HP Envelope Printer	Printer	Free	Federal Hill Software	800-846-4319; 410-356-5592
Huge Array DLL 9/11/92	Programming	Free	Microsoft (Mods By Scherer)	
Huge Array DLL 9/16/92	Programming	Free	Microsoft (Mods By Seale)	
Huge Array Support	Language Extension	Free	Microsoft	206-882-8080; 800-992-3675
Huge Grid 1.0	Language Extension	Free	Ford, Nelson	CIS:71355,470
Huge String Array Manager	Programming	Free	Marquis Computing, Inc.	203-963-7065; 800-818-1611
Huge Variable And Fixed String	Language Extension	$30 SW	Vi Qual Software	
Hypertext For VB	Help	Free	Martin, Wendell	CIS:73737,1237
Hypertext Printer 1.1	Printer	$5	Dass, Beena	
HyperVB Multifont Text DEMO	Text	$70	Data Preference	313-278-4187; CIS:70162,1037
I Declare API/Multimedia Decla	Programming	$20 SW	Mullin, Dan	719-599-7477; CIS:72644,2423
ICOBMP	Icon Utility	Free	Campbell, George	CIS:71571,222; BBS:805-528-3753
Icon Browser	Programming	Free	Bonner, Paul	CIS:76000,13
Icon Chooser 1.3	Icon Utility	$15 SW	Ledbetter, Keith	804-674-0780; CIS:72240,1221
Icon DLL	Icon Utility	Free	Curran, James M.	CIS:72261,655
Icon Extract	Graphics	Free	Tisoft S.A.	33-1-4320 5108; CIS:100412,2653
Icon Extract	General	Free	Hill, Tim	
Icon Extractor	Icon Utility	Free	Mulks, Charles	CIS:70612,1117
Icon Extractor	Icon Utility	Free	Germelmann, Christian	49-6421-45457;CIS:100520,2644
Icon Extractor	Icon Utility	$15 SW	Valley Programming	210-650-9515
Icon Grabber	Icon Utility	Free	AndyD	Internet:AndyD@Pragmatix.Com

Name	Type	Price	Vendor	Phone/E-mail
Icon Selector	Icon Utility	Free	McNamee, Tom	
Icon To Bitmap Converter 3.2	Graphics	$15 SW	Germelmann, Christian	49-6421-45457; CIS:100520,2644
Icon Viewer	Icon Utility	Free	Evers, Dave	217-224-3615
IconLook	Icon Utility	Free	Pitts, David	
IList Custom Control	Custom Control	$25	Taylor, Ian	44-706-353-412; CIS:100025,557
ImageKnife/VBX Demo	DLL - Graphics	$199	Media Architects, Inc.	503-297-5010
ImageKnife/VBX Demo	Graphics	Unknown	Media Architects, Inc.	503-297-5010
Improved Notepad With Macros	Text	Free	Gordon	CIS:72567,3416
IMPVB 2.0 Code Printing	Program Utility	$15 SW	Tisoft S.A.	33-1-43205108; CIS:100412,2653
Index For Data Access Guide	Reference	Free	Microsoft	206-882-8080; 800-992-3675; 800-277
IndexTab And Ruler CC Demo	Custom Control	Unknown	VideoSoft	510-704-8200; 800-547-7295; CIS:715
Info Dialog Form	Form	Free		
Info Recall 1.1	Database	$70 SW	Curtram Consulting	416-502-1311
InFocus Status Line CC	Custom Control	$20 SW	Hanson, Mark	CIS:72773,71
InfoSoft VBTables	Custom Control	$32	InfoSoft	414-282-0535; CIS:70403,3412
InfSpy 2.10	System Utility	$10 SW	Dean Software Design	
INI Custom Control	Custom Control	$12	Stubbs, Scott	CIS:73474,313
INI File Custom Control 3.2	Custom Control	$5	Mabry Software	206-634-1443; CIS:71231,2066
INI Manager	Program Utility	$12 SW	Owens, Mike	404-472-9017 CIS:75037,2625
INI Navigator 3.1	Program Utility	Free	Di Bacco, Daniel	CIS:100140,1156
INI.VBX Custom Control	Custom Control	Free	Dexter, Walter F.	CIS:76450,663
Inifile	Prog. - Sys. Util.	Free	Hegerty, Chad	CIS:71212,1045
Inifile - INI File Wrapper 3.0	Programming	Free	Petersen, Karl E.	CIS:72302,3707
Inimagic 2.2	Custom Control	$30 SW	Bits & Bytes Solutions	206-328-1523; CIS:72603,1674
INIUPD INI File Source Code	Programming	Free	Jniblack	Internet:Jniblack@Ix.Netcom.Com
Install Master (DEMO)	Setup	$99	Poseidon Software, Ltd.	800-931-1221; CIS:74244,1616
Installigence Demo	Setup	$295	Instance Corporation	206-836-0111 800-494-0550
InstallWare 4.02	Program Utility	$0–$35	Dolan, Bob	716-865-8248; CIS:71075,3256
IntelliPrint DEMO	Program Utility	$50	Alliance Software Specialists	414-859-2124; AOL:AllianceSS

Name	Type	Price	Vendor	Phone/E-mail
Internet	Communications	Unknown		
IPPort Control	Communications	$25	DevSoft Inc.	CIS:75244,2736; AOL:Devsoft
IPX And SPX Custom Control 2.0	Data Access	$30 SW	Wiltbank, Lee	CIS:71776,1274
ISAM Emuilation For VB	Database	Free	Eibl, Gunter	011-49-89-609-7046; CIS:10012,1323
ISFILE Function	File Finder	Free	Carr, J. Frank	404-880-5762; CIS:75120,2420
Italian Codice Fiscale Calcula	Calculator	Free	Sorrentino, Silvio	CIS:100265,1725
ITGraph	Graphics	$80 SW	Indra Technology, Inc.	800-735-7776; CIS:74214,1576
Jeopardy Scorekeeper	Game	$5 SW	Persky, Jonathan D.	Internet:jonpersky@aol.com
Jet 2.0/VB 3.0 Compat. Notes	Text	Free	Microsoft	206-882-8080; 800-992-3675
Jet Database Engine White Pape	Reference	Free	Microsoft	206-882-8080; 800-992-3675
Jet Inspector Benchmark Data	Text	Free	Mercury Interactive Corp.	800-837-8911; 408-523-9900
JET Inspector Test Drive	Database	$495	Mercury Interactive Corp.	800-837-8911; 408-523-9900
Jet Vs. Visual Basic	Database	Free	Weber, Phil	CIS:72451,3401
Journal Program	Business	$25 SW	Smith, Gordon	703-759-4415
Joystick Custom Control 1.3	Custom Control	$15 SW	Mabry Software	206-634-1443; CIS:71231,2066
Joystick Status	Special	Free	Six, Raymond W.	CIS:70530,433
Joystick Status Source Code	Special	Free	Six, Raymond W.	CIS:70530,433
Joystick.VBX	Special	Free	Thomas, Zane	206-297-8012; CIS:72060,3327
Junque - Open-Ended Activity	Programming	Free	Merriman, Dave	
Kalendar Custom Control	Custom Control	$25 SW	Parachute Software	415-737-0870; CIS:71662,205
KeyState (CapsLock And NumLock	System Utility	Free	Bridge, Inc.	
Keytest	Prog. - Sys. Util.	PD	Mosher, Sue	
KillDLL	Programming	Free	Brown, Carl	
Knight's Tour Chess Problem	Game	Free		
Knob Control	Custom Control	$40	Global Majik Software	CIS:73261,3642
KnowledgeBase 4/95	Reference	Free	Microsoft	206-882-8080; 800-992-3675
Label Turn Text Rotation	Custom Control	$10 SW	Digital PowerTOOLS	601-932-5931; CIS:74547,23
Labtab	Programming	Unknown		
Lcl4B V 4.2(1)	Communications	$65 SW	MarshallSoft Computing, Inc.	205-881-4630; BBS:205-880-9748

Name	Type	Price	Vendor	Phone/E-mail
LEADTOOLS Imagehandler Demo	Graphics	Free	LEAD Technologies	704-332-5532; 800-637-4699x1
LED Code Module	Graphics	$10	Anno Domini, Inc.	
LED Custom Control	Custom Control	$15 SW	Mabry Software	206-634-1443; CIS:71231,2066
LED Custom Control 2.0	Custom Control	$40	Global Majik Software	CIS:73261,3642
LED Display Control	Custom Control	$22 SW	Syncom, Inc.	800-457-7884; CIS:72632,345
Leong Profile CCs 1.02	Custom Control	$25 SW	Leong, Mabel	44-1462-454703; CIS:100332,3614
Let's All Get Sick	Desktop	Free	Smythe, William	CIS:74640,637
LFStatus Custom Control	Custom Control	$14 SW	Lake Forest Software	CIS:74361,22
Liberty Basic 1.1	Programming	$35 SW	Shoptalk Systems	508-872-5315
Liberty Basic Document	Text	Free	Shoptalk Systems	508-872-5315
Life	Game	Free	Ivory Tower Software	310-370-7045; CIS:76427,2611
Link Demo	Listbox	Free	Presley, Jack	CIS:70700,166
Link Manager 2.0	Program Utility	$10 SW	Praxis Software Developments	CIS:100265,1064
Linked List Demo	Data Access	Free	Weiss, Thomas R.	CIS:75000,327
Linked Text Box And Smartfill	Programming	Free	Presley, Jack	CIS:70700,166
List Box With Bitmaps CC 2.0	Listbox	$20 SW	Mabry Software	206-634-1443; CIS:71231,2066
Listdrag	Programming	Unknown		
Lister Box	Program Utility	$10	Gallino, Jeff	
Load Time Problem Solution	General	Free		
Loan DB Manager 4.0	Finance	$25 SW	Soft Solutions	
LocalDim	Program Utility	Free	Denenberg, Steve	CIS:71630,1265
Lock - Disable Task-Switching	System Utility	Free	Hengelhaupt, Thomas	CIS:100120,115
Locker API DLL 1.0 Demo	DLL - Communication	$245	Hampshire Software	800-NetSoft; 617-826-4208
Log Window	Communications	$30	Solution Studios Inc.	309-692-9162; CIS:74454,117
Logfile 1.0	Program Utility	$10	Raffel, Matthew P.	404-394-8373; CIS:73113,2625
Lookie Here Fonts	Fonts	$5 SW	Jackson, Jacob A.	
LostFocus Field Validation	Form	Free	Price, N.	CIS:100063,3363
Lottery Numbers	Programming	Free	Riley, Ian	CIS:100445,2626
LRPAD String Padding	Text	Free	Harbolt, Martin L.	AOL:MartyDarts

Name	Type	Price	Vendor	Phone/E-mail
LstGrid	Listbox	Free	Gamber, Mark	CIS:76450,2754
LZH Compression DLL	Language Extension	Free	Taylor, Ian	44-706-353-412; CIS:100025,557
LZPACKIT.DLL	File Compression	Free		
Mabry Software Info And Produc	Text	Free	Mabry Software	206-634-1443; CIS:71231,2066; Inte
Macro Manager	Program Utility	$25	Ruzicka, John	415-566-9225; CIS:75160,2376
Mailslot.Vbx	Custom Control	$25	Mabry Software	206-634-1443; CIS:71231,2066
Make GRID.VBX Editable	Form	Free		
Mantec Code Library 1.5 Demo	Program Utility	$10	Mantec Development Group	
Many Things Screen Saver 3.0	Graphics	Free	McLean, Bruce	CIS:71413,2664
Mapping With Visual Basic	Graphics	$19	Educational & Business Systems	CIS:71003,1670
Marketing Demo	Programming	Free	Landau & Associates	
Marquee	Graphics	Free	Campbell, George	CIS:71571,222; BBS:805-528-3753
MaskDemo	Programming	Free		
Masked Input Using Text Box	Input Routines	Free	Craig, Bob	
Math Expression Evaluator	General	Free	Big Dog Software	908-885-1513; CIS:70744,1624
MathFlash	Educational	$15 CR	Kaufman, Brad	CIS:76330,1156
MC Bundle	DLL - General	Unknown	Renard, Michael	CIS:100042,3646
MCursor 2.0	Custom Control	$30	SoftLand Inc.	215-741-2030; CIS:73321,1525
MDB Guru 4.0	Database	$30 SW	Zero-1 Software	64-3-352-6481; CIS:100032,40
MDI Background Demo	Program Control	Free	Petersen, Karl E.	CIS:72302,3707
MDI Child Form From Dialog Box	Form	Free	Rutledge, Thomas	CIS:72223,1637
MDI Demo	Form	Free	Radford, Andrew	CIS:74151,2317
MDI Standard Application Shell	Form	Free	Blessing, John	CIS:100444,623
Media ID	Disk Utility	Free	Renard, Michael	CIS:100042,3646
MediaPlayer	Sound	$15	Mundy, Ward	BBS:706-746-5109
MemCheck	Program Utility	Unknown	Hawkes, Peter R.	Internet:prhawkes@msn.com
Memory Match 2.0	Game	Free	Marino, Lou	609-243-4979
Menu Embedding Demo	Menu	Free	Stewart, David	CIS:72122,3562
Menu Enable/Disable	Menu	Free		

Name	Type	Price	Vendor	Phone/E-mail
Menu Event Custom Control 3.2	Custom Control	$10 SW	Mabry Software	206-634-1443; CIS:71231,2066
Menu Help Text Custom C. 3.0	Help	$18 SW	Weimar Software	408-268-6638
Menudemo Custom Control	Custom Control	$15	Becker, Jeff	
MenuWatch Custom Control	Custom Control	$15 SW	Lathrop, Steve	CIS:70540,370
Mergewav	Sound	$25	Thomas, Neville W.	61-8-2967745; CIS:100026,1461
Message Blaster 2.2	Program Control	Free	Microsoft	206-882-8080; 800-992-3675
Message Box Boss	Form	$10	Burke, Eric	Internet:Ericburke@Aol.Com
Message Box Creator	Form	Free	Wallette, Nick	907-753-9263; CIS:71756,1207
Message Box Designer 1.9	Form	$15	Burnham, Gordon	502-363-5136
Message Box Editor	Listbox	$15 SW	Durocher, James	CIS:76061,3515; AOL:JDurocher
Message Box Generator 1.1	Programming	$10 SW	Taylor, Rick	CIS:70472,115
Message Box Helper	Form	Free	Hernandez, J. M.	CIS:70323,1772
Message Box Wizard	Program Utility	Free		
Message Spy Custom Control 2.1	Custom Control	$20 SW	Anton Software Limited	44-0-81-302-4373; CIS:100265,2172
Message.VBX 1.75	Programming	$10 SW	Digital PowerTOOLS	601-932-5931 CIS:74547,23
MessageBox Magic 1.0a	Form	$6	Extreme Software	602-494-4724; AOL:extremsoft
MessGbox 2.0	Program Utility	$7 SW	Collado, Louis	CIS:7220,1272
Meter	Program Control	Unknown		
Meter Bar Control	Custom Control	$12	Stubbs, Scott	CIS:73474,313
Metrix	Custom Control	Free	Wilkinson, Robert	602-493-0196; CIS:72730,3433
MicroHelp Demo Communications	Communications	Free	MicroHelp, Inc.	800-922-3383; 404-516-0899
Microsoft Jet Engine 2.0 Overv	Text	Free	Microsoft	206-882-8080; 800-992-3675
Microsoft Multimedia Viewer	Help	Free	Microsoft	206-882-8080; 800-992-3675
Microsoft Support Services 2.2	Text	Free	JSH Scientific	CIS:722030,1073
Microsoft Word 6.0 Viewer	Special	Free	Microsoft Product Support	206-454-2030
MIDI For Visual Basic	Sound	Free	Mainat, Josep M.	CIS:100414,1026
Midi MPU-401 Music Demo	DLL - Sound	Unknown	Graves, Michael Love	CIS:72240,1123
Midi Time Code Read/Write	Sound	Free	Mainat, Joseph M.	CIS:100414,1026
Minifile - INI File Help	Program Control	Free		

Name	Type	Price	Vendor	Phone/E-mail
MiniHelp Plus 3.2	Help	$25 SW	Arnote, Paul	Internet:Aerosolman@Aol.Com
Minimize Program Manager	Program Utility	Free	Warning, Mike	
MLISTBOX.VBX	Programming	Free	Grier, Dick	CIS:76244,1145
Modem Configuration Example	Communications	Free		
Module API Functions	System Utility	Free		
Module For 3D Effects.	Form	Free		
Moneybox Custom Control 1.79	Finance	$20 SW	Richards Software & Consulting	CIS:72262,1315
MoreAPI	Language Extension	Free		
Mouse Pointer Push and Pop	Misc.	Free	Bridge, Inc.	415-737-0870; CIS:71662,205
MouseKeeper 1.0b	Custom Control	$30 SW	JOSWare, Inc.	516-293-8915; CIS:71222,3522
Move Form Without Title Bar	Form	Free	Fawcette Technical Publication	415-917-7650; MCI:jfawcette
Movtxt	Programming	Free	Funk, Keith B.	CIS:72240,2020
MPopup 1.0	Custom Control	$15 SW	McKean Consulting	CIS:72622,1403
MQUERY	Database	Free	Smythe, Robert E.	CIS:71174,430
MRB Drop 'n' Comp	Programming	Free	Barnes, Nic	44-81-694-0110; CIS:100111,3452
MS Mega Pack 1.1	Custom Control	$90 SW	Mabry Software	206-634-1443; CIS:71231,2066
MSGBOX Code Generator	Form	Free	Bunton, Vernon	415-883-1503
MsgBox Editor	Program Utility	Free	GeoDuck Systems	206-324-9024; CIS:70671,1501
MsgBox Editor 2.1	Program Utility	Free	Pewitt, Woody	214-283-8426; CIS:71670,3203
MSGBOX Replacement - Non-Modal	Form	Free	Kornbluth, Aaron	
MsgBox3D - 3D Message Box 3.0	Custom Control	$19 SW	Bridge, Inc.	415-737-0870; CIS:71662,205
MSGDemo	Programming	Free	Campbell, George	CIS:71571,222; BBS:805-528-3753
MSLOT - W4WG Mailslot CC 1.2	Custom Control	$30 SW	Mabry Software	206-634-1443; CIS:71231,2066
MSlot.Vbx	Mail	Unknown	Thomas, Zane	206-297-8012; CIS:72060,3327
Multi Language Messenger VBX	Custom Control	$37 SW	PTAHSoft	CIS:75240,664
Multi-Button Control	Custom Control	Free	Gamber, Mark	CIS:76450,2754
Multi-Purpose Combobox Control	Listbox	$10 SW	McKean Consulting	CIS:72622,1403
Multi-Select List Box	Listbox	Free	Hamilton, Peter	CIS:73774,3661
Multicolumn Listbox	Listbox	Free	PC HELP-LINE	909-797-3091; CIS:72357,3523

Name	Type	Price	Vendor	Phone/E-mail
Multicolumn Listbox VBX 4.55	Listbox	$10 SW	McKean Consulting	CIS:72622,1403
MultiFSR Meter 1.0	System Utility	$12	Griffith, Matthew W.	CIS:76531,2651
Multigrid	Form	Free	Desai, Anand	
Multimedia Button VBX 1.3a	Custom Control	Unknown	Boelzner, Edward J.	CIS:71740,3121
Multimedia Demo	Graphics	Free	Trimble Technologies	619-599-0733; CIS:76306,1115
Multimedia Help Viewer	Help	Free	McGregor, Rob	
Multimedia VBX Button Demo	Custom Control	$38 SW	Stedy Software	
Multipic	Buttons	Free	Gamber, Mark	CIS:76450,2754
Multipik	Programming	Free		
Multiple App Project Launcher	Program Utility	Free	Truesdale, Greg	CIS:74131,2175
Multiple Language Resource DLL	Internationalizatn	Unknown	Little, Thomas	CIS:100016,2355
Multiple Selection File List	Buttons	Free	Guardalben, Giovanni	39-45-592966
Multiple Server Example	Communications	Free	Johnson, L. J.	
Multisel	Listbox	Free	Gamber, Mark	CIS:76450,2754
MultiText	Text	$25 SW	Bannister, Steve	44-01604-719413
MWATCH.DLL	Programming	$73	User Friendly, Inc.	202-387-1949; CIS:76702,1605
MyMemory Game	Game	Free	Rogers, Dirk	
Naming Conventions	Text	Free	Dolson, Jim	
NavButton Custom Control	Custom Control	$5	Theis, H. Eric., Jr.	CIS:76270,1533
NCALC Keyboard Handling	Calculator	Free	Smaby, Marcus	CIS:72571,3126
NetCode Control 1.30	Custom Control	$30	DevSoft Inc.	CIS:75244,2736 AOL:Devsoft
NetPrn	Programming	Free	Krumsee, Art	CIS:76702,1526
NetVBX	Communications	$35 SW	Huon, Benoit	
NetWare API Test For VB	Data Access	Free	Novell Inc.	512-794-1488; 800-733-9673
Netware Bindery Browser	Communications	Free	Johnston, Scott	CIS:72677,1570
NetWare Interface For VB	Data Access	Free	Novell Inc.	512-794-1488; 800-733-9673
Network Control VBX	Custom Control	$35 SW	Wright Futures, Inc.	
New Composite Controls	Programming	Free		
Newstart	System Utility	Free	Elkins, Jeff	

Name	Type	Price	Vendor	Phone/E-mail
NiftoMeter Custom Control	Custom Control	$7 SW	Noonan, Timothy D.	416-261-7866; CIS:70751,1647
Nisus Missile Master 2.70	Game	$17	Nisus Development & Technology	CIS:73730,761
NoBeep	Listbox	Free	Leckkett, Blaine	
NOBOOT - Ctrl-Alt-Del Disable	System Utility	Free	Mabry Software	206-634-1443; CIS:71231,2066
Nodes Database Grid	Database	Free	Macedob, Antonio	CIS:75210,3332
NoGhost	Program Control	Free	Blaum, Greg	CIS:71212,1763
Nomove Example Unmovable Form	Form	Free	Marquette Computer Consultants	415-459-0835; CIS:70413,3405
Number	Language Extension	Free	Marquis Computing, Inc.	203-963-7065; 800-818-1611
Number Crunch	Game	$5 SW	Persky, Jonathan D.	Internet:jonpersky@aol.com
Number To Text	Language Extension	Free	Martinez, Brad	AOL:BradDuder
Numbers Game	Game	Free	Huss, Dennis L.	
NUMWIN HWND Finder CC 3.8	Custom Control	$18 SW	Weimar Software	408-268-6638
Object Library 1.2	Program Utility	Unknown	Exile Software	CIS:100267,546
ODBC Sniffer For Windows 1.1	Data Access	$295	Mercury Interactive Corp.	800-837-8911; 408-523-9900
Odometer - System Resource Mon	Desktop	Free		
Odometer Custom Control 2.0	Custom Control	$40 SW	Global Majik Software	CIS:73261,3642
Ogmess Network Lan Messaging	Communications	$5	Chavez, Steven R.	
OLE Destination Example	Communications	Free	Febish, George J.	201-816-8900
OLE Object-To-Bitmap 1.3	Graphics	Free	McCreary, Jeremy	CIS:72341,3716
OLE To ODBC2 Using VB3 Objects	Database	Free	Kosten, Michael	CIS:71520,161
OLE-Obj <-> Database Tables	Data Access	Free	Schloter, Martin	
On Top - Keeps One Form On Top	Form	Free	Sigler, John	CIS:71631,776
One Note Midi	Sound	Free	Artic Software	800-892-0677; 414-534-4309
Orbital Motion	Graphics	Free	Brown, Nathan	
Order Form	Programming	Free		
Orient	Printer	$10 SW	Poellinger, Paul F.	CIS:70732,3576; AOL:Pfpelican
Other Fonts In Menu	Fonts	Free	PTAHSoft	CIS:75240,664
Outline Control 1.3	DLL - General	$75 SW	Abel, Todd J.	CIS:73611,1023
Outline Control Sorting	Programming	Free		

Name	Type	Price	Vendor	Phone/E-mail
OutReach For Windows DEMO	Custom Control	Unknown	InterGroup Technologies	206-643-8089
OXButton 2.1c	Custom Control	$19 SW	Opaque Software	CIS:70621,3034; CIS:74777,3227
OXDisplay 1.0b	Programming	$22 SW	Opaque Software	CIS:70621,3034; CIS:74777,3227
OXDisplay 1.0b	Programming	$22 SW	Opaque Software	CIS:70621,3034; CIS:74777,3227
Pack	Program Utility	Free	Summers, Judy	CIS:70771,1444
Paradox Engine Demo	Database	Unknown	Jaster, John	CIS:73770,2233
Paradox Engine Interface	DLL Interface	Free	Dooley, Sharon F.	CIS:70740,2330
Parameter Queries	Reference	Free		
PARAMS	Form	Free	Carr, J. Frank	404-880-5762; CIS:75120,2420
Parse Demo Project 2.0	Text	Free	Reynolds, Paul	CIS:71011,2040
Parser - Evaluate Formulas	Calculator	Free	Tricaud, Christophe	33-1-43-20-51-08; CIS:100412,2653
Passing Character String DLL	Language Extension	Free	Aylor, Bill	
Passing Selection Formulas-CRW	Reference	Free	Crystal Services	604-681-3435; 604-681-2934
Password	Programming	$5	Janes, Matthew	
Patch Kit for Access Apps.	Misc.	Unknown	Hanson, Michael E.	CIS:75143,126
Patterns	Graphics	Free	Speranza, Paul	
PBClone Windows Library 2.0	DLL - General	$12 SW	Hanlin III, Thomas G.	
PC Mag Guide To API Updates	Reference	Free	Desaware	408-377-4770; CIS:74431,3534
PCDone.DLL Status Bar	DLL - General	$18 SW	Abri Technologies Inc.	304-947-7129; CIS:72345,1623
PCSSave Screen Saver	Graphics	Free	PCSWare (Paul Coombes)	CIS:100413,155
PDOComm For Windows Demo	DLL - Communicatio	$149	Crescent Software Inc.	203-438-5300; CIS:72657,3070
Peacock - Color By Name Databa	Programming	$23SW	Maplerow Brothers Software	CIS:72047,2134; Internet:Phila@Sgte.com
Peeper 1.15 Version Info	System Utility	$23 SW	Fineware Systems	CIS:70650,2022
Peer Evaluation System	Business	Unknown	Gibson, Steve	
Percentage Bar Control 2.6	Custom Control	$10 SW	Mabry Software	206-634-1443; CIS:71231,2066
PerfectTAB 1.0	Form	Free	Bytes & Letters	49-6831-506534; CIS:100275,3554
Personal Helper	Help	$15	FAR, Inc.	CIS:70043,1652
Pic Clip Tool (For VB2Pro)	Graphics	Free	Freel, Fred	CIS:70642,673
PicClip Viewer	Graphics	Free		

Name	Type	Price	Vendor	Phone/E-mail
PicScroll -Scroll Picture DEMO	Graphics	$50	Bennet-Tec Information Serv.	516-433-6283; CIS:71201,1075
PICTAB Picture Box Tabs	Form	Free	Crouse, Aaron P.	614-235-5341; CIS:72123,1243
Picture Boxes As Controls	Form	$5	Pozharov, Vitaliy	AOL:VitaliyP
Picture Button CC 1.1	Custom Control	$15	Mabry Software	206-634-1443; CIS:71231,2066
Picture-Button Demo	Programming	Free		
Pizazz 1.3 Custom Control	Custom Control	$30	Visual Bits	CIS:70402,3651
Pointers.DLL 1.1	Language Extension	Unknown	Blaum, Greg	CIS:71212,1763
Polygon	Graphics	Free	Mack, Jim	CIS:76630,2012
Popup Calendar 3.00	Calendar	$10	Wessex Systems	CIS:100112,2164; 44-1202-546466
Popup Help VB Source	Help	Free		
Popup Lunar Calendar Demo 3/95	Calendar	$15 SW	Crazy Rides	905-712-9824; CIS:74072,3600
Popup Menu Custom Control	Custom Control	$30 SW	Mullins, Robert	
Popup Menu Problem Fix	Menu	Free	Liblick, Dathan	CIS:74663,1364
PopUp Menu Reentrancy Problem	Form	Free		
Port I/O For Visual Basic	Custom Control	Free	Venema, John E.	CIS:100033,1415
Power Buttons	Program Control	Free	Tanner, Ron	303-689-0720; CIS:75170,176
Power Page 1.09	Communications	$25 SW	Haynes, Chris	CIS:73642,3626
Power Toolz Code Manager	Program Utility	$50 SW	BKMA Inc.	CIS:71251,1771
Power.DLL	DLL Interface	$20 SW	Bytes & Letters	49-6831-506534; CIS:100275,3354
PowerTABLE 1.1 Data Manager	Database	$49 SW	Dart Communications	315-841-8106; Internet:sales@dart.com
PowerTCP Demo	Communications	$598	Poellinger, Paul F.	CIS:70732,3576
PpFont	Fonts	$10 SW	Poellinger, Paul F.	CIS:70732,3576
PPRTR 4.4	DLL - General	$10 SW	Aardvark Software Inc.	201-833-4355; 800-482-2742
Pretty Print For VB 2.1	Program Utility	$86	Aardvark Software Inc.	201-833-4355; 800-482-2742
Pretty Printer Notes	Text	Unknown	Barnett, Clifford	
Print Clip CB	Program Utility	Free	Barnett, Clifford	
Print Clipboard	Printer	Free	I.I.G. Development	
Print Code As You Want 3.0b	Program Utility	$45	Nolte, Barry	604-689-8345; 604-689-8997
Print DLL Test Application	Printer	Free		

Name	Type	Price	Vendor	Phone/E-mail
Print Manager Switch 1.3	System Utility	Free	Morris, Jeffrey	CIS:70751,1565
Print Multiline Textbox	Printer	Free		
Print Preview DEMO	Printer	$30	Phase II Software	206-216-0772
Print Previewer 2.0 DEMO	Graphics	$30	Lee, Joseph	CIS:74013,3316
PrintClip	Printer	Unknown	Krumsee, Art	CIS:76702,1526
PrintEnvelope	Envelopes	$29 SW	Maurer Associates	CIS:74017,2140
Printer Lines Per Page	Printer	Free	Obeda, Ed	510-713-0814; CIS:72537,163
Printer Pick / Printer Cancel	Printer	Free	PC HELP-LINE	
Printer SetUp	Printer	Unknown	Programmer's Warehouse	602-443-0580; CIS:73240,2734
Printer Setup	Programming	Free	Palmer, Joe	
Printer Setup (CK)	Printer	Free	Kitsos, Costas	CIS:73667,1755
Printers' Apprentice 5.8	Fonts	$20 SW	Lose Your Mind Software	215-275-7034; CIS:70564,2372
PrintFile Altern. To Spoolfile	Printer	Free	Johnston, Scott	CIS:72677,1570
PrintForm DEMO	Printer	Unknown	KWG Software	49-531-72982; CIS:100010,204
Printing Forms	Printer	Free	Tisoft S.A.	33-1-43205108; CIS:100412,2653
PrintVB	Program Utility	$15	Brant, Kyle	317-297-9801; CIS:74220,2420
ProEssentials 1.5	Graphics	$395	Gigasoft, Inc.	817-431-8470
Professional Toolkit Control C	Custom Control	$10	Obeda, Ed	510-713-0814; CIS:72537,163
Profile	Language Extension	Free		
Profile	Programming	Free	Hegerty, Chad	CIS:71212,1045
ProgGuide	Programming	Free		
Program Manager Example	Program Control	Free	Conger, Scott	
Program Picker	Programming	$5	Force 12	203-444-7954; CIS:70740,2472
Programmatic Database Creation	Database	Free	Dirigible Software	310-614-9466; AOL:PROGRAM396
Programmers Icon Pack Vol. 1	Icon Utility	Free	Creativision Graphics	817-656-5970; CIS:70404,3014
Programmers Tool Kit	Educational	$28	Influential Technologies, Inc.	
Programming Conventions (MS)	Programming	Unknown	Microsoft	206-882-8080; 800-992-3675
Project Doc 2.2	Program Utility	$20 SW	Software Factory UK Ltd.	CIS:100023,3177
Project Manager For VB Win 3.2	Program Utility	$40 SW	A.F. Street Consulting	705-292-5502; CIS:72152,333

Name	Type	Price	Vendor	Phone/E-mail
ProjectSnap 1.0	Program Utility	$25	Caladonia Systems, Inc.	206-759-2325; CIS:70711,3300
Prompt Control	Custom Control	$15 SW	Dean, Andrew S.	404-874-6938; CIS:71233,1412
Properties On Top	Program Utility	See docs	Sauve, Eric	CIS:73304,3541
Propview.VBX	Program Control	Unknown	Merriman, Loren	CIS:76701,156
PS-Out 1.0	Graphics	Free	Stephen Cramp	
PSetup	Programming	Unknown		
PSound	Prog. - Sound	Unknown		
Pulsar	Printer	$15 SW	Tesserax Information Systems	714-840-8822; CIS:72247,1463
Pushbutton Control	Custom Control	Free	Gamber, Mark	CIS:76450,2754
PX Create	Programming	Unknown	OutRider Systems	713-726-0386; 800-845-0386
Q+E Database/VB Documentation	Reference	Unknown	Intersolv/Q+E Software	919-859-2220; 800-876-3101
QB-VB Converter	Program Utility	Unknown	TransSend Technology	CIS:72457,2444
QCARDS.DLL	Graphics	Free	Murphy, Stephen	CIS:70661,2461
Qsearch.Dll	Disk Utility	Free	Simms, Jeff	301-593-6067; CIS:72200,3173
QSetup	Disk Utility	$10	Stillwater Systems	CIS:72643,604
Query Def Utility 1.2	Database	$10 SW	Winworks Software Corp.	CIS:74211,2503
Queue Watch	Printer	Unknown	Landgrave, Tim	800-223-8720; CIS:71760,12
Quick And Dirty Help 3.0	Help	$49 SW	Allen, Phil	CIS:72047,2134
Quickform Form Generator 2.0	Form	$20	Mass, Martin	418-624-9596; CIS:75034,1755
Quickhelp Tooltip VBX	Custom Control	Free	Steingraeber Fachverlag	49-431-563212; CIS:100111,3245
QuitWin	System Utility	$9 SW	MarilynSoft	
RandGrid 1.0	Language Extension	Unknown	Ford, Nelson	CIS:71355,470
RAS (WFW) Declarations	Communications	Free	Zieglar, Adam	CIS:72147,2221
RASCall 1.0	Communications	Free	Zieglar, Adam	CIS:72147,2221
RASVBX RemoteAccessServer 1.34	Custom Control	$45	Cutting Edge Consulting Inc.	716-271-6391; CIS:74362,2163
RDB Clipboard Tool	Custom Control	$5 SW	Thomas, Zane	206-297-8012 CIS:72060,3327
RDB Library 1.4	Programming	Free	Bacon, Royce D.	414-462-3418 CIS:70042,1001
Rdonly.Dll	General	Free	Simms, Jeff	301-593-6067; CIS:72200,3173
ReadForms	Program Utility	Free	Ludwig, Bill	CIS:76516,1274

Name	Type	Price	Vendor	Phone/E-mail
Reading And Writing INI Files	File Management	Free	Marquette Computer Consultants	415-459-0835; CIS:70413,3405
Record Numbers Demo	Database	Free		
Reformat Utility	Data Access	Free		
Refresh Demo	Form	Free	Hartquist, Peter	
Register Management	Setup	Free		
Registration Creator	Language Extension	$41	Hutchings, Donathan	
Registration Information	Program Utility	Free	Renard, Michael	CIS:100042,3646
Registration Key 3.1	Security	$24	Pirie, Brian	FIDO:1:243/8; Internet:Brian@bpecom
Report Generator For VB	Programming	Free	Hobson, Graham	
Resistor Color Codes	Graphics	Free	Sheppard, Brian	
Resize And Move Controls	Buttons	Free		
ReSize Custom Control 2.0	Custom Control	$34	Larcom And Young	CIS:70555,312
Resource Bar	Desktop	$2	Denihan, Timothy J.	817-468-8237; CIS:70600,745
Resource Monitor VBX 1.1	Custom Control	Free	Stefanik, Michael J.	CIS:72202,1427
Resource-Only DLL For Bitmaps	Graphics	Free	ImageSoft Inc.	516-767-2233; 800-245-8840
Restricting Mouse Movement	Form	Free	Leckett, Elaine	CIS:73730,761
Retrieve Disk Volume Serial #	Disk Utility	Free	Mohler, David S.	CIS:76450,1642
Revisited Generic Application	Programming	Free	Perrin, Charles L.	
RI-VB Database Toolkit	Database	$34	MIS Resources International	404-640-3400; CIS:75350,205
RIGHTMOUS Help Text CC 3.8	Help	$19 SW	Weimar Software	408-268-6638
RoboHELP DEMO Animation	Help	Free	Blue Sky Software	619-459-6365; 800-677-4946
Roll'em	Game	$1 CR	Lewellen, Kirk	BBS:615-890-8715
Rosettes Screensaver	Misc.	Unknown	Bennis, Robert G.	Internet:rgb7795@aol.com
Rotate.Dll	Graphics	$25 SW	Dragon Software	304-584-4143; BBS:304-363-2252
Rotated Label CC 2.0	Custom Control	$15	Mabry Software	206-634-1443; CIS:71231,2066
Rotato	Pen Windows	Unknown	Michael	CIS:74237,151
Round Function	Calculator	Free	Grabe, Marcus O. M.	49-89-346916;: CIS:100120,1405
RPN Calculator	Calculator	PD		
RTFMagic Help File Generator	Help	$20 SW	Bainbridge Knowledge Mgmt.	CIS:71251,1771

Name	Type	Price	Vendor	Phone/E-mail
Runfix - Minimizes Apps	Program Utility	Free	Mezaros, Mike	CIS:75300,1642
Ruthie	Educational	$5 CR	Murdoch, John	CIS:71507,1212
Sam Spade Runtime Debugger	Program Utility	$10 SW	KnowledgeWorks	CIS:72310,2614
Sample	Database	Unknown		
Sample MDI With Child Windows	Form	Free	Schmitt, Hans-Jochen	Internet:hajo@bwl.bwl.th-darmstadt.de
Save Me	Programming	Free	Irwin, Gregg	CIS:72450,676
ScaKey Custom Control	Custom Control	Free		
Scale Custom Control	Custom Control	Free	Venugopalan, Vivek	CIS:73512,3675
Scary Time	Clock / Fonts	Free	Zeitman, Dan	
SCFILE 2.0	Program Utility	$30 SW	Garrison, Gary P.	612-541-0144; CIS:76400,3555
Schedule	Productivity	Free	Kosten, Michael	CIS:71520,161
Scoper	Program Utility	$19	ISES, Inc.	CIS:72417,627
Scraper VBX 1.1	Custom Control	$55 SW	Northeast Data Corp.	716-247-5934
Screen Saver	Language Extension	Free	User Friendly, Inc.	202-387-1949; CIS:76702,1605
Screen Saver DEMO	Graphics	$20	Hudson, James A.	CIS:75317,232; AOL:JHoudini
Screen Saver Demo	Graphics	$20 SW	INside	
Screen Saver Launcher	Special	Free	Coope, Geoff	
Screen Size Template	Form	Free	MJ-Datatechnic GbR	CIS:100442,644
Screen Tester Utility 2.0	Form	Free	Carr, J. Frank	404-880-5762; CIS:75120,2420
Scroll	Programming	Unknown		
Scroll Demo	Form	Free		
Scroll Text	Form	Free		
SCRTEST Demo Of Browser/Scroll	Database	Free	Whittaker, Ross	CIS:100275,317
Search A List Box	Listbox	Free		
Searching For Windows	Language Extension	Unknown		
SearchHistory	Language Extension	$15	Chiselbrook, Craig	CIS:74650,3571; AOL:CraigChis
Security Example	General	Free	Miller, Bill	
See VB 0.99	Program Utility	Free	Collier, Jim	CIS:71064,130
Seek Table Object From Listbox	Listbox	Free		

Name	Type	Price	Vendor	Phone/E-mail
Selector/Knob VBX 2.0	Custom Control	$40	Global Majik Software	CIS:73261,3642
Self Expanding Grid	Form	Free	O'Roarke, Peter	
Sending Escape Sequences	Programming	Free	Hutmacher, Dave Th.	CIS:100012,74
Sendmessage API Listbox	Programming	Free		
Serialization	Setup	Free	JSS Inc, Steve Shiavo	
Setparent Demonstrations	Form	Free	Barrett, Simon	44-0-874-636835; CIS:100102,1247
SETUP Enhancement By Barrett	Program Utility	$12	Indigo Rose Corporation	800-665-9668; 204-668-8180
Setup Factory 3.03	Program Utility	$250	Chevron, Denis	33-1-40726483; CIS:100333,27
Setup Studio 2.4	Program Utility	$50 SW	Venugopalan, Vivek	CIS:73512,3675
Shaded Blue Setup	Program Utility	Free	Weimar Software	408-268-6638
Shadowbox Popup Window CC 3.8	Custom Control	$18 SW	Snyder, James Wj	CIS:75141,3544 AOL:JamesWJS
SHARE Install During Setup	Setup	Free	Caughran, Mike	C.S:71034,2371
Shell And Wait	Program Control	Free	Wykes, Harry	CIS:100014,2573
Shell Sort Example	Programming	Free		
Sheridan Datagrid Cut/Copy	Text	Free	PDA, Inc.	CIS:71150,3407; AOL:MailPDA
Show - VBX Demos	Custom Control	Free	Allen, Phil	CIS:72047,2134
Show Environment	System Utility	$10 SW	Geron, Israel	
Shrink Icon Capture Utility	Icon Utility	Free	Falconer, Jay J.	CIS:72074,2677
Shrink VB EXE Up To 50%	Program Utility	Free	Elkins, Jeff	GEnie:J.ELKINS1
Simon1	Game	Free	Liedtke, Brian	49-6181-47710; CIS:100140,2534
Simple 3D VBX	Custom Control	$18 SW	De Bruijn, Michiel	CIS:100021,1061; Internet:Mdb@Vbd.NI
Simplfax - Link Winfax Pro	Communications	Free	Raike, William	CIS:100236,1656
SIZ Form Sizer Custom Control	Custom Control	$15 SW	Anton Software Limited	44-0-81-302-4373; CIS:100265,2172
Skeleton VBX Source Code	Custom Control	$50 SW	Page, Preston	CIS:71712,1473
Sleepless Nights Fx CCs	Custom Control	$35 SW	Skisoft Software	CIS:73042,3371; Internet:skibby@aol.com
Slide Show 1.0	Graphics	$10 SW		
Slider	Program Control	$10 SW	Northeast Data Corp.	716-247-5934
Slider VBX Control 2.2	Custom Control	$55 SW	Global Majik Software	CIS:73261,3642
Slider/Meter VBX 2.0	Custom Control	$40		

Name	Type	Price	Vendor	Phone/E-mail
SmartDoc 1.2	Help	$25 SW	Oakley Data Services	44-0270-759359; CIS:100024,1763
SmtHlp	Help	Unknown	Bytes & Letters	49-6831-506534; CIS:100275,3554
Snatch	Programming	Free	Bergh, Arild	
Sndbite Wave Embedding CC	Sound	$28 SW	Maplerow Brothers Software	CIS:72047,2134; Internet:Phila@Sgtec.com
SocketWrench Custom Control	Communications	Free	Catalyst Software	818-879-1144; CIS:72202,1427; AOL:M
Softcraft Graphic CC DEMO	Graphics	$295	Softcraft, Inc.	608-257-3300; 800-351-0500
Some Information About Windows	Prog. - Sys. Util.	Free	Phares, Wayne	Internet:Phares@Rsi.Prc.Com
Sort Demonstration	Special	Free		
Sorts	Programming	Free	Dacon, Tom	CIS:71062,426
Sound	Sound	Free		
Soundex	Language Extension	Free	User Friendly, Inc.	202-387-1949; CIS:76702,1605
Soundex And Metaphone CC 1.4	Text	$10	Mabry Software	206-634-1443; CIS:71231,2066
Soundex Word Matching CC 3.8	Custom Control	$18 SW	Weimar Software	408-268-6638
SoundEX/Metaphone VBX	Custom Control	Free	Porter, Todd	CIS:102024,3256
Source Code Tool Box DEMO	Database	$25	Bear Hug, The	
SourcePrinter 1.20	Program Utility	$25 SW	Ansuini, Doug	CIS:74012,2555
SpaceTime	Program Utility	Free	Paul James Barrett	CIS:71020,2624
Spell Checker API Sample	Special	Free		
Spelmate Spell Checker 1.2	Text	$50 SW	Herron, James	44-41-762-0967
Spin Control Plug In Code	Form	$10	Anno Domini, Inc.	
Spinlist Demo	DLL - Graphics	Unknown	OSoft Development Corporation	404-233-1392
Splash Libraries	Form	$20 SW	HSC Software Developers	314-530-7647
Splash Screen Demo	Form	Free	SoftCircuits Programming	CIS:72134,263
SpSound Routines	Sound	Free	Giordano, Alfred J.	914-783-2526; CIS:76407,143
SPush VBX Demo	Custom Control	Free	Jwpc, Inc.	Internet:JwpcEMail@Aol.Com
SPY:FRX Graphics Recovery	Program Utility	Free	Koot, Andre	CIS:100120,2360
SQL 2 Variable	Database	Free	Ferguson, Jim	919-799-4396; CIS:71477,2345
SQL Data Administrator 1.3 DEM	Data Access	Unknown	DataTools	800-987-0421; 615-987-0421
SQL Sniffer For Windows	Data Access	$295	Blue Lagoon Software	818-345-2200; BBS:818-343-8433

Name	Type	Price	Vendor	Phone/E-mail
SQL Test	Data Access	See docs	Weaver, Peter R.	
SQLsmts: SQL Statements	Database	Free		
StarBar For Windows	Sound	Unknown	Gerton, David	
Statbar Status Bar VBX	Custom Control	$10	WingedAxe Software, Inc.	CIS:73764,3540
Status	Program Utility	$10	Staffin, Ed	908-253-0246
Status Bar	Language Extension	$10 SW	Staffin, Ed	908-253-0246
Status Bar Custom Control	Custom Control	$20	Mabry Software	206-634-1443; CIS:71231,2066
Status Bar Demo 2.0	General	Free	Rodriguez, M. John	CIS:100321,620
StatusBar Control	Custom Control	Free	Beekes, Bernd	CIS:100031,2063; 49-2261-55369
StatusFX V2.5 Standard Edition	Custom Control	$35 SW	Megabyte Services	800-242-4775; CIS:73422,3565
StatusFX V3.0 Itn'l. Edition	Custom Control	$45	Megabyte Services	800-242-4775; CIS:73422,3565
Steve's Find And Replace	Text	Free		
Steve's OLE 2.0 ProgMan	System Utility	Free	Peschka, Steve	CIS:71722,55
Steve's VB Spell	Spellcheck	Free	Peschka, Steve	CIS:71722,55
STMOUS Help Text CC 3.8	Help	$18 SW	Weimar Software	408-268-6638
Stock Index	Communications	Free	Visual Basic Programmer's Jrnl	800-848-5523; 415-917-7650
Stom.Dll	File Compression	$25 SW	Dragon Software	3C4-584-4143; BBS:304-363-2252
Store/Display Pictures In MDB	Graphics	Free	Luhring, Mark	AOL:MLuhring
Stretch	Graphics	Free	Crouse, Aaron P.	614-235-5341; CIS:72123,1243
StrField	Programming	Free	Williams, Cris	
String Encryption	Language Extension	Free	Albrecht, Karl D.	AOL:Karl25
String To Bitmap	Language Extension	Free	Monasterio, Jorge	CIS:72147,2674
String.DLL String Manipulation	DLL - General	Free	INside	
Strip	Program Utility	Unknown	Quarles, Mark J.	601-932-5931; CIS:74547,23
StrPlus.DLL	DLL - General	$10 SW	Digital PowerTOOLS	44-376-517-206; CIS:100116,1031
Subdoc 2.1	Program Utility	$35 SW	Fox, Peter	202-387-1949; CIS:76702,1605
Subform Simulation Sample	Form	Free	User Friendly, Inc.	
Suite Of Calculators Demo	Calculator	$15	Owens, Mike	404-472-9017; CIS:75037,2625
SuperButton	Custom Control	$58	Manfred Walmeyer	

Name	Type	Price	Vendor	Phone/E-mail
SuperSpin	Buttons	Free	Slagman, Herman	CIS:100101,131
Switch	Game	$5 SW	Persky, Jonathan D.	Internet:jonpersky@aol.com
Syscolor Module	Form	Free	Bamber, Gordon	CIS:74437,672
System Color Finder	Desktop	Free	Conger, Scott	
System Info	System Utility	$10	Mundy, Ward	BBS:706-746-5109
System Sound Shuffler Part One	Prog. - Sound	Free	Stine, Brian D.	CIS:73617,323
System Sound Shuffler Part Two	Sound	Free	Stine, Brian D.	CIS:73617,323
Tab Demo	Form	$10 SW	Gamesman Inc.	204-475-7903; 800-670-8045
Tab/VBX Demo	Custom Control	Contact	FarPoint Technologies, Inc.	919-460-1887; 800-645-5913
Tabbed Dialog Box Control	Form	$35	Ashton Information Services	
Tabbed Dialog Box Example	Form	Free	Eke, Richard	CIS:100031,233
Tabbed Dialogs	Form	Free	Fehr, Andreas	CIS:100042,2070; Internet:afehr@itr.ch
TabFrame 1.4 Demo	Form	$40 SW	GC Consulting Services Ltd.	44-335-370562; CIS:100113,2774
TabFrame 1.4.1 Upgrade	Form	Unknown	GC Consulting Services Ltd.	44-335-370562; CIS:100113,2774
TabFrame, ToolTip, Toolbar Dem	Custom Control	$85	GC Consulting Services Ltd.	44-335-370562; CIS:100113,2774
Table Doc	Database	Free	Nelson, John R.	CIS:70641,3562
Tablenette	Game	Free	Sycomp Limited	
Tabs2	Form	Free	Crawford, Ross	CIS:100354,677
Tag Environment Subsystem	Programming	Free	Dacon, Tom	CIS:71062,426
Task Killer	Program Utility	$15 SW	Hyperion Microsystems	CIS:76370,3353
Taskbar Like Win'95	Misc.	SW	Lee, Joseph	CIS:74013,3316
Tasklist 1.0 Revised	System Utility	Free	De Bruijn, Michiel	CIS:100021,1061; Internet:Mdb@Vbd.Nl
TBAR21 Toolbar Custom Control	Custom Control	$20 SW	McKean Consulting	CIS:72622,1403
Template MDI Demo	Program Utility	$15 SW	INside	
Test For Calculator Bug	Calculator	Free	Holland, Sarah	CIS:70620,1425
Test Pentium	Reference	Free		
TestIni	Programming	Free	Tisoft S.A.	33-1-43205108; CIS:100412,2653
TestLay	Listbox	Free	Bridge, Inc.	415-737-0870; CIS:71662,205
Testres	Program Utility	Free	MJ-Datatechnic GbR	CIS:100442,644

Name	Type	Price	Vendor	Phone/E-mail
Text Editor	Programming	Free	Huskins, Douglas A.	
Text File To VB Help	Help	Free	Rivers, Jerry	
Text Justification Function	Listbox	Free	Trimble, Daniel	
TextBox Plus 1.0	Listbox	Free	Irwin, Gregg	CIS:72450,676
Textbox Styles	Listbox	$17	SNS Software	CIS:72640,1442
The Creator	Programming	Free	Forbes, Garry	CIS:76207,333
The Nag	Program Utility	Free	Integrated Data Systems, Inc.	818-223-3344; CIS:73700,1622
Thermometer Demo	Program Control	Unknown	Thunder Island Inc.	CIS:74777,2544
Thunder Bars Bar Codes DEMO	Custom Control	$33	Software Savants	CIS:70404,1563
Thunderbolt For VB 1.04	Program Utility	Free	Renard, Michael	CIS:100042,3646
Time 2 Win Hints	Text	$65 SW	Leaning Birch Computer Cons.	207-443-1664; CIS:72617,1770
Time And Billing For Windows	Business	$25 SW	ISbiSTER International	
Time And Chaos	Productivity	$1	John Galt Software	
Time And Date Stamp	Program Utility	Free	Snider, Charles K.	CIS:73730,1315
Time Bandits	Productivity	$5S W	Leithauser Research	
Time It	Productivity	$61	Renard, Michael	CIS:100042,3646
Time To Win (615)	DLL - General	$43	Renard, Michael	CIS:100042,3646
Time To Win Light	DLL - General	Free	Jaster, John	CIS:73770,2233
TimeTrak	Database	$20	Marquis Computing, Inc.	203-963-7065; 800-818-1611
Tip Of The Day	Programming	$5	Graham, Glenn	CIS:72662,2733
Tip Of The Day With Editor	Form	$15 SW	Mabry Software	206-634-1443; CIS:71231,2066
Tips - Tool Tips VBX	Custom Control	$24	Anno Domini, Inc.	
Tips Of The Day	Educational	$40	SoftLand Inc.	215-741-2030; CIS:73321,1525
TitleSpy 5.0	Custom Control	Unknown	Noble, Jason R.	
TLBox	Misc.	$6 SW	Schoeffel, Dave	
To Do List	Productivity	$40 SW	Global Majik Software	CIS:73261,3642
Toggle Switch Control 1.02	Custom Control	Free	Shiavo, Steve	
Togglprt	Printer	Free	Bassal, Thomas	49-89-772291; CIS:100276,1324
Tom's Happy Constants	Program Utility			

Name	Type	Price	Vendor	Phone/E-mail
Tool Palette Program Launcher	Desktop	SW	Lee, Joseph	CIS:74013,3316
Toolbar Button & Statusbar CCs	Custom Control	$60	Westacott, Andrew	CIS:100023,702
Toolbar Custom Control 1.1	Custom Control	$20 SW	Washington, Winefred	CIS:72070,3713
Toolbar Custom Control 3.0	Custom Control	$7	McKean Consulting	CIS:72622,1403
Toolbar Demonstration	Programming Demo	Free	Milbery, Jim	
Toolbar Demonstration	Desktop	Free		
Toolbar Source 1.1a	Desktop	Free	Fehr, Andreas	CIS:100042,2070
Toolbox	Program Control	Free	Williamson, Gary	CIS:70600,1751
Toolbox On Top	Program Utility	Free	Carr, J. Frank	404-880-5762; CIS:75120,2420
Toolbox With Mini Title Bar	Desktop	Free	Barham, Tim	Internet:expired
ToolButton 2.0	Custom Control	Free	Foster, Brett	
Tools On Top 1.0	Program Utility	$10	Bits & Bytes Solutions	206-328-1523; CIS:72603,1674
ToolTip Demo 1.4	Custom Control	$40	GC Consulting Services Ltd.	44-335-370562; CIS:100113,2774
Tooltips Bar Sample	Language Extension	Free	Crouse, Aaron P.	614-235-5341; CIS:72123,1243
TPW2VB	Programming	$20 SW	Opaque Software	CIS:70621,3034; CIS:74777,3227
Trace Plus ODBC 2.0	Communications	$110	Systems Software Technology	818-346-2784; CIS:70233,2504
TrafficLight	Entertainment	Unknown	Brody, Evan	
Trap Access Error	Database	Free	Okapi (Pat Hayes)	805-257-3377; CIS:74437,134
Trapper 2.1	Programming	$10	Presley, Jack	CIS:70700,166
Tree	Disk Utility	Free	Aaerdeus, Inc.	415-325-7529
TreeList 1.0	Form	Free	Fehr, Andreas	CIS:100042,2070; Internet:afehr@itr.ch
Trig	General	Free	Gorman, Robert	CIS:75010,754
TriviaTron Trivia Game	Game	$14 SW	Nannini, Stephen F.	617-444-9061; CIS:75031,1262
True Grid Demo	Database	$69	Apex Software Corporation	412-681-4343; 800-858-2739
TrueType Font Specifications	Fonts	Free		
TT Editor Rev. A	Form	Unknown	Thorp, Ron	CIS:72557,3632
Turbo DXF	DLL - Graphics	$50 SW	Ideal Engineering Software	
TurboPack 1.0	Custom Control	$120	SoftLand Inc.	215-741-2030; CIS:73321,1525
TX Text Control (DEMO)	Custom Control	$249	European Software Connection	913-832-2070

Name	Type	Price	Vendor	Phone/E-mail
Txthook.DLL	Programming	Free	Simms, Jeff	301-593-6067; CIS:72200,3173
Tynee-Calc	Productivity	Unknown	Wilson, Michael	CIS:71261,63
UDPPort Control 1.01	Custom Control	$30	DevSoft Inc.	CIS:75244,2736; AOL:Devsoft
UFLHTS String Formatting	DLL - General	Free	Heritage Technology Solutions	310-374-7748
Unload	Programming	Free	Sax Software	CIS:75470,1403; CIS:74774,710
Update ODBC Driver	Programming	Free	Microsoft	206-882-8080; 800-992-3675
Updated MSCOMM.VBX	Custom Control	Free	Microsoft	206-882-8080; 800-992-3675
Updated VBRUN300.DLL (301)	Run Time Library	Free	Microsoft	206-882-8080; 800-992-3675
Updated XBS110.DLL	DLL - Database	Free	Microsoft	206-882-8080; 800-992-3675
User Defined Labels For Crysta	Language Extension	Free	Johnston, Robert J.	415-697-1945; CIS:71611,1370
Using Borland C++ For VB Contr	Language Extension	Free	Langley, Brent K.	CIS:70312,2142
Using BWCC.DLL Message Box	DLL Interface	Free	Duhamel, Guy	CIS:100334,2130
Using CTL3DV2.DLL	Reference	Free		
Using DDE With Access Basic	Communications	Free	Tissington, Mike	CIS:100430,614
Using WinAPI Calls With WinHep	Help	Free	Arnote, Paul	Internet:Aerosolman@Aol.Com
Utility Custom Control	System Utility	Free	Dotson, Bill	CIS:73512,3675
Valet 1.0	Program Utility	$15	English, Donald R.	CIS:70724,2576
Variable Naming And Coding Gui	Reference	Free		
VB 3.0 Setup Bug Fixes	Language Extension	Free	Microsoft	206-882-8080; 800-992-3675
VB 3.0 Stack Patch	Program Utility	Free	Monro, Chris	CIS:74250,1327
VB Add File Utility 1.0.5	Program Utility	$10 SW	Manoogian, Paul J	CIS:76646,3542
Vb Add-On Witch (BETA)	Program Utility	See docs	Mey & Westphal	49-0-40-22-17-23; CIS:100111,305
VB Add-Ons 1.02	Language Extension	Free	Stewart, Michael	CIS:76234,3314
VB Addins 1.5	Program Utility	$15 SW	Margraff, Tom	909-980-7344; CIS:71165,2623
VB AHA!!! 1.23	Help	$50	Villalon, Craig	Internet:villalon@crl.com
VB And Jet 2.0 Demo	Database	Free		
VB API Assistant 1.0	Program Utility	Free	Fry, Brian W.	2C3-571-5206; CIS:70732,1327
VB Assistant	Program Utility	Free	English, Donald R.	CIS:70724,2576
VB Backup 1.0	Program Utility	$10	Gentils, David M.	CIS:75543,1402

Name	Type	Price	Vendor	Phone/E-mail
VB Backup And Restore	Program Utility	Free	Kearney, Stephen	510-547-3189
VB Bar	Programming	$15 SW	Rathwick, Zane / Addsoft	
VB Bookmark	Program Utility	$25	Peopleware	800-959-2509
VB Button Clock	Clock	Free		
VB Clean	Program Utility	Free	Hite, David	CIS:72130,2400
VB Clock	Productivity	Free	Gagliano, Jim	CIS:74017,3342
VB Code Analyst	Program Utility	Unknown	Bergmann, Ken	206-557-4279; CIS:74441,163
VB Code Flush 1.1	Programming	$4 SW	Moccia, Lou A.	
VB Code Manager 1.7	Program Utility	$15 SW	Burnham, Gordon	502-363-5136
VB Code Print	Printer	$10	Thornton, Michael	AOL:Frogware
VB Code Wizard 1.1	Program Utility	$40	Taylor, Jonathan B.	214-328-4276
VB Comment Potato 1.0	Program Utility	$6 SW	Stewart, David	CIS:72122,3562
VB Compile	Program Utility	Free	Buchholz, Elliot C.	CIS:71034,2464
VB Compress	Programming	Free	Buchholz, Elliot C.	CIS:71034,2464
VB Compress Pro 3.11 Demo	General	$60	WhippleWare	617-242-2511; 800-241-8727
VB CONSTANT.TXT Help File	Programming	Free	Buhrer, Richard	CIS:70671,1501
VB Controls	Custom Control	Free	Gamber, Mark	CIS:76450,2754
VB Convert	Program Utility	$25	CC Advies	
VB Data Companion 2.1	Database	$50	MM Technology	201-612-8222; CIS:71155,1010
VB Documentation Errors	Reference	Free	Microsoft	206-882-8080; 800-992-3675
VB Documentor 2.1	Program Utility	$50 SW	Lake St. Clair Publishing	206-456-7000; CIS:76376,737
VB Drag-Drop 1.0	Custom Control	Free	Gamber, Mark	CIS:76450,2754
VB Error Handler 3.0	DLL - General	$34	Renard, Michael	CIS:100042,3646
VB Escort For Windows 2.0	Program Utility	$19.95 SW	Full Sail Software	817-292-1852; CIS:73521,3353
VB File Listboxes 1.0	Custom Control	Free	Gamber, Mark	CIS:76450,2754
VB Global Help File	Program Utility	Free	Thorp, Rick	CIS:72077,1701
VB HelpWriter 2.0c	Help	$59 SW	Teletech Systems	CIS:72260,2217
VB HelpWriter Dictionary	Help	Unknown	Teletech Systems	CIS:72260,2217
VB Icon Browser 2.2	Desktop	$20 SW	Valley Programming	210-650-9515

Name	Type	Price	Vendor	Phone/E-mail
VB Icon Extraction	Programming	Free		CIS:100020,2452
VB Install	Programming	Free	Kallonen, Jari	
VB Jigsaw	Game	Unknown		
VB Key Code Generator	Programming	$30 SW	Reinstein, Robert	CIS:76702,2075
VB Label 1.0	Custom Control	Free	Gamber, Mark	CIS:76450,2754
VB Language Manager Demo	Internationalizatn	$100+	WhippleWare	617-242-2511; 800-241-8727; CIS:723
VB Librarian 2	Program Utility	Unkown	Bergmann, Ken	206-557-4279; CIS:74441,163
VB Listbox Controls 1.1	Custom Control	Free	Gamber, Mark	CIS:76450,2754
VB Make 1.11	Program Utility	Free	Irwin, Gregg	CIS:72450,676
VB Menu Potato 1.1	Menu	$5 SW	Stewart, David	CIS:72122,3562
VB Menu Printer	Program Utility	Free	Transact Software	
VB Message Box Builder 1.0	Form	Free	Hot Chilli Software	CIS:100035,3510
VB Messenger - Owner-Draw LB	Programming	Free	JOSWare, Inc.	516-293-8915; CIS:71222,3522
VB Messenger - Subclassing CC	Custom Control	$30 SW	JOSWare, Inc.	516-293-8915; CIS:71222,3522
VB MIDI Piano Demo	Sound	$99	Artic Software	800-892-0677; 414-534-4309
VB Print 1.3	Program Utility	$25 SW	In Touch Software	CIS:75330,746
VB Progress Bar Code	Graphics	Free	Kraft, Rob and Jeff Trader	AOL:RobKraft
VB Project Analyzer 0.3 Beta	Program Utility	Unknown	Chapman, Mike	CIS:100030,351
VB Project Analyzer 0.3 Beta 2	Program Utility	Unknown	Chapman, Mike	CIS:100030,351
VB Project Analyzer 0.3 Beta 3	Program Utility	Unknown	Chapman, Mike	CIS:100030,351
VB Project Analyzer 0.3 Beta 4	Program Utility	Unknown	Chapman, Mike	CIS:100030,351
VB Project Backup	Program Utility	$6	U-Turn Productions	AOL:Jason T668
VB Project List Spy	Program Utility	Free	Stewart, David	CIS:72122,3562
VB Project Protector	Program Utility	$30 SW	Professional Software Systems	CIS:71554,357
VB Quick Reference To Win API	Reference	$15	Stillwater Systems	CIS:72643,604
VB RecentFiles	Program Utility	Free	Joyce, Ben	CIS:100101,36
VB Runtime Library Version	Run Time Library	Free	Germelmann, Christian	49-6421-45457; CIS:100520,2644
VB Setup Kit 1.00.02	Program Utility	Free	Jwpc, Inc.	Internet:JwpcEMail@Aol.Com
Vb Shade Selection Assistant	Program Utility	Free		

Name	Type	Price	Vendor	Phone/E-mail
VB SNR - Global Change Automat	Program Utility	Unknown	TARDIS DP Consultants	CIS:73337,2472
VB SNR Search And Replace	Program Utility	$8	TARDIS DP Consultants	CIS:73337,2472
VB Space	Program Utility	Free	Irwin, Gregg	CIS:72450,676
VB Squeeze	Program Utility	Free	Irwin, Gregg	CIS:72450,676
VB Task Switcher	Desktop	Free	Morris & Steinwart	CIS:72447,1545; CIS:73647,1613
VB Tech Journal Writer's Guide	Special	Free	VB Tech Journal	800-234-0386; 503-747-0800
VB Tips 07/02/94	Programming	Free	Ford, Nelson	CIS:71355,470
VB Tips And Tricks '94 And '95	Programming	Free	NicheWare	CIS:74777,447; AOL:DPMCS
VB Tips Viewer	Programming	Free	Ford, Nelson	CIS:71355,470
VB To Excel	DDE	Free		
VB To Visual C++ Forms Convert	Programming	Demo	PractiSys	818-706-8877
VB Toolbox Pro 3.0	Programming	$25 SW	Jurcik, Hal	CIS:71042,1566
VB Tracer/Profiler 3.0	Program Utility	$43	Renard, Michael	CIS:100042,3646
VB TrueCal 2.2	Calendar	$12 SW	IntuiTech Systems, Inc.	
VB Witch	Program Utility	$10 SW	Ling, Sui	CIS:100267,546
VB Wizard 3.13	Custom Control	$35 SW	Pocket Change Software	CIS:71441,1264
VB Wizard 3.X System Files	Misc.	Unknown	Pocket Change Software	CIS:71441,1264
VB WNet* Functions And Example	Communications	Free	Computer Technologies, Inc.	704-634-1766; CIS:71163,2657
VB*Alyzer	Programming	Free	Woodhouse, Mike	
VB-ASM 1.3	DLL - General	Free	SoftCircuits Programming	CIS:72134,263
VB-Awk	Language Extension	$25 SW	SYNERGY Software & Services	203-761-0749; CIS:73467,3661
VB-Clip Space Saver	Program Utility	Free	Stewart, Robert W.	CIS:72632,3004
VB-Drop (Dust Bin)	File Management	Free	Computer Technologies, Inc.	704-634-1766; CIS:71163,2657
VB-Switch	Program Control	Free	Computer Technologies, Inc.	704-634-1766; CIS:71163,2657
VB-Tools 1.0 Toolbar	Program Utility	$25 SW	Disk And Desk Software	414-744-9263; CIS:76753,127
VB/DLL Internet Procedure Call	Programming	$249	DataObjects Inc.	615-987-0421
VB/Rig Standard 1.0c	Program Utility	$29-$59	PC HELP-LINE	909-797-3091; CIS:72357,3523
VB_APPS	Programming	$30 SW	Resolutions Now	312-994-6450
VB3 For Dummies Example	Programming Demo	Free	Wang, Wallace	CIS:70334,3672

Name	Type	Price	Vendor	Phone/E-mail
VB3 Initial Blank Record	Database	Free	Hamilton, Peter	CIS:73774,3661
VBA Array Sorter	Data Access	Free	Hamilton, Peter	CIS:73774,3661
VBA Disable Break On Errors	Programming	Free	Bostwick, Marshall	216-864-1778; CIS:76646,2552
VBAPI Help 2.1 Program	Help	Free	Kitsos, Costas	CIS:73667,1755
VBArray	Programming	Free	RUW-Computer	049-2358-7760; CIS:100116,1532
VBBACKUP.VBX	Custom Control	Unknown	Visual Basic Programmer's Jrnl	800-848-5523; 415-917-7650
VBBK08 Listing Of Books, Etc.	Reference	Free	Scott, Dennis	803-650-7460; CIS:71360,3701
VBBook 1.2	Printer	Free		
VBBtrv	Database	Free		
VBcheck 1.01	Program Utility	$15 SW	Colton, J. E.	CIS:70620,1425
VBClock 2.1	Clock	$15 SW	Holland, Sarah	
VBCtl3D 1.51	Custom Control	$29 SW	Simms, Jeff	301-593-6067; CIS:72200,3173
VBDB	Database	$50 CR	Marquis Computing, Inc.	203-963-7065; 800-818-1611
VBDOS	Programming	Unknown		
VBDOS5	System Utility	Unknown		
VBE Enhancements	Program Utility	$15 SW	Northington, Otha L.	
VBench Data Access Benchmark	Data Access	Unknown	Fawcette Technical Publication	415-917-7650; MCI:jfawcette
VBFlip	Game	Free		
VBForm Custom Control	Custom Control	Free	Venugopalan, Vivek	CIS:73512,3675
VBHelper Integrated Help DEMO	Help	$25	Disk And Desk Software	414-744-9263; CIS:76753,127
VBINST Install Program 1.30	Programming	Free	Kallonen, Jari	CIS:100020,2452
VBIO Disk And File VBX	Disk Utility	Free	Broeze, Arjen	Internet:Vbx_Dev@Shear.laf.Nl
VBLaunch	Misc.	$149	VideoFax Ltd.	44-1440-783789
VBMail	Productivity	Free		
VBMem 3.2	Prog. - Sys. Util.	Free	Snider, Charles K.	CIS:73730,1315
VBMEM V3.1	Programming	Free	Snider, Charles K.	CIS:73730,1315
VBMenu	Programming	Free		
VBMoreControl For Mouse 0.9	Custom Control	Free	Brown, Tim	CIS:73557,3461
VBossAPI Function Lib 1.0/2.01	DLL - General	$21 SW	Truesdale, Greg	CIS:74131,2175

Name	Type	Price	Vendor	Phone/E-mail
VBPaths	Programming	Free	Brown, Tim	CIS:73557,3461
VBPJB2 VB And Access Books Etc	Reference	Free	Fawcette Technical Publication	415-917-7650; MCI:jfawcette
VBPlus	Program Utility	$20 SW	Gottlieb, Daniel	CIS:73552,1460
VBPLUS Toolbar	Program Utility	$25 SW	Pennington, Bill	CIS:72154,167
VBproFX Animated Demo	Graphics	$129	Advance Animation Systems	
VBPtr	Language Extension	Free	User Friendly, Inc.	202-387-1949; CIS:76702,1605
VBQuirk	Programming	Free	MicroHelp, Inc.	800-922-3383; 404-516-0899
VBrotary Rotary Card Printing	Printer	Free	Antony, P. Scott	CIS:74002,2373; AOL:PSAntony
Vbrowser	Database	Free	ETN Corporation	717-435-2202
VBScript 1.1	Program Utility	$20 SW	Simmons, Jason	CIS:70254,2017
VBSort	Programming	Free	Ford, Nelson	CIS:71355,470
VBstrAPI Huge String Array	DLL - General	$20 SW	Truesdale, Greg	CIS:74131,2175
VBTerm	Communications	Free	McGuiness, Charles	CIS:76701,11
VBToolbox	Programming	$10 SW	Jurcik, Hal	CIS:71042,1566
VBTools Demo	Language Extension	Unknown	MicroHelp, Inc.	800-922-3383; 404-516-0899
VBTrace 2.0e	Program Utility	Free	Stuart, Chuck	CIS:76560,51; AOL:ChukStuart
VBUSE - VB Usage Reader	Program Utility	$5 SW	Mabry Software	206-634-1443; CIS:71231,2066
VBUtils	Programming	Free	White, George M.	CIS:71511,1072
VbValet Print 1.2	Program Utility	$30 SW	Haduch, Robert Wydler	41-01-3121062; CIS:100116,3443
VBVoice DEMO	Sound	$395	Pronexus	613-839-0033; CIS:71054,3225
VBWerx 2.0	Program Utility	Free	Joyce, Ben	CIS:100101,36
VbWin Programmer Magazine #10	Text	Free	Schoonover, Mark	Internet:Schoone@Cts.Com
VbWin Programmer Magazine #11	Text	Free	Schoonover, Mark	Internet:Schoone@Cts.Com
VbWin Programmer Magazine #12	Text	Free	Schoonover, Mark	Internet:Schoone@Cts.Com
VbWin Programmer Magazine #8	Text	Free	Schoonover, Mark	Internet:Schoone@Cts.Com
VbWin Programmer Magazine #9	Text	Free	Schoonover, Mark	Internet:Schoone@Cts.Com
VbWin Programmer Magazine 1/95	Text	Free	Schoonover, Mark	Internet:Schoone@Cts.Com
VbWin Programmer Magazine 2/95	Text	Free	Schoonover, Mark	Internet:Schoone@Cts.Com
VBWsk - Winsock Custom Control	Custom Control	Free	Syme, Brian	Internet:Gxlr07@Udcf.Gla.Ac.Uk

Name	Type	Price	Vendor	Phone/E-mail
VBX Control Development Wizard	Programming	$25 SW	Bish Programming	CIS:100257,3010
VBX Generator 2	Custom Control	$50SW	Pagett, Paul	
VBX Interface To Intel 8255PPI	Custom Control	$15	DB Technologies	813-378-3760
VBX Studio 1.2	Custom Control	$55+SW	Chevron, Denis	33-1-40726483; CIS:100333,27
VBX Wizard	Programming	$70	Zeitlin, Eli And Dani	972-2-793-895; CIS:100274,1321
VBX Wizard For MS C++	Programming	Free	Sax Software	CIS:75470,1403; CIS:74774,710
VBXpress Custom Controls Demo	Custom Control	Unknown	AJS Publishing	800-992-3383; 310-215-9145
VBXRef Demo	Programming	Free	MicroHelp, Inc.	800-922-3383; 404-516-0899
VBXtasy Volume 1 DEMO	Form	$149	Spinoza Ltc.	310-231-9770; 800-700-2217
VBXtras Catalog Winter 1995	Inspiration	Free	VBxtras	404-952-6356; 800-788-4794
VBZ Electronic Journal	General	$73	User Friendly, Inc.	202-387-1949; CIS:76702,1605
VER Version Info / File Instal	Program Utility	$20 SW	Mabry Software	206-634-1443; CIS:71231,2066
VerInfo Demo	Program Utility	Free	De Palma, John R	CIS:76076,571
Version Browser 1.0	Program Utility	Free	WINDOWS Magazine	
Version Information 2.0	Program Utility	$10 SW	Jones, Graham	CIS:100010,2164
Version Viewer 1.0	Program Utility	$10 SW	Lose Your Mind Software	215-275-7034; CIS:70564,2372
Versions/VB 1.1c DEMO	Program Utility	$99	StarBase	714-442-4400; 800-891-3262
VEXE 1.0b EXE File Embedding	Program Utility	$104	Versatile Control Systems Inc.	407-881-9050; CIS:75144,3111
VGASize Form Template	Form	Free	Dover, Bob	512-578-9100
VideoMaster For Windows	Database	$10 SW	BMH Software	
VideoSoft Custom Controls Libr	Custom Control	$45 SW	VideoSoft	510-704-8200; 800-547-7295
Virtual Desktop	DLL - General	$17 SW	Rathwick, Zane / Addsoft	
Virtual List Box	Listbox	Free	Craig, Bob	
Virtual Text Browser 0.9	Listbox	Free	Risholm, Bob	CIS:76030,270
Virtual VsView Printer Demo	Printer	Free	Hayes, Brain C.	CIS:74653,1760
VisEFEX	Graphics	$49 SW	Advance Automation Systems	310-530-3938
Visible Serialization (tm) 1.1	Setup	$19.95	RCCO Research Associates	
Visual Basic 2.0 Primer Editio	Programming Demo	Free	Microsoft	206-882-8080; 800-992-3675
Visual Basic 3.0 Runtime	Run Time Library	Free	Microsoft	206-882-8080; 800-992-3675

APPENDIX

C

Name	Type	Price	Vendor	Phone/E-mail
Visual Basic Access Key Potato	Program Utility	Free	Stewart, David	CIS:72122,3562
Visual Basic Backgrounder	Reference	Free	Microsoft	206-882-8080; 800-992-3675
Visual Basic Conventions & Gd.	Reference	Free	Rother, Jim	CIS:71064,130
Visual Basic For Apps Tips	Text	Free	Microsoft	206-882-8080; 800-992-3675
Visual Basic Message Potato	Listbox	$5	Stewart, David	CIS:72122,3562
Visual Basic Naming Convention	Text	Free	Brewer, Dirk	Internet:expired
Visual Basic Office 1.03	Program Utility	$40 SW	Marquette Computer Consultants	415-459-0835; CIS:70413,3405
Visual Basic Office Descript.	Reference	Free	Marquette Computer Consultants	415-459-0835; CIS:70413,3405
Visual Basic Project Manager	Program Utility	Free	Kallonen, Jari	CIS:100020,2452
Visual Basic Project Tools	Programming	Free	Dombroski, Bob	215-287-6484
Visual Basic Run Time 1.0	Run Time Library	Free	Microsoft	206-882-8080; 800-992-3675
Visual Basic Run Time 2.0	Run Time Library	Free	Microsoft	206-882-8080; 800-992-3675
Visual Basic Shareware Rev. #2	Text	Free	TANSTAAFL Software	303-989-7389; CIS:73700,3053
Visual Basic Shareware Review	Text	Free	TANSTAAFL Software	303-989-7389; CIS:73700,3053
Visual Basic To C Resource	Programming	Free	SoftBit Enterprises	703-421-0225
Visual Basic To Document	Text	$25	Juden, Eddie V.	CIS:72154,1324
Visual Basic Toolbar 2.0	Program Utility	Free	Germelmann, Christian	49-6421-45457; CIS:100520,2644
Visual Basic Toolbar 2.0a	Menu	Free	Germelmann, Christian	49-6421-45457; CIS:100520,2644
Visual Basic Vs. PowerBuilder	Text	Free	Green, William	CIS:71203,1414
Visual DLL DEMO Program	Programming	Cal vend	Simply Solutions	800-355-2405; 310-575-5047
Visual Help 2.1i	Help	$49	WinWare	CIS:70272,1656; BBS:714-363-9802
VPFade Form With Gradient	Form	Free	Pozharov, Vitaliy	AOL:VitaliyP
Vprint 2.2	Program Utility	$15	Pazur, Scott	CIS:74457,2772
VSVBX Library 5.0	Custom Control	$45	VideoSoft	510-704-8200; 800-547-7295
VSView 1.07	Printer	$99	VideoSoft	510-704-8200; 800-547-7295
VXBase 1.07	DLL - Database	$59.95 SW	VXBase Systems	403-488-8100; 800-992-0616
VxBase Assistant	Database	$15	Purcell, Tim	358-0-5022542
VXBase Documentation	DLL - Database	Unknown	VXBase Systems	403-488-8100; 800-992-0616
VxC	Database	$100 SW	VXBase Systems	403-488-8100; 800-992-0616

Name	Type	Price	Vendor	Phone/E-mail
Waldo Animation	Graphics	Free	Melanson, Leo M.	CIS:74130,2141
Wallpaper Changer	Programming	Free	Hitchings, Tim	
Wampus Tracker	Programming	Free	Fuller, H. L.	510-704-8200; 800-547-7295
WAV Files From PC Speaker	Sound	Free	VideoSoft	
WAV Playing/Info VBX	Sound	$15	Mabry Software	206-634-1443; CIS:71231,2066
Wave After Wave 2.01	Sound	$5 SW	Iyer, Sunil	CIS:expired
Wave Maker 1.5 Demo	Custom Control	$20 SW	Washingtor, Winefred	CIS:72070,3713
Wave Sound Control	Sound	Free	Gamber, Mark	CIS:76450,2754
Waveform Spectrum Plot	Sound	Free		
WavePlayer	Sound	Free	Asensio, Pete	CIS:70143,467
Waving Demo Of A Bitmap	Graphics	Free	Rossow, Frank	CIS:100074,1756
WavPlus 2.0	Sound	$10 SW	Digital PowerTOOLS	601-932-5931; CIS:74547,23;
Wemory 1.0	System Utility	$5 SW	Porcaro, Jeff	
WGLIB 1.01	DLL - General	Unknown	InfoSoft	414-282-0535; CIS:70403,3412
What's My Number	Game	$5 SW	Persky, Jonathan D.	Internet:jonpersky@aol.com
WhizNotes S2.00	Help	$50 SW	Advanced Support Group Inc.	CIS:70304,3642;
Win Help Builder	Help	$20	McFall, Pete	
WIN5x5 Solitaire	Game	$15 SW	Hilgart, John	
WinAPI	Programming	Free	Microsoft	206-882-8080; 800-992-3675
WinBack 3.0	Disk Utility	$15 SW	Jurcik, Hal	CIS:71042,1566
WinBasic 1.2	Programming	$30	Zimmer Informatik	CIS:100276,3020
WinBrowse 1.6	Data Access	$22.50 SW	Q&D Software Development	201-635-1824; CIS:76336,3271
Wind Chill	Calculator	Free	Huss, Dennis L.	
WindChill	Science	Free	Trunck, James P.	
Window Info	Program Utility	Free	Bonner, Paul	CIS:76000,13
Window Treatments 1.0 Demo	Form	$17	Lee, Joseph	CIS:74013,3316
Windows 3.1 APIs	Reference	Free	Microsoft	206-882-8080; 800-992-3675
Windows API Functions Cardfile	Reference	Free		
Windows Help Magician Demo 3.0	Help	$199	Software Interphase	401-397-2340

Name	Type	Price	Vendor	Phone/E-mail
Windows LZSS Compression Lib	Language Extension	$25 SW	Eschalon Development Inc.	604-520-1543; CIS:76625,1320
Windows Online VB Column #16	Reference	Free	Marquette Computer Consultants	415-459-0835; CIS:70413,3405
Windows Online VB Column #17	Reference	Free	Marquette Computer Consultants	415-459-0835; CIS:70413,3405
Windows Online VB Column #18	Reference	Free	Marquette Computer Consultants	415-459-0835; CIS:70413,3405
Windows Online VB Column #19	Reference	Free	Marquette Computer Consultants	415-459-0835; CIS:70413,3405
Windows Online VB Column #21	Reference	Free	Marquette Computer Consultants	415-459-0835; CIS:70413,3405
Windows Online VB Column #22	Reference	Free	Marquette Computer Consultants	415-459-0835; CIS:70413,3405
Windows Process Status	System Utility	Free		
Windows Quick Help	Help	$15 SW	SMI Enterprises Corp	918-560-9536
Windows'95 Dialog Box Wizard	Misc.	Free	Allcock, Alun	CIS:100255,1506
Windows95 Style Tab Controls	Graphics	Free	Dompier, Jim	CIS:73501,445
WinfoXL System Control API	DLL - General	$20	Digital PowerTOOLS	601-932-5931; CIS:74547,23
Wing3D - #D Made Simple	Form	$3	Silverwing Systems	904-668-8530; CIS:70254,613
Wingine	System Utility	$15 CR	Software Shop	
WinHelp 1.10	Program Utility	Free	Torralba, George R.	206-781-7622
WinHelp Extension Library 3.2	Help	$20	Arnote, Paul	Internet:Aerosolman@Aol.Com
WinLock	System Utility	Free	Zeitman, Dan	
WinMsg	Custom Control	$25 SW	SoftBit Enterprises	703-421-0225
WinPRT 1.0	Program Utility	$10 SW	Shaw, Kevin	CIS:74002,315
WinPS Control Flow DLL	Program Control	$18SW	Muehlenweg, Ulli	CIS:100331,1413
Winptr	Program Utility	$20 SW	Poellinger, Paul F.	CIS:70732,3576; AOL:Pfpelican
WinSend 1.5	Communications	Free	Larcombe, Andrew	
WinShark Poker	Game	Free	Tyminski, James D.	CIS:76376,2375
Winsock RCMD.DLL	DLL - Communication	$35SW	Denicomp Systems	CIS:71612,2333
Winsock RCP.DLL	DLL - Communication	$35SW	Denicomp Systems	CIS:71612,2333
WINstall	Program Utility	$43 SW	Dovcom	801-221-4527; CIS:74552,1027
Wintab	Form	Free	Stewart, Robert W.	CIS:72632,3004
Wintrace	Prog. - Sys. Util.	$20SW	Bridges, Steve	CIS:71507,1033
Wiper	Program Utility	Free	Pleas, Keith R.	CIS:72331,2150

Name	Type	Price	Vendor	Phone/E-mail
Wire Frame Maze Demo	Game	$25	Krystal Cat Software	Internet:KrysCat@Aol.Com
WMF To BMP Converter	Graphics	Free	Campbell, George	CIS:71571,222; BBS:805-528-3753
Wmfpix	Graphics	Unknown		
Write VBX Control Using MFC2.0	Programming	Free	Microsoft	206-882-8080; 800-992-3675
Writing Custom Controls W/MFC	Language Extension	Free		
Writing DIF Files From VB	Finance	Free		
WSHELP Help Text CC	Help	$45 SW	Weimar Software	408-268-6638
WSIHLP Custom Controls	Custom Control	$75 SW	Weimar Software	408-268-6638
X World Clock	Clock	Free	Kienemund, Wilfried	49-211-203490; CIS:100015,2550
X-Ray/WINSOCK 1.2	DDE	$80 SW	Systems Software Technology	818-346-2784; CIS:70233,2504
X10WIN	Device Control	Unknown	Tenholder, Edward J.	CIS:76447,1030
Xantippe	Help	$15 SW	IRIS Media Systems	510-256-4673
XFile Custom Controls 2.5 DEMO	Custom Control	$399	BC Soft AB	46-8-657-91-90; CIS:70630,1337
XLabel 2.2	Fonts	$15 SW	Hanson, Mark	CIS:72773,71
Xtal Report Field Scaler 3.1	Database	$26	Johnston, Robert J.	
XTASK.DLL Monitors Termination	Programming	Free	Stam, Pieter	
Zip Code Database	Database	$18 SW	HELP Software	816-331-5809; CIS:73720,2530
ZIP File Into CC 1.2	Data Access	$15	Mabry Software	206-634-1443; CIS:71231,2066
Zip Master	File Compression	Free	Saucedo, Rosary	
Zip Server 1.4	File Compression	$40 SW	Redei Enterprises Inc.	310-832-6984; CIS:71744,3633
ZZHot.Vbx	Custom Control	Unknown	Solid Software Inc.	Internet:gat@csn.org

IDG Books Worldwide License Agreement

prohibited by applicable law. If the Software is an update or has been updated, any transfer must include the most recent update and all prior versions. Each shareware program has its own use permissions and limitations. These limitations are contained in the individual license agreements that are on the software discs. The restrictions include a requirement that after using the program for a period of time specified in its text, the user must pay a registration fee or discontinue use. By opening the package which contains the software disc, you will be agreeing to abide by the licenses and restrictions for these programs. Do not open the software package unless you agree to be bound by the license agreements.

4. **Limited Warranty.** IDG warrants that the Software and disc are free from defects in materials and workmanship for a period of sixty (60) days from the date of purchase of this Book. If IDG receives notification within the warranty period of defects in material or workmanship, IDG will replace the defective disc. IDG's entire liability and your exclusive remedy shall be limited to replacement of the Software, which is returned to IDG with a copy of your receipt. This Limited Warranty is void if failure of the Software has resulted from accident, abuse, or misapplication. Any replacement Software will be warranted for the remainder of the original warranty period or thirty (30) days, whichever is longer.

5. **No Other Warranties.** To the maximum extent permitted by applicable law, IDG and the author disclaim all other warranties, express or implied, including but not limited to implied warranties of merchantability and fitness for a particular purpose, with respect to the Software, the programs, the source code contained therein and/or the techniques described in this Book. This limited warranty gives you specific legal rights. You may have others which vary from state/jurisdiction to state/jurisdiction.

6. **No Liability For Consequential Damages.** To the extent permitted by applicable law, in no event shall IDG or the author be liable for any damages whatsoever (including without limitation, damages for loss of business profits, business interruption, loss of business information, or any other pecuniary loss) arising out of the use of or inability to use the Book or the Software, even if IDG has been advised of the possibility of such damages. Because some states/jurisdictions do not allow the exclusion or limitation of liability for consequential or incidental damages, the above limitation may not apply to you.

7. **U.S.Government Restricted Rights.** Use, duplication, or disclosure of the Software by the U.S. Government is subject to restrictions stated in paragraph (c) (1) (ii) of the Rights in Technical Data and Computer Software clause of DFARS 252.227-7013, and in subparagraphs (a) through (d) of the Commercial Computer—Restricted Rights clause at FAR 52.227-19, and in similar clauses in the NASA FAR supplement, when applicable.

Index

Code window, 81–108
  basic description of, 83–87
  splitting, 87–89
  syntax checking and, 96–98
  Visual Basic text editor and, 89–92
collections
  of built-in forms, 504
  creating/using, 460–462
  definition of, 463
  developing, 454–570
  organizing, 463
  overview of, 443–484
colon (:), 303
Color dialog box, 388
colors
  for charts, selecting, 354–355
  displaying code in, 89, 90, 91, 94, 98
colReminderPages, 455, 460–463, 469
ColumnByRegion, 353, 354, 355, 369–370, 588–591
ColumnByYears, 353, 354, 355, 367–369, 588–591, 642, 644, 646–652
Columns method, 566
ColumnWidth property, 566
combo box buttons
  adding, 37–38, 42, 50–52
  defining properties and, 64–67, 69–74
  flashing vertical cursor inside, 65
  Sub procedures and, 128–129
comma, 235, 300
command buttons
  adding, 40, 41, 42, 50
  defining properties and, 62–64, 66, 69–71, 74–76
  setting captions for, 62–64
comments
  display of, in green, 90, 91
  including, 89, 90–91
Comments box, 165, 173, 181
Comments field, 403, 404
Common Dialog control, 388, 390
  mnuSaveAs_Click and, 403–404, 408–410
  setting properties and, 406–408
  using, overview of, 405–410
  working with, in code, 408–410
Common Dialogs Control Properties box, 407–408
comparison operators, 145, 225–227, 229–230, 235, 238
concatenation, 144–145, 180
conditions
  decisions as, 223, 224–225
  loops and, 238
Connect property, 611, 613

● D ●

● **E** ●

• **T** •

Visual Interface Design

The commonly accepted wisdom of the post-Macintosh era is that graphical user interfaces, or GUIs, are better than character-based user interfaces. This is generally a true statement but, while there are certainly GUI programs that dazzle us with their ease of use, the vast majority of GUI programs irritate and annoy us in spite of their graphic nature. Why is this?

Visual Software

It's not merely the graphic nature of an interface that makes it better. Using a bit-mapped system to render the lines and characters of a character-mode program doesn't change the essential nature of the program. It's very easy to create a program with a "graphical user interface" that has the same extreme difficulty-of-use as a CP/M, DOS or UNIX application.

The qualities that make a user interface good are user-centric and not technology-centric. "Graphicalness" is a technology-centric concept. There are two really important user-centric qualities: the "visualness" of the software and the program's vocabulary.

741

Most humans process information better visually than they do textually. Sure, we learn by reading, but we learn much more, much faster by seeing things whole and in context. In order to realize the advantages of the technology, the interaction with the user must become visual. The issue isn't the graphic nature of the program, it's the visualness of the interaction. Instead of GUI, it's a visual user interface—a VUI—that we are looking for. Software that recognizes this is called visual interface design. When done well, a VUI has a feeling of fluency, of moving along smoothly and effortlessly towards the user's goals without hitching or stopping on confusing little problems of comprehension.

Visual processing

The human brain is a superb pattern-processing computer. It uses this strength to make sense of the dense quantities of visual information we are bombarded with from the moment we open our eyes in the morning. The acuity of the human eye is tremendous, and if our brain couldn't impose some management system on what our eyes report, we would collapse from overload. Look out the window. See the trees, the water, the waves, the clouds, the people, the windows, the people in the windows, the guy carrying the box, the name printed on the box, the letters in the name.... If we had a difficult time with visual complexity, the sheer quantity of visual information we take in when we look out the window would put us in a state of shock. But we clearly aren't bothered by this visual complexity. When we look out the window, our eyes encompass a huge scene filled with constantly changing terabytes of complex information. Our brain manages the input by unconsciously discerning patterns, and by using these patterns to manage what we are looking at. Our brains establish a system of priorities for the things we see that allow us to consciously analyze the visual input.

Text, when viewed from a distance, forms a recognizable pattern and shape that our brains categorize. This is a different act from reading, where we scan the individual words and interpret them. Even then, we use pattern-matching more than we actually sound out each syllable the way we did as children. Each word has a recognizable shape, and this is why WORDS TYPED IN ALL CAPITAL LETTERS ARE HARDER TO READ than upper/lower case—our familiar pattern-matching hints are absent in all capitals, so we must pay much closer attention to decipher what is written. This same pattern-processing talent explains why body text in books is always in a relatively standard, serif typeface like the one you are looking at now. However, if this book were printed using a sans serif font, or a font with unusual proportions, you would find it not a strain on the eyes, but a strain on the brain.

When we look at the complex scene out the window, our brain gathers big chunks of the view into manageable pieces—building, street, ocean, sky—and lets our conscious processes grapple with higher-level issues.

If, for example, we find ourselves taking a second look at one person in the crowd on the street below, it is because our subconscious pattern-matching equipment got a hit. We next study the person's face, searching for details in order to make a positive identification. We go through the identical process when we read documents. Our unconscious mind is constantly reducing visual input to patterns, and our conscious mind is constantly ordering those patterns into hierarchies. When our eye-brain-pattern system reports an "envelope," our brain-hierarchy system isolates it and examines it for our name. The pattern system detects the envelope pattern; then the conscious system disambiguates that pattern into either a letter for us or a letter for someone else.

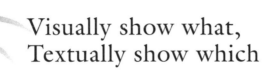

Visually show what, Textually show which

If our unconscious mind could not classify the pattern as an envelope, we would have to get our conscious mind involved in the preliminary processing. It is much faster when our unconscious mind provides the first cut because pattern-matching is so much faster and more efficient than having to think about it.

Visual patterns

If our conscious mind had to grapple with every detail of what our eyes saw, we would be overwhelmed with meaningless detail. The ability of our unconscious mind to group things into patterns based on visual cues is what allows us to process visual information so quickly and efficiently. Understanding and applying this model of how the human mind processes visual information is one of the key elements of visual interface design. The philosophy is to present the program's components on the screen as recognizable visual patterns with accompanying text as a descriptive supplement. The user can choose, on a purely pattern-matching, unconscious level, which objects to consider consciously. The accompanying text only comes into play once the user has decided it's important.

You build an effective visual interface from visual patterns. Notice that I did not say pictures or images or icons. Representational images are useful, but patterns are the engine of unconscious recognition. For the user to discern a particular icon from a screenful of similar but different icons is just as difficult as discerning a particular word from a screenful of similar but different words. Icons that must be consciously recognized or deciphered are no better—and possibly much worse—than plain text.

A visual interface is based on visual patterns

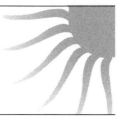

The pecking order of visual understanding always regards visual pattern-matching as superior to verbal or pictographic reading. Pattern-matching is unconscious and reading is conscious. Our visual user interface must create readily recognizable patterns. It will certainly include text, but only in a secondary role of distinguishing between objects with similar patterns.

We create patterns in very simple ways. Possibly the simplest is by creating recognizable graphic symbols and giving them value by association. As you drive down the highway, you read all of the signs you see. After a while, you begin to notice a pattern. Every time the highway you are on is identified, its number is accompanied or even enclosed by the symbol "⬡." You probably don't pay much attention to this trivial detail, and why should you? You are usually well aware of what highway you are on. Your unconscious mind filters out the ⬡ signs. Then one day you are on an unfamiliar highway and you want to know exactly which one you are on. Your conscious mind wants to know this, so your unconscious mind alerts you to the presence of each ⬡ it sees. Your conscious mind then reads the numbers on the sign to separate it from all of the other ⬡s you have seen. The ⬡ is not representational. It is not metaphoric. It is idiomatic: you learn the shape from the context in which it is used, and from then on it represents its context.

This is exactly what you do with visual interface design. You create symbols for the objects in the interface. If the program you are creating manages a restaurant, for example, you will find that tables, checks, orders, specials, and waitpersons are the fundamental elements—the building blocks—with which you must create the interface. In other words, these are the objects that the users will manipulate to achieve their goals. What you need to do is create a recognizable visual symbol for each of these primary types:

◯   Tables

✎   Checks

◪   Orders

🍁   Specials

🦆   Waitpersons

The symbols don't have to be representational, but it doesn't hurt. If you do choose a representational image, don't kid yourself about its value as a teaching tool. On the other hand, don't ignore the value of mnemonics. Each user can form his own mental cues to help him remember what the symbols represent: factories and tables both produce value; ducks and waitpersons both fly from place to place.

In order to drive home the connection between symbol and object, you must use the symbol everywhere the object is represented on the screen. Whether the object is an item in a listbox, an entire dialog box, a mention in text, or a gizmo on the toolbar, it must be accompanied by the visual symbol. You don't have to spell this out to the user: you are teaching it to his unconscious mind, and its presence alone over time is sufficient to do that. I call this a **visual fugue**.

If you have a list of waitpersons, prefix each one with the 🦆 symbol as in Figure 4-1.

The power of this technique is even greater if you have a listbox filled with heterogeneous objects. Imagine a similar listbox filled with both tables and orders as shown in Figure 4-2.

Our minds differentiate each line—each object—by its visual symbol, and once we have identified the type we are interested in, we read the text to separate it from its siblings. We don't have to read about objects we are not interested in. This type of processing is very natural to humans and we can perform it rapidly and with little effort.

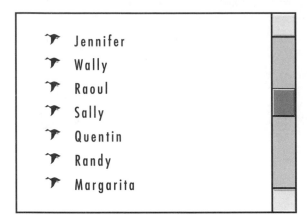

Figure 4-1

This listbox is filled with several objects of one type. You can see that unconsciously, because your mind discerns the identical symbols associated with each entry. It will probably take some additional reading to disambiguate which object is which, but without the symbols, we'd have to read them all just to know what they are and that they are all the same type. Symbols should always be associated with text in visual user interfaces.

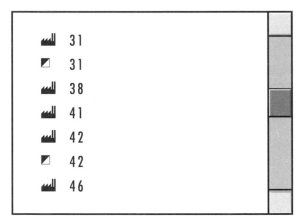

Figure 4-2

This listbox is filled with objects of two different types. Without the symbols to differentiate between tables and orders, it would be impossible to make sense of the list. We would have to label each entry with text, "Table 31," "Order 31," and so on. The symbols are much faster, letting our unconscious minds recognize the patterns before our relatively slow conscious minds even have to pay attention.

Restricting the vocabulary

When graphical user interfaces were first invented, they were so clearly superior that many observers credited their success to their graphics. This was a natural reaction, but it was only part of the story. One of the most important reasons why those first GUIs were better was that they were the first user interfaces to restrict the range of their vocabulary for communicating with the user. In particular, the input they could accept from the user went from a virtually unrestricted command line to a tightly restricted set of mouse-based actions. In a command line interface, the user can enter any combination of characters in the language—a virtually infinite number. In order for the user's entry to be correct, he needs to know exactly what the program expects. He must remember the letters and symbols with exacting precision. The sequence can be important. The capitalization can be vital.

In the GUI, the user can point to images or words on the screen with the mouse cursor. Using the buttons on the mouse, the user can click, double-click or click-and-drag. That is it. The keyboard is used for data entry, not for command entry or navigation. Instead of 26 letters, 10 digits and a couple of dozen other keys available in an infinite number of combinations in the command line interface, the user has just three basic actions to choose from. The number of atomic elements in the user's input vocabulary dropped from millions to just three, even though the range of tasks that could be performed by GUI programs wasn't restricted any more than that of command-line systems.

The more atomic elements there are in a communications vocabulary, the more time-consuming and difficult the learning process is. Vocabularies like the English language take at least ten years to learn thoroughly, and its complexity requires constant use to maintain fluency. Of course, English is a fantastically expressive language and, in the hands of an artist, can be a most compelling medium. Our users aren't artists, though, and they shouldn't have to invest that much effort in becoming effective with our software. Merely restricting the number of elements in the vocabulary reduces the expressiveness of it, so that alone is not the solution. The answer lies in the way we build our vocabularies—some parts are restricted in size, while others can be huge.

A properly formed vocabulary is shaped like an inverted pyramid. All easy-to-learn communications systems obey this pattern. It is so fundamental that I call it the canonical vocabulary. You can see a picture of it in Figure 4-3.

The Canonical Vocabulary

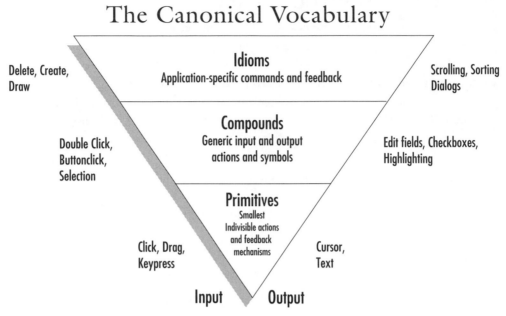

Idioms
Application-specific commands and feedback

Delete, Create,
Draw

Scrolling, Sorting
Dialogs

Compounds
Generic input and output
actions and symbols

Double Click,
Buttonclick,
Selection

Edit fields, Checkboxes,
Highlighting

Primitives
Smallest
Indivisible actions
and feedback
mechanisms

Click, Drag,
Keypress

Cursor,
Text

Input   **Output**

Figure 4-3

The main reason GUIs are so much easier to use is that they were the first platform to enforce a canonical vocabulary. It has very little to do with graphics. All vocabularies follow this archetypal form.

At the lowest level is a set of primitives from which all else is constructed. Generally, the set of primitives shouldn't exceed four elements. The middle layer consists of more complex constructs built from combinations of the primitives. The upper-level idioms are compounds with the addition of domain knowledge.

The bottom segment contains what I call the **primitives**, the atomic elements of which everything in the language is comprised.

Paraphrasing Albert Einstein, this set should be as small as possible, but no smaller. In a GUI, it consists of pointing, clicking and dragging. A set of primitives of two to four items is about right. More than that leads to trouble.

The middle trapezoid contains what I call the **compounds**.

These are more complex constructs created by combining one or more of the primitives. Nothing else is added; they are built exclusively from elements below them in the pyramid. In a GUI, it contains such actions as double-clicking, click-and-dragging and manipulable objects like push-buttons and checkboxes.

The uppermost layer of the pyramid contains what I call the idioms. Idioms combine compounds with knowledge of the problem under consideration, known as domain knowledge. Domain knowledge is information related to the user's application area and not specifically to the computerized solution. The set of idioms opens the vocabulary to information about the particular problem the program is trying to address. In a GUI, it would include things like OK buttons, caption bars, listboxes and file icons.

Any language that does not follow the canonical form will be very hard to learn. Many effective communications systems outside of the computer world follow canonical vocabularies. Street signs follow a simple pattern of shapes and colors: Yellow triangles are cautionary, red octagons are imperatives and green rectangles are informative.

Our telephone system has a tiny set of primitives consisting of simple audio tones. Hearing a buzz—a dial tone—means the system is available. When the buzz alternates with silence, it means the number is busy. A warble means the phone is ringing. Silence means we have failed to enter valid numbers, or there is some other problem and we should try again.

Designing for users

Successful user interfaces are those that focus on the user's goals even if they have to ignore the technology of the implementation. Professional software designers are the primary group today acting as advocates for the user.

To create effective visual interfaces, designers must create interaction from a canonically formed vocabulary that is expressed visually. This vocabulary follows the user's mental model, even if it diverges from the physically correct model. As Frederick Brooks says, "The [designer] sits at the focus of forces which he must ultimately resolve in the user's interest."

VBASIC UTILITY LIBRARY

- ***The Ultimate Programmer's Resource***

The VBASIC Utility Library CD-ROM from EMS Professional Shareware is an indispensable tool for every Visual Basic programmer, from the beginner to the most sophisticated developer. The August '95 edition contains over 1,440 public domain and shareware products chosen for programmers using MS-Visual Basic for Windows™.

The products are neatly organized in an indexed database directory, which includes a search program to locate programs by their name, vendor, type, release date and more. The directory lists over 65 types of products including: Buttons, Calculator, Calendar, Clock, Communications, Custom Control, Data Access, Database, DDE, Desktop, Device, DLL (for Communication, Database, Graphics, Telephone, others), DLL Interface, Educational, File Compression, File Management, Finance, Fonts, Form, Graphics, Icon Utility, Input Routines, Listbox, Mail List, Menu, Printer, Productivity, Program Control, Programming, Reference, Run Time Library, Science, Security, Setup, Sound, Spellcheck, System Utility, Text, Timer, and many more.

- ***Special Low Price for Purchasers of This Book***

You can get the current edition of the VBASIC Utility Library CD-ROM for just $29.50 (over half off list price) + shipping and handling. Just send in this coupon (or a copy and proof of purchase) and payment. Call EMS for current release date.

ORDER FORM

☐ Yes, send me the current edition of the VBASIC Utility Library on CD-ROM for just $29.50 + Shipping & Handling (UPS Ground/US Air Mail: $5 US, $10 CAN, $15 other).

Name:_____ Phone:_____

Address: _____ Fax:_____

_____ E-Mail:_____

_____

Visa/MC/AMEX/**Discover** #_____EX_____

Check # _____ Enclosed

☐ Please send me information on the VBASIC Library and other EMS technical shareware collections.

Send form and payment to: **EMS Professional Shareware**
4505 Buckhurst Court
Olney, MD 20832-1830
301-924-3594 Fax:301-963-2708
ems@wdn.com http://www.wdn.com/ems

Order Center: **(800) 762-2974** *(8 a.m.–6 p.m., EST, weekdays)*

5/8/95

Quantity	ISBN	Title	Price	Total

Shipping & Handling Charges

	Description	First book	Each additional book	Total
Domestic	Normal	$4.50	$1.50	$
	Two Day Air	$8.50	$2.50	$
	Overnight	$18.00	$3.00	$
International	Surface	$8.00	$8.00	$
	Airmail	$16.00	$16.00	$
	DHL Air	$17.00	$17.00	$

*For large quantities call for shipping & handling charges.

**Prices are subject to change without notice.

Ship to:

Name _____

Company _____

Address _____

City/State/Zip _____

Daytime Phone _____

Payment: ☐ Check to IDG Books (US Funds Only)

☐ VISA   ☐ MasterCard   ☐ American Express

Card # _____ Expires _____

Signature _____

Subtotal _____

CA residents add
applicable sales tax _____

IN, MA, and MD
residents add
5% sales tax _____

IL residents add
6.25% sales tax _____

RI residents add
7% sales tax _____

TX residents add
8.25% sales tax _____

Shipping _____

Total _____

Please send this order form to:

IDG Books Worldwide
7260 Shadeland Station, Suite 100
Indianapolis, IN 46256

Allow up to 3 weeks for delivery.
Thank you!

IDG BOOKS WORLDWIDE REGISTRATION CARD

RETURN THIS REGISTRATION CARD FOR FREE CATALOG

Title of this book: Foundations of Visual Basic 4 for Windows 95 Programming

My overall rating of this book: ❏ Very good [1] ❏ Good [2] ❏ Satisfactory [3] ❏ Fair [4] ❏ Poor [5]

How I first heard about this book:

❏ Found in bookstore; name: [6] _____

❏ Advertisement: [8] _____

❏ Word of mouth; heard about book from friend, co-worker, etc.: [10]

❏ Book review: [7] _____

❏ Catalog: [9] _____

❏ Other: [11] _____

What I liked most about this book:

_____

_____

What I would change, add, delete, etc., in future editions of this book:

_____

_____

Other comments:

_____

Number of computer books I purchase in a year: ❏ 1 [12] ❏ 2-5 [13] ❏ 6-10 [14] ❏ More than 10 [15]

I would characterize my computer skills as: ❏ Beginner [16] ❏ Intermediate [17] ❏ Advanced [18] ❏ Professional [19]

I use ❏ DOS [20] ❏ Windows [21] ❏ OS/2 [22] ❏ Unix [23] ❏ Macintosh [24] ❏ Other: [25]_____
(please specify)

I would be interested in new books on the following subjects:
(please check all that apply, and use the spaces provided to identify specific software)

❏ Word processing: [26]

❏ Data bases: [28]

❏ File Utilities: [30]

❏ Networking: [32]

❏ Other: [34]

❏ Spreadsheets: [27]

❏ Desktop publishing: [29]

❏ Money management: [31]

❏ Programming languages: [33]

I use a PC at (please check all that apply): ❏ home [35] ❏ work [36] ❏ school [37] ❏ other: [38] _____

The disks I prefer to use are ❏ 5.25 [39] ❏ 3.5 [40] ❏ other: [41]_____

I have a CD ROM: ❏ yes [42]   ❏ no [43]

I plan to buy or upgrade computer hardware this year: ❏ yes [44] ❏ no [45]

I plan to buy or upgrade computer software this year: ❏ yes [46] ❏ no [47]

Name: _____ Business title: [48] _____ Type of Business: [49] _____

Address (❏ home [50] ❏ work [51]/Company name: _____)

Street/Suite# _____

City [52]/State [53]/Zipcode [54]: _____ Country [55] _____

❏ **I liked this book!** You may quote me by name in future
IDG Books Worldwide promotional materials.

My daytime phone number is _____

IDG BOOKS

®

THE WORLD OF COMPUTER KNOWLEDGE

☐ **YES!**

Please keep me informed about IDG's World of Computer Knowledge.
Send me the latest IDG Books catalog.